# HEALTHY ACTIVE LIVING
## Keep Fit, Stay Healthy, Have Fun

Information on how to obtain copies of this book may be obtained from:

Website: http://www.thompsonbooks.com

E-mail:             publisher@thompsonbooks.com

Telephone:          (416) 766–2763

Fax:                (416) 766–0398

**Library and Archives Canada Cataloguing in Publication**

Temertzoglou, Ted, 1964–
Healthy active living : keep fit, stay healthy, have fun / Ted Temertzoglou.

Includes index.
ISBN 978-1-55077-150-3

1. Health—Textbooks.  I. Title.
GV341.T475 2006       613       C2006-903908-9

Publisher: Keith Thompson
Managing Editor: Jennie Worden
Book design concept: Elan Designs, Inc.
Cover design: Tibor Choleva
Page design, graphic art, and special effects: Tibor Choleva
Photo editors: Kristen Pedersen Chew, Katy Harrison, and Tibor Choleva
Copyeditor: Christine Hobberlin
Proofreader: Gillian Faulkner
Permissions Editor: Katy Harrison
Illustrations: Bart Vallecoccia
Senior Editor: Rachel Stuckey
Editorial Assistants: Crystal J. Hall, Katy Harrison, and Megan Burns

Every reasonable effort has been made to acquire permission for copyrighted materials used in this book and to acknowledge such permissions accurately. All credits for re-printed material can be found on pages 491-92. Any errors or omissions called to the publisher's attention will be corrected in future printings.

We acknowledge the support of the Government of Canada through the Book Publishing Industry Development Program for our publishing activities.

Printed in Canada.  2 3 4 5    12 11 10 09 08

# HEALTHY ACTIVE LIVING
## Keep Fit, Stay Healthy, Have Fun

## Ted Temertzoglou

Birchmount Park Collegiate Institute
Toronto District School Board

Thompson Educational Publishing, Inc.
Toronto

# Healthy Active Living—Author Team

## Lead Author

**Ted Temertzoglou**
*Birchmount Park Collegiate Institute, Toronto District School Board*

## Contributing Authors

**Andy Anderson**
*Ontario Institute for Studies in Education, University of Toronto*

**Pauline Auty**
*Canadian Safe School Network*

**Heidi Bates**
*Registered Dietitian, University of Alberta*

**Alyson Beben**
*Educational Specialist, Peel Region*

**John Griffin**
*Fitness and Lifestyle Management, George Brown College of Applied Arts and Technology*

**Beau Kent**
*Fitness and Lifestyle Management, George Brown College of Applied Arts and Technology*

**Justin Maloney,** MD
*Ottawa Hospital and Medical Director of the Ottawa Base Hospital Program*

**Linda McCarger**
*Department of Agricultural, Food and Nutritional Science, University of Alberta*

**Gary Roberts**
*Canadian Association for School Health*

## Ontario Physical and Health Education Association

The writing and publishing team would like to thank the management and staff at Ophea (the Ontario Physical and Health Education Association) for their support at every stage of this project—from our early discussions about developing a textbook to match the curriculum, to their input during the writing and reviewing process, to their endorsement and widespread promotion of the text. Without Ophea's support and assistance, the completion of this textbook and its supporting materials would not have been possible.

## Advanced Coronary Treatment Foundation (ACT Foundation)

The writing and publishing team would also like to thank the management and staff of the ACT foundation for their support and permission to reproduce the  ACT High School Student CPR Manual as an appendix to this resource.

## The Society of Obstetricians and Gynaecologists of Canada

The writing and publishing team would also like to thank The Society of Obstetricians and Gynaecologists of Canada for permission to reproduce their tables as an appendix to this resource.

## The Canadian Safe School Network

The writing and publishing team would also like to thank The Canadian Safe School Network, a national, chartitable organization dedicated to reducing youth violence and making our schools and communities safer, for their support in the development of the Conflict Resolution and Personal Safety unit.

# Reviewers

We are immensely grateful to all of the following individuals who kindly reviewed all or parts of this resource prior to publication. Responsibility for any errors or omissions rests with the author and the publisher.

## Ophea Reviewers

- Sean Appleton, Algoma District School Board
- Patricia Coburn, Michael Power/St Joseph High School, Toronto Catholic District School Board
- Gerry Cockburn, Dufferin-Peel Catholic District School Board
- Deb Courville, Halton District School Board
- Marilyn Cowie, Centre Wellington District High School, Upper Grand District School Board
- Nathaniel Dufresne, St Benedict Catholic Secondary School, Waterloo Catholic District School Board
- Tara Feeney, Trenton High School, Hastings & Prince Edward District School Board
- Nancy Gould, Lambton Kent District School Board
- Catherine Johnson, Lambton Kent District School Board
- LeLand McQuarrie, Rainbow District School Board
- Elizabeth Mulholland, Northeastern Catholic District School Board
- Kelly Pace, St. Clement's School, Conference of Independent Schools
- Dave Paddington, Lakehead District School Board
- Tony Petitti, Toronto Catholic District School Board
- Karen Podlatis-Brown, Near North District School Board
- Nancy Popovich, Hastings & Prince Edward District School Board
- Michael Pus, Waterloo Catholic District School Board
- Sarah Robertson, E.C. Drury High School, Halton District School Board
- Nancy Schad, Toronto District School Board
- Shane Verbiski, Waterloo Catholic District School Board
- Richard Ward, Toronto District School Board
- Jeff Weddig, Erin District High School, Upper Grand District School Board

## Institute for Catholic Education

- Staff from Thompson Educational Publishing, Inc. requested suggested modifications from the Institute for Catholic Education for use of this text in Ontario Catholic schools.

## Educational Consultant Reviewers

- Sandra Clarke, The ACT Foundation
- Mary Cunningham, Kenora Catholic District School Board
- Mary Ann Fratia, Peel District School Board
- Diahne Graham, Kawartha Pine Ridge District School Board
- George Kourtis, Toronto District School Board
- Louise Lannan, Algonquin and Lakeshore Catholic District School Board
- Debbie Lawlor, Ottawa-Carleton Catholic District School Board
- Ron Lopez, District School Board of Niagara
- Jayne McCullough, Thames Valley District School Board
- Sophie O'Brien, Toronto District School Board
- Barb O'Connor, Halton Catholic District School Board
- Ivan Saari, Renfrew County District School Board
- Mike Sheahan, Niagara Catholic District School Board
- Connie Smart, The ACT Foundation
- Debbie Sprentz, Hamilton-Wentworth District School Board
- Bob Thomas, Ottawa-Carleton Catholic District School Board
- Lisa Verge, Catholic District School Board of Eastern Ontario

## Teacher Reviewers

- Sheila Allen, Havergal College, Conference of Independent Schools
- Jennifer Aziz, Lincoln M Alexander Secondary School, Peel District School Board
- Lorna Bradley, Bell High School, Ottawa-Carleton District School Board
- Bruce Briard, L'Amoreaux Collegiate Institute, Toronto District School Board
- Sarah Bruce, Havergal College, Conference of Independent Schools
- Jeff Bumstead, Laurelwood Public School, Waterloo Region District School Board (former Provincial Consultant, Health & Physical Education)
- Carolyn Cameron, Peterborough Collegiate and Vocational School, Kawartha Pine Ridge District School Board
- Catherine Casey, Vice-Principal, Sir William Mulock Secondary School, York Region District School Board
- Jane Clark, Gananoque Secondary School, Upper Canada District School Board
- David Clipper, Huron Heights Secondary School, York Region District School Board

**Healthy Active Living**

- Dean Crites, McKinnon Park Secondary School, Grand Erie District School Board
- Jen Crites, Brantford Collegiate Institute and Vocational School, Grand Erie District School Board
- Chris Deighan, Cardinal Carter Secondary School, York Catholic District School Board
- Danielle Dutchak, Robert Bateman High School, Halton District School Board
- Andrew Fair, Don Mills Collegiate Institute, Toronto District School Board
- Sofia Fox, Westmount Secondary School, Hamilton-Wentworth District School Board
- Steve Friesen, St James Catholic School, Wellington Catholic District School Board
- Karen Gannon, Atikokan High School, Rainy River District School Board
- Elizabeth Gibson, Cobourg District Collegiate Institute West, Kawartha Pine Ridge District School Board
- Peter Glaab, St James Catholic School, Wellington Catholic District School Board
- Derek Graham, Westdale Secondary School, Hamilton-Wentworth District School Board
- Rob Greco, East York Collegiate Institute, Toronto District School Board
- Jason Henderson, Gananoque Secondary School, Upper Canada District School Board
- Dave Inglis, H B Beal Secondary School, Thames Valley District School Board
- Ellen Irving, Iroquois Ridge High School, Halton District School Board
- Jeff Kennedy, Great Lakes Christian College, Unaffiliated Schools
- Bill King, Sacred Heart High School–Walkerton, Bruce-Grey Catholic District School Board
- Angeline Lacasse, Colonel By Secondary School, Ottawa-Carleton District School Board
- Pat Lacasse, Colonel By Secondary School, Ottawa-Carleton District School Board
- Andrew Macallum, Cameron Heights Collegiate Institute, Waterloo Region District School Board
- Dan McFadden, Earl Haig Secondary School, Toronto District School Board
- Tim McAlpine, Lindsay Collegiate and Vocational Institute, Trillium Lakelands District School Board
- John Morelli, Father Michael McGivney Catholic Academy High School, York Catholic District School Board
- Jamie Nunn, Vice-Principal, Westmount Secondary School, Hamilton-Wentworth District School Board
- Doug Osborne, Parry Sound High School, Near North District School Board
- Rob Pacas, Birchmount Park Collegiate Institute, Toronto District School Board
- Bev Palen, Wexford Collegiate Institute, Toronto District School Board
- Kim Parkes, Westdale Secondary School, Hamilton-Wentworth District School Board

- Kari Platman, Havergal College, Conference of Independent Schools
- Kim Potter, Streetsville Secondary School, Peel District School Board
- Jennifer Powles, Trinity College School, Conference of Independent Schools
- Tonya Reesor, Resurrection Catholic Secondary School, Waterloo Catholic District School Board
- Dale Roberts, Elmira District Secondary School, Waterloo Region District School Board
- Randy Ruttan, Principal, Gananoque Secondary School, Upper Canada District School Board
- Cindy Seligman, Middlefield Collegiate Institute, York Region District School Board
- Judy Selinger, Geraldton Composite High School, Superior-Greenstone District School Board
- Paul Solarski, Brebeuf High School, Toronto Catholic District School Board
- John Spicer, St Theresa of Lisieux Catholic High School, York Catholic District School Board
- Myra Stephen, Vice-Principal, St. Andrew's Junior High School, Toronto District School Board (former Provincial Consultant, Health & Physical Education)
- Tracy Streutker, College Avenue Secondary School, Thames Valley District School Board
- Carolyn Temertzoglou, Havergal College, Conference of Independent Schools/Ontario Institute for Studies in Education (OISE), University of Toronto
- Lorna Tremonti, Dryden High School, Keewatin-Patricia District School Board
- Michele Van Bargen, Strathroy District Collegiate Institute, Thames Valley District School Board
- Martha Wenn, Huron Heights Secondary School, York Region District School Board (former Health & Physical Education consultant to the Waterloo Region District School Board)
- Bessie Zaravinos, Pine Ridge Secondary School, Durham District School Board

## Safety Reviewers

- Bob Soroko, Ophea Safety Consultant, Health & Physical Education
- Dr. Stuart McGill, Faculty of Kinesiology, University of Waterloo

## Literacy Reviewers

- Sandy Haliburton, York Region District School Board
- Joanne Walsh, Iroquois Ridge High School, Halton District School Board

## Medical/Science Reviewers

- Dr. Brian Roy, Department of Physical Education & Kinesiology, Brock University
- Dr. Dee Ballyk, Faculty of Medicine, University of Toronto
- Dr. Tim Rindlisbacher, Sports Medicine Physician/Cleveland Clinic, Canada

**Keep Fit, Stay Healthy, Have Fun**

# Table of Contents

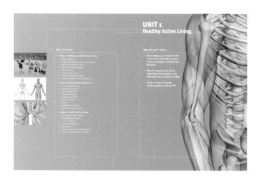

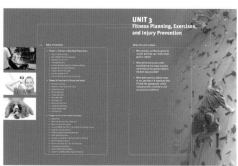

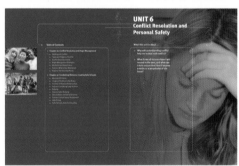

# Introduction

**I**t is no secret. Students who are physically active are healthier ... and they have more fun. They perform better academically, they make better decisions, and they feel better about themselves.

That's exactly why you should take Health and Physical Education throughout high school.

## Your "Health and Phys-Ed" Book

The book you are holding is your "Health and Phys-Ed" book. There is no resource quite like it, anywhere. In reality, it is three books in one:

> ➢ the first third of this book (Units 1–3) will help you *keep fit*,
>
> ➢ the second third (Units 4–7) will help you *stay healthy*, and
>
> ➢ the final third (Unit 8) will encourage you to *have fun*.

Health and Physical Education may be the most important course you will take in high school. You will assess your current fitness level and learn how to design a personal fitness program. In this course, you will learn about sexuality, substance use and abuse, conflict resolution, and healthy eating. You will also learn how to participate in a variety of sports and physical activities that you can pursue for a lifetime.

Three for one—what could be better than that?

*Healthy Active Living* is your book. We hope you will enjoy it and that you will return to it often.

Meanwhile, *keep fit, stay healthy, and have fun being active*!

**Ted Temertzoglou**
*Birchmount Park Collegiate Institute*
*Toronto District School Board*

*Take care of your body with steadfast fidelity. The soul must see through these eyes alone, and if they are dim, the whole world is clouded.*

**Johann Wolfgang von Goethe**

German poet, novelist, playwright, and natural philosopher

**Healthy Active Living**

# Acknowledgements

The creation of this book was a team effort, but I would like first to thank Keith Thompson. Without his passion for creating quality resources for our students, this textbook would not have been possible. Further thanks to Faye Thompson for her constant support, encouragement, and friendship.

A special thanks goes to the editorial team for their tireless efforts at making this resource better. Thanks to Elizabeth Phinney and Paul Challen, who helped with the early stages, and especially to Managing Editor Jennie Worden and Katy Harrison, Crystal J. Hall, Rachel Stuckey, and Megan Burns. A special thanks also goes to our graphic designer Tibor Choleva for his artistic abilities and to Bart Vallecoccia for his outstanding anatomical illustrations. Additional thanks go to Tanya Winter for taking so many great pictures of our students, and to the staff at Colborne Communications.

We are especially grateful to the Institute for Catholic Education for their cooperation and always constructive involvement with us. In particular, thanks are due to Sister Joan Cronin and Sharron McKeever who always made time for us when we needed to consult with them. This resource is far better as a result of their involvement, and we sincerely hope that it meets their high expectations.

I would also like to thank the following individuals for the helping hand they gave me: Jane Fjeld and Sharon Labonte-Jacques, Centre for Addiction and Mental Health; Pauline Poon, Canadian Health Network; Dr. James Mandigo, Brock University; Greg Schell, Toronto Maple Leafs Youth Hockey Development Program; Sherry Doiron, Field Hockey Canada; Jennifer Bolton, Canadian Curling Association; Joanne Shulist, Sexuality reviewer; Kyle Hunter, Badminton Canada; Ramesh Jagoo, Canadian Cricket Association; Stan Tzogas, head coach of Canada's 2004 Olympic Greco Roman Wrestling Team; Karen Hume (Principal), Peter Paputsis (Vice-Principal), Michael Perovic, and Tom McDonell at East York Collegiate Institute; Nick Rowe, Toronto District School Board; Georgia Gallagher (Principal), Bill Mackay, and Ronda Sinclair (Office Administrator) at Birchmount Park Collegiate; Michael Dwyer, Westwood Middle School; Neil Dalgarno, Pope John Paul II; John Renzetti, Victoria Park Collegiate Institute; Richard Bass, Emery Collegiate Institute; Deb Townsley, North Middlesex District High School; Mira Wong and Roger Bernardes, York Mills Collegiate Institute; Tom Lazarou (Principal), Sir Oliver Mowat Collegiate Institute; Jim Spyropoulos, (Principal) Newtonbrook Secondary School; Jim Veltman, Agincourt Collegiate Institute; Carter Livingstone, West Hill Collegiate Institute; Diane Reed, Maplewood High School; Jan Green, Sir William Osler High School; Robert Lee, West Hill Secondary School; Rasa Augaitis, St Mary's Catholic Secondary School, Ultimate Frisbee reviewer; Dave Holt, Toronto District School Board (retired), Badminton reviewer; Shanna Davy, Gymnastics reviewer; Randy Ruttan, Enzo Rocca (in memory), Gary Reilly, Don Hibbert, Greg Hughes, Terence Green, John Bratina, Casey Zaph, Ron Whiteside, mentors and former colleagues at East York Collegiate Institute; and to all my students for trusting me to be their teacher.

Last, but not least by any means, I wish to express my gratitude to my wife Carolyn, as well as to Rebecca and Zachary whom I hope one day will consider this resource to be a trusted friend.

# Literacy Skills

Outlined in the next few pages are some proven strategies to help you become better at reading, writing, and studying. Remember, if you continue to practise, you are certain to improve. Improving on these basic skills will serve you a lifetime.

## Read for Better Results

As the old saying goes, "Those who don't read are no better off than those who can't read." Try following these strategies to help you become a better reader:

> **Before you read.** Be an active reader. Before you read an article or a book, ask yourself questions such as the following: What do I know about the topic? What do I need to know about the topic? Can I predict what the text is trying to say to me? This will put you in the right frame of mind and allow you to get the most out of your reading.

> **As you read.** Active reading does not stop there. As you read, ask yourself more questions to ensure you know what the writer is trying to say: Does the information connect to what I already know? Work through tricky parts as you read—pause and think about what you are reading and take a closer look at what the writer is trying to say. Consult a dictionary if you run into unfamiliar words. There is no point in just going through the motions of reading. Be sure you understand what you read. Visualize what you read by creating a mental picture of it. Make connections between what you read and other sources, such as other books, past experiences, movies, or newspaper articles. Sometimes what you are reading may not be clearly written. This will take even more effort. Take notes and use visual organizers (see page xv), symbols, or colour-coded markings to record what you have learned.

> **After you read.** It's not over yet. After you read, ask yourself more questions: What was the most important part or main message? What clues or features helped me understand more about what I've read (graphics, images, clear definitions)? After you read, you may have additional questions about what you have read. If you do, write them down in your notebook. You can always ask your classmates or raise them in class, which will help you get more out of your reading.

Where you read can be just as important as how you read. Be sure to choose a quiet spot that is both comfortable and free of distractions. If you have a great deal to read and are feeling overwhelmed, try breaking it up into manageable parts and taking quick breaks between sections to help you maintain your focus.

## Better Presentations

Having good communication skills is critical to getting across your ideas.

Below is a list of strategies to help boost your presentation skills.

### Listening and Speaking

- Do not jump to conclusions—keep an open mind.
- Let people finish what they are saying before adding your ideas.
- Respond with a question to clarify what was asked.
- Avoid sarcasm and put-downs.

### Presentation Skills

- Know your subject.
- Have a beginning, middle, and end.
- Repeat and rephrase key messages.
- Use visual aids where possible.
- Rehearse your delivery.
- Prepare for questions you might be asked.

Like most things, developing good presentation skills requires practice. Practise often, keep smiling, and above all have fun.

## Write for Better Results

Although it might sound obvious, the best way to learn how to write well is to write often. Of course, reading on a regular basis also helps, especially if what you read is engaging and well written.

To help you organize your writing, you can use this well-known writing process as your guide:

➤ **Generate your ideas.** In point form, jot down everything you know about the topic.

➤ **Develop your ideas.** Use other resources such as reliable Web sites or textbooks, or conduct interviews with experts.

➤ **Organize your ideas.** Be sure your introduction and conclusion are clear. Stay on topic and choose words that suit the audience.

➤ **Revise your work.** Make sure your point of view is clear. Check that your spelling, punctuation, and grammar are correct.

Becoming a better reader and writer will inevitably help you become more "marketable" in the future. No matter what you decide to do in your life, having good literacy skills will serve you well.

Study in a quiet area that is free of distractions.

## Skimming and Scanning
### Read More

**B**efore you read (and even after you read), it may be helpful to practise a little skimming and scanning.

Experienced readers skim and scan all the time. Here's how it is done:

- **Skimming** is a technique used to get the main idea of a paragraph, page, or chapter as quickly as possible.
  To skim effectively, you can read the first and last sentence of the paragraphs, look at the pictures, graphs, or diagrams, and read the captions to get the main ideas.

- **Scanning** involves moving your eyes down a page to find one specific detail (such as facts, dates, names, or key terms) quickly.
  To scan effectively, try to predict where you might be able to find the information you are seeking. It might be in the glossary, index, or in a box or sidebar separate from the text. Also, you can focus on headings, diagrams, sidebars, or bolded words to guide you.

### To Read or Not to Read—That is *Not* the Question

Skimming and scanning are not substitutes for actual reading. They are techniques to help you focus your time and effort. They are particularly useful when there is a great deal of information to cover.

We live in an information age, and there are no quick substitutes for reading. Skimming and scanning are simply ways to help you keep ahead of the game.

## Studying for Success

**M**any of the concepts taught in health and physical education can't be learned in one class, let alone overnight. As with any subject you take in school, your understanding depends on how hard you study and practise the skills or concepts taught.

In health and physical education classes, you need to study many different things: from learning the proper steps of an overhand serve in volleyball, to understanding how to eat healthily, to learning the various stages in designing a personal fitness profile. Developing good study habits, such as the ones outlined below, can help you with your learning.

### Smart Studying

When you sit down to get some serious studying done, you should do it in a quiet environment. Any quiet area at home or at school will do, as long as you are free of distractions, such as television, phone calls, friends, or siblings.

Once you have found a quiet area, establishing a study routine is important. Follow these steps to get started:

➤ Keep your study area organized, with all your files, books, and magazines stored in a place that is easily accessible.

➤ Establish a work area that includes all the tools that you need, such as books, workbooks, and writing materials.

➤ Make sure you have a desk that is big enough to write on and hold a computer (if needed). Also, make sure your chair is comfortable.

➤ Do all your readings well before class time. This will help you stay informed and ahead of the class.

➤ Use graphic organizers such as concept maps, placemats, or Venn diagrams (described on the next page).

➤ Once you have learned a concept or skill, teach it to a friend or classmate. One of the best ways to gain a deeper understanding of something is to teach it.

➤ Throughout the course, mark terms or ideas that you think are important with sticky notes or highlighters. That way, when it comes time to review, all the main ideas will be easier to find.

➤ Make sure you have time set aside each day for studying so you don't leave it until the last minute.

Your success in any class depends on how hard you work and how much you study. Using these "Smart Studying" tips will help you start on your way to developing good learning habits for life.

Being in the right frame of mind can help you get more out of reading.

## Organize Your Thoughts Graphically

"Graphic organizers" are tools that can help us organize our ideas. There are many kinds of graphic organizers. Let's look at these two types to see how you can use them:

➢ **Venn diagrams.** These are used to contrast and compare two or more ideas or concepts. They are made up of two or more circles that overlap, with the commonalities of the comparison placed in the middle and the differences placed in the appropriate circles.

➢ **Concept maps.** These are used for brainstorming or recording vital bits of information that you read. They are a series of shapes, clouds, or squares where the main idea or topic is placed in the top shape. All related ideas or concepts are connected to the main topic, and to each other, by arrows or lines.

To the side and below you will find examples of each. Give them a try yourself. There are plenty of other ways to visually organize ideas, so if there's another method that works for you, by all means use it.

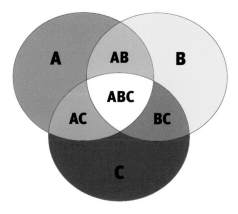

Venn diagrams are used to contrast and compare two or more ideas or concepts.

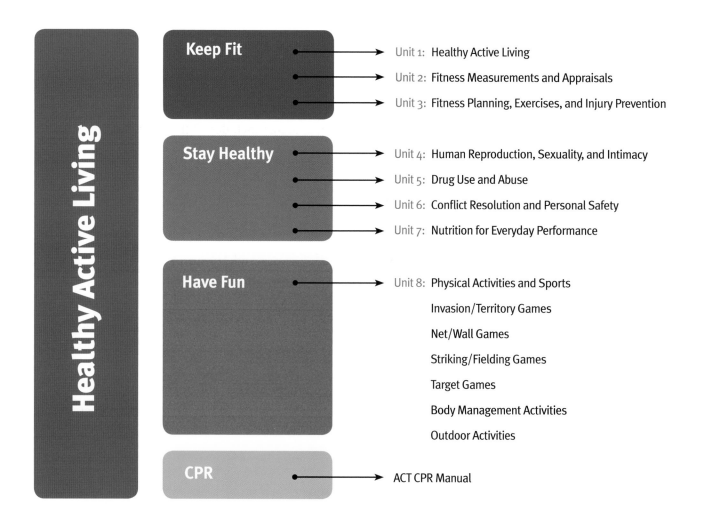

**Keep Fit**
Unit 1: Healthy Active Living
Unit 2: Fitness Measurements and Appraisals
Unit 3: Fitness Planning, Exercises, and Injury Prevention

**Stay Healthy**
Unit 4: Human Reproduction, Sexuality, and Intimacy
Unit 5: Drug Use and Abuse
Unit 6: Conflict Resolution and Personal Safety
Unit 7: Nutrition for Everyday Performance

**Have Fun**
Unit 8: Physical Activities and Sports
Invasion/Territory Games
Net/Wall Games
Striking/Fielding Games
Target Games
Body Management Activities
Outdoor Activities

**CPR**
ACT CPR Manual

Creating a concept map is a good way to sketch out the main ideas of something that you read.

# Using the World Wide Web

**T**hanks to the Internet, it is now easier than it has ever been to get information on any range of health topics. The problem is that too many people believe that if it is on the Internet, it must be true. This is not always the case.

One great site for Canadians is the **Health Canada**.

## What Health Canada Has to Offer

**Health Canada** is the department of the federal government that is responsible for national public health. The home page for Health Canada (www.healthcanada.ca) is a good bilingual resource for Canadians that offers lots of up-to-date information on a variety of health issues that affect Canadians.

From the Health Canada site, you can also link to numerous other Canadian health resources like the Public Healthy Agency of Canada, and national and provincial/territorial non-profit organizations, as well as universities, hospitals, libraries, and community organizations.

**Best of all, it is 100 percent Canadian!**

## Credible, Practical Information

Health Canada's goal is to improve the life of all Canadians by improving the longevity of Canadians as well as improving the lifestyles of Canadians and their use of public healthcare.

Health Canada offers Canadians information on a number of topics including the following health issues:

➢ Consumer Product Safety

➢ Diseases and Conditions

➢ Drugs and Health Products

➢ Emergencies and Disasters

➢ Environmental and Workplace Health

➢ First Nations and Inuit Health

➢ Food and Nutrition

➢ Health Care System

➢ Healthy Living

➢ Science and Research

Check it out at: **www.healthcanada.ca**

---

## Health Canada's Goal

**A**ccording to their mission and vision, Health Canada's goal is for Canada to be among the countries with the healthiest people in the world.

In order to achieve this goal, Health Canada:

- Relies on high-quality scientific research as the basis for their work

- Conducts ongoing consultations with Canadians to determine how to best meet their long-term health care needs

- Communicates information about disease prevention to protect Canadians from avoidable risks

- Encourages Canadians to take an active role in their health, such as increasing their level of physical activity and eating well

View the page in English or French

For information on a variety of health topics, search Health Canada or look in the A-Z index

Drop down menus to help you find the information you are looking for:

- "I'm looking for" leads you to coomonly requested information
- "Get Involved!" leads to public involvement opportunities
- "Partner Sites" links to other health-related sites run by the federal government

Health information by topic

Featured health topics

The "Explore" Menu provides quick links to the A–Z index, the site map and health topics sorted by demographic

Health topics in the news

Quick Links to some of the most visited sections on the site

Highlights of items posted recently on the site

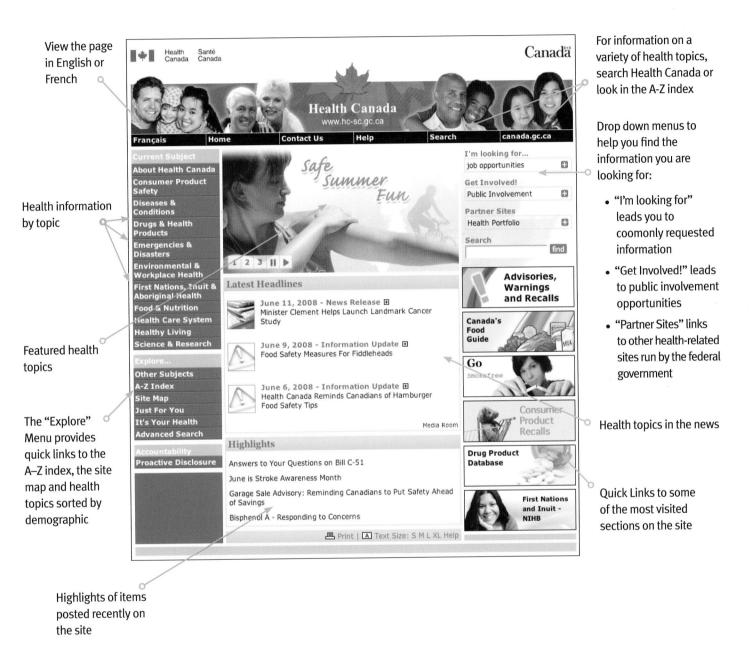

In the past Canadians could also get health information on the internet through the Canadian Health Network (CHN). The CHN has now been consolidated with the Public Heath Agency of Canada, a branch of Health Canada.

**www.healthcanada.ca**

Source: (Health Canada Webpage), Health Canada, Reproduced with the permission of the Minister of Public Works and Government Services Canada, 2008.

**Keep Fit, Stay Healthy, Have Fun**

# Decision-Making Skills

## See, Judge, Act, and Evaluate

**T**his way of making decisions gets you to think over the steps involved in making choices very carefully. The emphasis is on helping you improve your decision-making skills for the long run.

The key components are:

- **See.** Recognize the issues involved and ask how you and others might be affected by the decision. Determine if the decision is in agreement with your own moral code (religious or ethical beliefs).

- **Judge.** Analyze the options and alternatives, and the consequences of each. Consider which options would be thoughtful and considerate ones and call upon your conscience (your sense of right and wrong).

- **Act.** Decide to do what a kind and respectful person would do, and ask for guidance (divine, spiritual, parental) in putting these decisions into action. Divide your decision into small steps and then carry out your plan, one step at a time.

- **Evaluate.** Assess how your decision worked out, identify what effects your decision has on your life or on those around you, ask yourself what you learned, and how you feel about your decision.

The ability to make good decisions separates leaders from followers. During your high school years, you are confronted with some pretty important decisions, and how you deal with them can change the course of your life. Therefore, it is important to learn how to make decisions that are beneficial to you and that don't violate the law or put your family, friends, or others in difficult positions.

Making decisions does not have to be a random, disorganized process. There are several proven methods of arriving at sound decisions, which you can use whenever you need to determine the best option in a given situation. Two of the most commonly used models are "See, Judge, Act, and Evaluate," which appears in the sidebar on this page, and the "IDEAL" method, described on the next page.

Next time you are stuck in a situation and don't know what to do, try them out. If they don't work the first time, try them again.

Throughout this textbook, you will be introduced to many topics that will require you to make informed decisions based on the choices that are available to you. Refer to the facing page to see the IDEAL model in action.

After all, as the old saying goes, "If you don't decide for yourself, it's likely someone else will decide for you."

The IDEAL method of arriving at decisions is particularly effective when you're faced with a difficult problem or situation. It can be used in many different circumstances to help you sort through your options, prioritize them, and then make the best possible decision.

The key components of the IDEAL method are as follows:

I    Identify the problem

D   Discuss options

E    Evaluate options; prioritize concerns

A   Act on the best choice

L    Learn from the experience

Here is how the IDEAL method might play out if, for example, you're trying to decide whether you should go to a late-night party with an older group of friends:

### I—Identify the problem

My friends want me to go, and there will probably be some cool older kids, but I'm sure there will be alcohol and drugs.

I want to go because it will be cool to hang out with these older students, but if my parents ever found out, they would definitely be angry about it and I would get into trouble.

Well, the problem seems to be that going to the party means I will have to lie to my parents, which is wrong, and I could get in trouble for it. It might also cause other problems, like I might have trouble getting up early the next morning if I stay up too late.

### D—Discuss options

I could go to the party and not tell my parents.

I could stay home.

I could try to negotiate with my parents. Maybe they will let me go if I promise to act responsibly at the party and if I promise to be home by a certain time.

### E—Evaluate options, prioritize concerns

Lying to my parents is not a good thing to do.

Staying at home will make my parents happy, but I will end up sitting at home doing nothing.

Do I want to go to this party because I'm hoping to become friends with these people, or is it a way for me to fool myself into thinking I'm cool?

### A—Act on the best choice

It's more important in the long run to have a good relationship with my parents. Lying to them so I can brag to my friends that I went to a party with older students is not worth it. Knowing that my parents trust me is important.

### L—Learn from the experience

Sometimes decisions are difficult. Making the right decision might feel like I gave something up, but it showed me that I am a strong person who does what is right.

Besides, there will always be another party.

## Table of Contents

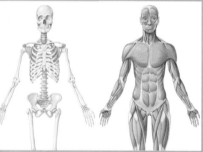
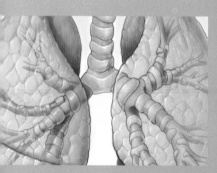

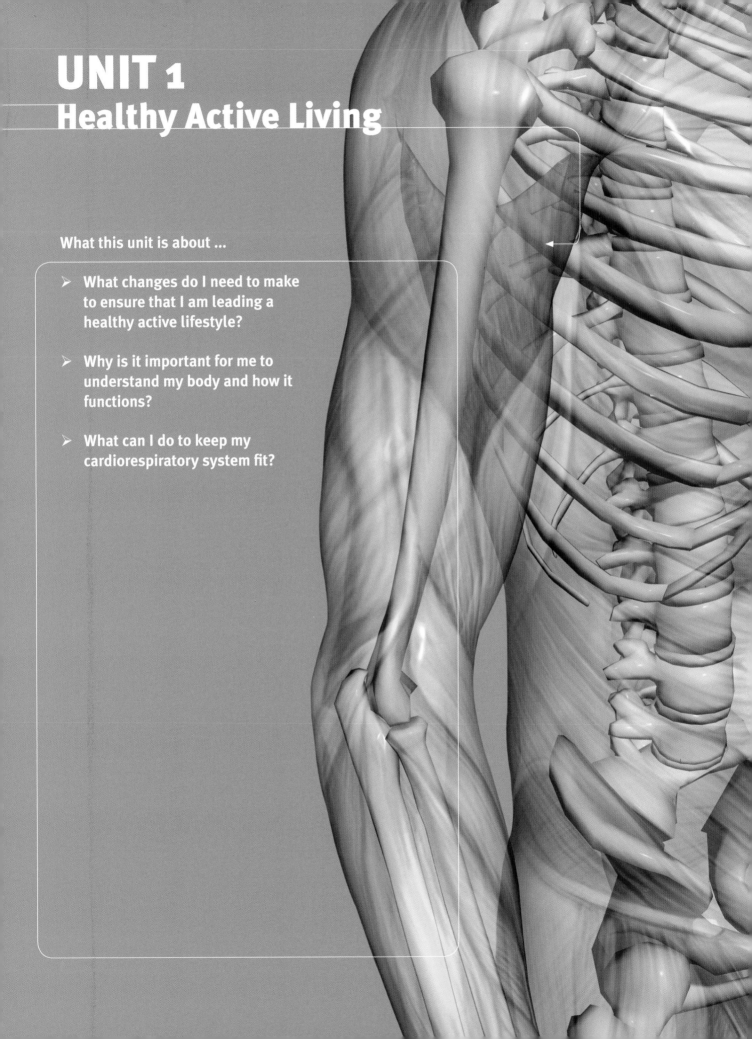

# UNIT 1
## Healthy Active Living

**What this unit is about ...**

➢ **What changes do I need to make to ensure that I am leading a healthy active lifestyle?**

➢ **Why is it important for me to understand my body and how it functions?**

➢ **What can I do to keep my cardiorespiratory system fit?**

# 1

# Wellness and Healthy Active Living

**I**n this book, you will learn about healthy active living—about making important choices here and now that will improve the way your body and mind work for the rest of your life. Few things can be as important as this.

**Healthy active living** means not simply thinking about your health some of the time, but actively doing something about it all the time. It also means learning how to develop healthy relationships, dealing with stress and difficult situations, and helping to improve not only yourself but also your community. In other words, heathy active living is not for the faint of heart—it requires effort.

This chapter looks at the dimensions of healthy active living and how you can begin to take steps now towards a lifelong commitment to a healthy active lifestyle.

## Chapter Objectives

In this chapter, you will:

➢ Explore the "wellness–awareness continuum" as a way of thinking about your own lifelong health

➢ Examine the physical, mental, social, and spiritual dimensions of a "healthy active lifestyle"

➢ Examine the growing problem of obesity in our society and what can be done about it

➢ Distinguish between health-related and skill-related fitness and understand the benefits of each

➢ Investigate the role of the federal and provincial governments in helping to improve the health of Canadians

➢ Learn about the role of the Canadian Physical Activity, Fitness & Lifestyle Approach (CPAFLA) in assessing the overall fitness of Canadians

➢ Reflect on the importance of health and physical education (H&PE) classes in our schools

> *I have been impressed with the urgency of doing. Knowing is not enough; we must apply. Being willing is not enough; we must do.*

**Leonardo da Vinci**

Italian Renaissance painter, architect, inventor, and musician

## Key Terms

➢ healthy active living
➢ wellness
➢ wellness–awareness continuum
➢ healthy lifestyle
➢ overweight
➢ obesity
➢ fitness
➢ health-related fitness
➢ skill-related fitness
➢ Medicare
➢ Canadian Physical Activity Fitness & Lifestyle Approach (CPAFLA)
➢ Health Benefit Zones

# What Is Wellness?

In general, **wellness** means being in "a state of good health." However, there is much more to it than that. Wellness is not for the short term— it is a commitment to a way of living.

Wellness requires that you be:

➢ **Health conscious.** You must be aware of the overall state of your health and what you need to do to improve it.

➢ **Health active.** You must actually do something about your health, not just talk about it—wellness doesn't just "happen."

➢ **Health wise.** You must be aware of the areas that you need to improve (such as diet, exercise, and goal setting).

➢ **Health committed.** You must be prepared to "stay fit, keep healthy, and have fun" for the rest of your life.

The **wellness–awareness continuum** is a way of measuring your attentiveness to your wellness and level of activity. What stage are you at now? Where would you like to be by the end of the current school year? What about the end of your high school career, and beyond?

Having a support system that includes good friends can help you achieve a sense of wellness.

## The Wellness–Awareness Continuum
### Keeping Healthy and Active

**Conscious**
You must be aware of the overall state of your health and what you need to do to improve it.

**Active**
You must actually do something about your health, not just talk about it.

**Wise**
You must be aware of the areas that you need to improve.

**Committed**
You must be prepared to "keep fit, stay healthy, and have fun" for the rest of your life.

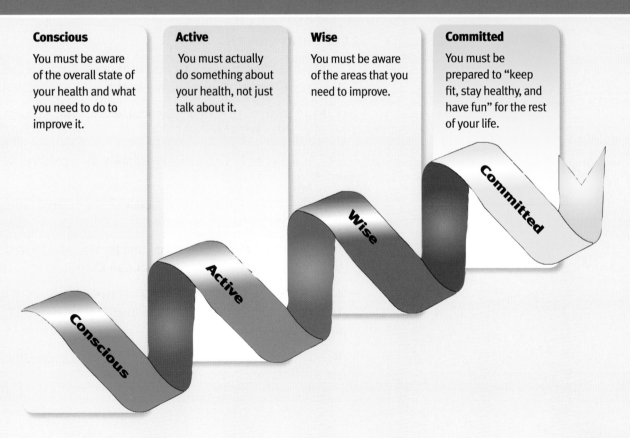

# What Is Healthy Active Living?

Healthy living means making choices to improve your health and minimize controllable illnesses and diseases. Active living is doing physical activities in order to improve your fitness level. The two go together. Choosing a healthy active lifestyle will enhance all aspects of what we generally call "health" or "wellness."

## Four Components of Healthy Active Living

There are four dimensions to healthy active living, and they are all closely interconnected. Moreover, each of them is under your own control.

You can consider yourself to have a **healthy lifestyle** if you have good physical, mental, social, and spiritual health.

1. Good **physical health** is a result of all your body's important functions working well together. A person in good physical health can more easily:

   ➢ fight off disease;
   ➢ recover from illness; and
   ➢ perform daily routines without feeling tired.

2. Good **mental health** is a result of positive feelings about yourself and about others. Your mental health can influence your decisions. A person in good mental health can more easily:

   ➢ deal with stress;
   ➢ cope with change; and
   ➢ maintain a positive outlook on life.

3. Good **social health** is a result of your interactions with others and of coping well with social situations. Social health can be built through friendships, participation in community groups, and volunteer work. A person in good social health can more easily:

   ➢ feel close and connected to other people;
   ➢ understand his or her own self-worth; and
   ➢ cope with life's ups and downs.

4. Good **spiritual health** gives peace of mind. Spirituality can be gained and expressed in the way you play a musical instrument, dance, work with art materials, or through religion. It can also be apparent through reaching out to help others in ways that restore their dignity and self-worth. Good spiritual health can:

   ➢ give your life a purpose;
   ➢ provide you with stress relief; and
   ➢ help you develop support systems.

Focusing on each of these dimensions, and continually striving to improve in each area, is one of the keys to a long and happy life.

---

## Preparing for Everyday Life

The benefits of healthy active living extend to many aspects of your life, including:

- Increased self-confidence
- Increased energy
- Increased concentration
- Improved study habits
- Better marks in school
- Easier weight management
- More intense participation in sports, now and in the future
- Improved sense of well-being
- Improved sleeping habits
- Healthier food choices
- Stronger relationships with others
- Increased enjoyment of life
- Better approach to goal setting and achievement
- Increased willingness to try new things
- More enjoyment of leisure time

## Benefits of Healthy Active Living

A healthy, active approach to life brings with it both short-term benefits (benefits you can see and feel right away) and long-term benefits (benefits you will be able to see for many years to come). Both are important:

> **Short-term benefits.** Healthy active living enables you to enjoy each day with more energy for the things you like to do on a daily basis.

> **Long-term benefits.** A healthy active lifestyle also ensures that the body and all its important parts continue to work as effectively as possible. The friendships and skills developed through pursuing such a lifestyle can last a lifetime.

Just remember that a healthy active lifestyle is not something that happens overnight. Nor is it always self-evident how best to pursue a more healthy way of life. For example, with the pressure of completing all your academic courses in high school, you might be uncertain as to the merits of taking health and physical education. Yet, the skills and lessons that you learn in H&PE class will help you lead a healthy active lifestyle for years to come.

A healthy active lifestyle can benefit anyone.

**Physical Health**
- Fight off disease
- Recover from illness
- Perform daily routines without feeling tired

**Social Health**
- Feel connected to people
- Understand your own self worth
- Maintain good support systems
- Cope with life's ups and downs

## Healthy Active Living

**Mental Health**
- Deal with stress
- Cope with change
- Overcome negative feelings
- Maintain a positive outlook on life

**Spiritual Health**
- Give your life a purpose
- Provide you with stress relief
- Help you develop support systems

Maintaining a balance: the components of healthy active living.

# Maintaining a Healthy Weight

Many Canadians, young and old, do not engage in enough regular exercise and pay too little attention to what they eat. As a result, **overweight** and **obesity** have become serious public health issues.

The terms "overweight" and "obese" are often used interchangeably, but it is important to distinguish between the two:

> **Overweight.** Being overweight means having excess body fat for one's size and build—a condition that will lead to health problems. The main way to address an overweight condition is to choose a better diet and to be more physically active.

> **Obesity.** Being obese is more of a "chronic" condition—meaning that one is overweight to the point where it is a danger to one's health. The condition may require action on many fronts, including professional intervention by a physician or other medical professionals.

Of the two conditions, overweight is by far the more prevalent, though both are on the rise in Canada and other industrialized countries. Being overweight does not always lead to obesity, but it does require action before one's health is affected for the worse.

## Health Risks

Carrying excess weight places unnecessary strain on the body. Such people are at increased risk for certain diseases and health problems:

> **Hypertension (high blood pressure).** The heart of an obese person has to work very hard to pump blood and oxygen, and the extra stress can lead to heart disease or stroke.

> **Type II diabetes.** A form of diabetes that usually occurs at an older age, but is now beginning to show up among young adults as a result of poor eating habits and physical inactivity.

> **Osteoarthritis.** Excess weight places stress on the joints, which damages the cartilage and causes pain.

> **Sleep apnea.** A condition that often occurs in obese people, and causes them to stop breathing for short periods during the night, interrupting sleep patterns, and causing fatigue.

> **Cancer.** Obesity increases the chance of developing cancer, including colon, breast, gallbladder, ovarian, and prostate.

Overweight or obese individuals may not only face problems with their physical health, but also with their mental, spiritual, and social health. Obesity can result in feelings of low self-esteem, especially if the individuals feel their identity and self-worth are linked closely to their weight. Obese individuals may also turn to dieting products as a quick way to lose weight—not necessarily for health reasons, but simply so they can feel accepted by others.

## Behind the Statistics

Health scientists have a rough-and-ready way of measuring overweight and obesity across large population groups.

When comparing nations, for example, they generally use "Body Mass Index" (BMI) scores (a simple calculation using height and weight). This is because measures of weight and height are more readily available to the statisticians. According to the statisticians, obesity is a BMI score of 30 or more.

However, while BMI scores may work well when used to compare whole populations (taken in aggregate), they are not always reliable when looking at particular individuals. BMI can be affected by many factors (such as body type, or amount of muscle) and they do not work at all for certain large groups (the young and the old, for example).

So one must always be careful when interpreting BMI results at the individual level.

## Active Living and Healthy Eating

Researchers have identified three main causes of overweight and obesity: (1) insufficient physical activity; (2) excessive food intake; and (3) heredity (our genetic make-up).

Of course, we can't control our genes. We can do something about the first two—how much we exercise and what we eat:

Choose healthy snacks such as fresh fruits or vegetables .

➤ **Active living.** The first step to prevention is being physically active. This includes participating fully in H&PE classes. The goal of H&PE class is to teach you about fitness through games, activities, and sports and to teach you how to design a healthy active lifestyle plan. Try to spend at least 30 minutes every school day on physical activities, with at least 10 minutes involving vigorous activities.

➤ **Healthy eating.** Choose your fuel wisely. A balanced food plan includes three or more meals per day that target all the food groups. If you find yourself lacking energy during the day, choose healthy snacks such as fresh fruits (bananas, apples, and pears) or fresh vegetables (carrots, celery sticks, and broccoli).

Physical activity is one of the first steps to preventing obesity and achieving good health.

# What Is Fitness?

**Fitness** is achieved by regular exercise, proper diet, and adequate rest. However, your level of fitness may vary over time. Indeed, at any point in time, you may be fit in one respect, but not especially fit in another. For example, you may have good muscular strength but weak cardiorespiratory fitness. You may also decide at different times to work on improving your level of fitness in one area or another.

It is helpful to think of the term "fitness" as having two dimensions. One pertains to overall health; the other focuses more on performance and skill. If you are generally "health fit," then you can probably look forward to a long life—all the important body parts (heart, lungs, muscles, bones) are in good working order and are exercised regularly.

If you are also "performance fit," you are able to call up the skills required for a high level of involvement in a particular sport or some other kind of rigorous physical activity.

## Health-Related Fitness

**Health-related fitness** is generally assessed in five main areas:

1. **Cardiorespiratory fitness** is the ability of the heart and lungs to supply oxygen and energy to the muscles. It is critical because it builds the endurance needed to accomplish day-to-day activities, such as climbing stairs or running for the bus. Some activities that build this aspect of fitness include running, swimming, and dancing.

2. **Muscular strength** is the ability to exert force or lift a heavy weight. We use it on a daily basis, for example, in pushing or pulling a heavy door to open it. Some activities that build strength include ice hockey, football, and resistance training.

3. **Muscular endurance** is the ability of muscles to work over a long period of time, such as hitting a ball over and over again in a long game of tennis. Some activities that build muscular endurance include wrestling, aquatics, cycling, and cross-country skiing.

4. **Flexibility** is the ability of the muscles to stretch. It prevents injuries when the body is pushed beyond its usual limits, such as during a fall while skateboarding. Some activities that build flexibility include martial arts, dance, and yoga.

5. **Body composition** refers to the distribution of muscle and fat throughout the body. A healthy body composition means that the body has enough fat to provide it with energy and enough muscle to perform a variety of activities. Of course, this aspect of fitness focuses on whether one is generally maintaining a healthy weight range, regardless of actual physical appearance.

The chart on the following page is a rough guide to how one or more of these health-related components of fitness are emphasized in various kinds of organized physical activity.

Physical activities that build cardiorespiratory fitness include running, swimming, and dancing.

Muscular strength and endurance is important in wrestling, football, and resistance training.

Activities that increase your flexibility include martial arts, dance, and yoga.

## Health Fit

A rough guide to the main health-related components of fitness emphasized in the sports, games, and activities described in Unit 8.

| | CARDIORESPIRATORY | MUSCULAR STRENGTH | MUSCULAR ENDURANCE | FLEXIBILITY |
|---|:---:|:---:|:---:|:---:|
| **INVASION/TERRITORY GAMES** | | | | |
| Soccer | ✓ | ✓ | ✓ | ✓ |
| Basketball | ✓ | ✓ | ✓ | ✓ |
| Ultimate Frisbee | ✓ | ✓ | ✓ | ✓ |
| Ice hockey | ✓ | ✓ | ✓ | ✓ |
| Field hockey | ✓ | ✓ | ✓ | ✓ |
| Rugby | ✓ | ✓ | ✓ | ✓ |
| Canadian football | ✓ | ✓ | ✓ | ✓ |
| Lacrosse | ✓ | ✓ | ✓ | ✓ |
| **NET/WALL GAMES** | | | | |
| Volleyball | ✓ | | ✓ | ✓ |
| Badminton | ✓ | | ✓ | ✓ |
| Tennis | ✓ | | ✓ | ✓ |
| Table tennis | ✓ | | ✓ | |
| **STRIKING/FIELDING GAMES** | | | | |
| Baseball/softball | | ✓ | ✓ | ✓ |
| Cricket | | ✓ | ✓ | ✓ |
| **TARGET GAMES** | | | | |
| Curling | | | ✓ | ✓ |
| Golf | | | ✓ | ✓ |
| **BODY MANAGEMENT ACTIVITIES** | | | | |
| Track and field | ✓ | ✓ | ✓ | ✓ |
| Wrestling/combatives | ✓ | ✓ | ✓ | ✓ |
| Gymnastics | | ✓ | ✓ | ✓ |
| Aquatics | ✓ | ✓ | ✓ | ✓ |
| Aerobics | ✓ | | ✓ | ✓ |
| Yoga and Pilates | | ✓ | ✓ | ✓ |
| Dance | ✓ | | ✓ | ✓ |
| **OUTDOOR ACTIVITIES** | | | | |
| Orienteering | ✓ | | ✓ | |
| Skiing | ✓ | | ✓ | ✓ |

## Skill-Related Fitness

In the context of physical activity, a skill is the ability to do something efficiently and well. For example, you may be skilful at serving in tennis or doing a jump shot in basketball. If you notice you're improving in a particular sport, it usually means you're improving in several skill areas at once.

Skills are developed over time with practise. Learning how to perform a particular action better also develops patience and discipline. While health-related fitness focuses on "core health" (the heart and lungs, muscular strength and endurance, flexibility, and body composition), **skill-related fitness** usually centres on the following six components:

Snowboarding, dancing, and soccer are some of the sports that require agility.

Balance is crucial in activities such as yoga, skiing, and fencing.

1. **Agility** is the ability to change direction rapidly and accurately. Basketball and hockey players are very agile; their feet go one way, their upper bodies go another and their hands yet another. Activities that need agility include dancing, football, and soccer.

2. **Balance** is the ability to maintain equilibrium when moving or standing still, such as the ability to avoid falling over when playing racquetball or even when just walking a straight line. Activities that build balance include yoga, skiing, and fencing.

3. **Coordination** is the ability to combine balance and agility while moving. Doing two unrelated tasks at the same time, such as running and dribbling a basketball, takes coordination. Sports that build coordination include field hockey, handball, and gymnastics.

4. **Power** is the ability to apply maximum effort in as short a time as possible. For example, the start of a downhill ski race or a roundhouse karate kick need power to get a person or body part moving at maximum speed. Activities that require power include a sprint start in track and field, a basketball lay-up, and a swimming race start.

5. **Reaction time** is the ability to respond to a situation in as short a time as possible. For example, in soccer or hockey, goalies are expected to react to an oncoming ball or puck in fractions of a second. Sports that need quick reaction time include table tennis, badminton, and karate.

6. **Speed** is the ability to cover a short distance as quickly as possible. It is generated by a combination of all the skills listed so far. At a competitive level, speed is obviously the most important skill, such as in a swimming or a cycling race. Sports that require speed include baseball, soccer, and road hockey.

Coordination can be improved by participating in field hockey, badminton, or gymnastics.

The chart on the following page is a rough guide to how one or more of these skill-related components of fitness are emphasized in various kinds of organized physical activity.

## Skill Fit

A rough guide to the main skill-related components of fitness emphasized in the sports, games, and activities described in Unit 8.

| | AGILITY | BALANCE | COORDINATION | POWER | REACTION | SPEED |
|---|---|---|---|---|---|---|
| **INVASION/TERRITORY GAMES** | | | | | | |
| Soccer | ✓ | ✓ | ✓ | ✓ | ✓ | ✓ |
| Basketball | ✓ | ✓ | ✓ | ✓ | ✓ | ✓ |
| Ultimate Frisbee | ✓ | ✓ | ✓ | ✓ | ✓ | ✓ |
| Ice hockey | ✓ | ✓ | ✓ | ✓ | ✓ | ✓ |
| Field hockey | ✓ | ✓ | ✓ | ✓ | ✓ | ✓ |
| Rugby | ✓ | ✓ | ✓ | ✓ | ✓ | ✓ |
| Canadian football | ✓ | ✓ | ✓ | ✓ | ✓ | ✓ |
| Lacrosse | ✓ | ✓ | ✓ | ✓ | ✓ | ✓ |
| **NET/WALL GAMES** | | | | | | |
| Volleyball | ✓ | ✓ | ✓ | ✓ | ✓ | |
| Badminton | ✓ | ✓ | ✓ | ✓ | ✓ | ✓ |
| Tennis | ✓ | ✓ | ✓ | ✓ | ✓ | ✓ |
| Table tennis | ✓ | | ✓ | | ✓ | ✓ |
| **STRIKING/FIELDING GAMES** | | | | | | |
| Baseball/softball | ✓ | ✓ | ✓ | ✓ | ✓ | ✓ |
| Cricket | ✓ | ✓ | ✓ | ✓ | ✓ | ✓ |
| **TARGET GAMES** | | | | | | |
| Curling | | ✓ | ✓ | | | |
| Golf | | ✓ | ✓ | ✓ | | |
| **BODY MANAGEMENT ACTIVITIES** | | | | | | |
| Track and field | ✓ | ✓ | ✓ | ✓ | ✓ | ✓ |
| Wrestling/combatives | ✓ | ✓ | ✓ | ✓ | ✓ | |
| Gymnastics | ✓ | ✓ | ✓ | ✓ | | ✓ |
| Aquatics | | | ✓ | ✓ | ✓ | ✓ |
| Aerobics | | ✓ | ✓ | | | |
| Yoga and Pilates | | ✓ | ✓ | | | |
| Dance | ✓ | ✓ | ✓ | | ✓ | |
| **OUTDOOR ACTIVITIES** | | | | | | |
| Orienteering | | | | | | ✓ |
| Skiing | ✓ | ✓ | ✓ | | ✓ | |

# Health Canada and You

We Canadians are fortunate. The Canadian health care system, known as **Medicare**, guarantees quality medical care to all of us. The fees associated with medical care are paid through the taxes all Canadian citizens pay.

Helping Canadians stay healthy can relieve much of the financial stress on the Medicare system. Therefore, money is also invested by various levels of government in many health programs that emphasize disease and injury prevention. These initiatives include such things as *Canada's Food Guide to Healthy Eating* and *Canada's Physical Activity Guide to Healthy Active Living*.

Pressures on the health care system, such as the rise in cost of treatment and the increase in number of users, are causing debates over the future of Medicare. Some would like to have people start paying for services; others would like the government to divert more tax money towards Medicare and to extend Medicare coverage to dental services and medication.

## The Health Card

The key to the public health care system is the health card (called CareCard in some provinces). Your health card allows you to access the public health care system and acts as a way of keeping track of health care spending. The rules for getting and using a health card vary by province. In general, each province issues a health card to each resident, and the card allows him or her to receive health benefits.

When you go to your doctor, you show your health card and get treated. Your doctor sends his or her fees to the provincial government for payment. If you travel to another province and get sick, you can use your card to get the health care you need there, and the fees are eventually transferred to your home province.

All essential health services are covered under the *Canada Health Act*, but the exact coverage permitted is determined by each province. Each province has its own list of eligible procedures that it will cover. Services that are considered non-essential, such as massage therapy and orthodontics, or dental and eye-care, are usually not covered and require the patient to pay an additional fee.

It is important for all of us to be in good health so as not to tax the system too much. Learning to maintain a healthy lifestyle will help accomplish this goal.

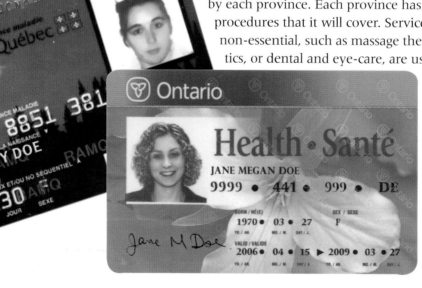

# Assessing the Nation
## Canadian Physical Activity, Fitness & Lifestyle Approach (CPAFLA)

**M**ost of the fitness appraisals you will be reading about in this book are adapted from the **Canadian Physical Activity, Fitness & Lifestyle Approach (CPAFLA)**. The CPAFLA standards for fitness appraisals were developed under the guidance of the Canadian Society for Exercise Physiology (CSEP).

### The Appraisals

The CPAFLA appraisals outline the procedures for fitness assessment for persons aged 15 to 69 emphasizing health benefits of physical activity. They measure physical health by assessing your fitness in the following categories:

- **Blood Pressure and Heart Rate**—how high your blood pressure and heart rate are
- **Body Composition**—how much of your body is made up of fat
- **Aerobic Fitness**—heart and lung capacity
- **Musculoskeletal Fitness**—the strength and endurance of your muscles and bones
- **Back Fitness**—the endurance of your back muscles

Within each category, the various tests have ratings (or "norms") associated with them, so that you can see where you fall.

Many H&PE teachers are certified fitness consultants from CSEP and most will have an excellent understanding of the CPAFLA appraisals.

### Health Benefit Zones

After performing the CPAFLA tests, you can find your own "health rating" for each test or each series of tests. Your rating can then be located on a "Health Benefit Zone" chart. **Health Benefit Zones** provide an indication as to where you stand with respect to fitness standards for your group.

The five zones are:

- **Excellent**—associated with optimal health benefits
- **Very Good**—associated with considerable health benefits
- **Good**—associated with many health benefits
- **Fair**—associated with some health risks
- **Needs Improvement**—associated with considerable health risks

When you perform some of these appraisals, keep in mind that they are only estimates of your current fitness level. Do your part, track and record your results. Later, you can use your results as benchmarks in order to build a personal fitness program that is perfectly suited to your own individual needs. The CPAFLA manual, available from Canadian Society for Exercise Physiology, fully outlines the proper procedures for assessment and counselling and it includes a "Personal Plan for Active Living" booklet. The manual also provides information on certification as a CSEP–Certified Fitness Consultant (CFC).

| HEALTH BENEFIT ZONES FOR FITNESS | | |
|---|---|---|
| **Excellent** | ↑ | Your fitness falls within a range that is generally associated with optimal health benefits. |
| **Very Good** | ↑ | Your fitness falls within a range that is generally associated with considerable health benefits. |
| **Good** | ↑ | Your fitness falls within a range that is generally associated with many health benefits. |
| **Fair** | ↑ | Your fitness falls within a range that is generally associated with some health risk. |
| **Needs Improvement** | ⬆ | Your fitness falls within a range that is generally associated with considerable health risk. |

The large arrow indicates the zone where improvements represent the greatest gains to your health.

**Source:** Reproduced with permission of the Canadian Society for Exercise Physiology.

# Why Take Health and Physical Education?

The H&PE classes you take in school are all about you. Your teacher will want you to learn the names of muscles and try new activities, but the ultimate reason for taking H&PE is to gain knowledge about how to take care of your body and to help you get excited about playing sports and participating in physical activities. Best of all, you do not have to be a great athlete to get a good mark—just work hard and participate fully.

Health and Physical Education classes will:

➤ Help you learn and develop new activity skills

➤ Prepare you to make better decisions about your health now and as you grow older

➤ Improve your physical, mental, social, and spiritual health

➤ Give you a regular opportunity to be active

➤ Prepare you to lead—H&PE students learn how to be educators and leaders as well as participants

Taking H&PE will not only allow you to gain knowledge about how to take care of your body but can also help get you excited about sports.

Active participation is crucial to obtaining the full benefits of H&PE class.

## Choosing to Participate

You can't expect to benefit from, or even enjoy, what you are doing in class unless you go out of your way to actively get involved. If you actively participate each day, the gains will be obvious. It all begins with the right attitude; bringing yours to class each day will surely lead to a positive environment and a high level of achievement.

If you make the choice to participate, here are a few examples of ways to increase your success and enjoyment in class:

➤ **Be on time.** Being on time is an everyday routine for most successful people.

➤ **Dress appropriately for class.** Come to class with running shoes, cotton socks, shorts or sweat pants, a T-shirt or a sweat top. Wear a hat, gloves, track pants, sunscreen, sunglasses, and proper footwear when appropriate. Do not wear your school clothes to your physical education class.

➤ **Play fair.** It is essential to try as hard as you can, keep moving, and encourage your classmates to do the same. Play within the rules laid out by your teacher.

➤ **Play safe.** The gymnasium can be a hazardous place if you aren't careful. Listen to your teacher and follow the simple rules of the game, and the environment you play in will be safer.

➤ **Practise good social skills.** Contribute to positive social interactions. Avoid putting classmates down and using inappropriate language. A positive attitude will lead to a strong sense of well-being and self-worth for both you and your classmates.

➤ **Have fun!** Do not be afraid to try and learn new activities.

## Questions for Study and Review

### Things to Think About and Explore

1. Define "wellness" and explain what is meant by the "wellness–awareness continuum."

2. Give examples of indicators of good "mental," "social," "physical," and "spiritual" health.

3. Identify four health risks that can result from being overweight or obese.

4. Describe what is meant by the terms "healthy living" and "active living."

5. Explain the differences between "health-related fitness" and "skill-related fitness."

6. Describe the roles that the federal and provincial governments play in helping to improve the health of Canadians.

### Things to Do and Practise

7. Recreate the wellness–awareness continuum graph (page 3). Under each heading, write, using a black pen or marker, what you are currently doing to lead a healthy active lifestyle. Over the period of this course, write under each heading, using a red pen or marker, what you have done to improve or maintain your healthy active lifestyle.

8. Create a bulletin board using cut-outs from various magazines showing teenagers leading healthy active lives.

9. Choose a sport or activity from the Health Fit and Skill Fit tables on page 9 and page 11. Try it out either by joining an intramural team in your school, or a recreational facility in your neighbourhood that offers the sport or activity. Keep a journal about your experiences, challenges, improvements, and personal enjoyment.

10. Over the next five days, record in your activity journal the amount of time that you spend on maintaining or improving your overall fitness. Focus on activities outside your normal routine as well as any changes in your diet.

11. Using a pedometer—a device used to count the steps you take—record the number of steps it takes to walk/jog or run one kilometre. Keep track of your step count during H&PE classes during the term. After the school term is over, compute how many kilometres you covered in your H&PE classes during the term.

12. Find people with a healthy active lifestyle that you admire and interview them about how they stay motivated, who has helped them to achieve their fitness goals, and what advice they can offer on how to stay active.

### WWWeblinks

Name ➤ Health Canada

URL ➤ www.healthcanada.ca

The official site for Health Canada, the federal department which aims to help Canadians maintain and improve their health.

Name ➤ Pause to Play

URL ➤ www.pausetoplay.ca

Developed by the Government of Ontario, this website contains information on how to get involved in sports and other activities.

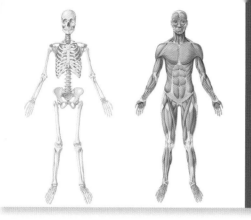

# 2

# Healthy Bones and Muscles

**A** car has a steel frame to protect its vital parts and an engine to give it the power to move. Similarly, our bodies are protected by a frame called a skeleton, which is made up of hundreds of bones, and our muscles to help us move.

If you understand how your body works, you will be in a much better position to look after it and avoid injury.

In this chapter, you will be introduced to the major parts of the skeletal and muscular systems. You will learn what each component does and how to keep them healthy for a lifetime.

## Chapter Objectives

In this chapter, you will:

➤ Distinguish between *anatomy* and *physiology*

➤ Identify the main features of the "anatomical position," the standard reference point used to describe the location and relationship of body parts

➤ Learn about anatomical "planes" and "axes" using the anatomical position

➤ Examine the main functions of the human skeleton

➤ Identify the major bones of the human body and distinguish between the axial and appendicular skeleton

➤ Investigate how muscles work and examine the main components of skeletal muscles

➤ Identify the major skeletal muscles of the human body

➤ Explore the main types of joints and identify the special characteristics of synovial joints

➤ Distinguish the main types of synovial joints in the human body

➤ Identify the terms used to describe the main types of movement at synovial joints

## Key Terms

➤ anatomy/physiology
➤ anatomical position
➤ anatomical axes and planes
➤ axial skeleton/appendicular skeleton
➤ smooth muscle/cardiac muscle/skeletal muscle
➤ muscle contraction
➤ sliding filament theory
➤ neuromuscular junction
➤ joints
➤ muscle pairs

# Anatomy and Physiology

The famous *Gray's Anatomy of the Human Body* was first published in England 150 years ago (in 1858–59). This landmark publication was the first scientific work to describe, in great illustrated detail, the bones, muscles, and internal systems of the human body. Revised editions of this work continue to be published to this day.

## Structure and Function

Of course, great strides have been made in our knowledge since Henry Gray's time. Scientists now know not only what exists (*anatomy*), but how just about everything works as well (*physiology*). The two fields—anatomy and physiology—are closely linked areas of study. The distinction is an important one:

> ➤ **Anatomy** is the branch of science concerned with describing the bodily structure of humans, animals, and other living organisms.

> ➤ **Physiology** is the branch of biology that is concerned with how the various body parts function and work together.

As you read through the early chapters of this text, it may be useful to keep in mind that you will be examining not only the *structure* of such organs as the heart and lungs (their anatomy) but also how each of these organs *functions* (their physiology).

Engaging in different activities throughout the year will help strengthen your bones and muscles.

# The Anatomical Position

Every body of science has its own language and conventions. Anatomy and physiology are no different.

The **anatomical position** is a common starting point from which scientists view, describe, and analyze body parts and body movements. The anatomical position is used to describe the body in the same way a compass (north, south, east, and west) is used to indicate direction and location.

When demonstrating the anatomical position:

➢ The person is standing erect with his or her head, eyes, and toes pointing forward.

➢ The feet are together and the arms are slightly out to the side.

➢ The palms of the hands are facing forward.

From this fixed starting point, you can describe positions and movements in a way that will be understood by everyone.

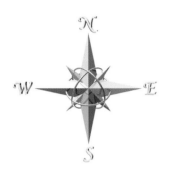

The anatomical position is used to describe the locations of things on your body the way a compass is used to describe the locations of things in geography.

## Describing Positions and Relationships

Here are some of the terms used to describe locations and relationships of body parts, starting from the anatomical position.

### Anterior/Posterior

➢ **Anterior** refers to locations on the front of your body; **posterior** refers to locations on the back of your body. Your rectus abdominis muscle is anterior to your spine.

### Superior/Inferior

➢ **Superior** means above, or towards your head; **inferior** means below, or towards your feet. Your nose is superior to your mouth while your chin is inferior to your mouth.

### Medial/Lateral

➢ Something that is **medial** is closer to an imaginary line, called the midline, that divides your body in equal halves; **lateral** means something is farther from the midline. Your chest muscle is medial and your shoulder muscle is lateral.

### Proximal/Distal

➢ **Proximal** refers to portions of limbs that are closer to your body; **distal** refers to parts and locations further from your body. Your foot is at the distal end of your leg, while your thigh is at the proximal end.

These are the basic terms of anatomy and physiology, and they will come up time and time again as you pursue your health and physical education studies. You should try to use these terms so they become second nature to you.

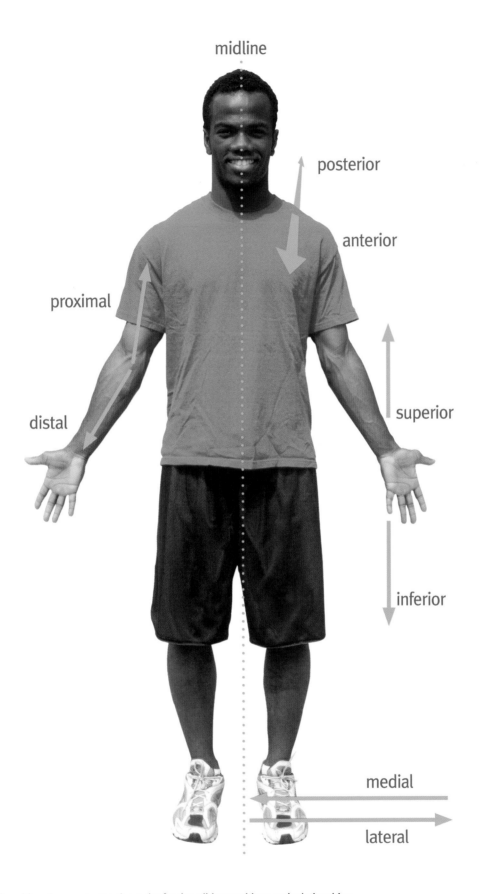

The anatomical position: A common starting point for describing positions and relationships.

# Describing Movement

Starting from the anatomical position, it is also possible to identify anatomical axes and anatomical planes. These are the imaginary lines and flat planes that are used to describe movement.

## Anatomical Axes and Planes

**Anatomical axes** are imaginary lines around which rotation occurs. They skewer the body—horizontally, from back to front, and vertically. The three anatomical axes are:

All forms of human movement can be described using the terms on this page.

> **Horizontal axis (bilateral axis).** This line passes laterally (from side to side) through the body. For example, a whole body rotation around this axis would be a forward or backward somersault.

> **Anteroposterior axis.** This line passes through the body from front to back. For example, a whole body rotation around this axis would produce a cartwheel.

> **Polar axis (vertical axis).** This line passes lengthwise (top to bottom) through the body. An example of a body rotation around this axis would be when a figure skater performs a spin.

**Anatomical planes**, on the other hand, are like sheets of glass placed through the body that show the dimension in which a movement occurs.

Using correct anatomical terms can make describing position and movement much easier.

The three anatomical planes are:

> **Sagittal plane.** This plane divides the body into right and left portions (side to side).

> **Frontal plane (coronal plane).** This plane divides the body into anterior and posterior portions (front to back).

> **Transverse plane (horizontal plane).** This plane divides the body into superior and inferior portions (top to bottom).

## A Rule of Thumb

A good tip to remember is that the axes and planes are always at right angles to each other. Experiment with these terms and you will quickly discover how useful they are in allowing you to describe all forms of human movement.

## The Relationship Between Axes and Planes

| AXIS OF ROTATION | PLANE OF MOVEMENT | EXAMPLE |
|---|---|---|
| Horizontal | Sagittal | Flexing your biceps |
| Polar | Transverse | Figure-skater's spin |
| Anteroposterior | Frontal | Jumping jacks |

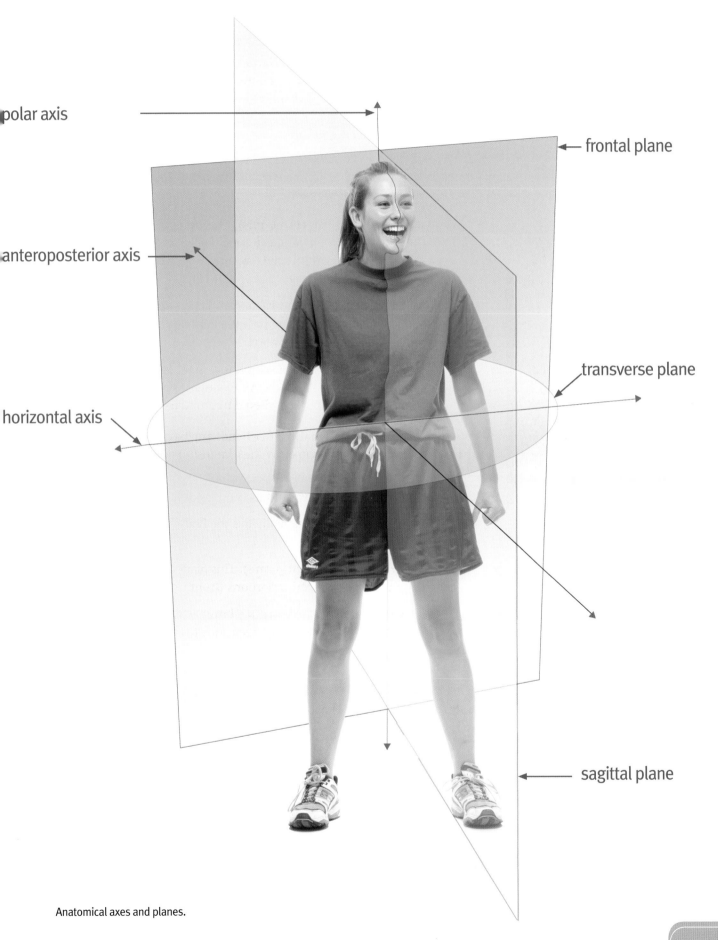

polar axis

frontal plane

anteroposterior axis

transverse plane

horizontal axis

sagittal plane

Anatomical axes and planes.

# The Skeletal System

We are born with more than 300 bones. As we get older, many of these bones join or fuse together to form 206 bones. Our bones account for approximately 14 to 20 percent of our total body weight.

## The Parts of the Skeleton

The skeleton can be divided into two major segments or parts: the axial skeleton and the appendicular skeleton. The illustrations on pages 24 and 25 illustrate these two divisions.

> **Axial skeleton.** The axial skeleton is similar to the frame of a car in that all the major parts are attached and connect to it. It consists of 80 bones which are located in the skull, spinal column, sternum, rib cage, and the sacrum.

> **Appendicular skeleton.** The appendicular skeleton consists of the bones that connect to the axial skeleton, the way doors do on a car's frame. It consists of 126 bones found in the arms, shoulder blades, forearms, hands, pelvic girdle, legs, and feet.

## Types of Bones

Bones come in many shapes and sizes. Below is a breakdown of the types of bones and where they can be found in the body.

❶ **Long bones** are found in the arms and legs. The femur in your upper leg is an example of a long bone.

❷ **Flat bones**, as the name implies, are flat. The individual bones in the roof of your skull are examples of flat bones.

❸ **Irregular bones** include the bones of the vertebrae.

❹ **Sesamoid bones** are small, flat bones wrapped within tendons. The patella (kneecap) is the largest sesamoid bone in the body.

❺ **Short bones** are found in the wrists and ankles. The carpal bones in your wrists are examples of short bones.

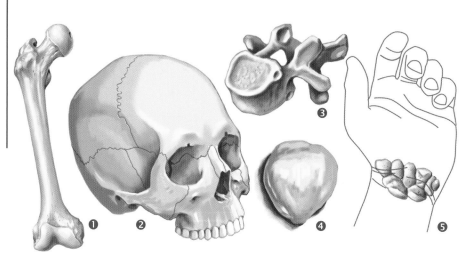

Types of bones.

# The Anatomy of a Long Bone
## Built Tough

**B**ones are very strong. In fact, in a lab test, the tibia bone, located in the lower leg, was able to support 900 kg without breaking.

Examining some of the key components of bones will give us an understanding of the factors that contribute to this strength and durability.

The following is a list of the main structures of bone:

- **Cartilage** is located on both ends of long bones and is referred to as articulating cartilage. It allows smooth movement (articulation) within joints while protecting the ends of bones.

- The **periosteum** is the connective tissue that covers the entire length of the bone. Ligaments and tendons connect to bone through this lining.

- The **diaphysis** is the name given to the shaft of a long bone.

- The **medullary cavity** is found inside the bone shaft and contains bone marrow: red marrow (where blood cells are made) and yellow marrow (which is mostly made of fat cells). Generally, children have a higher concentration of red marrow in their long bones, and as they grow into adulthood, it changes to yellow marrow.

- **Compact bone** is a dense part of the bone, which is responsible for the bone's strength. Compact bone is thickest along the diaphysis.

- **Cancellous, or spongy bone**, has many honeycomb-like spaces which are filled with marrow. Cancellous bone will strengthen with resistance exercise, such as weightlifting.

- The **epiphysis** is located at the end of the diaphysis. The outer surface of the epiphysis articulates (moves) with other bones.

- **Epiphyseal plates**, commonly called "growth plates" are the site of growth. If they are not present, growth has stopped and epiphyseal lines appear. Next time you have an X-ray done on a long bone ask your doctor to see if she or he can show you these plates or lines.

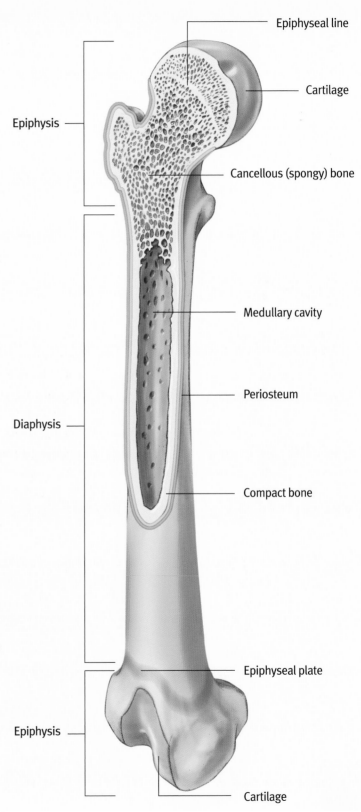

Epiphyseal line

Cartilage

Epiphysis

Cancellous (spongy) bone

Medullary cavity

Periosteum

Diaphysis

Compact bone

Epiphyseal plate

Epiphysis

Cartilage

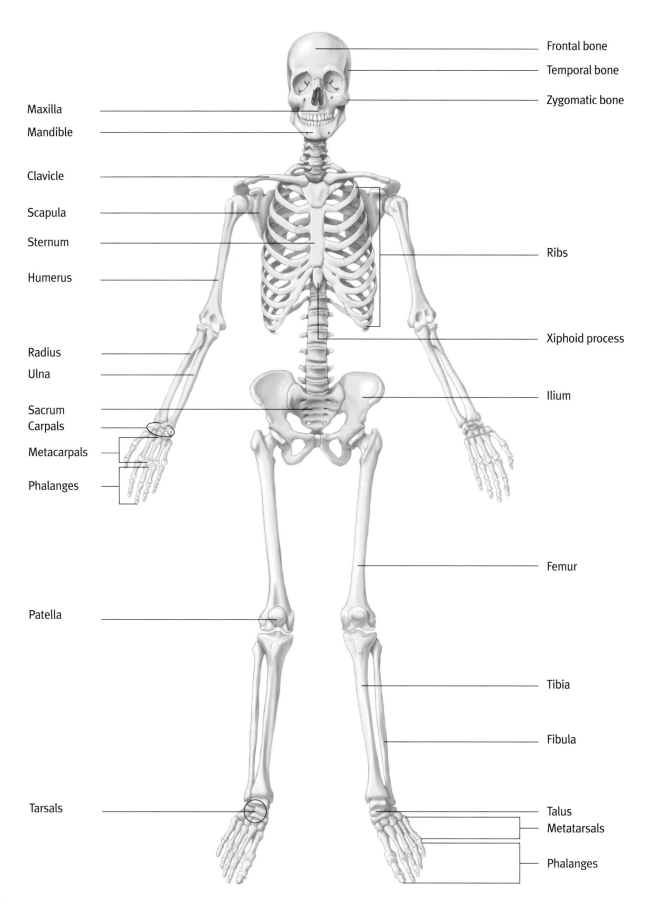

Frontal bone

Temporal bone

Zygomatic bone

Maxilla

Mandible

Clavicle

Scapula

Sternum

Humerus

Ribs

Radius

Ulna

Xiphoid process

Sacrum

Carpals

Ilium

Metacarpals

Phalanges

Femur

Patella

Tibia

Fibula

Tarsals

Talus

Metatarsals

Phalanges

Anterior view of the human skeleton.

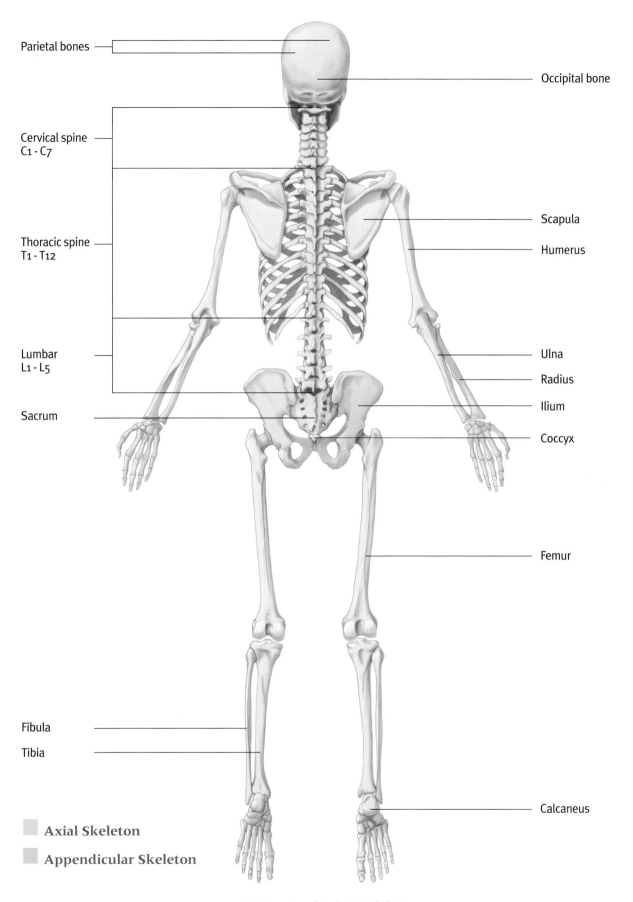

Parietal bones

Occipital bone

Cervical spine
C1 - C7

Scapula

Humerus

Thoracic spine
T1 - T12

Lumbar
L1 - L5

Ulna

Radius

Ilium

Sacrum

Coccyx

Femur

Fibula

Tibia

Calcaneus

Axial Skeleton

Appendicular Skeleton

Posterior view of the human skeleton.

# The Muscular System

Our bodies have over 600 muscles, which together make up half of our body weight. We use muscles in all kinds of ways, from performing athletic skills, to eating, talking, and dancing. Muscles burn plenty of calories both when they are being used and when they are resting, and they burn even more when they are "in shape."

## Muscle Types

There are three major muscle types. Each type has distinct characteristics and functions, as listed below.

> **Smooth muscles** are involuntary and contract automatically. The central nervous system adjusts its contraction as required. These muscles do not tire easily and can stay contracted for a long period of time. This is important because the walls of our esophagus, stomach, intestines, and blood vessels are composed of smooth muscle.

> **Cardiac muscle**, as the name implies, is the specialized muscle tissue that comprises the heart. It is also involuntary. (Certain people— for example, deep-sea divers—can lower their heart rates to very low levels, which helps them adapt to underwater conditions.)

> **Skeletal muscles** are connected to bones by tendons. They are voluntary, meaning that we have control of them. Skeletal muscles are the engines that pull on bones, causing joints to move.

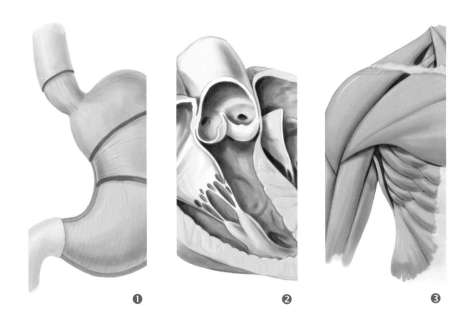

Types of muscle:  ❶ Smooth muscle  ❷ Cardiac muscle  ❸ Skeletal muscle

Cylindrical **muscle fibres** are individual skeletal muscles in which contraction occurs.

**The perimysium** is a connective tissue that surrounds the fascicle.

**The epimysium** is a protective, connective tissue that surrounds the entire muscle holding it all together.

**The muscle belly** is the region of the muscle that is widest in diameter.

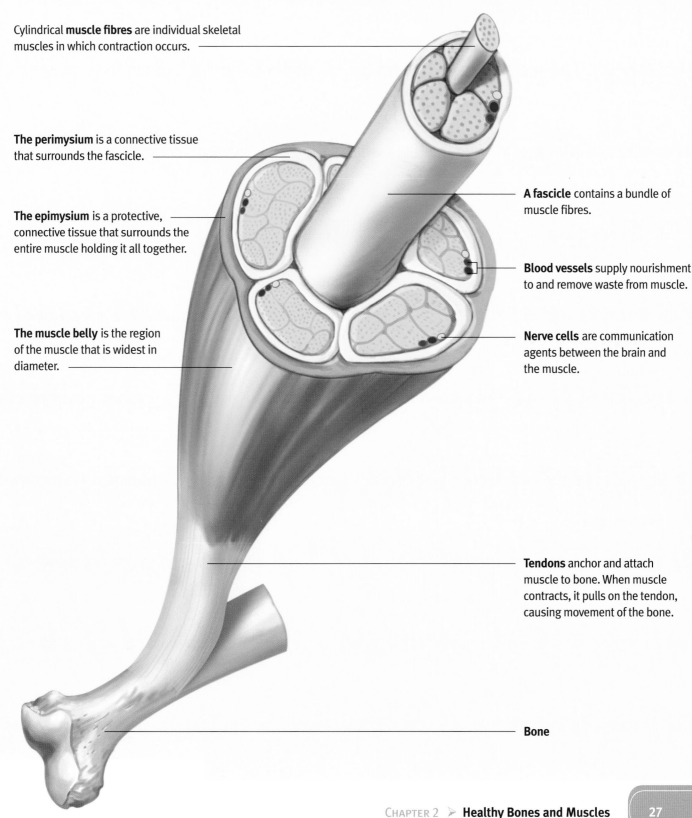

**A fascicle** contains a bundle of muscle fibres.

**Blood vessels** supply nourishment to and remove waste from muscle.

**Nerve cells** are communication agents between the brain and the muscle.

**Tendons** anchor and attach muscle to bone. When muscle contracts, it pulls on the tendon, causing movement of the bone.

**Bone**

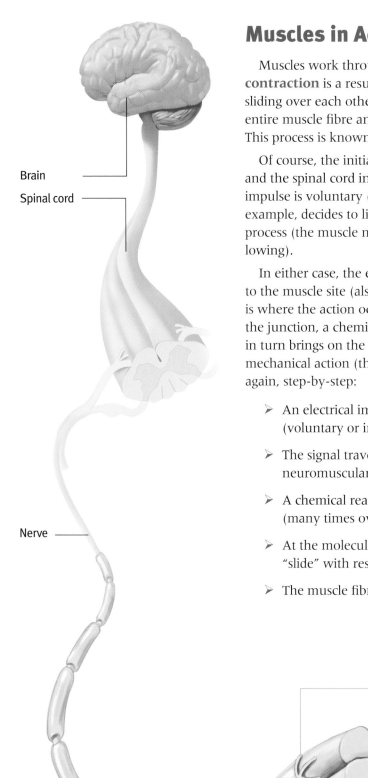

Brain

Spinal cord

Nerve

Neuromuscular junction

## Muscles in Action

Muscles work through a process called contraction. **Muscle contraction** is a result of the filaments deep within the muscle fibre sliding over each other. This process occurs simultaneously across the entire muscle fibre and, as a result, the entire muscle fibre contracts. This process is known as the **sliding filament theory**.

Of course, the initial "instruction" always comes from the brain and the spinal cord in the form of an electric impulse. Sometimes, the impulse is voluntary (the person decides to contract the muscle—for example, decides to lift a weight); at other times, it is an involuntary process (the muscle moves automatically—for example, when swallowing).

In either case, the electrical signal (impulse) is transmitted via nerves to the muscle site (also known as the **neuromuscular junction** which is where the action occurs). Once the impulse attempts to jump across the junction, a chemical reaction takes place in the muscle fibre, which in turn brings on the sliding of the filaments and ultimately the desired mechanical action (the full contraction). Let's follow that sequence again, step-by-step:

➤ An electrical impulse comes from the brain or spinal cord (voluntary or involuntary).

➤ The signal travels along the nerve to the muscle site (the neuromuscular junction) and attempts to jump the gap.

➤ A chemical reaction takes place deep within the muscle fibre (many times over), affecting the entire muscle group.

➤ At the molecular level, the reaction causes the filaments to "slide" with respect to each other in a ratchet-like fashion.

➤ The muscle fibre contracts.

Nerve ending

Thick filament (myosin)

Thin filament (actin)

Muscle

# Types of Muscle Contraction
## Concentric, Eccentric, and Isometric

The main function of skeletal muscle is to get our skeletons moving through a process called contraction. There are three types of contraction. Understanding these contraction types will help you use them in your resistance and fitness programs.

- **Concentric contraction** occurs when your muscle shortens while working. To see it in action, bend your elbow and watch what happens to your biceps muscle. You will notice that it has rolled up into a ball as it contracts.

- **Eccentric contraction** is the opposite of a concentric contraction. It occurs when your muscle lengthens while working. To see it in action, fully flex your elbow and then slowly straighten out your arm. This slow, controlled movement is the result of the biceps muscle lengthening.

- **Isometric contraction** occurs when a muscle force is equal to resistance and the muscle doesn't change in length. For example, as you push or pull against an immovable object, such as a wall, your muscles will contract but they will stay the same length.

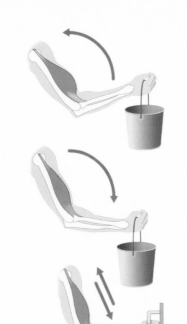

CONCENTRIC CONTRACTION

ECCENTRIC CONTRACTION

ISOMETRIC CONTRACTION

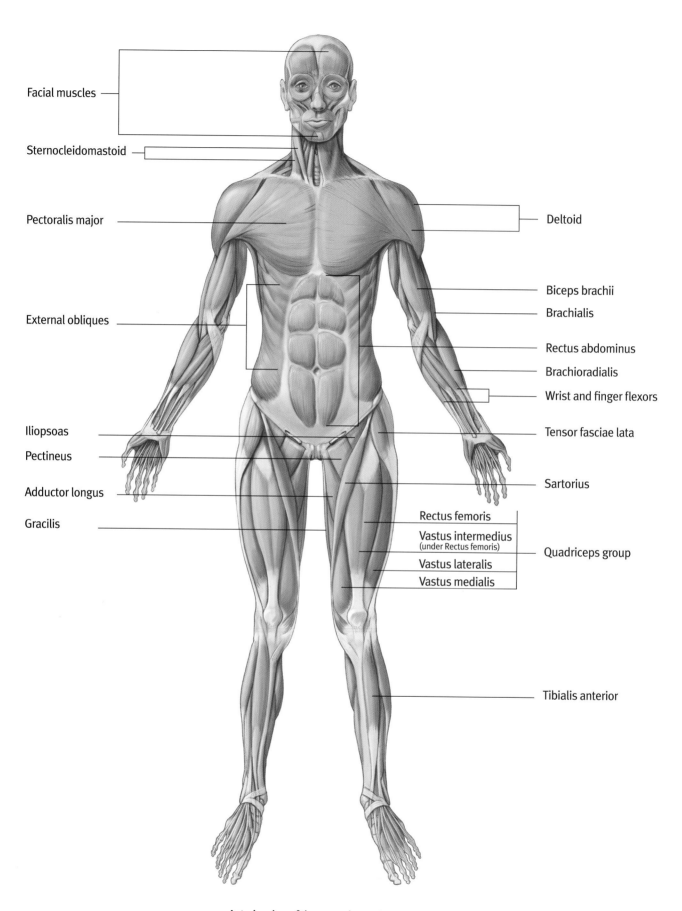

Facial muscles

Sternocleidomastoid

Pectoralis major

External obliques

Iliopsoas

Pectineus

Adductor longus

Gracilis

Deltoid

Biceps brachii

Brachialis

Rectus abdominus

Brachioradialis

Wrist and finger flexors

Tensor fasciae lata

Sartorius

Rectus femoris

Vastus intermedius
(under Rectus femoris)

Vastus lateralis

Vastus medialis

Quadriceps group

Tibialis anterior

Anterior view of the muscular system.

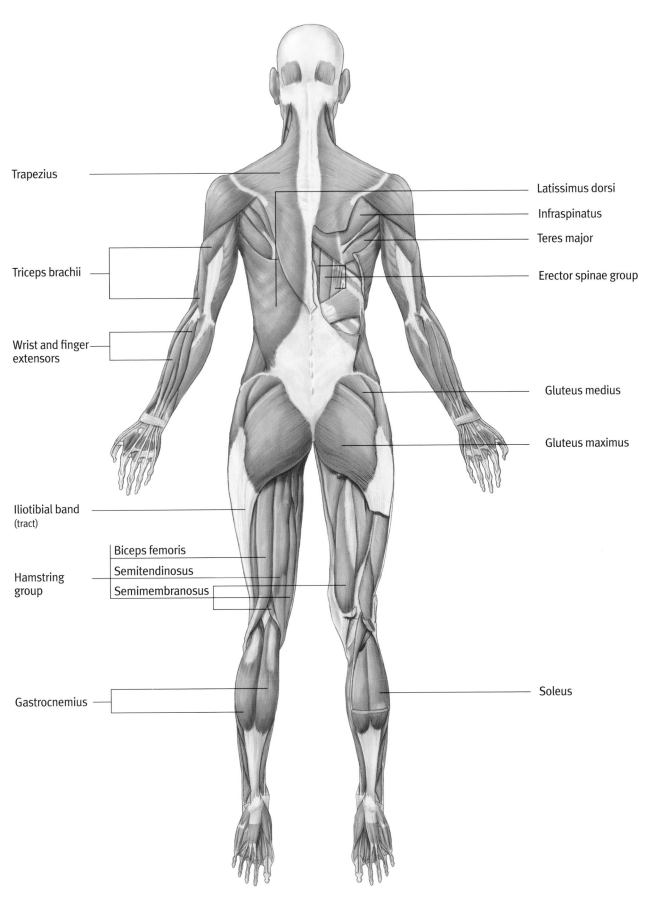

Trapezius

Triceps brachii

Wrist and finger
extensors

Iliotibial band
(tract)

Hamstring
group

Biceps femoris

Semitendinosus

Semimembranosus

Gastrocnemius

Latissimus dorsi

Infraspinatus

Teres major

Erector spinae group

Gluteus medius

Gluteus maximus

Soleus

Posterior view of the muscular system.

# Joints

Bones are connected at areas called **joints** which are held together by various connective tissues including ligaments and muscles. Elbows, knees, and knuckles are commonly-known joints, but there are many more. In fact, we have over 140 joints in our bodies.

Most bones are connected to one or more other bones by joints. One bone, the hyoid bone, which helps protect the voice box in your throat, is the only bone in the body which does not connect to another bone. In fact, it anchors your tongue in your mouth.

## Types of Joints

Joints are classified by their structure and function. There are three major types of joints.

➤ **Fibrous joints** (or immovable joints) are held together by strong, fibrous, connective tissue and, as the name suggests, they permit no movement. Examples of fibrous joints include: where your teeth are anchored in the jawbone, and where the bones of the skull come together.

➤ **Cartilaginous joints** (or slightly moveable joints) are connected by cartilage and allow partial movement. The stacked vertebrae bones in your spine, for example, are held together by cartilaginous joints.

➤ **Synovial joints** (or freely moveable joints) provide the most movement and are the most common of all joints found in the body. Some examples include: the shoulders, elbows, wrists, hips, knees, and ankles. See "The Synovial Joint" on the next page for more information on how a synovial joint works and "Types of Synovial Joints" on pages 34 and 35 for more information on the different types of synovial joints in our bodies.

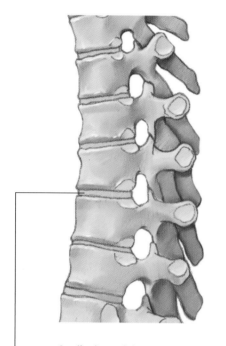

Cartilaginous joint

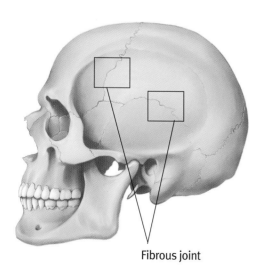

Fibrous joint

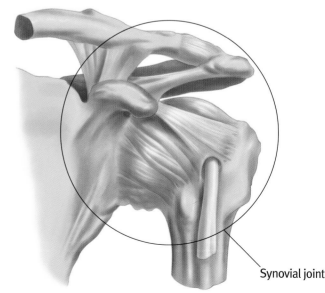

Synovial joint

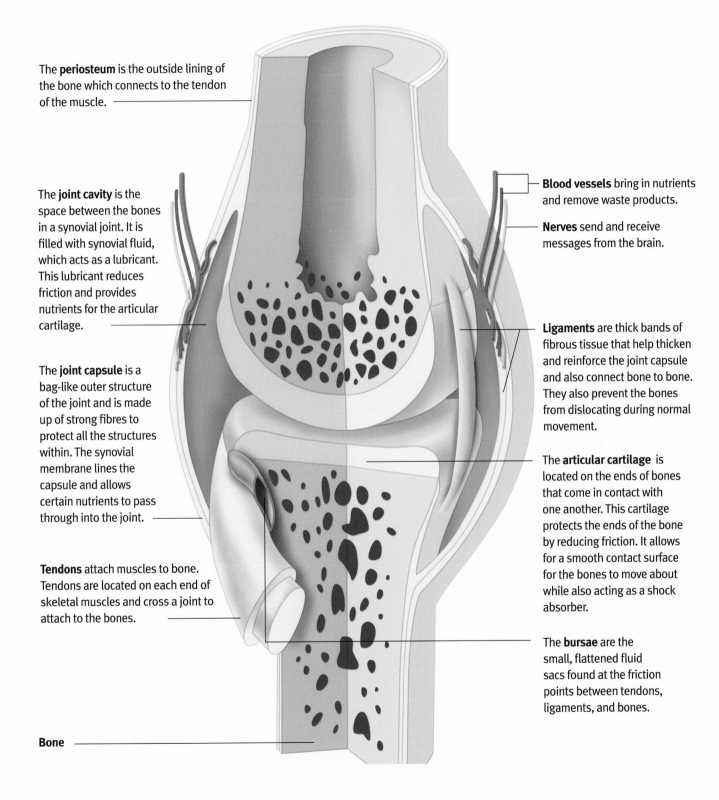

The **periosteum** is the outside lining of the bone which connects to the tendon of the muscle.

The **joint cavity** is the space between the bones in a synovial joint. It is filled with synovial fluid, which acts as a lubricant. This lubricant reduces friction and provides nutrients for the articular cartilage.

The **joint capsule** is a bag-like outer structure of the joint and is made up of strong fibres to protect all the structures within. The synovial membrane lines the capsule and allows certain nutrients to pass through into the joint.

**Tendons** attach muscles to bone. Tendons are located on each end of skeletal muscles and cross a joint to attach to the bones.

Bone

**Blood vessels** bring in nutrients and remove waste products.

**Nerves** send and receive messages from the brain.

**Ligaments** are thick bands of fibrous tissue that help thicken and reinforce the joint capsule and also connect bone to bone. They also prevent the bones from dislocating during normal movement.

The **articular cartilage** is located on the ends of bones that come in contact with one another. This cartilage protects the ends of the bone by reducing friction. It allows for a smooth contact surface for the bones to move about while also acting as a shock absorber.

The **bursae** are the small, flattened fluid sacs found at the friction points between tendons, ligaments, and bones.

## Types of Synovial Joints

There are basically six types of synovial joints. These are usually distinguished by the kind of movement they allow. Some types allow for limited movement (one direction), while others allow for maximal movement (multi-direction).

Outlined below are some of the key characteristics of the different types of synovial joints. On the next page, there are illustrations of the six types.

> **Ball-and-socket joints** provide the most movement of all the synovial joints. As the name suggests, one end of a bone has a ball shape that fits into a bone with a socket shape. The shoulder and hip are types of ball-and-socket joints.

> **Gliding joints** connect flat or slightly curved bone surfaces. Examples of gliding joints include joints in the foot and in the hand.

> **Hinge joints** have a convex portion of one bone fitting into a concave portion of another, and allow movement around one axis. The elbow, the knee, and the joints between the bones of the fingers are examples.

> **Pivot joints** also allow movement around one axis. A rounded point of one bone fits into a groove of another. An example is the joint between the first two vertebrae in the neck (the axis and the atlas), which allows the rotation of the head from side to side.

> **Ellipsoid joints** allow movement around two axes. The wrist is an example of an ellipsoidal joint.

> **Saddle joints**, like ellipsoid joints, allow movement around two axes. A key saddle joint is found at the base of the thumb.

Proper warm-ups, cool-downs, and stretches help your joints stay strong and healthy.

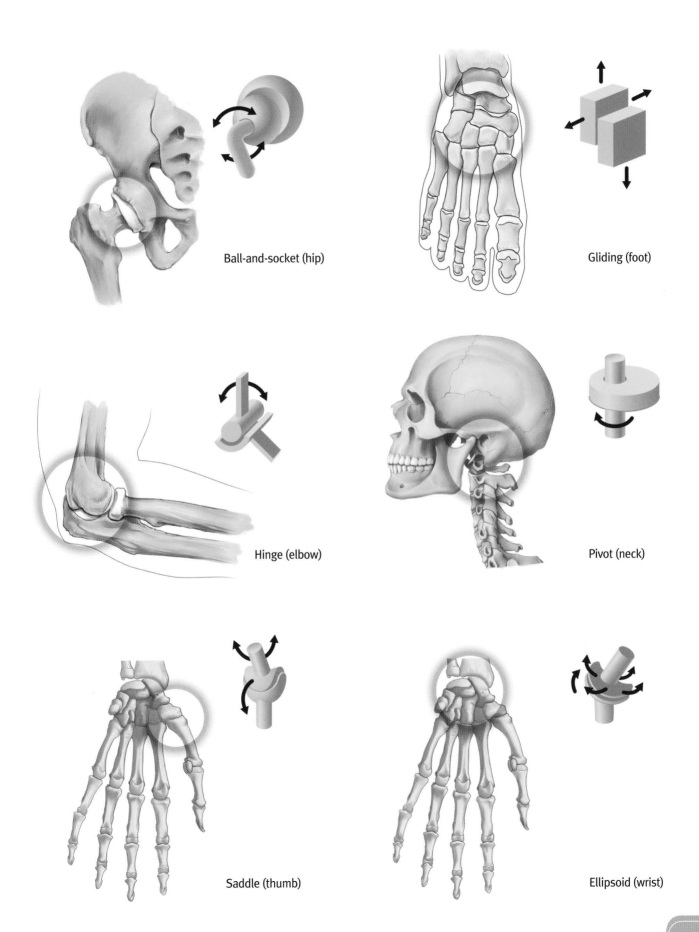

Ball-and-socket (hip)

Gliding (foot)

Hinge (elbow)

Pivot (neck)

Saddle (thumb)

Ellipsoid (wrist)

# Types of Movement at Joints

Starting from the anatomical position, the following terms are used to describe the types of movement at joints. Each type of movement is illustrated on the next page.

illustrated on the next page.

> **Flexion** is the action of bending at a joint such that the joint angle decreases. An example of flexion is when you bend your elbow to bring your palm up towards your face (the angle between your upper and lower arm gets smaller).

> **Extension** is the opposite of flexion. It occurs when you increase the joint angle. When you straighten your arm from the flexed position, you are extending your arm.

> **Abduction** occurs when you move a body segment to the side and away from your body. An example of abduction is when you move your arm out to the side and bring it level with your shoulder.

> **Adduction** is the opposite of abduction and occurs when you move a body segment towards your body. You adduct your arm when you bring it back down to your side.

> **Supination** is rotating the wrist such that the palm of your hand is facing forward. When you catch a softball underhanded with one hand, you must supinate your wrist.

> **Pronation** occurs in the opposite direction of supination. When you dribble a basketball, you first have to pronate your wrist.

> **Dorsiflexion** is specific to the ankle joint. It occurs when you bend at the ankle to bring the top of your foot closer to your shin. It is essential when walking, jumping, or sprinting.

> **Plantar flexion** is also specific to the ankle joint. It occurs when you point your toes.

> **Inversion** is associated with the ankle joint. Inversion is a result of standing on the outer edge of your foot. It is normally what happens when you twist your ankle.

> **Eversion** also is associated with the ankle joint. Eversion is a result of standing on the inner edge of your foot.

> **Internal rotation** results when you twist or turn a body part inward towards the midline. You internally rotate your foot when you turn your toes inward.

> **External rotation** results when you twist or turn a body part outward from the midline. You externally rotate your foot when you turn your toes outward.

> **Circumduction** is a combination of flexion, extension, abduction, and adduction all wrapped up into one movement. An example of this occurs in softball, when a pitcher throws the ball with a windmill action.

## Muscle Pairs

Some muscles work together as **muscle pairs**. For example, if one muscle performs a flexing action, the other performs an extending action.

Below are examples of muscles that work in pairs:

- The biceps brachii flexes the elbow and triceps brachii extends it.

- The deltoid muscle abducts the arm and latissimus dorsi adducts it back.

- Two small muscles (not illustrated on pages 30 and 31) located on the deep surface of the forearm, called supinator and pronator teres, supinate and pronate your hand.

- Tibialis anterior, located on the front of your lower leg, dorsiflexes your foot while gastrocnemius (the major muscle in the calf at the back of your lower leg) plantar flexes it.

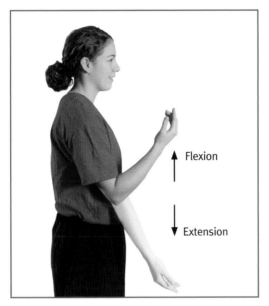

Flexion

Extension

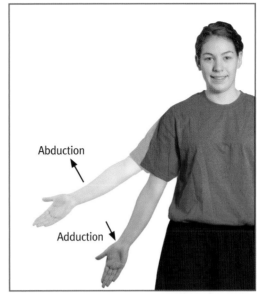

Abduction

Adduction

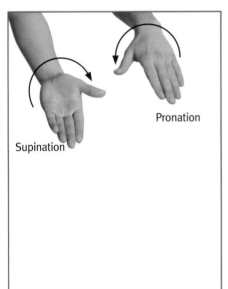

Pronation

Supination

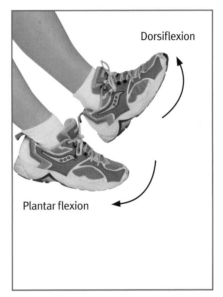

Dorsiflexion

Plantar flexion

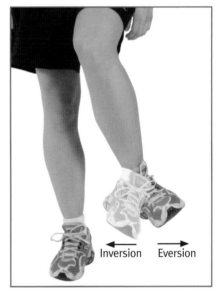

Inversion    Eversion

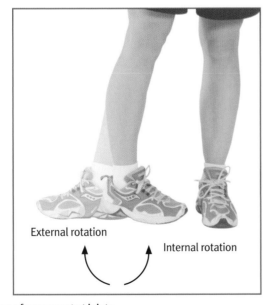

External rotation

Internal rotation

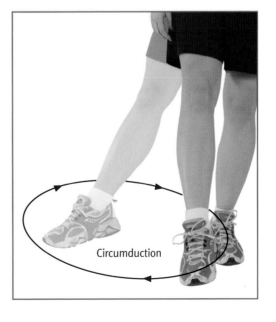

Circumduction

The basic types of movement at joints.

## Derek Call
### Be an example to others ...

Setting goals and discovering what motivates you not only helps you in H&PE class but in other academic areas as well. Derek Call knows this and it's made him a better all-around student. Derek went to East York Collegiate Institute in Toronto and now attends York University.

### What was the most important thing you learned in H&PE class?

I learned how passionate I could be about something that interests me. I now find myself wanting to learn more about my studies, whereas before I would only do the minimum I had to do.

### Who were the people who helped you the most in achieving your goals?

My health and physical education teacher in Grade 11 helped me a lot. He was the first to expose me to the field of Kinesiology which I am now studying at university.

My parents have also had a profound impact on me. They allowed an outlet for my interests as a child by supporting the various baseball and hockey teams that I played for. I would be hard pressed to remember a game that neither of them attended.

### How have you transferred what you learned in H&PE class into other aspects of your life?

The biggest thing I took from H&PE class was the drive that is required to succeed. It has been my experience that if you want anything in life, the main factors in achieving that goal are hard work and a legitimate interest in whatever it is that you are doing.

### Friends and healthy relationships are important to any student. How have you and your friends supported each other in pursuit of your goals?

Friends and family have always been there for me when needed. Whether it's to remind me of the hard work that's required when I lose motivation or to provide competition to achieve some goal. The role friends and teammates have had upon my development as a person has been immense.

### What are your future goals in the area of healthy active living?

I plan to work in the field of sports medicine, hopefully as an orthopedic surgeon. In that role I will have the ability to work with athletes that are as interested as I am in healthy active living. I hope to be an example to others on how to incorporate a healthy lifestyle into your everyday routine.

### What message would you give students in Grades 9 and 10 about H&PE class?

The advice I would give to a Grade 9 or 10 student would apply not only to H&PE class but to all areas of school, sports, and life. Once you find a legitimate interest and develop a goal, only hard work and persistence will allow you to achieve it. Find things that make you curious, find answers to your questions, put that extra bit of work into everything you do, and you will find it that much more rewarding.

**Find a healthy activity that you love and try to incorporate it into your daily life. Healthy behaviour will build upon itself and make you feel much better about yourself in the long run. Small things now will have a huge effect on your life later.**

# Chapter Review

## Questions for Study and Review

### Things to Think About and Explore

1. Investigate the four main functions of the human skeleton.

2. Distinguish between the three different types of muscle in the human body and give examples of each type.

3. Describe how skeletal muscle contraction takes place, beginning with an electrical impulse coming from the brain or spinal cord.

4. Compare the three different types of muscle contraction and give examples of each type (other than those given in this textbook).

5. Explain how bones are connected together at joints.

6. Describe the basic types of movement that occur at joints by giving examples of each type of movement.

### Things to Do and Practise

7. Take a digital photo of yourself standing in the anatomical position (or draw a basic diagram) and label the standard reference points.

8. Draw a rough illustration of a long bone and highlight the following parts: the diaphysis, the epiphysis, the medullary cavity, the periosteum, ephiphyseal plates, and articular cartilage.

9. Draw a rough illustration of a skeletal muscle and highlight the following parts: the muscle fibre, the fascicle, the perimysium, the epimysium, and the muscle tendon.

10. Make and mold a joint using Plasticine, or any form of molding clay. Label the joint and explain its movement.

11. Draw a rough illustration of a synovial joint and highlight the following parts: the joint cavity, the joint capsule, the articulating cartilage, the bursae, the ligaments, and the tendons.

12. Create a pamphlet entitled "How to Keep Your Joints Healthy and Strong." Use one specific sport or activity as your focus. Include illustrations or pictures as well as guidelines and any other resource material that may relate to your pamphlet.

## WWWeblinks

Name ➤ Active 2010

URL ➤ www.active2010.ca

A Government of Ontario program that aims to increase participation in sport and physical activity throughout the province.

Name ➤ HealthNet Canada

URL ➤ www.healthnet.ca

A means of communication for all Canadian health care workers but one that is especially useful for those in rural areas. The site also offers health news and resources.

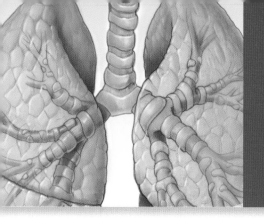

# 3
# Healthy Heart and Lungs

**O**ur bodies can go without food for many days, but without oxygen we die within minutes. The heart and lungs team up to perform a vital role in our bodies, which is to transport oxygen to every cell. This is all the more reason to keep them as healthy as possible.

The cardiorespiratory and energy systems are fundamental to every aspect of our daily lives. Gaining knowledge as to how these systems interact with one another is the first step in staying fit and preventing disease.

This chapter provides an overview of the heart and lungs, how they work, and some tips on how to go about keeping them fit. We will also look at how our bodies create the energy we need for everyday activity and for high performance.

## Chapter Objectives

In this chapter, you will:

➢ Explore the overall workings of the cardiorespiratory system, consisting of the heart, the lungs, and associated organs

➢ Distinguish between pulmonary and systemic circulation

➢ Investigate how the "double pump" action of the heart enables blood to circulate throughout the body

➢ Examine how the respiratory system moves air in and out of our bodies using differences in air pressure

➢ Investigate the role of the alveoli and capillaries in exchanging oxygen from the air we breath with carbon dioxide from our blood

➢ Explore the relationship of the aerobic and anaerobic energy systems and the role of each system in producing the energy we need for daily activity

➢ Identify ways to help keep the cardiorespiratory system fit

## Key Terms

➢ cardiorespiratory system
➢ artery/vein
➢ cardiovascular system
➢ pulmonary/systemic circulation
➢ cardiac control centre
➢ cardiac cycle
➢ blood pressure
➢ respiratory system
➢ alveoli
➢ adenosine triphosphate (ATP)
➢ aerobic system
➢ anaerobic system
➢ lactic acid
➢ aerobic activity

# The Cardiorespiratory System

The **cardiorespiratory system** is comprised of the heart, lungs, and all their supporting structures, including the blood vessels. If the cardiorespiratory system is neglected, you can—and almost certainly will—develop serious health problems. Unhealthy behaviours that affect this system, such as smoking and lack of exercise, often result in high blood pressure, heart and lung disease, and premature death.

Fortunately, keeping the cardiorespiratory system in strong working order is largely within our own control.

## Heart and Lung Awareness

Air pollution, for example, may be a risk that is difficult to avoid today, but finding ways to reduce this risk to yourself and others (hybrid cars that use gasoline and electricity, for example) is a small but important step. Other risk-avoiding behaviours are easier to accomplish on one's own—not smoking being the first, of course.

It is also important that you are proactive and not just reactive. This means going out of your way to ensure that your heart and lungs have a regular workout every day.

Air filter masks help reduce the effects of air pollution while exercising.

Working your heart and lungs every day is part of being proactive rather than reactive.

# The Cardiovascular System

The **cardiovascular system** refers to the heart, blood vessels (the network of arteries, veins, and capillaries), and blood. This system enables oxygen and nutrients to be distributed throughout the body, and for blood to be returned to the heart and lungs for replenishment.

At the centre of this system is a highly specialized muscle, the heart muscle. Its main functions are to pump oxygen-poor blood to the lungs, where it is replenished with oxygen, and to pump oxygen-rich blood out to the body.

## Pulmonary and Systemic Circulation

The important thing to remember is that there are two circulation systems at work. The "lung cycle" (the movement of blood to the lungs for re-oxygenation and back to the heart) is referred to as pulmonary circulation. The "body cycle" (the movement of blood to and from the body) is referred to as systemic circulation.

> **Pulmonary circulation.** Deoxygenated blood is pumped to the lungs and newly oxygenated blood is returned to the heart.

> **Systemic circulation.** Oxygenated blood is pumped out to the body and deoxygenated blood is returned to the heart.

The pulmonary and systemic circulation systems work in unison with one another. Blood circulates to the lungs (where it is replenished with oxygen), and to the body (where it supplies oxygen to the tissues).

## The Double Pump

The flow of blood is brought about by the contractions of the two upper chambers (atria) and then, the two lower chambers (ventricles).

The heart contracts automatically, without any input from the nervous system. This is because of the specialized cells of the sinoatrial (SA) node and atrioventricular (AV) node, which control the basic rate of contraction of the heart. A specialized centre in the brain (the **cardiac control centre** of the medulla oblongata) sends impulses to the heart to adjust this basic rate of contraction to meet the body's demands for oxygen at any point in time.

The signal sent from the SA node to the AV node forces the two upper chambers (atria) to contract simultaneously. As a result, the right atrium pumps deoxygenated blood (from the body) into the right ventricle and the left atrium pumps oxygenated blood (from the lungs) into the left ventricle.

From the AV node, the signal passes into the walls of the two ventricles, causing them to contract simultaneously. This contraction causes the right ventricle to pump deoxygenated blood to the lungs and the left ventricle to pump oxygenated blood to the body.

In an instant, the ventricles relax, the atria again fill up and the sequence is continued.

## Arteries and Veins

In the pulmonary cycle, deoxygenated blood going out to the lungs from the heart, travels through the pulmonary arteries.

Oxygenated blood returning from the lungs arrives at the heart through the pulmonary veins.

The rule to keep in mind is that:

- **Arteries** carry blood away from the heart (whether the blood is oxygenated or deoxygenated).

- **Veins** bring it to the heart (again, whether it is oxygenated blood or deoxygenated blood).

## In a Heart Beat

The **cardiac cycle** is the term used to refer to the series of events that occurs through one heart beat. There are two basic phases in the cardiac cycle:

➢ In the diastolic phase, the ventricles are relaxed.

➢ In the systolic phase, the ventricles contract and push blood out into the arteries.

## Blood Pressure

**Blood pressure** refers to the force exerted by the blood against the walls of the artery. It is measured in millimetres of mercury (mmHg), and it is usually stated as being systolic pressure (the contraction phase) over diastolic pressure (the relaxation phase)—for example, 120/80 mmHg is considered normal.

Poor diet and lack of exercise can cause a hardening of the arteries (arteriosclerosis or atherosclerosis) and result in high blood pressure (hypertension).

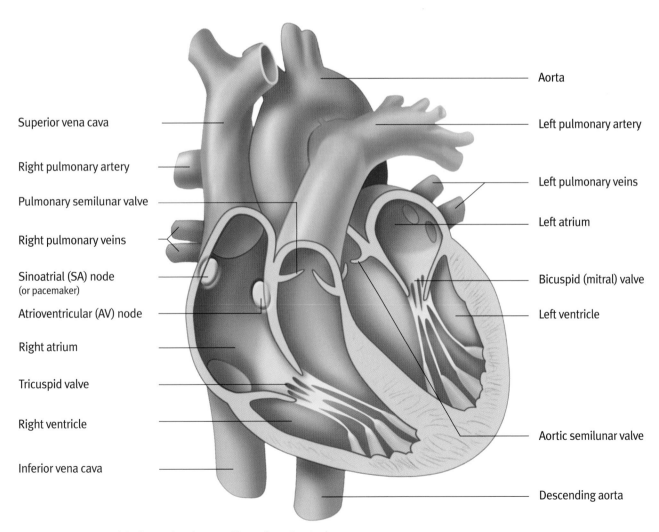

The main structures of the internal and external heart (anterior view).

# The Path of Blood

We could start at any point in the cardiac cycle, but let's start with deoxygenated (oxygen-poor) blood arriving from the body and oxygen-rich blood arriving simultaneously from the lungs.

## Phase 1

The deoxygenated blood enters the heart at the upper-right chamber (the right atrium). Simultaneously, oxygen-rich blood arrives at the upper-left chamber (the left atrium). Both upper chambers fill.

With the contraction of the upper chambers, the deoxygenated blood is forced through the tricuspid valve to the lower-right chamber (right ventricle). Simultaneously, the oxygenated blood is forced through the bicuspid valve to the lower-left chamber (left ventricle).

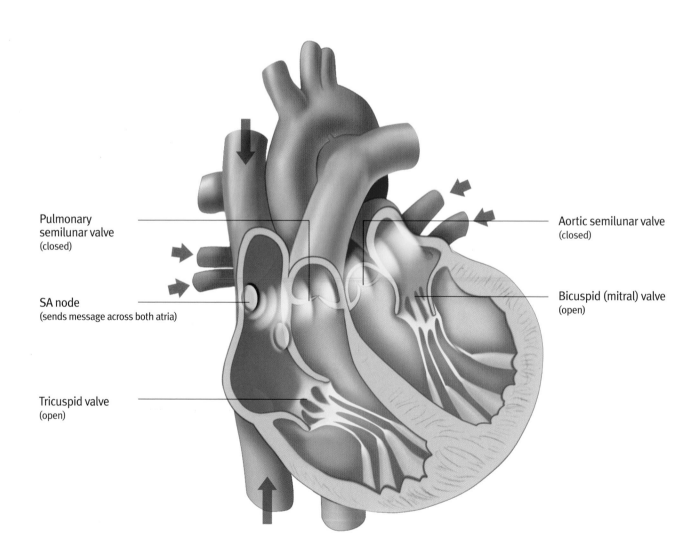

Pulmonary semilunar valve (closed)

SA node (sends message across both atria)

Tricuspid valve (open)

Aortic semilunar valve (closed)

Bicuspid (mitral) valve (open)

Contraction of the upper chambers (atria) forces blood into the lower chambers (ventricles). The tricuspid and bicuspid valves then close.

## Phase 2

The deoxygenated blood is now located in the lower right chamber and the oxygenated blood is in the lower left chamber. Next, the left and right lower chambers contract, causing the pressure in these chamber to rise. This has two effects:

First, it causes the bicuspid and tricuspid valves to close, preventing blood from re-entering the atria. The first "lub" sound you hear when listening to your heart is the sound of the tricuspid and bicuspid valves closing. Second, the contraction of the ventricles causes the pulmonary and aortic valves to open. Thus, simultaneously, deoxygenated blood is pumped out through the pulmonary valve to the pulmonary arteries, which lead to the lungs, and oxygen-rich blood is pumped through the aortic valve and out to the body through the aorta.

When the ventricles relax, the pulmonary and aortic valves close. The second "dub" sound you hear when listening to your heart is the sound of the pulmonary and aortic valves closing after the blood has left the chambers.

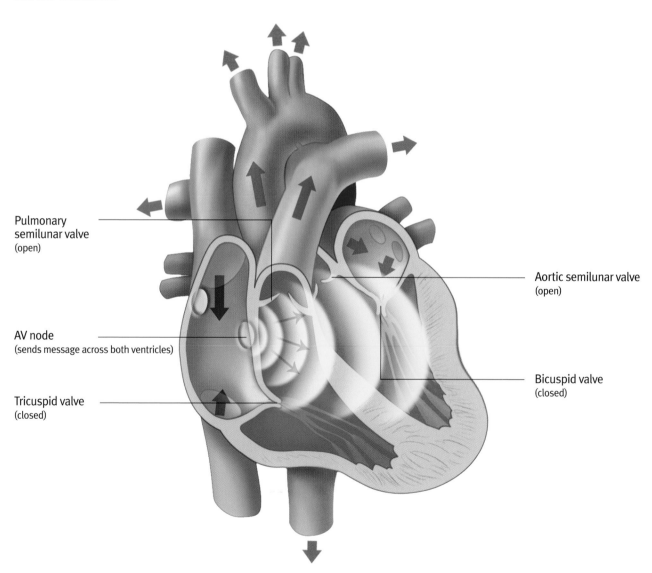

Pulmonary semilunar valve (open)

Aortic semilunar valve (open)

AV node (sends message across both ventricles)

Bicuspid valve (closed)

Tricuspid valve (closed)

Contraction of the lower chambers (ventricles) forces blood out to the body and the lungs. The pulmonary and aortic valves then close.

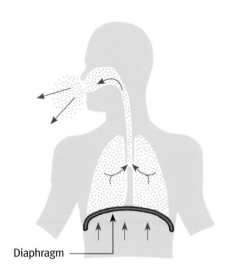

Diaphragm

As we breathe in, the expanding rib cage draws air into the lungs.

Diaphragm

When we breathe out, the rib cage contracts to move air out of the lungs.

# The Respiratory System

The **respiratory system** allows for the passage of air from outside the body to the lungs as well as the exchange of oxygen and carbon dioxide. Each time you breathe, oxygen ($O_2$) is taken in from the air and carbon dioxide ($CO_2$), a waste gas, is exhaled.

The respiratory system can be divided into two main zones:

> **Conductive zone.** The conductive zone refers to the area where air enters the lungs.

> **Respiratory zone.** The respiratory zone is where the gas exchange occurs.

## Conductive Zone (Breathing)

In order to take air into your body, the diaphragm, the muscle that separates your chest cavity from your abdominal cavity, contracts to increase the volume of your chest cavity. This causes the air pressure inside of your lungs to become lower than the air pressure outside of your body. Since air moves from areas of high pressure to areas of low pressure, the air outside will rush into your lungs through your mouth or nose.

To send air out of your lungs, or to exhale, your diaphragm muscle relaxes, causing your chest cavity to return to its normal size. This increases the air pressure in your lungs, making it higher than the air pressure outside your body, and forces the air in your lungs back into the air around you.

## Respiratory Zone (Gas Exchange)

Deep within the lungs, the exchange of oxygen and carbon dioxide are the responsibility of **alveoli**, which are shaped like microscopic bunches of grapes. We have 600 million or so of these tiny alveoli within our lungs. Each alveoli is surrounded by hundreds of capillaries. These capillaries allow oxygen and carbon dioxide to be exchanged through a process called diffusion.

During the diffusion process, the two gases simultaneously change places. The carbon dioxide from the blood diffuses into the alveoli and is eventually exhaled. The oxygen from the lungs diffuses to the red blood cells and is then transported back to the heart and pumped out to the body.

This diffusion process happens over our entire lives and if it stops, clearly, we cease to exist. Keeping your lungs healthy is literally a matter of life or death.

The alveoli are very fragile and easily damaged or destroyed. If these delicate parts are unable to function properly, there is a less efficient exchange of gases. This disease is known as emphysema. Smoking is a major cause of emphysema. Smoking, combined with other environmental factors, has caused an increase in the number of people with this deadly disease.

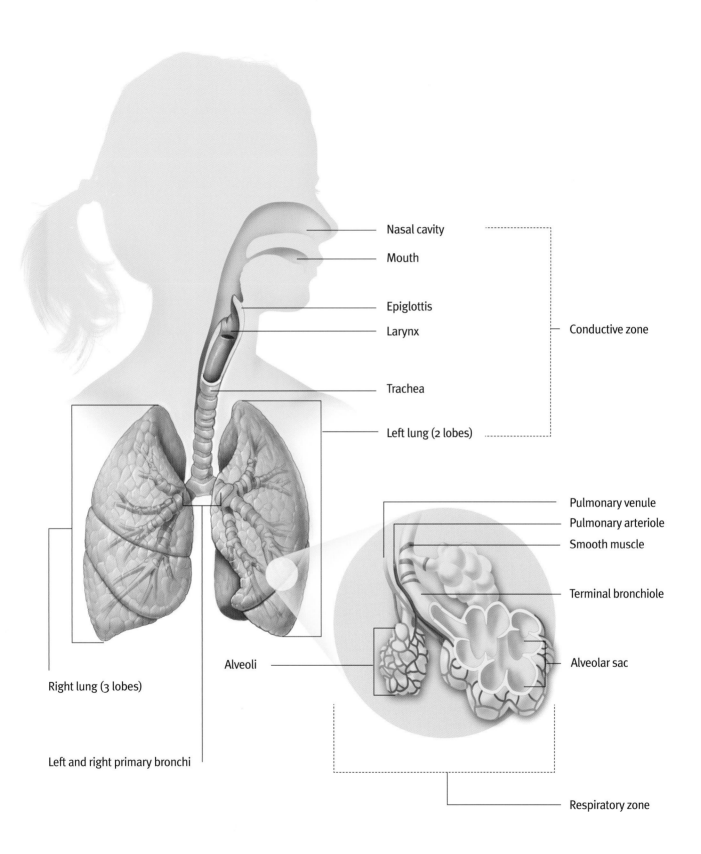

Nasal cavity

Mouth

Epiglottis

Larynx

Conductive zone

Trachea

Left lung (2 lobes)

Pulmonary venule

Pulmonary arteriole

Smooth muscle

Terminal bronchiole

Right lung (3 lobes)

Alveoli

Alveolar sac

Left and right primary bronchi

Respiratory zone

The main components of the respiratory system.

# Energy Systems

Our body creates energy from the nutrients we eat and the air we breathe. The energy we use to move around takes the form of an "energy molecule" called **adenosine triphosphate (ATP)**.

The way the body creates ATP is complex. It is easiest to think of there being two overlapping energy systems: the aerobic system and the anaerobic system.

## The Aerobic System

You may have heard the term "aerobic activity." In this context, the word aerobic means "requiring oxygen." Distance running is often used as the classic aerobic activity, but almost every activity of any duration requires drawing on the large amounts of ATP produced through aerobic means.

The **aerobic system**—the breakdown of food nutrients (carbohydrates, fats, and sometimes protein) in the presence of oxygen—is the primary way our body produces the energy we need. The aerobic system is the one that allows us to perform over longer periods of time at a fairly balanced intensity. Deep breathing is the most obvious sign that the aerobic system is at work for us.

Keeping that aerobic system healthy, starting with the lungs and heart, is a major concern. In general, the more you keep regularly active, the better you will be able to do what you have to do, and the better you will feel.

## The Anaerobic System

Our bodies are also able to create smaller amounts of ATP, when needed, without using oxygen. In the **anaerobic system**, the amount of ATP produced is much less than the amount created by the aerobic system. However, anaerobic energy is especially important in short- and medium-duration activities, such as weightlifting or a long shift in hockey.

To make things a little more complicated, there are two different anaerobic energy "pathways":

➤ **ATP–CP.** For very short-term needs, the ATP–CP pathway involves a rapid chemical reaction in the muscle fibre itself and does not require the breakdown of food nutrients. It is essential for short bursts of intense activity.

➤ **Glycolysis.** Glycolysis is a more complex process involving the partial breakdown of glucose. Glycolysis involves eleven separate chemical reactions and produces four times as much ATP than the ATP–CP system. If oxygen is present, this pathway leads to the aerobic system. Glycolysis comes into prominence for medium-duration activities, such as an intense shift in hockey or a 400-metre run.

## Cellular Respiration

Another term for aerobic energy system is "cellular respiration," because the process takes place deep within our cells.

Cellular respiration is our main source of energy. Our lungs and heart allow this process to take place.

- The lungs take in oxygen and filter it to the blood.
- The heart moves oxygenated blood to the cells and moves de-oxygenated blood from the cells back to the lungs.
- The lungs allow us to dispose of carbon dioxide.

That is why you do so much aerobic activity in health and physical education class.

## Lactic Acid

As we have seen, there are two distinct energy systems at work, the aerobic and anaerobic systems. The former yields large amounts of ATP; the latter is important for short, intense activities. The complexity comes when you try to grasp the link between the two systems.

Take an activity such as a long shift in hockey. After 2 or 3 minutes, the body cannot breakdown glucose quickly enough to keep up. A substance known as **lactic acid** builds up inside the muscle fibres and the participant is forced to stop or, at least, slow down. This lactic acid is associated with the extreme pain normally felt on such occasions.

In less intense forms of physical activity where the body can access sufficient oxygen easily—for example, distance running—the full breakdown of food nutrients continues at the cellular level (that is, aerobically). In a sense, therefore, and this is the complex part to grasp, the process is continuous. In the presence of oxygen, glycolysis becomes the first stage of the aerobic process. The aerobic process enables the activity to continue longer. If the balance is right, the activity can continue much longer (e.g., distance running).

The illustration below shows the energy systems in simplified form, and some of the sports and activities that tend to use one source of energy more than the others. For the most part, these three "energy pathways" work in unison and we shift in and out of each during most physical activity we perform.

Hockey is an example of a sport that can cause lactic acid build up.

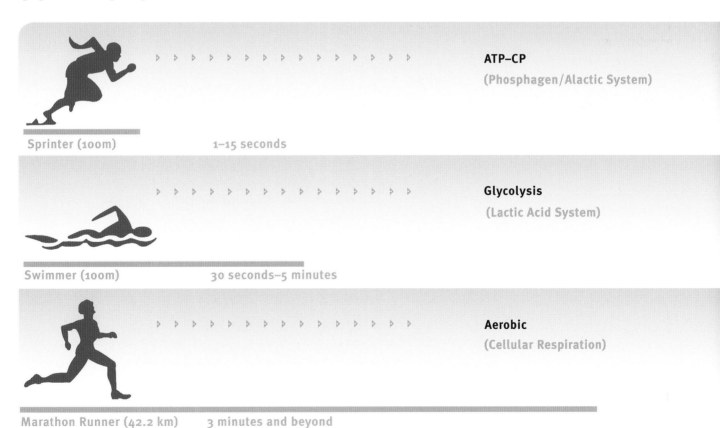

Sprinter (100m) 1–15 seconds

**ATP–CP**
(Phosphagen/Alactic System)

Swimmer (100m) 30 seconds–5 minutes

**Glycolysis**
(Lactic Acid System)

Marathon Runner (42.2 km) 3 minutes and beyond

**Aerobic**
(Cellular Respiration)

A simplified depiction of the three energy systems. In everyday activities, the three systems are overlapping and interdependent.

# Keeping the Cardiorespiratory System Fit

Clearly, a strong and healthy cardiorespiratory system is vital to everyday performance. Here is a look at some of the factors that can help keep your cardiorespiratory system fit.

## Exercise

Typically, in most H&PE classes, you will be asked to do some form of **aerobic activity**—swimming, jogging, skipping, cross-country skiing, running, or through a variety of activities and sports in which you are involved.

By definition, aerobic activities require many muscles to move at the same time. This requires the body to burn many calories and use large amounts of oxygen. As you perform exercises, your system will respond by becoming more efficient, and work that once seemed difficult will seem easier.

## Nutrition

What you put into your body is just as important as how hard you work in class. In Unit 7, you will learn about proper nutrition and how it helps to improve daily performance.

Ensure your breakfast, lunch, dinner, and snacks are healthy and that they come from a variety of food sources, as outlined in Canada's Food Guide to Healthy Eating. Above all, avoid unhealthy foods—over time, foods high in saturated fats, for example, can damage your arteries and heart. Unhealthy eating can lead to many health problems.

The key to balanced food consumption is to eat a variety of foods in moderation.

## Smoking

There are thousands of chemicals found in both tobacco and marijuana smoke, none of which are beneficial to the body, especially to the cardiorespiratory system. Tar from tobacco and marijuana damages the cilia—the hair-like structures that protect the lungs from harmful invaders. These chemicals also damage the delicate walls of alveoli causing them to break down.

Smoking can also damage the lung cells themselves causing the healthy cells to die off, only to be replaced by cancer cells.

## Stress

Stress can also be damaging if it is not managed and controlled. Too much stress can cause high blood pressure and lead to cardiovascular disease. Stress also weakens the immune system, making it harder for the body to fight off disease. Exercising to help manage stress may enable you to avoid unhealthy alternatives such as smoking. Aerobic exercise also releases hormones, called endorphins, which give you a healthy "high" feeling, sometimes referred to as "runner's high."

In most H&PE classes, you will be asked to do some form of aerobic activity—running, swimming, jogging, skipping, cross-country skiing, or bike riding.

Eating healthy foods that come from a variety of food sources is recommended in *Canada's Food Guide to Healthy Eating*.

## Keep Your Heart and Lungs Fit

Thousands of Canadians die each year from heart attacks and other cardiorespiratory malfunctions. In fact, it is the number one killer in Canada, even though most early deaths from cardiorespiratory problems are largely preventable.

Keeping your cardiorespiratory system fit and healthy can help prevent many short-term problems related to the heart, lungs, and circulatory systems. Moreover, healthy heart habits formed early in life will decrease the likelihood of heart- and lung-related health problems as you get older.

Maintaining a high level of heart and lung fitness will put you at a lower risk for many common health problems, and help you:

> Avoid excess weight gain,

> Reduce or prevent high blood pressure,

> Lessen the risk of coronary artery disease, and

> Reduce the risk of stroke.

Each time we exercise our heart and lungs, our systems become stronger and better than the day before.

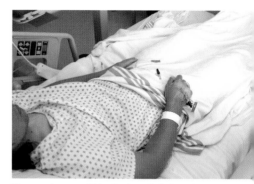

The number one killer in Canada is heart disease. Medical research tells us that most deaths from cardiorespiratory problems are preventable.

There are many benefits to being physically fit and active, particularly if you start when you are young.

## Being Active with a Disability
### Everyone can benefit from being active

People with disabilities face different challenges when attempting to lead a healthy active lifestyle. However, thanks to advancements in modified equipment and increasing awareness of mobility issues, most can still engage in almost any activity they wish. People with disabilities can and do participate in all sorts of activities such as basketball, dance, horseback riding, and skydiving.

### Being Active in a Wheelchair

There are many exercises that wheelchair users can do in their own home in order to maintain or improve the strength and fitness of their upper body. Even something as basic as arm lifts (either with or without weights) can go a long way towards working your upper body.

There is also specialized equipment available. Arm bikes (also known as hand cyclers or arm ergometers) can provide either strength and endurance training or cardiorespiratory exercise.

Participating in one of the many wheelchair sports is another good way to maintain a healthy active lifestyle.

### Being Active as an Amputee

There are a huge number of sports and activities available to amputees. Some amputee athletes compete using prosthetic limbs or modified equipment. Depending on the nature of the amputation, these devices may not always be necessary.

If you have a disability, physical activity may help to:

- Reduce aches and pains caused by long periods of sitting
- Improve circulation and prevent swelling in the legs for those in wheelchairs
- Maintain a healthy weight (which can help you move around more easily)
- Ease the physical and mental stresses of a disability
- Prevent relapses of certain disabilities
- Improve stamina and muscle strength (especially in people with chronic, disabling conditions)
- Improve your posture (which in turn can lead to a reduction in the aches and pains that can occur from sitting for long periods)
- Improve your balance and flexibility
- Enhance quality of sleep

### Tips for Getting Started

- Always consult your doctor before starting a new fitness plan.
- Think about your needs and goals. Is there a specific activity or a specific area of the body you would like to work on?
- Find out if your chosen activity requires any specialized or modified equipment.
- Try to be more active in your everyday activities.
- Investigate what community resources are available to help you.

### Web Resources

- Active Living Alliance for Canadians with a Disability
  **www.ala.ca**
- Active Living Resource Centre for Ontarians with a Disability
  **www.getactivenow.ca**
- Ontario Cerebral Palsy Sports Association
  **www.ocpsa.on.ca**
- Amputee Sports Links
  **www.amputee.ca**

# Chapter Review

## Questions for Study and Review

### Things to Think About and Explore

1. Identify and describe the major components of the cardiorespiratory system.
2. Define the terms "pulmonary" and "systemic" circulation. In this context, explain the difference between an artery and a vein.
3. Describe the functions of the two components of the respiratory system.
4. Explain the basic mechanics of breathing.
5. Investigate how oxygen and carbon dioxide are exchanged in the lungs.
6. Explain how the aerobic and anaerobic energy systems come into play during various types of sports and physical activities.

### Things to Do and Practise

7. Produce a schematic drawing to show the path of blood through the heart.
8. Investigate how the heart pumps blood to the lungs and to the body. Use a concept map to illustrate this process.
9. While resting comfortably on a chair, count how many times you breathe in or out in one minute. Now jog on the spot for one minute and count your breaths. Give two reasons why your rate of breathing increases when you are jogging as opposed to sitting down.
10. Using a tracking sheet over a one-week period, record the various activities that you did to improve the efficiency of your cardiorespiratory system.
11. Organize and prepare arguments on "the negative effects of smoking on the cardiorespiratory system."
12. Prepare a list of things, ranked in order of importance, that you and your friends can do now to help each of you ensure that your heart and lungs are healthy for a long time to come.

## WWWeblinks

Name ➤ Heart and Stroke Foundation

URL ➤ www.heartandstroke.ca

This site emphasizes keeping your heart healthy and has tips and tools for everyone, from people with high blood pressure to people just trying to be more active.

Name ➤ Lung Association

URL ➤ www.lung.ca

The official site for the Lung Association with information on various lung diseases and suggestions on what you can do to keep your lungs healthy.

Name ➤ Canadian Association for Cardiac Rehabilitation

URL ➤ www.cacr.ca

The official site for this organization focuses on cardiac disease prevention, cardiac rehabilitation, and the enhancement and maintenance of good cardiovascular health.

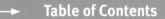

## Table of Contents

# UNIT 2
# Fitness Measurements and Appraisals

What this unit is about ...

➢ Why is it important for me always to stay within my Target Heart Rate Zone when I am involved in various physical activities?

➢ What is musculoskeletal fitness, and why is it important for me to partake in musculoskeletal appraisals?

➢ How can assessing my body composition help me to understand my fitness needs?

# 4
# Cardiorespiratory Appraisals

*To keep the body in good health is a duty ... otherwise we shall not be able to keep our mind strong and clear.*

**Buddha**

Integral figure of Buddhism

**Y**ou don't have to be a great athlete to perform fitness appraisals, or to become fit. Moreover, you don't need to worry if you don't perform well the first time. Fitness appraisals simply allow you to find out where your fitness level is now. They are intended to help you set your fitness goals.

Many of the appraisals that will be introduced to you in this unit have been developed by the Canadian Society for Exercise Physiology (CSEP). They are known as the Canadian Physical Activity, Fitness & Lifestyle Approach (CPAFLA, pronounced "Cee-Paf-La"). The CPAFLA appraisals are standardized for ages 15 to 69 and cover all health-related aspects of fitness.

When performing these appraisals over the next few years, keep in mind that your results will fluctuate. Your fitness scores will depend on your physical growth, as well as on whether you have been exercising regularly and whether you have been careful about what you eat.

## Chapter Objectives

In this chapter, you will:

➢ Understand the importance of finding a cardiorespiratory fitness test that is just right for you

➢ Explore the concept of "aerobic fitness" and the idea behind cardiorespiratory appraisals

➢ Identify the safety guidelines that must be followed when performing cardiorespiratory appraisals

➢ Learn how to find your "Resting Heart Rate," and from this how to calculate your "Maximal Heart Rate," your "Heart Rate Reserve," and finally your "Target Heart Rate Zone"

➢ Learn about the Modified Canadian Aerobic Fitness Test (mCAFT) and how to calculate your "Aerobic Fitness Score (AFS)"

➢ Explore three other common (non-CPAFLA) cardiorespiratory appraisals—the "12-Minute Run," the "Talk Test and Breath Sound Check," and the "Beep Test"

## Key Terms

➢ cardiorespiratory appraisals
➢ aerobic fitness
➢ VO$_2$ MAX
➢ Resting Heart Rate
➢ Target Heart Rate Zone
➢ Modified Canadian Aerobic Fitness Test (mCAFT)
➢ 12-Minute Run
➢ Breath Sound Check and Talk Test
➢ Beep Test

# Cardiorespiratory Fitness

**Cardiorespiratory appraisals** are probably the most important of all fitness appraisals. These appraisals gauge the efficiency of your heart and lungs.

When you increase your cardiorespiratory fitness, you can complete your daily activities easily. The increased feeling of energy you get also will lead to a more positive outlook on life, which in turn can lead to an increase in your self-esteem.

## Finding Appraisals That Are Right for You

Most of the appraisals outlined in this chapter are appropriate for all levels of fitness—from people who view themselves as being in excellent shape to those who are in poor shape. The most important thing is to find the appraisals that are appropriate for you. If you are not sure which appraisals are best for you, consult your physical education teacher.

If there are medical reasons why you cannot participate in any of these cardiorespiratory appraisals, let your teacher know well ahead of time. If there are no health issues, bring your activity handbook to class and get ready to have some fun.

Once you have completed an appraisal, you can refer to the sidebars to see where you stand. If the results of the appraisal are not quite as good as you expected, fear not. Improvement is easy—it just takes practice.

Engaging in aerobic sports such as basketball, hockey, or ultimate Frisbee does much to improve your overall health.

Staying in your Target Heart Rate Zone is essential to improve your cardiorespiratory fitness.

# What Is Aerobic Fitness?

Performing highly aerobic physical activities (such as basketball, cross-country skiing, or ultimate Frisbee) improves the overall health of your heart and lungs. However, before you strap on the running shoes, you first need to know the condition of your cardiorespiratory system.

### VO₂ MAX

**Aerobic fitness** is a general term that refers to the overall efficiency of the heart, lungs, blood vessels, and exercising muscles. In effect, it refers to one's ability to sustain prolonged physical effort.

Aerobic fitness results in an increase in the amount of oxygen that is delivered to your muscles. This, in turn, allows them to work harder and longer. Assuming there are no health concerns, any activity that moderately raises your heart rate and keeps it up for a period of time will improve your aerobic fitness.

The common indicator of aerobic fitness is the amount of oxygen consumed during intense ("maximal") effort. Exercise scientists call this **VO$_2$ MAX**. A high VO$_2$ MAX score indicates that you have a strong cardiorespiratory system. This means that your working muscles are able to receive and use more oxygen.

Playing a sport like basketball, either on a team or recreationally, can improve the overall health of your heart and lungs.

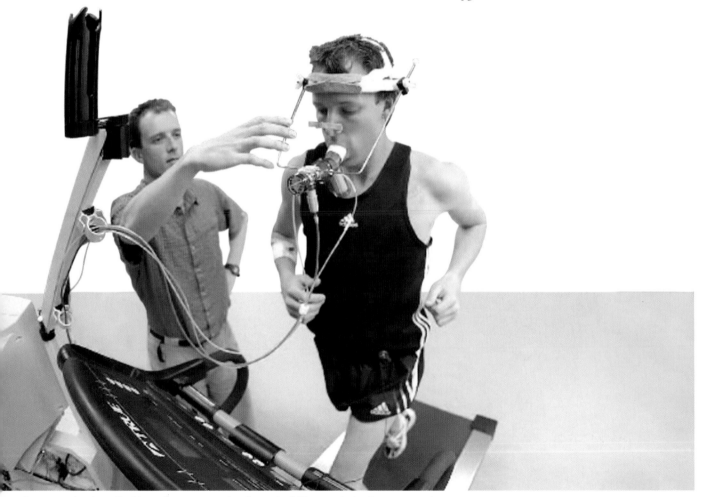

Oxygen and carbon dioxide analyses are used to determine VO$_2$ MAX during intense exercise.

## Finding Your Resting Heart Rate

Heart rates vary from person to person, but the average **Resting Heart Rate** (the number of times your heart beats per minute when you are at rest) is between 70 and 80 beats per minute (bpm).

Having a Resting Heart Rate of 60 to 50 bpm generally means that you have a strong heart. Some endurance athletes such as Olympic-level cross-country skiers have Resting Heart Rates in the low 40s.

The difference between a Resting Heart Rate of 60 beats per minute and one with 75 beats per minute is the strength of the left ventricle. Remember, the left ventricle is the chamber that pumps oxygen-rich blood to the body (see Chapter 3).

To be sure, genetics play a role in determining one's Resting Heart Rate. Nevertheless, you can still do much to improve the strength of your heart with regular aerobic exercise and a better diet. Doing aerobic exercise causes the left ventricle to become stronger over time.

Heart rate monitors, which provide constant feedback on changes in your heart rate, are a safe and convenient way to keep track of your aerobic effort during exercise.

## Finding Your Pulse

To find your Resting Heart Rate you first need to find your pulse. The two main locations are the carotid artery on your neck and the radial artery on your wrist. Once you have found one of these sites, count each time over the course of a minute that the artery "pulses" against your fingers (or count for 10 seconds and multiply by six). Be sure to use your index and middle finger and not your thumb since your thumb has its own pulse.

The most accurate way is to take your resting pulse three mornings in a row, just after waking up. Add them together and divide by three to get the average.

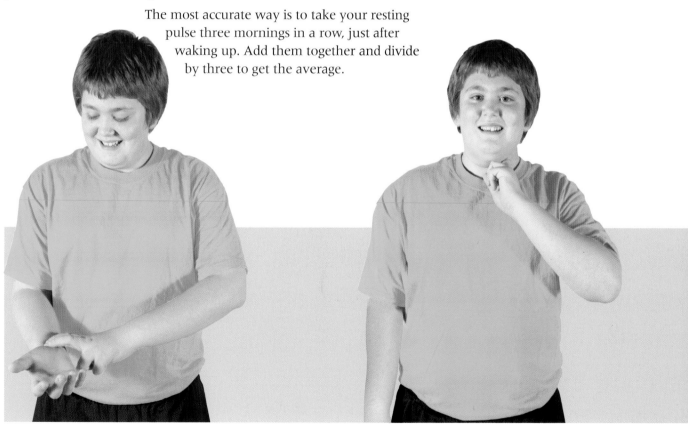

Finding your pulse at the radial artery.

Finding your pulse at the carotid artery.

## Staying in the Zone

To get the most out of an aerobic exercise session, you need to determine the range within which you should aim to exercise your heart. This is known as your **Target Heart Rate Zone.** If you are exercising within this range, you are getting the maximum aerobic benefit from your workout session.

### Heart Rate Reserve

The common way to find your Target Heart Rate Zone is to use the Heart Rate Reserve method. You can think of your Heart Rate Reserve (HRR) as the additional capacity of your heart to pump blood to your body over and above what is otherwise required when you are at rest.

To find your HRR all you need is your Resting Heart Rate (RHR), your Maximal Heart Rate (MHR), and a simple calculation.

➤ **Maximal Heart Rate.** You can find your Maximal Heart Rate by subtracting your age from 220.

$$MHR = 220 - age$$

For example, 15-year-old Jasmine's MHR is 205 bpm (220-15).

➤ **Heart Rate Reserve.**
To find your Heart Rate Reserve, simply take your MHR and subtract your Resting Heart Rate.

$$HRR = MHR - RHR$$

Jasmine's RHR is 75 and her MHR is 205. Therefore, her Heart Rate Reserve is 130 bpm (205-75).

Working hard during various activities and games in H&PE class will ensure that you are in your Target Heart Rate Zone.

Staying in your Target Heart Rate Zone is essential to improve your cardiorespiratory fitness.

## Target Heart Rate Zone

To get the maximum health benefit from an aerobic workout, CPAFLA recommends that you should normally aim to exercise at 50 percent to 85 percent of your HRR. In Jasmine's case, this would be between 65 bpm (.50 × 130) and 110.5 bpm (.85 × 130).

Once you have your HRR, you can easily find your Target Heart Rate Zone. To get the lower limit, add your RHR to the lower limit of your HRR. To get the upper limit, add your RHR to the upper limit of your HRR.

> Target Heart Rate Zone (Lower Limit) = (50 percent of HRR) + RHR
> Target Heart Rate Zone (Upper Limit) = (85 percent of HRR) + RHR

So, for example, in Jasmine's case, her Target Heart Rate Zone is between 140 bpm (65 + 75) and 185.5 bpm (110.5 + 75). In other words, at the end of an active aerobic session, Jasmine should have a heart rate between 140 and 186 (rounded up from 185.5) beats per minute to ensure that she is exercising at a healthy aerobic intensity.

Above that range, she may be working too hard; below that range, she will not get the maximum benefit from her exercise session.

Exercising at 50 percent to 85 percent of your HRR ensures that you get the maximum health benefit from an aerobic workout.

## Finding Your Zone
### Getting the Most out of an Aerobic Workout

If you work your heart and lungs "all out" all the time, you may cause yourself serious harm. Yet, if you work below your limits, you will not make the health and fitness gains you are seeking.

To get the most out of your workout, you must stay within your Target Heart Rate Zone. Work within your zone and you will begin to see significant improvements in the health of your cardiorespiratory system.

### The Key Formulae

Here are the basic formulae for finding the upper and lower limits of your Target Heart Rate Zone:

- Maximal Heart Rate (MHR) = 220 bpm – age
- Heart Rate Reserve (HRR) = MHR – Resting Heart Rate (RHR)
- Target Heart Rate Zone:
      Lower limit = 50% HRR + RHR
      Upper limit = 85% HRR + RHR

After each appraisal period, re-calculate these values. If you have worked hard, your heart and all its supporting structures will have become stronger.

### Working Example

**Question:** Jeff is 14 years old. His Resting Heart Rate is 70. What is Jeff's MHR, his HRR, and his Target Heart Rate Zone?

**Answer:**

| | | |
|---|---|---|
| Jeff's **Maximal Heart Rate** = | | 220 – 14 = 206 |
| Jeff's **Heart Rate Reserve** = | | 206 – 70 = 136 |
| Jeff's **Target Heart Rate Zone** | | |
| Lower Limit | = | 50% HRR + RHR |
| | = | .50 × 136 + RHR |
| | = | 68 + 70 |
| | = | 138 bpm |
| Upper Limit | = | 85% HRR + RHR |
| | = | .85 × 136 + RHR |
| | = | 115.6 + 70 |
| | = | 186 bpm (rounded up from 185.6) |

During an active aerobic session, Jeff should have a heart rate between 138 and 186 beats per minute to ensure that he is exercising at a good aerobic intensity. Initially, Jeff should start on the lower end of his Target Heart Rate Zone, progressing to the higher ranges as he becomes more fit.

# Modified Canadian Aerobic Fitness Test

A good appraisal for estimating your overall aerobic fitness is the **Modified Canadian Aerobic Fitness Test (mCAFT)**. It is the only aerobic fitness test in the CPAFLA appraisals. The mCAFT is a "sub-maximal" appraisal—meaning that you will not be going "all out" or "full blast" during the appraisal. It is most appropriate for beginners and those who see themselves as currently being relatively unfit. Like other CPAFLA appraisals, mCAFT is standardized for persons 15 years and over.

For the mCAFT appraisal, the Ceiling Heart Rate (see page 64) is set at 85 percent of the Maximal Heart Rate for your age group. CPAFLA recommends that a heart rate monitor is used during the administration of this appraisal.

If there are medical reasons that you cannot take this or any other appraisal, you should notify your teacher well ahead of time.

## Getting Started

You will complete one or more sessions of three minutes of stepping until you reach your predetermined Ceiling Heart Rate for your age group. The pace at which you perform the mCAFT appraisal is determined for you by a recording.

The recording also tells you when to stop and take your pulse to see if you have reached your ceiling. This is a built-in safety feature of the mCAFT appraisal. You should never proceed to the next stage once you have reached your Ceiling Heart Rate.

You have two choices on how to climb the steps: the "two-step" or "one-step" technique. The "one-step" variation is more suitable for taller individuals or those that see themselves as being more fit. Both techniques are illustrated on the opposite page.

## Practise the Movements First

To get accurate results, you will want to perform the appraisal under the best conditions possible. Before proceeding to take the actual test itself, you should:

➤ Practise the stepping sequence first without, and then with, the recording.

➤ Ensure you practise the stepping motion so that both feet end up on the top step with legs extended, and your back straight.

➤ Ensure that you can maintain a constant stepping tempo.

➤ Practise finding your heart rate within the window of time allowed on the recording.

Remember, if you have any concerns as to whether you should undertake the mCAFT appraisal, consult with your physical education teacher beforehand. Be sure to review the safety guidelines before undertaking the appraisal.

## Safety Guidelines

Before participating in any cardiorespiratory appraisal, follow the safety guidelines below to make your experience a safe and beneficial one:

- Any individual with joint injuries or cardiorespiratory illness should not participate in the appraisal without medical clearance
- Do not eat two hours before, or drink fluids 15 minutes prior to, the appraisal session
- Wear appropriate footwear and clothing during the appraisal
- Do not exercise six hours prior to the appraisal or perform heavy exercise the day before
- Do not perform the appraisal in hot and humid weather
- Do not eat, smoke, or have a caffeinated drink for two hours before the appraisal
- Listen and follow the safety guidelines outlined by your teacher

## The Two-Step Test

## The One-Step Test

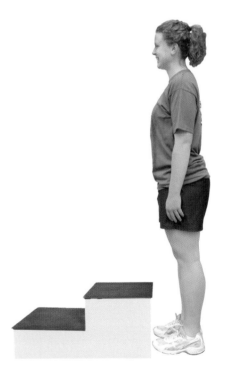

**B**elow are the starting stages and Ceiling Heart Rates for the mCAFT appraisal for persons 15 years of age and older. Pay close attention to the values and do not exceed them.

**Starting Stage.** The starting stages for females and males, ages 15 to 19, are

- **Females:** Stage 3
- **Males:** Stage 4

**Ceiling Heart Rate.** The Ceiling Heart Rate for males and females ages 15 and 16 are

- **Age 15:** 29 beats in a 10-second count (or 174 on your heart rate monitor)*
- **Age 16:** 28 beats in a 10-second count (or 173 on your heart rate monitor)*

If you touch or surpass the Ceiling Heart Rate for your age at any time during the appraisal, you must immediately stop. Record the last stage completed in your activity handbook.

*Note:* If you are using a heart rate monitor, CPAFLA sets the Ceiling Heart Rate at 173 for persons aged 16 (instead of 168, which would be the case if you simply multiplied the 10-second count by six).

## mCAFT—Ready, Set, Go!

Now that you have had some practice with the stepping sequence and finding your heart rate, you are ready to begin the mCAFT appraisal.

Listen carefully to your teacher and follow the instructions below. Once the appraisal begins, listen to the cues on the CD or cassette tape as to when to start and stop to take your pulse.

➤ From the sidebar on this page, obtain your Ceiling Heart Rate and the starting stages for your age and sex.

➤ Stop the test if you begin to stagger, feel dizzy, have extreme leg pain, or feel nausea or chest pain.

➤ Stop when your heart rate is equal to or above your Ceiling Heart Rate.

## Oxygen Used (O₂ Cost)

With your mCAFT result, you can calculate an "Aerobic Fitness Score" based on the final stage you were able to reach. Each stage represents a different stepping cadence (steps per minute).

Essentially, you note your $O_2$ cost (the amount of oxygen you consumed) and plug it into the standard formula that has been developed for this purpose by CPAFLA.

Your $O_2$ cost can be determined from the table below.

An example of how to find your Aerobic Fitness Score is provided on the following page.

### Finding Your "O₂ Cost" Based on Your mCAFT Results

| mCAFT | FEMALES | | MALES | |
|---|---|---|---|---|
| STAGE COMPLETED | STEPPING CADENCE | O₂ COST | STEPPING CADENCE | O₂ COST |
| 1 | 66 | 15.9 | 66 | 15.9 |
| 2 | 84 | 18.0 | 84 | 18.0 |
| 3 | 102 | 22.0 | 102 | 22.0 |
| 4 | 114 | 24.5 | 114 | 24.5 |
| 5 | 120 | 26.3 | 132 | 29.5 |
| 6 | 132 | 29.5 | 144 | 33.6 |
| 7 | 144 | 33.6 | 118* | 36.2 |
| 8 | 118* | 36.2 | 132* | 40.1 |

* Single-step test. O2 cost is measured in ml.kg-1.min-1

**Source:** Reproduced with permission of the Canadian Society for Exercise Physiology.

## Finding Your Aerobic Fitness Score (AFS)

Using your mCAFT results, you can calculate your Aerobic Fitness Score (AFS) quite easily. Here is how you do it.

First, from the table on the previous page, find the amount of oxygen you used (your $O_2$ cost) based on the last stage you completed. Then, plug that number into the AFS formula below.

$$AFS = 10 \times [17.2 + (1.29 \times O_2 \text{ cost}) - (0.09 \times \text{weight in kg}) - (0.18 \times \text{age})]$$

Once you have your raw AFS, you can locate your Health Benefit Zone using the table in the sidebar. Be sure to record your rating in your activity handbook.

## A Working Example

Let's take a real-life example, using Jasmine's mCAFT results:

| | |
|---|---|
| Jasmine's age | 15 years old |
| Jasmine's weight | 66 kg |
| Final stage completed | 6 |

From the table on the previous page, we see that the $O_2$ cost at Stage 6 for a female is 29.5.

Therefore, Jasmine's AFS is

$$
\begin{aligned}
AFS &= 10 \times [17.2 + (1.29 \times 29.5) - (0.09 \times 66) - (0.18 \times 15)] \\
&= 10 \times [17.2 + 38.055 - 5.94 - 2.7] \\
&= 10 \times 46.615 \\
&= 466.15
\end{aligned}
$$

From the table on the right, you can see that Jasmine's Aerobic Fitness Rating (a female aged 15 who reached Stage 6 in the mCAFT appraisal) is "very good."

Full participation in H&PE class can help improve your AFS.

### How Well Did You Do?

Find your Aerobic Fitness Rating using the table below. Record your score and your rating in your activity handbook.

| AGES 15 TO 19 | FEMALES |
|---|---|
| Excellent | $\geq 490$ |
| Very Good | 437–489 |
| Good | 395–436 |
| Fair | 368–394 |
| Needs Improvement | < 368 |

| AGES 15 TO 19 | MALES |
|---|---|
| Excellent | $\geq 574$ |
| Very Good | 524–573 |
| Good | 488–523 |
| Fair | 436–487 |
| Needs Improvement | <436 |

You can refer back to the Health Benefits Zones table on page 13 to interpret your rating. The greatest health improvement is to move from a "fair" to a "good" rating.

Remember, regardless of your score, participating fully in your physical education classes will improve your results next time.

**Source:** Reproduced with permission of the Canadian Society for Exercise Physiology.

# The 12-Minute Run

The **12-Minute Run** (also known as the Cooper Test) was designed for military use by the American researcher Dr. Kenneth H. Cooper in 1968. The 12-Minute Run sets out to determine one's aerobic capacity based on the distance completed over 12 minutes.

This appraisal is suitable for all fitness levels, but make sure you are properly warmed up first. Ideally, you want to pick a jogging or running pace that you are comfortable with, since this will ensure the greatest distance covered. Beginners or less-fit individuals may walk or jog during any part of the appraisal.

Again, if there are any medical reasons why you cannot take this appraisal, you should inform your health and physical education teacher well ahead of time.

## Ready, Set, Go!

All you need to perform this test is a partner and a running surface that is marked off by 100-metre markers. Your partner will keep track of your laps while waiting for his or her turn.

When the teacher signals you to start, select a pace that will enable you to run for 12 minutes. Usually, after each lap, your teacher will read off how much time you have been running. Try to adjust your speed so that you can last 12 minutes.

At the 10-minute mark, your teacher will give you a warning indicating the time remaining. Pick up the pace, if you can, until the whistle blows. Walk back and record the distance covered in laps and metres in your activity handbook.

Before you count for your partner, be sure to cool down until your heart rate returns to normal.

During your next appraisal period, you should try to increase the distance you covered.

The 12-Minute Run is suitable for all fitness levels.

# Breath Sound Check and Talk Test
## Simple Ways to Monitor Aerobic Effort

Developed by Professor Bob Goode and his team from the University of Toronto, the **Breath Sound Check** and **Talk Test** are alternative ways to monitor the intensity of aerobic activity.

### The Breath Sound Check

The Breath Sound Check is based on the idea that you should be able to hear your breathing while exercising aerobically. This ensures you have reached the minimum benefit level of aerobic exercise intensity.

Jog slowly or walk briskly for one minute. Gradually increase the pace so you can just start to hear your breathing and maintain that pace. You are now in the Breath Sound Check zone.

As you become more fit, you will have to jog faster or longer before you can hear your breathing. Now you are getting in shape.

### The Talk Test

The principle behind the Talk Test is quite simple: you should be able to carry on a conversation during your aerobic activity.

If you are out of breath and having difficulty talking, then you are working too hard.

Conversely, if you can carry on a conversation too easily, then you are not working hard enough.

## The Beep Test

In 1982, Dr. Luc Léger and his team at the University of Montreal developed a 20-metre shuttle-run appraisal. A sound from an audio recording determines how fast the participants will have to run. Today, this test is referred to as simply the **"Beep Test"** because of the beep sound made to indicate that the runner should change direction.

### A "Maximal" Appraisal

The Beep Test gives results that compare with the high-tech appraisals conducted under laboratory settings. It is a highly accurate way to measure your maximal oxygen consumption or $VO_2$ MAX.

The Beep Test is a "maximal" appraisal, which means that at some point you will be going all out. You should attempt this test only if you are in good physical condition and only under the supervision of qualified instructors. If you are in good condition, this is the test for you. Otherwise, you will likely struggle and last only a few stages.

Again, do not select this test if you have any medical condition or you do not feel completely comfortable with it. Your physical education teacher will have alternative appraisals better suited to your needs.

Before participating in any cardiorespiratory appraisal, be sure to read the "Safety Guidelines" found on page 62 to ensure a safe testing experience. If you have any questions or concerns, be sure to ask your teacher before you begin.

You can also use a pedometer to keep track of your total steps during the Beep Test.

The Beep Test is an accurate way to measure your maximal oxygen consumption or $VO_2$ MAX.

## Ready, Set, Go!

As noted on the previous page, the Beep Test is a "Maximal" fitness appraisal (and therefore, not for everyone). It is conducted over a 20-metre distance and can be performed in a gymnasium, hallway, or on a tennis court. Whichever surface you choose, make sure you use the same one to repeat the test later in the year. This will increase the accuracy and the consistency of the results.

Begin at the first pylon (the starting line) and briskly walk or lightly jog to the second pylon at the first beep sound. You must reach the 20-metre line (second pylon) before the next beep sound. If you get there before the next beep sound, wait! You cannot head back to the first pylon until you hear the beep sound again. Each minute the pace will pick up and soon you will be sprinting from pylon to pylon.

## How Did You Do?

The test ends when you have failed to reach a pylon for two consecutive beep sounds. At that point, record your final stage in your activity handbook and follow the instructions below to see how well you performed.

A feature of the Beep Test is that it requires no calculations. All you need is your age and the number of the last stage you completed. Determine your rating by locating the final stage you completed in the table below. Record your rating in your activity handbook.

Participate fully in physical education class in the months to follow, and you will undoubtedly raise your rating the next time you take the Beep Test.

Beginning with a brisk walk, the pace will pick up after each beep.

## Beep Test Standards

| RATING | MALES (NUMBER OF STAGES COMPLETED) | | | FEMALES (NUMBER OF STAGES COMPLETED) | | |
|---|---|---|---|---|---|---|
| | AGE 13 | AGE 14 | AGE 15 | AGE 13 | AGE 14 | AGE 15 |
| Excellent | $\geq 9.4$ | $\geq 9.9$ | $\geq 10.5$ | $\geq 7.0$ | $\geq 6.5$ | $\geq 7.0$ |
| Very Good | 8.1–9.3 | 8.6–9.8 | 9.4–10.4 | 5.6–6.9 | 5.1–6.4 | 5.5–6.9 |
| Good | 7.0–8.0 | 7.5–8.5 | 8.1–9.3 | 4.6–5.5 | 4.3–5.0 | 5.0–5.4 |
| Acceptable | 6.0–6.9 | 6.2–7.4 | 6.5–8.0 | 3.6–4.5 | 3.5–4.2 | 4.0–4.9 |
| Needs Improvement | $\leq 5.9$ | $\leq 6.1$ | $\leq 6.4$ | $\leq 3.5$ | $\leq 3.4$ | $\leq 3.9$ |

**Source:** Léger, L.A., Mercier, D., Gadoury, C., and Lambert, J. The Multistage 20 -m Shuttle Run Test for Aerobic Fitness. J. Sports Sci. 6: 93-101, 1988.
The Beep Test CD is available at the Quebec Branch of CSEP's Health and Fitness Program (info@kinesiologue.com).

## Career Focus
## Becoming a Personal Fitness Trainer

I f the fitness industry appeals to you, check the careers below to see which one might suit you.

- **Fitness Leaders**. Fitness leaders learn how to conduct aerobics, aquafit, or a variety of other fitness classes. Fitness leadership certifications can be acquired through many universities, colleges, and private fitness clubs.

- **Certified Fitness Consultant (CFC)**. As a CFC, you are recognized by the Canadian Society for Exercise Physiology (CSEP) and can administer the CPAFLA tests. CFCs provide people with feedback and can suggest how individuals can improve their current level of fitness.

- **Personal Trainers (Fitness Appraisers)**. The CSEP recently introduced its personal trainers certificate, called the CSEP-Certified Personal Trainer. With this certification you can administer the CPAFLA protocol and provide individuals with customized physical activity and lifestyle plans.

- **Professional Fitness Leadership Consultants (PFLC)**. In order to become a PFLC, you must have a university degree in health and physical education (also known as kinesiology, kinetics, or exercise science). A professional fitness leadership consultant can apply many more types of appraisals than the other trainers mentioned above.

When choosing a training agency, be sure to pick one that will give you the most information, keep you current (conferences, workshops, or online learning), and has qualified instructors.

Other factors to consider include:

- The cost of certification, fees for courses, and materials such as manuals and books

- Whether the certification includes insurance and how much coverage you will receive

Visit the links at **www.csep.ca** to find out about certification in your province or territory.

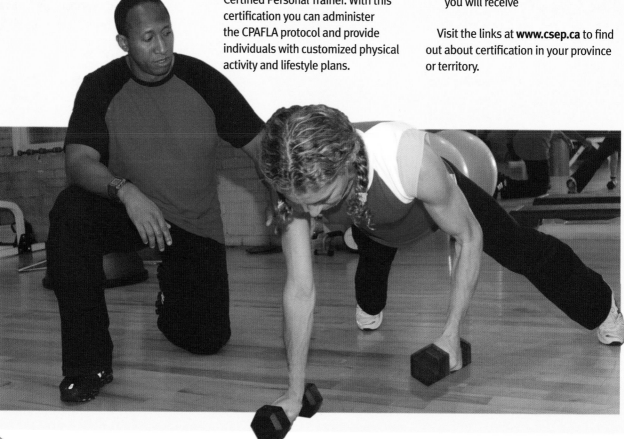

## Questions for Study and Review

### Things to Think About and Explore

1. Define what is meant by aerobic fitness.
2. Explain how the 12-Minute Run is suitable for all fitness levels.
3. Examine the importance of determining your Target Heart Rate, and describe the calculations you must make to find your Target Heart Rate Zone.
4. Investigate the advantages, for all levels of fitness, of doing the mCAFT appraisal.
5. Explain how you would go about determining your aerobic fitness score from your mCAFT appraisal.
6. Explain how the Talk Test and Breath Sound Check can be used to estimate the intensity of aerobic activity.

### Things to Do and Practise

7. Calculate your average Resting Heart Rate over a period of three mornings and record your findings. Once you have determined your average, calculate your Heart Rate Reserve to find your Target Heart Rate Zone.
8. Take your heart rate during a strenuous exercise session in class to see if you are exercising in your Target Heart Rate Zone. Explain why it is important to get your heart rate into this zone when exercising.
9. Choose three safety guidelines for the appraisals. Create a poster that presents compelling reasons as to why those three guidelines are in place.
10. Make an instructional booklet that describes the Beep Test and include all of the pertinent information regarding the Beep Test and results.
11. Based on your cardiorespiratory appraisal, create a list demonstrating the steps you need to take to improve or maintain your current level.
12. Interview someone who has chosen a career in the fitness industry. You may use a tape recorder, a video camera, or notation. Be prepared to present your interview to the class.

## WWWeblinks

Name ➤ Canadian Association for Health Physical Education Recreation and Dance

URL ➤ www.cahperd.ca

A national, charitable organization whose main goal is to influence the healthy development of children and youth by advocating for quality, school-based physical and health education.

Name ➤ Canadian Parks and Recreation Association

URL ➤ www.cpra.ca

A national organization dedicated to realizing the full potential of parks and recreation services as a major contributor to community health.

Name ➤ Youth Ontario

URL ➤ www.children.gov.on.ca

A Government of Ontario site that focuses on the concerns of young people in the province.

# 5
# Muscular Strength and Endurance Appraisals

T he appraisals in this chapter focus on muscular strength, muscular endurance, and flexibility. You can achieve many health benefits by addressing these aspects of your overall fitness. Most importantly, you will be able to perform everyday activities without fatigue or soreness. In turn, this will enhance your quality of life as well as your confidence.

These appraisals measure, with the aim of improving, overall musculoskeletal fitness. Some appraisals focus on specific muscles or muscle groups; others involve many muscles at one time. For sure, all these appraisals will give you a good workout, and you will see improvements after participating fully in your Health and Physical Education class.

Whichever appraisal you choose, your results can be used to design a program that addresses your individual fitness needs. (You'll learn all about developing a personal fitness program in Unit 3.)

> *The human body is made up of some four hundred muscles; evolved through centuries of physical activity. Unless they are used, they will deteriorate.*

**Eugene Lyman Fisk**

Chairman of the Life Extension Institute

## Key Terms

- ➢ musculoskeletal fitness
- ➢ muscular strength/endurance
- ➢ flexibility
- ➢ Grip Strength Appraisal
- ➢ Push-Ups
- ➢ Partial Curl-Ups Appraisal
- ➢ Sit-and-Reach Appraisal
- ➢ Vertical Jump Appraisal
- ➢ performance-level appraisals
- ➢ Dot Drill
- ➢ Illinois Agility Run
- ➢ Wall-Ball Toss
- ➢ 20- and 40-Yard Sprints
- ➢ Chin-Ups/Flexed-Arm Hang Appraisals

## Chapter Objectives

In this chapter, you will:

- ➢ Explore what is meant by the term "musculoskeletal fitness"
- ➢ Distinguish between "muscular strength" and "muscular endurance"
- ➢ Learn how to perform the following basic-level musculoskeletal fitness tests: grip strength, push-ups, partial curl-up, the sit-and-reach appraisal, and the vertical jump
- ➢ Learn how to interpret your musculoskeletal results using CPAFLA's scores and ratings
- ➢ Identify common "performance-level appraisals" that focus more on measuring (and improving) speed, agility, and coordination

# Musculoskeletal Fitness

**Musculoskeletal fitness** refers to muscular strength and muscular endurance as well as to the flexibility of your joints. Muscular strength and muscular endurance are often used interchangeably, but they are not the same.

> **Muscular strength** refers to the maximum force a muscle can exert in a single contraction.

> **Muscular endurance** refers to a muscle's ability to perform repeatedly without fatigue.

In the context of physical activity, **flexibility** simply refers to the ability of joints to bend through their full range of movement (ROM). The more flexible your joints, the more you will be able to perform physical activity effortlessly.

The musculoskeletal appraisals in the first part of this chapter are part of the Canadian Physical Activity, Fitness & Lifestyle Approach (CPAFLA). Whichever of these CPAFLA appraisals you choose, try your best (without overdoing it). As with most things, good effort usually yields good results.

As a bonus, at the end of this chapter, there are additional appraisals (performance appraisals) that you will find more challenging.

Musculoskeletal fitness appraisals measure muscular strength, muscular endurance, and joint flexibility.

Muscular strength refers to the force a muscle can exert in a single contraction.

# Grip Strength

The **Grip Strength Appraisal** uses a device called a hand-grip dynamometer. This device can be adjusted to suit your hand size. Readings are expressed in kilograms.

Even though this appraisal specifically measures the strength of your forearm muscles, research suggests that this is a good indicator of overall muscular strength. This makes perfect sense, since most of the intense physical work that we do requires a firm grip. Such activities include: carrying groceries, lifting boxes, shovelling snow, mountain biking, and rock climbing, just to name a few.

## Ready, Set, Go!

To use the dynamometer and get a measure of your grip strength, follow the instructions below and refer to the sidebar to obtain an overall rating:

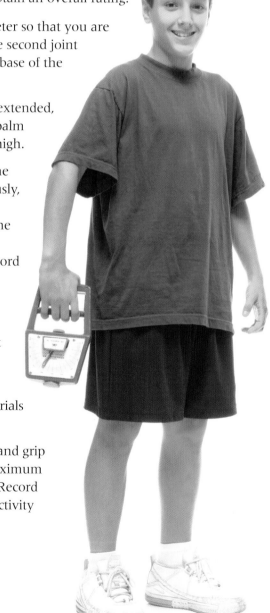

➤ Adjust the dynamometer so that you are holding it between the second joint of the fingers and the base of the thumb.

➤ Stand with your arm extended, away from the body, palm facing towards your thigh.

➤ Exhale and squeeze the dynamometer vigorously, without moving your arm position. Check the level attained on the dynamometer and record your results (in kg).

➤ Switch the dynamometer to the other hand and repeat as stated above.

➤ Measure both hands alternately, with two trials for each hand.

➤ In order to get your hand grip score, add the two maximum scores for each hand. Record these values in your activity handbook.

## How Well Did You Do?

The table below will provide you with your rating on the Grip Strength Appraisal.

| AGES 15–19 | FEMALES |
|---|---|
| Excellent | ≧ 68 kg |
| Very Good | 60–67 kg |
| Good | 53–59 kg |
| Fair | 48–52 kg |
| Need Improvement | ≦ 47 kg |

| AGES 15–19 | MALES |
|---|---|
| Excellent | ≧ 108 kg |
| Very Good | 98–107 kg |
| Good | 90–97 kg |
| Fair | 79–89 kg |
| Need Improvement | ≦ 78 kg |

You can refer back to the Health Benefits Zones table on page 13 to interpret your rating. The greatest health improvement is to move from a "fair" to a "good" rating.

Remember, regardless of your score, participating fully in your physical education classes will improve your results next time.

**Source:** Reproduced with permission of the Canadian Society for Exercise Physiology.

# Push-Ups

The **Push-Ups Appraisal** is a good all-round indicator of upper-body strength. The largest muscle used is your chest muscle (pectoralis major). Push-ups also work your shoulders and triceps.

There are two variations—the "modified push-up" and the "standard push-up." CPAFLA standardizes the scores for males and females separately, with females doing modified push-ups and males doing standard push-ups. In truth, of course, females can perform standard push-ups just as males can and, most likely, this out-dated feature of the appraisal will change in future releases.

## Ready, Set, Go!

The appraisal involves performing as many as you can consecutively, with no time limit. The appraisal ends when you are straining notice-ably or are unable to maintain proper technique over two consecutive repetitions.

Whether you are performing the standard or modified push-up, follow the instructions below:

➢ Lie face down on the floor or a mat, with feet together and hands under the shoulders, and with your chin just touching the floor.

➢ Push up until both arms are fully extended, keeping your body in a straight line.

➢ Return to the start position without touching the floor or mat and repeat up and down.

➢ Remember to keep your back straight. In standard push-ups, remember to keep your legs straight, too.

In your activity handbook, record the number of push-ups that you can perform and refer to the sidebar for your overall rating.

## How Well Did You Do?

**U**se the table below to find your overall rating on the Push-Ups Appraisal.

| AGES 15–19 | FEMALES (MODIFIED) |
|---|---|
| Excellent | ≧ 33 |
| Very Good | 25–32 |
| Good | 18–24 |
| Fair | 12–17 |
| Need Improvement | ≦ 11 |

| AGES 15–19 | MALES (STANDARD) |
|---|---|
| Excellent | ≧ 39 |
| Very Good | 29–38 |
| Good | 23–28 |
| Fair | 18–22 |
| Need Improvement | ≦ 17 |

You can refer back to the Health Benefits Zones table on page 13 to interpret your rating. The greatest health improvement is to move from a "fair" to a "good" rating.

Feel free to try both variations of this appraisal—if only for fun.

**Source:** Reproduced with permission of the Canadian Society for Exercise Physiology.

# Partial Curl-Up

In recent years, there has been much attention in the fitness community on the need to improve "core strength" (the muscles of the anterior and posterior trunk). These muscles largely are responsible, among other things, for maintaining proper posture.

The **Partial Curl-Up Appraisal** is a good test for "the core" because it measures the muscular strength and endurance of the anterior trunk—specifically, rectus abdominis (often referred to simply as the "abs"). Developing strong abdominal muscles will help to prevent back injuries and enable more efficient energy transfer from the legs to the upper body.

## Ready, Set, Go!

The partial curl-up appraisal is done to a 50-beat-per-minute count (set by a metronome). Your goal is to perform a maximum of 25 consecutive curl-ups in one minute. The appraisal ends when the minute is up.

Stop if you experience undue discomfort or if you are unable to maintain the pace or your technique over two consecutive sit-up repetitions. Follow the instructions and refer to the illustration below to begin your assessment:

➤ Lie on your back with your head resting on a mat. Keep your arms at your sides, palms in contact with the mat, with the middle finger of each hand on the 0-cm mark (indicated by a strip of tape on the floor).

➤ Keeping your heels in contact with the mat (do not anchor feet), curl up so that the middle finger of each hand reaches the 10-cm mark (indicated by a second strip of tape on the floor)

➤ Lower back down so that your shoulders and head touch the mat and tips of your index fingers touch the 0-cm mark.

➤ Repeat for one minute to the beat of the metronome.

In your activity handbook, record the number of curl-ups you are able to perform and refer to the sidebar to find your overall rating.

---

## How Well Did You Do?

The table below will provide your partial curl-up rating. Take the total number of repetitions completed in one minute and see how well you performed.

| AGES 15–19 | FEMALES |
|---|---|
| Excellent | $\geqq$ 25 |
| Very Good | 22–24 |
| Good | 17–21 |
| Fair | 12–16 |
| Need Improvement | $\leqq$ 11 |

| AGES 15–19 | MALES |
|---|---|
| Excellent | $\geqq$ 25 |
| Very Good | 23–24 |
| Good | 21–22 |
| Fair | 16–20 |
| Need Improvement | $\leqq$ 15 |

You can refer back to the Health Benefits Zones table on page 13 to interpret your rating. The greatest health improvement is to move from a "fair" to a "good" rating.

Remember, regardless of your score, participating fully in H&PE classes will improve your testing results next time.

**Source:** Reproduced with permission of the Canadian Society for Exercise Physiology.

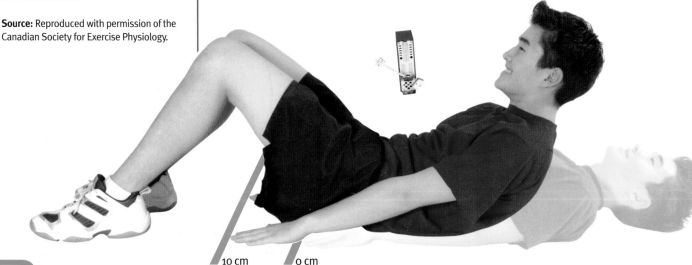

10 cm        0 cm

# Sit-and-Reach

The **Sit-and-Reach Appraisal** measures joint flexibility using a special device called a flexometer. The flexometer will allow you to measure how far you can reach forward from a sitting position.

A number of factors can affect flexibility, including the structure of the joint itself, the bulk of the muscle close to the joint, and the length of its ligaments and tendons. In young people, growth spurts also can affect flexibility. Muscle tightness also will compromise range of movement (ROM) and may lead to an increased risk of injury.

Your results on the sit-and-reach appraisal may be limited if you have poor flexibility in the hamstrings (back of the thigh) or back muscles.

## Ready, Set, Go!

Remove your shoes and make sure you are warmed up before trying this appraisal. Follow the instructions and refer to the illustration below:

➤ Sit in front of the flexometer, legs fully extended, with the soles of the feet against the box (approximately 15 cm apart).

➤ Slowly reach forward with both arms, palms down, keeping your legs fully extended.

➤ Hold for two seconds, then relax.

➤ Repeat this sit-and-reach twice, and record your position on the flexometer each time to the nearest 0.5 cm.

➤ If your knees flex, the trial is not counted, in which case you must repeat the appraisal.

➤ When finished, record the best result in your activity handbook and refer to the sidebar to find your overall rating.

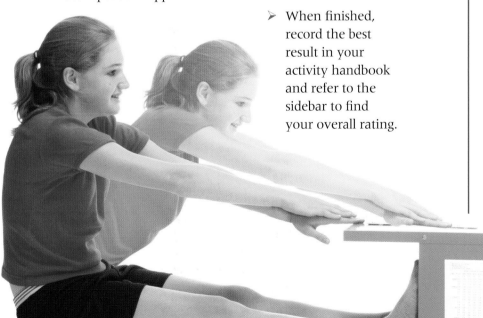

## How Well Did You Do?

**U**se the table below to find your sit-and-reach rating. Be sure to have a good warm up beforehand so as to avoid injury.

| Ages 15–19 | Females |
| --- | --- |
| Excellent | ≧ 43 cm |
| Very Good | 38–42 cm |
| Good | 34–37 cm |
| Fair | 29–33 cm |
| Need Improvement | ≦ 28 cm |

| Ages 15–19 | Males |
| --- | --- |
| Excellent | ≧ 39 cm |
| Very Good | 34–38 cm |
| Good | 29–33 cm |
| Fair | 24–28 cm |
| Need Improvement | ≦ 23 cm |

You can refer back to the Health Benefits Zones table on page 13 to interpret your rating. The greatest health improvement is to move from a "fair" to a "good" rating.

Improving your core flexibility is not as difficult as you might think. As with everything, it just takes a little practice.

**Source:** Reproduced with permission of the Canadian Society for Exercise Physiology.

Using the table below, you can now find the overall rating you achieved on CPAFLA's Vertical Jump Appraisal.

| Ages 15–19 | Females |
|---|---|
| Excellent | $\geq$ 40 cm |
| Very Good | 36–39 cm |
| Good | 32–35 cm |
| Fair | 28–31 cm |
| Need Improvement | $\leq$ 27 cm |

| Ages 15–19 | Males |
|---|---|
| Excellent | $\geq$ 56 cm |
| Very Good | 51–55 cm |
| Good | 46–50 cm |
| Fair | 42–45 cm |
| Need Improvement | $\leq$ 41 cm |

You can refer back to the Health Benefits Zones table on page 13 to interpret your rating. The greatest health improvement is to move from a "fair" to a "good" rating.

Again, remember, regardless of your score on this appraisal, participating fully in H&PE class will lead to improvements next time.

**Source:** Reproduced with permission of the Canadian Society for Exercise Physiology.

# Vertical Jump

A **Vertical Jump Appraisal** requires the use of almost all the major muscles in the body. The muscles that do the pushing and lifting are your gluteus maximus, quadriceps, and calfs. The upper-body muscles activated include the abdominals, the deltoids, and the back muscles.

This appraisal measures "muscular power" (the ability to exert a large amount of force quickly). Muscular power is especially important in sports and physical activities that involve jumping, throwing, and rapid lifting.

## Ready, Set, Go!

All you need to perform this appraisal is a partner, a wall, and measuring tape. Follow the instructions below and refer to the illustration on the opposite page to ensure a proper assessment:

> ➤ Stand sideways to a wall and reach as high as possible with your fingers fully extended; record this stand-and-reach height to the nearest 0.5 cm.

> ➤ Move away from the wall slightly. Bend your knees and bring arms down and back.

> ➤ Pause, then bend your legs and jump as high as possible, moving the arms forward and upward to touch the wall.

> ➤ Record how high you were able to reach in cm.

> ➤ Rest 10–15 seconds between each jump, and then perform two more trials.

> ➤ Subtract the stand-and-reach height from the best of the three trials and record the difference in your activity handbook.

## Estimating Your "Peak Leg Power" (PLP)

Your Peak Leg Power (PLP) also can be determined from the vertical jump appraisal by taking into account your body weight. Simply plug in the values and check the table to find your overall rating:

$$PLP = (60.7 \times \text{jump height in cm}) + (45.3 \times \text{body mass in kg}) - 2055$$

## Peak Leg Power (Watts )

| Ages 15–19 | Males | Females |
|---|---|---|
| Excellent | $\geq$ 4,644 | $\geq$ 3,167 |
| Very Good | 4,185–4,643 | 2,795–3,166 |
| Good | 3,858–4,184 | 2,399–2,794 |
| Fair | 3,323–3,857 | 2,156–2,398 |
| Need Improvement | $\leq$ 3,322 | $\leq$ 2,155 |

**Source:** Reproduced with permission of the Canadian Society for Exercise Physiology.

The Vertical Jump Appraisal provides a good estimate of muscular power in the legs.

# Performance-Level Appraisals

The group of fitness appraisals below focus on specific movement skills such as speed, agility, and coordination. They are referred to as **performance-level appraisals** because they are intended for measuring and improving particular aspects of performance (as opposed to overall health).

Many of the performance-level tests described here are used by universities and professional sports teams to identify and recruit athletes for certain sports.

## The Dot Drill

The **Dot Drill** is a part of the *Bigger, Faster, Stronger* (BFS) program developed by Dr. Greg Shepard. This appraisal assesses quickness, agility, and muscular endurance. It is performed on a configuration of painted dots forming a rectangle (as shown in the illustration).

The drill includes five patterns, each repeated six times consecutively in quick succession. Start the clock as soon as your partner begins the first pattern.

Don't forget to repeat all patterns six times, then check your rating and record it in your activity handbook. Here is the sequence:

### UP AND BACK

➢ Start with your right foot on A and your left foot on B.

➢ Now jump quickly to C with both feet coming together.

➢ Then jump and split feet to D and E.

➢ Return the same way backward.

### RIGHT FOOT

➢ At the end of "Up and Back" your feet should be on A and B.

➢ Now jump to C using only your right foot.

➢ Now jump in order to D, E, C, B and A.

➢ Then repeat the same pattern with your **left foot** then with **both feet**.

### TURN AROUND

➢ Both feet should now be on A. Now jump to C with both feet.

➢ Now jump to D and E, with your left foot landing on E and your right foot landing on D.

➢ Now quickly jump and turn 180-degrees clockwise so your left foot is now on D and your right foot is on E.

➢ Now jump to C with both feet and then to A and B with the left foot landing on A and the right foot on B.

➢ Now do a counterclockwise 180-degree spin, with your left foot landing on B and your right foot landing on A.

# Dot Drill Standards for Girls and Boys

| Girls | Less than 158 cm (5' 2") | 159–165 cm (5' 3"–5' 5") | 166–174 cm (5' 6"–5' 8") | 175 cm or more (5' 9" or more) |
|---|---|---|---|---|
| **Standard Build** | less than 56.5 kg (125 lbs) | 57–65.5 kg (126–145 lbs) | 66–72.5 kg (146–160 lbs) | 73–79.5 kg (161–175 lbs) |
| **Large Build** | 56.5 kg (125 lbs) or more | 65.5 kg (145 lbs) or more | 72.5 kg (160 lbs) or more | 79.5 kg (175 lbs) or more |

### Girls' Standards (in seconds)

| | Grade 9 | | Grade 10 | |
|---|---|---|---|---|
| | **Standard** | **Large** | **Standard** | **Large** |
| **Good** | 76–67 | 81–72 | 74–65 | 79–70 |
| **Great** | 66–57 | 71–62 | 64–55 | 69–60 |
| **All-Province** | 56–52 | 61–57 | 54–50 | 59–55 |
| **All-Canadian** | 51–47 | 56–52 | 49–45 | 54–50 |
| **World Class** | 46 or less | 51 or less | 44 or less | 49 or less |

| Boys | Less than 174 cm (5' 8") | 175–180 cm (5' 9"–5' 11") | 181–188 cm (6' 0"–6' 2") | 189 cm or more (6' 3" or more) |
|---|---|---|---|---|
| **Standard Build** | Less than 56.5 kg (125 lbs) | Less than 91 kg (200 lbs) | Less than 100 kg (220 lbs) | Less than 109 kg (240 lbs) |
| **Heavy Build** | 82 kg (180 lbs) or more | 91 kg (200 lbs) or more | 100 kg (220 lbs) or more | 109 kg (240 lbs) or more |

### Boys' Standards (in seconds)

| | Grade 9 | | Grade 10 | |
|---|---|---|---|---|
| | **Standard** | **Heavy** | **Standard** | **Heavy** |
| **Good** | 69–65 | 74–70 | 66–62 | 71–67 |
| **Great** | 64–60 | 69–65 | 61–57 | 66–62 |
| **All-Canadian** | 59–50 | 64–55 | 56–47 | 61–52 |
| **World Class** | 49 or less | 54 or less | 46 or less | 51 or less |

**Source:** Adapted from *Bigger, Faster, Stronger* by Dr. Greg Shepard, (Human Kinetics Publishers, 2003).

## Illinois Agility Run

**Agility** is the ability to change direction quickly and accurately without loss of balance. Sports such as squash, football, soccer, and tennis, to name just a few, require high levels of agility. Agility also is important in preventing injuries during many recreational activities.

Agility comes in many forms: changing direction quickly to avoid an object (or opponent), running backwards, and then quickly turning to run forward to catch a ball. Therefore, there is no one true test for agility.

The **Illinois Agility Run** is a good appraisal for sports or activities that involve changing direction and weaving around objects or opponents. It also makes for a fun obstacle course.

The course is laid out on a flat surface at least 15 metres long and 8 metres wide. Four cones are placed at the corners of a 10 × 5 metre rectangle to mark the start and finish and the two turning points. Four other cones are placed 3.3 metres apart along a line in the centre.

To perform the Illinois Agility Run appraisal:

➤ Lie face down (in a push-up position) at the starting point.

➤ On command, jump to your feet and sprint to the top corner cone, go around it and come back to the beginning of the middle set of cones. Then, without stopping, weave around the middle cones. Sprint to the other top corner, go around the cone, and then sprint to the finish (see illustration).

➤ In your activity handbook, record the time taken from the initial command to when you cross the finish line.

## Wall–Ball Toss

**Coordination** is the ability to use the nervous and musculoskeletal systems to control complex movements. It is a key skill in most sports and recreational activities and one that you should seek to improve upon.

The **Wall–Ball Toss** specifically measures hand-eye coordination. This skill is especially important in games such as tennis, baseball, and similar sports. If you are good at juggling, then you should do well on this test.

The Wall–Ball Toss requires you to throw a tennis ball against a wall, from waist level, and catch it with the opposite hand. If you are using a 30-second count, a score of 30 or above is considered "very good" to "excellent." Similarly, a score of 60 and above is considered "very good" to "excellent" for a 60-second count.

Mark a line on the floor 1.5 metres from a smooth wall—most gymnasium walls will work fine.

The Wall-Ball Toss measures hand-eye coordination, a skill that is important in sports such as table tennis, lacrosse, and baseball.

> ➤ Stand behind the line and underhand the ball against the wall, catching with the other hand.

> ➤ Alternate hands—throw left, catch right; throw right and catch left—for 30 or 60 seconds.

> ➤ Count each successful catch and do not use your body to catch the ball.

> ➤ If you drop or miss-catch the ball, pick it up as fast as you can and continue on to count the next completion.

> ➤ In your activity handbook, record the number of successful catches that do not hit the floor.

## 20-Yard and 40-Yard Sprints

One of the main performance-level fitness appraisals used to gauge one's ability to accelerate quickly is the **20- and 40-Yard Sprints** (or dash). This is an important appraisal because in many sports, athletes start from a stationary position and attempt to reach a high velocity as quickly as possible.

The 40-yard sprint was first developed by the Dallas Cowboys of the National Football League in the late 1960s. It is now not specific to any sport, but is widely used to test speed and acceleration. This appraisal can be performed indoors or outdoors.

Use a measuring tape to mark off 20 yards (18.29 metres) and 40 yards (36.58 metres). Two timers are required to record the 20- and 40-yard times:

➢ Stand at the start line in a sprint or standing position.

➢ On command, run as fast as possible past the 40-yard marker.

➢ Record your time taken at the 20-yard mark and again at the 40-yard mark.

➢ Record your score in your activity handbook.

Use your body size measurement from the Dot Drill to determine your build.

Now, compare your results against those in the table below to see how well you performed. If you did not perform as well as you thought you might, it is easy to show improvement. All it takes is practice.

## 20- and 40-Yard Sprint Standards

| 40 Yard | Grade 9 Girls | | Grade 9 Boys | | Grade 10 Girls | | Grade 10 Boys | |
|---|---|---|---|---|---|---|---|---|
| | Std* | Lar* | Std | Hev* | Std | Lar | Std | Hev |
| All-Canadian | 5.1 | 5.3 | 4.65 | 4.95 | 5.0 | 5.2 | 4.6 | 4.9 |
| All-province | 5.4 | 5.6 | 4.75 | 5.05 | 5.3 | 5.5 | 4.7 | 5.0 |
| Great | 5.7 | 5.9 | 4.95 | 5.2 | 5.6 | 5.8 | 4.9 | 5.1 |
| Good | 6.0 | 6.2 | 5.25 | 5.5 | 5.9 | 6.1 | 5.2 | 5.4 |
| **20 Yard** | | | | | | | | |
| All-Canadian | 3.2 | 3.4 | 2.65 | 2.95 | 3.1 | 3.3 | 2.6 | 2.9 |
| All-province | 3.4 | 3.6 | 2.75 | 3.05 | 3.3 | 3.5 | 2.7 | 3.0 |
| Great | 3.8 | 4.0 | 2.95 | 3.2 | 3.7 | 3.9 | 2.9 | 3.1 |
| Good | 4.1 | 4.3 | 3.25 | 3.5 | 4.0 | 4.2 | 3.2 | 3.4 |

\* See page 81 for definitions of "standard," "large," and "heavy" build.
**Source:** Adapted from *Bigger, Faster, Stronger* by Dr. Greg Shepard (Human Kinetics Publishers, 2003).

## Chin-Ups and Flexed-Arm Hang

Both the **Chin-Ups** and **Flexed-Arm Hang Appraisals** measure muscular strength and endurance of the forearms, arms, and shoulders. The major difference is that chin-ups (also called pull-ups) require movement. The flexed-arm hang, on the other hand, is an isometric contraction (involving no movement).

If you cannot yet perform 1 to 5 chin-ups on your own, it may be best for you first to try the flexed-arm hang appraisal until you are ready for the more difficult chin-up variation.

For both appraisals you will need a horizontal bar, approximately 3.81 cm (1.5 inches) in diameter, positioned at a height that allows you to hang without touching the ground.

For the Chin-Up Appraisal:

➢ Grasp the bar using an underhand grip (palms facing towards you, thumbs wrapped around the bar).

➢ Pull your body up until your chin rests over the bar and then lower yourself until your arms are straight.

➢ Perform as many repetitions as possible (without using your legs to gain momentum).

➢ Refer to the adjacent table to see how you performed on the test.

➢ Record the results in your activity handbook.

For the Flexed-Arm Hang appraisal:

➢ Grasp the bar using an underhand grip.

➢ With the help of two spotters, one in front and one in back, pull yourself up so that your chin is above the bar.

➢ Hold this position as long as possible.

➢ Stop the test if your chin touches the bar, if your head tilts backward to keep your chin above the bar, or if your chin falls below the level of the bar.

➢ In your activity handbook, record your time so the next time you do the test you can see if you have improved.

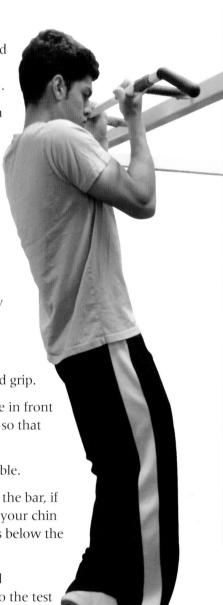

### How Well Did You Do?

No less than 10,275 students from 19 states took part in The National Children and Youth Fitness Study conducted by the Public Health Service of the U.S. Department of Health and Human Services.

The table below, adapted from this study, will give you an idea of how you fared in your chin-up appraisal.

| AGES 13–15 | FEMALES |
| --- | --- |
| Excellent | ≧5 |
| Very Good | 3–4 |
| Good | 1–2 |
| Need Improvement | 0 |

| AGES 13–15 | MALES |
| --- | --- |
| Excellent | ≧8 |
| Very Good | 4–6 |
| Good | 2–5 |
| Fair | 1–3 |
| Need Improvement | 0 |

**Source:** Adapted from *Exercise Testing and Prescription* by David C. Nieman, Appendix A, Section 1, Tables 3 and 4 (McGraw-Hill, 2003). Reproduced with permission of the McGraw-Hill Companies.

## Nicole Tritter
### A healthier lifestyle is not as hard as it seems

Some people may be naturally more athletic than others, but even the best athletes have to work at being fit and healthy. Nicole Tritter is a great example of how working hard and setting goals can take you further than you ever thought possible. Nicole attended Birchmount Park Collegiate Institute in Toronto and now attends the University of Connecticut.

**What were the most important things you learned in H&PE class?**
I learned to believe in myself; if I do that I can achieve anything. I also learned how important it is to set a goal, and to take action to achieve it. Hard work, dedication, and support can take you a long way.

**How did you overcome challenges?**
By staying positive during hard times. Rather than getting discouraged and down on myself, I realized that it's imperative to learn from mistakes and put them in the past. Hard times are inevitable, but it's how you react during those times that can make a difference.

**How have you transferred what you learned in class into other aspects of your life?**
Time management is always a challenge for students; the trick is prioritizing. It's very important to set your goals and then figure out what you need to do in order to achieve them. In order to reach my goal I had to give up some extracurricular activities and some Friday night parties.

**What are your future healthy active living goals?**
At the moment I have reached my goal of playing university ice hockey. My future goals, once I'm finished university, are to go home and play in the NWHL (National Women's Hockey League). Also, although I want to continue to play hockey all my life, I also want to give back to the sport either by coaching or by volunteering to help underprivileged children to play.

**What advice would you offer to high school students looking to lead healthier, more active lives?**
A healthier lifestyle is not as hard as it seems. Start by taking baby steps; little changes can make a big difference. Try doing it with a friend; it is much easier to lead a healthier lifestyle with someone helping you out.

**You don't need to aspire to play a sport professionally or obtain a sports scholarship to learn from Nicole. Decide what's really important to you, and what your healthy active living goals are. Then, figure out what you need to do (and maybe what you have to give up) to achieve them.**

## Questions for Study and Review

### Things to Think About and Explore

1. Distinguish between the terms "muscular strength" and "muscular endurance."

2. Identify possible reasons why the grip strength appraisal may be a good indicator of overall muscular fitness.

3. Investigate the importance of developing your core muscle strength.

4. Most of the musculoskeletal fitness appraisals in this chapter have different standards for boys and girls. Give reasons as to why you do, or do not think those overall differences between males and females will ever diminish.

5. Make a list of the various performance-level appraisals in this chapter and how they might be used to improve certain skills in different sports.

6. Evaluate the importance of performing muscular strength and endurance appraisals on a regular basis.

### Things to Do and Practise

7. In a journal, record how many push-ups you are able to do. Use the table on page 75 to determine your overall rating. On a weekly basis, perform push-ups and continue to record your results. At the end of the course look back through your journal and follow your progression. Record your thoughts about your standings. Do you see a marked improvement?

8. After performing your vertical jump appraisal, calculate your peak leg power using the equation given in this chapter.

9. Participate in the musculoskeletal fitness appraisals and record your results. On which fitness appraisal did you score the lowest? Determine what you can do to improve your results for the next round of tests.

10. Create a poster with illustrations that could be used to help students follow the sequence of the Dot Drill (as described on page 80).

11. In a journal, record how many successful catches you made with the Wall-Ball Toss Appraisal. For one month, perform the Wall-Ball Toss on a daily basis, and continue to record the number of successful catches. On the final day of the month, look back through your journal and view your results. Has your hand-eye coordination improved?

12. Make a collage of pictures that depict each musculoskeletal and performance-level appraisal covered in this chapter.

### WWWeblinks

Name ➤ Physical Activity Unit

URL ➤ www.phac-aspc.gc.ca

A Public Health Agency website detailing some of the Agency's inititatives to promote active living and physical fitness to Canadians.

Name ➤ Canadian Fitness and Lifestyle Research Institute

URL ➤ www.cflri.ca

The CFLRI conducts research about physically active lifestyles. Its vision is to have 50 percent of all Canadians active by 2020.

Name ➤ Go for Green

URL ➤ www.goforgreen.ca

A group that promotes active living in conjunction with a desire to preserve the environment. Its focus is on outdoor activities that protect, enhance, or restore the environment.

# 6

# Body Composition Appraisals

**B**odies come in different shapes and sizes, and so does fitness. For this reason, using body composition scores alone may not give an accurate picture of where you are with respect to overall fitness.

Body composition appraisals need to be used in conjunction with appraisals that focus on the other two main areas of fitness—the condition of your cardiorespiratory system and your muscular strength and endurance. Taken together, these three types of fitness appraisals will provide a fairly accurate assessment of your fitness needs.

## Chapter Objectives

In this chapter you will:

> Learn what is meant by the term "body composition"

> Learn why body composition may not always be a good indicator of overall fitness

> Evaluate the merits and shortcomings of "Body Mass Index" as one measure of body composition

> Explore the idea behind "body types" or "somata types" (endomorph/mesomorph/ectomorph)

> Learn about Waist Circumference and Waist-to-Hip ratio as alternative body composition indicators

*The person who enjoys good health is rich, though they know it not.*

**Italian Proverb**

## Key Terms

> body composition
> Body Mass Index (BMI)
> endomorph
> mesomorph
> ectomorph
> Waist Circumference (WC)
> Waist-to-Hip Ratio (WHR)

# Body Composition

Fat protects organs, insulates body tissue, provides energy, and helps break down certain vitamins—in other words, it is essential. However, serious health issues arise when we store more fat on our bodies than we really need.

## What Is Body Composition?

The term **body composition** refers to the relative distribution of fat throughout the body in relation to bone, muscle, and other tissue. The purpose of body composition appraisals is to get an idea as to whether there are any health issues that one should be considering.

Keep in mind, body appraisals have their limitations and do not work for everyone. The appraisals outlined in this chapter include:

➢ Body Mass Index (BMI)

➢ Waist Circumference (WC) + Body Mass Index (BMI)

➢ Waist-to-Hip Ratio (WHR)

With the help of your teacher, you can determine which of these body composition appraisals, if any, can work for you.

These are photographs of fat (yellow) and muscle (red). They both weigh 2.5 kg. As you can see, muscle is more dense and takes up less space than fat.

Body composition appraisals are most helpful when used in conjunction with appraisals that address other aspects of fitness.

# Body Mass Index (BMI)

The first appraisal in this series is one of the most widely used fitness measurements. **Body Mass Index (BMI)** gives a rough indication as to whether your body weight (mass) is appropriate for your height (it does not directly measure the amount of body fat).

BMI is very widely used; however, it does not work well for some people—especially children, teenagers, and the elderly. It also does not work well for very fit individuals, because BMI does not distinguish between body fat and dense muscle, nor does it take into account where this fat resides. For this reason, CPAFLA recommends that this appraisal be combined with the Waist Circumference appraisal, which is explained next.

## Calculating Body Mass Index

To find your BMI, follow the steps below. Use the worksheet in your activity handbook to record your calculations:

➢ Using a tape measure (or fixed-height wall chart), find your height in metres (m).

➢ Using a weighing scale, find your weight in kilograms (kg).

➢ To calculate your BMI, divide your weight in kilograms by your height in metres squared (m²).

In the illustration below, David is 1.68 m tall and weighs 83.5 kg. His BMI is 29.6 and is calculated as follows:

$$BMI = \frac{weight\ (kg)}{height\ (m^2)}$$

$$BMI = \frac{83.5}{1.68 \times 1.68} = 29.6$$

## BMI Rating

**B**ody Mass Index is widely used to assess health risk, but it is not always a reliable indicator. The standard BMI scoring is shown below.

| BMI (KG/M²) | BMI RATING |
|---|---|
| < 18.5 | Underweight |
| 18.5–24.9 | Normal |
| 25.0–29.9 | Overweight |
| 30.0–35 | Obese |
| > 35.0 | Morbidly Obese |

CPAFLA recommends that you can get a better indication of body composition by combining BMI with Waist Circumference. BMI does not distinguish body fat from dense muscle, nor does it take into account where the body fat resides.

For comparison, let's use David's values. His BMI is 29.6 kg/m². The BMI table above places David in the "Overweight" (bordering on "Obese") category. David is not overweight, but rather sturdy and muscular. If you were to use Waist Circumference in conjunction with BMI (next appraisal), David's score would be "Excellent."

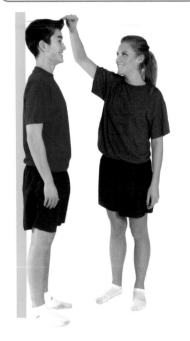

# What's Wrong with the Body Mass Index?
## We Are Not All the Same

Bodies come in a variety of shapes and sizes. Some research tells us that there are three main "somata types" (or body types). No one person fits any of these categories exactly—all of us are a little of each type.

The three body types are endomorph, mesomorph, and ectomorph. Below are the main characteristics of each category:

- **Endomorph.** This body type is a soft, round pear shape with excess fat around the hips and waist and little muscle definition.
- **Mesomorph.** This body type is naturally well muscled with broad shoulders and a narrow waist. People with this body type look fit even when out of shape and can put on muscle easily.
- **Ectomorph.** This body type is a very thin, long boned body type with little muscle or fat.

Keep in mind that these are not "true" types—no one person ever matches any one of these categories exactly. Rather, the three types are "forced exaggerations" that can help us think about body composition issues.

### BMI and Body Types

Your BMI value can be misleading, especially if you have a mesomorphic (more athletic) body type. For example, consider two 15 year olds, both of whom are 151 cm tall and weigh 64 kg.

The first teen participates in physical education class, eats a balanced diet, works out with weights, and jogs three times a week. This person is generally very fit. The other has been doing the exact opposite. According to their BMI scores, they're both overweight.

The reason for this is that muscle weighs more than fat. The amount of body fat varies greatly with age and other factors, and the BMI appraisal works for some individuals who have stopped growing and who have a predominately endomorphic body type. Furthermore, BMI alone may not accurately indicate health risk.

The good news is that regardless of your body type, you can still achieve good overall health. Your attitude and motivation will be assets or obstacles in achieving your health goals, not your body type.

# Waist Circumference (WC) + BMI

If you ask real estate agents what are the three most important criteria to look for when buying a home, their answer will be: "Location, location, location." Well, the same can be said about the distribution (or location) of fat on your body. Excess fat in certain areas of the body can pose serious health risks.

The **Waist Circumference** (WC) appraisal is effective in predicting the health risks that come with excess fat weight around your midsection. To get a pretty good indication of your body composition, combine your WC measurement with your BMI value (see sidebar). Below is an explanation on how to conduct a WC appraisal and how to combine it with you BMI score.

## Finding Your WC

The Waist Circumference appraisal is quite straight forward. All you need is a partner and a tape measure, then follow the steps below:

➢ While holding one end of a tape measure, reach around your partner and grasp the other end of the tape with your other hand, then join the two ends together.

➢ The tape should be perfectly horizontal and midway between the bottom of the rib cage and the hip bone (above the belly-button).

➢ Record the measurement to the nearest 0.5 cm.

➢ Now, with your BMI and WC values in hand, refer to the table in the sidebar to find out your rating.

➢ If you wish, record this rating in your activity handbook for future use.

In Unit 3, you will learn how to design a fitness program that suits your particular needs.

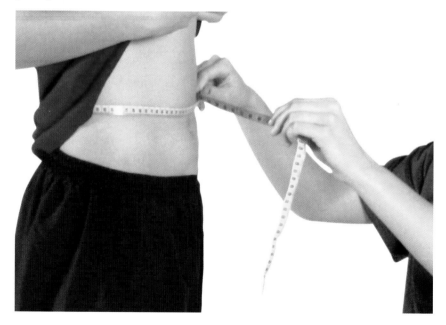

---

## BMI + Waist Circumference

The table below uses your BMI, WC, and your gender to determine your overall body composition rating.

| BMI (kg/m²) | WC (cm) MALES | WC (cm) FEMALES | RATING |
|---|---|---|---|
| < 18.5 | All Girths | | Very Good |
| 18.5–24.9 | < 94 | < 80 | Excellent |
| | 94–101 | 80–87 | Very Good |
| | > 101 | > 87 | Fair |
| 25.0–29.9 | < 94 | < 80 | Excellent |
| | 94–101 | 80–87 | Very Good |
| | > 101 | > 87 | Fair |
| 30.0–32.4 | < 94 | < 80 | Excellent |
| | 94–101 | 80–87 | Good |
| | > 101 | >87 | N.I. * |
| 32.5–35.0 | < 94 | < 80 | Excellent |
| | 94–101 | 80–87 | Good |
| | > 101 | >87 | N.I. * |
| > 35.0 | < 94 | < 80 | Excellent |
| | 94–101 | 80–87 | Good |
| | > 101 | > 87 | N.I. * |

* Needs Improvement

You can refer back to the Health Benefits Zones table on page 13 to interpret your rating. The greatest health improvement is to move from a "fair" to a "good" rating.

Regardless of your score on this WC + BMI appraisal, full participation in physical education class will improve your results next time.

**Source:** Reproduced with permission of the Canadian Society for Exercise Physiology.

# Waist-to-Hip Ratio
## Apples and Pears

All excess calories not used as energy are stored as body fat. Generally, we store fat either below or above our waist. However, where exactly fat is stored is associated with different levels of health risk.

Some people store fat above the waist (in the trunk or abdominal area, where many vital organs are located), giving them an "apple-like" appearance. Others tend to store excess fat below the waist on their hips and thighs giving them a "pear-like" shape.

Of the two, research suggests that the "apples" have a greater chance of developing cardiovascular diseases (high blood pressure, strokes, and heart attacks).

### Waist-to-Hip Ratio (WHR)

Some researchers believe that an alternative body composition measure, the Waist-to-Hip Ratio (WHR), is an excellent indicator of cardiorespiratory risk for adults. This is not one of the CPAFLA appraisals, but it is one worth knowing about and worth trying.

### Calculating Your Waist-to-Hip Ratio

The **Waist-to-Hip Ratio** looks at the relative proportion of fat stored around your waist and hips. It is a simple but useful measure of body fat distribution.

All you need to perform this appraisal is a partner and a measuring tape. Simply follow the steps below:

- Stand up straight, with your stomach relaxed.
- Find the narrowest point at your waist (usually just above your bellybutton).
- Record your waist measurement in either centimetres or inches.
- Find the widest point at your hips and buttocks and record your hip measurement.
- Divide the first measurement (your waist) by the second (your hips), and this is your WHR.

### Interpreting Waist-to-Hip Ratio

Research suggests that women should have a waist-to-hip ratio of less than 0.8, whereas a healthy WHR for men is less than 0.9. The higher the number, the greater the risk of developing a cardiovascular disease.

Of course, these studies were done on adult subjects, so more research is needed to determine accurate values for teenagers. People differ, and only a health professional, such as your physician, can tell for sure whether there is any associated health risk with your body type.

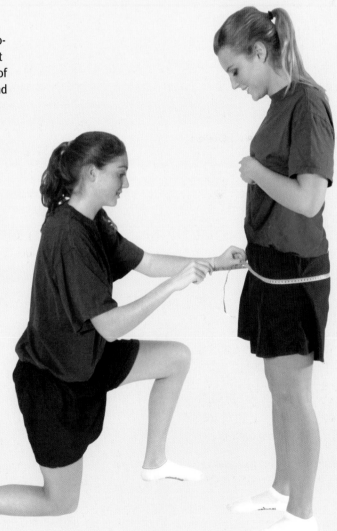

## Exercise-Induced Asthma
### What You Need to Know

A healthy active lifestyle is important for everyone, but perhaps especially so for those who suffer from Exercise-induced Asthma (EIA).

### What is Exercise-Induced Asthma?

Asthma occurs in the airways of the lungs and is characterized by laboured breathing and a wheezing sound. The triggers can include cat or dog hair, dust, cigarette smoke, mould, and even exercise. The result is inflammation and restricted airflow. The signs of an asthmatic attack are: shortness of breath, wheezing, tightness in the chest, and coughing.

At rest, we normally breathe through our nose, which filters, warms, and humidifies the air. When we exercise vigorously, we breathe through our mouths, so that we can take air in faster.

It is believed that the cooler, drier air going into the lungs during intense activity helps to bring about an asthmatic reaction for some individuals. Exercise-Induced Asthma is the name given to asthma that has been brought about by exercise.

### Physical Activity and Asthma

Paradoxically, exercise seems to be important for those who have Exercise-Induced Asthma. In general, exercise strengthens our breathing muscles, boosts our immune system, and improves the efficiency of our cardiorespiratory system.

The first step is to design an action plan with your doctor. He or she may suggest longer warm-ups and cool-downs and may prescribe a mild asthma medication. Your physician may also discourage you from exercising in conditions where the air is cool and dry, and discourage you from exercising too rigorously until your asthma is under control. Be sure to stop exercising if the problem persists.

With few exceptions, those who are able to control their Exercise-Induced Asthma can generally be as active as anyone else.

If famous athletes (such as Gary Roberts of the National Hockey League and Olympic gold medal sprinter Donovan Bailey) can control their asthma, then with the help of your physician, so can you.

## Chapter Review

### Questions for Study and Review

**Things to Think About and Explore**

1. Define what is meant by the term "body composition."

2. Identify four essential functions that fat performs in our bodies.

3. Identify reasons why one should or should not perform a body composition appraisal at your age.

4. Investigate why the "Body Mass Index" does not work for everyone.

5. Investigate the importance of combining Waist Circumference with BMI in the context of evaluating overall body composition.

6. Describe why the Waist-to-Hip Ratio appraisal might be fairly accurate in predicting cardiovascular disease.

**Things to Do and Practise**

7. Create a pamphlet that explains why our bodies should not accumulate excess fat and list the types of foods we should eat to keep healthy. Create a one-day meal plan as an example to follow.

8. Make a collage of pictures of people with different body types. Label each body type in the collage, classifying them as ectomorphs, mesomorphs, or endomorphs.

9. Participate in one body composition appraisal of your choice, record your rating, and then compare your performance with a second appraisal period.

10. Based on your body composition appraisal, what steps could you take to improve or maintain your current level? Create a guideline for you to follow.

11. Encourage some of your family members to participate in a body composition appraisal. Record their results and discuss if you were met with reluctance and why they may have been reluctant.

12. Make a presentation to your class explaining why body composition alone may not provide a complete picture of one's fitness level.

### WWWeblinks

Name ➤ CPAFLA

URL ➤ www.csep.ca

If you would like to learn more about the fitness appraisals outlined in this chapter or about other CSEP programs, visit this website.

Name ➤ Canadian Obesity Network

URL ➤ www.obesitynetwork.ca

This site offers educational resources, training programs, and data for health-care planning to aid people dealing with obesity.

Name ➤ Active Healthy Kids

URL ➤ www.activehealthykids.ca

A charitable organization that advocates the importance of quality, accessible, and enjoyable physical activity for children and youth.

## Table of Contents

# UNIT 3
# Fitness Planning, Exercises, and Injury Prevention

**What this unit is about ...**

> ➤ Why should I set fitness goals for myself, and how can I make those goals a reality?

> ➤ Why will knowing and understanding how my major muscles work help me to exercise them in the best way possible?

> ➤ What does exercise safety mean to me, and why is it important that I follow the appropriate safety measures when involved in various physical activities?

# 7
# Setting and Reaching Fitness Goals

*Obstacles are those frightful things you see when you take your eyes off your goals.*

**Henry Ford**

Inventor of the automobile

**W**hen setting fitness goals, we often start out with the best of intentions. Other things—commitments to school or work, video games, or peer pressure—often get in the way. However, if your goal setting is properly planned you can deal with the distractions and achieve your goals.

It is important to know that the goals you are setting are realistic and to know exactly why you are setting them. You also need to know the steps to take so that you can meet your goals. If you do not do your "homework" ahead of time, you will undermine your plan before you even begin.

In this chapter, we will look at goal-setting techniques and how they can be applied to your fitness and exercise routine.

## Chapter Objectives

In this chapter, you will:

➤ Distinguish between short-term and long-term fitness goals

➤ Explore the SMART approach to goal setting and how you can apply it to your own fitness and exercise routine

➤ Examine common barriers to reaching fitness goals and the kinds of strategies that can be used to overcome these obstacles

➤ Examine the principles associated with fitness training, specifically the "overload principle," "the progression principle," "the specificity principle," and the "reversibility principle"

➤ Learn how you can determine, with the help of your teacher, the maximum weight you can safely lift using the "multiple repetition maximum" method

➤ Learn how to utilize the FITT principle of fitness program design to help you develop a realistic fitness plan

➤ Elaborate your own personalized fitness plan using the strategies and techniques you have encountered in this chapter

## Key Terms

➤ short-term goals
➤ long-term goals
➤ SMART
➤ overload principle
➤ progression principle
➤ specificity principle
➤ reversibility principle
➤ multiple-repetition maximum
➤ FITT principle
➤ action plan

# Types of Fitness Goals

Habits can be difficult to break, but with clear goals and proper planning, you can change the way you do things. Setting reachable goals changes your focus from vague and general aims to very specific ones that are attainable. Knowing that you can succeed is a strong motivator to continue.

There are two types of goals:

> **Short-term goals.** Short-term goals are specific and can be completed in a few hours, days, or weeks. Short-term fitness goals may involve measuring your progress in a single workout, or comparing your progress over a series of exercise sessions.

> **Long-term goals.** Long-term goals specify what you want to achieve over a longer period of time. For example, long-term fitness goals could include reaching a particular body weight over a month, a semester, or even a few years.

In the context of goal-setting, "short" and "long" are relative terms. Short-term goals should be part of long-term goals, which in turn can be part of longer-term goals.

Long-term fitness goals could include reaching a desired number of repetitions over a month, a semester, or even a few years.

Inspirational sayings can help keep you motivated and focused on your goals.

# Being SMART about Goal Setting

Getting started can often be the hardest part of setting goals. To set goals you need a plan, and to make a plan you need motivation. To help find that motivation there is a strategy called **SMART**, which stands for **S**pecific, **M**eaningful and **M**easurable, **A**ction-oriented, **R**ealistic, and **T**ime-bound. Knowing these five key pieces of information will help you reach your goals more effectively.

## Specific—Is Your Goal Clear?

Your objectives must be clear and specific. Unclear and non-specific goals (such as "I want to get in shape.") do not give an indication of how to do it, or for what reason. They will not give you a clear motivation to act. A more specific and effective goal (such as "I want to run 20 minutes a day, non-stop, to prepare for my 5 km fun run.") will more effectively motivate you to go out and meet that goal.

## Meaningful and Measurable—How Will You Know?

Decide on goals that are meaningful to you. Measuring your results is also important. To achieve goals (such as "I want to run a road race by the end of the year, but I'm out of shape.") you need a series of progressive, measurable, short-term goals showing gradual improvement (such as "after one week I will not be out of breath when I run for 10 minutes straight"). To ensure that your goals are measurable, and that you are regularly measuring them, ask yourself, "What will be different once I accomplish my goal?"

## Action-Oriented—What Steps Do You Need to Take?

Your goal must require you to take action through a series of well-planned steps. A non-action-oriented goal would be, "I want to get in shape this year." An action-oriented goal would be, "To get into better shape this year, I will cut my consumption of junk food to once a week, and I will start having breakfast every day. I will also walk to school two times a week and join one intramural activity each semester."

## Realistic—How Likely Are You to Reach Your Goal?

Do not try to accomplish the impossible, for clearly that can't happen. A goal is realistic if it involves a convenient location and appropriate equipment, if it is within your physical and mental capabilities, and if it is something you want. It is important to set goals that are realistic.

## Time-bound—How Long Will It Take to Reach Your Goal?

You must know how long it will take you to reach your goal. It is harder to reach your goal if you do not have a firm timeline—how long it will take and the steps you need to take along the way—and a time or date you expect to reach the goal. Short-term goals that are successfully completed will boost your confidence.

---

## Setting Your Goals

Your goals must be personalized—that is, above all, they must apply to you. Consider the following factors when setting health and fitness goals:

- Your personal motivation
- Your current fitness level
- The influence of peers and friends
- Availability of equipment and facilities
- School, work, and family commitments

Taking health and physical education throughout your high school years can go a long way to helping you achieve a healthy active lifestyle.

## Tracking Your Goals

When you have determined that your particular goals are SMART, and when you have assessed all your strengths and weaknesses, you should combine these two elements into a successful goal-setting plan. One way to do this is to develop a goal-setting worksheet, such as the one in your activity handbook.

This worksheet identifies your long-term goals and all other short-term goals that are needed to reach the ultimate goal. Although it is not necessary to list everything at this early stage, you can examine your strengths and weaknesses. You can also identify the people whom you can call upon to support you and help you reach those goals.

As with most things, getting started early is usually the most important part of any exercise program. Writing things down, point-by-point, is an excellent way to begin a fitness program that you want to pursue and, ultimately, achieve. You also can review this worksheet from time to time to see how you are progressing, and you can update it as time goes on.

Writing things down will help you to focus on the tasks at hand and ensure that all your goals are SMART ones.

Setting SMART short-term goals will help you achieve the long-term ones.

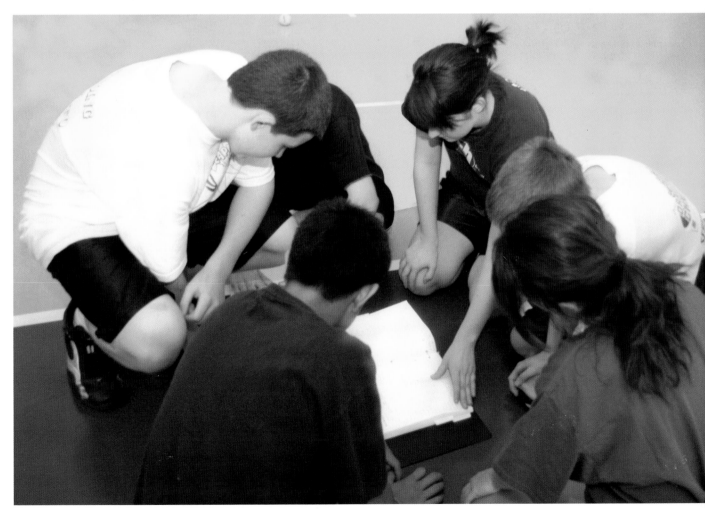

Surround yourself with classmates that will help you achieve your goals.

Taking H&PE throughout your high school years will help you reach all your fitness goals.

Being active with friends can help you stay motivated.

## Strategies for Success

It has probably happened to every one of us. In spite of our best intentions, our fitness plan is slow to take off, or starts to falter after a short time. What holds us back? What are the barriers that stand in the way, and how can we overcome them?

### Overcoming the Barriers to Reaching Your Goals

The first few days and weeks of a fitness program are critical. Once you are able to find the time, and overcome self-consciousness and the aches and pains, it becomes much easier.

Here are some strategies to help you overcome common barriers to healthy active living.

> **Barrier #1:** *"I just don't have the time to exercise."*
>
> *Possible solution:* Make exercise a higher priority—one that you need to fit into your day. Examine the inactive parts of your day to see if you can add exercise to them, such as walking to school instead of getting a ride. Look for sacrifices you can make, such as watching less television.

> **Barrier #2:** *"The facilities are too far away to use regularly."*
>
> *Possible solution:* Use distant facilities less often and find other areas you can use, such as your bedroom or the basement. The alternative, inactivity, is much worse.

> **Barrier #3:** *"I have heavy school and work commitments."*
>
> *Possible solution:* Review your timetable and find ways to fit H&PE into your timetable every year. Discuss it with your guidance counsellor or teacher. They may be able to help you organize your time better. If you are fit, you will be in better shape to perform at school and work.

> **Barrier #4:** *"I am never going to reach my goal!"*
>
> *Possible solution:* Think about revising your original goal, possibly scaling back a little. Write your goal(s) down and place them somewhere you will see them often (for example, in your locker). Look for people who can support you, such as friends, relatives, and training partners.

> **Barrier #5:** *"I am not in very good shape and feel embarrassed."*
>
> *Possible solution:* Focus on the positive health benefits rather than how you look to others. Spend time with a trusted friend or teacher discussing your goals and other concerns. There are always other people who will help you reach your goals.

> **Barrier #6:** *"This new exercise program is boring!"*
>
> *Possible solution:* Try different equipment (e.g., if you are working with weights, try using medicine balls). Listen to music to keep yourself motivated. Or, simply, vary your routine a little. Most of all, have fun.

## Assessing Your Strengths and Weaknesses

It is wise to surround yourself with a strong support team—teachers, family members, coaches, and friends. Of course, the most important support person is yourself—no one knows you as well as you do.

First, you have your own unique set of skills that you can call upon (determination, stamina, coordination, etc.). Using this textbook, you also are beginning to acquire a sound knowledge and understanding of fitness and health issues. You can bring all this information to bear when setting your goals.

Everyone has problems and weaknesses—even professional athletes who appear to be "super-fit." Over time, you will be able to overcome, or work around, any weaknesses, eventually weeding them out of your plan—and your life. Being frank about weaknesses in the early stages will only help you design a better fitness plan, one that is actually attainable.

With the fitness knowledge you have already acquired, and with the additional health information that you will encounter as you proceed through this textbook, you will have no trouble developing a fitness plan that works for you. You will also have no trouble following it through to the end.

The support of others is important, but not as important as supporting yourself.

With the information in this textbook, you will have no trouble developing a fitness plan that works for you.

# Training Principles

Your fitness program must be tailored to your own specific needs and goals, but the underlying principles of fitness training are similar for everyone. Understanding these principles will help you maximize the effectiveness of your fitness plan and minimize any potential harm you could cause yourself.

Let us briefly review four of these training principles.

Understanding the four training principles can help you design a better fitness program.

## The Overload Principle

When you give your body more to do than it is accustomed to doing, you create an "overload." This is known as the **overload principle** and it underlies most fitness activity. Unless there is some sort of overload, there can be no benefit to you.

Your body will gradually adapt to the additional demands put on it—whether it be your heart and lungs in response to aerobic activities, your abdominal muscles in response to sit-ups, or your legs in response to squats. In the course of all this, your cardiorespiratory system and your muscles become stronger and more efficient.

## The Progression Principle

Jogging or running can lead to aerobic improvements over time.

If you are just starting fitness training, you may see fairly rapid improvement (and probably soreness), but the rate of improvement will gradually slow down, and the gains will be more evenly paced. This is known as the **progression principle** of fitness training. It states that fitness improvements occur gradually by progressively adding to the overload. Miracles do not happen overnight.

In order to see further improvement, the amount of resistance must gradually be increased.

## The Specificity Principle

Whether you are exercising or doing another activity, you will improve in response to the type of activity that you are practising. Improvements in muscle strength come from lifting resistance objects such as weights; aerobic improvements come from activities such as cycling, swimming, or jogging; improvements to flexibility occur when you stretch. In sports, the maximum training effect comes when you mimic the effort required in the actual sport as closely as possible.

This is known as the **specificity principle**. It does not mean that some upper-body strength won't come from swimming, or that there are no aerobic benefits from a stretch and strength class. In fact, sometimes our favourite activities produce several specific fitness benefits. In general, however, you improve by practising a specific activity repeatedly.

The more the activity is specifically focused on improving a particular aspect of fitness or a particular muscle area, the more the benefit in that particular area.

## The Reversibility Principle

A short break in your routine is not a serious problem, providing you can get back at it as soon as possible. Sometimes, you may even need a short break in order to move on to larger goals. If you stop for a long time (a process sometimes called "detraining"), you will start to lose, or reverse, the gains you have made—your body's response to training is, unfortunately, not permanent.

This is known as the **reversibility principle**. Some strength gains may start to decrease in as little as three days. In a few months, without regular activity, you will revert back to where you were before starting your program.

The secret is to keep active on a regular basis to the point where energetic activity becomes an integral part of your lifestyle. That way you will always be in shape.

The reversibility principle is sometimes also referred to as the "use it or lose it" principle. If you do not exercise regularly, you will lose the gains you have made. Of course, this basic principle applies not only to fitness and fitness training, but has wider applications in other areas of life.

The secret is to keep active on a regular basis to the point where activity becomes an integral part of your lifestyle.

## Multiple-Repetition Maximum Method
### How Much Should You Lift?

For professional fitness trainers, one of the first steps in developing a resistance training program is having an idea as to the maximum amount of weight that a client can lift.

In resistance training, this is what is known as the "one-repetition maximum" or your "1-rep max." Finding your 1-rep max by going "all out" is definitely not wise or safe as you can risk injury to your bones, muscles, and joints, but there is an alternative.

Using the multiple-repetition maximum method, you can safely and effectively predict how much weight you can maximally lift once.

### Your Predicted One-Repetition Maximum

Knowing your predicted 1-rep max is important. As each week passes, your teacher might ask you to work within a certain percentage of your predicted maximums. This is done to prevent injury and over-training, while getting the maximum physical benefit from your workout.

Finding your estimated 1-rep maximum for each exercise will make your personal resistance program more efficient and more enjoyable.

### Finding your Multiple-Repetition Maximum

Under no circumstances should you try to lift more than is appropriate for you. Under the supervision of your H&PE teacher, and with the help of spotters, follow these steps:

- With three classmates of similar ability, select a resistance exercise that all of you wish to try (e.g., bench press).

- While one person is performing the lift, the others act as spotters to ensure safety at all times.

- As a warm-up exercise, add light weights that each of you can lift safely and easily for 15-20 rep. Take turns performing the warm-up—this will ensure that each person gets adequate rest.

- Now, estimate a weight that each of you think you can lift for 10 reps with some difficulty. Again, take turns lifting and spotting.

- Repeat until you find a load that you can lift for 10 reps with some difficulty.

Once you find your 10-repetition maximum, your teacher can refer to a standardized reference chart and give you your estimated one-repetition maximum.

# Designing Your Fitness Program

Your most important fitness goal should be to become committed to a healthy, active lifestyle. This means establishing a realistic balance of physical activity, good eating, and adequate rest.

## The FITT Principle

There are many factors to keep in mind when designing a fitness training program, and there is a well-known method that can help you. It is called the **FITT principle**. FITT stands for the four elements of any good training plan: **F**requency, **I**ntensity, **T**ime (or duration), and **T**ype of activity.

Let's take a look at the role of each of these FITT elements in developing a comprehensive fitness plan:

> **Frequency.** An exercise's frequency is simply how often you do it. How often you exercise is just as important as the type of exercise you do. There will be gains after a single exercise session, but to continue to build your fitness takes some form of regular, energetic activity, generally as often as three times a week or more.

> **Intensity.** The intensity of an exercise is a measure of how hard you are working while you are doing it. Scientists who study the effect of exercise on the body have come up with simple methods that can be used to determine just how hard one's heart, lungs, and muscles are working when they are exercised. For your cardiorespiratory system—your heart and lungs—these measurements are based on your heart rate. For your muscles, they are based on how much weight a given set of muscles can lift with proper technique.

> **Time.** Is there a magic number for how long you should spend at an activity? For aerobic benefits, it is best to spend at least 20 minutes of continuous activity on an exercise such as walking, jogging, or cross-country skiing. Even if you are far along in your exercise program, the duration of the activity will depend on the intensity, your goals, and how much time you have available.

> **Type of activity.** Any training program must not only specify how often, how intensely, and how long you should exercise, but also what type of activity you should be doing. Unless you are training for a specific type of activity or sport—and, therefore, need to be doing plenty of exercises specific to that sport—most experts recommend a training program that includes a variety of activities. Maintaining this variety will prevent you from becoming bored, and will help you stay motivated.

---

## A Balanced Fitness Program

**A**ny successful fitness program needs balance. It is important to include all the following phases in your activity design:

- **Warm-up.** To prepare the body for exercise, and to avoid injury

- **Aerobic conditioning.** To build strong lungs and heart, and improve cardiorespiratory fitness

- **Muscular conditioning.** To build strength through resistance training

- **Flexibility exercises.** To maintain muscle balance and range of motion, and to prevent injuries

- **Cool-down.** To allow recovery and relieve tightness

Remember the importance of adequate rest and good nutrition. After a long or difficult workout, you may need to wait one or two days before a similar workout.

# The FITT Principle
## How to Design a Balanced Fitness Program

FITT refers to frequency, intensity, time (or duration), and type of activity. Take all four into account when you plan your fitness program. The table below matches these four elements against the main components of a balanced fitness program.

| | CARDIORESPIRATORY | FLEXIBILITY | MUSCULAR ENDURANCE | MUSCULAR STRENGTH |
|---|---|---|---|---|
| **F** Frequency | 3–5 times per week<br><br>Increase frequency as you get into better shape | Should be a regular part of your warm-up and cool-down<br><br>Increase frequency as you get into better shape | Daily for some muscle groups<br><br>Perform 3–4 times per week<br><br>Increase frequency as you get into better shape | Perform 3 times per week<br><br>Different muscle groups each time you work out<br><br>Increase frequency as you get into better shape |
| **I** Intensity | 50%–65% of heart rate reserve<br><br>Increase intensity as you get into better shape | Stretch all major muscles and joints; hold for 15–30 seconds<br><br>Perform 1–3 repetitions<br><br>Increase intensity as you get into better shape | Less than 50% of your predicted 1-rep max<br><br>Start with body weight then add resistance<br><br>15 or more reps/1–3 sets<br><br>Increase intensity as you get into better shape | 60%–80% of 1–rep max<br><br>8–12 reps / 1–3 sets<br><br>Increase intensity as you get into better shape |
| **T** Time | 20–60 minutes of continuous activity<br><br>Increase the time as you get into better shape | 10–20 minutes<br><br>Increase the time as you get into better shape | 30–60 minutes<br><br>Increase the time as you get into better shape | 15–60 minutes<br><br>Increase the time as you get into better shape |
| **T** Type | Running, cycling, swimming, and activities that use large muscles | Perform static stretches and controlled dynamic stretches | Resistance training (body weight/tubing/medicine balls/free weights) | Resistance training (body weight/tubing/medicine balls/free weights) |

**Source:** Adapted with permission from "Ontario Health and Physical Education Curriculum Support: Grades K-10", Ophea (Ontario Physical Health Education Association), Toronto 2000, Grades 9–10, Resource Unit 2, p. 42.

# Creating an Action Plan

An **action plan** can help you achieve your health and fitness goals. It also can help you achieve any other changes you would like to make happen as well—from getting good grades to developing successful relationships.

An action plan involves four stages: (1) setting SMART goals, (2) developing action steps, (3) identifying barriers and solutions, and (4) identifying a final "success reward."

Visualize your goals and ask yourself if they meet the SMART criteria.

## Stage 1: Set SMART Goals

Sit down and try to visualize your goal or goals. The goal doesn't have to be large or difficult, but it has to be personal, something that serves your own purpose. Separate the short- and long-term aspects and determine how they relate to one another. Then ask: "Do my goals meet the SMART criteria?" Goals should be **S**pecific, **M**eaningful and **M**easurable, **A**ction-oriented, **R**ealistic, and **T**ime-bound.

## Stage 2: Develop Action Steps

In general, it is good to have a "game plan." Start by listing all the smaller things that need to happen in order for you to reach the larger goal. Develop flexible deadlines for each step. What will you do tomorrow? Next week? Next month? By the end of the school year? In relation to achieving your long-term goals, patience is a virtue.

Monitoring your progress allows you to see how far you have come and can help you to stay motivated.

## Stage 3: Identify Barriers, Find Solutions

There will be times when you cannot maintain your program for various reasons. Remember that sticking to it is not an all-or-nothing thing. You need to be flexible to allow for the unexpected things that happen in everyday life that may throw you off your schedule. Be prepared for setbacks. At the beginning of *Healthy Active Living*, on page xix, you read about the IDEAL model of decision making. This is a good sequence of steps to follow if you find yourself having to make some difficult decisions about how to continue your fitness program. Could someone help, or are there other resources from school, home, or the community that could lend a hand?

## Stage 4: Reward Success

Your planning should include monitoring your progress to keep track of how close you are to success. What will you be doing or what will be different when you reach your goal? Feedback and monitoring can come from keeping a log of test results or from people, such as H&PE teachers, coaches, supportive friends, or parents. If people see you trying, they will be there to help out, and you should welcome their advice. Finally, all your effort probably deserves some sort of reward for success—significantly changing your approach to health and fitness is definitely worth rewarding and celebrating. Even the most modest of rewards will encourage you to continue on your way to fitness success.

# Nothing Succeeds Like Success
## How to Get Yourself Motivated

**M**any people starting a fitness program notice that they make a great deal of progress in the first few weeks. Then, the grind begins.

For your personal fitness program to be successful, you must be able to motivate yourself and put in the effort. But, it is not always easy to exercise on a regular basis.

One of the biggest motivators comes from noticing that, over time, you are actually making some progress towards your goals. For this reason, it is a good idea to monitor your progress along the way so that you can see your results. For example, monitoring your Resting Heart Rate every morning over a four- to five-week period of aerobic training should reveal a drop of about five to ten beats per minute.

### Motivation and Effort

Motivation and effort go hand in hand. If you can motivate yourself to perform to the best of your ability, the effort will surely follow.

Likewise, if you perform to your best ability, the results that this effort brings will motivate you even more to continue.

Here are some suggestions to help you commit to, and follow through on, your fitness plan:

- **Ownership.** Make sure the goals are your own, not your friends' or your teachers'.
- **Options.** Provide yourself with a choice of activities. There are many ways to produce the same training results, and a variety of activities will help keep you motivated.

- **Reinforcement.** Praise yourself for any action taken towards your goal. Celebrate successes and promise yourself rewards as you meet your objectives.
- **Variety.** Think variety—a training partner, new exercises, a change of equipment (even workout time) can make the occasion more pleasant.
- **Challenge.** Think both big and small. Small victories towards your goal can feed the drive to achieve big things.
- **Revision.** Sometimes you will be successful, sometimes you will not be successful. In both cases, it is a good idea to stop and think: "Are the goals I had set originally still good ones?" If not, revise them.

## Mandi Gillies
## Set goals that are achievable ...

**W**anting to lead a healthier lifestyle is the first step, but knowing specifically how you can do it is crucial to seeing progress. Mandi Gillies demonstrates the importance of choosing achievable goals and utilizing tools like the FITT principle. Mandi is in Grade 10 at Grey Highlands Secondary School in Flesherton, Ontario.

### What was your healthy active living goal?

I had several specific goals; each geared to the five basic areas of fitness—cardiovascular, muscular endurance, muscular strength, flexibility, and body composition. To reach these goals, I designed a FITT program, which involved jogging three times a week; doing push-ups, crunches, chin-ups, oblique crunches, and stretches; and eating healthily. I was able to achieve all of my goals by sticking to my FITT plan—even though I did not always feel energetic about doing so!

### What was the most important thing you learned in H&PE class?

The importance of trying my hardest at any physical activity and not giving less than 110%. I also learned a lot about realistic expectations; specifically, that I should not expect immediate results from an improved diet and my FITT plan.

### Who were the people who helped you the most in achieving your goals?

My family (my mom, my dad, and my sister) helped a lot. They are my greatest supporters, and would do anything to help me achieve my goals. All of my coaches were also great at pushing me during practices and at games and they encouraged me to do my best.

### What was the biggest challenge you faced in achieving your goal? How did you overcome it?

I have had type-1 diabetes for five years, and my biggest challenge was not to let it affect my athletic performance and my will to be physically active. Diabetes can cause serious health problems, so I must do everything I can to prevent any complications from happening.

### What are your future goals in the area of healthy active living?

I hope to stay active in sports, and I want to continue to eat healthy foods and exercise on a regular basis. This will not only affect my physical condition but my emotional condition as well because I am always in a better mood when I am active.

### What advice can you offer to other students about how they can achieve their own healthy active living goals?

Set yourself achievable goals so you do not get discouraged. As you achieve your goals, set harder ones for yourself so that you really have to push to achieve them. This way, when you do achieve your goals, you will be proud of yourself and determined to push even harder the next time.

**Staying motivated can be the hardest part of incorporating more activity into your schedule, but try not to let the occasional bad day get you down. Be sure to use the SMART strategy when setting your fitness goals and don't let missing a day of activity turn into an excuse to stop altogether.**

## Questions for Study and Review

### Things to Think About and Explore

1. How would you distinguish between short-term and long-term fitness goals? In practice, what is the relationship between the two types of goals?

2. What is meant by each component of the SMART principle of goal setting? Give examples of each.

3. Investigate the main ideas behind the "overload" and "progression" principles in relation to fitness training.

4. Define what is meant by the "specificity" and "reversibility" principles in relation to fitness training.

5. Explain what is meant by the term "one-repetition maximum" in relation to resistance training. Describe why this particular benchmark is inappropriate at your age and grade level.

6. The FITT principle outlines the main factors to consider when developing a balanced fitness program. Describe what FITT stands for and present examples.

### Things to Do and Practise

7. Set yourself a fitness goal and then design a work-chart to follow and monitor your progress in reaching that fitness goal.

8. Give examples of the kinds of obstacles that one might encounter when trying to adhere to a fitness program. Create an instructional video or pamphlet that covers the specific steps that one could take to help to overcome these obstacles.

9. Apart from warm-up and cool-down, demonstrate through illustrations the three other components of a balanced fitness program.

10. Using the FITT principle, develop and monitor a program of exercises that specifically meets your needs and focuses on all four main components of fitness.

11. Nothing happens without an action plan of some sort. In a journal entry, apply the four stages of developing an effective action plan to improve your level of fitness. Through the duration of this course, monitor how closely you adhered to your action plan.

12. Try various methods (e.g. exercising to music, exercising with friends, introducing variety into all your workouts) to get yourself motivated to begin, and adhere to, a serious fitness program.

## WWWeblinks

Name ➤    Centre for Active Living

URL ➤    www.centre4activeliving.ca

This Alberta-based website is an active living affiliate of the Canadian Health Network.

Name ➤    YMCA Canada

URL ➤    www.ymca.ca

This site provides links to the closest YMCA in your community. Most YMCAs offer gym services and fitness classes.

Name ➤    In Motion

URL ➤    www.in-motion.ca

A Saskatchewan based health promotion strategy which encourages people to make regular physical activity part of their daily lives.

# 8
# Exercises for Fitness and Health

**T**his chapter introduces you to a series of exercises that work the major muscles of the body. Give them a try in your physical education class. With the help of your teacher, you will see an improvement in your levels of endurance and strength. You will feel better as well.

Each muscle performs a specific role. Knowing how particular muscles work will shed light on how you can exercise them in the best possible way. For this reason, this chapter also provides information about the individual muscles involved in each exercise.

With practice and proper supervision, in a short period of time you will be the expert.

## Chapter Objectives

In this chapter, you will:

➢ Discover the potential benefits of resistance training as part of an overall fitness program

➢ Explore the basic principles and key concepts of resistance training

➢ Become familiar with the basic recommendations that you should follow before beginning any strength-training program

➢ Examine and attempt a number of health-related fitness exercises that target the following muscles or muscle groups: deltoids, biceps, triceps, chest, back, abdominal, quadriceps, hamstrings, and calves

## Key Terms

➢ resistance training
➢ repetitions/sets
➢ deltoid
➢ biceps
➢ triceps
➢ pectoralis major
➢ trapezius
➢ latissimus dorsi
➢ erector spinae
➢ abdominal muscles
➢ quadriceps
➢ hamstrings
➢ gastrocnemius

# Resistance Training

**Resistance training** refers to exercising a particular muscle or muscle group by subjecting it to additional weight stress. The weight may be an external object, such as a dumbbell, or it can involve using your body weight as a form of resistance (such as with a push-up).

The objective of resistance training is to develop the targeted muscle or muscle group and make it stronger.

## Is Resistance Training Safe?

The weight need not be excessive to reap the benefits of resistance training. Indeed, any resistance will yield muscular strength and muscular endurance benefits. The important thing is to use resistance that is appropriate and will not result in injury to muscles and joints.

Of course, if you are in a weight room, you should always avoid maximal or near-maximal lifts. Lifting heavy weights or excessive resistance training is very dangerous. As long as you use moderate weights, and closely follow the directions of your teacher, resistance training can become a valuable part of your fitness plan.

Remember, too, that resistance training is only one part of a balanced fitness program. This program should include flexibility exercises (stretching), aerobic activities (walking, jogging, swimming, soccer, etc.), in addition to resistance training.

Resistance training develops muscular strength and muscular endurance.

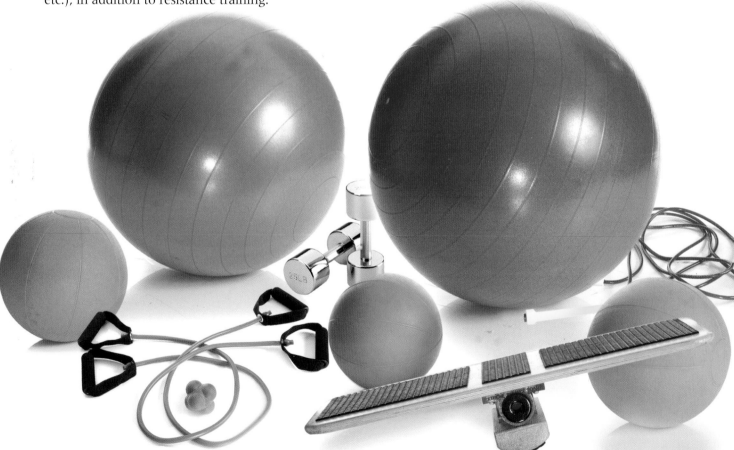

Using the right equipment will help you get more out of resistance training.

# Resistance Training Fundamentals

This chapter describes exercises that are commonly performed in health and physical education classes (H&PE) and in personal-training programs. Basic exercises are described on the left-hand page, and more advanced exercises are provided on the right-hand page. Background information about that particular muscle or muscle group—where it is located, and its function—is provided in the text box on the bottom of the right-hand page.

## Safety First, Always

Safety is an important issue. Here are some tips to keep in mind when attempting these exercises:

➤ **Maximize benefits, minimize risks.** Always ensure that the exercise is appropriate for you, that you are comfortable with any equipment that you may be using, and that the conditions under which you are performing the exercise are safe. To get the best results, practise the exercises shown on the left-hand pages throughout this chapter before attempting the more difficult ones (shown on the right-hand pages).

➤ **Proper technique.** Executing the proper exercise technique will help you get the most out of the exercise and minimize the risk of injury. There are four key training techniques:

- **Body position.** Maintaining proper body alignment is the best way to avoid injury. That is why most exercise instructors require you to "keep your back straight" or "not bounce or rock." If you cannot maintain the required technique, or feel discomfort or pain at any time, stop the exercise immediately and inform your teacher.

- **Breathing.** Do not hold your breath while training with resistance equipment. Holding your breath while using resistance places pressure on the major arteries in the chest and limits the availability of oxygen to your brain. This could cause you to pass out. The general rule is to breathe in before you begin your lift and during the non-lifting phase of the exercise, and breathe out slowly while performing the lift.

- **Grips.** Various exercises require the use of different grips. The two grips that are recommended are the **supinated grip** (underhand grip) and the **pronated grip** (overhand grip) These grips are shown on the next page. Both involve wrapping the thumb around the bar. The one grip that is not recommended under any circumstance is the so-called "monkey grip." This grip is unstable since your thumb is not wrapped around the bar. This could lead to the resistance weight falling and possible serious injury.

---

## Safety Precautions

Follow these guidelines and you will get the most out of your resistance-training program.

- Learn all the basic exercise techniques before moving to more challenging exercises.

- Initially, use only your own body weight as resistance and, when you master the technique, increase the resistance by using free weights.

- Perform 3 sets of each exercise and keep your repetitions between 10–15; avoid weight that you can only lift 1–5 times.

- Avoid using adult-strength training programs as they can lead to injury.

- Consult with your teacher or a certified strength and conditioning specialist before designing any sport-specific exercise programs.

- **Tempo and phases.** Each time you perform an exercise, be it a push-up or a squat, you should maintain a certain tempo or speed. Tempo is the amount of time it takes you to perform all phases of a lift. Take, for example, the push-up: up, top, and bottom are the three phases. The speed of this exercise or lift should be "1-0-1." The numbers represent the amount of time you should spend on each phase. In this case, one second to push "up," no pause at the "top," and one second on the "down phase."

## Repetitions and Sets

The terms **repetitions** and **sets** are used to describe the number of times you perform a certain resistance training exercise. They are often used as if they meant the same thing, but they do not.

Here is the difference:

➢ **Repetitions.** Repetitions (or reps) are the number of times you continuously perform an exercise. If you lift a barbell once, that is one rep. If you lift it 25 times consecutively, that amounts to 25 reps.

➢ **Sets.** Sets are the number of times you perform a certain number of reps. If you lift a barbell for 25 reps, then rest, then perform another 25 reps, combined you would have done 2 sets of 25 reps.

The number of repetitions and sets you perform will determine the endurance or strength gains that your muscles experience.

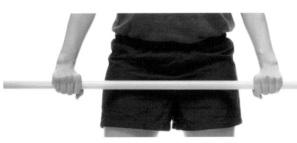

Pronated grip (overhand grip)

Monkey grip (thumb not wrapped around the bar)—not recommended under any circumstances

Supinated grip (underhand grip)

## Deltoid Exercises

**T**he deltoid is a small but powerful muscle on the end of each shoulder. It is named after the greek letter *delta*, which is triangular in shape.

### Lateral Shoulder Raise

The lateral shoulder raise is an excellent exercise for the beginner and expert alike. It works the outside, or lateral, part of the deltoid muscle, and can be done with a variety of equipment. Start off with lightweight tubing or lightweight dumbbells so as not to place undue stress on the deltoid muscle or other muscles in the area.

Follow the steps below to get started:

➢ Place light tubing securely under the middle of both feet while holding the ends firmly in both hands (use an overhand grip).

➢ Be sure never to lift your toes or heels off the ground as this may cause the tubing to slip.

➢ Keep your back straight, knees slightly bent, and feet shoulder-width apart.

➢ Raise both of your arms to shoulder height, continuing to keep your back and arms straight.

➢ Breathe normally throughout the entire exercise.

➢ Return to the start position slowly, keeping the tension on the tubing.

➢ Repeat for the required number of repetitions and sets.

➢ To increase the level of difficulty, use tubing that provides greater tension or heavier dumbbells.

## Rear Deltoid Raises

The posterior, or rear, of the deltoid muscle is probably the most neglected part of the muscle. The best way to train this area is by using lightweight tubing or lightweight dumbbells. Rear deltoid exercises should be incorporated into your routine to ensure that you are working all parts of the muscle.

The exercise is performed as follows:

> ➢ Step forward with one leg and place the tubing securely under your front foot while holding the end firmly in one hand.

> ➢ Bend over and place your non-lifting hand on your front knee, and keep your back straight throughout the entire motion.

> ➢ Begin by slowly extending your arm backward, moving only at the shoulder joint.

> ➢ Pause briefly at the top of the motion then return to the start position, keeping tension on the tubing at all times.

> ➢ Rest and repeat for the required number of repetitions and sets.

> ➢ To increase the level of difficulty, use tubing that provides greater tension or slightly heavier dumbbells.

## Deltoids
### Shouldering the Load

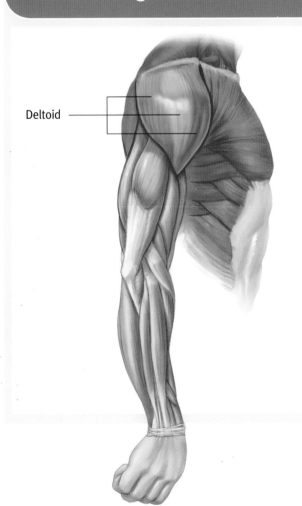

Deltoid

The **deltoid** muscle is made up of three distinct parts (or heads). Each head is responsible for specific movements that allow the shoulder to move in many different ways (from raising your hand to ask a question in class to lifting a spoonful of food to your mouth).

### Location

The broad base of the triangular-shaped deltoid wraps around your shoulder attaching to your clavicle (collar bone) on the front and your scapula (shoulder blade) on the back.

The tip of the deltoid attaches to your humerus, so when the muscle contracts, it lifts the arm in a number of directions.

### Function

The deltoid has three movements or functions. It flexes, abducts, and extends the arm. Thus, the deltoid raises your arm forward, raises your arm to the side and moves your arm towards the back of your body.

# Biceps Exercises

The elbow joint has four muscles that enable it to flex. The most powerful of these muscles is the biceps brachii (the "biceps"). Below are a few exercises that target the biceps and other muscles that work alongside it.

## Standing Tubing Curls

This exercise requires you to keep your back straight, and your knees slightly bent at all times. With your teacher's approval, after a few weeks of building this exercise into your regimen, you can slowly increase the load either by increasing the tubing tension (using thicker tubing) or switching to dumbbells or other free weights.

If it is your first time trying this exercise, begin with lightweight tubing and follow the steps below:

> Place the tubing securely under one foot, and move the other foot slightly back.

> Be sure never to lift your toe or heel off the ground as this may cause the tubing to slip.

> Extend your arms fully, and hold one handle firmly in each hand using an underhand (or supinated) grip.

> At all times, keep your back straight, a slight bend in your knees, and avoid rocking back and forth.

> Breathe normally throughout the entire exercise.

> Begin by slowly flexing your elbows until your hands are at approximately shoulder level, keeping your elbows close to your body.

> When lifting, be sure to bend only at the elbow, as this will ensure the maximal use of your biceps muscle.

> Slowly return back to the starting position, keeping tension on the tubing at all times.

> Repeat for the required number of repetitions and sets.

## Stability Ball Concentration Curls

The challenge in this variation, known as a "concentration curl," is to keep your upper body still. Do not perform this exercise until you can sit on the ball without losing your balance. Once you are balanced, follow the instructions below:

➢ Place yourself comfortably on the stability ball with your legs spread apart and a light dumbbell in hand.

➢ Bend forward and place your lifting elbow on the inner portion of your thigh and your non-lifting hand on the other thigh.

➢ Keep your back straight at all times and avoid rocking back and forth.

➢ Breathe normally throughout the entire exercise.

➢ Begin by slowly rasing the dumbbell towards your chest without taking your elbow off your thigh.

➢ Pause briefly at the top of the motion, then return to the start position.

➢ Repeat for the required number of repetitions and sets.

# Biceps Brachii
## Flexing Your Arm Muscles

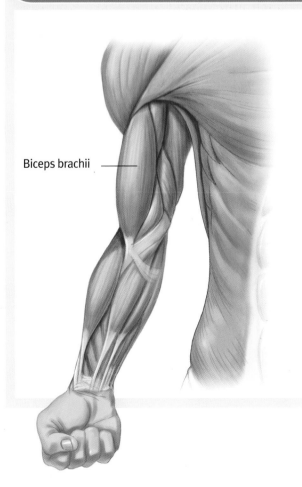

Biceps brachii

This "two headed" muscle, (*bi-* means two, *brachii* is Latin for arm) is likely the most recognized muscle in the body. The **biceps**, commonly referred to as "bis" or "pipes," rests on the anterior side of the upper arm.

Make a fist while bending your elbow and look at your upper arm. What you see popping out is your biceps brachii muscle.

### Location

The biceps brachii arises from two proximal points of attachment to the scapula (shoulder blade). The muscle forms a single belly whose tendon crosses the front of the elbow to attach to the radius.

### Function

Like most muscles in the body, the biceps brachii also has more than one function. As well as flexing the elbow, the biceps brachii also supinates the forearm.

The biceps brachii works in cooperation with the triceps (at the back of the humerus). The former flexes the elbow, while the latter extends the elbow.

## Triceps Exercises

There is no such thing as a three-headed monster, but there is a three-headed muscle. It is the triceps brachii, located on the back of your upper arm. Basketball, ultimate Frisbee, and tennis are activities that benefit from well-trained triceps. The exercises below are a good starting point for anyone looking to strengthen his or her triceps.

### Standing Triceps Extension

Similar to the standing biceps curl, this exercise requires you to maintain a straight back and a slight bend in your knees. Ensure that you fully extend your arm when performing the exercise.

To get the most out of this exercise, pick the tubing tension that best suits your needs and follow the steps below:

➢ Firmly grasp the tubing on one end and use an underhand grip to hold the other end securely at your chest.

➢ Your knuckles should be at ear level, with your arm bent at the elbow.

➢ Ensure that you only bend at the elbow in order to work the triceps muscle to its fullest.

➢ Slowly extend your arm upwards on a 45 degree angle.

➢ Breathe normally throughout the entire exercise.

➢ Pause briefly at the top, then slowly return to the start position (keeping tension on the tubing at all times).

➢ Repeat for the required number of repetitions.

➢ Repeat with the opposite arm.

➢ To increase the level of difficulty, use tubing that offers more resistance.

## Triceps Kickbacks

This exercise is sometimes referred to as "Donkey Kickbacks," and it can be performed with tubing or dumbbells. It may be helpful to use a wall mirror to ensure that you are adopting the proper technique. Here are the key steps:

➢ Bend forward slightly, with your legs slightly apart.

➢ Keep your back straight and place your non-lifting hand on your knee.

➢ Raise your lifting arm until you have achieved a 90-degree bend at your elbow.

➢ Keep your shoulder fixed in place and slowly extend your arm backward by bending only at the elbow.

➢ Breathe normally, and pause briefly at the top of the motion (at which point, your arm should be parallel to the ground).

➢ Slowly return the dumbbell back to the start position.

➢ After completing the required number of repetitions, switch positions and repeat on the other side.

## Triceps Brachii
### The Three-Headed Muscle

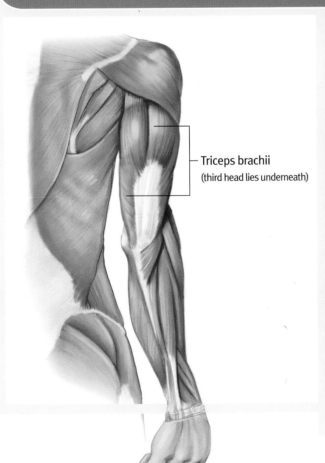

Triceps brachii
(third head lies underneath)

Like the biceps on the front of the upper arm, the triceps brachii is named after the number of heads it has (*tri-* means three). The **triceps** acts, as noted, in co-operation with the biceps brachii—when one contracts, the other relaxes and vice versa.

### Location

This horseshoe shaped muscle is located on the posterior side of your arm directly opposite your biceps. Its upper tendons attach to the scapula (shoulder blade) and humerus (upper arm). The lower tendon of triceps brachii crosses the back of the elbow and attaches to the ulna (one of two bones in the forearm) at the elbow.

The triceps brachii is quite a bit larger than your biceps muscle. You can feel the length of the muscle by simply grasping along the back part of your arm.

### Function

The triceps' primary function is to extend the elbow joint. This action occurs, for example, when throwing a dart or when shooting, passing, or throwing a basketball.

## Chest Exercises

**P**ectoralis major is the large, thick, fan-shaped muscle that covers the upper part of the chest. Pushing is what this muscle is all about. There are many exercises from which to choose when you are looking to increase the strength and endurance of your chest muscles. Here are two of them.

### Standard Push-Up

The "modified" and "standard" versions are the two most common types of push-ups. The modified push-up is done from a kneeling position, whereas the standard push-up is performed with your legs fully extended.

If you can perform three sets of 15 repetitions from the modified position without difficulty, then you are ready to progress to the standard push-up.

Follow these instructions for the standard push-up:

➢ Lie face down on the floor with your hands pointing forward and placed slightly wider than shoulder-width apart.

➢ Keeping your back, hips, and knees perfectly straight, raise your body from the floor.

➢ Breathe normally throughout the entire exercise.

➢ Once your arms are fully extended, slowly lower your body without touching the floor (stay approximately 6 cm from the floor).

➢ Keep your entire body—shoulders, torso, hips, and legs in a straight line, throughout.

➢ Repeat for the required number of repetitions and sets.

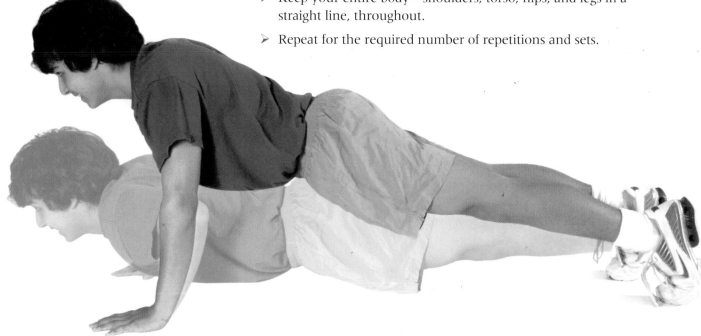

## Tubing Chest Press

Chest presses are another good way to exercise your chest muscles. First, select light exercise tubing that offers a resistance that is appropriate for you. Then, follow the steps below:

> Using a soft surface, such as a mat, kneel down on one leg and place the tubing around your back.

> Adjust the tubing to the desired tension by holding it below the handles (keep some tension on the tubing at all times).

> Breathe normally throughout the entire exercise.

> Looking straight ahead, and keeping your back and hips perfectly straight, extend your arms forward in a smooth, fluid movement.

> Slowly return to the starting position, keeping tension on the tubing, and your elbows parallel to the ground.

> Repeat for the required number of repetitions, switching leg positions after each set.

## Pectoralis Major
### The Major Muscle of the Chest

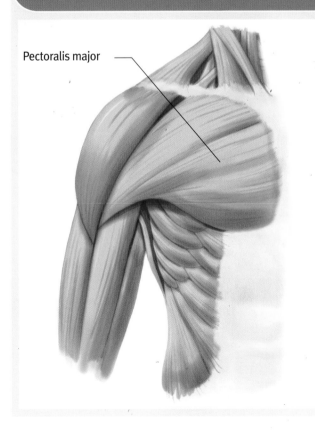

Pectoralis major

The **Pectoralis major** is a powerful chest muscle that is appropriately named after its size. It has a smaller "sibling" muscle that lives underneath it, called pectoralis minor. Pectoralis major and minor make up the pectoral muscle group. They are commonly referred to as simply the "pecs."

### Location

Pectoralis major starts from the middle of the chest where it attaches itself to the sternum and the clavicle. It then crosses the front of the shoulder joint and anchors itself onto the humerus.

To feel this muscle, place one palm flat on a table and push downward. Now, take the thumb and index finger of your other hand and grab the front part of your armpit. The part that you are grasping is your pectoralis major muscle.

### Function

Pectoralis major serves to adduct and flex at the shoulder joint. Strengthening this muscle will not only improve your forehand in tennis, but will also enable you to get out of the pool easier.

## Back Exercises

There are many large muscles and muscle groups in the back. These include trapezius, latissimus dorsi, and the erector spinae group. Each muscle group plays its own unique and important role. The exercises below generally utilize them all.

### Bird Dog

This exercise primarily targets the erector spinae group, the three powerful muscles that run up and down your spine (iliocostalis, longissimus, and spinalis). This group helps to keep our spines erect (as the name implies).

Ideally, this exercise requires the use of a mat. Be sure to keep one leg and one hand on the floor at all times.

Follow the instructions below:

➤ Place your hands and knees on a mat with your hands shoulder-width apart.

➤ Raise your right arm and left leg at the same time.

➤ Your back should be "table-top" flat, forming a straight line with your raised arm and leg.

➤ Breathe normally throughout the entire exercise.

➤ Hold this position for the required number of seconds, then rest.

➤ Repeat, this time raising your left arm and right leg.

➤ Perform this pair of "Bird Dog" exercises for the required number of repetitions and sets.

## Upward Row

This exercise is harder than it looks. It targets trapezius and latissimus dorsi (as well as the "rhomboids," two other muscles deep in the upper back). This exercise is not primarily intended for the biceps. The key is to start by pulling from the shoulder:

➢ Holding a dumbbell in one hand, spread your legs one behind the other, and place one hand on your front thigh.

➢ Slowly slide your hand down your thigh to the top of your knee by bending at the waist, keeping your back straight.

➢ The arm with the weight should be fully extended downwards.

➢ Keep your back straight throughout the entire movement.

➢ Begin by pulling your shoulder upwards, then follow-through by bending at the elbow until the dumbbell reaches chest level.

➢ Hold this position briefly, breathing normally, and return the dumbbell to the starting position.

➢ Repeat for the required number of repetitions, then switch position and repeat with the other arm.

## Major Back Muscles
### Protectors and Erectors

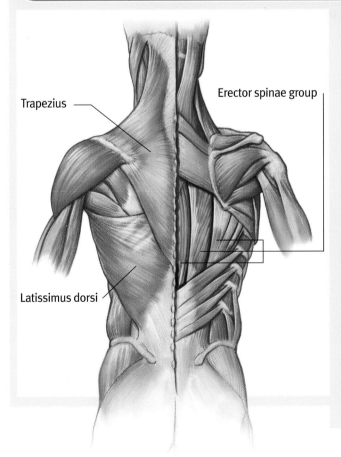

Trapezius

Erector spinae group

Latissimus dorsi

The major muscles of the back are **trapezius, latissimus dorsi, and the erector spinae** group. Trapezius, so-named because it is shaped like a trapezoid, covers the upper part of the back, while latissimus dorsi (the "lats") covers most of the lower back. The erector spinae group lies underneath all of them and runs along the length of your spine and the back of your ribs.

### Location

Trapezius has many attachment sites. It extends from the base of the skull and vertebral column to the scapula (shoulder blade). Latissimus dorsi, on the other hand, extends from your middle and lower vertebrae to the humerus.

The three erector muscles are firmly anchored on to your spinal column and ribs.

### Function

Trapezius raises and lowers the shoulders and extends the neck. Latissimus dorsi adducts and extends the arms. The erector spinae, as the name suggests, keeps our spines erect, and helps us maintain good posture.

# Abdominal Exercises

The abdominal muscles are commonly referred to as the "abs." Together with the deep back muscles they form the core muscle group. Collectively this group contributes to good posture and better sports performance. Below are common exercises used to target the abdominal area.

## McGill Crunch

The McGill Crunch is named after Dr. Stuart McGill, a professor of biomechanics and a world-renowned back specialist at the University of Waterloo in Ontario. This is an isometric exercise that works many of your abdominal muscles. It requires you to raise your shoulder blades off the ground in a slow, controlled manner, and hold the posistion for a few seconds.

Follow the instructions below to perform this exercise correctly:

> Lie on a mat, with your hands under your lower back (palms down) and one knee bent at 90 degrees.

> In a smooth motion, lift only your head and shoulders off the ground while breathing throughout the entire motion.

> Hold this position for the required number of seconds, then rest.

> Repeat for the required number of repetitions.

> To increase the level of difficulty, try raising your elbows off the floor along with your shoulders and head.

## Towel Crunch

Using a towel is a good way to learn the mechanics of the abdominal crunch. To get the maximum benefit, ensure your head is completely enclosed in the towel. Try to keep your arm motion to a minimum in order to focus the effort on the abdominal area:

➢ Place your towel on a mat and lie on it, making sure your head is completely on the towel.

➢ Grasp the ends of the towel with both hands, and bend your knees approximately 90 degrees.

➢ Use the towel to support your neck, but do not pull on it. Breathe normally.

➢ Slowly lift your body towards your knees and stop when your shoulder blades are off the ground.

➢ Slowly return to the starting position then repeat for the required number of repetitions and sets.

# The Abdominal Family
## Core Muscles

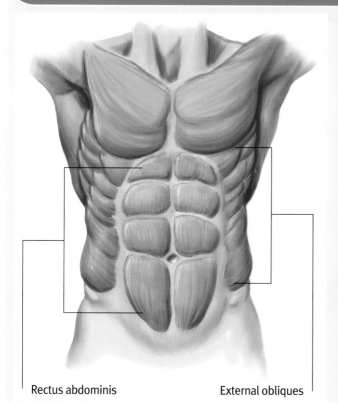

Rectus abdominis          External obliques

A common myth is that the more abdominal exercises you do, the more fat you will lose around your mid-section. In fact, the more abdominal exercises you do, the stronger your abdominal muscles will get. Fat reduction cannot be achieved by performing abdominal crunches alone. You must also take heed of how much, and what, you eat.

### Location

The two major **abdominal muscles** are rectus abdominis and the external obliques.

The rectus abdominis is located on the anterior surface of your torso. The external obliques are located on the sides of your body.

### Function

The abdominal muscles allow you to flex and rotate your upper body. The complimentary muscle group on the back is the erector spinae group.

Together these core muscles are essential for maintaining posture and a high level of performance in most sports and physical activity.

## Quadriceps Exercises

**T**he quadriceps is a group of four muscles located on the front of your thigh. They serve to extend (straighten) the knee. Each muscle originates in a different place, but all four come together at the quadriceps tendon. This tendon then wraps around the patella (knee cap), and inserts on the tibia (shin bone) by means of the patellar ligament.

### Tubing Squats

Initially, this exercise should be performed only with light tubing resistance. Once you have mastered the squatting technique, your teacher may ask you to move to tubing that offers more resistance, or to use free weights. If you ever use squat racks, be sure to have your teacher show you the proper technique, and never squat without spotters.

You should avoid any squatting exercises if you have knee pain or back injuries.

Here are the key elements of this exercise:

➢ With feet slightly wider than shoulder-width apart, place the tubing equally under both feet, and hold the ends at shoulder level.

➢ Keep your head and back straight and never lift your heels or toes off the ground.

➢ Breathe normally throughout the entire exercise.

➢ Slowly bend at the knees until your thighs are parallel (or almost parallel) to the ground, keeping your back straight.

➢ Make sure your knees never turn inwards.

➢ Return to the start position and repeat for the required number of repetitions and sets.

## Single-Leg Squats

Single-leg squats are extremely effective in strengthening the quads. Begin by bending only slightly at the knee, and progress lower as you get stronger. Start with your own body weight, then use other forms of resistance such as dumbbells:

➢ Stand on your right leg with your arms raised up to shoulder level and extended out to the sides. Your left leg should be raised off the floor throughout the entire exercise.

➢ Keep your head and back straight, and your right foot flat on the ground.

➢ Breathe normally throughout the entire exercise and always maintain your balance.

➢ Start by slowly bending at the knee and hips, while simultaneously bringing your arms forward.

➢ Pause briefly, then return to the upright position.

➢ Perform this exercise on one leg for the desired number of repetitions, then switch to your other leg and do the same.

# Quadriceps
## The Fantastic Four Extensors

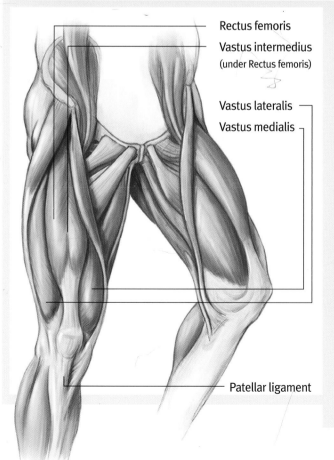

Rectus femoris

Vastus intermedius
(under Rectus femoris)

Vastus lateralis

Vastus medialis

Patellar ligament

The Latin name is musculus **quadriceps** femoris, but the common name is simply the "quads." This powerful muscle group is made up of four separate muscles: vastus medialis, vastus lateralis, vastus intermedius, and rectus femoris.

### Location

Three of the quadriceps are anchored on various locations on the anterior surface of the femur. The other is anchored on the hip bone (pelvis). They travel down the front of the femur, cross the front of the knee, and attach together below the patella on the tibia.

You can feel this attachment site if you run your fingers down your patellar ligament (the first bump you feel is the attachment site). That is why it is important to wear knee pads when in-line skating, skateboarding, or playing ice hockey. If damaged, you could end up with a lifetime of pain.

### Function

All of the quads act to extend the knee. Rectus femoris performs double duty as a hip flexor. Keep them in shape and they will keep you moving.

# Hamstring Exercises

**T**he hamstrings, on the back of the thigh, complement the quadriceps on the front. The hamstrings serve to flex the knee. Their unusual name derives from their string-like appearance, and because we get ham from the same muscles on a pig. The exercises listed here target this muscle group.

## Lunges

Lunges are an excellent all-round lower body exercise. You can exercise several muscle groups at once—the quadriceps, the hamstrings, the hip extensors (mainly gluteus maximus)—and if you use a medicine ball, you can strenghten muscles in your upper body as well.

As with most exercises, it is important to start off with no resistance other than your body weight. The key is not to lunge too far forward, nor to go too far down.

Here are the instructions for performing this exercise with the aid of a medicine ball:

➢ Start with a light medicine ball held above your head, with your feet shoulder-width apart.

➢ Keep your back straight to avoid any bending while lunging.

➢ Breathe normally throughout the entire exercise.

➢ Begin by taking a slow, controlled step forward covering about a metre in distance.

➢ Once the lead foot is firmly planted, bend with the same leg until your thigh is parallel to the ground. Lower your arms so they are also parallel to the ground.

➢ Do not allow your lead leg to bend more than 90 degrees. The back knee should not touch the ground.

➢ To return to the starting position, push off your lead leg; then repeat with the other leg.

➢ Repeat the sequence for the required number of repetitions and sets.

## Stability Ball Leg Curls

This is an advanced exercise and should be done only when you have mastered the lunge and the single-leg squat. Make sure your legs have had a good warm-up before you try this exercise. Use a mat as a cushion for your back and follow the instructions below:

➢ Lie on your back next to a stability ball, hands out to the side for balance.

➢ Raise your feet so that your lower calves and heals are on top of the ball.

➢ Keeping your hips high, breathe normally, and roll the ball towards your body by bending at the knees.

➢ Once your knees are bent to 90 degrees, slowly return to the starting position by extending your knees.

➢ Repeat for the required number of repetitions and sets.

# The Hamstrings
## Knee Flexors and Hip Extensors

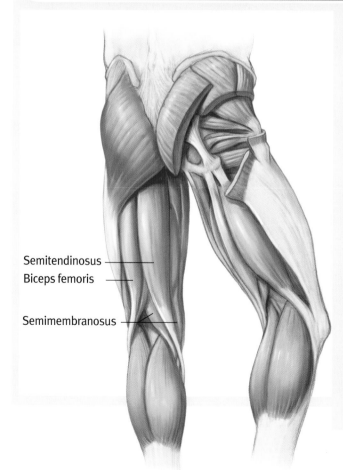

Semitendinosus
Biceps femoris
Semimembranosus

Three muscles make up the **hamstrings** muscle group: semitendinosus, semimembranosus, and biceps femoris. The two "semi" muscles are named after their appearance—one resembles a tendon, while the other resembles a flat membrane. Biceps femoris is named for having two heads (bi) and being located on the femur.

### Location

The "hams," as they are commonly called, reside on the posterior (or back part) of your femur. They all have a common anchoring point on the posterior aspect of the pelvic bones. They run down the leg, crossing the back of both the hip and the knee, to various attachment sites on your two lower leg bones (the tibia and fibula).

### Function

Collectively, the hamstrings flex the knee and extend the hip—both of which are extremely important movements in daily life, not to mention pretty well every sport. These hamstring muscles must be kept strong in order to keep up with the powerful "quads" on the front part of the femur (in this case, imbalance is not really an option). Keeping the hamstrings and quads fit will make many daily activities seem easy.

## Calf Exercises

The calf muscles have the unenviable task of carrying your entire body weight most of the time. Each time you plant your foot to take a step, your calf muscles shift into gear to get you to where you need to go. Here are a couple of fairly common exercises you can use to make this muscle more efficient.

### Calf Raises

A raised platform or step is all you need to perform calf raises. Although not essential, you can position your raised platform close to a wall or railing so you can use it to maintain your balance.

As you get better you can introduce other forms of resistance to this exercise, such as a light dumbbell or other object.

The instructions below will help you learn the key stages in executing a proper calf raise:

> Place both feet slightly apart on the edge of a step or raised platform.

> Breathe normally throughout the entire exercise.

> Allow your heel to drop slightly below the step without losing your balance (you may hold onto a railing or wall for added support).

> Slowly come up on your toes without bending at the knees or hips.

> Once you have reached the top of your movement, slowly return to the starting position, always maintaining a smooth movement (never bouncing).

> Repeat this motion for the required number of repetitions and sets.

## Single-Leg Calf Raises

The single-leg calf raise is more difficult than it looks. You can supplement the exercise by adding a light resistance weight, but in the beginning start off slowly, both in speed and in weight.

For this exercise you will need a railing or wall to help keep your balance. We have added a dumbbell to show you the next progression of the single-leg calf raise. Follow the instructions below:

➢ Holding a dumbbell at thigh level, place both feet on the edge of the platform (place your other hand on a wall for support).

➢ Slightly lift one foot off the platform while allowing the other heel to slightly drop below the platform.

➢ Breathing normally, slowly come up on the ball of your foot without bending at the knees or hips.

➢ Once you have reached the top of the movement, slowly return to the starting position.

➢ Avoid dropping your heel down too far, which might unnecessarily stretch your calf muscle (never bounce).

➢ Repeat for the required number of repetitions and sets.

## Gastrocnemius
### The Mighty Calf Muscle

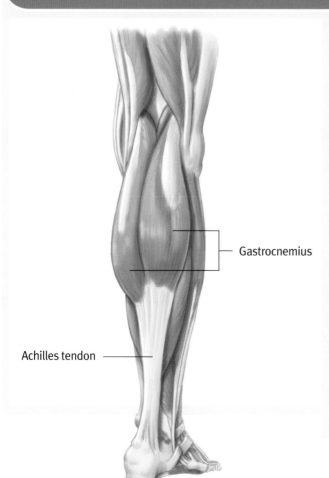

Gastrocnemius

Achilles tendon

Commonly called the "jumpers' muscle," the **gastrocnemius** is a powerful "plantar flexor" of the ankle joint. It has two major heads that resemble "tear drops."

### Location

The gastrocnemius muscle is on the posterior (back) of the leg. Situated just under the back of the knee, this muscle has three main points of attachment. It starts off from two sites at the back, lower end of the femur. It crosses the back of the knee and continues downward, attaching via the largest tendon of the body (the Achilles tendon) to the heel bone.

### Function

The function of the gastrocnemius is to "plantar flex" your foot. Simply stated, this muscle works each time you stand on your toes.

The muscle can easily be seen and felt. Grab the large muscle on the back of your lower leg. The muscle you are holding is the gastrocnemius. It is relatively small, but extremely strong. After all, it carries your entire weight for your entire life.

## Sanket Ullal
## Always crave improvement ...

**A**nyone can set goals and go through the motions of doing exercises, but really committing to a plan will make an active lifestyle that is much easier to achieve. Sanket Ullal has experienced first-hand the way that pushing yourself can lead to great things. Sanket attends Westdale Secondary School in Hamilton, Ontario.

### What was your healthy active living goal?

My main goal was to thrive in every single activity we did in H&PE class in Grade 10. I knew I had some weaknesses coming in from Grade 9, but by setting my sights high, increasing my effort and commitment, and being positive in every class, my goals were not out of reach.

### What was the most important thing you learned in H&PE class?

A key word in class was "improvement" and I have made that the basis of my efforts. I also made up an acronym, HEAP, based on what I learned in class, that stands for Hard work, Enhancement, Aspiration, and Perseverance. I made a checklist for myself, and every day that I achieved all the aspects of HEAP, I gave myself a check mark. That simple word really helped me stay motivated.

### Who helped you the most in achieving your goals?

I have definitely relied on family, friends, and teachers to help me achieve my goals. My friends have taught me to strive harder by pushing past the difficulties I have faced. My parents have opened all kinds of doors by having faith in me and allowing me to try new things. My teachers have helped by providing the tremendous guidance required for success.

### What was the biggest challenge you faced in achieving your goal? How did you overcome it?

One major obstacle was the lack of motivation I sometimes had. It's natural to want to give up sometimes and it can seem like an easy shortcut. Luckily, because of my family and my teachers, I felt inspired and felt that no matter how much I achieve there will always be more great things to accomplish.

### What are your future goals in the area of healthy active living?

I have always loved recreation and I intend to stay fit and healthy. My priorities may change, but keeping an hour aside each day for fitness will definitely continue to be a priority!

### What advice can you offer to other students about how they can achieve their own healthy active living goals?

In the course of picking your goals, it is crucial to decide exactly how you are going to achieve them. Always crave improvement, and never give up! Every goal is attainable and with effort, and faith in yourself, you will go a long way.

**It may seem difficult to find time to be active every day. If you do make the time, you will not only be in better shape but other aspects of your life will benefit as well. People who follow good nutrition guidelines and lead active lifestyles often sleep better, are more able to concentrate, and experience a greater sense of well-being. So, see if you can find a few hours a week for activity—it can only lead to good things.**

## Questions for Study and Review

### Things to Think About and Explore

1. Resistance training should be part of a balanced exercise program. Describe the other main components, and present examples for each type of training.

2. Investigate why safety is a major concern in relation to resistance training.

3. Write a paragraph explaining where the biceps brachii is located and what function it performs.

4. Examine where the pectoralis major is located, and what function it performs.

5. Investigate the three major muscles and muscle groups on the back and explain why they are given those names.

6. Identify the two main abdominal muscles and explain their functions.

### Things to Do and Practise

7. Create a poster about the five safety precautions (listed on page 114) that apply to all resistance training sessions.

8. Choose three of the exercises in this chapter and record in a journal the number of "reps" and "sets" that you do. Continue with these exercises for one month, recording your results each time. After one month, look back and compare the number of "reps" and "sets" that you have done each time you performed the exercises. Do you see any improvements? How do you feel?

9. The deltoid muscle rests on the ends of each shoulder. Demonstrate to the class the three functions it performs.

10. Research other resistance exercises that you can do to strengthen the quadriceps muscle group and demonstrate to the class either by performing the exercise or showing pictures or video clips.

11. The hamstring muscle group rests on the posterior surface of the femur (back of upper leg). Make a mold of this muscle group using Plasticine or another form of molding clay. Clearly indicate the muscle group, where it attaches, and what its function is.

12. Choose a resistance exercise routine that will help to develop a muscle group that is of interest to you (perhaps one that is emphasized in your favourite sport). Make a presentation to your class that describes and explains the steps involved in this exercise routine.

## WWWeblinks

Name ➤ Canadian Women's Health Network

URL ➤ www.cwhn.ca

A voluntary national organization that aims to improve the health and lives of girls and women in Canada and the world.

Name ➤ Canadian Men's Health Network

URL ➤ www.mensnet.ca

A site aimed at helping Canadian men lead healthier lives.

Name ➤ Coalition for Active Living

URL ➤ www.activeliving.ca

A national group of 80 organizations that focus on health promotion and disease prevention through physical activity.

# 9
# Injury Prevention and Safety

> **My body could stand the crutches but my mind couldn't stand the sideline.**
>
> **Michael Jordan**
>
> Legendary basketball player

**N**ot using the right protective equipment or using improperly fitted equipment is a leading cause of preventable injuries. Using the proper equipment in all types of physical activity is essential to preventing injuries both minor and catastrophic.

Any sport or physical activity can be risky. The choices you make with respect to exercise safety can help prevent serious injury and allow many years of healthy active living.

In this chapter, you will be introduced to some common sports injuries and ways to prevent them from happening.

## Chapter Objectives

In this chapter, you will:

> ➢ Be reminded of the importance of the "Safety First" principle in the gym and in the weight room

> ➢ Understand the importance of the warm-up and cool-down periods

> ➢ Identify the main types of muscle and tendon injuries: DOMS, muscle strains and tears, and tendonitis

> ➢ Learn how to identify and treat injuries using the acronyms SHARP and PIER as your guidelines

> ➢ Identify the main types of joint and ligament injuries: sprains, dislocations, and separations

> ➢ Learn how to distinguish the main types of bone and head injuries: fractures, shin splints, stress fractures, and concussions

> ➢ Identify various injuries associated with environmental conditions: heat cramps, heat exhaustion, heat stroke, hypothermia, frostbite, and sunburn

> ➢ Learn how to make exercising in the fitness or weight room an enjoyable experience by following proper "spotting" procedures

## Key Terms

- ➢ warm-up/cool-down
- ➢ dynamic stretching/static stretching
- ➢ strains
- ➢ DOMS
- ➢ tendonitis
- ➢ SHARP/PIER
- ➢ ligaments
- ➢ sprains
- ➢ dislocation/separation
- ➢ fracture
- ➢ shin splits
- ➢ stress fractures
- ➢ concussion
- ➢ weather-related injuries

# Safety First

Physical activity is not only good for our health, it also brings pleasure and enjoyment. However, to be able to enjoy the benefits of physical activity for a lifetime without serious injury, we must be safety conscious at all times.

Here are some of the essential pieces of equipment, and some preventive measures, that can help to prevent many common injuries:

> Wear the appropriate helmet made for skateboarding, hockey, biking, in-line skating, football, and baseball, to name a few.

> Wear eye protection in sports and activities that require it.

> Wear mouth guards to protect your teeth, and to help prevent and limit concussions.

> Wear wrist, knee, and elbow guards to prevent fractures and major cuts, as well as protective cups for hockey players.

Wearing properly fitted equipment decreases the chance of becoming seriously injured. Making that safety choice will allow you to enjoy the physical activities and sports you like for a long time.

Always remember to take the needed precautions when being physically active.

In order to prevent injuries, be sure to use the appropriate safety equipment.

# Warm-Up and Cool-Down Exercises

Before doing any type of physical activity, it's important to warm up the body. The **warm-up** gets the body ready for physical activity. Equally important as the warm-up is the cool-down exercise after participating in physical activity. The **cool-down** returns the body to its normal resting state.

Both warming up and cooling down may help reduce injuries and lessen the discomfort sometimes felt after physical activity.

## Warm-Up Exercises

For most recreational athletes and physical education students, the warm-up usually lasts about 10 to 15 minutes. This includes participating in a mild aerobic activity, such as a light jog around the track or gymnasium, followed by dynamic stretching.

**Dynamic stretching** is essentially stretching while moving. Current research tells us that this is effective in preparing the body for physical activity. Examples include "high knee walks," as shown in the picture below, and "lunges."

## Cool-Down Exercises

After vigorous physical activity, it is important to take a few minutes to cool the body down gradually. Stopping abruptly, such as lying down after an intense game of soccer or a long run, only hurts the body more.

A cool-down exercise is similar to a warm-up exercise, but usually is shorter and less intense. For example, a light jog or brisk walk for five minutes, followed by a total body stretch. Not only does a cool-down exercise routine return the body to its normal resting state, it also rids the body of waste material that was produced during exercise, such as carbon dioxide and lactic acid.

**Static stretching** is basically bending our joints until we feel a slight pull on the muscle(s) and holding that position for 15 to 30 seconds. Static stretches should be included in your cool-down exercises.

Below are some common static stretches you can use. Remember to perform these stretches only after your breathing rate returns to normal.

### Benefits of the Cool-Down

Here is a summary of the benefits of doing cool-down exercises after participating in any form of physical activity:

- Prevents blood from pooling in muscles which could cause dizziness or fainting
- Helps body discard adrenaline which increases heart rate during exercise
- Reduces muscle stiffness
- Helps remove some of the painful by-products of exercise, such as lactic acid

# Muscle and Tendon Injuries

The most common injures sustained to the body during physical activity are to the muscles and tendons. Here are some of the more common muscle- and tendon-related injuries.

## Muscle and Tendon Strains and Tears

**Strains** are caused by twisting or pulling a muscle or tendon. Depending on the severity of the injury, a strain may be the result of a muscle or a tendon being overstretched. If strains remain untreated, tears in the muscle or tendon fibres may worsen.

Strains can either be acute or chronic:

➢ **Acute strains** appear suddenly and can be severe. They can occur in contact sports or when improperly lifting heavy objects.

➢ **Chronic strains** occur over an extended period of time. They usually are the result of prolonged overuse and repetitive movement of the muscles and tendons while not giving them enough time to rest.

Strains and tears fall into three categories of severity: first-, second-, and third-degree. See "SHARP and PIER" on page 141 for tips on identifying the signs of injury:

➢ First-degree injuries are the least severe. They usually take a day or a few days to heal if proper care is taken.

➢ Second-degree injuries are moderate and more severe. They require physiotherapy treatment once diagnosed by a doctor.

➢ Third-degree injuries are the most severe and may require surgery and rehabilitation. They may take from six to twelve months to fully repair.

## Delayed Onset Muscle Soreness (DOMS)

This type of injury refers to the feeling of muscle pain a day or two after intense exercise. It is not the same as the immediate acute pain of a pulled or strained muscle.

**Delayed onset muscle soreness** is believed to be a result of microscopic tearing deep within the muscle fibres. The amount of soreness depends on the activity performed, and the intensity of the activity.

The important things to know about DOMS are:

➢ In addition to tearing, swelling can occur in and around a muscle.

➢ DOMS can be minimized by performing proper warm-up and cool-down exercises.

➢ If soreness continues for more than a few days, you should consult with your physician.

## Injury Intelligence

Some people believe that injuries are part of the game. Nothing could be further from the truth. Let's look at some of the things you can do to make your activities safer for yourself and others:

- Be or become fit for your specific activity or sport.
- Always begin with a warm-up and end with a cool-down.
- Use proper equipment that has been certified by the Canadian Safety Association.
- Wear the correct clothing and footwear.
- Keep shoelaces tied up to help prevent slips and poor shock absorption.
- Obey and follow the rules of the game or activity.
- Learn and apply the safety precautions for your sport or activity.
- Play within your physical limits—do not over-exercise.
- Look for potential hazards such as broken glass or pot holes on the playing field.
- Keep your equipment in perfect working order by having it serviced and checked regularly.

Taking that little extra time to address the guidelines above could keep you out of harm's way.

## Tendonitis

**Tendonitis** is the inflammation of a tendon caused by irritation due to prolonged or abnormal use. The Achilles tendon is a common site where tendonitis occurs.

Most tendonitis can be avoided with proper warm-up exercises, rest, and gradual increase in physical activity.

Symptoms of tendonitis may include:

➢ Pain or tenderness on the tendon near or around a joint

➢ Stiffness and pain on the tendon, which restricts movement

➢ Occasionally, mild swelling, numbness, or a tingling sensation at the joint

Tendonitis is usually named after the affected tendon or joint. For example, tendonitis of the Achilles tendon is known as "Achilles tendonitis." Similarly, tendonitis resulting from excessive strain in the forearm and elbow is often referred to as "tennis elbow."

Treatment of tendonitis involves rest, cold and heat therapy, and may also include casts and splints. A doctor may also prescribe oral medication for inflammation and pain.

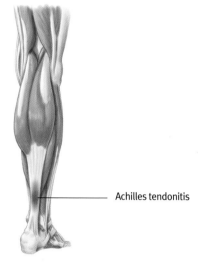

Achilles tendonitis

Tendonitis is an inflammation of a tendon caused by irritation due to prolonged or abnormal use. Common sites for tendonitis are the Achilles tendon and the patellar tendon.

## SHARP and PIER
### Identifying and Treating Injuries

**W**hen injuries do occur it's important to recognize the signs and take immediate action to stop further damage. Two well-known acronyms used for recognizing and treating minor injuries are SHARP and PIER.

### SHARP

A simple acronym to help you remember the signs of an injury is known as **SHARP**. When an injury happens one or more of the following signs will appear:

• **S**welling of affected area, instantly or over time

• **H**eat or increased temperature of the area

• **A**ltered joint (the area will not function properly)

• **R**edness in the affected area

• **P**ainful to move or touch the affected area.

The SHARP acronym will help you identify the type of injury and its severity. With that information, you will then be in a better position to help out or call for medical support if it is needed.

### PIER

The acronym **PIER** can help you remember the steps to take when treating an injury:

• **P**ressure in the form of a tensor wrap should be administered at the same time the ice is on the affected area.

• **I**ce should be placed on the affected area. A paper towel (or something similar) should be placed between the ice and the skin to avoid skin damage. Keep ice on for 10 to 20 minutes with a 10–20 minute break between repeated icings.

• **E**levate the injured area while it's being iced to help reduce the swelling.

• **R**estrict and rest the affected area with the use of tensors, slings, or crutches.

If a sports injury is sustained, keep in mind the PIER acronym and you will be able to limit the damage. If necessary, you should then quickly bring in a medical professional to treat the injured person.

# Ligament and Joint Injuries

In Chapter 2 (page 32), we learned about the structures and properties of joints. Here we will look at some of the injuries that these joints might sustain during physical activity or sport.

## Ligaments

**Ligaments** are a form of connective tissue that attach bone to bone. Similar to rope, they don't stretch much.

When ligaments are pulled to their limit they will tear, damaging some of their fibres. The severity of the tear depends on the amount of force placed on them. Once ligaments are torn, the entire joint can become unstable.

## Sprains

**Sprains** occur when a ligament is overstretched or torn. Similar to strains, which occur in muscles and tendons, sprains have a grading or severity of injury classified by degrees:

> A first-degree sprain can be treated easily since only a few fibres are torn.

> Second-degree sprains are the result of more widespread damage, and will require more attention.

> Third-degree sprains might require surgery to reattach the ligament to the bone, since the entire ligament usually is torn.

Sprains usually occur from a hit directly on the joint, as in hockey when two players collide knee-to-knee. Awkward landings also can produce sprains, such as going up for a lay-up basketball and landing on the outside of your ankle, commonly called "rolling over on your ankle."

## Dislocations and Separations

**Dislocations** occur when a bone is displaced from its joint. They are often caused by collisions or falls, and are common in finger and shoulder joints. Do not attempt to put the bone back into place as this could cause more damage.

Your collar bone (clavicle) is attached to your shoulder blade (scapula) by strong ligaments. When these ligaments are torn, as a result of a collision or an awkward fall, the bones may separate. This is known as a shoulder **separation** and is the most common type of separation.

Dislocation and separations vary in degree of severity depending on the amount of tearing the ligaments sustain. Be sure to inform your teacher, coach, or parents if you injure yourself.

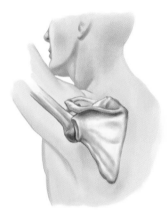

Ligaments don't stretch very far; so when they stretch too much, a sprain occurs. Sprains often occur in the ankle joints.

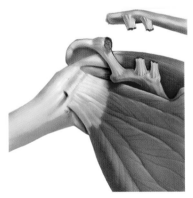

A rough collision or fall can cause a bone to be displaced from its joint. This is called dislocation and occurs often in shoulder or finger joints.

Your clavicle is attached to your shoulder blade by strong ligaments. When the ligaments tear due to a fall, the bones may separate. This is known as a shoulder separation.

# Growing Pains
## Osgood-Schlatter Syndrome

**A**s everyone knows, young people often experience growth spurts. It is at this point when many complain about swelling, tenderness, and aching pain underneath their knee cap—especially those involved in sports or other extra-curricular activities.

This condition was discovered by Dr. Robert Osgood and Dr. Carl Schlatter and is known as Osgood-Schlatter Syndrome (OSS) or Osgood-Schlatter disease.

### What Causes OSS?

This condition affects the growth plate (epiphyseal plate) on the front part of the tibia (shinbone). The specific location is called the tibial tuberosity. This tiny bump located below your patella (knee cap) is where the tendon from the patella attaches.

OSS occurs when this growth plate gets overused. The tendon from the patella pulls, irritating the tuberosity, which in turn causes it to become inflamed. Activities or sports that involve a great deal of running, jumping, and deep knee bending especially overload this area.

### Symptoms

The symptoms of OSS can vary depending on the severity of the condition. It may only occur during physical activity and the pain could be mild. On the other hand, you may feel tremendous pain hindering you from participating in any physical activity.

A physician familiar with sports medicine can diagnose OSS effectively. Below are a few of the common symptoms of Osgood-Schlatter Syndrome:

- Pain, swelling, and tenderness below the patella and on the tibial tuberosity
- Increased pain when jumping, running, or doing deep knee bends
- Limping after physical activity
- Relief from pain only when resting

### Treatment

The good news is that OSS usually goes away on its own once you get older. If you have symptoms, it is a good idea to apply the principles of PIER (see page 141) until you see your physician. It will help to lessen the pain and swelling, allowing the doctor to make a quick diagnosis.

Generally, OSS is treated with rest and anti-inflammatory drugs that help to reduce the inflammation.

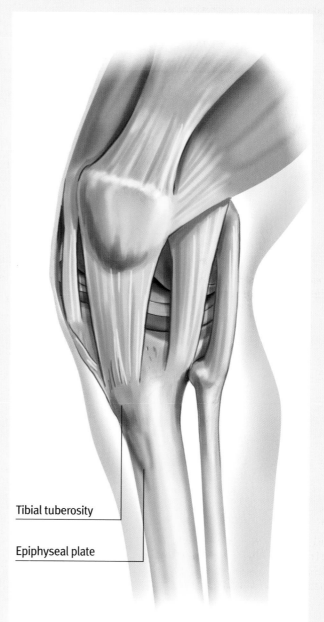

Tibial tuberosity

Epiphyseal plate

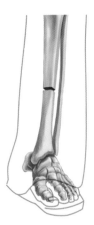

When a **simple** or hairline fracture occurs, a bone breaks but does not split apart; the break can only be seen on an X-ray.

If a bone breaks into separate pieces and protrudes through the skin, that is called a **compound** fracture.

If a bone breaks or shatters into many pieces, a **comminuted** fracture has occured.

# Bone and Head Injuries

Bones bear the weight of our bodies and, therefore, are highly vulnerable to breaking. The good news is that they usually heal well and rarely break in the same spot twice.

In this section, we will deal with two major sets of problems related to bones.

## Fractures

The medical term for a broken bone is **fracture**. The three types of fractures are summarized below:

> ➤ A **simple (or closed) fracture** occurs when a broken bone doesn't split apart or break the skin, but a break or crack can be seen on an X-ray.

> ➤ A **compound (or open) fracture** occurs when the bone breaks into separate pieces, usually the result of a hit or fall.

> ➤ A **comminuted fracture** occurs when the bone has been shattered into many pieces as might happen in a major automobile crash.

The main indications of a fractured bone include (1) hearing or feeling a crack or snap, (2) feeling sick or dizzy and vomiting, and (3) the limb may look deformed or break through the skin. A fracture will require medical attention.

## Shin Splints and Stress Fractures

There are two common lower leg injuries or conditions:

> ➤ **Shin splints** are the result of the tearing of the connective tissue between the tibia and fibula along the front shaft of the shin bone. Shin splints can lead to stress fractures which can take months to heal.

> ➤ **Stress fractures** are tiny cracks along the bone that are virtually undetectable by an X-ray. Like shin splits, stress fractures are very painful and can take a long time to heal.

Both stress fractures and shin splits have the same main causes: Going from small to large amounts of physical activity with little rest in between; running, jogging, or skipping on hard surfaces; and using inappropriate or worn out shoes.

If you seek medical attention early, you can avoid much of the pain and suffering associated with shin splints and stress fractures and also be able to return to your normal activity levels sooner. In the meantime apply the PIER principle to lessen the swelling and pain.

Of course, avoiding the main causes listed above will reduce the likelihood of you having to deal with these troublesome conditions in the first place.

## Concussions
### Use Your Head for Thinking

**W**hen you sustain a head injury, the brain literally bangs against the skull causing nerve damage and bruising from bleeding blood vessels attached to the brain. It results in a temporary loss of normal brain function and is known as a **concussion**.

Some physical activities, such as football, biking, skateboarding, lacrosse, and hockey, are termed "high risk" when it comes to the possibility of sustaining a concussion.

Even with the use of protective headgear, concussions can still occur. Concussions are always a serious matter and medical attention is always required.

### The Symptoms

Concussions can be mild or severe and it is often difficult to tell the difference. The best thing to do is be aware and be educated.

Here are some of the common symptoms of a concussion:

- Feeling nauseous
- Feeling dizzy or light-headed
- Having trouble remembering what happened before and after the injury occurred
- Headaches, blurred vision, or sensitivity to light
- Mumbled or slurred speech
- Difficulty concentrating, thinking, or talking sensibly
- Feeling unlike your normal self or acting out of character
- Feeling overly tired and just wanting to sleep.

### Grading Concussions

There are three basic grades of concussions:

- **Grade 1.** Classified as a mild concussion, the individual may experience some of the symptoms listed above without losing consciousness. The symptoms usually disappear after 10 to 15 minutes.

- **Grade 2.** As with a Grade 1 concussion, the individual doesn't lose consciousness but symptoms last longer. The individual should stop participating in the activity that caused the injury.

- **Grade 3.** This is the most severe concussion and results in the individual losing consciousness. Seek medical attention immediately even if the person only loses consciousness for a few seconds.

If someone you know sustains a head injury, inform the coach, teacher, or individual in charge right away. All concussions must be taken seriously and only trained personnel can properly diagnose the severity of one.

### Post-Concussion Syndrome

Post-Concussion Syndrome, or PCS, is a serious condition that occurs when concussions don't adequately heal after the injury.

People who have continuing problems after a concussion should see a doctor who may refer them to a rehabilitation specialist for additional help.

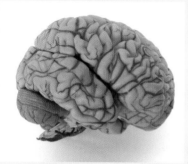

### Using Your Head

Even though preventing or reducing the severity of a concussion sounds easy, it's amazing how many people don't follow simple guidelines.

If you are smart (and want to stay smart), you can avoid very serious injury and continue your favourite sport for a long time.

Follow these simple rules:

- Always wear your seat belt when in a car.
- Always wear the appropriate CSA-approved headgear for the type of activity you are doing.
- Get proper treatment after you have sustained a concussion, and closely follow the doctor's instructions.
- Never get in a car with someone who is under the influence of alcohol or drugs.

Repeat—use your head for thinking, follow rules, wear the right gear, and advise your friends and loved ones to do the same.

You definitely don't want the mind-altering experience of a concussion.

# Weather-Related Injuries

Some, jokingly, characterize the weather patterns in Canada as ten months of winter and two months of poor skiing. We definitely live in a nation where weather seems to change in an instant.

Extreme heat or cold can result in **weather-related injuries**. Therefore, it is important that we learn how to protect ourselves from them. Below is a list of common injuries related to the environment:

> **Heat Cramps**: Water makes up 50 to 60 percent of our total body weight and close to 90 percent of our blood volume. Heat cramps are caused by dehydration through sweating and are characterized by the seizing up of muscles in the legs or abdominal area, and are often indicated by dark yellow urine. When we are dehydrated, we feel dizzy or light-headed and our mouth becomes dry and sticky.

> **Heat Exhaustion:** Heat exhaustion usually occurs when we exercise in a hot, humid environment without drinking enough fluids. This condition is more serious than heat cramps and is characterized by slow short breaths, a weak pulse, shivering or chills, and clammy skin.

> **Heat Stroke:** Sometimes referred to as sunstroke, this condition also occurs when we exercise in a hot, humid environment. Sweating allows our bodies to dissipate heat to keep our body's temperature at a normal level. However, when this system shuts down, our body's core temperature increases, and we become prone to heat stroke. Heat stroke is a life-threatening condition that requires immediate medical attention. Symptoms include high body temperature, clammy skin, and possible loss of consciousness.

> **Hypothermia:** This condition occurs when our body's core temperature drops below normal levels. Some symptoms include chills, shivering, confusion, slow movement, and poor coordination. To prevent hypothermia, be sure to wear appropriate clothing for cold days, such as wind- and cold-resistant fitness clothing, a hat, and mittens or gloves. Change into dry clothes immediately following activity.

> **Frostbite:** This condition usually appears on unprotected fingers, toes, and ears. When frostbite sets in, the affected area becomes frozen and, in severe cases, may require amputation of the affected area. Although it may be difficult to determine right away how bad the affected area has become, the best advice is to get out of the cold immediately. Mild frostbite shows up as grey or yellow patches on the skin. Advanced forms appear brown and are accompanied with discomfort and tingling in the affected area. If the discomfort or tingling persists after a half hour or so, you should seek medical attention.

## Locker Necessities

Some people believe that one T-shirt, a pair of socks, gym shorts, and a pair of running shoes is all they need to get them through the year in gym class. That is not entirely correct.

Most gym classes are a mixture of outdoor and indoor activities. Therefore, it is important to keep your locker well-stocked with the following items:

- Sweatshirts and sweatpants, especially in the fall and winter months

- Extra shorts, socks, T-shirts and running shoes

- A pair of cleats for participation in field sports such as football

- Hats and sunscreen (water- and sweat-proof) to protect you from the sun's harmful rays

- Toques or winter hats to keep you warm on cold days

- Personally labelled water bottles to stay hydrated when you are outside during class

It is best to keep all valuables at home. If you must bring them to school, store them safely in your locker.

## Sunshine 101
### One Hot Character

Few would deny that sunlight does wonders for our mood. It can also be beneficial to our health since our bodies can convert it into Vitamin D, a nutrient essential to bone development. Unfortunately, being exposed for too long can cause much more harm than good.

### UV Rays and Sunburns

Sunlight contains ultraviolet (UV) rays, which can be very harmful to the skin. The two forms of UV rays that make it through Earth's atmosphere are UVA and UVB and both can cause sunburn, skin damage, and skin cancer.

UVA rays provide us with natural light; unfortunately, they also penetrate the skin, causing wrinkles and other effects of aging to appear prematurely. UVB rays are 1,000 times stronger and are the main cause of sunburns. It can take as little as 12 minutes for your skin to burn and some evidence suggests that every sunburn you get increases your risk of developing skin cancer.

### Skin Cancer

Skin cancer is the most common form of cancer and while it is often treatable, it can still be fatal in some cases. Exposure to UV rays can alter the skin's normal cells causing them to mutate and become cancerous.

Despite the prevalent societal belief that tanned people look healthier than pale-skinned people, both tans and sunburns are signs that UV rays have damaged the skin. If you sunburn easily or have fair or freckled skin, you are more susceptible to developing skin cancer.

If you notice any abnormally dark or discoloured spots or patches on your body, or if you have any moles that change size, shape, or colour, or start to bleed or get crusty, see a doctor immediately as it could be a sign of skin cancer.

Ninety percent of all skin cancer is preventable. Taking a few simple steps towards protecting yourself can go a long way towards reducing this risk.

Whenever possible ...

- Keep your skin covered with loose fitting clothing that can breathe easily.
- Generously apply water- and sweat-proof sunscreen that has a Sun Protection Factor (SPF) of 15 or greater.
- Protect yourself with a hat or visor and sunglasses.
- Minimize your time in the sun, particularly between the hours of 10 am and 3 pm.

### Electric Sunlight

Using a tanning bed is just as dangerous (if not more dangerous) than exposure to the sun. The UV rays that come from tanning beds or sun lamps are identical to the ones in sunlight. In fact, according to Health Canada, tanning beds and lights can produce five times more UVA than the sun.

For this reason, the World Health Organization recommends that NO person under the age of 18 use artificial sources of tanning.

### Make Shade Your Friend

If you have to be outside for long periods, try to stay in the shade. You won't feel drained and your athletic performance won't be compromised. Wear sunglasses—they protect your eyes from harmful radiation.

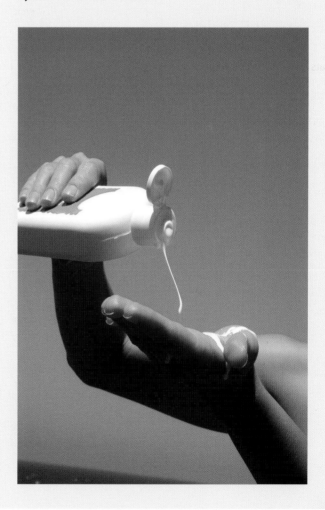

# Using Equipment Safely

Besides performing warm-ups and cool-downs to reduce the risk of injury, it is also important to be aware of other potential hazards in your playing area. Your principal, teachers, and the custodial staff try to make sure the school is kept free of hazards to ensure your safety. There is much that you can do, as well, to make your school and playing area safe.

Outlined below are some small, yet critical, things that you can do to help keep your gymnasium, weight room, and playing fields hazard-free. If you attend to the small things, the bigger things will begin to fall into place.

## Safety in the Gym

Custodians sweep and mop the gym floors to allow for maximum traction to help reduce the risk of slips and falls. You can help make their jobs easier by following some of these simple rules:

➢ Never consume food or soft drinks, or chew gum in the gym.

➢ Be sure to recycle all water bottles that you bring.

➢ Allocate a pair of running shoes to be worn in class and never outside. Do not use the gym as a "short cut" to get from class to class.

➢ Never be in the gym unsupervised.

➢ Carefully listen to all rules stated by your teacher and offer to help clean up after class.

## Safety on the Field

We share our fields with the entire community. Here are a few things to keep in mind:

➢ Check the field for any cans or bottles and report any broken glass to your teacher.

➢ Wear appropriate footwear, such as cleats, especially on wet fields.

➢ Do not be distracted by friends sitting in the stands.

➢ If you play on the field during lunch or after school, be considerate—clean up any waste you might have left behind and recycle your bottles and cans.

➢ Look for and report any irregularities in the field, such as holes.

By following these simple rules you will ensure a safe and enjoyable atmosphere in which to play.

Whether you are in the gymnasium, on the playing field, or anywhere else for that matter, always put safety considerations at the top of your list.

## Helping Hands

**W**eight-room "spotting" is when one or more individuals help the lifter perform his or her exercise properly and safely. Spotters provide assistance during lifts and ensure that the proper technique is followed.

Since you and your partner will often take turns spotting each other, it's important to keep the following in mind:

- Make certain you both know the proper lifting techniques, especially ones requiring the use of free weights such as the barbell bench press and squat.

- Listen carefully and learn the proper spotting technique as demonstrated by your teacher.

- Pay close attention to the person you are spotting and know exactly how many repetitions he or she wishes to complete.

- Stop the exercise if it's being performed incorrectly or if there is undue stress.

- Serious injuries can occur when spotters are distracted and standing too far from the lifter.

- Know the proper course of action if an injury occurs and inform your teacher immediately.

Following proper spotting procedure will make your weight-room experience an enjoyable one.

# Weight-Room Safety
## Make Your Weight-Room Experience Enjoyable

**K**nowing the proper exercise technique is only part of weight-room safety. There are many things that you can do to ensure your safety and that of your classmates:

- Listen carefully and apply the proper lifting and spotting techniques presented by your teacher.
- Check cables and resistance tubing for tears and rips, and report them to the teacher.
- Keep fingers and feet clear of moving machines and report all jammed weight stacks to the teacher.
- Do not attempt to clear weight jams by removing pins or plugs yourself.
- Return all free weights to their original location after you finish using them.
- Use a towel to wipe sweat from machines or mats.
- Wear suitable clothing, and use a weight belt as instructed by your teacher.
- Tie back long hair.
- If the weight room is left unlocked unintentionally, report it to your teacher.
- Never workout in an unsupervised weight room.
- Water bottles are the only foodstuff that should be brought into a weight room.
- Always work out with a "training buddy" and call upon others if additional spotters are needed.
- Respect your classmates' space and avoid "horseplay" at all times.

These are only some of the rules that will apply in your school. Be sure to listen carefully to your teacher when he or she describes the proper etiquette and weight-room safety guidelines.

Doing your part in the weight room will not only help your grade, it will also provide you and your classmates a safe environment in which to get into shape.

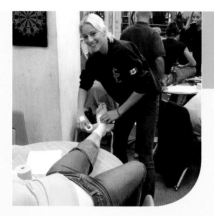

## Career Focus
## Who's Who in Sports Medicine

nevitably, along with all the activity, some of us get hurt. Below is a list of individuals that can help, and perhaps a career that you might be interested in pursuing:

- **Certified Athletic Therapist.** Athletic therapists help athletes prevent injuries by showing them how to select equipment, teaching them proper warm-up techniques, designing conditioning programs for them and showing them how to tape joints. The Canadian Athletic Therapist Association (CATA) website (www.athletictherapy.org) lists colleges and universities that offer Certified Athletic Therapy courses.

- **Physiotherapist.** Physiotherapy involves both the assessment of an injury or disease and its treatment through physical means. This includes exercises, stretches, and the use of specialized medical equipment. Many universities across Canada offer physiotherapy degrees.

- **Chiropractor.** Chiropractors do not prescribe drugs or perform surgery; instead, they rely on their hands to assess, diagnose, and treat patients. Chiropractors help treat people by manipulating the spine and other joints. To become a Chiropractor in Canada, you must first go to university, and then apply to a Chiropractic College.

- **Sports Medicine Specialist.** Sports Medicine Specialists are medical doctors that diagnose and treat activity- or sport-related injuries. To become a Sports Medicine Specialist in Canada, you must first become a medical doctor. Then, you must complete a sports medicine internship and pass a certification exam offered by the Canadian Academy of Sport Medicine (CASM).

If any of these careers in sports medicine interest you, ask your school's guidance counsellor for more information. If they can't help, they will know someone who can.

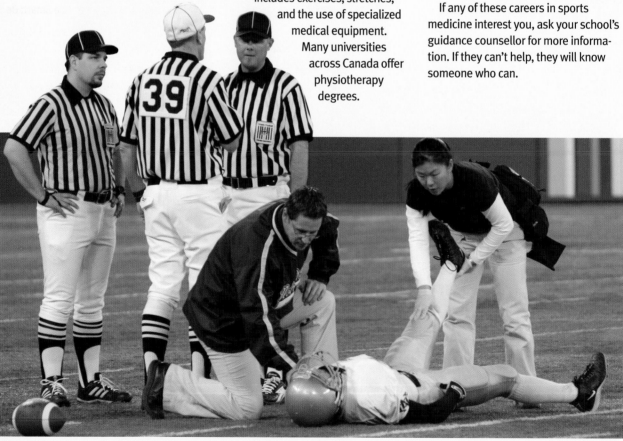

# Chapter Review

## Questions for Study and Review

### Things to Think About and Explore

1. Muscle and tendon strains usually are classified into three levels depending on their severity. Distinguish and compare the three levels of severity.

2. What is "tendonitis"? What are the main symptoms associated with tendonitis? Explain the treatment that usually is prescribed to someone who has tendonitis.

3. What is the difference between a strain and a sprain? Demonstrate an understanding of how one would apply the PIER principle in relation to treating a common strain or sprain injury.

4. Evaluate the difference between a shin splint and a stress fracture and investigate what treatment is usually prescribed if one experiences one of these injuries.

5. Describe the main signs that can indicate a concussion and explain the essential differences between Grade 1, 2, and 3 concussions.

6. What are the differences between heat cramps, heat exhaustion, and heat stroke? Provide examples of how athletes in various sports minimize the possibility of heat-related injuries.

### Things to Do and Practise

7. On a sheet of bristol board, illustrate and explain three warm-up exercises, and three cool-down exercises. Be prepared to teach the class your exercises.

8. Distinguish between the three types of fractures (simple, compound, and comminuted) through illustrations.

9. Create a pamphlet that focuses on the precautions a person should take when in the sun or other extreme weather conditions.

10. Describe the main responsibilities of the weight-room spotter and, using a specific weight-room exercise, demonstrate effective "spotting" technique in relation to that exercise.

11. Develop a series of posters that list the minimum precautions that students should take to help prevent injuries in the gymnasium, weight room, and on the field.

12. List three sports that are of particular interest to you and provide various examples (object, picture, etc.) of protective equipment or preventive measures that are commonly used to help minimize injuries.

## WWWeblinks

Name ➤ Canadian Academy of Sport Medicine

URL ➤ www.casm-acms.org

A national organization of sport medicine physicians with numerous position statements on sport injury management and prevention.

Name ➤ National Brain & Spinal Cord Injury Prevention Foundation

URL ➤ www.thinkfirst.ca

A site that targets youth in their campaign to raise awareness of brain and spinal cord injury.

Name ➤ Be Smart, Be Safe

URL ➤ www.besmartbesafe.ca

An organization that works with other injury prevention groups to keep Canadians safe on the road and at play.

## Table of Contents

# UNIT 4
# Human Reproduction, Sexuality, and Intimacy

**What this unit is about ...**

➤ **Why is it important for me to take good care of my reproductive system?**

➤ **What is sexual development, and how do I know if mine is normal?**

➤ **How can I make good decisions about sexuality and intimacy?**

# 10
# Caring for the Reproductive System

> *Every human being is the author of his own health or disease.*

**Buddha**

Integral figure of Buddhism

**H**uman reproduction requires the joining of sperm and egg. Most of the time, obviously, human reproduction involves sexual contact between women and men.

Certain infections, conditions, or diseases can jeopardize a person's ability to have children as well as threaten his or her health in significant ways. In addition to making sure you stay healthy now, taking good care of your reproductive system while you are young will limit the possibility of problems should you decide, later in life, to have children.

This chapter presents information about the female and male reproductive systems and how to care for them.

## Chapter Objectives

In this chapter, you will:

➤ Learn why caring for the reproductive system is important

➤ Identify the basic components of the female and male reproductive systems

➤ Identify problems that can arise when you do not care properly for your reproductive system

➤ Explore the role your family doctor can play in ensuring proper reproductive system care

➤ Learn how you can perform different types of self-examinations to ensure a healthy reproductive system

➤ Examine how to maintain your sexual reproductive health both now and for the rest of your life

## Key Terms

➤ female reproductive system
➤ vulvovaginitis/vaginitis
➤ yeast infections
➤ endometriosis
➤ ovarian cysts
➤ cervical and ovarian cancer
➤ breast cancer
➤ breast self-examination
➤ male reproductive system
➤ hernia
➤ testicular injury
➤ testicular and prostate cancer
➤ testicular self-examination

## Why It's Important to Care

Although you might find it embarrassing to talk about it, caring for your reproductive system is just as important as caring for any other part of your body.

If you had questions about your heart, lungs, or eyes, you would probably feel comfortable asking your parents, a teacher, or your family doctor. Asking questions about your reproductive system or sexuality may not be quite as easy, but, as with any other part of your body, problems that are not addressed can become more serious. As with most things, it is always better to attend to health problems early.

The material presented in this chapter will help you identify the key components of your reproductive system and the ways you can keep them healthy. Knowing how your reproductive system is supposed to work is important should it ever be necessary for you to ask questions or seek professional advice.

The remaining two chapters in this unit will provide you with an overview of some of the broader issues pertaining to sexuality and sexual health (Chapter 11) and to issues related to intimacy and sexual decision making (Chapter 12).

Caring for your reproductive system is as important as caring for any other part of your body.

Health class provides an opportunity to consider sexual health information that can help you throughout your lifetime.

# The Female Reproductive System

The **female reproductive system** is responsible for producing, nourishing, and transporting ova/eggs, and eventually carrying and delivering babies. It includes both external and internal parts, as well as glands and tubes that connect the different parts of the system.

## The External System

Vulva is the general name given to the external parts of the female genitals. It includes the mons pubis, the labia, the clitoris, the opening of the urethra, and the vaginal opening.

> **Mons pubis.** The skin and tissue that is located just above the top of a woman's vaginal opening. After a young woman goes through puberty, her mons pubis will be covered with pubic hair.

> **Labia.** The flaps of skin that surround the vaginal and urethral openings. The vulva includes two sets of lips—the labia minora (inner lips) and the labia majora (outer lips), which contain erectile tissue that fills with blood and swells when a woman is aroused.

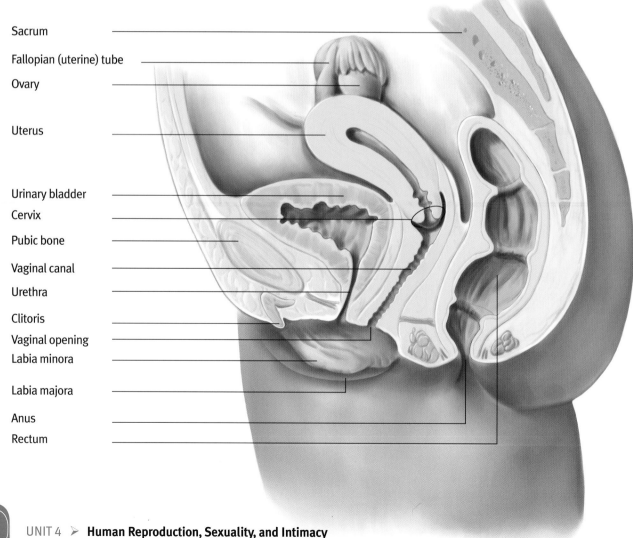

Sacrum

Fallopian (uterine) tube

Ovary

Uterus

Urinary bladder

Cervix

Pubic bone

Vaginal canal

Urethra

Clitoris

Vaginal opening

Labia minora

Labia majora

Anus

Rectum

- ➢ **Clitoris.** A sensory organ located towards the top of the vulva where the folds of the labia join. It is filled with nerve endings, making it the most sensitive spot on a woman's genitals—the organ that gives women sexual pleasure. Although it can vary in size, its exposed portion is approximately the size of a pea. The clitoris is made up of erectile tissue that swells and fills with blood when a woman is aroused.

- ➢ **Urethra.** The tube that carries urine outside of the body from the bladder. The opening is located between the labia, just below the clitoris.

- ➢ **Vaginal opening.** The vagina's opening to the outside of the body, located between the urethral opening and the anus.

## The Internal System

The internal parts of the reproductive system, located inside the entrance to the vagina, are the vagina, cervix, uterus, endometrium, fallopian tubes, and ovaries:

- ➢ **Vagina.** A muscular tube that extends from the vaginal opening, on the outside of the body, to the uterus, on the inside. It forms the birth canal (vaginal canal) through which babies travel during childbirth, and the opening into which the penis is inserted during vaginal sexual intercourse with a man. Approximately three to five inches in length in an adult woman, the vagina has muscular walls that allow it to expand and contract. These walls are lined with mucous membranes that protect the vagina. Normally, the vaginal walls rest comfortably against one another, but during sexual arousal they expand in size. This ability to become wider or narrower allows the vagina to accommodate something as slim as a tampon or something as wide as a baby.

- ➢ **Cervix.** The narrow lower and outer end of the uterus. The vagina connects with the uterus at the cervix. The cervix has strong, thick walls, and is located at the back wall of the vagina. The opening of the cervix is very small (no wider than a straw), which is why a tampon can never get lost inside the body. During childbirth, the cervix expands to allow a baby to exit the woman's body.

- ➢ **Uterus.** The hollow muscular organ located inside a woman's pelvic cavity (also known as the "womb"). This is where a fertilized egg implants and develops into a baby. The uterus is shaped like an upside-down pear. It has a thick lining and extremely muscular walls. In fact, the uterus contains some of the strongest muscles in the female body. These muscles expand to accommodate a growing fetus, and contract to help push the baby out during labour.

> **Endometrium.** The nutrient-rich lining of the uterus. If an egg is fertilized, the lining thickens in order to nourish the embryo. If fertilization does not occur, the lining is shed monthly during a woman's period, and is expelled through the vaginal opening.

> **Fallopian tubes.** The tubes located near the upper corners of the uterus that connect the uterus to the ovaries. They are only a few inches long and approximately the width of a piece of spaghetti. Each tube has a tiny passageway that is no wider than a sewing needle. One end of each Fallopian tube is attached to the uterus. At the other end of each Fallopian tube is a fringed area that looks like a funnel. This fringed area wraps around the ovary but does not completely attach to it. When an egg is released from the ovary, it enters the Fallopian tube. Once the egg is in the Fallopian tube, tiny hair-like structures in the tube's lining help push it down the narrow passageway toward the uterus.

> **Ovaries.** The two oval-shaped organs that are located to the upper right and upper left of the uterus. They produce, store, and release eggs into the Fallopian tubes in the process called ovulation. Each ovary measures approximately five centimetres (two inches) in an adult woman. The ovaries also produce female sex hormones, such as estrogen and progesterone.

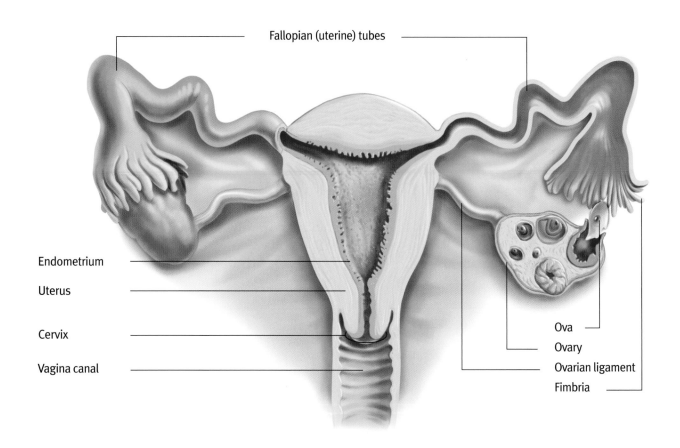

Fallopian (uterine) tubes

Endometrium

Uterus

Cervix

Vagina canal

Ova

Ovary

Ovarian ligament

Fimbria

# Caring for the Female Reproductive System

Most of the time, you can ensure a healthy reproductive system by good hygiene and, for those individuals who are sexualy active, the use of barrier contraceptives. However, certain conditions cannot be avoided. The most common problems are as follows:

## Vulvovaginitis

When irritating substances (such as soap or bubble bath) enter the vulva or the vagina, they can cause inflammation or infection. This itchy feeling in the vulva or vagina is called **vulvovaginitis** when it occurs in the vulva, or **vaginitis** when it occurs in the vagina. It is important to wash only the outside area of the genitals and to be careful when wiping after a bowel movement. Wearing cotton underwear, changing tampons every four to six hours, and avoiding highly perfumed cleansing products help to reduce the risk.

## Yeast Infections

Monilia (commonly known as a "**yeast infection**") is caused by the yeast fungus *Candida albicans*. Candida is found in every woman's normal, healthy vagina. However, sometimes too much of it grows inside the vagina, causing an infection. Symptoms include a thick, white discharge, which can cause extreme itching and discomfort. Some women are more prone to yeast infections than others. Factors that can encourage the growth of candida include the long-term use of hormonal contraception pills or antibiotics, diabetes, menstruation, douching, scented tampons or pads, sexual activity with an infected partner, and wearing non-cotton underwear. As unpleasant as it can be, a yeast infection can be easily diagnosed by a doctor and treated with creams and vaginal suppositories.

## Endometriosis

**Endometriosis** occurs when tissue normally found within the endometrium starts to grow on the ovaries, fallopian tubes, cervix, vagina, vulva, or other parts of the pelvic cavity. Endometriosis can cause abnormal bleeding, painful and lengthy periods, and pelvic pain. This fairly serious condition can lead to sterility if left untreated. Women with symptoms of endometriosis should seek medical attention from a physician.

## Ovarian Cysts

**Ovarian cysts** are non-cancerous sacs filled with fluid or semi-solid material. Fairly common among adult women, they are generally harmless; however, they can become a painful problem if they grow large enough to push on surrounding organs. Often these cysts will disappear over time and do not require treatment. However, if they are large and painful, a doctor might prescribe hormonal contraception pills to slow their growth, or suggest surgery.

### Problems Resulting from STIs

Sexually transmitted infections (STIs) can cause serious problems for a woman's reproductive system.

Many STIs have no symptoms in young women, but some can lead to major health problems. A doctor can treat most of these infections.

Early treatment may prevent the infection from spreading and causing such problems as pelvic inflammatory disease (P.I.D.), one of the most common causes of infertility in women.

Chapter 12 contains further information on sexually transmitted infections, which spread from one person to another mainly through sexual activity.

# Cancer in Women

Cervical, ovarian, and breast cancer pose serious health risks for women. Examinations and tests can detect these forms of cancer. It is up to you to monitor your health, and get tested in order to catch any problems while they can still be treated relatively easily.

## Cervical and Ovarian Cancer

**Cervical cancer** poses a particular risk for young Canadian women and seems to be linked to heterosexual vaginal intercourse. Doctors have found that young women who begin having vaginal intercourse before the age of eighteen are at higher risk for developing cervical cancer. As well, the more sexual partners a woman has, the greater her chances of developing cervical cancer. These findings suggest that cervical cancer likely occurs after H.P.V. (or human papilloma virus) is passed between partners during intercourse.

Once a woman has been sexually active, she should go to a doctor for a yearly Pap test. A Pap test can feel somewhat painful, but the discomfort does not last long. The test is highly accurate in identifying cell changes on the cervix and can detect cancer long before a woman experiences any signs or symptoms, at a stage when any irregular or cancerous cells can be treated and cured.

**Ovarian cancer** can be difficult to detect because the early stages have only mild symptoms. The causes of ovarian cancer are unknown but there is thought to be a hereditary influence. During a sexual health exam, the doctor will feel the ovaries to check for abnormalities or ovarian cysts. Some studies have indicated that the risk of developing ovarian cancer is reduced by taking oral contraceptives, breastfeeding, having at least one child, having a hysterectomy, or undergoing tubal ligation.

## Breast Cancer

**Breast cancer** is the most frequently diagnosed cancer in Canadian women. One in nine women is expected to develop cancer of the breast in her lifetime. Family history plays a role: The risks are higher for women whose grandmothers, mothers, aunts, or sisters have had breast cancer. However, researchers also believe that there are other causes for breast cancer, including smoking, diet, and possibly a virus.

Smoking, and exposure to second-hand smoke, can increase a woman's chance of developing breast cancer and other ailments. In countries where diets are low in saturated fats and contain plenty of fruits and vegetables, rates of breast cancer are lower than in North America. Preliminary studies have also found that a virus appears to be associated with severe forms of breast cancer. This is promising, because if a virus causes breast cancer, it is possible that a vaccine could be developed in the future.

---

### The Sexual Health Exam

**M**ost women do not have a sexual health exam (sometimes called a "Well Woman" appointment) until they become sexually active. Once a woman is sexually active, she should see a doctor annually for an exam. During the exam, women can expect the doctor to do some or all of the following:

- Visually examine the external parts of the genitals
- Put a speculum inside the vagina to examine the vaginal canal and cervix
- Use a swab to take samples of cervical cells, which are then placed on a slide and examined in a lab for abnormalities. This procedure is called a Pap test
- Take other swabs from the vagina and/or cervix
- Feel the ovaries and uterus by placing one or two fingers of one hand inside the vagina while placing the other hand on your stomach to detect abnormalities such as cysts or cancer
- Perform an internal exam of the rectum
- Ask for a urine sample and take a blood sample

Of course, if you notice anything unusual, you should talk to your doctor right away, and not wait for your regular appointment.

# Breast Self-Examination
## Early Detection Is the Key

**B**reast cancer is more likely to be treated successfully if it is detected in its early stages. All women should perform a monthly **breast self-examination** (BSE) seven to ten days after the start of their periods, when a woman's breasts are the least swollen and tender.

A good BSE involves examining and feeling the entire breast and chest area. You should check the entire breast, but remember that most breast cancers are found in the upper, outer portion of the breast, or in the area behind the nipple. Pay particular attention to these areas.

### Visual Inspection: In Front of a Mirror

Begin with your arms at your side, and look at your breasts in the mirror for any changes in their size or shape. If you are still developing, your breasts will probably change over time; you should look for unusual changes in size or shape, and rashes, scarring, dimpling, or puckering.

- Raise your arms above your head, looking for any changes in the size, shape, and contour of each breast. Inspect the areas around your breasts, including the region from the armpit to the collarbone and below the breasts.
- Examine your nipples for any signs of discharge or changes, such as swelling, or whether they have become misshapen or inverted.
- Lift your arms up, and put your hands behind your ears. Look at your breasts and under your arms.
- Lower your hands to under your nose, and push your palms together (see Figure A). Look again for any changes.

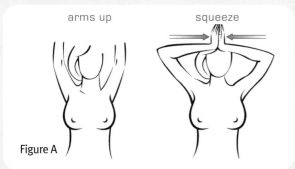

Figure A

### Manual Inspection: Standing

Continue your inspection by using the flat pads of your fingers to feel your breast and the surrounding areas.

- Use either a grid pattern (Figure B) or a circular pattern (Figure C) to make sure you check the entire breast.

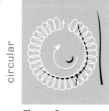

Figure B            Figure C

- Use the opposite hand from the breast (i.e, your left hand for your right breast).
- Using the flat pads of your fingers and holding your fingers together (see Figure D), press gently but firmly in small overlapping circles, starting below your collarbone.
- Carefully examine the area between the breast and the armpit: Relax your arm at your side, and slide your opposite hand under it.
- Make small circles, as you did with the breast.
- Switch arms and repeat with the other breast.

Figure D

correct            not correct

### Manual Inspection While Lying Down

Repeat the same procedure as above while lying on your back on a firm surface.

- Put one arm behind your head, and use the opposite hand to examine that breast.
- Use the techniques described above to check the entire surface of your breast.
- Use the pads of your fingers, and bend your wrists to cover the curves of your breasts.
- Switch hands and check the other breast.

Every breast has a unique texture, which may include some lumps or bumps. For this reason, it is important that you learn about your own breasts.

Checking every month is a good way to become familiar with what feels normal for your breasts, so that you know what represents a change. If you see or feel any changes or abnormalities in your breast or chest area, be sure to see your doctor.

# The Male Reproductive System

The **male reproductive system** is responsible for producing, nourishing, and transporting sperm. It includes both external and internal organs as well as internal glands and tubes that connect different parts of the system.

## The External System

The external parts of the male reproductive system are the parts you can see. They include the shaft of the penis, the glans penis, and the scrotum:

> **Penis shaft.** The penis is the passageway for both urine and semen. The main part of the penis is called the shaft. Inside the penis are three large columns that fill with blood during sexual excitement causing the penis to become hard or erect. For ejaculation to occur, the penis must be erect. The urethra, which runs through the penis to the outside of the body, carries urine or ejaculatory fluid.

> **Glans penis.** The glans penis is the sensitive tip of the penis. It may be covered by the foreskin, except when the foreskin has been removed by circumcision. The mechanics of how the penis works are the same, regardless of whether or not the foreskin has been removed.

> **Scrotum.** The scrotum is the sac of skin that holds the testicles. The wall of the scrotum consists of skin and smooth muscle. The fibres contract and relax in response to cold and heat, which helps to regulate the temperature of the testicles. This is important because in order to function properly, the testicles need to be kept slightly cooler than the rest of the body.

## The Internal System

The internal parts of the male reproductive system are the testicles, the duct system (the epididymis, the vas deferens, and the urethra), and the accessory glands (the seminal vesicles, the prostate gland, and the Cowper's glands):

> **Testicles (or testes).** Testicles are the male reproductive glands. During puberty, a boy's pituitary gland sends a message to the testicles to start releasing more testosterone. This causes the testicles to produce the male reproductive cells called sperm. This process, in which males produce functional sperm, is called spermatogenesis. While a man's testicles are approximately the same size, one usually hangs lower than the other.

> **Duct system.** The epididymis, the vas deferens, and the urethra make up the duct system. The epididymis is a set of long tubes that are attached to each testicle. They connect to the vas deferens—tubes that carry sperm from the testicles to the

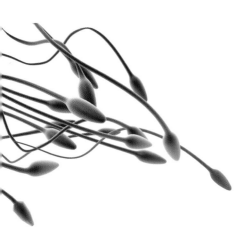

The male reproductive system is designed to produce, nourish, and transport sperm.

seminal vesicles. During an ejaculation, sperm produced in the testicles travels from the epididymis through the vas deferens to the seminal vesicles where they collect semen. The urethra then carries this fluid containing sperm through the penis to the outside of the body during an ejaculation.

➢ **Accessory glands.** The accessory glands, including the seminal vesicles, the prostate gland, and the Cowper's glands, provide fluids that lubricate the duct system and nourish the sperm. The seminal vesicles are sacs that are attached to the vas deferens. Below the seminal vesicles is the prostate gland. Both the seminal vesicles and the prostate gland produce semen. Before ejaculation occurs, the Cowper's glands (two small glands located below the prostate) secrete a small amount of clear fluid on the top of the penis to neutralize acid and allow for the safe passage of sperm.

**Semen** is a whitish–yellow fluid that nourishes the sperm. It is a combination of fluid produced from the three accessory glands: the seminal vesicles, the prostate, and the Cowper's glands. Contrary to what many people think, sperm only makes up about 1 percent of the ejaculatory fluid; the rest of the fluid is semen. Each ejaculation contains about 250 million sperm.

During an ejaculation, the semen exits through the urethra—the same tube that allows for urination. However, the urethra has a valve that shuts off the possibility of urination during ejaculation.

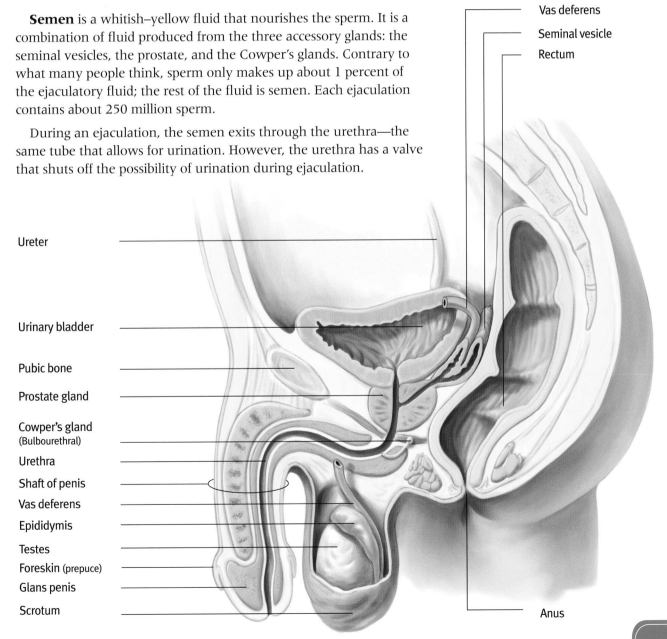

Vas deferens

Seminal vesicle

Rectum

Ureter

Urinary bladder

Pubic bone

Prostate gland

Cowper's gland
(Bulbourethral)

Urethra

Shaft of penis

Vas deferens

Epididymis

Testes

Foreskin (prepuce)

Glans penis

Scrotum

Anus

# Caring for the Male Reproductive System

Most of the time, young men have healthy reproductive systems. However, some men will experience reproductive system problems. Many of these problems can be avoided with good hygiene, by using barrier contraceptives, and by wearing protective equipment during strenuous activities to help support, or cover, the groin area.

## Hernia

A **hernia**, which normally looks like a bulge in the groin area, may occur when a portion of the intestine pushes through an opening in the abdominal wall and into the groin or scrotum. This painful condition requires minor surgery.

## Testicular Injury

**Testicular injury** is the most common problem associated with the male reproductive system. It usually results from an accidental blow to the testicles while a man is participating in physical activities.

Testicular injury also can occur when one of the testicles twists around, cutting off the blood supply to the entire region.

## Steroid Use

Steroid use can have particularly serious side-effects that are not often talked about, nor listed on the packaging labels. Using anabolic steroids to increase muscle volume can cause the male sex organs to shrink or atrophy. Steroids can also decrease the male sex drive, cause liver and heart problems, as well as breast growth.

## Problems Caused by STIs

While many STIs do not cause any signs or symptoms in young men, they can still cause serious health problems. For that reason, it is important for men to protect themselves when engaging in sexual activity, and to visit a doctor regularly for check-ups. Sexually transmitted infections (STIs) may cause symptoms including inflammation of the penis or the foreskin, sores, or genital warts. Chapter 12 contains extensive information on sexually transmitted infections.

## Testicular Cancer

Testicular and prostate cancer pose serious sexual health risks for men. If detected early, these cancers can usually be successfully treated. Regular check-ups and self-examinations can help detect abnormalities.

**Testicular cancer** represents one of the most common forms of cancer in men under the age of 40. It occurs when cells in the testicle divide abnormally to form a tumour.

If it is detected early, testicular cancer can be cured before it spreads to other parts of the body. To help with early detection, young men should perform regular testicular self-examinations (TSE).

---

### The Sexual Health Exam

Once males go through puberty, they need to start thinking about including sexual health exams in their regular health care routine.

Men should certainly talk to a doctor and begin having sexual health exams once they become sexually active.

Men can expect the doctor to do some or all of the following:

- Examine the external parts of the genitals
- Feel the testicles and penis
- Take a swab from the urethra
- Perform an internal exam of the rectum
- Take a urine and/or blood sample

While some of this may feel uncomfortable at first, you should consider your sexual health exam a normal part of your health routine.

---

## Prostate Cancer

**Prostate cancer** is the most frequently diagnosed form of cancer in Canadian men—over 20,000 Canadian men are diagnosed each year. One in seven men will develop prostate cancer.

The prostate gland is located below the seminal vesicles and plays a role in the process of fertilization (its main function is to supply fluid for the sperm during ejaculation). Prostate-specific antigen (PSA) is a protein produced by the prostate that may be found in an increased amount in the blood of men who have prostate cancer. Prostate examinations (rectal examinations) and prostate tests (PSA tests) are crucial, particularly in men over 40.

Symptoms of prostate cancer may include:

➢ Frequent, difficult, or painful urination

➢ Blood or pus in the urine

➢ Pain in the lower back, pelvic area, or upper thighs

➢ Painful ejaculation

If you experience any of these symptoms, you should contact your doctor for an examination.

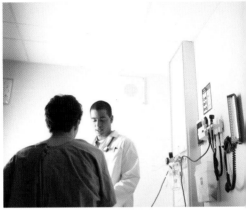

Even if you feel healthy, it is still advisable to have a yearly sexual health exam.

## Testicular Self-Examination
### Early Detection Is the Key

A testicular self-examination (TSE) is a simple 3-step process that can help you detect testicular cancer early. All men should perform a TSE regularly from the time they are 15 years old.

Ideally, you should perform the examination after a hot bath or shower because the warmth will cause your testicles to descend and the skin of your scrotum to relax, making it easier to feel any lumps, growths, or tenderness.

Stand in front of the mirror. Look for any swelling on the skin of your scrotum. Examine each testicle one at a time, placing your index and middle fingers of both hands on the underside of your testicle and your thumbs on the top side. Firmly roll your testicle between your fingers and thumbs, carefully feeling for any lumps, growths, or sensations of tenderness that don't feel normal. It is normal for one of your testicles to be larger than the other.

At the back of each testicle there is a soft cord. This is the tube that collects and carries your sperm. It is a normal part of your scrotum. After you have examined one testicle and cord, check the other side.

Become familiar with how your scrotum feels so you will be able to tell if there are any changes over time. Testicular cancer may not always create a noticeable lump on your testicle.

Other clues to look for include:

- Any change in size, shape, tenderness, or sensation of your testicles or scrotum
- A change in the consistency or swelling of your testicles or scrotum
- Pain in your testicles or scrotum
- A dull ache or heaviness in your lower abdomen
- Abnormal and persistent backache
- Unexplained weight loss
- Breast development

Regular testicular self-examination is an important health habit, but it cannot replace a doctor's examination. Your doctor should check your testicles when you have a physical exam. You can also ask your doctor to teach you how to do testicular self-examination. It is better to be safe than sorry.

# Surviving the Sexual Health Exam
## Questions and Answers

**M**ost people go for their first sexual health exam in their mid to late teens. Others may wait longer, until they are sexually active. Although you may not be excited about the prospect, knowing what to expect can help you feel more comfortable with the process.

If you have questions before your exam, see if you can talk with your doctor ahead of time, or speak with a public health nurse, to address any potential concerns.

- **You should feel comfortable with your doctor.** A sexual health exam involves sensitive parts of your body, which you may have been taught are private. You need to feel comfortable with the person touching and looking at them. Although all doctors—male or female—are familiar with both male and female anatomy, some people prefer to have sexual health exams done by a doctor of the same sex as they are. You may feel your family doctor knows you best, and that you are comfortable with him or her. Or you may feel that it's time to find a doctor different from the one you visited as a child. If you would rather not see your family doctor, for whatever reason, see if you can locate a sexual health clinic or walk-in clinic instead.

- **It's okay to ask questions.** Even if you were to try to think of a really strange question, chances are your doctor has heard some that are even stranger. Don't be afraid to ask your doctor questions—it's your body and your sexual health, and your doctor is there to help you care for and understand it. During puberty, both your body and your mind go through a lot of changes, and asking questions can make some of these changes easier to understand.

- **You don't have to go alone.** Some prefer to do these things alone, but if you feel you would be more comfortable taking someone along, then do so. Many young people find that it helps to have a friend around for moral support, in the doctor's office, or just in the waiting room.

- **Relax.** That may be tough to do but becoming tense and stressed out can make the process not only last longer but also feel more uncomfortable. No matter how unfamiliar things may seem to you, doctors generally have seen it all. Keep breathing, and try to relax your muscles as much as possible.

- **You will need to ask for specific tests.** Many people think that once they have had a sexual health exam, they will have been tested for STIs, but this is not the case. You must inform the doctor specifically if you wish to be tested for an STI. Don't worry about being judged—most doctors are more interested in helping you to maintain your health and that of your partner than in judging your behaviour. Regular testing is a good habit to develop, as many STIs can be present for long periods of time, with no symptoms.

- **Trust your instincts.** Doctors may have many years of training, but no one spends as much time with your body as you do. So, if your doctor tells you you're fine but you still feel like something is wrong, get a second opinion.

It's a good idea to get into the habit of going for regular sexual health exams. The sooner any potential problems are detected, the sooner they can be dealt with and put behind you.

## Questions for Study and Review

### Things to Think About and Explore

1. Itemize and briefly describe the main functions of the six internal and six main external components of the female reproductive system.

2. Itemize and briefly describe the main functions of the three internal and three main external components of the male reproductive system.

3. Give three reasons it is important to care about your sexual health as a teenager.

4. Write a paragraph explaining the possible consequences of women and men not receiving treatment for a sexually transmitted infection.

5. Describe some of the signs that might indicate a problem with the reproductive organs.

6. Investigate the cancer rates (cervical, ovarian, breast, testicular, or prostate) among Canadian women and men. How have these rates changed over the last 25 years? What factor(s) could explain these changes?

### Things to Do and Practise

7. Interview your family doctor (if they have the time available) or speak to a pubilc health nurse, and identify the role a family doctor can play in ensuring your reproductive health. Present your interview to the class.

8. In a small group, compare and contrast the experiences of women and men at a sexual health exam. What part(s) of the exam are most worrisome for women and men? Discuss some things you could do if you are nervous about your sexual health exam.

9. Investigate your family medical history to see if you might be at risk for certain types of cancer. Further investigate what type of lifestyle your family tends to lead. Make a guideline of what you can actively do to decrease your risk of developing certain types of cancer.

10. Imagine you are heading up a campaign to encourage young people to perform breast self-exams or testicular self-exams. Create an advertisement for teens promoting either breast self-exams or testicular self-exams.

11. There are plenty of events across the country aimed at raising cancer awareness as well as funds for research. Investigate those taking place in your community. What else do you think could be done?

12. Make a poster illustrating how cancer can hurt people other than the cancer victims themselves.

## WWWeblinks

Name ➤     Canadian Breast Cancer Foundation

URL ➤     www.cbcf.org

Breast cancer is the most common cancer among Canadian women. This is one of the many online resources dedicated to making breast cancer a thing of the past.

Name ➤     Canadian Cancer Society

URL ➤     www.cancer.ca

The official site for this nationwide organization which aims to both eliminate cancer and assist people living with cancer.

Name ➤     Prostate Cancer Research Foundation of Canada

URL ➤     www.prostatecancer.ca

The official site for this foundation which is dedicated solely to eliminating prostate cancer.

# 11
# Sexuality

**W**e are all exposed to information about sex and sexuality every day. Sexual images are used in advertising to sell everything from shampoo to cars. Yet, if you look at the content of these forms of media, it is clear that much of the sexual information presented is either incomplete or incorrect. Some of it can be demeaning and offensive.

If you are going to learn how to look after your reproductive system and make responsible sexual decisions, you need honest and accurate information. Among other things, this means knowing about the physical, emotional, and social changes you are likely to experience. It also involves thinking through the situations you will probably face throughout adolescence and later in life.

These are the topics of this chapter and the next. You will not find answers to all questions in these chapters, but the main topics are covered. After working through them, you should be able to begin to think things through for yourself, with your teacher, and with your parents and friends.

## Chapter Objectives

In this chapter, you will:

➢ Identify the stages of human sexual development

➢ Examine the physical and emotional changes associated with adolescence and puberty

➢ Explore the notions of gender roles and gender stereotypes and the factors that affect them

➢ Question the cultural influences shaping how we view gender roles and sexuality

➢ Explore how sex and sexuality are presented, and sometimes misrepresented, in the media

## Key Terms

➢ sexuality
➢ adolescence
➢ sex hormones
➢ menstruation/spermatogenesis
➢ sexual orientation
➢ heterosexual
➢ homosexual
➢ lesbian/gay
➢ bisexual
➢ transsexual/transgender
➢ Human Rights Codes
➢ sex
➢ gender/gender roles
➢ socialization
➢ media literacy

# What Is "Sexuality"?

What do you think of when you see or hear the word sexuality? Many people think simply of "sex" (meaning "sexual intercourse"). However, sexual intercourse is just one part of what is meant by the term "sexuality."

People use the term **sexuality** to refer to a number of related ideas:

➢ Physical development of sexual characteristics

➢ Gender roles and relations between the sexes

➢ Intimacy, love, and affection

➢ Sexual attraction

➢ Sexual contact

➢ Sexual decision making

In other words, sexuality includes everything that defines us as girls and boys, women and men. It encompasses our physical development, sexual knowledge, attitudes, values, and behaviours. It also involves making important decisions about intimate relationships.

Sexuality is shaped not only by our biology and psychology, but also by our culture, family history, education, and life experience.

## Sexuality
### One Term, Many Dimensions

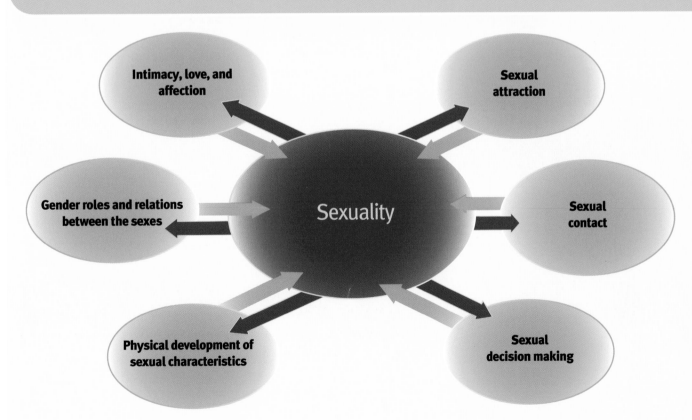

# The Stages of Human Sexual Development

Sexuality is always a part of our lives. As we progress through the stages of human sexual development, we learn more about ourselves as sexual beings and we express feelings of love, affection, and pleasure in different ways.

There are no exact times that these changes occur, but the broad outlines of the stages are summarized below and in the table on pages 172–73.

Stage 1: Infancy—Birth to age 2.

## Stage 1: Infancy (birth to age 2)

From birth until about two years old, infants are completely dependent on others. They learn about love through nurturing physical contact, including hugs, kisses, and snuggling with their caregivers. Infants begin to develop their gender identities by learning from and mimicking others.

It is at this early stage that infants begin to discover some of the socially expected behaviour differences between girls and boys, women and men.

Stage 2: Childhood—Ages 3 to 8.

## Stage 2: Childhood (ages 3 to 8)

Children, from the age of three until about eight years old, become increasingly curious about sexuality and about their bodies. They explore through role-playing games and begin asking questions about sex. Children at this stage learn they are either male or female. They also possess definite ideas, which are frequently stereotypical, about male and female roles.

They also begin to have a basic sexual identity and sexual orientation at this stage of development—they understand what it means to be a boy or girl, and may begin to develop an awareness of what they consider attractive.

Stage 3: Pre-Adolescence—Ages 9 to 12, people at this age are commonly called "tweens."

## Stage 3: Pre-adolescence (ages 9 to 12)

Between the ages of nine and twelve, young people often begin the important transition of puberty. As their bodies begin to produce more sex hormones, pre-teens may begin to experience sexual feelings and fantasies.

As their bodies change, pre-adolescents begin to change the way they think about themselves and others. Many children of this age feel awkward about their own bodies, therefore they become more modest and want increased privacy. They may also develop crushes on friends, classmates, older teens, and even teachers or rock stars.

Puberty comes at different times for different people, so pre-adolescents may find that they are changing more quickly or more slowly than their friends.

### Stage 4: Adolescence (ages 13 to 18)

**Adolescence** is a time during which people are faced with many physical, social, and emotional changes as they make the transition from childhood to adulthood. During this period their bodies continue to grow and change.

Many teens begin to date during this period, and develop intimacy with boyfriends or girlfriends. During your teenage years, you will likely experience increased sexual feelings and a desire to be physically close, or romantic, with a partner.

This is a time when many teens face peer pressure to be sexually active, and to experiment sexually, whether they feel ready or not.

Stage 4: Adolescence—Ages 13 to 18.

### Stage 5: Early Adulthood (ages 19 to 45)

Adults may have fully developed bodies, but as adults they still face many changes physically, emotionally, and socially, each of which can affect their sexual development.

In early adulthood, people often become comfortable with sexuality in general, as youthful embarrassment fades. They experience an increase in their desire for physical intimacy and sexual relationships. Younger adults often select long-term partners and make decisions about cohabitation and/or marriage, and sometimes about children.

By the time they reach their 30s, many adults have entered into long-term intimate relationships, and may have chosen to have children. By this stage, people are often quite comfortable with their sexual identity and sexual orientation, and in consequence they feel less pressure to behave in gender-specific ways. This, in part, explains why adults in this age group report increased satisfaction with their intimate relationships.

Stage 5: Early Adulthood—Ages 19 to 45.

### Stage 6: Later Adulthood (ages 46 and up)

In the first part of this stage (46–65), adults may continue to raise children with their partner or on their own. Some may experience physical and hormonal changes linked to menopause (when a woman's menstrual cycle stops) or andropause (when a man's testosterone level drops). Sexuality during this stage remains an important part of a person's identity.

In the second part of this stage (66 and up), adults almost always experience menopause or andropause, if they have not already done so. They also often struggle with negative stereotypes surrounding sexuality and aging.

Even if they decrease the amount of sexual activity in which they participate, most coupled adults continue to express feelings of love through sexual intimacy with their partner during the more mature stage of their lives.

Stage 6: Later Adulthood—Ages 46 and up.

## THE STAGES OF HUMAN SEXUAL DEVELOPMENT

| STAGE | PHYSICAL CHANGES | SOCIAL/BEHAVIOURAL CHANGES | EMOTIONAL/MENTAL CHANGES |
|---|---|---|---|
| **Stage 1: Infancy (Birth–2 years)** <br><br>During this stage, infants may … | • Have erections or lubricate vaginally <br> • Experience pleasure through genital stimulation | • Learn about love through nurturing, physical contact <br> • Discover socially expected behaviour differences between genders <br> • Explore bodies, including their own genitals | • Gain a sense of self-worth/self-esteem through exposure to kindness/physical closeness <br> • Understand the concept of trust through relationships with parents/caregivers <br> • Begin to notice differences between bodies of girls/boys and children/adults |
| **Stage 2: Childhood (3–8 years)** <br><br>During this stage, children may … | • Experience pleasure from exploring/touching their own bodies (e.g., masturbation) | • Discover female/male roles by observing others <br> • Have romantic attachments towards a parent—small children will often say that they wish to marry their mother or father <br> • Ask questions about birth or pregnancy <br> • Explore body/sexuality through role-playing games <br> • Mimic adult intimate behaviour <br> • Seek a strong relationship with same-sex parent/caregiver <br> • Develop strong friendships with/mimic children of the same sex <br> • Engage in name-calling and teasing | • Begin to use language to express needs/feelings <br> • Become curious about bodies and learn they are either male or female <br> • Enjoy learning/talking about body parts/functions, adult bathroom activities <br> • Use words related to sexuality, develop important attitudes about sex from listening to parents/caregivers <br> • Become aware of sex/reproduction and have basic sexual identity and orientation <br> • Possess definite (often stereotypical) ideas about male/female roles <br> • Begin to be affected by stories heard in media regarding sexual issues such as abuse |
| **Stage 3: Pre-adolescence (9-12 years)** <br><br>During this stage, pre-adolescents may … | • Experience an increase in the production of sex hormones <br> • Begin the changes of puberty including menstruation/sperm production <br> • Experience increased sexual feelings and fantasies <br> • Experience pleasure from exploring/touching own body <br> • Masturbate to orgasm | • Become more modest and want privacy <br> • Continue to value same-sex friendships <br> • Take part in sexual exploration with peers <br> • Increasingly influenced by peers, particularly with regards to self-image | • Struggle with mixed emotions, wonder if they are "normal" <br> • Feel awkward about their own bodies <br> • Acquire core values from parents and family <br> • Develop crushes—on friends, older teens, teachers, and/or rock stars <br> • Have romantic feelings for people of the opposite sex, same sex, or both <br> • Face decisions about sex and drugs |

| STAGE | PHYSICAL CHANGES | SOCIAL/BEHAVIOURAL CHANGES | EMOTIONAL/MENTAL CHANGES |
|---|---|---|---|
| **Stage 4:** **Adolescence** **(13–18 years)** During this stage, adolescents may … | • Complete the changes of puberty<br>• Experience increased sexual feelings and fantasies<br>• Desire physical closeness with a partner | • Begin to separate from parents<br>• Begin to date<br>• Experience relationship break-ups<br>• Face pressure to be sexually active whether or not they feel ready<br>• Exchange close friendships in favour of romantic relationships<br>• Be increasingly influenced by peers/partners/family/cultural community<br>• Sometimes engage in risk-taking activities, or face violence in relationships | • Have strong sexual identity/orientation<br>• Place great value on independence<br>• Be very concerned about their appearance/attractiveness<br>• Develop intimacy with boyfriends/girlfriends<br>• Make choices regarding sex |
| **Stage 5:** **Early Adulthood** **(19–45 years)** During this stage, adults may … | • Experience an increase in their desire for physical intimacy and sexual relationships<br>• Report increased sexual satisfaction in their relationships | • May experience break-up of relationship or divorce<br>• Less concerned with conforming to peer group members<br>• Develop adult relationship with parents<br>• Seek out friends of both sexes<br>• Complete self-examinations for good health (breast and testicular self-exams)<br>• Feel less pressure to behave in gender-specific ways in relationships | • Become more comfortable with sexual identity/orientation and sexuality in general<br>• Make decisions about cohabitation/marriage/children |
| **Stage 6:** **Later Adulthood** **(46 years and up)** During this stage, older adults may … | • Experience physical and hormonal changes linked to menopause or andropause<br>• Continue to explore sexual intimacy and sexual activity with partner(s) | • May experience relationship break-ups/divorces/death of loved ones<br>• Raise children with partner or on their own<br>• Make healthy decisions regarding safer sex<br>• May decrease amount of sexual intercourse/activity after age 65<br>• Enjoy relationships with adult children and grandchildren | • Choose to be single/to date/to have intimate relationships/to be married<br>• Become comfortable with sexual identity/orientation<br>• Struggle with negative stereotypes of sexuality/aging |

# Physical Changes During Adolescence

Puberty begins with the body's release of **sex hormones**—estrogens in girls and testosterone in boys. When the body is ready, the pituitary gland delivers messages to the ovaries and the testicles to start producing these hormones.

As these hormones increase, a number of physical changes commonly take place. The sebaceous gland enlarges and sebum (or oil) production accelerates, sometimes causing pimples, or serious acne. An increase in perspiration can cause body odour. Hair grows in new places, including under the arms, on the legs, and in the pubic area.

In addition, during puberty, people grow taller. Their hips, shoulders, and chests broaden. Young women's breasts grow and develop, while in young men, the penis, testes, and scrotal sac develop further. Even the larynx grows, causing everyone's voice to deepen. (This change is more noticeable for men, but everyone experiences it.)

## Changes to the Female Body

Baby girls are born with all the ova (eggs) they will need over their lifetime. At puberty these eggs mature, and hormones released from the pituitary gland send a message to the ovaries. As a result, the ovaries begin to release estrogens, which in turn leads to the release of female reproductive cells called ova or eggs.

This process, which occurs about once every month from puberty to menopause, is called ovulation. Once ovulation occurs, the egg is caught by the Fallopian tube and travels down to the uterus. In the uterus (or womb) a fertilized egg can develop into a fetus.

Throughout each month, the endometrium (the lining inside the uterus) thickens. If an egg is fertilized by a man's sperm cell, it implants itself in this nourishing lining in the uterus. Fertilization occurs during vaginal intercourse when the penis is inserted inside the vagina and an ejaculation occurs.

Women can become pregnant when sperm enters the vagina, even if vaginal intercourse does not take place. It is estimated that sperm can live inside a woman's reproductive system for three to five days. Therefore, if the egg is not present at that particular moment, the sperm may still be able to fertilize an egg released in the following days. Fertilization can also occur through artificial insemination or other forms of reproductive technology. A fertilized egg takes about 40 weeks to develop into a full-term baby.

However, most of the time a woman's egg will not be fertilized, the thick lining will not be needed, and it will be shed off the sides of the uterus and out of the body through the cervix and the vagina. This process is called **menstruation** or "having a period." Menstruation generally lasts between three and seven days. During this time, women can use tampons, sanitary napkins, or a specially designed "cup" (or "keeper") inserted into the vagina to catch menstrual blood.

## Wet Dreams

Many boys have wet dreams (so-called, "nocturnal emissions") during puberty. They become aroused in their sleep and ejaculate, waking up wet and sticky.

Girls also experience wet dreams, although their dreams are not as obvious in their results. Since women produce lubrication inside their bodies, when they become aroused in their sleep they may find vaginal secretions in their underwear or pyjamas the next morning.

While not everyone experiences wet dreams, they are very common in adolescents. They are a natural part of reaching sexual maturity, as young people develop sexual thoughts and feelings and their bodies respond to the increased sex hormones in their bodies.

## Changes to the Male Body

Baby boys are born with the capacity to produce sperm, but this process does not begin until puberty. At this time, the pituitary gland sends a message to the testicles to start releasing more testosterone. This, in turn, causes the testicles to produce male reproductive cells or sperm.

This process is called **spermatogenesis**. Sperm move from the testicles to the epididymis where they mature. During an ejaculation, sperm from the epididymis move through the vas deferens to collect semen. Semen nourishes the sperm.

For ejaculation to occur, the penis must be erect. Inside the penis are three large vesicles that engorge with blood during an erection. The penis becomes hard or erect because of this rush of blood. During puberty, erections can sometimes occur for no apparent reason and without warning.

The semen is ejaculated through the urethra—the tube that also allows for urination. A male cannot ejaculate and urinate at the same time because a valve closes off one opening or the other to prevent this from happening.

During puberty, many physical changes occur in response to the release of sex hormones—testosterone in males and estrogen in females.

# Personal Hygiene
## Keeping Clean

During and after puberty you will need to make sure that your hygiene keeps up with changes in your body.

### Skin

Since the sebaceous gland produces more oil, skin may become prone to acne. Taking care of your skin means eating well, drinking plenty of water, and exercising, as well as gently cleansing your face twice a day.

### Body Odour

Increased production of sex hormones in adolescence can cause body odour, but managing it is relatively simple. Be sure to shower or bathe regularly, change your clothes every day, and try using an anti-perspirant deodorant.

### Personal Hygiene

Good sexual health also includes washing your genitals with warm water and gentle soap. For men, this means cleaning the penis and testicles. Young men with circumcised penises can simply clean the whole genital area with a wash cloth. Boys and men with uncircumcised penises should clean the tip of the penis by pulling back the loose skin and washing underneath.

Young women need to wash their genital area very carefully, using warm water on the labia. Avoid putting soap near or in the vagina, as it can cause irritation and infections. There is no need to clean your vagina because it has natural fluids to keep it clean and healthy.

### Grooming

For many young people, looking nice becomes especially important during adolesence. How you look and what you wear are important to the image you portray to yourself and your friends.

Of course, all this is quite natural. It becomes unhealthy when, responding to outside pressures, an individual goes overboard, risking his or her own well-being just for the sake of appearance. As with most things, moderation and caution are useful guidelines in this department.

# Emotional and Social Changes During Adolescence

The sex hormones that begin the physical changes during puberty also affect the way you feel and the way you behave. This means that your teenage years will be a time of not only physical changes, but also emotional and social ones.

## Emotional Changes

During adolescence, people often experience intense emotions including happiness, love, anger, frustration, sadness, and sexual feelings. This is perfectly natural.

Most people start to become interested in romantic love and intimacy during their teen years. This is often accompanied by increased interest in their physical appearance. It is normal to want to look your best. Part of looking good is being healthy and clean and feeling strong. Eat a balanced diet, get regular exercise, shower and wash your hair regularly. Wear clothes that make you feel good.

It is fine to want to look good, but sometimes this desire becomes unhealthy. Most people who develop eating disorders report that their issues with weight, eating, and body image began during adolescence.

Some teens have unreasonable expectations about how they should look because we are surrounded by images of very thin or very muscular media figures, such as models and celebrities. It can feel upsetting to compare yourself to these figures, who are supposed to represent the most attractive people in our culture. You may feel as though you will never be thin enough or muscular enough. All this can be unhealthy. It is important to pay attention to the diet and exercise choices you make, and how you feel about your body and your appearance.

The good news is that you do not need to look like a celebrity in order to look attractive. As we will explore on pages 182–83, in everyday situations, most celebrities don't look the way they look on television or in advertisements. Quite often, their appearance has been altered—digitally or by other means.

During adolescence, most people also want increased independence, as they begin to feel like they can manage their own lives. This is perfectly normal. Parents or caregivers may be nervous about this new desire for independence because they care about you and want to protect you. What seems like overprotection on their part is normally just a genuine concern for your well-being.

In general, if you feel like you are always unhappy, stressed out, or anxious, talk with your friends, siblings, your parents, or a trusted adult. If you need more serious help, you could visit the guidance counsellor at your high school or see your family doctor. Either of these people can put you in contact with good community resources.

## Peer Pressures

Teens, like all people, feel pressure to be liked by their peers. However, this can leave young people in a bit of a bind.

On the one hand, they want to be true to their personal values and beliefs; on the other hand, they want to go along with their peers.

Of course, if your peers share your ideals, this is less of an issue. However, if they hold opposing views, you will need to clearly communicate what you are willing and not willing to do.

Being honest with yourself will result in self-respect and positive self-esteem.

## Social Changes

During this time, your friends, peers, and teachers will likely play an increasingly important role in your life. This change is very important. Many of the friendships and loyalties you develop during adolescence will remain with you for the rest of your life. Ensuring that your friends share the same ideals and values as you do is especially important.

That said, during this period it is also important to keep the lines of communication open with your parents or caregivers. This way, you can explore your individual identity, friendships, and relationships while still remaining emotionally and socially connected to your immediate family.

Eventually, each of us develops our own sense of self as we move through adolescence and into adulthood. Our past experiences as children, our personalities, our family values, our education, our cultural standards, information received via the media, and our spiritual beliefs—all of these will influence how we view such things as sex and sexuality. As we grow and mature, as one might expect, our beliefs and feelings change to reflect the new ideas and new experiences that we encounter.

Trusted friends, as well as trusted adults, can help you deal with some of the changes that adolescence brings.

## Finding Help
### Where To Go with Questions

Parents, doctors, friends, teachers, counsellors, and religious advisors can often answer your questions about sexuality.

Sometimes, though, you may wish to remain anonymous. You can get anonymous, reliable help and information on the phone and online.

### Kids Help Phone

Kids Help Phone at 1-800-668-6868 is a toll-free, anonymous help line for young people. Kids Help Phone counsellors can talk with you about any sexual health matter (including sexual assault, sexual abuse, sexual orientation, pregnancy) or more general health-related issues (bullying, drug addiction, physical abuse, suicide).

Professional counsellors at Kids Help Phone can also give you information or refer you to other sources.

At the Kids Help Phone website (**www.kidshelpphone. ca**), you can browse through sexual health topics (and many other subjects) or send your question to a counsellor via e-mail.

### Resources on the Internet

Some internet resources are better than others. In fact, some material found online is actually wrong, so it is important that you visit reputable, trusted sites.

You can find good, reliable information at the following web sites, as well as at those listed at the end of each chapter in this book.

- **www.sexualityandu.ca**—Society of Obstetricians and Gynaecologists of Canada
- **www.hc-sc.gc.ca**—Health Canada
- **www.yesmeansyes.com**—Sexual Assault Centre, Victoria, B.C.
- **www.livepositive.ca**—HIV/AIDS Information for Canadian Teens and Teachers
- **www.cdnaids.ca**—Canadian AIDS Society

## Sexual Orientation

Sexuality is complicated: People vary in terms of their sexual attraction towards others. These differences are described as a person's sexual orientation. Sexual orientation becomes evident, for most people, during puberty. This is because your body, and your brain, begin to change in significant ways at this time. Once your pituitary gland sends signals to your sex glands to start working, these glands send out sex hormones. The sex hormones are chemical substances that flow through your bloodstream. When this happens, not only will your body develop, but you will also begin to have feelings about sexuality and your sexual orientation generally becomes evident.

**Sexual orientation** refers to an individual's sexual attraction towards a particular group of people. Most people describe themselves as heterosexual. Someone who experiences his or her sexuality as **heterosexual** feels an exclusive or predominant sexual attraction toward persons of the opposite sex (woman to man, man to woman).

Sexual orientation becomes evident, for most people, during puberty. This is because your body, and your brain, begin to change in significant ways at this time.

Essentially, sexual orientation is an individual's sexual attraction towards a particular group of people.

### Respecting Diversity

Essentially, sexual orientation is an individual's sexual attraction towards a particular group of people. The majority of people describe themselves as heterosexual. However, approximately 10 percent of people are not heterosexual.

Someone who experiences his or her sexuality as a **homosexual** feels a sexual attraction towards persons of the same sex. A **lesbian** is a woman who is attracted to other women. A **gay** man is attracted to other men. The term **bisexual** refers to people who are attracted to both women and men. **Transsexual** people feel a consistent and overwhelming desire to live as members of the opposite sex, and most consider or pursue hormonal therapy and surgical changes in order to make the transition from man to woman or woman to man. People who identify as **transgender** feel a consistent desire to live as a member of the opposite sex, and often choose to dress and present themselves as members of the opposite sex without undergoing Sexual Reassignment Surgery.

People who self-identify as "questioning" are often, but not always, young. These people generally feel some confusion about their sexuality and are unsure of their sexual orientation.

In the last thirty years, members of several groups use the term "queer" as both a means of self-identification as well as a way of declaring they are not heterosexual. This form of self-identification is political—it is meant to empower members of this community. That being said, if people outside the group (i.e., heterosexuals) use the term "queer," it may be considered offensive or hateful.

This information may seem confusing or surprising to you. The most important thing to remember about sexual orientation is that all human beings share the same desire to be loved in the context of an intimate relationship regardless of their sexual orientation.

## Canadian Human Rights Codes

In the past, sexual orientation was a taboo subject. The good news is that social attitudes are changing rapidly. Today, most young people respect the rights of others to live freely according to their sexual orientation.

In Canada, the Canadian Human Rights Act (federal legislation) and the various provincial **Human Rights Codes** strictly prohibit discrimination or harassment on the basis of sexual orientation. Sexual orientation is a serious issue when a person's legal rights are denied, when someone is discriminated against, or when that person is persecuted or injured because of his or her sexual orientation.

Even though federal and provincial legislation makes it illegal, individual and institutional discrimination on the basis of sexual orientation still occurs in Canada. This kind of discrimination falls under the category of a "hate crime." (For more on hate crimes, see Chapter 17, pages 284–85.)

As a democratic and humane society, it should be our goal to eliminate all forms of injustice and inequality. Learning to be tolerant and accepting of all people, regardless of individual differences, benefits all Canadians.

The Canadian Human Rights Act and provincial Human Rights Codes prohibit discrimination or harassment on the basis of sexual orientation.

# Sex Versus Gender

Even though some people use the terms sex and gender interchangeably, they are quite different. The term **sex** refers to the qualities by which people are categorized by their reproductive organs and functions. Our sex is determined on the basis of our biology. In contrast, the term **gender** applies more to social factors than to physical ones.

## Gender Roles

**Gender** is the condition of being female or male as defined by society. Gender differences in people arise from variations in the way they grow up—their family, education, or culture. Right from birth, each of us learns about "appropriate" gender roles as we observe the people around us. As we grow up, we discover more about what it means to be a girl or a boy, a woman or a man.

**Gender roles** are sets of behaviours that project an image of femininity or masculinity. They are, essentially, patterns of behaviour by which women and men are expected to live.

In terms of sexuality, stereotypes about gender roles dictate how women and men are supposed to act; for instance, women are believed to be sexually passive while men are expected to be sexually aggressive. Rigid gender roles like these are harmful because they can pressure us to behave according to stereotypical rules instead of being true to ourselves.

## Cultural Considerations

Unfortunately, our culture, like many others, often looks for differences between females and males to highlight the ways one is superior to the other. Women are said to be naturally superior at some tasks, men at others.

While people often show tremendous fascination with pointing out differences between the sexes, in most ways, women and men from the same cultural group are more biologically alike than they are different. Variations are most often the results of differences in socialization and environment, not biology. The findings in academic studies about gender tend to illustrate very small differences, with a large degree of overlap, between the sexes.

Differences in behaviour that are based on gender occur because of the ways people are raised in various parts of the world. When researchers complete cross-cultural studies, they often find that what it means to be a woman or man differs greatly depending on the country and area in which people live. For example, women in Japan have different ideas about gender than do women in Canada. From an early age, girls in Japanese cultures are taught that the appropriate speaking style for women is extremely polite and quiet. Adult women in Japan tend to speak softly and cover their mouths when laughing in circumstances when men would not.

Gender is the condition of being female or male as defined by society.

Many occupations traditionally regarded as either "male" or "female" are now open to men and women.

## Changes Over Time and Place

The time and place in which a person lives also affects how males and females are expected to behave. Imagine a woman or man from medieval times. Do you think they would have held similar ideas about gender and sexuality as you do today?

Even what is considered attractive varies from place to place, and from time to time. For instance, historically, most women did not shave their underarms. Hair was considered a sign of fertility and sex appeal. In Canada today, beauty standards dictate that, in order to be considered attractive, women should shave their underarms. In contrast, in certain European countries such as France, many people still consider it sexy for women to have underarm hair.

The important point is that ideas about gender and sexuality change over time. **Socialization** is the term that captures this notion. Socialization is most strongly enforced by family, school, and peer groups, and is a process that continues throughout an individual's lifetime.

Passing on the customs, attitudes, and values of a social group, community, or culture helps to ensure that these beliefs and customs will be passed on to new generations.

Many differences in behaviour occur simply because of the ways people are raised.

Times change. Do you think the family members above would have held similar ideas about gender and sexuality to those you hold today?

# Gender, Sex, and the Media

"The media" is any form of communication that distributes information. The media includes television, radio, music, movies, newspapers, magazines, billboards, and the Internet, as well as many other forms of communication. All forms of media are directed at a specific audience. That audience is often targeted on the basis of sex and age—girls, women, boys, or men.

The commercial media often uses stereotypical notions of femininity or masculinity to tell us what is appropriate and desirable for women and men. This includes what we should look like and what roles we should play in relationships, among other things.

## Sex as a Sales Tool

Issues surrounding sexuality in the media are often quite troublesome. Sexual images of young women and men tell us that being sexy is a goal that can be achieved by wearing certain clothes or using specific products, such as diet aids, perfume, cologne, lotion, body wash, deodorant, and makeup.

Not only are sexual images used to sell clothing and personal items, they are also used to sell almost everything else, including compact discs, cars, food, cigarettes, and alcohol.

## Double Standards in Sexuality

Television shows, newspapers, magazines, billboards, music videos, and websites are full of sexual images. In particular, they are full of sexual images of young women. This leaves young women in a difficult situation. They experience enormous pressure to appear "sexy," while at the same time receiving a message that sexual activity should be avoided.

In everyday life, sexual activity is often discouraged for women and, at the same time, encouraged for men. Young men are supposed to be highly interested in sex and the sexual attractiveness of young women. The media often promotes this double standard. Ideas such as these about what we are "supposed to be" lead to the creation of stereotypes about how young women and men should behave.

Unfortunately, these stereotypes become part of our society's definitions of gender roles regarding sexuality. Recent studies demonstrate that while teens are aware of the trouble with this kind of stereotyping, they continue to be influenced by it. This may be because it is difficult for individuals to find a clear sense of sexuality when faced with so many inaccurate messages and contradictions.

It is important to be aware that our ideas about sex, gender, femininity, and masculinity are heavily influenced by what we view and read in the media. Often these messages are out of touch with reality or they are heavily biased. Being aware of this will help you make decisions that are best for you and your friends, rather than relying on stereotypical views or media-created gender roles.

---

## Stereotyping

Stereotypes are generalized portrayals of groups that are usually oversimplified, such as "all women are nurturing," or "all men are aggressive."

In a recent Canadian study, high school students were asked to help define femininity and masculinity. The teens chose five categories to define femininity and masculinity.

The results for "femininity" were:

- Physical beauty
- Sexuality
- Motherhood
- Domesticity
- Kindness

The results for "masculinity" were:

- Strength
- Independence
- Intelligence
- Wealth and financial success
- Athletic ability

Consider the different ways media advertising portrays women and men. Where do you see these stereotypes about gender roles best being illustrated?

**Source:** For more information on this study of sexual stereotypes, check out *A Barbie Who Puts Out* by Alyson Beben (Toronto: York University, 2003).

## Looking Good: Beauty Myths

Have you ever noticed that when you look at pictures in magazines all the people look perfect? Well, it is important to remember that the images you see in the media often are not real. Not only do advertisers consistently use models who represent a stereotypical version of North American beauty (white, young, tall, and fit), they also use a variety of techniques to alter the images to make the models look flawless.

Make-up covers acne. Wardrobe tricks (such as taping body fat) are used to hide imperfections. With computer enhancement, breasts can be enlarged and muscles defined. Wrinkles and cellulite are easily airbrushed away. Teeth are instantly whitened. Computer technology makes it possible to "touch up" images of models and actors in order to eliminate any physical flaws. So many changes can be made that the final photographs look radically different from the actual person.

Today, the standards of beauty and attractiveness in the media go far beyond good health and grooming. When average people compare themselves to these images, they often feel inadequate. Even though these idealized versions of femininity and masculinity are unattainable (they are fake, after all), they continue to influence us. Both women and men feel pressure to spend enormous amounts of time and money trying to improve their physical appearances.

It is difficult to find your own bearings when you are faced with many inaccurate messages and outright contradictions in the media.

It is important to remember that the images you see in the media are often not real. The left side of this photo shows the enhancements to the original image on the right.

## What Is Media Awareness?
### Deconstructing Messages

You have probably heard the term "literacy" used many times to describe a person's ability to read. While "media literacy" involves reading, it goes much farther than that.

**Media literacy** is the ability to sift through and analyze the messages that inform, entertain, and sell things and ideas to us every day. It is the ability to be a critical thinker when you consume (watch, listen, read) all forms of media—from television to billboards, from the Internet to music videos.

When taking in media messages, there are some central ideas that you should keep in mind. Consider the following:

- **All media are constructions.** This means that somebody (or some group) created them. Remember that everything in media has been carefully crafted to send specific messages. Ask yourself some important questions. Who is supposed to receive this message? Who wants to reach this audience, and why? From whose perspective is this story told? Whose voices are heard, and whose are absent?

- **The media construct reality.** We learn about the world, in large part, by consuming media. This means that our "reality" is shaped by messages that have been pre-constructed and have built-in attitudes, interpretations, and conclusions.

- **Audiences find meaning in the media.** Individual factors such as age, race, ethnicity, socio-economic status, sexual orientation, family, and cultural background all play a part in shaping the way we receive media messages.

- **The media is big business.** All media are influenced by commercial considerations—that is, they are all out to make money. This goal, of earning a profit, affects the entire process of making and distributing media. Worse yet, since huge corporations own many forms of media, a relatively small number of individuals control what we watch, read, and hear in the media.

- **Media contain value messages.** All media products are advertising, in some sense, in that they portray values and ways of life. Messages about sexuality and gender are particularly evident in most forms of media.

- **Media have social and political implications.** The media have great influence on politics and on forming social change. Media sources help us learn about local, national, and global concerns, therefore affecting the world both socially and politically.

**Source:** John Pungente, S.J. Adapted from *Media Literacy Resource Guide* by Barry Duncan et al. (Toronto: Ontario Ministry of Education, 1989).

# Chapter Review

## Questions for Study and Review

### Things to Think About and Explore

1. Itemize the various components of the term "sexuality" and assess what they mean to you.

2. Outline the factors that make the adolescent stage so important to sexual development.

3. Distinguish between the terms "sex" and "gender."

4. Think about the ways strict gender roles affect both women and men. Judge how things might improve for both if these restrictions no longer existed.

5. Assess the impact that media portrayals of sexuality have on men and women. Explain how different stereotypes are used to give conflicting messages about sex and sexuality, and men and women.

6. Explain the relationship between "the media" and "reality." How does each affect the other?

### Things to Do and Practise

7. In your library or over the Internet, locate a copy of the Canadian Human Rights Act and your province's Human Rights Code. Find and compare the clauses in each legal document that specifically prohibit discrimination and harrassment on the basis of sexual orientation.

8. In a group, discuss the current standards of physical attractiveness for both women and men. Compare the standards for women with standards for men and discuss how realistic they are.

9. In a group, discuss how your cultural background (race, ethnicity, religion, nationality, etc.) affects your views of sexuality and beauty.

10. Search through some teen magazines for examples of advertisements directed at young women and men. Create a chart with the headings "femininity" and "masculinity." Under each heading, write the words found in the ads that relate to each term.

11. Search the Internet and the telephone book for community resources for teens in your area. If you were experiencing stress, depression, or other emotional issues, where could you turn for help?

12. While watching television, monitor how many gender stereotypes you witness. Try to include at least two different types of shows and discuss which you think is closer to reality.

# 12

# Intimacy and Sexual Decision Making

> *It is our choices that show what we truly are, far more than our abilities.*

**J. K. Rowling**

Author of the Harry Potter series

## Key Terms

- ➢ healthy relationships
- ➢ sexual intimacy
- ➢ self-esteem
- ➢ sexual decision making
- ➢ abstinence
- ➢ sexually transmitted infections (STIs)
- ➢ Human Immunodeficiency Virus (HIV)
- ➢ Acquired Immune Deficiency Syndrome (AIDS)
- ➢ methods of contraception

**A**dolescence is a period of change for young people. Gradually, teens become more independent, take greater responsibility for their own decisions, and are faced with choices that will have profound consequences for their adult lives. As part of this process, teens are confronted with choices about relationships and sexuality.

In order to make good decisions about sex, we all require comprehensive information about sexual health, time to consider possible choices, and opportunities to practise our decision-making skills. While you may not yet be prepared to engage in sexual activity, you can begin to think about how you want to make decisions of this kind, what you want for your future, and how choices about sexuality may affect you.

In this chapter, you will find information and ideas to help you in this process.

## Chapter Objectives

In this chapter, you will:

- ➢ Explore what constitutes sexual intimacy
- ➢ Examine the characteristics of healthy and unhealthy relationships
- ➢ Learn how to make good decisions about sex and sexuality
- ➢ Consider how your decisions about sex can affect you and others
- ➢ Identify effective communications skills and when to use them
- ➢ Examine the possible consequences of sexual decision making including sexually transmitted infections, HIV/AIDS, and pregnancy

# Up Close and Personal

It is definitely a little odd. It has been with us since life began—sex, that is—and we still have difficulty discussing it openly. What's the fuss all about?

## Thinking Through the Consequences

Your sexuality encompasses an important part of who you are—your body, thoughts, values, ideals, morals, and personality. Since it is so important, decisions about sex and sexuality need to be made with all the possible consequences in mind. Some sexual behaviour, for example, can have serious long-term consequences that will affect the options available to you in the future. Making good choices is therefore important.

When making these decisions for yourself, above all, make sure to listen to your own "gut instinct" about what is right and wrong. You can rely on your family and friends for advice and guidance. As you get older, it will be up to you to decide what values you hold with respect to sex and sexuality at each stage of your life, and what choices you make for yourself along the way.

Once we are enjoying healthy relationships, we need to make choices about intimacy.

You are the only person who can decide what is comfortable for you in terms of your sexuality.

# Healthy Relationships

Responsible sexual and intimate decisions are most easily made within healthy relationships. How you feel when you are in a relationship is a sign of whether or not the relationship is healthy for you.

Generally, **healthy relationships** cause people to feel good about themselves, while unhealthy relationships cause people to feel unhappy. In healthy relationships, partners respect themselves and one another. They consider and show concern for each other's feelings. Often, in unhealthy relationships, one partner mistreats the other. Occasionally, both partners treat each other badly. Sometimes, people who are not being treated well in a relationship do not recognize it.

When people make a commitment to one another, and invest time and energy in a relationship, they can feel as though they have to remain in that relationship even if it hurts them. They might also feel powerless to improve the relationship or they might want to leave it but feel afraid to do so. They might feel that any relationship at all is better than being alone.

The following chart lists qualities of both healthy and unhealthy relationships. Read through it and consider which qualities apply to your relationships.

Healthy relationships help people to feel good about themselves, while unhealthy relationships can have the opposite effect.

| HEALTHY RELATIONSHIPS VERSUS UNHEALTHY RELATIONSHIPS | |
| --- | --- |
| **IN HEALTHY RELATIONSHIPS, PARTNERS ...** | **IN UNHEALTHY RELATIONSHIPS, PARTNERS ...** |
| Feel happy and relaxed | Feel unhappy |
| Are confident | Manipulate one another to get what they want |
| Have positive self-esteem | Pressure the other person to do something that she or he does not want to do |
| Act with mutual respect | Use intimidation or threats |
| Are considerate of one another | Disagree and frequently argue over fundamental issues |
| Feel appreciated | Are unsure of themselves |
| Build intimacy through an honest exchange of ideas | Have negative self-esteem |
| Communicate openly and honestly | Act with disregard for the other person's feelings |
| Listen to each other | Feel disrespected and unappreciated |
| Attempt to understand one another | Do not communicate well |
| Demonstrate trust | Are dishonest or feel like they have to lie in order to be loved or safe |
| Enjoy equality | Do not attempt to understand one another |
| Hold positive body images | Hold negative body images |
| Have the ability to talk about sexuality | Do not talk about sexuality |
| Make sexual decisions together | Do not make sexual decisions together |
| Spend time together and time apart | Hurt or harm each other |
| Demonstrate independence | Act needy and depend on the other person for emotional stability |

# The SHARE Qualities
## The Components of Healthy Relationships

Every relationship is unique, but healthy relationships always have some things in common—these are sometimes referred to as the SHARE qualities.

- **Safety.** A healthy relationship means both people feel safe—neither person worries about being physically or emotionally hurt by the other. You feel comfortable making a decision—such as whether or not to have sex—without being afraid of how your partner will react.

- **Honesty.** You and your partner tell each other the truth at all times, even when you know that you disagree, or that the truth may not be pleasant. Each of you can share your opinion without worrying that you will be made fun of or ignored. You resolve problems honestly and openly, and you are able to admit when you have made a mistake.

- **Acceptance.** You accept each other for who you are. You know that your partner has different qualities than anyone else, and you like them for being this way. Neither of you tries to "fix" the other, and neither of you tries to make the other more like your friends' partners or like some other ideal. If your partner has qualities you really don't like, you probably shouldn't be with that person.

- **Respect.** You respect your partner's right to have his or her own opinion, and your partner gives the same respect to you. You do not feel inferior or superior to your partner; you each think highly of the other for being who they are, even if you don't always agree.

- **Enjoyment.** A healthy relationship should be enjoyable—otherwise, why are you with that person? You have fun together, and feel happy and energized when you are with each other. You can play or be serious together, but you enjoy each other's company no matter what you are doing. Even when things aren't perfect, even when you disagree, you still feel comfortable with each other and enjoy each other's company.

Sometimes, a person knows that he or she is not happy in a particular relationship, but that person may not know exactly what to do about it. If you are in this situation, tell a parent, school counsellor, doctor, social worker, or anyone else you trust. They can help find the right kind of counselling for you.

If you think you are in an unhealthy relationship, you probably are. Unhealthy relationships damage your self-esteem. Help yourself by getting out.

# Intimacy and Relationships

From the moment of our births we long for intimate contact: the touch of a hand, a loving cuddle, the sound of a caring voice, or just the sight of a familiar face looking lovingly at us. Intimacy is the expression of a deep, faithful love. It is the foundation of good friendship and is essential in a truly loving relationship.

You probably have trusted friends with whom you share your deepest secrets. This closeness and trust is what we call intimacy. Sexual activity is just one expression of intimacy that can take place between loving and committed persons.

## What Constitutes Sexual Intimacy?

As we establish intimate relationships, we make choices about how intimate we wish to be. This can include how much personal information we share with our partner, how we communicate, and how we want to be physically close to one another. **Sexual intimacy** represents a way of expressing intimate feelings for another person.

You can think of sexual activity as a progression—something that begins slowly, with less intimate acts, and over time may move towards more intimate acts. For the majority of couples, a new relationship will begin with a period of sexual abstinence, during which they get to know each other and become emotionally close. Couples may see each other socially and privately, talk and chat, hold hands, and become comfortable with each other's company.

Over time, romantic relationships often progress and become more intimate in nature. As they become closer, some couples may choose to enter a long-term, committed relationship and/or get married, and increase their levels of intimate and sexual activity.

## Healthy Decisions

This process could take years to complete or it could happen fairly quickly. The speed at which a couple moves through the steps of intimacy will depend on a wide variety of factors including their age, the amount of time they have spent together, and their personal values.

All too often young people rush through the steps of intimacy. This is unfortunate for a number of reasons—the experience of getting to know another person closely, falling in love, and engaging in intimate behaviour with that person is really special. When people move rapidly through the steps, they do not allow themselves to grow as couples and strengthen their relationship overall.

Since you and your partner will be making decisions about sex together, it is important that you take the time to become comfortable discussing your beliefs, thoughts, fears, and hopes, with trust and respect.

## Evaluating Relationships

Relationships do not have to involve physical violence to be unhealthy. If you feel that you have to do anything you don't want to do in order to make someone like or love you, then you should question the relationship.

Many studies demonstrate that girls are at greater risk for sexual or physical assault than boys. In Canada, research suggests that about one in four women between the ages of 18 and 24 experience violence at the hands of their partners.

If you or someone you know is living with violence or abusive behaviour in a relationship, help is available. You can talk with your parents, a family member, a guidance counsellor, or another trusted adult.

As well, you can always call your local health department or Kids Help Phone at 1-800-668-6868.

# Defining Your Limits
## Practise Your Communication Skills

It is up to you to consider the possible consequences of choices that you may make about sexual activity. You will also need to decide what level of intimacy is acceptable to you. When the time comes for you to make these decisions, you will want to consider the beliefs and values of the people most important to you.

Good communication skills are essential.

- **Refusal**. This means you say "no" and you stick to it. Though this can sometimes be difficult, it is important to remember that you are refusing to participate in a particular activity—you are not rejecting the other person.

- **Delay**. You might need time to think things over before deciding, or you might already know that you are not ready to engage in a particular activity. It is always okay to say "I am not ready for this yet." In effect, you are telling your partner that you want to wait and that your partner must respect your decision.

- **Negotiation**. When partners respect each other's needs and wishes, they can sometimes find solutions by negotiating. Negotiation involves give and take, looking for common ground, and ensuring that both partners can be happy with a joint decision. When negotiating your participation in intimate activities, you need to find things with which you are both comfortable. Negotiation works when both partners are respectful and mature.

- **Acceptance**. You are responsible for setting clear boundaries. It is best to do this before you are in the position of having to enforce them. Stating them consistently and clearly will help to ensure that your boundaries are understood and respected.

Practise your communication skills so that they become second nature to you and you will be able to handle most situations.

# The Importance of Self-Esteem

Since sexuality is so personal, it has a great effect on a one's self-esteem. **Self-esteem** is a feeling of pride in yourself and a sense of self-worth.

When people respect themselves and act according to their beliefs and values, they generally feel positive about themselves. In terms of sexuality, people with a healthy and strong sense of self are more likely to communicate what they want and need to their partner. They are less likely to compromise their values, or act in ways that are unsafe or degrading to their own sense of morality.

When we act in ways that are in accordance with our beliefs, we normally feel good. This can positively affect our self-esteem. It is only when we build our self-esteem that we can also build healthy romantic and sexual relationships.

When people engage in risky behaviours, it can mean that they do not value themselves, their health, or well-being enough to make smart choices to protect themselves. When we act in ways we think are "wrong" and ignore our feelings about sexual and moral decisions, we tend to feel badly about it. This can have a negative impact on our self-esteem. We might feel embarrassed or as if someone has taken advantage of us.

## Making Good Decisions

**Sexual decision making** entails making conscious choices about your sexual activity. When making these choices, you have much to consider. First, you will need to decide what this term means to you right now. Sexual activity covers a broad spectrum of activities that promote intimacy in healthy and loving relationships, and can include all activities that are intimate, romantic, or sexual in nature.

Research shows us that young people who have positive relationships with their parents, who participate in extra-curricular activities, and who possess a good education about sexuality are best able to make responsible sexual decisions:

➤ Having strong relationships with your parents or guardians suggests that you feel loved and that you care about what they think. In this way, they have already equipped you with the ability to think about the ways your actions affect your family.

➤ Participating in extra-curricular activities requires you to make a commitment to yourself and to a group. This can indicate that you have goals for the future and clear priorities.

➤ Having accurate sexual health information is essential to making decisions that have healthy, positive outcomes. If you do not know the risks and benefits that your choices bring, then you won't have much on which to base a decision. Sexuality education is all about giving you the facts you need in order to make responsible, fully-informed choices.

## Factors Affecting Sexual Decision Making

- Increased sex hormones after puberty
- Your age
- The quality of your relationship
- Parents, siblings, teachers
- Personality
- Culture, ethnicity
- Friends and peers
- Self-esteem
- Religious or spiritual beliefs
- Sexual experiences
- Personal sense of morality
- Knowledge about sexuality
- Health factors
- Plans for the future
- Legal concerns: whether or not your actions break the law
- Love
- Seeking physical and/or emotional closeness with another person
- Curiosity about sex
- Sense of loyalty in a relationship
- Pressure to conform to the media's definitions of sexuality
- Attempting to gain status (popularity or socio-economic)
- Rebelling against parents
- Drugs and/or alcohol

# It's Okay to Wait ...
## Sexuality and You

Pressure to have sex (or not to have sex) comes from all directions—the media, friends, family, religious and community leaders, and partners. You will need to sift through all these influences carefully, weigh them against your beliefs, and discuss your choices with those closest to you, before making such an important decision for yourself.

### What's the Rush?

Certainly, if you are thinking about having sex, especially for the first time, or even of increasing your level of intimacy with a partner, you should ask yourself why you want to take such a big step, and why now.

Are you trying to fit in with a group? Are you trying to make someone else happy? Is your partner pressuring you? These reasons may lead you to regret your decision in the future.

In situations such as this, it doesn't really matter what your friends are doing—you have to make your own decisions based on your own values. Making decisions for yourself is a sign of maturity; sexual activity is not.

Remember, it's always okay to wait, since what you choose can affect the way you live your life, how you feel about yourself, and what options are available to you in the future.

### Reasons to Wait

The following are some perfectly legitimate reasons why many people decide to wait:

- Religious beliefs about the nature of marriage and sexuality (no sex before marriage)
- Wanting to avoid a bad reputation
- Concerns about pregnancy
- Concerns about disease
- Lack of trust in your partner or the relationship
- Waiting for the right person
- Feeling somehow that you are not really old enough
- Simply not feeling ready

You will need to think about all your feelings, your personal reasons to wait, and the potential consequences of your decision before making your choice.

Make sure your decision is right for you.

# Understanding the Health Risks

Close, intimate relationships are, quite simply, a natural part of being human. Most people look forward to sharing close relationships in their lifetime. There is nothing scary about close relationships—they are to be cherished, perhaps above all else.

Sexual health education is about giving you the information you need in order to understand the possible consequences of your actions, so that you can make responsible choices, when you are ready. This includes telling you about the inherent risks in sexual activity.

We have already examined some of the components of healthy relationships. The remainder of this chapter surveys the potential physical health risks associated with sexual intercourse and other kinds of intimate sexual relations.

## Watching Out for Yourself

In matters pertaining to sex, you need to be alert and smart. You need to understand, weigh, and make decisions based on the potential risks, just as you do in many other aspects of your life. You need to know what you want, and where your limits are—preferably before you are faced with a decision.

Sexual activity carries the possibility of several serious health risks:

➢ Sexually transmitted infections (STIs), including HIV/AIDS

➢ Becoming a parent when you are not yet prepared or able to be one

Either of these outcomes will influence the choices that will be available to you for the rest of your life:

➢ If you contract an STI, you will require medical treatment. Some infections cannot be cured. Some have other unpleasant consequences.

➢ If you become a parent before you are ready to, you will face some very difficult choices. Taking care of a child places many demands on a parent, and you may find that your desired career or other plans for the future are more difficult to arrange.

As you begin to think about sexual intimacy, keep in mind the choices you want to have available to you in the future. Consider the positive and negative consequences in the table on the facing page. How do these apply to you and to your life?

Becoming a teenage parent or contracting an infection may affect the choices that are available to you throughout the rest of your life. Making sure you know everything you need to know to take care of yourself and your partner, and waiting until you feel ready for a specific activity, or a specific set of possible consequences, is never a bad idea.

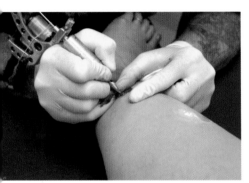

Genital herpes is a very common sexually transmitted infection caused by a virus.

Did you know that getting a tattoo or piercing can put you at risk for acquiring HIV or hepatitis?

# Abstinence

Most people will have some sexual contact at some point in their lives. Therefore, it is important to know how best to avoid becoming a parent before you are ready to, or contracting an infection. Although abstinence is the only sure way to avoid pregnancy or infection, you should be aware of what other methods and precautions exist, as well as the risks that they may pose.

**Abstinence** from sexual activity means refraining from any form of sexual activity that could result in pregnancy or the transmission of an STI, including all forms of intercourse. Generally, when couples are abstinent, they may hug, kiss, and cuddle but avoid more intimate sexual activities that could involve the transfer of bodily fluids.

Abstinence, when practised correctly, offers the best protection against STIs, HIV/AIDS, and 100-percent protection against unwanted pregnancy. Although some STIs (such as HIV/AIDS and herpes) can be spread by other means, young people who practise abstinence, and who generally live healthy lives, should be safe from infections.

Because it is the only sure-fire way of avoiding both infection and unplanned pregnancy, many young people choose abstinence. For some, it may not always be an easy choice, but it is the most effective way to avoid many of the negative consequences associated with sexual activity.

Make sure you know and understand the risks associated with sexual activity.

## CONSEQUENCES OF SEXUAL DECISION MAKING

| Possible Desirable Consequences | Possible Undesirable Consequences |
| --- | --- |
| Feelings of responsibility and pride | Unplanned pregnancy |
| Maintaining parental trust | Sexually transmitted infections |
| Avoidance of pregnancy | Increased stress and worry |
| Avoidance of sexually transmitted infections | Feeling badly about yourself |
| Maintaining moral convictions | Unhappiness about your reputation among your peers |
| Positive self-esteem | Conflict with partner |
| Self-respect | Pressure from partner |
| Happiness about your decisions | Loss of partner |
| Developing good communication skills and habits | Parents not agreeing with your choices; loss of parental trust |
| | Regret |

# Knowing the Options

Since physical intimacy can be an important part of close relationships (and because it can be difficult to make decisions on the spot), it's a good idea to consider what you are willing to do before it is an issue. Values and long-term goals will influence your choices.

You should also consider what health risks may be associated with any sexual activity. Some couples may choose to engage in less risky sexual activities, and avoid any form of intercourse. Sex education specialists often call this "outercourse." Of course, "outercourse" activities carry greater risks than abstinence because they may result in the inadvertent transfer of bodily fluids or infections.

When deciding what activities you are comfortable with, be aware that the more intimate the physical contact the more aroused participants are likely to become, increasing the risk of going beyond the limits they have set for themselves.

## Contraceptive Methods and Barriers Against Disease

Some methods of contraception, such as condoms, offer protection against HIV/AIDS and other STIs. Most protect only against unplanned pregnancy, either by blocking the sperm from reaching the egg or by preventing ovulation. No method of contraception is 100 percent effective in preventing pregnancy or infection; but they can significantly reduce the risks associated with sexual activity.

Condoms for males or females are widely available without prescription. They physically block the exchange of bodily fluids during sexual contact. Used correctly, condoms have a high success rate in both preventing pregnancy and in blocking the transmission of infections including HIV/AIDS.

Dental dams are latex barriers used during oral sex to prevent the spread of STIs (such as herpes, genital warts, or HIV).

## Hormonal Methods of Contraception

Hormonal methods, such as the Pill, the Patch, or contraceptive injections, work by preventing ovulation—if a woman does not ovulate, she cannot become pregnant. To obtain any of these contraceptives, you must visit your doctor to have a physical examination and obtain a prescription.

These methods need to be used correctly. The risk of pregnancy increases if a woman fails to follow her doctor's instructions, or if she takes medication that can interfere with the form of contraception (such as antibiotics). In addition, they provide no protection against infection, and can have side-effects. At the moment, birth control pills for men are not available. Anyone considering hormonal contraception should discuss the decision with a doctor. Taken properly, with a doctor's prescription, these methods can work effectively to prevent conception and help to regulate an irregular menstrual cycle.

## Stepping Back

At some point in our lives, we all make decisions we regret. We can always decide to stop doing something if the behaviour makes us unhappy. It is possible to decide to stop smoking or to stop eating french fries for lunch, and benefit from a healthier choice.

Similarly, it is possible to decide to step back from a sexual decision, and benefit from a choice that works better for you.

You may change or re-evaluate your personal boundaries. You may decide to re-affirm abstinence either within your current relationship or as a fresh start with a new partner. Your partner should respect whatever choice you make.

The important thing is to be honest with yourself and your partner about how you feel and what you need in order to feel good about yourself.

## Natural Methods of Contraception

Some women and couples choose to practise "natural" (non-mechanical, non-hormonal) methods of birth control or "fertility awareness." The most effective methods, the Billings method and the Sympto-thermal method, require a women to pay attention to the symptoms that indicate ovulation, such as body temperature and amount of cervical mucous. Couples avoid sexual intercourse on days on which an egg is available to be fertilized.

➢ Neither method is recommended for a young woman whose reproductive system has not fully matured. Her ovulation cycles will not be regular enough to predict when she is likely to be fertile.

➢ Neither method is recommended outside of a long-term relationship in which partners are committed to each other and accept the possibility that an error may result in a pregnancy.

➢ Neither method protects against STIs and both require a great deal of care, attention, and discipline from both partners.

When practised correctly by an adult couple who have been properly trained, these techniques can be effective in both avoiding unplanned pregnancy and in conceiving a child when the time is right.

Fertility awareness can be effective in both preventing pregnancy and helping couples to conceive, when practised by a couple who are committed and properly trained.

## Just the Facts
### Myth Busting

There's a great deal of inaccurate information about contraception—some is outdated and some of it is simply wishful thinking.

Here are a few facts so that you will know the myths when you see them:

• **FACT:** A woman can get pregnant the first time she has intercourse.

• **FACT:** "Pulling out" (withdrawing the penis prior to ejaculation) is not an effective way to prevent pregnancy or infection, as some semen is present prior to ejaculation.

• **FACT:** Vaginal cleansing (douching) after intercourse will not prevent pregnancy or infection, no matter what a woman uses to douche.

• **FACT:** Spermicidal lubricants will help reduce the risk of pregnancy; however, they do not prevent the transmission of HIV/AIDS.

• **FACT:** The birth control pill does not protect against sexually transmitted infections.

• **FACT:** Having sex standing up, or jumping up and down after sex, does not prevent pregnancy.

• **FACT:** Women ovulate at different times during their menstrual cycle. For many young women, the time of ovulation will fluctuate.

• **FACT:** Anyone can get HIV/AIDS, no matter his or her race, gender, or sexual orientation.

• **FACT:** Sexually transmitted infections can be transmitted during oral sex.

• **FACT:** At this point, there is no vaccine or cure for HIV/AIDS.

• **FACT:** Loving someone and being ready to have sex with them are two different things. If someone you love is pressuring you to have sex, and possibly even threatening to dump you if you don't, it says a great deal about his or her feelings for you.

# Think First—Sexually Transmitted Infections (STIs)

Sexually transmitted infections (STIs) are exactly what the name suggests—infections caused by bacteria, viruses, or parasites, which are transmitted through semen, vaginal fluid, blood, or other body fluids during sexual activity.

The term STI is now commonly used instead of STD (sexually transmitted disease) because it is more precise and covers a broader range of conditions. STI includes infections that may be "asymptomatic" (may not have any recognizable symptoms).

Some STIs have fairly minor consequences, such as itching, rashes, or sores. Many can be easily treated and have few lasting consequences if they are treated early. Other infections, however, can lead to serious health consequences. Some, such as HIV and herpes, cannot be cured, although many researchers are working to find effective treatments.

## How STIs Are Spread

Sexually transmitted infections can be spread in several different ways, not always involving direct sexual contact:

> STIs are usually spread through sexual contact or intercourse because the bacteria or viruses travel in semen, vaginal fluids, and blood. Saliva (or spit) can spread some STIs if you have a tiny cut in or around your mouth, allowing the infection to enter the bloodstream.

> Infected blood (on needles and syringes, for example) can spread certain STIs.

> Infected women can pass some STIs to their babies during pregnancy, at childbirth, or during breastfeeding.

Many people who have been infected show no symptoms, and therefore may not know they are infected. When symptoms do appear, they can show up in different ways—some symptoms are more severe than others.

The only sure way to avoid contracting an STI is to avoid risky behaviour. Condoms and dental dams reduce the risk of exposure to infections, but they do not ensure protection.

## Getting Tested

Learning about the signs and symptoms is helpful so that you can get medical treatment quickly. Since some sexually transmitted infections do not have symptoms, it is important to get tested regularly if you become sexually active.

Untreated STIs can cause serious health problems for both sexes, so it is important to get tested and treated early.

---

## How Will I Know?

Some people with an STI have few or no symptoms at all; others have very obvious symptoms. Be aware of any changes in your health, or symptoms such as:

- Different or heavier discharge from the vagina
- Discharge from the penis
- A burning feeling when urinating
- Sores, particularly in the genital or anal areas
- Itchy feeling around the sex organs or anus
- Appearance of a rash
- Swollen glands in the groin

These symptoms might appear alone, or in combination.

Since many STIs do not cause obvious symptoms, anyone who has had any sexual contact, or who might have come into contact with an infection (for example, by getting a tattoo or piercing from an unsterile needle) should be tested regularly for STIs.

## Getting Treatment

Because each STI is caused by a different microorganism (bacterial or viral), different tests are needed to determine the precise infection. Some infections can be completely cured with medication, while others can only be controlled—medication can reduce the effects of the symptoms, but will not make the disease go away.

➤ Bacterial infections, such as chlamydia, gonorrhea, and syphilis, can be cured using various antibiotics, but will require different types of medication; that is, no single drug is effective against all bacteria. Furthermore, some bacteria now show resistance to standard treatments.

➤ Viral infections, such as hepatitis B, genital herpes, genital warts, and HIV/AIDS, often do not have a cure; however, treatment may be available to reduce the symptoms.

If you think you may be infected, talk to your doctor, visit a clinic, or contact the local public health department. You owe it to yourself and your partner. All the information you give will be kept private.

To find a clinic, check your telephone book under "Sexual Health" in the white pages or under "Health" in the blue pages.

If you are sexually active, get tested for STIs. Allowing them to go untreated can lead to serious health problems.

See your doctor or visit a clinic if you have any concerns about your sexual health.

| NAME | HOW IT IS TRANSMITTED | SYMPTOMS | TREATMENT |
|---|---|---|---|
| **Chlamydia** | • unprotected sex*<br>• mother to infant at birth<br>• can be spread through hand to eye contact | • usually no symptoms<br>• genital discharge or inflammation<br>• pain during urination and/or intercourse<br>• pain in testicles or abdomen | • antibiotics (there are various antibiotic treatments; check with your doctor) |
| **Gonorrhea** ("the clap") | • unprotected sex*<br>• mother to infant at birth | • often no symptoms<br>• genital discharge<br>• pain during urination and/or intercourse<br>• pain in genitals or abdomen | • antibiotics prescribed by a doctor (those diagnosed are often treated for chlamydia at the same time) |
| **Herpes Simplex Virus (HSV)** (genital herpes) | • unprotected sex*<br>• direct contact with facial or genital sores (touching, kissing, skin-to-skin contact)<br>• mother to infant at birth | • usually no symptoms<br>• facial or genital sores, blisters<br>• flu-like symptoms including achiness, fever, and swollen glands<br>• pain during urination or inability to urinate | • there is no cure, but antivirals and topical creams can relieve symptoms<br>• in most cases, outbreaks become fewer and weaker over time |
| **Hepatitis B** | • unprotected sex*<br>• sharing items such as needles, razors, eating utensils, or toothbrushes<br>• mother to infant at birth | • close to half of those infected show no symptoms<br>• flu-like symptoms (abdominal pain, fatigue)<br>• darkened urine<br>• yellowed skin | • preventative vaccine<br>• there is no cure, but there are treatments that can prevent infection and, in some cases, it disappears on its own |

* Unprotected sex includes all forms of intercourse (vaginal, oral, and anal).

| NAME | HOW IT IS TRANSMITTED | SYMPTOMS | TREATMENT |
|---|---|---|---|
| **Syphilis** ("Miss Siff," "Pox," "Great Pox") | • unprotected sex* <br> • direct contact with sores/kissing <br> • mother to infant before birth | • Stage 1: small red bumps, liquid in genital area (chancres) <br> • Stage 2: rash, flu-like symptoms, hair loss, genital growths | • antibiotics, but only if it is caught early <br> • if not treated early, medication cannot repair damage already done |
| **Human Papiloma Virus (HPV)** (genital warts) | • unprotected sex* <br> • skin-to-skin contact | • usually no symptoms <br> • genital warts <br> • some links to cervical cancer | • there is no cure <br> • warts can be removed but the virus stays in the body |
| **Trichomonas** (trich) | • unprotected sex* or sexual contact | • vaginal discharge and odour <br> • pain or itching (during urination) <br> • spotty bleeding, frequent urination | • antibiotics for infected person and his or her partner(s) |
| **Human Immunodeficiency Virus (HIV) and Acquired Immune Deficiency Syndrome (AIDS)** | • unprotected sex* or exchange of fluids (blood/semen/vaginal fluids/breast milk) <br> • sharing needles <br> • mother to infant at birth | • often none <br> • weight loss, fatigue, flu symptoms | • no cure, but medication may slow progress from HIV to AIDS |
| **Pubic Lice** ("crabs") | • sexual contact <br> • contact with infected items (linens, towels, clothes) | • itching or irritation around genitals (or infested area) <br> • greyish coloured rash | • lice killed with a special shampoo <br> • eggs must be removed by shaving pubic hair or with a fine-toothed comb |

# HIV/AIDS

**Human Immunodeficiency Virus (HIV)** is an STI that can be transmitted through the exchange of bodily fluids passed through mucous membranes during sex, or by other means, such as intravenous drug use and blood transfusions.

Over time, HIV can lead to **Acquired Immune Deficiency Syndrome (AIDS)**. AIDS occurs when a person's immune system has become so weak that it can no longer successfully fight off infection. People who have AIDS do not normally die from it. Instead, their immune systems will be so damaged because of AIDS that another illness, even something very common like a cold, may kill them.

## What You Need To Know About HIV/AIDS

Although HIV starts growing in the body fairly quickly, the virus can live in a person's body for ten years or longer before any signs of it appear. However, some people develop symptoms within months of contracting HIV. There is no sure way of knowing whether someone has contracted HIV without a blood test.

For infection to occur, HIV has to pass from the body fluids of an infected person to the body fluids of another person. The fluids that have been shown to contain HIV are blood, semen, vaginal fluids, breast milk, and any other body fluids containing blood.

Most people who contract HIV do so during sexual activity or by sharing needles used to inject drugs. However, these do not represent the only methods of transmission. A mother can pass the infection to her baby in the womb, during childbirth, or through breastfeeding. HIV can also be transmitted by infected blood products to recipients of blood transfusions or organs.

You cannot tell if people have HIV/AIDS by looking at them or by talking with them. If the person you are sexually intimate with has ever had sexual contact with another person, your partner could be carrying the virus. Since HIV/AIDS may exist in the body without any symptoms for years, it is important that anyone who might have come into contact with the virus (through sexual activity, sharing needles, piercings, or any other activity in which blood, semen, or mucous passed from one person to another) get tested.

The initial symptoms of HIV infection, for both women and men, feel like the flu. They can include fever, diarrhea, weight loss, dry cough, and swollen glands. For this reason, most people fail to recognize them as a sign of something more serious. Over time, the symptoms become more severe and can include night sweats, rapid and unexplained weight loss, extreme fatigue, persistent dry cough, pneumonia, and purple blotches on the skin.

Many advances have been made in the treatment and management of this disease. While there is no cure for HIV/AIDS, people infected with HIV are now living longer active and fulfilling lives.

## HIV/AIDS in Canada

It is estimated that close to 15,000 Canadians have HIV/AIDS but do not know it. That's about one-quarter of the estimated 58,000 Canadians living with the virus at the end of 2005.

More Canadian women are being diagnosed with HIV and AIDS than in the past. Women accounted for an estimated 27 percent of all new infections in 2005. Twenty percent of HIV/AIDS patients are now women.

Native people are also over-represented in the epidemic, being almost three times more likely than other Canadians to be infected.

The number of Canadians living with HIV infection will likely continue to increase in the years to come as more people become infected and survival rates improve.

### Living with HIV in Canada

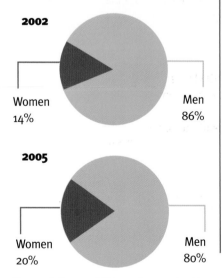

**2002**

Women
14%

Men
86%

**2005**

Women
20%

Men
80%

**Source:** *Estimates of HIV Prevalence and Incidence in Canada*, 2005. Public Health Agency of Canada, News Release, July 31, 2006.

# The Global HIV/AIDS Pandemic
## A Health Risk for Us All

Since 1981, the World Health Organization estimates that HIV/AIDS has killed more than 25 million people worldwide.

First identified in 1981, HIV/AIDS was originally thought to affect only gay men. However, by 1982, the medical community realized that nearly half of the people who were diagnosed with the condition were not homosexual. Like any virus, it affects people who come into contact with it, without any regard for sexuality, gender, age, or lifestyle.

### The Death Toll in Sub-Saharan Africa

HIV/AIDS can be contracted by anyone, regardless of where they live or whether they are rich or poor. People who live in what is known as sub-Saharan Africa have been hit particularly hard.

An estimated 2.7 million adults and children in the region became infected with HIV during 2005. This brought the total number living with HIV/AIDS in the region to 24.5 million.

While the virus does not discriminate, extreme poverty, lack of access to sexual health education and medical facilities, war, and sexual violence have all contributed to the spread of the disease among the very poorest people in Africa. HIV/AIDS has affected African women and mothers such that, by 2010, there will be 71 million fewer people on the continent.

### A Worldwide Problem

While HIV/AIDS has certainly hit Africa the hardest, it is on the rise in other parts of the world as well and has become a worldwide pandemic, taking an immense toll on people around the world:

- According to estimates from the UNAIDS/WHO Global Report (May 2006), around 36.3 million adults and 2.3 million children were living with HIV at the end of 2005.

- During 2005, some 4.1 million people became infected with HIV.

- That year also saw 2.8 million deaths from AIDS—a high global total—despite the development of antiretroviral (ARV) therapy, which helps people who have access to the drugs avoid viruses.

- By the end of 2005, the epidemic had left behind 15.2 million AIDS orphans—children aged 18 and under who have lost one or both parents to AIDS.

- It is estimated that 1.3 million people are living with HIV in North America and 720,000 in Western and Central Europe.

You can read more about the worldwide HIV/AIDS pandemic at **www.unaids.org**.

---

### Myths and Facts about HIV/AIDS

- **MYTH**: HIV and AIDS are the same thing.
  **FACT**: HIV is the virus that causes AIDS. AIDS is a collection of medical conditions to which people who have HIV are vulnerable. A person can have HIV, but not AIDS.

- **MYTH**: HIV only affects gay men and drug users.
  **FACT**: HIV is a virus. It does not care about the practices, sex, sexual orientation, or drug use of the people it infects. It can affect anyone who comes into contact with blood, semen, or other body fluids that carry the virus.

- **MYTH**: People diagnosed with HIV die quickly.
  **FACT**: Before doctors knew how to treat HIV/AIDS, many people diagnosed with the disease did not live very long. While nobody has found a cure for HIV/AIDS, people who are now diagnosed with the virus can receive drugs and medical treatment, and live out a reasonable lifespan, in a healthy, productive way.

- **MYTH**: You can get HIV/AIDS by kissing, shaking hands with, or sharing a toilet with a person infected with HIV/AIDS.
  **FACT**: HIV can only be spread if the blood or semen of an infected person comes into contact with the blood or semen of another person. Casual contact, such as hugging, kissing, and shaking hands will not transmit the virus. For the same reason, you cannot contract the disease simply by sharing a toilet.

- **MYTH**: A specific diet (such as eating a lot of garlic) or medicine (such as a herbal remedy) will cure HIV/AIDS.
  **FACT**: While medications can control the progress of HIV, nobody has been successful in finding a cure for the virus. At this point in time, once a person is infected with HIV, he or she will carry the virus for the rest of his or her life, regardless of diet.

# A global view
## 39 million people

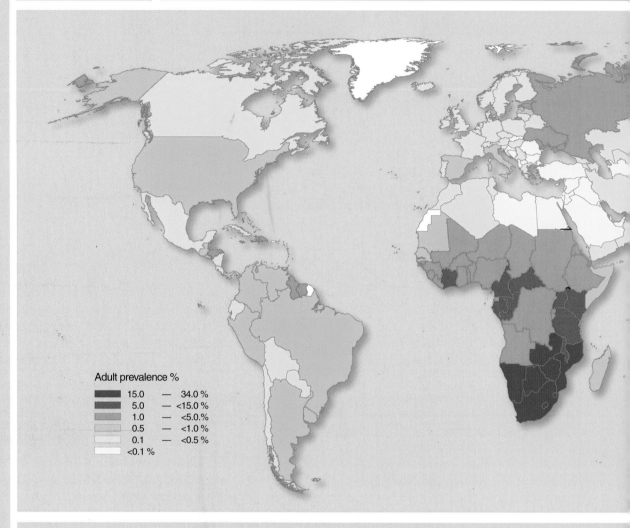

Adult prevalence %

- 15.0 — 34.0 %
- 5.0 — <15.0 %
- 1.0 — <5.0.%
- 0.5 — <1.0 %
- 0.1 — <0.5 %
- <0.1 %

**1990**

Adult prevalence %
- 2.0 — 5.0 %
- 1.0 — <2.0 %
- 0.5 — <1.0.%
- 0.1 — <0.5 %
- <0.1 %

**1995**

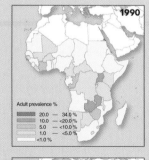

**1990**

Adult prevalence %
- 20.0 — 34.0 %
- 10.0 — <20.0 %
- 5.0 — <10.0 %
- 1.0 — <5.0 %
- <1.0 %

**199**

**2000**

**2005**

**2000**

**200**

UNHCR  UNODC
UNICEF  ILO
WFP  UNESCO
UNDP  WHO
UNFPA  WORLD BANK

JOINT UNITED NATIONS PROGRAMME ON HIV/AIDS

## Estimated adult (15–49) HIV prevalence (%) for countries in 2005.

| Country/Region | Estimate | [low estimate–high estimate] |
|---|---|---|
| **Sub-Saharan Africa** | | |
| Angola | 3.7 | [2.3–5.3] |
| Benin | 1.8 | [1.2–2.5] |
| Botswana | 24.1 | [23.0–32.0] |
| Burkina Faso | 2.0 | [1.5–2.5] |
| Burundi | 3.3 | [2.7–3.8] |
| Cameroon | 5.4 | [4.9–5.9] |
| Central African Republic | 10.7 | [4.5–17.2] |
| Chad | 3.5 | [1.7–6.0] |
| Comoros | <0.1 | [<0.2] |
| Congo | 5.3 | [3.3–7.5] |
| Côte d'Ivoire | 7.1 | [4.3–9.7] |
| Democratic Republic of the Congo | 3.2 | [1.8–4.9] |
| Djibouti | 3.1 | [0.8–6.9] |
| Equatorial Guinea | 3.2 | [2.6–3.8] |
| Eritrea | 2.4 | [1.3–3.9] |
| Ethiopia [1] | ... | [0.9–3.5] |
| Gabon | 7.9 | [5.1–11.5] |
| Gambia | 2.4 | [1.2–4.1] |
| Ghana | 2.3 | [1.9–2.6] |
| Guinea | 1.5 | [1.2–1.8] |
| Guinea-Bissau | 3.8 | [2.1–6.0] |
| Kenya | 6.1 | [5.2–7.0] |
| Lesotho | 23.2 | [21.9–24.7] |
| Liberia | ... | [2.0–5.0] |
| Madagascar | 0.5 | [0.2–1.2] |
| Malawi | 14.1 | [6.9–21.4] |
| Mali | 1.7 | [1.3–2.1] |
| Mauritania | 0.7 | [0.4–2.8] |
| Mauritius | 0.6 | [0.3–1.8] |
| Mozambique | 16.1 | [12.5–20.0] |
| Namibia | 19.6 | [8.6–31.7] |
| Niger | 1.1 | [0.5–1.9] |
| Nigeria | 3.9 | [2.3–5.6] |
| Rwanda | 3.1 | [2.9–3.2] |
| Senegal | 0.9 | [0.4–1.5] |
| Sierra Leone | 1.6 | [0.9–2.4] |
| Somalia | 0.9 | [0.5–1.6] |
| South Africa | 18.8 | [16.8–20.7] |
| Swaziland | 33.4 | [21.2–45.3] |
| Togo | 3.2 | [1.9–4.7] |
| Uganda | 6.7 | [5.7–7.6] |
| United Republic of Tanzania | 6.5 | [5.8–7.2] |
| Zambia | 17.0 | [15.9–18.1] |
| Zimbabwe | 20.1 | [13.3–27.6] |
| **East Asia** | | |
| China | 0.1 | [<0.2] |
| Democratic People's Republic of Korea | ... | [<0.2] |
| Japan | <0.1 | [<0.2] |
| Mongolia | <0.1 | [<0.2] |
| Republic of Korea | <0.1 | [<0.2] |
| **Oceania** | | |
| Australia | 0.1 | [<0.2] |
| Fiji | 0.1 | [0.1–0.4] |
| New Zealand | 0.1 | [<0.2] |
| Papua New Guinea | 1.8 | [0.9–4.4] |
| **South and South-East Asia** | | |
| Afghanistan | <0.1 | [<0.2] |
| Bangladesh | <0.1 | [<0.2] |
| Bhutan | <0.1 | [<0.2] |
| Brunei Darussalam | <0.1 | [<0.2] |
| Cambodia | 1.6 | [0.9–2.6] |
| India | 0.9 | [0.5–1.5] |
| Indonesia | 0.1 | [0.1–0.2] |
| Iran (Islamic Republic of) | 0.2 | [0.1–0.4] |
| Lao People's Democratic Republic | 0.1 | [0.1–0.4] |
| Malaysia | 0.5 | [0.2–1.5] |
| Maldives | ... | [<0.2] |
| Myanmar | 1.3 | [0.7–2.0] |
| Nepal | 0.5 | [0.3–1.3] |
| Pakistan | 0.1 | [0.1–0.2] |
| Philippines | <0.1 | [<0.2] |
| Singapore | 0.3 | [0.2–0.7] |
| Sri Lanka | <0.1 | [<0.2] |
| Thailand | 1.4 | [0.7–2.1] |
| Timor-Leste | ... | [<0.2] |
| Viet Nam | 0.5 | [0.3–0.9] |
| **Eastern Europe and Central Asia** | | |
| Armenia | 0.1 | [0.1–0.6] |
| Azerbaijan | 0.1 | [0.1–0.4] |
| Belarus | 0.3 | [0.2–0.8] |
| Bosnia and Herzegovina | <0.1 | [<0.2] |
| Bulgaria | <0.1 | [<0.2] |
| Croatia | <0.1 | [<0.2] |
| Estonia | 1.3 | [0.6–4.3] |
| Georgia | 0.2 | [0.1–2.7] |
| Kazakhstan | 0.1 | [0.1–3.2] |
| Kyrgyzstan | 0.1 | [0.1–1.7] |
| Latvia | 0.8 | [0.5–1.3] |

| Country/Region | Estimate | [low estimate–high estimate] |
|---|---|---|
| Lithuania | 0.2 | [0.1–0.6] |
| Republic of Moldova | 1.1 | [0.6–2.6] |
| Romania | <0.1 | [<0.2] |
| Russian Federation | 1.1 | [0.7–1.8] |
| Tajikistan | 0.1 | [0.1–0.7] |
| Turkmenistan | <0.1 | [<0.2] |
| Ukraine | 1.4 | [0.8–4.3] |
| Uzbekistan | 0.2 | [0.1–0.7] |
| **Western and Central Europe** | | |
| Albania | ... | [<0.2] |
| Austria | 0.3 | [0.2–0.5] |
| Belgium | 0.3 | [0.2–0.5] |
| Czech Republic | 0.1 | [<0.2] |
| Denmark | 0.2 | [0.1–0.4] |
| Finland | 0.1 | [<0.2] |
| France | 0.4 | [0.3–0.8] |
| Germany | 0.1 | [0.1–0.2] |
| Greece | 0.2 | [0.1–0.3] |
| Hungary | 0.1 | [<0.2] |
| Iceland | 0.2 | [0.1–0.3] |
| Ireland | 0.2 | [0.1–0.4] |
| Italy | 0.5 | [0.3–0.9] |
| Luxembourg | 0.2 | [0.1–0.4] |
| Malta | 0.1 | [0.1–0.2] |
| Netherlands | 0.2 | [0.1–0.4] |
| Norway | 0.1 | [0.1–0.2] |
| Poland | 0.1 | [0.1–0.2] |
| Portugal | 0.4 | [0.3–0.9] |
| Serbia and Montenegro | 0.2 | [0.1–0.3] |
| Slovakia | <0.1 | [<0.2] |
| Slovenia | <0.1 | [<0.2] |
| Spain | 0.6 | [0.4–1.0] |
| Sweden | 0.2 | [0.1–0.3] |
| Switzerland | | |
| The former Yugoslav Republic of Macedonia | <0.1 | [<0.2] |
| United Kingdom of Great Britain and Northern Ireland [2] | 0.2 | [0.1–0.4] |
| **North Africa and Middle East** | | |
| Algeria | 0.1 | [<0.2] |
| Bahrain | ... | [<0.2] |
| Cyprus | ... | [<0.2] |
| Egypt | <0.1 | [<0.2] |
| Iraq | ... | [<0.2] |
| Israel | ... | [<0.2] |
| Jordan | ... | [<0.2] |
| Kuwait | ... | [<0.2] |
| Lebanon | 0.1 | [0.1–0.5] |
| Libyan Arab Jamahiriya | ... | [<0.2] |
| Morocco | 0.1 | [0.1–0.4] |
| Oman | ... | [<0.2] |
| Qatar | ... | [<0.2] |
| Saudi Arabia | ... | [<0.2] |
| Sudan | 1.6 | [0.8–2.7] |
| Syria Arab Republic | ... | [<0.2] |
| Tunisia | 0.1 | [0.1–0.3] |
| Turkey | ... | [<0.2] |
| United Arab Emirates | ... | [<0.2] |
| Yemen | ... | [<0.2] |
| **North America** | | |
| Canada [3] | 0.3 | [0.2–0.5] |
| United States of America | 0.6 | [0.4–1.0] |
| **Caribbean** | | |
| Bahamas | 3.3 | [1.3–4.5] |
| Barbados | 1.5 | [0.8–2.5] |
| Cuba | 0.1 | [<0.2] |
| Dominican Republic | 1.1 | [0.9–1.3] |
| Haiti | 3.8 | [2.2–5.4] |
| Jamaica | 1.5 | [0.8–2.4] |
| Trinidad and Tobago | 2.6 | [1.4–2.4] |
| **Latin America** | | |
| Argentina | 0.6 | [0.3–1.9] |
| Belize | 2.5 | [1.4–4.0] |
| Bolivia | 0.1 | [0.1–0.3] |
| Brazil | 0.5 | [0.3–1.6] |
| Chile | 0.3 | [0.2–1.2] |
| Colombia | 0.6 | [0.3–2.5] |
| Costa Rica | 0.3 | [0.1–3.6] |
| Ecuador | 0.3 | [0.1–3.5] |
| El Salvador | 0.9 | [0.5–3.8] |
| Guatemala | 0.9 | [0.5–2.7] |
| Guyana | 2.4 | [1.0–4.9] |
| Honduras | 1.5 | [0.8–2.4] |
| Mexico | 0.3 | [0.2–0.7] |
| Nicaragua | 0.2 | [0.1–0.6] |
| Panama | 0.9 | [0.5–3.7] |
| Paraguay | 0.4 | [0.2–4.6] |
| Peru | 0.6 | [0.3–1.7] |
| Suriname | 1.9 | [1.1–3.1] |
| Uruguay | 0.5 | [0.2–6.1] |
| Venezuela | 0.7 | [0.3–8.9] |

To calculate the adult HIV prevalence rate, the estimated number of adults (15–49) living with HIV in 2005 was divided by the 2005 population (aged 15–49).

Depending on the reliability of the data available, there is more or less certainty surrounding any one estimate. Therefore we present ranges, called 'plausibility bounds' around the estimates. The wider the bound, the more uncertainty there is surrounding the country's estimate. The extent of uncertainty depends mainly on the type of epidemic, and the quality, coverage and consistency of a country's surveillance system and in generalized epidemics, whether or not a population-based survey with HIV testing was conducted. A full description of the methods used to develop plausibility bounds can be found in Morgan M et al, Sexually Transmitted Infections, 2006, 82 (Suppl).

These estimates are the product of UNAIDS/WHO. The estimates have been shared with national AIDS programmes for review and comments, but are not necessarily the official estimates used by national governments.

The designations employed and the presentation of the material in this map, including tables and colouring of country areas, do not imply the expression of any opinion whatsoever on the part of UNAIDS or WHO concerning the legal status of any country, territory, city or area or of its authorities, or concerning the delimitation of its frontiers or boundaries.

1. Ethiopia: important new data from a national community-based survey and from rural surveillance sites had become available in Ethiopia. At the time when this report went to press, those new data had only partially been analysed. As a result, the estimates for Ethiopia in this report should be considered preliminary. UNAIDS and WHO will make new estimates, based on a comprehensive analysis of all data, available on their websites as soon as possible.
2. United Kingdom: These ad hoc preliminary estimates for 2005 are based upon the official UK estimates for 2004—the official estimates will be published in late 2006 once all the relevant surveillance data for 2005 have been analysed.
3. Canada: These are preliminary estimates. Final estimates for 2005 will be available in mid-2006.

1990

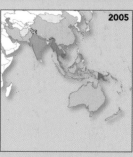

1995

2000

1995

2005

Prevalence %
| | | |
|---|---|---|
| 1.5 | — | 3.0 % |
| 1.0 | — | <1.5 % |
| 0.5 | — | <1.0 % |
| 0.1 | — | <0.5 % |
| <0.1 % | | |

World Health
Organization

Source: 2006 Report on the global AIDS epidemic, May 2006. UNAIDS.

# Values, Beliefs, and Decision Making

When deciding what sexual decisions are right for you, consider whether a choice will make you feel ashamed or that you have something to hide. If you feel that you have to lie about a decision, that is a pretty good indication that you should think twice about that course of action.

Since the choices you make about sexuality can have serious long-term consequences, it is important to think about them before you are "on the spot." If you decide that you are not ready for sexual involvement, this is probably a good time for you to examine your feelings, beliefs, and choices, so that you will have the information you need and a better idea of what you want.

Many teens look to their family and friends for advice about relationships and sexual decisions. Parents, siblings, or other relatives may play a role, as may other trusted adults—teachers, guidance counsellors, and religious or spiritual leaders. The views and experience of these people can help you shape your own choices as you think about the personal, social, and health consequences of each option.

## Think First—Pregnancy

The information presented in this unit is not intended to tell you what to do, but to encourage you to think for yourself on the basis of your own beliefs, good background knowledge, and firm facts. You need to know how to look after yourself—and the possible health consequences if you do not.

Most adolescents will tell you that they do not wish to have a child during their teenage years. Some are ensuring this cannot happen by choosing abstinence. Others use contraception to avoid pregnancy. If you are thinking about having sex and using birth control to prevent an unwanted pregnancy, be sure to learn about any possible side effects.

**Methods of contraception** (birth control) are designed to impede the union of the sperm and egg and prevent pregnancy. In order to make a thoughtful and mature decision, you need to know how each method works and the potential risks associated with each approach.

One of the key things to remember about any form of contraception is that its effectiveness depends on proper use. For example, if a woman forgets to take birth control pills in a given month, and has intercourse, her risk of pregnancy is significantly higher. If a condom tears or does not completely cover the penis, semen can leak into the vagina.

If you should choose to use a method of contraception, be sure that you know how to use it properly, and read all the packaging information. For more information, see Appendix 2 on pages 472–75.

## Teen Pregnancy

In 2003, the Canadian Council of Ministers of Education coordinated The Canadian Youth, Sexual Health and HIV/AIDS Study to examine what teens think and do when it comes to sex. The study gave some disturbing findings about teens and pregnancy:

- **Teen Mothers.** Over 42,000 young women (ages 15 to 19) become pregnant in Canada each year. For most of these young women, pregnancy will result in either abortion or single parenthood. 86 percent of teenaged mothers are single. Between 50 and 70 percent quit school and apply for social assistance. Teenagers are at greater risk for some health problems during pregnancy and after labour and birth.

- **Teen Fathers.** It is common for teen fathers to struggle with irregular school attendance, poor academic performance, and low aspirations, and to put goals on hold working in low-paying jobs to support their child(ren).

- **Teen Marriages.** Seventy-five percent of teen marriages end in divorce.

| **BIRTH CONTROL SUMMARY CHART** | |
|---|---|
| **ABSTINENCE** | Abstinence is choosing not to engage in any form of sexual intercourse. Some people choose this method because they do not want to have intercourse at this stage of their lives. Other reasons that people may choose abstinence may include cultural and religious beliefs. |
| **BARRIER METHODS**<br>• Male condom<br>• Female condom<br>• Diaphragm<br>• Cervical cap<br>• Spermicides (foam, film, and jelly)<br>• Vaginal sponge | Barriers can physically stop sperm from entering the uterus (such as a condom), or impede the egg from implanting in the uterus (such as the IUD). Chemical barriers, such as spermicidal foam, films, and jelly, kill sperm once they enter the vaginal canal. The vaginal sponge does both. |
| **HORMONAL METHODS**<br>• Birth-control pills<br>• Transdermal patch<br>• Vaginal ring<br>• Injectables | Hormones are taken either intravenously (injected with a needle), orally, or placed on the body and absorbed through the skin. These hormones are similar to the ones produced naturally in the women's body.<br><br>Some hormonal methods work by preventing the egg from being released from the ovaries (ovulation). Others affect the lining of the uterus (endometrium) making it difficult for the egg to implant itself in the uterus, and some cause changes in the cervical mucus so that sperm cannot easily pass through it. |
| **INTRAUTERINE METHODS**<br>• Intrauterine device (IUD)<br>• Intrauterine system (IUS) | There are two types of intrauterine methods, the IUD and IUS. Both are small, plastic devices that are inserted by a physician and remain inside the uterus for up to five years. The IUS has a copper wire coiled around the stem of its "t-shape" as well as hormones. Both methods rely on chemical reactions to inhibit pregnancy. |
| **NATURAL FAMILY PLANNING**<br>• Calendar<br>• Ovulation<br>• Sympto-thermal<br>• Post-ovulation | Natural family planning has been called "the rhythm method," "safe period," or "fertility awareness." It is not one method but rather a variety of them. Natural family planning methods rely heavily on the couple's knowledge of the women's menstrual cycle. Intercourse is avoided during the time of ovulation, when the woman is most fertile. |
| **STERILIZATION METHODS**<br>• Male sterilization (vasectomy)<br>• Female sterilization (tubal ligation) | Both of these methods involve some form of surgery. Vasectomy is reversible within a specific period of time after the initial surgery; for the most part, tubal ligation is irreversible. |
| **EMERGENCY**<br>• Emergency contraceptive pill (ECP) | The ECP delays or prevents ovulation with the use of hormones. It is not a form of birth control, but rather a last resort to prevent pregnancy. ECP will not terminate a pregnancy nor harm the fetus if you are pregnant. |

NOTE: For details on various contraception methods, see Appendix 2, pages 472–75.

This interview was conducted by Matthew Grier, a 16-year-old student at Glenforest Secondary School in Mississauga, Ontario. At the time of the interview, Alyson Beben was a Sexuality Education Specialist in Peel Region.

**Why did you choose to be a sex educator as a career?**

I became a Sexuality Education Specialist for two reasons. First, I wanted to help students become empowered to make good decisions regarding their sexual health and relationships. When I attended high school health classes, we barely talked about sexual health. Because many of us didn't talk with our parents about it either, we did not receive very much information about really important issues in sexual health.

Second, as a teacher, I realized that few of us received proper training to teach sexual health and that the resources available to us were often of poor quality and outdated. I hoped that by being a Sexuality Education Specialist, I could create curriculum documents that would be helpful to both teacher and students— educators could be more confident when teaching sexual education, and students could get the information they deserve.

**What are the responsibilities of a sex educator?**

This will depend on where you work. As a sexual health educator, you could work at a local health department, a college or university, a public or private clinic, or at a provincial or federal organization.

Most sex educators who work with health departments in Canada visit classrooms and teach sexuality to students directly. They work in co-operation with teachers to ensure that the health curriculum, which deals with puberty, sexuality, and relationships, is provided to students.

Other sex educators work with parents and teachers, helping them to build the skills to talk with kids about sex. They might write curriculum documents or parent guides and will likely run training sessions.

Some educators make presentations to students assemblies or to members of community groups. Others work one-on-one with university or college students or with clients in a clinic. There is no standard job description in this career— but that makes it interesting!

**What education do you need in order to work as a sex educator?**

People who are sexual health educators have various educational backgrounds. Some, like me, are teachers, so they have a Bachelor of Arts or Sciences and a Bachelor of Education. Some have a nursing degree, while others have a degree in social science or health science.

Though it may not be necessary in some regions of the country, most sexual health educators in Canada do have degrees from a university. In fact, many also hold Masters Degrees or PhDs. Every organization will decide what education is required for the position. When a position becomes available, these requirements will be posted on the job description.

**Why do you think it's important that people become sex educators?**

I believe that sexual health is an essential part of our overall well-being. In order for us to learn how to protect our sexual health, we need someone to teach us. This is why sexual health educators, of all kinds, are so important

When we are sexually healthy, we can have happy and rewarding personal relationships, great physical health, and feel good about ourselves and our choices.

## Questions for Study and Review

### Things to Think About and Explore

1. What do you think makes an intimate relationship healthy? Identify ten components of a healthy relationship that are important to you.

2. List three reasons why making responsible sexual decisions would benefit you and your health.

3. Outline all the ways sexually transmitted infections can be passed from person to person.

4. Choose five factors from the "Factors Affecting Sexual Decision Making" list on page 192 and describe why they are most important to you in your decision-making process.

5. Compare and contrast two different methods of contraception in terms of effectiveness, how they work, advantages, and disadvantages.

6. Investigate what is being done about the AIDS crisis in Africa and what implications it has for the worldwide AIDS situation.

### Things to Do and Practise

7. In a small group, discuss what could be done to educate Canadian teens and adults about the dangers of unprotected sexual activity. Describe some ways the media might be used to send more positive messages about sexuality and sex.

8. Write a two-minute speech explaining how self-esteem is related to sexual decision making. Be prepared to present in class.

9. Write a letter to someone who has influenced your sexual decision making. You can use a fictitious name and you don't have to send the letter; just use it to explain how this person has affected your decision.

10. Develop a poster that encourages teens to make responsible sexual decisions.

11. Write a script of a conversation between two partners—one who wants to have sexual intercourse now, and the other who wants to wait.

12. Discuss with your school principal and parent council about the possibility of having a community "teach-in" on the worldwide AIDS crisis—and offer to help your principal, teachers, parents, and staff to organize this community event.

### WWWeblinks

Name ➤ Sex Information and Education Council of Canada

URL ➤ www.sieccan.org

This site offers a number of resource documents put together by SIECCAN, a national non-profit organization that educates both the public and professionals about human sexuality.

Name ➤ Teen Health Website

URL ➤ www.chebucto.ns.ca/Health/TeenHealth/

A website, by an organization based in Nova Scotia, with good information on issues that affect teens, such as sexuality, drugs, and physical activity.

## Table of Contents

# UNIT 5
## Drug Use and Abuse

What this unit is about ...

➢ Why do some people use harmful drugs and what are the possible health consequences?

➢ What are the short- and long-term health effects of tobacco and alcohol on the body?

➢ What are the illegal drugs and what options are available for those who have become dependent on them?

# 13
# Types of Drugs and Their Effects

**L**ike most teens, you have probably heard a great deal about drugs. You have almost certainly heard that when drugs are overused or abused they can create serious problems for the user. You may think that you have already heard everything you need to hear about drugs, so why does everyone keep telling you about them?

> *In the course of history, many more people have died for their drink and their dope than have died for their religion or their country.*

**Aldous Huxley**

Author of *Brave New World*

**L**ike most teens, you have probably heard a great deal about drugs. You have almost certainly heard that when drugs are overused or abused they can create serious problems for the user. You may think that you have already heard everything you need to hear about drugs, so why does everyone keep telling you about them?

People keep telling you because they know that, as a teenager, you are more likely to confront decisions about alcohol, tobacco, and illegal drugs. In order to make safe, sensible decisions, you need to know as much as you can.

Drugs have been with us throughout history, and drug problems in our communities can be serious. Regardless of age, we all need to understand how we can prevent substance abuse in our own lives, in our families, and in our communities.

## Chapter Objectives

In this chapter, you will:

> Identify the main types of mood-altering drugs available in Canada today

> Investigate the "continuum of drug use" in the context of substance use and abuse

> Investigate reasons why drug use begins and why young people in particular may be at risk

> Identify the likely consequences of substance use and abuse

> Identify gambling as a separate but related dependence issue for Canadians

> Explore the main features of the Canadian government's policy for dealing with the widespread use of drugs

> Begin to understand the special problems associated with the lack of quality control with respect to illegal drugs

## Key Terms

> drugs
> psychoactive drugs
> marijuana (cannabis)
> hallucinogens
> depressants
> stimulants
> anabolic steroids
> continuum of drug use
> bingeing
> physical dependence
> psychological dependence
> Canada's drug policy

# What Are Drugs?

**Drugs** are substances, other than food, that affect a person's mental, emotional, or physical state. **Psychoactive drugs** (mood-altering drugs) affect our mental and emotional state.

A person who uses drugs is not usually trying to cause damage to his or her lungs, brain, or other vital organs. However, many drugs have harmful side effects, and such damage can occur.

## Making Decisions about Drugs

Legal and illegal mood-altering drugs are increasingly available in Canada, and the pressures to use such drugs are widespread. This is especially true for young people, who are experimenting with new levels of independence and responsibility, and who may experience pressure from friends, peers, the media, and other sources.

The same decision-making skills you use to make other health-conscious decisions can be applied to decisions about substances. All you need is good information. People with good information are more likely to make sound decisions, and they will pass this information on to their friends as well.

Young people often feel pressure from friends, peers, and the media to try drugs.

Psychoactive (mood-altering) drugs are those that affect a person's mental and emotional state.

# Types of Drugs

Mood-altering drugs affect the body's central nervous system (CNS), which sends information about what we are sensing or feeling to the body. We can classify mood-altering drugs according to the specific effects they have on our minds and bodies.

## Marijuana (Cannabis)

**Marijuana**, the most popular form of cannabis, is placed in a class of its own because it acts mostly as a hallucinogen, but also has depressant effects (it slows response time and affects memory) and a stimulant effect (it raises the heart rate). Common sources of cannabis are marijuana, hashish, hash oil, and tetrahydrocannabinol (THC).

## Hallucinogens

**Hallucinogens** alter users' perceptions of the world around them, causing distortions in the way they sense their surroundings. While overdoses are rare, these drugs can pose a risk of accidents and injuries because they distort what the user experiences. Users also may experience flashbacks later in life. Hallucinogens include LSD, psilocybin (magic mushrooms), mescaline, ecstasy, and peyote.

## Depressants

**Depressants** slow down the CNS and reduce inhibitions. Like stimulants, many depressants can be easy to obtain; however, this does not make them harmless. Examples of typical depressants are alcohol, solvents (for example, glue or gasoline); opiates (such as heroin); pain-killers; and tranquilizers and sleeping pills, including the "club drugs" GHB, and Rohypnol®.

## Stimulants

As the name implies, **stimulants** speed up body systems such as the CNS and the cardiorespiratory system, delay fatigue, and may produce hyperactivity. Some stimulants are prescribed for certain medical conditions. Common stimulants include nicotine, caffeine, diet pills, Ritalin, cocaine, crack, speed, methamphetamine, some of the so-called "club drugs," and other illegally manufactured amphetamine-type drugs.

## Anabolic Steroids

**Anabolic steroids** are commonly used to treat certain medical conditions. Non-medically, steroids can help increase training endurance and build muscles, and so people use them to enhance athletic performance and body image. They are a controlled substance; using them without a prescription is illegal. Anabolic steroid use is linked to a range of problems, both physical and psychological, which may continue even after a person stops using the steroids. Sports authorities worldwide ban the use of steroids as a form of cheating. For more information on steroids and their side effects, see pages 254–55.

---

## Risky Business

There are three main factors to keep in mind when considering the risk of using drugs: the drug itself, the user, and the context.

- **The drug.** The way a drug is prepared (for example, weak vs. strong dosage), the way it is used (swallowing, sniffing, inhaling, or injecting), and the actual amount of drug taken, all play a large role in determining risk level.

- **The user.** The physical traits of the person using the drug (such as weight, gender, metabolism, and state of health) can all play a role in determining risk levels. Risk also increases when a person drinks or uses drugs to cope with anger, stress, or sadness rather than to enhance an enjoyable situation.

- **The context.** The context is the setting or situation in which people use drugs. Certain contexts always pose a high risk and should be avoided: before driving a car, boat, ATV, or snowmobile, or using other machinery; before playing sports or doing other physical activity; before engaging in sexual activity (lack of inhibition may lead to unsafe practices); or when sick or using medication or other substances.

# The Continuum of Drug Use
## Weighing the Hazards of Substance Abuse

Using drugs for non-medical reasons almost always poses a degree of risk. Risk can range from very low to very high, and harm can occur even if it is your first time.

The continuum of drug use is a way of measuring your potential drug use and the risks associated with it.

### Levels of Use

There are different types or levels of drug use, and each of these has a certain level of risk that accompanies it:

- **Non-use.** It is estimated that about ⅓ of young Canadians choose not to use tobacco, alcohol, or any illegal substance. Non-use is the healthiest choice, because it involves zero risk.

- **Experimental use.** Experimental use occurs because of curiosity and may not occur again. The risk usually is low, but it depends on several factors: the drug taken, how it is taken, and how much of it is taken; the user's personality, mood, and expectations; and the surroundings. The risks can be higher for inexperienced users, who may accidentally take too much or not know how to handle the drug's effects.

- **Social use.** This is ongoing drug use with moderate consumption. The risk can be low to moderate depending on the particular drug and how it is used.

- **Binge use.** This is use of a large amount of a substance at one time. Even on a single occasion the risk of harm is high.

- **Frequent, heavy use.** This is ongoing drug use that leads to problems in one or more areas of a person's life (e.g., study, work, friendships, family relations). Risk of significant and lasting harm is high.

- **Dependent use.** This is compulsive and excessive drug use that continues despite problems in various life areas (for example, employment, relationships, etc.). Risk of significant and lasting harm is very high.

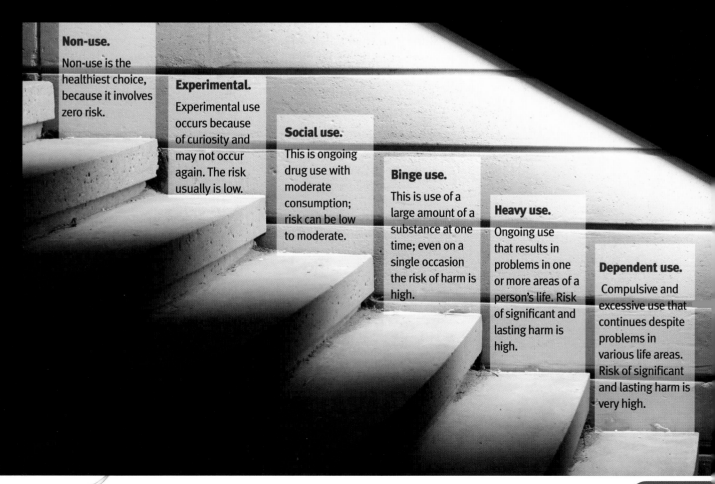

**Non-use.**
Non-use is the healthiest choice, because it involves zero risk.

**Experimental.**
Experimental use occurs because of curiosity and may not occur again. The risk usually is low.

**Social use.**
This is ongoing drug use with moderate consumption; risk can be low to moderate.

**Binge use.**
This is use of a large amount of a substance at one time; even on a single occasion the risk of harm is high.

**Heavy use.**
Ongoing use that results in problems in one or more areas of a person's life. Risk of significant and lasting harm is high.

**Dependent use.**
Compulsive and excessive use that continues despite problems in various life areas. Risk of significant and lasting harm is very high.

Often we hear rumours of celebrities using illegal substances. You may know some people who use drugs and don't seem to be harmed. Indeed, some drugs, such as alcohol, and tobacco, are legal for adults, therefore it's easy to wonder what the fuss is all about.

Society does not present a very consistent message about the risks of substance use and abuse. All drugs, including the readily available, socially acceptable ones, carry risks for users and abusers, but not all drugs carry the *same* risks.

## Safety Concerns

Most substances (e.g., alcohol, cannabis, amphetamines) affect the user's judgment and motor coordination. Intoxication can cause users to make unsafe choices. This makes any kind of physical activity, such as using equipment or machinery, or even playing sports, very dangerous.

## Long-Term Physical Health Problems

Introducing a foreign substance into the body on a regular basis may have long-term physical effects. The risks associated with some substances, such as tobacco, decrease greatly when a person stops using them. With other substances, such as methamphetamine, it is not clear whether the effects are reversible. With still other substances, such as anabolic steroids, some of the effects are clearly not reversible.

## Mental Health Problems

Casual use of some drugs such as amphetamines, ecstasy, and crystal meth can cause short-term anxiety and other negative feelings. Longer-term use can lead to more serious mental health problems. People with mental health problems often use substances to "self-medicate" their condition, but this is ultimately self-defeating because the highs and lows of intoxication will likely aggravate mental health problems.

## Cognitive Problems

Some substance use has a clear effect on the way users perceive and understand what is going on. For example, even short-term use of cannabis, cocaine, and ecstasy has been shown to impair short-term memory and the ability to concentrate. These effects can make it difficult for young people to develop a strong, positive identity, and to learn the coping skills they need.

## Violence and Crime

Many substances reduce inhibitions, give users a sense of self-confidence and invulnerability, and impair judgment. These effects can lead to violent behaviour. Alcohol has the strongest link with violent acts—an estimated 40–50 percent of the violent crimes committed by inmates in Canadian correctional facilities involved alcohol.

---

## Use and Abuse

**W**hat is the difference between drug use and drug abuse?

- If a person's substance use makes it difficult to carry on with the rest of his or her life, then that person is abusing the substance.

- If a person is using a substance in order to "cope" with other problems, such as stress, shyness, or pain, that person is abusing the substance.

- If a person is using a substance for a medical purpose without medical supervision, or in a way that doesn't match the prescription, that person is abusing the substance.

Many people consider any illegal drug use to be drug abuse.

## No Quality Control for Illegal Drugs

Although it is a serious criminal offense, new illegal drugs are constantly being developed. Many of the drugs currently available, such as crystal meth and MDMA (ecstasy), are manufactured in secret labs found in barns, mobile homes, motel rooms, houseboats, storage units, and basements by drug dealers, not chemists. There is no quality control over their production and, unlike real pharmaceutical laboratories, these labs have no guidelines for cleanliness or scientific procedures. During the manufacturing process, it is easy to make errors that can cause poisoning. Even if no impurities are purposely added to the drug, it may become contaminated because of poor or dirty facilities.

Most substances affect the user's judgment and motor coordination, making any kind of physical activity very dangerous.

## The Risk of an Overdose

The risk of an overdose is also always present. Users of opiates, such as heroin, develop a tolerance to the drug. This increases the risk of overdose because users have to take larger doses to get the same effect, until they have taken so much of the drug that their bodies can't cope. Injecting a drug holds a greater risk than swallowing a drug. Mixing drugs can greatly increase the possibility of overdose because the drugs may work together to produce a stronger reaction.

# Binge Use of Substances
## Risking It All

When young people in Canada drink alcohol or use another substance, they are more likely than adults to do so past the point of intoxication. Young people also may feel that they haven't had the full experience unless they have consumed to excess.

This is known as **bingeing**.

With alcohol, a female is considered to be bingeing when she has four or more drinks per drinking occasion. A male is considered to be bingeing when he has five or more drinks per drinking occasion.

The limit is higher for males because women's bodies have a higher proportion of fat tissue than men's, so their bodies absorb alcohol more quickly. With drugs other than alcohol, bingeing is not so easy to measure, but it is still defined as using a substance past the point of intoxication.

Combining drugs such as marijuana and alcohol, or alcohol and certain pharmaceutical drugs, can have a multiplier effect. Much less of each substance may be necessary to intoxicate an individual than would otherwise be the case if either substance was used alone.

### Bingeing Is Dangerous

Bingeing is a major cause of death and injuries due to accidents or violence; often a result of impaired judgment or an overdose. Bingeing on alcohol can also result in fetal alcohol spectrum disorder (FASD) if the binger is pregnant.

This pattern of substance use can also contribute to problems with parents, trouble with authorities, poor performance in school, unwanted and unprotected sexual activity, and an increased risk of HIV infection.

# How Drug Use Begins

People often believe that using mood-altering drugs will make them feel better or contribute to their enjoyment of sensory stimulation. Other factors also influence some young people to use substances.

## Culture and Media

Popular culture, which sometimes glamorizes the use of alcohol and other drugs, influences young people in Canada and around the world through the Internet, television, and movies. An example of this is the powerful advertising messages that link the consumption of alcoholic beverages with images of good times, popularity, and success.

## Curiosity

Drug issues are often in the news and frequently a topic of conversation among adults and teenagers. Curiosity is natural in young people (and most often a positive trait), so it is not surprising that some teens become curious enough to experiment with alcohol or other drugs.

## Social Acceptance

Some young people may feel pressure to smoke, drink, or use other substances if their friends do, and some believe that substance use is a way to gain acceptance to a particular social group.

## Lack of Knowledge About the Risks

Information is important. Young people may use a new drug heavily before good information is available about its risks. Conversely, fewer young people will choose to use a potentially harmful drug if they have believable, accurate information about its risks.

## Celebrations and Religious Observances

Drugs (alcohol, for example) are often a part of family or community celebrations and religious services. These are events in which people tend to value drugs more for their symbolic importance than for their effect.

## Everyday Emotional Pressures

Mood-altering substances hold the promise of temporarily improving feelings. That is why some stressed or anxious people—young or old—may find legal and/or illegal substances appealing.

## Mental Health Problems

Up to 15 percent of Canadian children and adolescents may experience clinical mental health problems such as anxiety disorder, attention deficit hyperactivity disorder (ADHD), depression, or schizophrenia. People with such problems are at risk for substance abuse because they may look to various drugs to "self-medicate" for the distress they feel.

Advertising often sends the wrong message by linking drugs with good times, popularity, and success.

The desire to be accepted into a social network or the pressures of friends is a reason young people may drink or try other substances.

# Myths and Facts about Drugs
## Why Someone Might Use Drugs ... and Why They Should Not

| WHY SOMEONE MIGHT | WHY THEY SHOULDN'T |
|---|---|
| I want to satisfy my curiosity. | You may satisfy your curiosity but at what price? Many people have satisfied their curiosity and had really bad experiences. Can you learn from them? |
| I'm bored and I need something to do. | It may be exciting once or twice, but the excitement will soon wear off and then what if you can't stop? Furthermore, there's always a risk involved. |
| I want to rebel against my parents and get their attention. | Is this really the kind of attention you want? Is negative attention worth losing their trust and endangering your health? |
| I want to avoid my problems and forget about them for a while. | Drugs can't solve problems. Even if you do forget about them for a while, the problems will still be there when you are sober. They may even be worse. |
| I'm lonely and stressed out. | Drugs can have a negative effect on your emotions and moods, turning you into the kind of person no one wants to be around. |
| I want to fit in with my friends OR I want to make new friends. | If your friends will only accept you because you do drugs, they're likely not the kind of people who will be good friends in the long run. |
| I'm too shy and I want more confidence. | Drugs only give you a false sense of confidence and courage and may even give you too much of it, causing you to say or do something you will regret later. |
| I want to feel comfortable in large groups and be able to talk to people I don't know. | Drugs can make you act like a fool or act in bizarre ways; do you really want that to be someone's first impression of you? |
| I want to be the "real" me. | Drug use can lead to mistakes (such as driving while impaired, getting into risky sexual situations, or letting people take advantage of you). Is that how you see the "real" you? |
| I need to stay awake and have an edge. | What if you can't sleep when you decide you want to or you can only sleep restlessly? Is it worth that risk? |
| I want to feel more creative. | Drugs can make you less motivated to do well in school or at work. What good is being creative if you have no desire to do anything about it? |
| I want to be able to focus and concentrate better. | Your ability to concentrate and remember things can be negatively affected by drugs. |
| I want to avoid living up to too many pressures. | The lack of emotional control that drugs give you can lead to negative consequences, such as failing in school or losing your job. Wouldn't that kind of pressure be much worse? |
| I need illegal drugs to control pain. | Self-medicating is never a good idea and can lead to chemical dependence which can be very tough to beat. |
| I need illegal drugs to control my weight. | Trying to control your diet with drugs can go one of two ways, neither of which are good: you can become undernourished which can lead to health complications, or your appetite may increase causing you to eat too much. |
| I need illegal drugs to gain the muscle mass I want. | Using drugs this way can cause females to become masculine looking and males to grow breasts. These effects may not go away even if you quit. |
| If I'm careful, what's the problem? | Even if you are careful, the lack of regulations around illegal drugs means you can never know for sure that you are safe. For example, using needles can lead to contracting HIV/AIDS or hepatitis. |
| I'm old enough to make my own choices. | No one is denying that it's your choice. You are old enough to think about the consequences of your choices, too. Do you really want to choose to behave in a way that can severely damage your major organs and body systems? |

# Targeting Teens

As part of the normal process of becoming adults, young people begin to establish their own identity apart from their parents or care-givers in the early- and mid-teen years. This means that often they test new ideas that don't always match those of their parents and other authorities.

This developmental phase is an important time for experimentation, but some experimentation can lead to harm to themselves or others.

## Questioning Authority

Demonstrating independence, and trying out new, exciting, and possibly risky experiences, are some of the needs and desires that often go with establishing identity. It is easy to see how substances such as alcohol, tobacco, or marijuana can satisfy these kinds of needs. In addition, these substances are readily available, and taking them doesn't require any particular skill.

All substance-use decisions should involve weighing the perceived benefits against the risks. However, many people often act on impulse, without thinking realistically about options or consequences, and this type of impulsive decision making can lead to problems.

People use substances for many reasons, including:

> Relief of stress

> Coping with boredom

> Heightened enjoyment

> Easier social situations

However, the two main reasons for substance use are the influence of the media and that of peers. These influences are interconnected.

## Media and Popular Culture

We hear a great deal about how the media—television, movies, advertising, music, music videos, and even computer games—affect society. Images from advertisers linking products such as alcohol and tobacco with a certain image or lifestyle are all around us.

Less obvious is the way the media can help shape our ideas of what is normal or desirable behaviour. When you watch a movie, look at an advertisement, or listen to a popular song that refers to drugs or drinking, ask yourself some questions:

> Is drug use (including smoking/drinking) portrayed as normal?

> What sort of person is shown using?

> What images accompany references to drugs or alcohol?

> In your experience, do these portrayals match the effects of alcohol or drugs as you have read or learned about them?

Experimentation during your teen years is natural, but no one says it has to include experimenting with drugs or alcohol.

Generally, you select the peer group you prefer to join—and, to some extent, you will be selected by this group.

## Peer Influence and Decision Making

By the time a person is in a social situation where alcohol or another substance is being used, he or she may already have formed an opinion on substance use. Yet, it may still be difficult for them to refuse when the situation arises. There are several reasons for this, including:

- ➢ Not wanting to be a bystander during the occasion
- ➢ Not wanting to miss bonding experiences with friends
- ➢ Not wanting to be mocked
- ➢ Not wanting to hurt someone's feelings
- ➢ Not knowing how to get out of the situation

You need to decide how you are going to respond to such pressures well before you are in a social situation where alcohol or other substances are being used.

Remember, too, that peer pressure is a two-way street—as a friend or classmate, you are also in a position to influence your peers. You can do so by encouraging them to avoid illegal substances and especially by helping them to avoid situations (e.g., drinking and driving) that will be dangerous to them, to yourself, and to others.

Decide whether you want to consume alcohol before you are in a situation where it is likely to be used.

# Drug Dependence

One of the most frequently discussed risks of drug abuse is that of dependence (or addiction). Drug dependence is the continued compulsive use of a substance, even in the face of growing problems in a number of life areas (e.g., work, family, legal problems). Somebody is said to have a drug dependence problem when they cannot stop using a substance.

Different drugs carry different risks, and different people may be more at risk than others. You have probably come into contact with enough people who drink alcohol socially to know that not everyone who drinks becomes dependent on alcohol. You may also know other adults who have become severely addicted to alcohol, or you may know of a situation where alcohol dependence has negatively affected that person's own health and has even disrupted his or her family life.

Being physically active and playing sports is extremely dangerous if someone is taking drugs of any kind.

Cannabis, cocaine, and ecstasy can negatively affect short-term memory and the ability to concentrate.

## Physical Dependence

**Physical dependence** explains why some people continue to use drugs. Once their bodies become accustomed to the drug, they experience physical symptoms of withdrawal if they try to go without it.

Using some substances over a long period of time can cause the body to tolerate them. When users develop a tolerance for a substance, they find that they need to take larger amounts of the substance in order to feel the same effects. Some drugs, such as alcohol, tobacco, and heroin, can produce severe physical dependence, whereas others cannot. All mood-altering substances can create a psychological dependence or craving.

Illegal drugs, as well as alcohol and tobacco, can cause withdrawal symptoms when a regular user stops using them. Symptoms often include depression, cravings, and anxiety. These symptoms can occur from hours to days after the last time the user took the substance. Withdrawal symptoms can serve as a serious barrier to quitting a drug habit.

Even prescription drugs such as anti-depressants can cause withdrawal symptoms. This is why patients are told to check with their doctor before they stop taking their medications.

Some drugs that cause withdrawal symptoms after regular, long-term use include:

➢ Caffeine

➢ Alcohol

➢ Nicotine

➢ Opiates (such as morphine and heroin)

## Psychological Dependence

Drug use may become a habit that the user finds difficult to break, even in the absence of physical cravings. Some people who use drugs—drugs that do not usually cause physical dependence—may find that their drug use begins to play a larger part in their lives, and that they cannot find an easy way to quit.

Such people have a **psychological dependence** on that drug. Psychological dependence is another serious form of addiction.

Despite the lack of physical withdrawal symptoms, psychological addiction can be extremely difficult to overcome. That person's addictive behaviour is driven by an overwhelming desire to repeat the effects of the drug rather than by the physical need to relieve the pain of withdrawal.

People who are psychologically addicted feel they have no choice in taking the substance, and therefore, they are in serious need of help and professional counselling. Like those who are physically addicted, people who have a psychological addiction feel so overcome by the desire to have that drug that they may even steal or become involved in other illegal means to get it.

Since they are not regulated, you can never be completely sure what illegal drugs contain.

## Gambling Addiction
### Teens Are Also at Risk

Although gambling is not a drug, gambling addiction is fast becoming as great a concern as substance addictions. People with a gambling addiction gamble compulsively and often end up in serious trouble.

Before 1969, virtually all forms of gambling were illegal in Canada. There are now numerous casinos, racetracks, and Internet gambling sites, as well as tens of thousands of slot machines and video lottery terminals (VLTs). Nowadays, gambling brings in almost as much revenue to governments as taxes on alcohol and tobacco combined.

### Ripple Effects

For the majority of Canadians, gambling is a form of entertainment that has no negative impact. However, gambling problems are on the rise in this country. Between 3 and 5 percent of gamblers develop a gambling problem. This means that between 600,000 and 1 million Canadians are problem gamblers.

As with a drug dependence, the effects ripple beyond that individual to include family and marital problems, serious financial problems, employment or workplace disruptions, criminal activity, depression, and in extreme cases, suicide.

### Teen Gambling

A high percentage of high school students report having gambled for money during the past year. It is estimated that 4 to 8 percent of adolescents presently have a serious gambling problem, while another 10 to 14 percent are at risk for developing a serious gambling problem.

# Canada's Drug Policy

The federal government has developed a strategy to address the harms linked to alcohol and other drugs in Canada.

**Canada's drug policy** has the following five objectives:

- ➤ To reduce the demand for drugs.
- ➤ To reduce drug-related deaths.
- ➤ To improve the effectiveness of, and accessibility to, substance abuse information and interventions.
- ➤ To restrict the supply of illicit drugs and reduce the profitability of illicit drug trafficking.
- ➤ To reduce the costs of substance abuse to Canadian society.

Health Canada is the leading agency for implementing Canada's drug policy. It is responsible for providing information to Canadians about all aspects of drug use and abuse as well as other important health matters.

Other groups and organizations also are involved in Canada's efforts to deal with the drug problem. These include various federal departments; provincial, territorial, and municipal governments; addiction agencies and counsellors; non-governmental organizations; a variety of professional associations; law enforcement agencies; the private sector; and community groups.

Canada's drug policy attempts to restrict the supply of illicit drugs and reduce drug trafficking.

## Making Smart Choices

No matter how much fun or how difficult they are, the teen years are about moving on and going somewhere.

You may already know exactly what you want to be doing later in life, or you may just know that you want to be happy and able to take care of yourself.

Whatever your aims, ask yourself "Are the things I am doing now helping me to get where I want to go?"

When you ask this question about substance use, it becomes pretty clear that the use of substances is not going to help you get where you want to go.

Knowing the harms that can arise from using substances can put you in a good position to develop a balanced view of the kind of role you would like to see substances play in your life.

## Questions for Study and Review

### Things to Think About and Explore

1. Describe the four main types of mood-altering drugs and give examples of each.

2. Outline three reasons why someone might try using drugs, and for each reason, present an argument against using drugs.

3. Explore how the lack of regulation in illegal drug labs make these drugs even more dangerous.

4. Define bingeing as it relates to alcohol and explain why it is especially dangerous.

5. Compare drug addiction and gambling addiction. Consider how they are similar, how they differ from one another, and whether you feel one is more dangerous than the other.

6. Research Canada's drug policy and how it is enforced. Investigate how it compares to the drug policy of another country (for example, the United States or the United Kingdom).

### Things to Do and Practise

7. Draw the Continuum of Drug Use (page 215) in another format of your choice. Incorporate into your diagram the three main factors that need to be taken into account when assessing drug use and abuse (the drug, the user, and the context).

8. Make a collage that clearly demonstrates the disadvantages of using the illegal drugs discussed in this chapter. Feel free to use pictures, literature, or graphics.

9. Divide into groups and discuss the various ways in which television, movies, or popular music tend to glamorize drug use.

10. Imagine you have a friend who has decided not to take drugs (either for religious, moral, or other reasons). Pair up with a classmate and take turns suggesting ways you could support his or her decision in the following situations:

    (a) You are at a party and your friends are using drugs.
    (b) You are in the cafeteria and friends are talking about drugs they have tried.
    (c) You are with a group that wants to watch a movie that features drug use that you know will make your friend uncomfortable.

11. Choose one specific illegal drug that is widely known and make it the focal point of a poster that can be used to dissuade teens from using this and other drugs.

12. Your class has been put in charge of promoting drug awareness in your school. List four key themes that can be emphasized over and over again to convince your peers to avoid using drugs.

## WWWeblinks

Name ➢ **Canadian Centre on Substance Abuse**

URL ➢ **www.ccsa.ca**

The CCSA is Canada's national addictions agency. This site offers links to addiction aid groups as well as treatment options in Canada. There are also statistics about various kinds of addiction.

Name ➢ **Council on Drug Abuse**

URL ➢ **www.drugabuse.ca**

The Council on Drug Abuse (CODA) is an organization that focuses on preventive drug and alcohol programs.

Name ➢ **George Chuvalo's Fight Against Drugs**

URL ➢ **www.fightagainst drugs.ca**

Former heavyweight boxer George Chuvalo lost a wife and three sons to substance abuse. He now travels coast to coast detailing, firsthand, how much drug problems can cost you or your family.

# 14
# Tobacco and Alcohol

**T**obacco and alcohol are the only controlled mood-altering substances permitted for non-medical use in Canada. Using either one has risks, but public support for tobacco has decreased steadily over the years, while alcohol still is widely accepted and used.

As with caffeine, which is not controlled at all and widely available, perceptions of alcohol may be different than those of illegal drugs. Many people believe that alcohol can be used responsibly by adults. Nevertheless, alcohol, like tobacco, causes many health and social problems.

Choosing to smoke or drink can have serious long- and short-term effects on you and those around you. In this chapter, you will learn what these substances contain, what they do to your body, and the consequences of using them. With this information, you can make informed decisions about your health.

## Chapter Objectives

In this chapter, you will:

> Identify reasons that young people try tobacco and/or alcohol

> Discover where tobacco and alcohol come from and what ingredients these substances contain

> Learn about the immediate physiological effects of tobacco and alcohol on the body

> Describe the likely long-term effects of continued tobacco and alcohol use

> Learn about some of the practices of the tobacco and alcohol industries that have had the effect of increasing tobacco use by youth

> Learn about the potential impacts of tobacco and alcohol dependence for individuals and their families

> Investigate the law in Canada related to tobacco and alcohol consumption

## Key Terms

> tobacco
> cardiovascular diseases
> respiratory diseases
> second-hand smoke
> alcohol
> blood-alcohol content (BAC)
> fetal alcohol syndrome
> liquor control regulations
> legal liability
> alcohol abuse
> alcohol dependence
> Mothers Against Drunk Driving (MADD)

# Why Some People Smoke and Drink

Tobacco and alcohol are often the first two mood-altering substances that young people try, probably because they are legally available for adults and relatively easy for teens to get. However, legal doesn't mean healthy, for either group.

Alcohol and tobacco are subject to only a few restrictions that prevent young people from buying them. They are not illegal for adults and many people, mistakenly, see them as harmless substances. When asked, people give many reasons for having tried a drink or a smoke:

➢ They are curious.
➢ People they like and respect do it.
➢ They don't see how it will do any harm.
➢ People in positions of authority have told them not to do it.

## Why Some People Do Not

Many young Canadians are happy not to drink or smoke. Some don't want to spend their money to support the liquor and tobacco industries. Others have a family member or a friend struggling with alcohol or tobacco dependency and don't want to fall into that pattern.

As for smoking, it is increasingly difficult to find a place to "light up" as more and more Canadian jurisdictions ban smoking in public places. Many teens are put off by bad breath and stained fingers. Those involved with athletics understand that smoked tobacco is a "performance-reducing" substance, which keeps them from staying in top physical condition.

For some young people, drinking and smoking goes against their values and their commitment to health.

More and more Canadian towns, cities, and provinces are banning smoking in workplaces, restaurants, bars, and other public places.

# Tobacco

**Tobacco** is the shredded, dried leaf of the tobacco plant, which can be smoked in cigarettes, cigars, pipes, or chewed. Tobacco is the only natural source of nicotine, one of the most addictive substances known to scientists.

It is difficult to believe, but tobacco smoke contains more than 4,000 chemicals. Many are harmful industrial chemicals, including carbon monoxide, benzene, toluene, formaldehyde, acetone, ammonia, cadmium, nicotine, and nickel. Smoking tobacco forms a tar that causes a variety of serious health problems. For example, more than 40 of these chemicals are carcinogens—that is, they are known to cause cancer in humans.

## Teens and Tobacco: Don't Even Start!

The choices you make right now, and throughout your teen years may affect you for the rest of your life. In Canada, the average age a person smokes their first whole cigarette is now 13 years old. Just remember: if you don't start smoking in your teens, it is unlikely that you will ever start.

The percentage of students who smoke (as with just about all drug use) increases significantly from Grade 7 to Grade 12. For example, the percentage of students who have used tobacco daily in Ontario ranges from 3 percent of Grade 7 students to 22 percent of Grade 12 students.

The consequences of smoking are apparent right away, even in young people. Grade 12 students who are regular smokers and who began smoking by Grade 9 are twice as likely as non-smoking students to report poorer overall health, coughs with phlegm or blood, shortness of breath when not exercising, and wheezing or gasping.

Some good news is that, thanks to education and awareness, young people aren't as likely to smoke as they once were. Student smoking rates are now at the lowest they've been since they were first measured in 1977. For example, 7 percent of Ontario Grade 9 students smoked daily in 2005, compared to 19 percent in 1995, and 24 percent in 1977.

## Did You Know?

The anti-smoking website **www.stupid.ca** gives many compelling reasons to quit smoking. Here are just a few:

> Unless they quit, up to half of all smokers will die from smoking, most of them before their seventieth birthday and only after years of suffering a reduced quality of life.

> The average smoker will die about 8 years earlier than a similar non-smoker. Life expectancy improves after a smoker quits.

> In Ontario alone, 44 people die every day as a direct result of smoking—16,000 a year, in just one province.

The leaves of the tobacco plant are shredded and dried to make tobacco that can be either smoked or chewed.

## The Hazards of Smoking

Remarkable as it may seem, smoking is the greatest cause of poor health in Canada and other industrialized nations. It causes over 40,000 deaths every year in Canada—over 21 percent of all deaths.

It gets even more shocking. Health Canada estimates that more than 50 percent of today's 15-year-old smokers will die before age 70 because of their tobacco use. By comparison, just 6 percent of those same smokers will die early because of traffic accidents, suicides, murders, and HIV/AIDS combined.

## The Short-Term Effects

Because nicotine is extremely addictive, even experimental use is risky. Once you start to smoke with any regularity, it's very difficult to stop, and equally difficult to remain an occasional smoker.

When you smoke one cigarette, your heart rate and blood pressure go up and your breathing gets faster. First-time smokers may feel dizzy and may experience diarrhea and vomiting. An immediate effect is reduced fitness and athletic ability. Smoker's breath is also a problem that you (and others) will notice right away.

Smoking just one cigarette can cause your blood pressure and heart rate to rise and your breathing to get faster.

## Anatomy of a Cigarette
### When You Smoke, What Are You Really Smoking?

Did you know that there are over 4,000 chemicals in tobacco smoke and that at least 40 chemicals found in tobacco smoke are known to cause cancer?

Of particular concern are:

- Tar (also found on paved roads and roofs)
- Nicotine (comes from the tobacco plant and is carcinogenic)
- Carbon monoxide (found in exhaust from cars)

- Methane (sewer gas)
- Formaldehyde (used to preserve dead bodies)
- Hydrogen cyanide (used in dyeing and explosives)
- Benzene (toxic and a known carcinogen)

In Canada, tobacco companies are required by law to indicate on tobacco packages how much of each of these is found in tobacco emissions (the exhaled smoke).

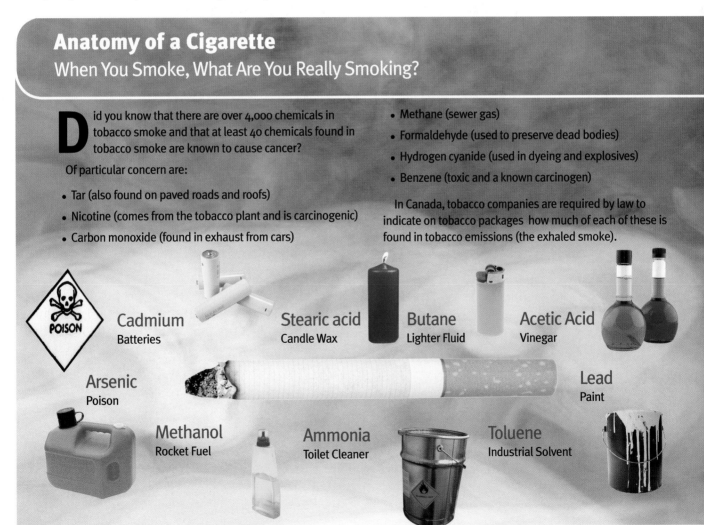

POISON

Cadmium
Batteries

Stearic acid
Candle Wax

Butane
Lighter Fluid

Acetic Acid
Vinegar

Arsenic
Poison

Lead
Paint

Methanol
Rocket Fuel

Ammonia
Toilet Cleaner

Toluene
Industrial Solvent

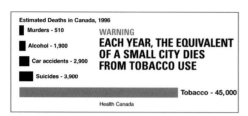

Estimated Deaths in Canada, 1996

| | |
|---|---|
| ■ Murders - 510 | **WARNING** |
| ■ Alcohol - 1,900 | **EACH YEAR, THE EQUIVALENT OF A SMALL CITY DIES FROM TOBACCO USE** |
| ■ Car accidents - 2,900 | |
| ■ Suicides - 3,900 | |

Tobacco - 45,000

Health Canada

Smoking is the greatest cause of poor health in Canada and in other industrialized nations. It causes over 40,000 deaths every year in this country—more than 21 percent of all deaths.

**WARNING**
**CIGARETTES CAUSE LUNG CANCER**
Every cigarette you smoke increases your chance of getting lung cancer.
Health Canada

Over 13,000 people in Canada die of lung cancer caused by smoking each year, and smoking can cause other cancers as well.

**WARNING**
**YOU'RE NOT THE ONLY ONE SMOKING THIS CIGARETTE**
The smoke from a cigarette is not just inhaled by the smoker. It becomes second-hand smoke, which contains more than 50 cancer-causing agents.
Health Canada

Health Canada estimates that more than 1,000 deaths from heart attacks and lung cancer in Canadian non-smokers each year are caused by second-hand smoke.

# Tobacco: The Long-Term Effects

Most smokers are physically and psychologically dependent. They smoke frequently and have trouble quitting. Smoking regularly places them at risk for a number of serious health problems, including:

> Cancer of the lungs, mouth, and throat

> Respiratory disease

> Heart attack

> Stroke

> Stomach ulcers

Smoking increases blood pressure, reduces vitamin C levels, keeps skin wounds from healing normally, and decreases the body's ability to fight disease. While there are always health benefits to quitting, some damage may be permanent. So, the earlier one quits, the better.

## Cardiovascular Disease

**Cardiovascular diseases** are diseases and injuries of the heart and blood vessels (veins and arteries). They are responsible for more than 35 percent of all deaths in Canada. More than 18,000 Canadians die each year from these cardiovascular diseases as a result of smoking.

Although these diseases have many forms, in all forms of cardiovascular disease, the supply of oxygen and the necessary nutrients carried by blood is slowed or blocked. Smoking, or even breathing someone else's smoke, forces the heart to work harder than it should.

## Cancers

In Canada, 13,000 deaths occur each year due to lung cancer caused by smoking. Lung cancer is a very deadly disease; over half of patients die within five years of being diagnosed. Smoking can also lead to cancer of the oral cavity, pharynx, larynx, esophagus, pancreas, kidney, bladder, cervix, large intestine, and to some forms of leukemia.

## Respiratory Diseases

Each year, smoking causes more than 9,000 deaths in Canada from **respiratory diseases** that attack our lungs and the other parts of the body that we use to breathe. People with these conditions often have difficulty being physically active. Smokers are more likely to develop respiratory infections, such as pneumonia and influenza, and according to recent research, even the common cold.

## Dental Health

Smokers are more likely than non-smokers to have lost some or all of their natural teeth, to have remaining teeth that are decayed, and to have significant gum disease. Smoking has even been linked to gum disease in young people.

# The Long-Term Health Effects of Smoking Tobacco
## Leaving No Body Part Unharmed

### Heart and Circulatory System

- Reduces fitness level and athletic ability
- Increases risk of heart disease
- Increases risk of heart attack
- Increases blood pressure
- Hardens arteries and decreases blood flow
- Leads to poor blood circulation in extremities that could lead to amputations

### Lungs

- Reduces the rate of normal lung growth
- Increases risk of emphysema and bronchitis
- Destroys tiny hair-like structures in the trachea ("cilia") that filter bacteria and other harmful substances, reducing immunity to diseases
- Leads to phlegm build up and excess coughing
- Increases the risk of lung cancer

### Reproductive Systems

#### Male
- Decreases sperm count
- Decreases sperm movement
- Lowers sex drive

#### Female
- Adversely affects menstrual cycle
- Increases risk of cervical cancer
- Increases risk of breast cancer
- Leads to early onset of menopause
- Leads to low-birth-weight babies
- Can affect infant growth, intellectual development, and behaviour

### Brain

- Increases risk of stroke
- Greater risk of stroke for women using the "pill"
- Can lead to nicotine addiction
- Kills brain cells

### Mouth and Throat

- Increases risk for mouth, throat, and tongue cancer
- Increases risk for larynx and esophagus cancer
- Stained teeth and tooth decay

### Skin

- Increases dryness
- Speeds up aging of skin
- Causes wounds to heal slowly

### Stomach and Intestines

- Increases risk of ulcers
- Leads to bleeding of the stomach lining
- Increases risk of stomach and intestinal cancer

### Bone

- Increases the risk of osteoporosis

Over the years, many of these effects of tobacco can be reversed if the individual quits smoking.

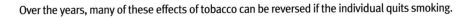

## Second-Hand Smoke

The idea that smokers are only harming themselves is simply not true. **Second-hand smoke**, sometimes called environmental tobacco smoke (ETS) or "passive smoking," happens when exhaled smoke from the smoker, or smoke from the smoldering cigarette, or the mouth end of the cigarette, is inhaled by another person.

Scientific evidence about the effects of second-hand smoke has encouraged laws to be passed that limit where people can smoke. Most jurisdictions across Canada now outlaw smoking within and, in some cases even outside, public premises. Restaurants and bars generally do not allow patrons to light up.

Not only do these "No Smoking" laws make for a more pleasant atmosphere, but a few more lives are saved as well.

### The Risks of Second-Hand Smoke

A person exposed to second-hand smoke is more likely to have respiratory problems (such as coughing, phlegm, and chest discomfort) than a person who is not exposed.

Health Canada estimates that more than 1,000 deaths from heart attacks and lung cancer in Canadian non-smokers each year are caused by second-hand smoke.

It is increasingly clear that second-hand smoke leads to heart disease in non-smokers. It is a special problem for people with allergies, and those with heart or lung disease. Children whose parents smoke tend to have more ear infections, chest infections, and other lung problems (such as asthma) than children of non-smokers.

Cigar smoke contains the same levels of carcinogens as cigarette smoke.

---

### Other Forms of Tobacco Use

- **Smokeless tobacco (snuff and chewing tobacco).** Like tobacco smoke, smokeless tobacco contains nicotine, carcinogens, and other harmful substances, leading to addiction and other health problems in some users. Smokeless tobacco is a cause of mouth cancer and other serious problems affecting the mouth, teeth, and gums.

- **Light or low-yield cigarettes.** These so-called light or low-yield cigarettes have less tar and nicotine than regular cigarettes. However, many smokers make up for the lower tar and nicotine levels by smoking more cigarettes, taking more puffs on each cigarette smoked, inhaling more deeply, and smoking more of the cigarette.

- **Pipes and cigars.** The levels of carcinogens are the same in pipe, cigar, and cigarette smoke, so pipe and cigar smokers can experience the same range of health problems as cigarette smokers. Although their risks are slightly lower because they tend to use less tobacco and inhale less, long-term pipe smokers still face particular risks, such as mouth and lip cancer.

## The Rewards of Not Smoking

While quitting smoking can be very difficult, the rewards are great. Compared to continuing smokers, people who have quit smoking have a reduced risk of lung cancer, other cancers, heart attack, stroke, chronic lung disease, and other conditions.

For example, stopping smoking reduces the risk of smoking-related cardiovascular disease by about 50 percent within one year. Five years after having quit, the risk goes down to the same level as people who have never smoked.

Other good reasons to quit are:

➢ You have more money in your pocket for other things.

➢ You withdraw your support of the tobacco industry.

➢ You can participate in physical activities more comfortably.

➢ You no longer have foul-smelling smoker's breath.

➢ You likely won't be visiting your doctor as often.

➢ You won't have to freeze outside in Canadian winters to have that smoke, since smoking is no longer allowed indoors.

Quitting smoking can quickly reduce your risk of cancer, heart attack, stroke, and chronic lung disease.

## Dealing with Tobacco Addiction
### Get Psyched, Get Smart, Get Support, Get On With It

Many young people say they would like to quit smoking and have tried to do so. Of current smokers aged 15 to 19 in Canada, 64 percent reported one or more attempts to quit in the 12 months before being surveyed.

The state of tobacco addiction occurs when someone has a physiological and psychological need for cigarettes.

The problem is that nicotine is powerfully addictive. Experts rank nicotine as more addictive than alcohol, cocaine, or heroin.

### Withdrawal

Addiction to nicotine produces withdrawal symptoms when a person tries to stop smoking. Long-term smokers who have stopped smoking for as little as 24 hours can be hostile, aggressive, and take longer to recover from stress.

So, quitting is very difficult, and after quitting there is always a possibility of relapsing (starting to use again) later on.

### Support groups

People at school, such as the school nurse or the guidance counsellor, and at the doctor's office, can put someone who wants to quit smoking in touch with people and resources that can help. Some schools have support groups to help students quit smoking.

### Online Resources

As an alternative, someone who wants to quit may wish to link up with a virtual support group or an online quitting buddy.

Here are a few online resources:

● **Quit 4 Life:** Q4L is a Canadian, web-based program to help young people quit smoking. It's organized around four central steps: Get Psyched, Get Smart, Get Support, Get On With It. **www.quit4life.com**

● **Ontario Smoker's Helpline:** Free support and advice at 1-877-513-5333.

● **Health Canada: E-Quit Program:** Sign up to receive daily support e-mails. **www.gosmokefree.ca**

# Alcohol

**Alcohol** is produced by fermenting or distilling various fruits, vegetables, or grains. In beverages, pure ethyl alcohol, which is clear and colourless, is mixed with other ingredients that affect the colour and reduce the alcohol content.

Aside from caffeine found in coffee, tea, and colas, alcohol is the most used substance in Canada and around the world. Because it is widely and legally available, alcohol often is not viewed as a harmful drug (even though potentially it is). Although many people do not drink alcohol (either by choice or because of cultural or religious reasons), it forms a part of the lifestyle of many Canadians. For instance, many young people have their first drinking experience at a family event.

Drinking alcohol may seem low-risk, but alcohol problems are a major public health issue in Canada, and alcohol-related accidents and violence among young people are a big reason for concern.

## Just How Alcoholic Is It?

The effects of any alcoholic drink depend on the amount of pure ethyl alcohol consumed. Spirits such as whiskey and gin usually contain 40 percent (or 80-proof) pure alcohol; table wine, 12 percent; regular beer, 5 percent; and spirit- and wine-based coolers, 5 percent.

In Canada, a typical serving (standard drink) of alcohol contains 17 ml of absolute alcohol—the amount contained in a 12-ounce (341 ml) bottle of regular beer, 5 ounces (142 ml) of table wine or 1.5 ounces (43 ml) of 80-proof liquor.

The manufacturing process may be more sophisticated nowadays, but there are reports of alcohol production and use from as early as 8000 BC.

# Alcohol Content of Standard Drinks

**A** standard drink contains the same amount of alcohol, 17 ml (0.6 oz) regardless of the type of beverage.

Each of these is the equivalent of one standard drink:

- Regular Beer (5%)—340 ml (12 oz)
- Light beer (4%)—426 ml (15 oz)
- Wine (12%)—142 ml (5 oz)
- Fortified Wine (18%)—85 ml (3 oz)
- Spirits (40%)—43 ml (1.5 oz)
- Coolers (5%)—340 ml (12 oz)

Most of these beverages also come in "extra strength" versions. The extra strength versions are potentially more dangerous because smaller amounts achieve the same effect.

12 OZ          5 OZ          1.5 OZ

# The Short-Term Effects

The effects of using alcohol depend on how it is used—the amount consumed, the mood and expectations of the person, and the situation. Alcohol is categorized as a depressant because it has the effect of depressing or slowing down the central nervous system.

## Blood-Alcohol Content (BAC)

The amount of alcohol in the bloodstream is called the **blood-alcohol content (BAC)** and is a measure of how much a person will be affected by the alcohol consumed. BAC depends mostly on the amount consumed in a given time period, but also on size (smaller people reach a higher BAC from the same quantity of alcohol), gender (women generally will reach a higher BAC from the same amount than men), and metabolism.

The amount of alcohol in the breath is directly related to the amount of alcohol in the blood, so BAC (a person's level of intoxication) can be measured with a breath test using a "breathalyzer." A number of factors will affect the level of intoxication:

Drivers with a BAC of 0.10 are seven times more likely to cause a motor vehicle accident because their judgment is impaired.

> ➤ **Age.** People with little or no experience with alcohol may not be able to predict its effects. They may make bad decisions while intoxicated, or drink to the point of alcohol poisoning.

> ➤ **Mood.** People who drink when they are angry or depressed often do not pay attention to the signs of intoxication.

> ➤ **Other substance use.** Signs of intoxication can be missed if other substances affect a user's self-perception.

> ➤ **Food.** A hungry person will metabolize alcohol more quickly.

A "breathalyzer" test determines your BAC by measuring the amount of alcohol in your breath.

## How a High BAC Affects the Body

A single drink will result in a BAC of about 0.02 gram percent (about 0.02 grams per 100 ml of blood). Inhibitions will be depressed and the drinker usually will feel relaxed. Drinking small amounts can also cause drowsiness, dizziness, and reddening of the face. Drinking can make some people feel sociable and possibly more self-confident, but others will become angry, depressed, and withdrawn.

Even when consuming below a BAC of 0.08 percent (the legal limit for driving in Canada), a person's judgment, ability to judge distances, and reaction time can be impaired. Studies have shown that drivers with a BAC above 0.10 are seven times more likely to cause a crash, because both their hand-eye coordination and judgment are impaired. At BACs over 0.20, a normal person is very intoxicated. They stumble when they walk and slur words when they speak.

A BAC above the range of 0.40 to 0.60 is usually fatal, typically because that much alcohol blocks the brain's control over breathing. This is called alcohol poisoning. A person who has used another depressant drug, such as a tranquilizer or painkiller, may overdose with a much lower BAC because the two drugs multiply each other's effects.

# Alcohol: The Long-Term Effects

Heavy, long-term drinking (more than two drinks a day on average for men, less for women) leads to a number of serious health problems, including: liver damage, heart disease, ulcers, certain types of cancer, blackouts (loss of memory), brain damage, and sexual problems. Women generally suffer these effects sooner than men.

## Dependence

With long-term, heavy use, a person's "tolerance" for alcohol increases, and the person may drink steadily without appearing to get drunk. When a person's body becomes used to alcohol it doesn't respond to it as strongly right away. These drinkers are likely to be physically and psychologically dependent. When a person stops drinking after long-term, heavy use, withdrawal symptoms can include sleeplessness, sweating, vomiting, tremors, seizures, and hallucinations. Withdrawal can lead to death if the symptoms are severe enough.

## Other Effects of Alcohol Abuse

Even though it is a legal substance, alcohol plays a prominent role in a range of serious social problems. Alcoholism, or alcohol dependency syndrome, can lead to troubles with the law (for drinking and driving or other illegal behaviour while intoxicated), problems with money (for spending too much on alcohol), and problems on the job (for missing work because of a hangover). Injuries, from car accidents, drowning, falls, fire, work-related accidents, or fights, also are consequences of alcohol abuse (even death in some cases).

## Alcohol and Violence

The relationship between alcohol and violence is complex. Alcohol lowers inhibitions, reduces judgment, and can feed anger, so it is easy to see how alcohol is strongly linked to many violent situations. A large number of people who have committed (and been victims of) serious violent crimes, such as domestic assault, rape, murder, and suicide, have been under the influence of alcohol. A 2004 study found that 11 percent of Canadians aged 15 years and over had been pushed or shoved by someone who has been drinking, while 3 percent were more physically assaulted.

## Alcohol and Driving

Driving while under the influence of alcohol is a major cause of injury and death in Canada. During 2001, 38 percent of all Canadian drivers killed in road accidents had been drinking, and each year close to 1,000 people a year die in alcohol-related road crashes in Canada. Many boating and snowmobile deaths also involve alcohol.

The good news is that recent Canadian research (2004) shows that teenage drivers account for only 5 percent of impaired driving trips, which is far less than any other age group.

---

### Fetal Alcohol Syndrome (FAS)

**W**omen of childbearing age need to be aware of the risks associated with drinking during pregnancy. It is a concern for young women because they might not realize they are pregnant until their pregnancy is well along. During this period, they could be exposing their fetus to alcohol without knowing it, causing serious damage.

Exposing a fetus to alcohol can result in a range of life-long effects. One of the worst is **fetal alcohol syndrome (FAS)**, which can cause the child to have reduced growth, mental disabilities, and a different facial makeup. People with FAS need plenty of support, and some may never be able to live independently.

Research suggests that most women who have children with serious problems, such as fetal alcohol syndrome, are binge drinkers (they drink more than 4 or 5 drinks per sitting). Public health authorities are concerned that binge drinking is more common among adolescent and young adult women.

---

# The Long-Term Health Effects of Alcohol
## Leaving No Body Part Unharmed

### Heart and Circulatory System

- Damages heart muscle and can lead to heart failure
- Weakens the heart's ability to pump blood
- Increases risk of high blood pressure
- Increases risk of heart attack
- Increases risk of stroke
- Reduces the production of red and white blood cells

### Liver

- Increases risk of developing cirrhosis (where scar tissue is formed in the liver as a result of dead liver cells)
- Increases risk of liver cancer
- Promotes excess fat to build up in the liver blocking the flow of blood to liver cells causing liver damage
- Can cause liver failure leading to coma or death

### Reproductive Systems

#### Male

- Decreases sperm count
- Leads to impotence

#### Female

- Increases reproductive problems such as irregular periods
- Drinking during pregnancy could lead to fetal alcohol syndrome

### Brain

- May lead to physical and psychological dependence on alcohol
- Leads to memory loss
- Disturbed sleep patterns
- Kills brain cells
- Affects normal growth patterns
- Impairs ability to think clearly
- May lead to mood swings and violent behaviour

### Pancreas

- Leads to inflammation of the pancreas. This blocks the entry to the small intestines, stopping pancreatic chemicals from entering the small intestines. These pancreatic chemicals begin to kill the pancreas. Death can result in severe cases.

### Stomach and Intestines

- Leads to ulcers, inflammation, and bleeding
- Leads to loss of appetite and vitamin deficiencies

### Bone

- Interferes with calcium absorption
- Leads to osteoporosis

Over the years, many of these long-term effects of alcohol can be reversed if the individual quits drinking.

## Alcohol and the Law

In Canada, all provinces and territories have **liquor control regulations** that govern the sale and advertisement of alcohol. Among other things, these laws set the age at which young people are allowed to drink. Currently, the drinking age is 19 years old in all provinces and territories, except for Quebec, Manitoba, and Alberta, where the age is 18 years.

These regulations also prohibit selling alcohol to underage, intoxicated, or disruptive persons. Restaurants and bars must obey these regulations because courts have sent a message to licensed establishments that they must not serve a guest to the point of intoxication.

### Legal Liability

Understandably, the courts have taken the issue of **legal liability** quite seriously—individuals in positions to make a difference have been held responsible for their actions where they have been negligent in looking out for the safety of the public or those under the influence of alcohol.

The national legal limit for impaired driving is 0.08 grams per 100 ml of blood. To drive with a BAC over this limit is a Criminal Code of Canada offence, which means that a person will have a criminal record if convicted. In addition, all provinces, except Quebec, have laws that allow a police officer to suspend a driver's license immediately for a short period of time (12 or 24 hours), if the driver has a BAC of .05 or greater (.04 in Saskatchewan).

### How to Get Help

People with alcohol dependence often are reluctant to change their harmful patterns. Newer professional treatment programs exist to help motivate a person to quit drinking before they hit "rock bottom."

A doctor or public health office will be able to make recommendations to anyone who feels his or her drinking is a problem. School guidance counsellors and nurses also have resources for teens.

Groups such as Alcoholics Anonymous provide important support for those with alcohol dependence by organizing meetings and discussions with others in similar situations and through their "12-step program."

These kinds of programs help people identify situations that trigger the desire to drink, teach ways to cope, and help with other life skills needed in order to live without alcohol.

More information can be found at the following website: **www.alcoholics-anonymous.org**.

# Alcohol Abuse and Dependence

**Alcohol abuse** is using alcohol in a way that causes problems for the individual or for others around that person. A person may abuse alcohol without actually being alcohol dependent; for example, when driving, during pregnancy, or when taking certain medications. Some problems linked to alcohol abuse include:

> ➢ Inability to meet work, school, or family responsibilities
> ➢ Arrests for drunk-driving and car crashes
> ➢ Drinking-related medical conditions
> ➢ Loss of non-drinking friends
> ➢ Loss of interest in activities that do not involve alcohol

Social situations that encourage drinking can lead a person to become alcohol-dependent.

Also known as alcoholism, **alcohol dependence** is very difficult (but not impossible) to break out of without help. The signs of alcohol dependence include:

> ➢ Drinking in larger amounts or over longer periods than intended
> ➢ Attempting to quit drinking without success
> ➢ Spending a great deal of time drinking or obtaining alcohol
> ➢ Neglecting daily activities

The dependent person deals with the many problems that result from drinking by drinking more. It is difficult for family and friends to understand and observe the vicious cycle.

Alcohol-dependent persons exist at all levels of society.

## Factors that Can Lead to Alcohol Dependence

Sometimes we think of alcohol-dependent persons as those on "skid row;" however, successful executives, senior citizens, and mothers at home are also the "face" of alcoholism. No single cause exists, but factors that increase a person's chance of dependency include:

> ➢ Frequent social situations that encourage drinking
> ➢ Mental health problems
> ➢ Excessive stress and unhappiness in one or more areas of life
> ➢ One or both parents dependent on alcohol
> ➢ Alcohol abuse in early teen years

Alcohol dependence is an addiction and can have the same serious, life-changing consequences that any addiction has. As with any drug, a person's tolerance for the drug increases as they consume increasing amounts. Therefore, a person suffering from alcohol dependence will need to drink more and more just to feel the effects.

Because alcohol dependency is a serious and widespread problem, many community resources are available to help people overcome drinking problems.

**MADD**
Mothers Against Drunk Driving™
Les mères contre l'alcool au volant™

**M**others Against Drunk Driving (MADD) may have been started by a mother but it has grown to include fathers, siblings, friends, and anyone else who would like to see drunk driving and drunk driving fatalities become things of the past.

The organization was started by Candy Lightner in California in 1980 after her 13-year-old daughter was killed by a drunk driver. MADD later expanded its focus from preventing drunk driving fatalities to ceasing impaired driving of any kind.

In 1990, the Canadian branch of the organization was created from a previously existing anti-impaired driving group known as PRIDE (People to Reduce Impaired Driving Everywhere).

MADD Canada's 70 chapters are composed of nearly 7,500 volunteers across the country.

### Did you know ...

- Each day in Canada there are approximately 4 deaths and approximately 190 injuries from crashes involving alcohol or drugs.
- Each year, close to 75,000 Canadians have their lives changed in some way by impaired drivers.

- Even though it's estimated that nearly 12.5 million impaired driving trips occur each year, only about 70,000 of them result in impaired driving charges.

One of MADD Canada's most visible activities is presentations in schools with the aim of educating children and teens about the dangers associated with impaired driving before they find themselves in risky situations. They also run programs for university and college students since people of that age are thought to be more at risk for impaired driving.  This focus is not unwarranted; in fact, 45 percent of teen drivers who are killed in road crashes are later found to have been drinking.

MADD Canada has also run several successful advertising campaigns. These have focused on (1) the people who get hurt by impaired driving crashes other than the victims themselves, and (2) how drinking can impair a driver's abilities even though the driver may not realize it.

For more information, or if you would like to volunteer, visit MADD Canada's website at **www.madd.ca.**

**Source:** MADD Canada (www.madd.ca).

## Questions for Study and Review

### Things to Think About and Explore

1. Identify two reasons why you think a teen might start to smoke and give three reasons why they shouldn't.

2. Youth smoking rates have gone down considerably in the last 30 years. List things that can be done to further reduce youth smoking rates in this country.

3. Outline three long-term health risks of smoking, besides cancer, and examine the ways in which each would decrease your quality of life.

4. List and describe four negative consequences of alcohol use and abuse.

5. Define BAC and explain why it is a useful measuring tool.

6. List four indicators of alcohol dependence and five factors that can lead to alcohol dependence.

### Things to Do and Practise

7. Cigarette warning labels and anti-smoking slogans have become more visual and graphic in recent years. Create another graphic image and slogan that the government could use to discourage people from starting to smoke or encourage them to quit.

8. Investigate the laws regarding tobacco and alcohol in your province or territory and evaluate whether or not you feel they are adequate.

9. Think about advertisements that you have seen for tobacco or alcohol that make these products seem appealing. Now create either a magazine advertisement or write a script for a television advertisement that discourages people from using tobacco or alcohol.

10. Start a debate in your class about the advantages and disadvantages of making alcohol completely illegal (prohibition).

11. Research the various techniques used in addiction counselling and decide which you think would be most effective in helping people quit smoking or drinking.

12. Imagine someone close to you has a dependency on tobacco or alcohol. Investigate the resources in your community that they could draw upon to help them quit.

## WWWeblinks

Name ➤     Al-Anon and Alateen

URL ➤     www.al-anon.alateen. org

Al-Anon and Alateen aim to help people who are close to those suffering from alcoholism. The site can help you find a group in your area.

Name ➤     P.A.R.T.Y.

URL ➤     www.partyprogram.com

The acronym P.A.R.T.Y. stands for *P*revent *A*lcohol and *R*isk related *T*rauma in *Y*outh. The P.A.R.T.Y. Program is an injury awareness and prevention program run by Sunnybrook and Women's College Health Sciences Centre.

Name ➤     Leave the Pack Behind!

URL ➤     www.leavethepack behind.org

A site that provides assistance to students and other young people trying to quit smoking.

# 15
# Marijuana and Other Illegal Drugs

**T**his chapter discusses the origins and effects of a range of psychoactive drugs that commonly are available to young people in Canada, as well as the laws regulating their use. These drugs will be presented according to how they are classified by Health Canada.

The first substance discussed is marijuana, which is presented in its own category because it produces several kinds of effects. The other drugs discussed will be presented in the following categories: hallucinogens (LSD, MDMA or ecstasy), depressants (heroin, inhalants), stimulants (amphetamines, cocaine, crystal meth) and performance-enhancing drugs (anabolic steroids).

## Chapter Objectives

In this chapter, you will:

➢ Identify the origins and chemical composition of cannabis (marijuana) and explore the factors influencing some people to smoke or not smoke the substance

➢ Understand the immediate and long-term health effects of smoking marijuana

➢ Learn that marijuana is classified as an illegal drug in Canada and that those caught with it in their possession may be subjected to criminal prosecution and a criminal record

➢ Distinguish the main types of hallucinogens and the dangers associated with them

➢ Distinguish the main types of illegal depressants and the dangers associated with them

➢ Distinguish the main types of illegal stimulants and the dangers associated with them

➢ Distinguish the main types of illegal anabolic steroids and the dangers associated with them

➢ Begin to understand how to deal with the problem of substance abuse and other forms of dependence

## Key Terms

➢ *Cannabis sativa*
➢ Gateway Theory
➢ Controlled Drugs and Substances Act (CDSA)
➢ club drugs
➢ lysergic acid diethylamide (LSD)
➢ ecstasy
➢ date-rape drugs
➢ heroin
➢ inhalants
➢ CNS depressants
➢ amphetamine-type stimulants (ATS)
➢ cocaine
➢ performance-enhancing drugs

# Cannabis and Marijuana

*Cannabis sativa* (Latin for "cultivated hemp") is the plant from which marijuana, hashish, sinsemilla, and hash oil are produced. Tetrahydrocannabinol (THC) is the major psychoactive ingredient in cannabis, and marijuana is its most popular form. It is the most commonly used illegal drug in Canada and around the world.

In Canada, cannabis is the subject of a great deal of debate, mostly concerning the possible medical uses of marijuana and the laws governing its use.

The desire to escape stress or negative thoughts is among the many factors that may lead a person to use marijuana.

## Who Is Saying "No" to Marijuana?

Less than 3 percent of teens in Canada report using marijuana daily. Among the relatively small number of regular users are people who use for a variety of reasons: to escape stress or negative thoughts, to relax, or simply because they like the way it makes them feel. Some may see it as a ticket into a certain social network; others may use it because it has a "forbidden" quality or because they wish to experiment.

For many young people who are active in sports or other activities, marijuana simply doesn't fit their lifestyle. It reduces reaction time and causes drowsiness. Other young people are concerned about the effects on their health that come from smoking any substance.

*Cannabis sativa* (Latin for "cultivated hemp") is the plant from which marijuana, hashish, sinsemilla, and hash oil are produced.

# Consequences of Marijuana Use

The effects of smoking marijuana are almost immediate and last from 2 to 4 hours. If the drug is eaten, effects appear more gradually, lastlonger, and can be more intense.

Typically, use of marijuana or cannabis causes red eyes, dry mouth and throat, increased appetite, and problems with concentration and short-term memory. Although basically a hallucinogen, marijuana also produces a mix of depressant effects, such as relaxation, and stimulant effects, such as increased heart rate. Sensory perception seems enhanced, and sense of time and space is distorted.

Some people experience more intense, unpleasant effects including hallucinations, anxiety, and depression, while a few experience panic, paranoia, or an increase in psychiatric symptoms that already existed.

## Physical and Psychological Effects

With most drugs, including marijuana, the longer and more heavily a person uses, the more likely it is that he or she will suffer from long-term effects:

> **Respiratory system.** Like tobacco smoke, marijuana smoke damages the respiratory system. Both contain many of the same carcinogens (cancer-producing chemicals), but marijuana smoke contains more tar and higher amounts of carcinogens. Marijuana smokers inhale more deeply and hold the smoke in their lungs longer—as a result, respiratory problems can occur from smoking less cannabis than tobacco.

> **The mind.** Long-term, heavy use of marijuana leads to problems with memory, concentration, and the brain's ability to organize and process complex information. Lack of motivation and lack of interest in life also seem to go hand in hand with regular, long-term marijuana use (although no one knows for sure if this is a direct effect of using, or a reason that a person might start using).

> **Mental and emotional health.** Recent important research has shown that marijuana use can make symptoms of schizophrenia (a serious mental disorder) worse in people who already have it. It also can bring on the disorder if a person is predisposed to it. Long-term marijuana use also may bring on schizophrenia in a person who has no predisposition to it.

> **Pregnancy.** Marijuana should not be used by pregnant women. Studies have shown that marijuana use during pregnancy can have a negative effect on the mental development of a child.

> **Dependence.** Users can develop a tolerance and will gradually need more to get the same effect. Treatment programs in Canada report that marijuana is the drug of choice for an increasing number of their patients.

---

## Marijuana Use and Driving

In Canada, the use of marijuana and other forms of cannabis has risen in the past number of years, and so have concerns over people driving under the influence of the drug.

Cannabis use before driving (or involvement in any other activity that requires coordination, such as using machines or playing sports) is dangerous. Cannabis use reduces motor coordination, especially when used in combination with alcohol.

THC, the major psychoactive ingredient in cannabis, has been found in the bodies of many fatally injured drivers and pedestrians in Canada and the United States.

## Dealing with Marijuana Dependence

Contrary to what some believe, psychological and physical dependence on marijuana, and other forms of cannabis, does occur in people who use these substances regularly and heavily. Users also develop a tolerance to marijuana and, as a result, they gradually need more to get the same effect.

Withdrawal symptoms may be relatively mild compared to other substances, but they include anxiety, irritability, sleeping problems, sweating, and loss of appetite. These withdrawal symptoms and psychological cravings can make it difficult for long-term marijuana users to stop using the drug. As with any drug, dependence on marijuana is characterized by compulsive use, increased focus on acquiring and using it, and continued use despite growing problems.

Treatment for marijuana dependence is much like treatment for other substance dependencies, and it usually involves learning the skills to live well without the use of any substance. Although some people may be able to learn to control their marijuana smoking and remain occasional users, a person who has developed a full dependency usually will find it very difficult to control.

Lack of motivation and lack of interest in life have been linked to marijuana use.

| IMMEDIATE, SHORT-TERM, AND LONG-TERM EFFECTS OF MARIJUANA USE | | | |
|---|---|---|---|
| EFFECT | IMMEDIATE | SHORT-TERM | LONG-TERM |
| Red eyes | ✓ | | |
| Dry mouth/throat | ✓ | | |
| Short-term memory loss | ✓ | ✓ | |
| Enhanced sensory perception | ✓ | | |
| Paranoia | ✓ | ✓ | |
| Lack of coordination | | ✓ | |
| Increased heart rate | ✓ | | |
| Anxiety | ✓ | ✓ | |
| Concentration problems | ✓ | ✓ | |
| Trouble with problem solving | ✓ | ✓ | |
| Cancer | | | ✓ |
| Respiratory problems | | | ✓ |
| Mental health problems | | | ✓ |
| Dependence | | | ✓ |

# Marijuana and the Law

Currently, all forms of cannabis are subject to the **Controlled Drugs and Substances Act (CDSA),** and unlawful possession is a criminal offence. The police and legal authorities will charge and prosecute individuals caught in possession of even small amounts of cannabis, and these individuals risk having a criminal record for life.

In addition to the possibility of a criminal record, possession of small quantities is subject to a fine of $1,000 or imprisonment for up to six months, or both. Penalties increase for larger amounts and subsequent offences. Trafficking, cultivation, and importing or exporting of cannabis products all carry jail terms, which vary depending on the amounts involved and the circumstances.

## Still a Criminal Offence

Possession of cannabis is a criminal offence in Canada and those caught in possession are likely to be prosecuted to the full extent of the law.

Until recently, the law pertaining to possession of small quantities appeared to be in a state of flux in Canada. The Canadian government had signalled its intention to change the law to reduce the penalty for possession of small amounts and to increase the penalties for growing and selling. The idea was to create a better balance between the nature of the offence and the severity of the penalty. In proposing this change, the government made it clear that it did not condone or wish to encourage marijuana use.

The new federal government elected in 2006 took this issue off the government's agenda. Possession of cannabis remains a criminal offence in Canada.

Unlawful possession of marijuana is a criminal offence under the Controlled Drugs and Substances Act (CDSA).

---

## The Gateway Theory

The **Gateway Theory** proposes that someone who uses marijuana is more likely than a non-user to go on to use drugs such as cocaine and heroin. Two main facts are usually cited to support this theory:

- Almost all people who used both marijuana and "hard" drugs used marijuana first.

- Marijuana users are more likely to try other drugs.

Those on the other side of the debate say that these facts may also be explained by other factors. For example:

- Opportunities to use marijuana arise earlier in life than the opportunities to use other drugs.

- Some individuals are simply more likely to use drugs in general (any drug).

- The vast majority of marijuana users do not go on to use heroin or cocaine.

In other words, the available evidence provides no clear conclusion on the question of whether marijuana is a "gateway" to more serious drugs.

The facts are consistent with the Gateway Theory, but there are alternative explanations that are also consistent with the evidence.

**Source:** Adapted from "Cannabis" produced by the BC Partners for Mental Health and Addiction Information, September 2003.

# The Classification of Illegal Drugs—The Risks and Effects

| CLASS AND EXAMPLES | EFFECTS<br>(CAN HAVE AT LEAST ONE OF THESE EFFECTS) | HARMS/DANGERS<br>(CAN INCLUDE SOME OF THESE) |
|---|---|---|
| **CANNABIS** | | |
| Marijuana | Drowsiness, relaxation | Impaired driving |
| Hash | Feelings of well-being, euphoria | Linked to schizophrenia |
| Hash oil | Increased appetite | Panic reactions |
| **HALLUCINOGENS** | | |
| Mescaline | Altered/distorted body image | Panic reactions |
| Ecstasy | Feelings of enhanced mental capacity | Psychosis |
| Phencyclidine (PCP, "angel dust") | Muscle twitches | Flashbacks |
| Lysergic acid diethylamide (LSD) | Dizziness, nausea, vomiting | Anxiety and depression |
| Psilocybin ("magic mushrooms") | Out of touch with reality | Memory and thinking problems |
| | Visual and auditory distortions, hallucinations | Poor judgment leading to serious accidents or death |
| **CENTRAL NERVOUS SYSTEM DEPRESSANTS** | | |
| Alcohol | Decreased inhibitions | Respiratory depression |
| Solvents, inhalants | Increased confidence | Seizures |
| Minor tranquilizers (Valium®, Ativan®) | Relaxation | Liver disease |
| Sleeping medications (Halcion®, Imovane®) | Intoxication | Heart disease |
| Barbiturates (Tuinal®) | Poor judgment | Increased risk of cancer |
| | Slurred speech | Fetal alcohol spectrum disorder |
| | Impaired memory/thinking | Fatal overdose |
| | Decreased motor skills | Brain damage |
| **OPIATES/NARCOTICS ( A SUB-CLASS OF CNS DEPRESSANTS)** | | |
| Various prescription pain killers | Pain killer (analgesia) | Hepatitis (from sharing needles) |
| Morphine | Drowsiness | HIV/AIDS (from sharing needles) |
| Codeine | Intoxication followed by euphoria | Increased risk of some cancers |
| Heroin | Constipation | Brain damage |
| | Decreased breathing rate | Pulmonary problems |
| | Pinpoint pupils | Fatal overdose |
| **CENTRAL NERVOUS SYSTEM STIMULANTS** | | |
| Amphetamines (including crystal meth) | Euphoria | Paranoid psychosis |
| Ritalin® (methylphenidate) | Increased energy | Depression |
| Cocaine and crack | Increased heart rate, blood pressure | Seizures |
| Nicotine | Decreased appetite | Insomnia |
| Caffeine | Dilated pupils | Sexual disinterest |
| | Feelings of enhanced sociability, sexuality, and confidence | HIV/AIDS (from sharing needles) |
| | | Heart attacks/stroke |
| | | Extreme anxiety, panic states |
| | | Hallucinations |

# Hallucinogens

The **hallucinogens** include a wide range of both naturally occurring substances (e.g., mescaline, peyote, psilocybin) and synthesized substances (e.g., LSD, PCP, MDA, MDMA or ecstasy). Hallucinogenic drugs greatly distort the senses and, as their classification implies, can cause hallucinations. Most of these substances are taken orally.

## LSD

**LSD (lysergic acid diethylamide)**, commonly known as "acid," is one of the most common hallucinogenic drugs. It is manufactured from lysergic acid, which is found in a fungus that grows on rye and other grains. It is very powerful; there are 3,000 doses of pure LSD in a pill the size of an aspirin. Pure LSD is a tasteless, odourless, fine white powder that is sold in capsules or tablets.

As is the case with other drugs, the effects of LSD are unpredictable. Usually, the user feels the first effects of the drug 30 to 45 minutes after taking it. Emotional reactions vary greatly. Users may feel several emotions in quick succession—euphoria (a feeling of extreme well-being) can quickly change to sadness or fear, and then back again. It is not uncommon for users to experience disorienting sensations that can lead to a "bad trip" involving anxiety, and terrifying thoughts and feelings. Because LSD trips last 12 hours or more, a negative experience can be extremely disturbing.

A person cannot overdose or become physically dependent on LSD, but regular users can experience upsetting flashbacks in which they feel the effects of LSD without taking the drug again.

## Ecstasy

**Ecstasy** (methylenedioxymethamphetamine, or MDMA) is considered a hallucinogen but it also has stimulant effects. It is made in illegal drug labs and goes by other names such as E, XTC, Adam, Euphoria, X, MDM, and Love Doves. It comes usually in gelatin capsules or tablets. The pills can be any colour, and they may have a design on one side such as a dove or a diamond. Ecstasy can also come as a powder that users snort or, less commonly, dissolve and inject.

As is the case with other drugs, the effects from ecstasy have a great deal to do with the state of mind and health of the user. Initially, users' pupils become dilated, their jaw tightens, and often they experience nausea, sweating, and dry mouth and throat—effects that are common with other stimulants. Their blood pressure and heart rate increase and they often lose their appetite. Some users also report a heightened sense of their surroundings, greater appreciation of music, and a heightened sensual experience.

The effects of long-term ecstasy use include impairment in short-term memory, depression, mood changes, and disrupted sleep patterns. Users also may experience flashbacks or psychosis. The signs of an overdose include eye-rolling, chest pain, and seizures.

---

## What are "Club Drugs"?

The term **club drugs** refers to a range of illegal and dangerous substances associated with some nightclubs and other dance or party venues.

Little is known about the long-term effects of these substances. A major concern is that often they contain unknown additives or impurities. This means that the results can be unpredictable and potentially very harmful, especially when these substances are used in combination with alcohol or other drugs.

In addition to LSD, ecstasy, crystal meth, and speed (discussed in this chapter), this group of illegal substances includes ketamine, GHB, and Rohypnol®.

The latter are the so-called "date-rape drugs" that are sometimes used intentionally to sedate unsuspecting victims. The victims are then sexually assaulted.

Date rape is a form of violent, sexual assault and is a very serious criminal offence.

# What Are Date-Rape Drugs?
## Stay Safe and Be in Control

**D**ate-rape drugs is a term given to any drug that is used for the purpose of getting someone intoxicated to the point where forced or non-consensual sexual activity can take place with little to no resistance. This is a severe form of physical and sexual assault and a serious criminal offense.

Generally, illegal or pharmaceutical drugs (such as Rohypnol ®, GHB, and ketamine) are thought of as date-rape drugs. However, far more unwanted sexual encounters take place when one or both parties are under the influence of alcohol than with prescription or street drugs.

- **Rohypnol®.** When mixed with a drink, Rohypnol® is colourless, tasteless, and odourless, which makes it especially easy to go undetected when slipped into a beverage. After the drug has worn off, Rohypnol® often leaves people with little or no memory of what has happened to them while on the drug.

- **GHB (also known as liquid E).** At higher doses, GHB can cause extreme fatigue and unconsciousness. However, the difference between a high and low dose can be extremely difficult to measure. GHB can taste slightly salty, so if your drink tastes funny to you, throw it away.

- **Ketamine (Special K, K).** Originally and still used as a veterinary anaesthetic, ketamine produces numbness and paralysis, and can also (depending on the dose) make you feel like you are out of your own body. High doses can lead to unconsciousness and can leave the user open to assault.

### How do I protect myself?

The best way to protect yourself is to constantly be aware of your drinks and your surroundings. You should also:

- **Always party with friends.** Be sure to keep close tabs on your friends; don't let them leave with strangers or anyone who makes you uncomfortable. It is a good idea to have one friend stay sober for the evening to keep an eye out for those who choose to drink.

- **Know who is pouring your drink.** Watch your drink being poured by professional bar staff, or pour your own drink.

- **Watch your drink.** Keep your drink with you and don't leave it unattended. Give your drink to a friend to hold if you are going outside or to the bathroom.

- **Tell someone you trust.** If you feel like you are overly intoxicated or have lost control of yourself, tell someone you trust. Tell them to stay with you until you feel better. If you are with someone who is out of control, do not leave them alone.

- **Don't plan to go home by yourself.** Plan to go home as a group or with someone you trust.

While these rules are not infallible, they will help make any partying situation safer. You will feel safer and more in control.

**Source:** Adapted from "Health Education and Promotion: Date Rape and Club Drugs." Copyright 2006 © York University.

# Depressants

**Depressants** have the effect of depressing the activity of the central nervous system (CNS) and slowing down bodily systems. This class of drugs includes alcohol (Chapter 14); opiates (e.g., heroin and morphine); inhalants (e.g., gasoline and glue); and various prescribed medications (e.g., barbiturates and tranquilizers).

## Heroin and Other Opiates

**Heroin** and other opiates are highly addictive. Some opiates (e.g., opium and morphine) are natural drugs that come from the seedpod of the Asian poppy, *Papaver somniferum*. Others (e.g., codeine, Demerol®, Dilaudid®, or Percodan®) are synthetic drugs produced in laboratories.

Heroin (variously referred to as H, horse, junk, or smack) is opium that is refined into a fine white or brown powder. It can be sniffed, smoked ("chasing the dragon"), taken orally, or injected under the skin ("skin popping"), but it usually is injected directly into a blood vessel ("mainlining"). The synthesized opiates have valuable medical uses as painkillers (e.g., oxycodone) or cough suppressants (e.g., codeine), but they should only be used under medical supervision.

Heroin and other opiates slow down body functions and suppress or reduce both physical and emotional pain. In addition to reducing pain, lower doses of these drugs also can produce dizziness, reduced mental alertness, and drowsiness. Initial use can result in unpleasant reactions such as nausea and vomiting, but these fade with regular use. Feelings of warmth, relaxation, and detachment, as well as a lessening of anxiety, are common effects of opiates.

At higher doses, opiates produce increased euphoria, impaired concentration, slower breathing and lower blood pressure, contraction of pupils, and constipation. In some cases, they cause a rapid and irregular heart rate. Large doses can produce stupor, coma, or even death from respiratory failure.

Because opiates, including legal medications, are quite addictive, it is not uncommon for a person to become dependent on an opiate-based medication (e.g., Percodan®, or OxyContin®). People do successfully give up long-term use of heroin and other opiates, but coming off and staying off these drugs is very difficult.

## Inhalants

**Inhalants** produce feelings of euphoria and light-headedness, while slowing down bodily systems. Examples include paint thinners, modelling glue, gasoline, and cleaning fluids. Their use can result in brain damage, suffocation, and death.

Abusers of inhalants tend to be children and younger teens. The number of students abusing inhalants tends to decrease through the high school years.

Not all drugs are created in labs; some opiates are natural drugs that come from the seedpod of the Asian poppy, *Papaver somniferum*.

The dangerous practice of injecting heroin or another drug directly into a blood vessel is called mainlining.

## Prescribed CNS Depressant Medications

**CNS Depressants** include a number of prescribed medications such as barbiturates and tranquilizers. Barbiturates ("downers") were developed to treat sleep problems, anxiety, tension, high blood pressure, and seizures. Some also are used as anesthetics.

Many disorders now are treated with tranquilizers called benzodiazepines, which usually are prescribed to treat anxiety, nervousness, sleep problems, and to relax muscles. Although they are safer and have fewer side effects than barbiturates, they generally are recommended only for short-term use because they can lead to dependence.

You should always follow the directions of your doctor and pharmacist when taking any prescribed medication.

CNS depressants should never be combined with any substance that causes drowsiness, including alcohol, opiate pain medicines, and certain over-the-counter cold and allergy medications. Combining such drugs can multiply each other's effects, slowing down breathing and heart rate to the point of death.

Discontinuing prolonged use of a CNS depressant medicine can lead to withdrawal. Because they work, in effect, to slow down the brain, when one stops taking the drug, a possible consequence is that the brain rebounds and seizures can occur. Before ending a course of treatment, a patient should consult a qualified medical practitioner with respect to the possible effects.

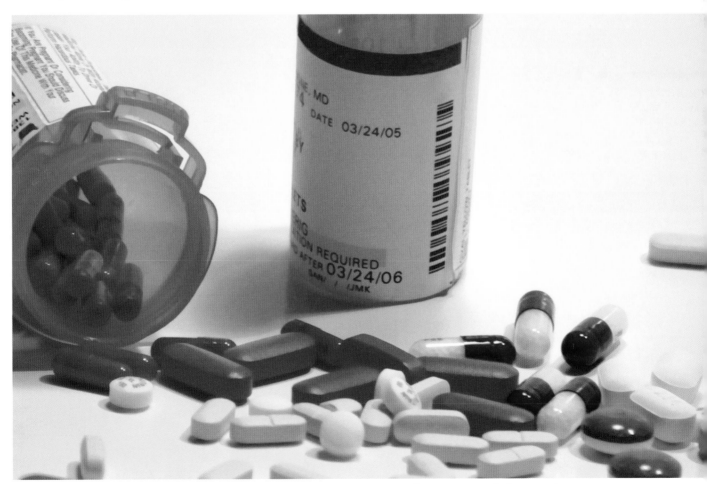

Overdoses of CNS depressants produce effects similar to alcohol overdoses. The person becomes extremely drowsy and passes out.

# Stimulants

**Stimulants** speed up or excite the central nervous system. Examples include caffeine, nicotine, cocaine, amphetamine-type stimulants, and a medication called methylphenidate (Ritalin®). Stimulants generally are used for their ability to increase alertness, decrease appetite, delay fatigue, and produce feelings of well-being. For people diagnosed with attention-deficit hyperactivity disorder (ADHD), methylphenidate produces a calming rather than stimulating effect.

Use of stimulant drugs can result in severe psychological and physical dependence, which can make it difficult to stop using them.

## Amphetamine-Type Stimulants (ATS)

**Amphetamine-type stimulants (ATS)**, such as crystal methamphetamine, are potent drugs with similar chemical structures. Most are made by illegal labs for non-medical purposes.

The effects of these powerful and dangerous stimulants are similar to those of cocaine. They include increased alertness and energy, a feeling of well-being, decreased appetite, rapid heart beat and breathing, increased blood pressure, sweating, dilated pupils, and dry mouth. A person may become talkative, restless, or excited; feel powerful, superior, aggressive, or hostile; or behave in a bizarre, repetitive fashion. Higher doses may cause euphoria.

ATS drugs can produce a strong dependence, making it very challenging to quit using them.

## Cocaine and Crack

**Cocaine** (variously called C, coke, snow, blow) is a powerfully addictive stimulant drug processed from the leaves of the South American coca bush. In Canada, the most common form of cocaine is a fine white crystalline powder that is often diluted with another similar material, such as sugar, cornstarch, or talcum powder. It can be sniffed, absorbed through other mucous membranes (such as those found in the mouth), smoked, or injected.

"Crack" is a smokable, freebase form of cocaine made by adding baking soda to a cocaine solution and allowing the mixture to dry. Freebase is a form of cocaine purified with ether that also can be smoked. Some users add crack and freebase to tobacco or marijuana cigarettes; others inhale the vapours from heated glass pipes.

## How Cocaine Becomes Addictive

People who try cocaine may get hooked on the quick feelings of euphoria and increased energy it produces. People addicted to cocaine are said to "chase the high," meaning they continue to use cocaine, trying to experience the effects they felt the first time they used it.

Cocaine addicts will never feel this high in the same way again, and this addiction can lead to insanity and death.

## Effects and Consequences of Cocaine

Cocaine users describe a range of effects from cocaine, saying they feel more alert, energetic, confident, physically strong, and intelligent. Although they may perceive those benefits, they actually are experiencing numerous negative psychological and physical effects, including rapid heart beat and fast breathing, dilated pupils, sweating, and decreased appetite.

Large doses can cause severe agitation, paranoid thinking, erratic or violent behaviour, muscle spasms, tremors, twitching, hallucinations, headache, pressure in the chest, nausea, blurred vision, fever, convulsions, and death. Impurities in street cocaine can bring on a fatal allergic reaction. People typically experience depression and extreme tiredness as a "hangover" from cocaine use.

Repeated use of cocaine may cause long-lasting problems with memory, attention, and behaviour. Chronic users, who alternate cocaine "binges" with crashes (periods of abstinence), often experience mood swings, restlessness, extreme excitability, sleep disorders, suspiciousness, hallucinations and delusions, eating disorders, weight loss, constipation, and sexual problems. People who inject cocaine get a short-lived high, so they need to inject a number of times a day to maintain the high. If they share needles, this greatly increases the risk of contracting HIV and/or hepatitis.

Caffeine is a common stimulant that speeds up or excites the central nervous system.

Repeated cocaine use leads to use of larger amounts because of the tolerance for the drug that regular users develop.

# A Reality Check on Steroids

When you think of steroids, you may think of Olympic scandals or professional athletes. Studies are telling us that about 83,000 young Canadians between the ages of 11 and 18 have tried steroids, at least once. Most of these are young males who are using steroids to improve their performance in sports, and to change their physical appearance. Steroids are performance-enhancing drugs that have many physical, psychological, and even legal consequences.

## What Are Anabolic Steroids?

Anabolic steroids belong to a class of drugs known as ergogenic, or **performance-enhancing drugs**. They include both the naturally occurring male sex hormone, testosterone, and synthetic drugs chemically related to testosterone. These drugs have a few medical uses, including combating body wasting in patients with AIDS and other diseases that result in loss of muscle mass.

**Anabolic steroids** are known on the street or in school by different names such as "roids," "juice," "gym candy," "pumpers," "stackers," "weight trainers," or "hype." They are a synthetic form of the male hormone testosterone. Testosterone is responsible for the growth and development of bones, muscles, facial hair, and a deeper voice.

Steroids are prescribed by doctors in certain cases to treat specific injuries, illnesses, and other medical conditions. They only are available with a doctor's prescription. Steroids obtained through any other means could possibly be impure, leaving the door wide open to a host of other health risks. Steroids can come in the following forms: pills and capsules, muscle injections, and gels and creams that are rubbed into the skin.

## What Are the Side Effects?

There are many very real, and very dangerous side effects to steroids. Part of the problem is that they do not show up right away. You may not know what you are in for until much later. If you are getting advice from friends or other users, remember that they may not know or be able to tell you about the dangers and side effects, especially if they have not yet experienced them:

> **Your physical appearance.** Some of the physical side effects of steroids can change the way you look in ways you may not have considered. Severe acne of the face and body and hair loss can occur. In teenagers, steroids can stop bones from growing, which means you may not grow to your full height. Some effects are gender-specific. Girls who use steroids may have more body hair, smaller breasts, a deeper voice, and a larger clitoris, all of which usually are permanent if steroids are used often enough. Boys can see breast growth and tenderness, which also could be permanent with frequent, long-term use.

## Enhancing Performance?

Today, some athletes and others abuse anabolic steroids to enhance performance and improve physical appearance.

These drugs increase lean muscle mass, strength, and endurance, but they have not been found to improve agility, skill, cardiovascular capacity, or recovery time after activity.

The governing bodies of most professional and amateur sports (including track and field, weight lifting, and football) have banned the use of anabolic steroids.

- **Your physical health.** Steroids can be very dangerous to your overall health. For example, if you inject steroids and share your needles or vials, you can become infected with Hepatitis B and C. You also put yourself at serious risk of getting HIV/AIDS. Some of the other side effects are just as serious, and can include high blood pressure, damage to the liver (and liver cancer), damage to the kidneys, and high cholesterol (leading to heart attack or stroke).

- **Your reproductive health.** Steroids can wreak havoc on your reproductive organs. In boys, steroids can shrink the testicles and cause impotence (difficulty in achieving erection). In girls, steroid use can cause irregular periods. In both girls and boys, it can cause infertility.

- **Your psychological health.** Your personality can undergo a number of changes as well. You can experience uncontrollable bursts of anger and aggressiveness, or even violence, which is known as "roid rage." You can experience depression, mood swings, nervousness, or edginess. You can even impair your learning and memory.

Long-term effects of steroids include shrunken testicles, impotence, severe acne, liver damage and stunted growth.

## Effects of Steroids on the Body
### More than You Bargained for ...

Steroids have a number of effects on the sexual characteristics of both males and females, which can change the user's appearance, sometimes drastically. They can also affect your physical, psychological, and reproductive systems.

Long-term use of steroids can cause the following changes to the user's body:

### Specifically in Boys and Men

- Shrunken testicles, leading to impotence
- Impaired sperm production, leading to infertility
- Breast growth and tenderness
- Hair loss

### Specifically in Girls and Women

- Irregular periods, or loss of periods, leading to infertility
- Deepening of the voice
- Growth of facial and body hair
- Shrinkage of breasts
- Growth of clitoris

### In Men and Women

- Severe acne
- Stunted growth
- Muscle spasms
- Decreased flexibility
- Water retention
- Nose bleeds
- Kidney damage
- Liver damage
- Weakened immune system
- Increased blood pressure
- Increased cholesterol

# Dealing with Dependence

All substance use presents the potential for problems. Even a single drinking or drug-using experience, or a pattern of so-called "experimental" use, can result in serious problems: an overdose, an accident, and, in the case of illegal drugs, criminal prosecution. Nevertheless, most teens who do experiment with alcohol and other substances do not go on to become dependent on drugs.

When does a substance-use pattern cross the line into something that is clearly not healthy—that is, a **substance dependence**? The simple answer is that if a person's substance use is causing problems and they continue to use, then they have developed a dependence. Trained physicians, psychologists, and social workers can assess this by asking questions such as:

If a person's substance use is causing problems and they continue to use, then they have developed a dependence.

People with a dependence can benefit from the help of a friend, classmate, co-worker, or family member who often will see the problem before the user does.

> ➢ Are you taking larger amounts of the substance or using over a longer period than was intended?

> ➢ Have you tried but failed to cut back or control your substance use?

> ➢ Do you spend a great deal of time on activities to obtain the substance, use the substance, and recover from its effects?

> ➢ Are you giving up or reducing important social, occupational, or recreational activities because of substance use?

> ➢ Are you continuing to use a substance even though you suspect it is causing problems in various areas of your life (e.g., family, school, social, financial, legal, work)?

> ➢ Do you keep using in order to avoid withdrawal symptoms?

On the basis of this kind of assessment, the doctor or counsellor would rate the level of severity of the person's dependence and work out a course of action with the person.

It usually is quite difficult for a person to admit that something that once gave them pleasure has become a problem.

## Finding Help

It is usually quite difficult for a person to admit that something that once gave them pleasure has become a problem. That is why people with a dependence can benefit from the help of a friend, classmate, co-worker, or family member, who often will see the problem before the user does. You can check the resources on the following page ("Kicking Addictions") to learn more about alcohol or drug dependence and how best to deal with it.

Talking to the user about your concerns and noting what you are seeing or feeling works better than pointing fingers in a blaming way. If the user is willing to go for help, support them. Help him or her contact a guidance counsellor, call the local addiction services office to talk to an addictions counsellor, or encourage them to go to a 12-step meeting such as Alcoholics Anonymous or Narcotics Anonymous.

Sometimes those close to a person with an alcohol or drug dependence try to cover up the problem, which often makes matters worse. If you are in such a situation, dealing with the problem effectively not only means making changes, it also means changing your response and possibly getting help for yourself.

## The Sooner, the Better

If substance use is beginning to cause problems, it is important to deal with it immediately and not allow the situation to worsen. When individuals start drinking or using a substance, they are not setting out to develop an alcohol or drug problem, but patterns of use can shift very easily.

In the past, some people believed that addicted individuals needed to "hit bottom" (or lose something very valuable to them) before they could be helped. Most counsellors are now trained in motivational approaches that can help people at any stage of a dependence.

Sometimes people with a substance abuse problem can deal with a dependence on their own, but if the problem becomes severe, or if they feel that they need support, it is important to seek help. Different kinds of help are available, including brochures, books, videos, and public information sessions. Trusted teachers, guidance counsellors, clergy, and family doctors are all possible resources, and most communities have addiction counselling offices nearby.

A substance abuse counsellor will talk to the user about the substance abuse and work with the user on a plan that starts him or her on a healthy new path. Nowadays, there are also many online resources that can be consulted privately either by a friend or by the person with the dependence problem, or by both together. Some of these resources are listed at the end of this chapter.

Substance dependence is a serious problem, one that often requires the help of professionally trained counsellors and medical professionals with experience in this area. Acting sooner to address a substance abuse problem is always better.

### Harm Reduction Approach

North America's first legal, supervised injection site (SIS) opened in 2003 in Vancouver's Downtown East Side, one of Canada's poorest neighbourhoods and home to nearly 5,000 injection drug users.

The SIS, known as Insite, is a clean, lower-risk environment where users can inject their own drugs under supervision. The purpose of the site is to reduce the spread of infectious diseases, reduce public disorder caused by street injecting, and increase contact between drug injectors and health services personnel.

The SIS is an example of a harm-reduction approach: It aims to reduce problems linked to drug use without insisting that clients stop using. For people suffering from drug dependencies who are not likely to accept treatment, this is viewed as a practical and humane approach.

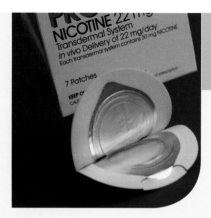

## Kicking Addictions
### Know the Options

For those who have decided to try to overcome an addictive behaviour, there are a number of treatment options available to them.

### The "Cold Turkey" Method

Some believe the simplest way to quit an addiction is to stop altogether. This is called going "cold turkey," a term that evolved from the fact that addicts going through withdrawal often break out in cold sweats and goose bumps. This method can be extremely difficult and, in cases of severe addictions, can be dangerous—so it's advisable to check with a doctor before beginning.

### The Anti-Craving Medication Method

In some cases, controlled medication can help wean people off addictive substances. Some people use either nicotine patches or nicotine gum to wean themselves off cigarettes. That way, they get small doses of the ingredient without the harmful additives. Some heroin addicts are treated with methadone, which decreases the withdrawal symptoms.

### The 12-Step Method

A key component of any 12-step program is the idea of group meetings with others who suffer from similar addictions. Groups are "anonymous" and participants use only their first names. They feel safe acknowledging their problems without worrying about their reputations outside the group. Alcoholics Anonymous (AA), formed in 1935, was the first 12-step group.

### Motivational Counselling

Strategies that focus on motivational counselling seek help a person to see the benefits of changing their relationship with substances. Motivational strategies avoid labelling a person, and do not necessarily require that person to quit the substance altogether.

**There is no surefire way to stop an addictive behaviour. Anyone looking to quit an addiction should start by talking to a doctor or a counsellor in order to assess the different options that are available.**

## Questions for Study and Review

### Things to Think About and Explore

1. Outline the possible legal implications of being caught in possession of marijuana by a law enforcement officer.

2. List the known physical and psychological consequences of prolonged marijuana use.

3. The Gateway Theory proposes that use of marijuana leads to use of other drugs. Debate whether or not the same could be said for alcohol or tobacco use.

4. Distinguish between depressants and stimulants and give examples of each of these types of drug.

5. Caffeine is a stimulant that nearly everyone has ingested at some point. Express an opinion as to whether or not you feel caffeine should be more closely regulated.

6. Imagine a friend is intending to use illegal drugs for the first time. Give three examples of ways that it can put your friend in danger and two examples of ways it can put you in danger.

### Things to Do and Practise

7. Write a letter to your Member of Parliament in which you express an opinion on the proposed decriminalization of marijuana. State whether or not you feel it might encourage or discourage young people to try using it. Be sure to consider both sides of the issue.

8. Choose one of the classes of drugs. Create a pamphlet listing the effects of this type of drug and how these effects will negatively impact a user if they are:
   (a) a parent with young children,
   (b) a teenager, or
   (c) a professional athlete.

9. Divide into groups and debate the issue of whether or not all drugs should be legal, but regulated. Be sure to consider both sides of the argument.

10. Apply what you have learned from this chapter to make a poster discouraging young people from trying illegal drugs.

11. Insite, the supervised injection site in Vancouver, has now been open for a few years. Write a paragraph detailing your position on the "harm reduction approach" in the case of severely addicted drug users.

12. Imagine you have a close friend or relative with a serious drug dependency. Draw up a list of services available in your community and online (individuals, associations, websites, etc.) that can help this person move away from the dependency.

## WWWeblinks

Name ➤ Centre for Addiction and Mental Health

URL ➤ www.camh.net

The Centre for Addiction and Mental Health is Canada's leading addiction and mental health teaching hospital. CAMH is committed to providing comprehensive, well-coordinated, accessible care for people who have problems with mental illness or addiction.

Name ➤ Narcotics Anonymous

URL ➤ www.na.org

Narcotics Anonymous (like Alcoholics Anonymous) uses a group support dynamic to help people overcome addictions to narcotic substances. Their site can help you find locations of meetings in your community.

## Table of Contents

# UNIT 6
## Conflict Resolution and Personal Safety

What this unit is about ...

➢ Why will understanding conflict help me to deal with conflict?

➢ What forms of violence have I witnessed in the past, and what can I do to ensure that I don't become a victim or a perpetrator of violence?

# 16
# Conflict Resolution and Anger Management

## Key Terms

- conflict
- internal conflicts
- interpersonal conflict
- intra-group conflict
- inter-group conflict
- conflict resolution skills
- mediation
- peer mediation
- adjudication

**C**onflict is a part of life, and it affects everyone. Your reactions and methods of dealing with conflict are important. Understanding the roots of conflict will give you the tools to respond effectively.

Conflict is inevitable in life and often can be constructive. Unfortunately, conflict sometimes can become destructive and lead to violence. Negative conflict arises when you don't have the proper tools to deal with a disagreement. The more you concentrate on winning a conflict, the less chance you have of understanding the person on the other side. Without understanding, it is impossible for both parties to walk away from a conflict feeling satisfied.

At other times, however, conflict can stimulate personal and intellectual growth for both parties. In this sense, "productive" conflict is actually an interaction between people or groups that can lead to something positive.

## Chapter Objectives

In this chapter, you will:

- Explain the difference between positive and negative conflict
- Investigate the possible types and triggers of conflict among individuals and groups
- Explore ways that you can cope and manage or resolve conflict in conflict-ridden situations
- Investigate a number of strategies for managing anger
- Explain how mediation and adjudication techniques can be used to relieve conflict situations

# Dealing with Conflict

**Conflict** is any clash between two or more people or groups. In some ways, it is an essential part of learning and growing. Even at the best of times, dealing with conflict can be difficult.

If a conflict arises, there are two basic approaches that you can take:

➤ **The positive approach** involves solving the problem in a collaborative way, taking responsibility for your actions, and thereby building stronger relationships and communities. This does not mean abandoning your own beliefs, but rather opening your mind to the opinions of others and trying to make informed decisions together, and moving on.

➤ **The negative approach** is to be aggressive and confrontational. With this approach, there is no sense of personal responsibility and no shared understandings emerge from the conflict situation—there are only winners and losers.

The positive approach to conflict resolution is always more productive, but it requires practice. In this chapter, you will learn about conflict management using this approach.

Not all conflict is bad, but dealing with it can still be difficult.

## Solving Conflicts
### Positive and Negative Ways to Resolve Disputes

| Collaboration | Negotiation | Mediation | Confrontation | Aggression |
| --- | --- | --- | --- | --- |
| Solving differences together is always preferred—shared understandings emerge and both parties are better off. | Most conflicts can be sorted out by negotiation between the parties—a little "give and take" on all sides is all it takes. | Mediation allows for a third party to give direction to the disputants. This can be an independent mediator or a peer. | Confrontation risks escalating a conflict to the point where there may be no way out except the next stage, aggression. | Aggression is what you want to avoid at all costs. At this point, there are only winners and losers (or perhaps neither). |

Positive Approaches                    Negative Approaches

# Types and Triggers of Conflict

Differences in beliefs, values, principles, or goals are often at the root of many conflict situations. It is how you respond in such situations that determines how events will unfold. In most situations, it is possible to resolve disputes calmly and in a way that both sides benefit.

There are four different types of conflict situations.

## Internal Conflicts

**Internal conflicts** are the opposing emotions you often feel within yourself. Sometimes, it is difficult to decide what to believe, especially when you can see both sides of an issue and you must choose which path to take, whom to support, or where to draw the line. For example, those with strong beliefs about cruelty to animals may have difficulty trying to reconcile those beliefs with an action like buying something made of leather or fur.

Such internal conflicts may cause you to question some of the core values and beliefs you learned in childhood. They can also help you clarify your moral values by revealing misconceptions and biases that you may have previously held.

## Interpersonal Conflict

An **interpersonal conflict** is a dispute that you have with someone else. You and a friend may have completely different views on, for example, the latest current event. In such situations, it is important to try to understand what your friend thinks about it, as well as what others think about it.

Whether you live, work, or study with someone, you will not agree on everything, and these differences of opinion can lead to conflict. Listening to, and fully accepting the views of a friend or family member, may sometimes be difficult. How you react will be influenced by the relationship you have with that person and your feelings about him or her.

## Intra-Group Conflict

Conflict among members of a group or team falls under the category of **intra-group conflict**. In these types of conflicts, members within a group disagree on some point or issue. Consider the example of a group of friends who are hosting a party together. Some may want to play a certain type of music all night, whereas others may want a variety of music. Their choice may be based either on loyalty to their friends or on their own personal feelings. Whatever the case, a conflict of sorts can arise within the group.

The key to getting along in a group, small or large, is to go out of your way to find compromises that work for everyone. Since the group is usually together for other reasons (e.g., classmates and friends), there is every reason to want to resolve such disputes quickly and amicably.

---

### Your Role in the Conflict

When conflict arises, it is easy to criticize the behaviour of others. Blaming the other party may be a natural first instinct, but it often makes sense to look at your own role in the situation too.

Think about how you handled yourself in recent conflict situations, large or small.

- Are you the one who initiated the conflict?
- Are you the one who was victimized in the situation?
- Are you the one who mediated the conflict so that it was resolved amiably?
- Are you the one who aggravated the conflict to the point where it could not be resolved calmly?

Include yourself in any assessment of a conflict situation. This way no variables are left out, and the solutions may then become clearer.

# Inter-Group Conflict

**Inter-group conflict** occurs when two groups (or teams) find themselves in opposition to one another. In sports, as in life, healthy competition is normal. However, if it is not handled properly, a dispute can have serious consequences. This is why team sports have umpires and referees to ensure that conflicts are properly managed.

Inter-group conflicts also happen outside of sports, but the "referees" have different names. In the business world, professional mediators often are hired to negotiate disputes between management and employees when the two opposing groups cannot agree.

Other kinds of real world "referees" include moderators, arbitrators, judges, mediators, and negotiators. Sometimes an entire organization exists just to act as a mediator. The United Nations, for example, negotiates world order among its member nations.

In severe cases, however, no such mediator exists to negotiate the peace between rival groups. Indeed, the opposing groups may consider a peaceful settlement as a sign of weakness. Often, this leads to a dangerous situation where differences are settled by violent means in order to assert power and control.

Having a different opinion on a current event than your classmate is an example of an interpersonal conflict.

When two groups of people disagree, umpires and referees are often needed to keep things under control.

# Conflict-Resolution Skills

Some people have an uncanny ability to find workable solutions, even in the most difficult of conflict situations. Such individuals usually bring an open mind to the dispute along with an intense search for novel solutions that work for everyone.

These special **conflict-resolution skills** and abilities can be learned and practised, and will come in handy in any conflict in which you become involved. Below are a few of the important ones:

> **Empathy.** Perhaps the most basic skill of all is the ability to put yourself in the other person's shoes. This is called empathy. When you show empathy, you recognize that other people's needs are as important to them as yours are to you. Empathy is a matter of treating others with the same degree of respect that you want from them and identifying with their concerns. Empathy is very important in conflict situations because it leads to a greater level of understanding on both sides. It opens the possibility of an outcome that exceeds the expectations of either side in the dispute.

> **Patience and tolerance.** If you are patient and tolerant, you are less likely to react quickly, and more likely to think before you speak or act. Being patient and tolerant simply means giving others the time to explain their case to you, and giving yourself time to assess all aspects of the situation. In conflict situations, as elsewhere in life, patience and tolerance are virtues. They help to prevent situations from escalating and getting out of control.

> **Clear and direct messages.** It is an invaluable skill to be able to express yourself clearly and in a non-threatening way, not just in a conflict, but all the time. Too often, discussions are cut short and the tension quickly rises. If you are able to articulate your feelings and possible solutions, the chances increase that you will settle the dispute without too much fuss. In general, the longer the talking can go on, the better.

> **Creative thinking.** In the end, of course, you have to resolve the issues. To do so, it is often helpful to be able to think creatively and to come up with imaginative solutions. "Thinking outside of the box," as the saying goes, allows you to approach problems from different viewpoints. You may find new solutions that have not been tried before. If both parties are able to "brainstorm" solutions together, even better.

> **Critical thinking.** In any dispute, you also have to try to get a firm understanding of all the issues. This involves being able to think through all aspects of the problem at hand. This is what is meant by critical thinking—critical, in the sense of not accepting things at face value but rather digging deeper, if necessary, to find the root causes and workable solutions.

---

## How to De-Escalate a Conflict

**W**hen you attempt to manage or resolve any type of conflict, there are a few basic guidelines that you can apply in working towards a solution.

Use the following steps as the basis for your conflict-resolution strategy:

- State the problem.
- Be assertive and direct, and avoid personal attacks or laying blame.
- Define the scope of the problem.
- List areas of agreement and disagreement.
- Brainstorm possible solutions.
- Together, create a list of ways the problem could be solved, without judging the effectiveness of any solution.
- Identify the consequences of each solution.
- Discuss and jointly choose the solution that seems to be the most effective and acceptable to both parties.

> **Assertiveness.** None of this means that you should shy away from issues that you feel strongly about or that you should not always state your views directly. You need to be assertive without being aggressive or abusive. If necessary, repeat your message so that it is understood by the other party. Always use "I messages" to say what you think, but be sure to listen to the other side too. It helps in these situations to maintain eye contact, use confident body language, and always remain in control.

> **Active listening.** Active listening lets the other person know that you are paying attention and genuinely want to find a solution. It may involve simply giving an indication that you are listening—perhaps short responses that do not interrupt the flow of the other person's thought, the occasional "uh huh" or "that's interesting," or body language to show that you are receiving the message loud and clear (such as eye contact or the occasional nod). When it is your turn, summarize the other person's points to show that you understood them. It seems pretty clear that, if there is no active listening, there is no active debate—and if there is no debate, there will be no solution to the dispute.

Active listening can be as simple as a nod to demonstrate that you understand what the person is saying.

# Anger-Management Strategies

Conflict can be accompanied by many emotions, but the most common one is anger. How well a conflict is resolved will be influenced by how well you channel both your own anger and other people's.

Behind most anger is fear. You have probably heard the expression "fight or flight." This means that, when feeling threatened, a person can choose to react with anger (fight) or run away (flight).

Anger, which comes from a Latin word meaning "to choke or strangle," literally chokes off the blood supply to the brain, which reduces the ability to think clearly. When most people become angry, they begin to breathe more rapidly, and their pulse rates increase. They may raise their voices, clench their fists, feel sweaty, or feel a tightness in their chests.

When angry, some people feel they cannot hear, focus their attention, process information, or make good choices. It is not surprising that the level of violence and aggression increases dramatically in such situations.

## Dealing with Anger

You can deal with anger using anger-management strategies, some of which are listed below:

> **Determine the causes.** When trying to control anger, first try to figure out what is causing it. You can often control the anger once you identify the cause or causes.

> **Use relaxation techniques.** Using relaxation techniques— such as deep breathing, counting backward, going for a walk, or getting some exercise and relaxing your muscles—will help to control your physical reactions. Once you take a break and "cool off," it is easier to control what you do and say than when you are feeling angry.

> **Avoid triggering conflict.** Sometimes, people behave in ways that make others angry. In some relationships, such as between siblings, this can be done intentionally (and is known as "picking a fight"). Try to be aware of situations where emotions are escalating because of something you or someone else said or did. In some cases, the conversation may need to be stopped temporarily to avoid emotions getting out of control.

> **Keep your feelings in check.** If you cannot avoid the things that trigger your anger, you can manage your reactions better by knowing which anger-management strategies work best for you. The six steps to reducing anger (which are listed on the left) may also be helpful in these situations.

In other words, when you become angry, stop and think before you react. When you do this, you will almost certainly be able to find your way out of difficult situations.

---

### Six Steps to Reducing Anger

For people who find it difficult to keep their feelings of anger in check, the following six-step approach for letting go will help:

- Stop blaming yourself.
- Try not to take things personally.
- Deal with your feelings.
- Put yourself in the other person's shoes.
- Make peace with the past.
- Seek professional help.

If anger is taking over your life, and you are finding that the first five steps are not effective, talking to a mental health professional may be a solution.

Remember, help is just a phone call away. Kids Help Phone: 1-800-668-6868.

---

## Taking Responsibility for Your Actions

You can also avoid conflict situations by taking more responsibility for your actions and behaviour. This could be as simple as improving your planning and organizational skills, which may reduce the potential for angry flare-ups. By being more organized, you will be less likely to overlook important dates or events, or forget commitments—actions that often lead to conflicts.

Improving your organizational skills will also allow you to set and accomplish goals more effectively.

## Chilling Out

Walking away from a conflict (even if just for a little while) sometimes can be the smart approach. After the cooling-off period, you will have time to calmly express your anger in ways that are not aggressive or confrontational.

When anger clouds your perspective, and all else fails, perhaps take yourself away from the situation temporarily. Go off by yourself or, better yet, talk to a friend or a trusted adult. Try not to avoid important issues for too long, since they may get worse.

Anger is the most common emotion accompanying conflict. If you avoid the triggers of anger, you will likely be able to avoid the conflict as well.

If you feel that anger is affecting your judgment during a conflict, it is often best to walk away until you feel more in control.

## Mediation and Adjudication

Often, two people or groups of people find that they cannot resolve a conflict on their own. In these cases, it is useful for both sides to bring in a third party who can help them reach a solution.

There are two main ways of achieving a third-party conflict resolution: (1) mediation (including the process known as "peer mediation"), and (2) adjudication.

### Mediation

**Mediation** is a good way to manage and resolve conflicts that seem unsolvable. It requires a trained person to help the conflicting parties work out a solution. To be an effective mediator, a person needs to build mutual respect between the parties and encourage problem solving.

Before a solution can be found, the people involved must have a chance to cool off, set their anger aside, and end their hostilities. The mediator then follows six problem-solving steps:

➢ Establish the ground rules

➢ Hear both sides of the story, taking into account each person's point of view and how each is feeling

➢ Find out whose best interests are being served by the possible outcomes of the conflict

➢ Come up with two or three solutions that serve the interests of both sides

➢ Evaluate each option using objective criteria

➢ Arrive at an agreement that is acceptable to both sides

**Peer mediation** programs often are successful in reducing conflict in schools (see the next page). An objective third-party, who is also a peer (a close friend, classmate, or colleague), is used to help two conflicting parties understand one another. Many believe that conflict-resolution skills provide lifelong benefits and should be taught and practised more widely.

### Adjudication

Negotiation and mediation sometimes fail. In these situations, an adult, usually one in a position of authority, can be brought in to decide on an appropriate solution using a process called **adjudication**. In the case of adjudication, the person acting as an adjudicator (or arbitrator) listens to both sides of the story, asks each person what they think the best solution is, and considers the consequences of each solution.

In the end, the adjudicator makes the final decision, which both parties have previously agreed to accept. Adjudication is a good way to resolve disputes that have reached an impasse when both sides are ready to sort things out and move on.

Occasionally people or groups of people find that despite everyone's best efforts, they can't solve a conflict on their own.

Conflict in schools can be reduced by using peer mediators.

# What Is Peer Mediation?
## Finding Peaceful Solutions

Peer mediation is a voluntary, confidential process that can be used to settle differences or disputes between students. The peer mediator is also a student who is trained to help other students solve their conflicts.

The mediator's job is not to decide who is right or wrong, or to tell either student what to do, but to help students find their own solutions.

### What Is the Purpose of Peer Mediation?

The purpose of peer mediation is to help students to:

- Understand conflict
- Deal with conflict in a positive way
- Receive training and skills to solve problems
- Learn healthy ways to solve their own problems
- Develop a different way of thinking
- See alternate ways to resolve problems

### Why Mediate Using Peers?

Peer mediation gives students the opportunity to settle their differences on their own, and in a neutral setting, without adults or authority figures involved.

Mediation is an alternative to:

- Adult involvement
- Adult decision making
- Fighting, detention, or suspension

### What Kinds of Conflicts Can Be Mediated?

Some issues or concerns that arise between students that can be brought to mediation are:

- Rumours
- Friendship and relationship issues
- Misunderstandings
- Personal property grievances, etc.

Situations involving physical or sexual abuse, drugs, and weapons are not cases for mediation. They should be referred to the proper authorities.

### How Does the Program Help?

Peer mediation has many benefits in school. It can help:

- To resolve peer disputes
- To increase student participation
- To develop leadership skills
- To build self-esteem
- To improve communication skills
- To promote a sense of community among students

**Source:** Adapted from "Peaceful Resolutions: Peer Mediation Program" by the National Crime Prevention Centre In Partnership with AESB District School, Community Mediation Services, The Mennonite Central Committee, and The John Howard Society of Newfoundland.

# Kids Help Phone—1-800-668-6868
## Keeping Young People Safe

Sometimes, you may feel that you can't quite figure out a problem on your own.

If you need some help, the Kids Help Phone is a place where you can get the answers to your questions. If they cannot help, they will find a local community or social service agency that will.

### About the Kids Help Phone

The Kids Help Phone is not just for little kids—it can help young people of all ages with all sorts of problems, concerns, or issues.

Kids Help Phone counsellors answer calls and online questions from all across Canada. They provide immediate help—both in English and French—24 hours a day, 365 days a year.

They are well prepared for any question on any topic that concerns you; such as sex, drugs, bullying, violence, abuse, and friendship or family problems, to name a few.

### What to Expect

Here's what you can expect when you call the Kids Help Phone:

- A caring professional who is there to help you with your question
- Your anonymity is protected and your call is confidential—you do not even have to give your name.
- Calls are not traced and they do not have call display
- Posters, brochures, and music videos supporting Kids Help Phone can be downloaded from their website
- Your call is free

If you or a friend are confronted with a difficult situation, don't be afraid to ask for help. That's exactly what many successful people of all ages do.

For more information on the Kids Help Phone, visit their website at **www.kidshelpphone.ca**.

## Questions for Study and Review

### Things to Think About and Explore

1. Distinguish between the four different types of conflict and give examples of each type.

2. List and describe the kinds of skills and personal abilities that can be especially useful in assessing and resolving conflict situations.

3. Describe some of the ways you can show someone you are actively listening during a conversation.

4. List the advantages (and any possible disadvantages) of peer mediation as a way of resolving disputes among students.

5. Outline a conflict you had with another person and list the steps you took to work through it.

6. Describe the main difference between the role of a mediator and that of an adjudicator.

### Things to Do and Practise

7. Write a public speech explaining how conflict, if properly managed, can lead to a better understanding of an issue or a situation, as well as a better solution for everyone involved.

8. Create a plan for reducing conflict in each of the following situations:

    (a) You have two classmates who disagree on just about everything.
    (b) Your siblings are arguing about what to watch on television.
    (c) Your best friend disagrees with your views on premarital sex.

9. List the various techniques that can be used to reduce anger. How well do you apply these techniques when you are angry—tick off the ones that you think work for you.

10. Monitor the conflicts you encounter (both ones that involve you and ones that do not) over a few days or a week. List the coping skills and anger management skills that were used (or not used) and explain how they were put into effect (or could have been put into effect).

11. Role play in groups of three. Two of you are in disagreement over a particular issue (for example, who gets to use a school computer first) and the third member in the group must conduct peer mediation. Choose another issue and rotate the roles in the group so that each person tries mediating. Discuss the challenges of mediating and the responsibilities it entails.

12. Prepare a report for your teacher and principal on how your school and community could benefit from working with organizations like the Kids Help Phone or the Canadian Safe School Network (CSSN).

## WWWeblinks

Name ➤ Canadian Safe School Network

URL ➤ www.canadiansafe schools.com

By raising awareness, developing youth programs and resources, and building partnerships, CSSN promotes student empowerment, self-advocacy, caring, and respect.

Name ➤ Safe Communities Foundation

URL ➤ www.safe communities.ca

A Canadian national organization working to improve the safety of workers and people in every community.

Name ➤ Canadian Institute for Conflict Resolution

URL ➤ www.cicr-icrc.ca

An organization designed to help people at home and abroad with conflict resolution.

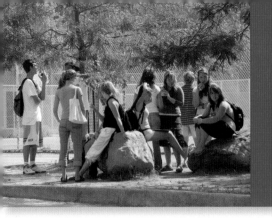

# 17
# Combatting Violence, Creating Safe Schools

## Key Terms

➢ abuse
➢ violence
➢ gang violence
➢ bullying
➢ cyber-bullying
➢ dating violence
➢ sexual harassment
➢ hate crime
➢ racism
➢ ethnic violence
➢ homophobia

**A**buse and violence have countless damaging effects on the individual and on the spirit of a society. Although you may not have been directly involved in an abusive or violent incident, it is likely that you have seen one in some form—maybe even in your own school.

The intent of this chapter is not to alarm you, but rather to make you aware of some of the reasons abusive and violent behaviour have become a part of life today. You will also learn about the different types of violence and how to prevent them.

In these matters, as in all others, we need to be proactive, and not simply reactive. We need to combat all forms of abuse and violence wherever they occur, as a precondition for safe schools and safe communities.

## Chapter Objectives

In this chapter, you will:

➢ Investigate the potential sources of violence in our society and the factors that may contribute to violence

➢ Consider the pervasiveness of violence in the mainstream media (television, movies) and how one should respond to it

➢ Examine the problem of gang violence and what to do about it

➢ Explore the problem of bullying and how to combat it

➢ Explore the problem of cyber-bullying and related violence on the Internet

➢ Explore the problem of hate crimes, especially racism and homophobia, and what can be done to eliminate them

➢ Explore the problem of sexual harassment and violence directed against women and what can be done about it

➢ Examine possible ways to make our schools and neighbourhoods safer

# Abuse and Violence

Abuse and violence are not the same, but they are closely related. When someone is a victim of abuse, they are being mistreated. Violence is often only a few steps beyond.

> **Abuse.** Abuse involves mistreating someone verbally, physically, or emotionally. Abuse may be direct and overt or it may be disguised and covert.

> **Violence.** Violence refers to acts of aggression and abuse that cause, or are intended to cause, injury or harm to another person.

## Forms of Abuse and Violence

Abuse and violence do not just happen mysteriously. They have definite causes, and there is much you can do to prevent them from occurring. Abuse and violence can take various forms, including: violence in the media, abuse and violence in personal relationships, bullying, dating violence and sexual harassment, and hate crimes.

This chapter looks at each of these in turn.

Violence can be as simple as a threat to injure someone.

## The Continuum of Violence
### Finding Better Ways to Resolve Disputes

**Non-abusive Relationships**

Healthy relationships are non-abusive and non-violent. Each partner respects and appreciates the other and seeks to work with the other person to resolve differences.

**Emotional and Verbal Abuse**

Emotional and verbal abuse may be direct or disguised, and sometimes is a precursor to threats of violence or overt violence.

**Threats of Physical Violence**

Frequently, physical violence is preceded by verbal and emotional abuse, as well as by threats to injure or harm the other person.

**Direct Physical Violence**

Direct physical violence involves acts of aggression intended to cause injury and harm to another person.

**Severe Physical Violence and Abuse**

This is the extreme form of physical violence and abuse directly intended to cause very serious injury and harm to the other person.

| -2 | -1 | 0 | 1 | 2 | 3 | 4 | 5 | 6 | 7 | 8 | 9 | 10 | 11 | 12 |
|----|----|---|---|---|---|---|---|---|---|---|---|----|----|----|

**Non-violence**

**Severity of abusive and violent behaviour**

# Images of Violence in the Media

We rely on the various forms of media—television, radio, the Internet, newspapers, and advertising billboards—for all kinds of information and for our entertainment. Unfortunately, the media also can be a source of violent images and language.

Even more unfortunate, continued exposure to such images can make violence seem like an acceptable way to solve problems.

## Video Games

The graphic content and interactive nature of violent video games are widely believed to have harmful effects on people who spend a great deal of time playing them. Because violent games are played repeatedly, some think that they may be even more dangerous than violent television images.

Many of these video games require the players to shoot, bomb, or defeat opponents in hand-to-hand combat in order to advance in the game. The concern is that this encourages "gamers" to view violence as exciting and, even worse, without consequence (since no "real" person gets hurt).

In 1994, the video game industry created the Entertainment Software Rating Board to classify games by age-appropriateness. A rating icon now appears on game packages, indicating the suggested minimum age for players, along with a brief description of any potentially controversial content.

In provinces such as Manitoba, Ontario, and Nova Scotia, for example, it is now illegal to sell or rent games marked "M for Mature" to anyone under 17 years old.

## Television and Movies

Young people spend a great deal of time watching television. This can lead to continued exposure to negative and violent images which, in turn, can make young people more fearful of the world around them.

In Canada, the government and the entertainment industry have created a classification system for television shows and movies to help protect young people from viewing disturbing scenes. These classifications are based on the level of physical violence, gore, nudity, strong language, or drug use contained in the show or movie.

Depending on the content, the show or movie is given a rating that indicates roughly the appropriate viewer age level. (For more information on this and other entertainment rating systems, see the box on the next page.)

All movies are rated. However, news shows, broadcasts of sporting events, documentaries and other information programming, talk shows, music videos, and variety programs on television are all exempt from the rating system.

The media presents violence on television, in movies, in music and music videos, and in video games.

Video games are now subject to a rating system similar to the one used to rate movies.

## Music and Music Videos

Some musicians write and sing songs that use vulgar language or sing about topics in a way that tends to glorify violence and anti-social behaviour. When accompanied by a video along the same lines, these can act as powerful examples to young listeners and viewers.

Of course, most young people can see through the profane lyrics and the explicit images, but they can be influential to others—especially a young person who may be going through a difficult time and who may be more socially isolated and vulnerable.

## Pornography

Because it depicts the subjects (usually women) in degrading ways, pornography is offensive. Simply seeing pornographic images—on the Internet, for example—can be frightening. Pornography that contains violence is especially offensive.

Pornography is regulated in the traditional media (newspapers, magazines, television, and film), but, in the new media (video and the Internet), it is difficult to contain. Regulators are grappling with the problem, but as yet there are few regulations in place.

Not everyone who plays violent video games will exhibit violent behaviour, but continued exposure to violent and aggressive imagery can desensitize people.

## Media Content Ratings
### What Do They Mean?

Video games, movies, and music are subject to warnings and ratings designed to let consumers know what kind of content they can expect. Below is a breakdown of the rating systems for various forms of media:

- **Computer and Video Games:** Ratings for computer and video games are assigned by the Entertainment Software Rating Board. Their six levels indicate for which games are suitable for which ages. The rating icon always appears on the front of the game with a description of any questionable content on the back.

- **Television:** In Canada, there are both English and French systems in place for rating television shows. The English system contains the following ratings: E (exempt from ratings), C (suitable for children), C8+ (suitable for ages 8 and up), G (general—suitable for all ages), PG (parental guidance—may not be suitable for those under 14), and 18+ (only suitable for adults).

- **Movies:** Several movie rating systems are in use across Canada. The most common are: G (general audiences), PG (parental guidance), 14A (persons under 14 should be accompanied by an adult), 18A (persons under 18 must be accompanied by an adult). You can find more information at **www.media-awareness.ca** .

- **Music:** Music that contains questionable language or violent, vulgar, or derogatory lyrics must have an advisory label on it. There is no rating system for music videos.

# Violence in Personal Relationships

Almost any relationship can become abusive or violent. Often, the situation seems to make no sense at all. A parent or guardian may abuse one child but not another. A boss or manager may pick on some of his or her employees but not others. Also, violent or abusive relationships are not always overt, and they can be difficult to identify if you are not directly involved.

In these situations, you may be hesitant to speak up because the person inflicting the abuse or violence is either an authority figure or someone who is supposed to take care of you. Nevertheless, it is important to remember that abuse in any form is never the victim's fault. The person inflicting the violence is in the wrong, and it is unlikely that they will stop on their own.

If a parent or guardian is physically or verbally abusing you, tell an adult you can trust.

Watching your parents or guardians be abusive can be damaging, but remember that you can't control the behaviour of those around you.

## People in Positions of Authority

Because disciplining practices have changed, abuse and violence from people in positions of authority (for example, an employer or coach) is less common now than it was in the past. But it is still a possibility. If you feel an authority figure has been physically or emotionally abusive, you can tell a co-worker, your principal, or a parent or guardian so that the issue will be dealt with promptly.

## Extended Family Members or Friends

Abuse or violence can also come from a relative or family friend. If the perpetrator is a relative, it may be especially difficult to tell your parent that someone whom they trust is hurting you. In such situations, seeking the advice of other family members, other relatives, church leaders, or professional counsellors is a wise choice. By reporting this violence, you are not betraying anyone—you are just taking an active step toward putting an end to it.

There are professionals who will listen and help find a solution to family violence situations. The staff at the Kids Help Phone (1-800-668-6868 or **www.kidshelpphone.ca**) or your own province's teen outreach service are available to help in such situations.

## Family Members

Sometimes, physical or verbal abuse and violence may be directed against one or more children by a parent, guardian, or caregiver. Siblings also can act in an abusive or violent way toward each other. While many siblings argue and get angry, it is never acceptable to be physically or verbally abusive.

Family members may also witness violence between other family members, which can be very emotionally upsetting. In such instances, trying to control the situation by oneself can often make things worse.

In the family context, it may not always be possible for a victim to talk to someone at home about abuse and violence. If that is the case, a teacher or another trusted adult should be able to help.

## Low Self-Esteem

People of all ages tend to model their behaviour on what they see around them. In this way they learn how to treat others. No doubt, some abusive and violent behaviour is learned from the media and society at large, and much of it is instilled at a very early age.

People who experience family violence are especially at risk of copying these abusive behaviours as they get older. Those who have had a difficult family situation often become abusers themselves, unless they have more positive role models helping them move in another direction.

Some people also have a low sense of self-worth or self-esteem. This is especially the case with people who are, or have been, victims of abuse or violence. Mistakenly, they believe that by exerting power and control over others, they can make themselves feel better or stronger. In such situations, their self-esteem only gets worse.

It can be difficult for people in such situations to change their ways without the support of friends, family, and professional counselling. By learning how to resolve conflict constructively, they can begin to rebuild their self-esteem and be able to pass positive messages on to their children and their children's children.

Everyone needs to feel a sense of belonging. You can fulfill this need by being a contributing member of a family, a team, a group, or a club.

# Combatting Gang Violence
## Providing More Opportunities for Young People

The issue of **gang violence** has become a major concern in many parts of Canada. But what exactly does it mean to be part of a "gang" and how can we reduce gang violence? Experts have identified three distinct groups as gangs:

- Highly sophisticated criminal organizations with formal structures.

- Semi-organized groups who engage in planned and profitable criminal behaviour or organized violence against rival gangs (often called street gangs).

- Unstructured groups of young people who become involved in spontaneous social activity and impulsive criminal activity; including collective violence against other groups of youth (sometimes called "wannabe" gangs or youth gangs).

Unfortunately, innocent bystanders have been injured or killed by members of rival gangs waging violence against each other.

### Providing Alternatives

Experts have attempted to understand why young people join gangs. Some argue that gangs offer a sense of belonging to people who have not joined other groups, such as sports teams or clubs. Others maintain that, in low-income areas, gangs offer a chance to earn an income, even if the money comes from illegal activities such as stealing or dealing drugs.

Most experts believe that the solution is simple: create chances for young people to join positive groups and increase social and economic opportunities, particularly for youth living in low-income areas.

# Bullying

**Bullying** takes place when a person or a group holds power over someone and uses that power in intimidating, aggressive, or violent ways. People who act this way believe their victims are worthless, stupid, unpopular, or just different. We used to think that bullying was an elementary-school phenomenon, but we now know it occurs among people of all ages.

As the abuse continues, the perpetrator feels increasingly powerful, while the victim feels more miserable. The people watching provide an audience for the bully, which supports his or her perception of power. Whether you are the victim of bullying, or a witness to it, you can take steps to stop it. For a start, make sure that your school recognizes the problem. If your school doesn't have a policy against bullying, start a committee that promotes and plans for school safety.

## Male and Female Bullying

In the past, bullying by males tended to consist of more direct, physical aggression. Now that such aggressive forms of bullying have been identified as serious and are prohibited, males are turning to more indirect methods of bullying, such as taunts, threats, intimidation, extortion, and exclusion.

Bullying by females typically seems to be more indirect. Some young women become experts at excluding peers, spreading rumours, and using emotional blackmail, ostracism, and manipulation to torment others.

**Cyber-bullying** (bullying over the Internet) also seems to be on the rise for both males and females. It is especially difficult to detect and control. (For more on cyber-bullying, see the next page.)

## If You Are Being Bullied

Many victims of bullying are too afraid of their intimidators to tell anyone what is happening or to fight back. They sometimes feel as if telling an adult will make the situation worse. Sometimes they have a good reason to feel this way—adults don't always do a very good job of recognizing the seriousness of bullying.

There are a number of positive steps you can take if you or a friend are being bullied. For example, it is usually a good idea to walk away from the situation and ignore the person. It may be difficult because sometimes losing your temper is often easier than showing restraint.

Telling an adult or an authority figure is important. This person might be a parent, teacher, school counsellor, or principal. Bullying is not a problem that you should have to handle on your own.

Being bullied can destroy your self-confidence. Try to find people who share your interests and spend time with them. If you and your friends support and stick up for one another, a bully is more likely to leave you alone. Above all, don't blame yourself—bullies often choose their victims at random.

---

### Bullying: What To Do

If you are being bullied, there are several ways to help prevent the violence from escalating into further conflict. Here are some tips:

- Stay calm and act confident, even if you don't feel that way. Someone acting violently towards you is less likely to continue if you project self-confidence.

- Don't use derogatory names or become aggressive. It will only make the situation worse, and it may provoke further violent action.

- Don't carry a weapon. Carrying a weapon is illegal, and you won't feel any safer. The weapon may end up being used against you or someone with you.

- Tell someone. School counsellors, a trusted friend, teachers, or adults can often rectify the situation. If you want to remain anonymous, you can call the Kids Help Phone (1-800-668-6868), or go to: **www.kidshelpphone.ca**.

Remember, if you are being bullied, the best plan is one that prevents the conflict from becoming worse.

## If Someone Else Is Being Bullied

If you see someone being bullied, or hear that something of this nature is being planned, tell an adult or a person in a position of authority right away. If you know the person who is doing the bullying, consider talking to this person about his or her actions. If the bullying has already occurred, encourage the victim to talk to an adult. Lending support will let the victim know that he or she is not alone.

Unkind comments, repeatedly made, are no longer considered harmless, but rather a form of taunting or harassment. Scratching, pushing, slapping, and hitting is assault, and gossiping and spreading rumours are slanderous acts. Part of the bully's power comes from having an audience. Don't participate! Don't let the bully provoke you into taunting someone else and don't laugh at what's happening.

If bullying is not stopped and corrected, it can lead to more serious forms of abuse, including physical, sexual, or racial harassment; dating violence or gender abuse; or even gang activity. The consequences of using personal power to humiliate or injure another person become more serious for bullies as they get older. They then become legally accountable for any harm caused.

There are many forms of bullying, but any form is always unacceptable.

## Cyber-Bullying
### Violence Perpetrated Over the Internet

Cyber-bullying is the use of information and communication technologies to bully others. Cyber-bullies use websites, e-mail, and phone or text messaging to threaten, intimidate, or antagonize others.

Breaking into e-mail accounts, using e-mail to spread hurtful gossip, spamming, and creating demeaning websites are the cyber-bully's new weapons.

Cyber-bullying is often hidden from adults. Some adults may not be familiar with these technologies and are unable to adequately supervise their use. Because the bullying can take place anonymously and reach a large audience, it can cause damage with little risk to the perpetrator.

There is also a wide variety of violent content on "the Net." This includes:

- Violent or vulgar song lyrics
- Sites depicting gore and murder
- Sites that perpetuate sexist or racist stereotypes

- Sites where sexual predators can connect with potential victims
- Sites that promote violent activity, such as those showing how to make homemade bombs
- Sites that entice people to join hate groups, such as white supremacist organizations

The police and Internet authorities are gradually getting on top of the most gratuitous forms of on-line bullying and abuse. By becoming aware of this type of violent content online, you can be your own "regulator" and help others as well.

The simple solution is to avoid websites with disturbing and violent content and to report any that you come across.

# Sexual Abuse and Dating Violence

In healthy relationships, partners enjoy each other's company, share each other's hopes, dreams, and successes, and try to make each other feel special.

In abusive relationships, anger, jealousy, possessiveness, cruelty, and manipulation prevail. The abuser may be easily frustrated and prone to violent or dangerous behaviour. The abused partner might become depressed, and may start missing school or withdrawing from friends. He or she may have difficulty sleeping or concentrating on schoolwork and may have unexplained injuries, such as bruises, cuts, or bite marks.

Victims of an abusive relationship are often afraid of what their partner may do if he or she ends the relationship. Some victims worry that if they break up with their partner, they will never find someone else. Unfortunately, the results of staying in an abusive relationship are potentially much worse.

Anyone can be at risk of being involved in an abusive relationship. However, individuals who have experienced some form of violence or abuse in the past may be more prone to falling victim to dating violence, or being the violent partner in relationships.

## Dating Violence

**Dating violence** is any sexual, physical, or psychological attack made on one partner by the other in a dating relationship. Dating violence can happen in heterosexual and same-sex relationships.

Dating violence is astonishingly common. Statistics have shown that one in nine high school students reports being involved in an abusive relationship. That is why it is important that you understand and recognize what an unhealthy dating relationship entails, and how to end it.

Dating violence is often motivated by sexist stereotyping, a lack of respect for a partner, a lack of skills needed to manage healthy dating relationships, jealousy, insecurity, or an imbalance of power between the dating partners. People who are prone to act violently towards their partner can be set off by external factors such as stress, or a substance abuse problem. However, there is no excuse for this type of violence.

The harm caused by dating violence can affect the victim for the rest of his or her life. It can damage self-esteem, confidence, and one's overall sense of well-being. Individuals caught in this type of relationship may find it difficult to express what they want or don't want. They may find themselves pressured into sexual acts or taking risks with their sexual behaviour that they would not normally take in a healthy relationship.

If you are a victim of dating violence, talk to a parent or guardian, or a school counsellor. Also, get involved with activities that build your confidence, your sense of well-being, and your self-esteem. Don't ever let anyone rob you of those qualities.

---

## A Friend in Need

If a friend tells you he or she is being treated badly in a dating relationship, or if you witness your friend being abused in some way, there are several things you can do to help out:

- Listen to your friend's concerns and take them seriously.

- Reassure your friend that no one deserves to be abused.

- Support your friend in looking at the risks and the impact of the violence.

- Suggest that your friend talk to a trusted adult or call an agency in your community for advice (many agencies can be called anonymously).

- Help your friend to realize that the situation will not change overnight.

## Combat Sexual Harassment
### Protect Yourself and Protect Your Rights

**S**exual harassment is any unwanted sexual behaviour of any kind. This may involve suggestive remarks of a sexual nature; unwelcome sexual invitations or requests; inappropriate touching; or unwelcome or repeated remarks about a person's body, appearance, or sexual orientation.

Sexual harassment is demeaning, degrading, and causes negative self-esteem. Sexual harassment often causes the victim to feel powerless in the situation and cannot be tolerated.

A victim of sexual harassment can be male or female, and it can occur between individuals of the same sex or opposite sex. Victims can also be any individual who may not be the target of the harassment, but who are affected by the offensive conduct.

A victim of sexual harassment should not ignore it. Ignoring it will not make it go away, and the behaviour can lead to violence.

Some examples of sexual harassment are:

- Unwanted sexual comments or remarks
- Whistling, cat calls, gestures, or noises
- A display of sexually offensive pictures
- Winking, throwing kisses, or licking of the lips
- Sexual gestures
- Inappropriate touching
- Emails of a sexual nature
- Unwelcome sexual invitations or requests for sexual favours
- Exposing herself or himself

If you are being sexually harassed, tell the person to stop. If they do not stop, report the behaviour immediately to a school counsellor, a parent or guardian, or an adult you can trust.

# Hate Crimes

According to the Criminal Code of Canada, a **hate crime** is a crime that is committed against a person or group of people because they are members of an "identifiable group." This means crimes directed against any section of the public who can be distinguished by colour, race, religion, ethnic origin, or sexual orientation. The two most common forms of hate crime are racism and homophobia.

Hate crimes are illegal, but sometimes even the threat of sanctions doesn't stop someone from committing a heinous act. Schools need to be proactive on these matters. They need to focus on strategies that will prevent harassment, not just increase the severity of the punishment. Students also need to take part in supportive programs that teach tolerance. Find out what your school's policies are and, if they are weak, work with your fellow students and teachers/principals to make them stronger.

Whatever happens, do not ignore the crime, since it is not likely to stop without some form of action. As difficult as it may be, your first step might be to tell the person to stop. If your friends or other people have witnessed the incident, find out whether any of them would be willing to back up your story.

Documenting everything may seem like too much work, but it helps to make teachers and parents aware of the seriousness of the problem. The recorded details give them a better chance of helping you put an end to the aggression.

## Anti-Racism

**Racism** is the belief in the superiority of a particular race and the prejudice, antagonism, or violence shown towards other races as a result of this attitude. Sometimes people can even become violent towards other groups, based on differences of religion or culture— when this happens, it is called **ethnic violence**.

When people focus their own fears and hatred on a specific group, the targeted group is treated as less than human. This can open the door to acts of violence or degradation towards this group.

Of course, racist attitudes and behaviours never stand up to the test of reason. This is because they are not based on facts but rather on ignorance and prejudice. That is why they need to be challenged on every occasion.

Remember too, that Canada takes pride in being a genuine multicultural society. Our population reflects a vast diversity of cultural heritages and racial groups—the result of centuries of immigration to this country. In Canada, we can keep our identities, take pride in our ancestries, and feel a sense of belonging. We are able to choose our friends based on who they are, not what they look like or their ethnic background. Around the world, Canada is seen as a kind and tolerant nation, one where racism is completely unacceptable.

## Canadian Charter of Rights and Freedoms

The Canadian Charter of Rights and Freedoms was adopted by the federal government in 1982. Under Canadian law, the Charter guarantees the fundamental rights of every Canadian citizen.

The Charter promises that, along with the right to vote, every citizen has the same "fundamental freedoms."

These fundamental freedoms include:

- the freedom of conscience and religion
- the freedom of thought, belief, opinion, and expression
- the freedom of peaceful assembly
- the freedom of association

## Eliminating Homophobia

The term **homophobia** refers to the fear of, or contempt for, other people because of their sexual preference or gender identification. Like racism, homophobia is considered a hate crime in Canada.

You can help prevent homophobic violence in the following ways:

Kindness and acceptance are important steps in reducing homophobia.

➢ Accept that there are students in your school who identify as lesbian, gay, bisexual, transgendered, or transsexual (LGBTT).

➢ Think about how you and your friends formed your attitudes and try to acknowledge and discard any prejudices you may have learned. Homosexuality is not contagious—you can't catch it by acknowledging that it exists.

➢ Keep your language free of biased terms. Use the words "gay," "lesbian," and "bisexual" rather than derogatory terms.

➢ Show kindness and acceptance. Speak to students who are being tormented, and listen to what they have to say.

By being proactive in this way, you can make your school and community a safer place for all students, and free from prejudice and discrimination of all kinds.

Create safe communities. Combat all forms of hate whenever and wherever they occur.

# Safer Schools, Safer Communities

Here are some ways to help protect yourself and your friends, and to keep your community free of mindless conflict and violence:

➢ **Be inclusive.** You can make a huge difference by simply reaching out and acknowledging all students, whether they are part of the in-crowd or not. This will make them feel included and less vulnerable. Once they see you making these gestures, they will feel more inclined to do the same.

➢ **Lead by example.** Never walk past an act of aggression without doing something positive to prevent it, even if it means simply reporting it. When you report someone just to get that person in trouble, that is ratting. When you tell someone in authority about an act of aggression, that is reporting.

➢ **Tell someone you trust.** It takes courage to tell someone that you feel hurt or threatened, and finding the right person to trust is tough. Having an adult that you can talk to—be they a coach, guidance counsellor, religious leader, parent, or relative—can make it much easier to deal with a tough situation.

➢ **Take advantage of school and community resources.** You can build a sense of community within your school by holding class meetings, planning "get to know one another" activities, and sharing stories. In your community, there will be many agencies and groups with anti-violence programs and resources that will be interested in working with you to make your school and community safer.

Just being inclusive can go a long way towards creating an environment that's free of violence.

Safe schools and safe communities go hand in hand.

# Chapter Review

## Questions for Study and Review

### Things to Think About and Explore

1. List five TV shows that you watch and record their ratings. Indicate whether or not you think the ratings assigned to them are appropriate.

2. List three potential sources of violent behaviour and indicate whether or not you have ever witnessed them in either your school or community.

3. Outline how male bullying can differ from female bullying.

4. Compare racism and homophobia; consider how they are the same and how they differ.

5. Describe some of the traits a person could possess that could lead to dating violence.

6. Explain how having an inclusive attitude can contribute to reducing violence.

### Things to Do and Practise

7. In small groups or pairs, discuss where you feel the most violent media images are found and what can be done about them.

8. Make a banner or a poster that captures the diversity within Canadian society, and illustrate how tolerance and inclusion can strengthen communities.

9. Create a plan that will encourage students in your school to report any incidences of violence or harassment.

10. Distinguish between sexual harassment and sexual abuse.

11. Investigate your school's policy on harassment and consider whether you think any improvements could be made to make it more effective or more widely known.

12. Devise a plan that you could use to help a friend in the following abusive situations and investigate the school or community resources available in such a situation:

   (a) A friend has just started a new job and has a boss who has made inappropriate and unwanted sexual comments. Your friend is worried about putting his or her job in jeopardy. What would you advise?

   (b) One of your friends is constantly being ridiculed at school by a group of three or four other students and you are the only witness. What should you do and how can you advise your friend?

   (c) Your best friend is involved in his or her first serious relationship with someone who is constantly putting him or her down in front of you. Your friend seems to think this is normal and not a big deal. What should you do to help?

## WWWeblinks

Name ➤ Bullying.org

URL ➤ www.bullying.org

An anti-bullying site that offers advice and support for victims of bullying as well as ways to help if someone you know is being bullied.

Name ➤ Canadian Charter of Rights and Freedoms

URL ➤ http://laws.justice. gc.ca/en/charter/

If you would like to read the *Canadian Charter of Rights and Freedoms* in its entirety, you can do so on this Department of Justice site.

Name ➤ Entertainment Software Rating Board

URL ➤ www.esrb.org

This site provides more information on the ratings assigned to video games, including how they are assigned and what they mean.

## Table of Contents

# UNIT 7
## Nutrition for Everyday Performance

**What this unit is about ...**

➤ What tools can I use to ensure that I am achieving the right nutritional balance for me?

➤ Why are there nutrition labels on food packages and why do I need to know how to interpret them?

➤ How does my body image affect my self-esteem and my eating habits?

# 18
# Nutrition and Healthy Eating

**A** race car requires high-octane fuel and good quality motor oil if the driver is going to be able to finish the race. So too, does your body. Your body runs on the food you eat. The better the quality of the fuel you take in, the smoother the ride over the long haul (and the longer that haul) will be.

Achieving the right nutritional balance is the trick. This means providing your body with all the right foods it needs to build and repair itself, which, in turn, will allow you to do the things that you want to do. Above all, it requires close attention to detail about what exactly you are eating, and establishing good eating habits early.

This chapter, the first of three, reviews the basics of nutrition—the science of how our body uses the components in our food to grow, maintain, and repair itself. Special attention is paid to the so-called energy nutrients, those that allow us to move about. One of the most useful tools in this respect is *Canada's Food Guide to Healthy Eating*. In the following chapter, you will learn about another tool—the nutrition label—and how, by using nutrition labels, you can take charge.

## Chapter Objectives

In this chapter, you will:

➢ Review the basic concepts underlying nutrition science

➢ Distinguish between macronutrients and micronutrients

➢ Examine the three macronutrients (carbohydrates, proteins, and fats) that provide us with energy or calories

➢ Explore the idea behind the "energy balance equation" and its value in helping us maintain a healthy lifestyle

➢ Investigate the pros and cons of vegetarianism as a possible alternative way of eating

➢ Consider the concerns of health care professionals about the use of dietary supplements

➢ Review *Canada's Food Guide to Healthy Eating* and *Canada's Physical Activity Guide to Healthy Active Living* and how they can be used to your advantage

## Key Terms

➢ nutrition
➢ macronutrients (carbohydrates, proteins, and fats)
➢ micronutrients (vitamins and minerals)
➢ calorie
➢ energy balance equation
➢ Total Daily Caloric Need
➢ Harris Benedict formula
➢ Resting Metabolic Rate (RMR)
➢ vegetarianism
➢ dietary supplements
➢ Canada's Food Guide to Healthy Eating
➢ Canada's Physical Activity Guide to Healthy Active Living

# What Is Nutrition?

**Nutrition** is the science behind how your body uses the components of food to grow, maintain, and repair itself. Nutrients are the chemical elements and compounds that are essential to the growth and maintenance of life. Your body needs more than 50 nutrients on a daily basis in order to function properly. Each nutrient helps your body perform a specific task.

The 50 nutrients belong to one of six general categories. These categories are:

- Carbohydrates
- Fats
- Proteins
- Minerals
- Vitamins
- Water

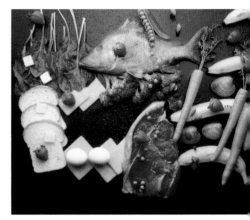

A balanced diet is the best way to ensure that your body is receiving all the nutrients it needs.

With the exception of water (*water* is just *water*), the nutrients within each category all have a similar chemical make-up, but they differ in terms of how they work within the body. For example, within the vitamin category, there are 13 different types of vitamins (each with a particular function). Similarly, there are 20 different amino acids (the building blocks of proteins), again with each protein having a unique role to play in the body.

Achieving the right nutritional balance means providing your body with all the right foods it needs to build and repair itself and to allow you to do the things that you want to do.

# Macronutrients

**Macronutrients** are the nutrients that we need in relatively large amounts every day. In addition to water, the macronutrients are carbohydrates, proteins, and fats (these three are also known as the "energy nutrients" because they provide us with energy or calories).

## Carbohydrates

**Carbohydrates** are the preferred source of food energy for your body. Over 50 percent of your total daily caloric intake should come from carbohydrate-rich foods. The body converts carbohydrates into a sugar called glucose, which it can use to fuel physical activity. The body also uses glucose to burn fat. There are two types of carbohydrates: simple and complex.

Orange juice is a source of simple carbohydrates.

> **Simple carbohydrates** are also called sugars and occur naturally in fruit, milk, yogourt, and fruit juices. Simple carbohydrates are also used in less nutritious foods such as soft drinks, candy, and some baked goods (such as cookies and cakes). These carbohydrates provide the body with a quick source of energy because they can easily be digested and absorbed into the bloodstream.

> **Complex carbohydrates** come from starches found in grain products (bread, pasta, cereal, rice), vegetables, and legumes (beans, peas, lentils). The word "complex" describes the structure of the molecules in this type of carbohydrate. Complex carbohydrates are made up of long chains of glucose molecules. This, in turn, means that your body takes longer to break them down. They provide a slow, steady source of energy.

Grain products (bread, pasta, cereal, rice), vegetables, fruit, and legumes are among the sources of complex carbohydrates.

**Fibre** is a type of complex carbohydrate that the body cannot digest and that is not a source of calories. Fibre helps you stay healthy because it takes some cancer-causing chemicals out of your body. It also helps to remove the building blocks of cholesterol, a type of fat that increases the risk of heart disease.

As well, fibre can help you manage your weight. When fibre attaches itself to water, it expands and makes you feel full, which means you are less likely to overeat. People who choose fibre-rich foods have an easier time achieving and maintaining a healthy body weight.

Rich sources of fibre include whole grain products (whole wheat breads and pastas, whole grain cereals), vegetables, fruit, and legumes.

## Proteins

**Proteins** can be found in all the cells in our bodies: muscles, tendons, ligaments, hair, skin, and nails. Proteins also play a role in sight, hearing, taste, and smell. Proteins are the building blocks of enzymes that help digest food, fight infection, and build blood. Proteins can act as an energy source; however, this normally happens only if our bodies are short of carbohydrates.

Proteins are complex nutrients made up of smaller sub-units called amino acids. Of the 20 different amino acids, the human body can produce 11; the other nine must be obtained from food:

> **High-quality protein sources**. Foods that contain all nine of these essential amino acids are considered to be high-quality protein sources. Examples include eggs, meat, fish, poultry, and milk products.

> **Low-quality protein sources**. Foods that are lacking in one or more essential amino acids are referred to as low-quality protein sources. Examples of low-quality protein sources include cereals, grain products, legumes, and nuts.

## Fats

**Fats** are a concentrated source of energy, and they are especially useful during prolonged physical activity. Fats are not bad. You should think of fats as a nutrient that the body needs to stay healthy. They are, to repeat, important sources of concentrated energy. They also help in the absorption of the fat-soluble vitamins that your body needs (more about vitamins on the next page).

People are often confused about the role that fats play in their diets. Choosing too many higher-fat foods too often can increase a person's risk of heart disease, diabetes, obesity, or some types of cancer. Fats do play an important role in maintaining good health; all that is needed is a little moderation and a little planning. Essentially, one should always try to choose higher-fat foods that also provide other nutrients (granola bars, peanut butter, cheese, meats), rather than higher fat, less nutritious foods (hot dogs, French fries, potato chips).

Fish contains all nine essential amino acids which means it is considered a high-quality protein source.

Nuts are an example of a low-quality protein source since they lack one or more of the essential amino acids.

| FUNCTIONS AND SOURCES OF MACRONUTRIENTS | | |
|---|---|---|
| **MACRONUTRIENT** | **FUNCTION** | **FOOD SOURCES** |
| Protein | ➢ Development and maintenance of body cells, tissues, and structures<br>➢ Provide energy or calories | ➢ Meat, poultry, fish, eggs, legumes, milk and milk products, vegetables, grains |
| Carbohydrate | ➢ Provide energy or calories | ➢ Breads, cereal, pasta, rice, fruit, fruit juices, vegetables, milk, yogourt |
| Fat | ➢ Provide energy or calories<br>➢ Carries fat-soluble vitamins | ➢ Meat, poultry, fish, milk and milk products, nuts and seeds, oils, butter, margarine, salad dressing |
| Water | ➢ Nutrient transportation<br>➢ Temperature regulation<br>➢ Waste product removal | ➢ Drinking water, all foods that contain fluid (milk, juices, fruits, soups) |

# Micronutrients

Those essential nutrients that are needed by our bodies only in small amounts are called **micronutrients**. Although we need less of each nutrient, these nutrients still play an important role in the way our bodies function.

Unlike carbohydrates, proteins, and fats, vitamins and minerals do not provide energy or calories. Rather, these "non-energy nutrients" help the body utilize the energy provided by carbohydrates, proteins, and fats.

## Vitamins

**Vitamins** are chemicals that the body needs to build and maintain its cells and to release energy from macronutrients. The two types of vitamins are water-soluble and fat-soluble:

> ➤ **Water-soluble vitamins.** Our bodies cannot store water-soluble vitamins, so we need to eat foods that contain these vitamins on a daily basis. For example, vitamin C, found in fresh fruits and vegetables, is a water-soluble vitamin that helps the body build collagen (the tissue in earlobes, tendons, bones) and fight disease.

> ➤ **Fat-soluble vitamins.** Fat-soluble vitamins are absorbed in the small intestine and then stored in the liver. We need smaller amounts of them. Vitamin D is a fat-soluble vitamin; it helps maintain strong bones because it aids in the absorption of calcium. Vitamin D is added to milk, but your body also makes it on its own when your skin is exposed to sunshine.

## Minerals

Aside from helping the body get energy from macronutrients, **minerals** help make bones, proteins, and blood. Minerals are inorganic substances needed by the body for good health. For example, calcium, which the body obtains from dairy products, is part of the structure of bones and teeth; while iron, found in some meat and some dark-green vegetables, plays a role in carrying oxygen to body tissues.

Electrolytes are minerals that carry an electrical charge when dissolved in the body. They are in all the fluids in your body—in the blood, and in and around the cells. Electrolytes balance fluid levels in the body, maintain blood pressure, and conduct nerve impulses.

The three types of electrolytes are sodium, chloride, and potassium. You get all the sodium and chloride your body needs from salt, and you can get potassium from vegetables and fruit.

---

## Balance, Variety, Moderation

When it comes to eating, there are three things to keep in mind:

- **Balance.** This means choosing foods that contain all the nutrients our bodies need for fuel and for restoring and repairing bones and tissue.

- **Variety.** Let's face it, it is much more enjoyable eating a variety of foods than eating the same thing all the time. As well, eating a variety of foods will ensure you get a good balance of nutrients.

- **Moderation.** When it comes to your diet, the old saying "Everything in moderation" certainly holds true (and not only during holidays). Moderation is especially important when eating those tempting foods that have little nutrient value.

## FUNCTIONS AND SOURCES OF MICRONUTRIENTS

| MICRONUTRIENT | FUNCTION | FOOD SOURCES |
|---|---|---|
| Vitamin A | ➢ Growth and maintenance of skin<br>➢ Wound healing and vision<br>➢ Acts as an anti-oxidant to protect cells from damage | ➢ Mango, cantaloupe, apricot, green leafy vegetables (e.g., spinach, kale, turnip greens) carrots, sweet potatoes, pumpkin, liver, fluid milk |
| Vitamin B1 (thiamin) | ➢ Helps release energy from carbohydrates<br>➢ Aids in growth of nerve and muscle tissue | ➢ Pork, wheat germ, whole and enriched grain products |
| Vitamin B2 (riboflavin) | ➢ Helps body capture and use released energy from food<br>➢ Promotes tissue repair and growth | ➢ Milk, cheese, and yogourt, eggs, organ meats, green leafy vegetables |
| Vitamin B3 (niacin) | ➢ Helps body capture and use released energy from food<br>➢ Maintains normal nervous function | ➢ Lean meats, poultry, peanuts, organ meats, fish |
| Vitamin B12 (cobalamin) | ➢ Aids in normal red blood cell development<br>➢ Nervous system maintenance | ➢ Liver, kidney, meat, poultry, eggs, milk and milk products, fish |
| Biotin | ➢ Helps body manufacture proteins fats and glycogen<br>➢ Helps maintain a steady blood sugar level | ➢ Liver, kidney, milk and milk products, egg yolk, mushrooms, bananas, strawberries, grapefruit, watermelon |
| Vitamin C (ascorbic acid) | ➢ Acts as an anti-oxidant to protect cells from damage<br>➢ Fights infection and heals wounds<br>➢ Formation of collagen<br>➢ Helps absorb iron and copper | ➢ Strawberries, grapefruits (and grapefruit juice), oranges (and orange juice), melons, mangos, broccoli, bell peppers, tomatoes (and tomato juice) |
| Vitamin D | ➢ Growth and maintenance of bones<br>➢ Helps absorb calcium and phosphorus | ➢ Fluid milk, fortified soy and rice beverages, higher fat fish (e.g., halibut, cod), margarine |
| Vitamin E | ➢ Acts as an anti-oxidant to protect cells from damage<br>➢ Stops LDL cholesterol from attaching to artery walls | ➢ Wheat germ, vegetable oils, beef liver, eggs, nuts |
| Folate | ➢ Helps red blood cells develop normally<br>➢ Neural tube development during pregnancy | ➢ Liver, green leafy vegetables, legumes (e.g., dried beans, peas, and lentils), asparagus, broccoli, fortified flour and grain products, nuts, oranges and orange juice |
| Vitamin K | ➢ Blood clotting<br>➢ Bone growth and maintenance | ➢ Vegetable oils, green leafy vegetables, liver |
| Calcium | ➢ Builds and maintains bones and teeth<br>➢ Helps muscles and nerves work properly<br>➢ Blood clotting | ➢ Milk and milk products, canned salmon (with bones), fortified soy and rice beverages, fortified fruit juices, turnip and collard greens, kale |
| Chloride | ➢ Maintains proper water balance in the body<br>➢ Aids in digestion | ➢ Table salt (and foods that contain table salt) |
| Chromium | ➢ Helps use glucose and fats<br>➢ Helps insulin regulate blood sugar | ➢ Meat, cheeses, eggs, whole grains |
| Copper | ➢ Assists the body in using iron and oxygen<br>➢ Aids in growth, immunity and brain development | ➢ Liver, kidney, shellfish, nuts, legumes, raisins, chocolate |
| Fluoride | ➢ Maintenance of bones and teeth | ➢ Fortified drinking water, fish |
| Iodine | ➢ Helps to regulate thyroid hormones and energy use | ➢ Seafood, iodized table salt |
| Iron | ➢ Attaches to red blood cells to form hemoglobin and carry oxygen | ➢ Liver, meat, poultry, oysters, legumes, green leafy vegetables, fortified cereals, dark molasses |
| Magnesium | ➢ Forms part of teeth and bones<br>➢ Nerve impulse transmission | ➢ Whole grains, nuts, legumes, milk |
| Phosphorus | ➢ Builds and maintains bones and teeth<br>➢ Energy production | ➢ Meat, poultry, fish, eggs, milk and milk products, nuts, legumes, bananas, potatoes |
| Potassium | ➢ Body fluid balance<br>➢ Blood pressure regulation<br>➢ Muscle contraction | ➢ Fruits (orange juice, bananas, and dried fruits in particular), potatoes, milk, meat |
| Selenium | ➢ Acts as an anti-oxidant to protect cells from damage | ➢ Whole grains, onions, meat, seafood |
| Sodium | ➢ Body fluid balance<br>➢ Blood pressure regulation<br>➢ Aids in muscle and nerve activity | ➢ Table salt (and foods that contain table salt), found in varying amounts in almost all foods |
| Zinc | ➢ Helps to form the hormone insulin<br>➢ Wound healing and immune response | ➢ Meat, liver, eggs, seafood, grains, nuts |

# What Are Calories?

Of the six categories of nutrients, the body can use only three as sources of energy: carbohydrates, proteins, and fats. Together, these three macronutrients provide us with all the energy our bodies use.

## Calorie Counting

Nutritionists measure how much energy we get from the three energy nutrients in units called *calories*. Of all the terms used in the nutrition context, none arises as often as this term. The term calorie is a measure of heat—technically, it is the amount of energy needed to raise the temperature of 1 gram of pure water by 1 degree Celsius.

In the dietary context, what is called a **calorie** is, in fact, a kilocalorie (1000 calories). Calories are a measure of the amount of energy that food will produce as it passes through the body. Energy can also be measured in joules, which is the metric unit of measurement for energy—one food calorie equals 4,186 joules.

The three energy nutrients supply energy (calories) in different amounts:

> 1 gram of carbohydrate provides 4 calories

> 1 gram of protein provides 4 calories

> 1 gram of fat provides 9 calories

It is generally recommended that we get 45–65 percent of our calories from carbohydrates, 10–35 percent from protein, and 20–35 percent from fats.

Body size, physical activity level, age, and genetic or family history all determine energy and nutrient levels needed for optimum health.

| SUBSTITUTE WITH A HEALTHIER CHOICE | |
| --- | --- |
| INSTEAD OF ... | TRY THIS ... |
| Potato chips, taco chips | > Pretzels, baked crackers, popcorn (use small amounts of butter or margarine, and salt to season), raw vegetables and lower-fat dip |
| Pop, fruit drinks, slushes | > Water, 100% fruit juices, milk, chocolate milk, or soda water |
| French fries | > Tossed salad with the salad dressing on the side or a baked potato (use only small amounts of butter, margarine, or salad dressing to season) |
| Large hamburger | > Small hamburger, or a chicken burger or turkey burger (order any special sauces "on the side;" use only small amounts of sauce) |
| Sugary cereals | > Whole grain cereals (use small amounts of sugar or dried fruits to sweeten) |
| Breaded, fried chicken burger | > Roasted chicken burger (order any special sauces "on the side;" use only small amounts of sauce) |
| Loaded meat pizza | > Thin-crust vegetarian pizza, whole-wheat crust, made with minimal oil and cheese |
| Deli meat submarine sandwich | > Ask for a whole-wheat bun; avoid sausage-type deli meats; choose leaner meats such as ham, roast beef, chicken or turkey; use mustard, relish, cranberry sauce, or salsa to season |

## The Energy Balance Equation

The key to achieving and maintaining a healthy body weight is to balance our energy intake with our energy expenditure. The **energy balance equation** treats our caloric intake as "energy in." The amount of calories we burn over the course of an entire day is called our "energy expenditure." It follows that:

➤ When energy intake is equal to energy expenditure, our bodies' energy needs are met and our body weight does not change. We are said to be in "neutral energy balance."

➤ If we take in fewer calories than we burn off through activity, we will lose weight. This is called "negative energy balance."

➤ In contrast, we sometimes take in more food than we balance out with physical activity. This is called "positive energy balance" and results in weight gain.

Obviously, physical activity significantly increases energy expenditure, making it easier to balance energy intake from foods. For this reason, people who are physically active are much less likely to be overweight or obese.

The secret, therefore, is to be active, to eat reasonably well, and to enjoy yourself.

Achieving the right nutritional balance means providing your body with all the right foods it needs to build and repair itself, thus allowing you to do the things that you want to do.

Caloric intake is "energy in" and should be balanced with activity or "energy expenditure."

# Understanding Your Caloric Needs

Obviously, no two people are exactly alike when it comes to the amount of calories they need each day. Gender, body size, genetics, age, and physical activity level all will influence your **Total Daily Caloric Need**. For example, a teenage male athlete needs more calories than an inactive elderly woman. Similarly, because they are still growing, teenage girls need more calories than older women or young children.

The **Harris Benedict formula** is a widely established way to help estimate the amount of energy your body uses when it is at rest. This is known as your **Resting Metabolic Rate (RMR)**.

You can multiply your RMR by an activity factor (how much activity you generally do each day) to arrive at your Total Daily Caloric Need. The process is described fully on the next page using the Harris Benedict formula.

## Quick Estimate of Resting Metabolic Rate

There is also a "quick formula" for estimating your Resting Metabolic Rate. This quick calculation is intended for adult males and females, but give it a try and then compare the results with the Harris Benedict calculation.

To estimate your RMR, simply multiply your weight in kilograms by 24.2 for adult males or by 22.0 for adult females. Here are examples of how this quick calculation works for Mark (68.4 kg) and Jillian (55 kg):

> Mark's RMR = 68.4 × 24.2 = 1,655 calories/day
> Jillian's RMR = 55.0 × 22.0 = 1,210 calories/day

Gender, body size, genetics, age, and physical activity level all influence how many calories each person will need.

# The Harris Benedict Formula
## Different People Have Different Caloric Needs

The Harris Benedict formula can be used to calculate your Resting Metabolic Rate (RMR). Once you have your RMR, you can easily estimate your Total Daily Caloric Need.

### Resting Metabolic Rate

Resting Metabolic Rate refers to the amount of energy your body uses when it is completely at rest. Obviously, this will vary between individuals, especially individuals of different heights, weights, and ages. Through rigorous testing under laboratory conditions, the Harris Benedict formula has been found to accurately estimate an individual's RMR.

Researchers have also found that whether that individual is male or female also needs to be taken into account. Accordingly, there is a different weighting in the basic formula for women and men.

Once your RMR has been estimated, computing your total daily caloric need is fairly straightforward—it is a simple multiple of that figure, depending on your particular level of activity. Researchers have come up with a set of multipliers that can be used to compute your total daily caloric need.

### Total Daily Caloric Need

To estimate your Total Daily Caloric Need, simply multiply your RMR by the appropriate activity factor, as follows:

- If you are sedentary (little or no exercise):
  Multiply your RMR × 1.2
- If you are lightly active (light exercise/sports 1–3 days/week):
  Multiply your RMR × 1.375
- If you are moderately active (moderate exercise/sports 3–5 days/week):
  Multiply your RMR × 1.55
- If you are very active (hard exercise/sports 6–7 days a week):
  Multiply your RMR × 1.725
- If you are extra active (very hard daily exercise/sports):
  Multiply your RMR × 1.9

You can use this calculation to ensure that you are taking in the right amount of calories every day.

## The Harris Benedict Equation

**For Mark (160 cm tall, 68.4 kg in weight, and 14 years of age):**

Resting Metabolic Rate = 66.5 + (5 × height in centimetres) + (13.7 × weight in kilograms) - (6.8 × age in years)

$$= 66.5 + (5 \times 160) + (13.7 \times 68.4) - (6.8 \times 14)$$

$$= 66.5 + 800 + 937.08 - 95.2$$

$$= \textbf{1,708 calories/day}$$

**For Jillian (153 cm tall, 55 kg in weight, and 15 years of age):**

Resting Metabolic Rate = 655 + (1.9 × height in centimetres) + (9.5 × weight in kilograms) - (4.7 × age in years)

$$= 655 + (1.9 \times 153) + (9.5 \times 55) - (4.7 \times 15)$$

$$= 655 + 290.7 + 522.5 - 70.5$$

$$= \textbf{1,398 calories/day}$$

**To find Mark's and Jillian's Total Daily Caloric need, multiply his or her RMR by the appropriate activity factor.**

*Note*: The terms "Resting Metabolic Rate" and "Basal Metabolic Rate" are often used interchangeably, so you may encounter both terms. "Basal Metabolic Rate" is generally the preferred term when a very precise measurement is attempted under strict laboratory conditions.

# Understanding Vegetarian Eating

A growing number of people are taking a second look at their eating habits, and interest in becoming vegetarian has grown. Approximately 4 percent of Canadian adults follow vegetarian diets on a full-time basis, and another 30 percent of Canadians say that they choose meatless meals regularly.

## What Is a Vegetarian?

**Vegetarianism** is a term that describes many different types of eating styles that emphasize vegetables, grains, fruits, nuts, and seeds. There is no single way to correctly eat like a "vegetarian." While most vegetarians eliminate meat, fish, and poultry from their diets, many do not exclude all animal foods, and some vegetarians limit red meat only.

For example, vegetarians who follow what is called a lacto-ovo vegetarian diet will eat eggs, as well as milk and milk products, such as yogourt and cheese. In contrast, vegan (or total) vegetarians eliminate these foods and, depending on their reason for being vegetarian, may also eliminate honey, beer, wine, and refuse to wear or use leather, wool, or fur clothing.

## What Do They Eat?

People who follow a vegetarian diet find alternate food sources for the nutrients they would otherwise get from meat. A healthy vegetarian diet includes vegetables and fruits, grains, legumes and soy products (such as tofu and texturized vegetable protein), and nuts as sources of protein and other nutrients. As a general rule, most vegetarians should try to combine two different sources of protein each day.

Vegetarians who eat eggs, milk and milk products, such as yogourt and cheese, are called lacto-ovo vegetarians.

Vegetarians who eliminate lacto-ovo foods and honey, and who refuse to wear or use leather, wool, or fur clothing are called vegan (or total) vegetarians.

| COMMON VEGETARIAN EATING STYLES | | |
|---|---|---|
| **TYPE** | **FOODS SELECTED** | **FOODS AVOIDED** |
| Semi-vegetarian | ➤ Vegetables and fruit, grain products, milk and milk products, poultry, fish, shellfish, eggs, and meat alternatives (tofu, legumes, nuts) | ➤ Red meat |
| Lacto-ovo vegetarian | ➤ Vegetables and fruit, grain products, milk and milk products, eggs, and meat alternatives (tofu, legumes, nuts) | ➤ Meat, fish, poultry, and shellfish |
| Ovo vegetarian | ➤ Vegetables and fruit, grain products, eggs, and meat alternatives (tofu, legumes, nuts) | ➤ Meat, fish, poultry, shellfish, and milk and milk products |
| Lacto-vegetarian | ➤ Vegetables and fruit, grain products, milk and milk products, and meat alternatives (tofu, legumes, nuts) | ➤ Meat, fish, poultry, shellfish, and eggs |
| Vegan | ➤ Vegetables and fruit, grain products, and meat alternatives (tofu, legumes, nuts) | ➤ Milk and milk products, meat, fish, poultry, shellfish, and eggs |

People choose to become vegetarian for a variety of reasons. In some cases, people feel a strong ethical commitment to protecting animal rights. For others, vegetarian eating is a part of their religious beliefs. People may also choose to become vegetarian because they want to enjoy the health benefits this kind of eating style offers.

### Is Vegetarian Eating Healthier?

Well-planned vegetarian diets offer a number of health benefits. Research suggests that vegetarian diets may reduce the risk for a number of chronic diseases and health conditions such as obesity and overweight, heart disease, and some types of cancer. Planning a well-balanced vegetarian diet, that provides all of the nutrients needed for good health, is the key to reaping these benefits.

Poorly planned or overly restrictive vegetarian diets can lead to nutritional deficiencies. Shortages of iron, calcium, and zinc are the most noted drawbacks of vegetarian eating. Vegetarian teenagers and young adults, who are growing and active, can have higher than average needs for these nutrients, and need to be especially careful when it comes to planning their food choices.

### Can You Get All the Nutrients Needed for Good Health on a Vegetarian Diet?

The nutritional quality of a vegetarian diet depends upon the foods that a person chooses. Vegetarians who choose a variety of different foods each day, in adequate amounts, can obtain all of the nutrients needed for good health.

On the other hand, vegetarian diets that are planned haphazardly or those that eliminate entire groups of foods without adding back a vegetarian replacement, can lack nutrients and be quite unhealthy.

It's all about planning. A vegetarian diet can provide you with all of the nutrients you need if you do a little bit of planning and focus on choosing foods that offer the nutrients found in animal products.

### Where Can I Go to Learn How to Plan a Vegetarian Diet?

Planning a healthy vegetarian diet is fairly straightforward provided you start off with some reliable information and practical tips. A Registered Dietitian can help you learn more about vegetarian eating. Visit the Dietitians of Canada website to locate a dietitian in your area: **www.dietitians.ca**.

**Source:** Adapted from "Vegetarian Diets: Position of the American Dietetic Association and Dietitians of Canada, 2003." Dietitians of Canada/American Dietetic Association. www.dietitians.ca/news/highlights_positions.asp.

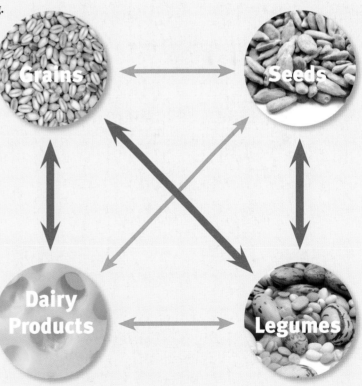

This diagram illustrates complementary proteins. For example, mixing grains with legumes (e.g., peanut butter on whole wheat bread) gives the body a complete protein. The wider red arrows show the best combinations.

# What Are Dietary Supplements?

**Dietary supplements** are products that you take by mouth, that contain a "dietary ingredient," and are intended to add to, or supplement, the foods that you eat. The "dietary ingredients" in these products may include: vitamins, minerals, herbs or other botanicals, amino acids, and substances such as enzymes, organ tissues, glandulars, and metabolites. Dietary supplements are sold in many different forms—from tablets, capsules, softgels, gelcaps, liquids, or powders to extracts or concentrates. Some are also sold as bars, drinks, or specialty cereals. However, supplements sold in these forms closely resemble traditional foods. Whatever their form may be, in Canada, dietary supplements are regulated as foods, not drugs.

The dietary supplement industry in both Canada and the United States is not well regulated. Unlike the system that is in place to ensure the safety of drugs, dietary supplements are only loosely controlled. As a result, the claims made by dietary supplements may not always be supported by scientific evidence. In addition, the contents of these products are not subject to the checking or scrutiny that drugs undergo.

There are literally hundreds of different dietary supplements sold in Canada. The table on page 304 reviews some of the more common supplements, their claims, and what we actually know about them.

## Buyer Beware!

Ultimately, we are all responsible for the health and lifestyle choices that we make. This is especially true where dietary supplements are concerned. Because these products are only loosely regulated, it is up to the buyer to learn more about a supplement before making a purchase. If you have an interest in using a dietary supplement, here are some do's and don'ts to help guide you.

> **Do: Research the product before buying**. Know exactly what the product contains and find out if any claims about the product are valid. Find information from reliable sources, such as Health Canada or your community pharmacist.

> **Don't: Believe everything that you read**. Information provided by health and fitness magazines, health food stores, or manufacturers is not always objective and reliable.

> **Do: Read labels**. Be sure you know exactly what you will be taking and how it might impact your body. Consider both the positive physical effects and any negative side effects. If there is something that you are unsure of, ask your doctor or pharmacist before taking the supplement.

> **Don't: Buy into phrases such as, "miracle product," "latest breakthrough," or "clinically proven."** Remember, if something seems too good to be true, it probably is. If a miracle health product has been discovered, you would have heard about it in the news or in your doctor's office.

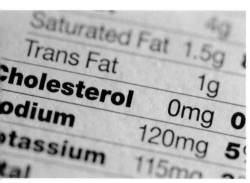

Make sure you read the ingredients and the nutrition label so you know how the nutritional supplement will affect your body.

Consult with your doctor or pharmacist before taking dietary supplements.

- ➤ **Do: Tell both your doctor and pharmacist exactly what you plan to take before you take it.** Some dietary supplements have powerful side effects. Others can interfere with other supplements or products you may be taking. Health care professionals can discuss the pros and cons of different dietary supplements with you and help you make an informed decision.

- ➤ **Don't: Take more than the recommended dose**. If you decide to try a dietary supplement, stick to the dosage recommended by your doctor or pharmacist. Do not take more than the recommended amount in the hopes of maximizing the benefits. It is possible to overdose on so-called "natural" products.

- ➤ **Do: Talk to your coach or team doctor if you are a competitive athlete and interested in trying a dietary supplement**. Most sport organizations recommend that athletes avoid ALL dietary supplements because there is no way to be sure that these products do not contain a banned substance.

- ➤ **Do: Report any side effects to your doctor immediately.** If you experience any unusual symptoms after using a supplement, contact your doctor. Even if the symptoms are mild, side effects are warning signs that something is wrong. Examples of symptoms that you should be concerned about include stomach upset, pain, headaches, rashes, dizziness, problems breathing, or tiredness.

Competitive athletes should consult with their coach or team doctor when considering supplements.

If you experience any side effects, tell your doctor, even if they are mild.

Choosing a balanced diet is the best way to meet your energy (caloric) and nutrient needs. Think "food first," and use supplements only after carefully considering all of the options.

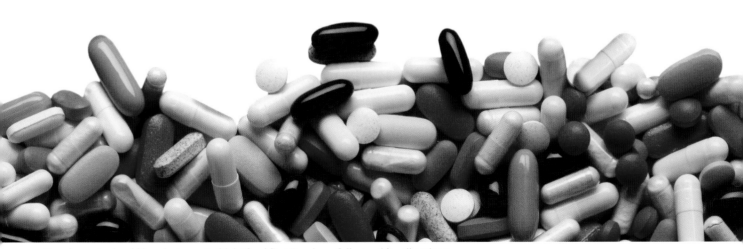

Supplements should be a last resort; think "food first," and carefully consider all options.

# Common Dietary Supplements

| SUPPLEMENT | CLAIMS | EVIDENCE | SIDE EFFECTS |
|---|---|---|---|
| **Protein Powders** | ➢ Claims to build bigger muscles.<br><br>➢ Supposed to be able to enhance exercise stamina and help the body repair faster. | ➢ Eating a balanced diet as outlined in Canada's Food Guide will give the variety of proteins that you need. | ➢ Side effects from protein powders include upset stomach, diarrhea, and elevated cholesterol.<br><br>➢ Excess protein is stored as fat in the body. |
| **Guarana** | ➢ Touted for its caffeine-like effects.<br><br>➢ Found in many "energy" supplements or "fat loss" supplements.<br><br>➢ Marketed as an appetite suppressant, stimulant, and energy enhancer. | ➢ Scientific support for the claims about guarana as a weight-loss aid is lacking.<br><br>➢ More research is needed to understand the effects of this herb. | ➢ Side effects of using guarana include: increased blood pressure, anxiety, headache, and cardiac stimulation.<br><br>➢ May interfere with prescription medication. |
| **Creatine** | ➢ Said to increase muscle mass and improve sport performance. | ➢ Scientific reports have been inconclusive.<br><br>➢ Results from some research studies suggest that creatine supplements may improve sport performance, while others do not. | ➢ Creatine has not been tested for safety or effectiveness in children or teenagers. |
| **Anabolic Steroids** | ➢ Said to increase muscle mass, improve sport performance, and help muscles repair quicker after exercise. | ➢ Scientific research shows that anabolic steroids are powerful hormones that increase muscle mass. | ➢ Anabolic steroids have been linked to life-threatening complications including liver damage, heart disease, sexual and reproductive problems, depression, and other forms of mental illness. |
| **Ephedra and Ephedra-Free Fat Burners** | ➢ Claims to be able to promote fat loss and enhance sport performance. | ➢ The effectiveness of ephedra-free fat burners is not supported by scientific research.<br><br>➢ The use of ephedra as a weight loss supplement in Canada is banned. | ➢ Ephedra has been linked to side effects including heart attacks and death.<br><br>➢ Ephedra can cause life-threatening side effects, particularly if combined with caffeine or guarana. |

**Source:** Adapted from "Dietary Supplement Dilemma: Helpful or Harmful?" Canadian Forces Health Services Group. National Defence. September 2004. www.forces.gc.ca/health.

# Energy Drinks
## Buyer Beware!

Energy drinks, as the name implies, are meant to provide mental and physical stimulation for a short period of time. Many people, particularly young people, drink them to keep up their energy late at night or during periods of intense physical activity.

The chemical mix bringing all this about is simple: caffeine, taurine (an amino acid), and glucuronolactone (a carbohydrate). In fact, these energy drinks may contain as much as 80 mg of caffeine, the equivalent of a cup of strong coffee.

The concern is that, if taken in larger quantities, and especially if used in the context of intense activity or mixed with alcohol, the combination may have unintended and unknown harmful effects.

### Energy Drinks Versus Sports Drinks

Many energy drinks are currently sold in Canada—in corner stores, gas stations, and supermarkets. Oddly, they are usually displayed alongside soft drinks, juices, and sport drinks. Yet, as many people point out, energy drinks are different from most soft drinks, juices, and sports drinks, such as Gatorade® or Powerade®.

Sports drinks are designed primarily to rehydrate the body after or during activity. By contrast, people drink energy drinks to keep up their energy and to quench their thirst. However, the caffeine in these drinks is a diuretic and, unless one is careful, rather than rehydrating, these drinks may actually cause serious dehydration.

### Dangerous When Mixed with Alcohol

There is also a concern that, when mixed with alcohol, the combination may be especially dangerous, and possibly even lethal.

Because energy drinks are stimulants and alcohol is a depressant, the stimulant effects can mask how intoxicated you are. No matter how alert you may feel, your blood alcohol concentration (BAC) will be the same.

### Regulation May Be Required

According to Health Canada, because of their composition and effects, some energy drinks may have to be brought under government regulations as natural health products, depending on their ingredients.

Health Canada advises caution when using these drinks, and to be aware of the following:

- Do not drink excessive amounts

- Do not mix with alcohol

- Ensure you drink enough water to rehydrate your system

- The safety of such drinks may not have been evaluated by Health Canada

- Report any adverse reactions

In short, buyer beware!

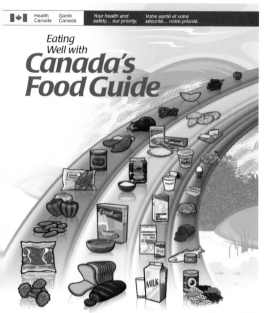

The new version of *Canada's Food Guide* was released in February 2007. You can now tailor your food guide based on your age and gender and new food examples have been added to reflect Canada's multicultural population.

# Canada's Food Guide to Healthy Eating

Eating balanced, nutritious meals, combined with regular physical activity, earns a number of benefits. It enables you to achieve and maintain a healthy body weight, have more energy, and have better overall health.

**Canada's Food Guide to Healthy Eating** is a simple tool to help people plan their food choices on a daily basis. It translates Recommended Dietary Allowances (RDAs) of nutrients into actual advice that people can use to change their eating habits.

## The Food Groups

The *Food Guide* is based on what nutritionists refer to as the "total diet" approach. This approach recognizes that no single food or single meal determines the quality of an individual's diet. Instead, the total diet approach focuses on a person's overall pattern of eating and the foods that they choose over time.

The *Food Guide* categorizes foods into four food groups:

➢ Fruit and Vegetables

➢ Grain Products

➢ Milk Products

➢ Meats and Alternatives

Foods that do not fit into any of these food groups belong to what previous versions of the *Food Guide* called the "Other Foods" category. Examples include: potato chips, corn chips, candies, soft drinks, and seasonings. Many of these foods are high in fat, salt, or sugar. These foods are not mentioned specifically in the new version of the food guide and should be consumed in moderation.

Remember ... no one food or meal determines the quality of an individual's diet. It is a person's food choices over time that impact his or her nutritional health.

## Combination Foods

Many foods contain a combination of ingredients that come from several different food groups. To evaluate these kinds of foods, you have to break them down into their various components.

A quarter-pound cheeseburger is a good example of this kind of "combination food." The hamburger bun represents two servings from the Grain Products group. The ground beef patty is approximately one serving from the Meats and Alternatives group. The cheese slice is approximately half a serving from the Milk Products group.

Each food group is essential because it provides its own set of nutrients.

## Using the Food Guide

Are you interested in changing your eating habits, but not sure where to start? *Canada's Food Guide* offers an easy-to-use "blue-print," or template for a healthy diet. It provides information on the kinds of foods to emphasize, portion sizes, and roughly how many servings of each kind of food you need in a day.

Unlike some diets or eating plans you will find in books, magazines, or on the Internet, the *Food Guide* is based on recent and reliable nutrition research. It can be used to assess how well you are currently eating and to develop a personal eating plan. Use the following tips to get started:

> **Create a food record.** Write down everything you have to eat and drink for 1–2 days or even longer.

> **Check and compare.** Compare your food record to *Canada's Food Guide to Healthy Eating.*

> **Set a healthy eating goal.** Changing your eating habits can be challenging.

> **Do a progress check.** After a week has passed, recheck your food choices.

> **Repeat the goal setting.** Revise your eating plan until you have created a balanced and healthy one that works for you.

*Canada's Guide to Healthy Eating* can help you achieve the proper balance in your diet.

## Food Servings
### What Does One Serving Look Like?

| GRAIN PRODUCTS | ½ bagel → hockey puck | ½ cup rice or pasta → light bulb or small fist | ¾ cup hot cereal → fist or cupped hand |
|---|---|---|---|
| **MILK PRODUCTS** | 1 cup milk → small measuring cup | ¾ cup yogourt → fist or cupped hand | 50g cheese → 2 thumbs or 2 processed cheese slices |
| **FRUIT AND VEGETABLES** | 1 medium-sized piece → tennis ball | ½ cup fresh, frozen, or canned → light bulb or small fist | ½ cup–1 cup beans or lentils → light bulb or small fist |
| **MEAT AND ALTERNATIVES** | 50–100g meat, poultry, or fish → deck of cards, computer mouse, or palm of hand | ½ cup–1 cup beans or lentils → light bulb or small fist | 2 tbsp peanut butter → ping pong ball |

# Canada's Physical Activity Guide to Healthy Active Living

Incorporate a variety of activities into your daily routine.

Research has shown that regular physical exercise can help people avoid some specific diseases and lead healthier lives. **Canada's Physical Activity Guide to Healthy Active Living** sets out guidelines about how much activity we should strive for every day.

For example, *Canada's Physical Activity Guide* recommends that Canadian children and youth who are not currently active should (1) increase the amount of time they currently spend being physically active by at least 30 minutes per day, and (2) decrease the time they spend on sedentary activities—such as watching TV, playing computer games, and surfing the Internet—by at least 30 minutes per day.

## Analyze Your Current Activity Level

Figuring out your current activity level is a good way to begin planning for a more active lifestyle. The *Physical Activity Guide* defines three main types of physical activities: aerobic activities (endurance and continuous movement), flexibility activities (stretching, reaching, and bending), and strength activities (using the muscles against resistance).

To analyze your current activity level, you can keep a diary of the activities that you do from the time you get up in the morning until the time you go to bed for seven consecutive days.

> ➢ Record all activities you do that involve continuous movement.
> ➢ Record the intensity of the activity—light, moderate, or vigorous.
> ➢ Be specific about duration.
> ➢ Estimate the time in minutes for each activity.
> ➢ Record the time of day you do each activity.

## Get Up, Get Out, and Get Active!

Increasing the amount of time you spend being physically active is not as difficult as you may think. Use the following tips to help you get up, get out, and get active everyday:

> **Walk more. Walk more often.** Pass up the ride and walk to school, to the mall, to the library, to games, or practices.

> **Use a pedometer or step counter.** Pedometers are relatively inexpensive devices that you wear on your belt. Pedometers track the number of steps you take. Aim to accumulate between 12,000 and 15,000 steps each day.

> **Plan an active getaway with friends.** Meet at a pool or beach and spend the day swimming. Hike or bike a scenic trail. Go canoeing or cross-country skiing.

> **Dance, dance—whoever you may be**. All forms of dance— from Irish dancing, to hip-hop, to ballroom—are great exercise and lots of fun. Sign up for a class or simply move to your favourite music with friends.

> **Step away from the box.** Balance time spent on the computer, watching TV, or gaming with physical activity. Take mini physical activity breaks every 20 minutes or so when you are watching TV or using the computer. Do push-ups, sit-ups, or go up and down the stairs.

> **Try something new.** You are more likely to be physically active on a regular basis if you do something that you truly enjoy. Experiment with a wide variety of different activities to find out what you like. Try yoga or Pilates. Go for a run with your local run club. Rock climb. There's no harm in trying, and many gyms and community groups offer complimentary services to people who want to try out their programs.

Dancing is a great way to exercise.

# The Fats of Life
## The Good, the Bad, and the Ugly

The fact is that we all need some fat—it is necessary for cell building, immune system response, hormone production, absorption of vitamins, such as A, D, E and K.

The mistake that most Canadians make is eating too much fat. High fat diets have been linked to high blood cholesterol, which leads to increased chances of heart attack and stroke.

### Let's Talk about Cholesterol …

Cholesterol is a waxy substance naturally manufactured by humans and animals, essential to body functions. Most cholesterol in your blood is produced by your own body and not obtained through food.

There is a difference between dietary cholesterol and blood cholesterol. The small amount of cholesterol contained in the foods we eat has very little effect on our blood cholesterol. So what raises blood cholesterol? Dietary fat. An excess of dietary fat is what causes cholesterol to build up in the blood vessels and cause heart problems.

### Blood Cholesterol

It is important to remember that there are two types of blood cholesterol:

- HDL: the "good" cholesterol
- LDL: the "bad" cholesterol

LDL is the cholesterol that builds up on the artery walls and increases the risk of heart problems. You want the level of LDL in your blood to be LOW.

HDL actually picks up the "bad" LDL in your blood and carries it to the liver to be excreted from your body. Generally, you want your HDL level to be HIGH.

### So How Do I Keep My Cholesterol Levels Balanced?

The way to ensure that you don't build up too much cholesterol in your body is to control your fat intake. This doesn't mean you can't eat any fat ever. It's all about moderation and variation. Your goal should be to reduce, not eliminate, fats in your diet.

**Source:** Reproduced from University of Ottawa, Health Services, www.uottawa.ca/health.

## Measuring Up: Fats and Their Effect on Blood Cholesterol
ALL FATS ARE NOT CREATED EQUAL. THERE ARE FOUR TYPES OF DIETARY FAT.

| Type | Function | Form | Found in |
| --- | --- | --- | --- |
| Polyunsaturated | Helps lower LDL | Liquid at room temperature | Corn, soybean, sunflower, safflower, sesame oils, soft margarines |
| Monounsaturated | Lowers LDL and raises HDL | Usually liquid at room temperature | Canola, olive, peanut oil, soft margarines containing these oils, seeds, and nuts |
| Saturated | Usually raises LDL | Solid at room temperature | Lard, meat, poultry, butter, cheese, palm oil, coconut oil, hard margarines |
| Trans fat | Raises LDL | Formed through the process of hydrogenation of shortenings | Baked goods, cookies, crackers, chips, some margarines, hydrogenated oils |

## Questions for Study and Review

### Things to Think About and Explore

1. Identify the three macronutrients that provide energy or calories.

2. Compare and contrast macronutrients and micronutrients. How are they similar? How do they differ?

3. Relate the concept of "energy balance" to body weight.

4. Identify three considerations that should be made before using a dietary supplement.

5. Demonstrate an awareness of the potentially negative side effects of dietary supplements by identifying three physical symptoms or warning signs.

6. Compare healthy eating and dieting. How are these practices different?

### Things to Do and Practise

7. Calculate your total daily caloric need using the Harris Benedict formula (adjusted for your personal activity level).

8. Stage a debate on the nutritional pros and cons of vegetarianism as a diet choice for teens.

9. Create a collage presenting examples of foods that would be found in the "Other Foods" category of Canada's Guide to Healthy Eating.

10. Use Canada's Physical Activity Guide to determine if your activity level meets current recommendations for health.

11. Create a script or a recording of a commercial describing five benefits of regular physical activity and healthy eating.

12. Create a one-day physical activity and food record. Analyze your record and compare your findings to Canada's Guide to Healthy Eating and Physical Activity.

## WWWeblinks

Name ➢ Canada's Guide to Healthy Eating and Physical Activity

URL ➢ www.phac-aspc.gc.ca/ guide/index_e.html

Check out this site if you would like more information on serving sizes or to obtain your own copy of CGHEPA.

Name ➢ Natural Health Products Directorate

URL ➢ www.hc-sc.gc.ca/ dhp-mps/prodnatur/ index_e.html

Before taking dietary supplements, check this site for information about which ones are safe, effective, and of high quality.

Name ➢ Canadian Food Inspection Agency

URL ➢ www.inspection.gc.ca

This Agency safeguards Canada's food supply and the plants and animals upon which safe and high-quality food depends.

# 19
# Nutrition Labels and Healthy Eating

**T**he new nutrition label completes a circle for healthy eating that began with two resources from the Government of Canada—*Canada's Food Guide to Healthy Eating* and *Canada's Physical Activity Guide to Healthy Active Living*. Together, these nutrition tools allow Canadians to enjoy a range of healthy food and look forward to a healthy life.

The new nutrition label requires manufacturers to include nutritional information directly on the food packages. No more guesswork is required of consumers.

Together, the new food label and *Canada's Food Guide to Healthy Eating* encourage us to achieve and maintain a healthy body weight by enjoying regular physical activity and healthy eating.

## Chapter Objectives

In this chapter, you will:

➢ Learn all about Canada's new nutrition labelling policy on food packaging

➢ Explore the details of the Nutrition Facts table and how to use it to your advantage when trying to choose healthy foods

➢ Understand the meaning of the term "Dietary Reference Intakes" and how Dietary Reference Intakes are used

➢ Understand the importance of the % Daily Value column on food labels and how this percentage is calculated

➢ Examine the kinds of "nutrition claims" that food manufacturers are now permitted to include on their packaging

➢ Examine what kinds of "diet and health claims" food manufacturers are now permitted to include on their packaging

➢ Learn how to use the nutrition label in conjunction with *Canada's Food Guide to Healthy Eating*

## Key Terms

➢ Nutrition Facts table
➢ % Daily Value
➢ 2000-calorie diet
➢ nutrient content claims
➢ diet and health claims

# First, Read the Label

Canada has a new system for providing nutritional information to its citizens. Canadian government regulations now make nutrition labelling mandatory on most food packaging. This will help Canadian consumers to make better-informed choices about the kinds of foods they buy and eat.

## Canada Leads the Way

The new **Nutrition Facts table** appears in a standard format so that it looks basically the same from one product to another. All of the main (core) nutrients are listed in the table. The same 13 core nutrients are always listed in the same order. The label may also contain a list of the ingredients. Health-related claims about the food and what it contains are also allowed on the labels of some foods.

Canada's food labelling policies are among the most advanced in the world. By reading the Nutrition Facts table, you will see the nutrients that are contained in that food as well as their proportions. Because you know what is in the package, you will be able to make informed and healthy decisions.

Nutrition information is available on almost every food product as a result of Canadian government regulations.

Become aware of which nutrients are in food and in what proportions.

## What Is on the Label

At the top of the Nutrition Facts table you will see the portion size, which tells you the amount of food on which the nutrient information on the label is based. On the label below, for example, you can see that one tray equals 262 grams.

Keep in mind that many products contain more than one serving in a package, so it is important to do the math correctly. If you eat two servings of a product, remember to double the calorie and nutrient values. Also be wary—some labels give information for half a serving. Check the amount stated at the top of the label for the serving size.

### The Nutrition Facts Table

The Nutrition Facts table lists the total calories along with 13 core nutrients. Using the label below, we can see that the food item (in this case a tray of food) contains 290 calories. You can also tell from this label that one serving contains 3.5 grams of fat, 19 grams of protein, and 45 grams of carbohydrates.

Most nutrients are shown in grams or milligrams. Vitamins and minerals are expressed only as a percentage of the Daily Value. The energy value is provided in calories.

Portion size is especially important—many packages contain more than one portion. The nutritional information on the label pertains to the portion size indicated (in the above case, one-quarter of a pizza).

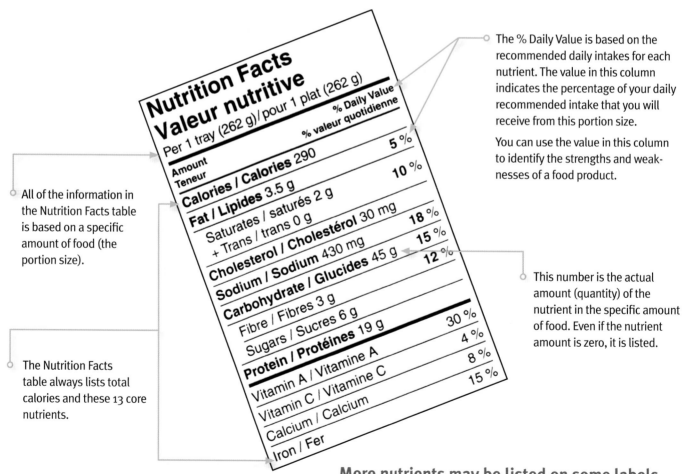

All of the information in the Nutrition Facts table is based on a specific amount of food (the portion size).

The Nutrition Facts table always lists total calories and these 13 core nutrients.

The % Daily Value is based on the recommended daily intakes for each nutrient. The value in this column indicates the percentage of your daily recommended intake that you will receive from this portion size.

You can use the value in this column to identify the strengths and weaknesses of a food product.

This number is the actual amount (quantity) of the nutrient in the specific amount of food. Even if the nutrient amount is zero, it is listed.

**More nutrients may be listed on some labels.**

# What Exactly Is "% Daily Value"?

The key to using the nutrient label on a daily basis is the column on the extreme right-hand side. The **% Daily Value** (% DV) column tells you how much, or how little, of a nutrient is contained in a particular food item or package in relation to what should be taken in on a daily basis. Because it is expressed as a percent, it works whether you know exactly what your daily nutrient requirements are or not.

Daily values for carbohydrates, total fat, and saturated and trans fat are based on a **2000-calorie diet**. Health Canada decided to base the % DV on a 2000-calorie diet because this level of calorie (or energy) intake meets the average needs of our population (this means the % DV can overestimate or underestimate the needs of some people). The % DV values for vitamins and minerals are based on the 1983 recommendations and represent the highest recommended intake for all ages and sexes.

The % DV information makes it easier to compare products, determine how nutritious a product is, manage special diets, and increase or decrease your intake of one or more of the listed nutrients. In other words, it provides consumers with information they need to eat right and stay healthy.

However, there are a few oddities in the table that need to be pointed out. These are described in the table below.

Knowing the percentage Daily Value (% DV) information is useful when trying to determine the nutritional value of food.

| LOOKING AT THE % DV COLUMN, YOU MAY HAVE NOTICED THAT ... | |
|---|---|
| There is one combined % DV for saturated and trans fats. Why? | They are combined because both types of fat have negative effects on blood cholesterol levels which increase the risk of coronary heart disease. |
| Optional % DV is allowed for cholesterol. Why? | While cholesterol represents a risk factor for heart disease, a reduction in saturated fat (found in meat and dairy products) will be accompanied by a reduction in cholesterol intake. |
| There is no % DV for sugars and protein. Why? | In the case of sugars, there is no generally accepted target recommendation for the healthy population. In the case of protein, research suggests that intakes are generally adequate and not a public health concern for Canadians who have access to a mixed diet. |
| Vitamins and minerals (other than sodium and potassium) are listed only as % DV. Again, why? | These other nutrients are usually expressed in different units. By using % DV, it is easier for consumers to understand the relative amounts present in the products. |

# Nutrient Content Claims

Manufacturers are permitted to use **nutrient content claims** on food labels to attract attention to their products. Generally, a claim is printed in bold or flashy type on the front of a food product package, and highlights a positive feature of the product that manufacturers hope will give them an edge over other brands with similar products. You have probably seen these nutrition claims before on products that advertise themselves to be "fat free," "low calorie," "high fibre," or "light."

The new government regulations set specific rules and standards that manufacturers must meet in order to be able to make a nutrition claim on their product. Even so, it's not a good idea for you to rely solely on the nutrition claims. Most often, these claims refer to only one of the elements on the Nutrition Facts table. Just because a product claims to be "low calorie," for example, does not necessarily mean that it is also "low fat" or "low cholesterol."

Another thing to keep in mind is that these claims also apply "per serving." For example, one serving of popcorn might be low in fat, but a whole bag might contain quite a bit of fat.

## Consumer Awareness

Some of the common nutrient content claims and their meanings, according to the new government regulations, include:

> **Free**—contains a nutritionally insignificant amount
>> Sodium free—less than 5 mg
>> Cholesterol free—less than 2 mg, and low in saturated and trans fat (but not necessarily low in total fat)

> **Low**—contains a very small amount
>> Low fat—3 g or less
>> Low in saturated fat—2 g of saturated and trans fat combined

> **Reduced**—contains at least 25 percent less of a specified nutrient when compared with a similar product
>> Reduced in calories—minimum 25 percent fewer calories than the food to which it is compared

> **Source**—contains a significant amount
>> Source of fibre—2 g or more
>> Good source of calcium—165 mg or more

> **Light**—products are reduced in fat or reduced in calories (when referring to a light taste, colour, or texture, the manufacturer must include explanatory text on the label.

A product that is deemed "trans fat free" contains a nutritionally insignificant amount of trans fat.

"Low fat" foods contain less than 3 g of fat or less than 2 g of saturated and trans fat combined.

A food that is "reduced" in something must contain at least 25% less of a specified nutrient than a similar product.

## Diet and Health Claims

Something else that food manufacturers are now able to do, provided that they meet the strict government-set criteria for nutritional content, is to highlight a relationship between diet and certain health conditions. These are called **diet and health claims**. You may now find one of the following on your food product packages:

> A healthy diet low in sodium and high in potassium may reduce the risk of high blood pressure.

> A healthy diet adequate in calcium and vitamin D may reduce the risk of osteoporosis.

> A healthy diet low in saturated and trans fat may reduce the risk of heart disease.

Having such diet and health claims printed right on the package is useful to consumers. However, once again, keep in mind that the manufacturers have an interest in promoting their own products. One claim may negate another—if a package stresses the importance of low sodium, it does not mean the food item contains low amounts of fat.

When in doubt, simply consult the Nutrition Facts table.

If a product is deemed a source of a nutrient, it must contain a pre-determined minimum amount.

There are many food choices available to us, so the more we know about what we eat, the better.

# A Guide to Action

Here are some recommendations from *Canada's Food Guide to Healthy Eating* with cross references to the new Canadian food label. You can see how the *Food Guide* directly relates to the nutrition label that you will find on most food packages today.

Choose healthier foods more often.

Eat a variety of foods to obtain the nutrients you need.

> **Canada's Food Guide recommends ...** *Choose lower fat foods more often.*

| CHECK THE LABEL | WHAT TO LOOK FOR ... |
|---|---|
| Nutrition Facts | Fat, saturated fat, trans fat |
| Nutrition claims | Low fat, reduced in saturated fat, trans fat-free<br>Health claim on saturated and trans fats and heart disease |
| Ingredient list | Sources of fat |

> **Canada's Food Guide recommends ...** *Choose whole grain and enriched grain products more often. Whole grain products, such as whole wheat, oats, barley, or rye, are suggested because they are high in starch and fibre.*

| CHECK THE LABEL | WHAT TO LOOK FOR ... |
|---|---|
| Nutrition Facts | Fibre, sugars, iron, fat, saturated fat, trans fat, sodium |
| Nutrition claims | Source of fibre, high in iron<br><br>Health claim on saturated and trans fats and heart disease |
| Ingredient list | Sources of whole grains, such as oats and whole wheat flour<br>Enriched grains will also include nutrients which have been added back to them (iron, niacin, riboflavin, thiamin, and folic acid) |

> **Canada's Food Guide recommends ...** *Choose dark green and orange vegetables and orange fruit more often. These foods are higher than other vegetables and fruit in certain key nutrients like vitamin A and folate. Fresh, frozen, and canned are all good choices.*

| CHECK THE LABEL | WHAT TO LOOK FOR ... |
|---|---|
| Nutrition Facts | Fibre, vitamin A, vitamin C, sodium |
| Nutrition claims | Source of fibre/iron<br>Excellent source of vitamin A/vitamin C<br>Health claim on vegetables and fruit, and reduced risk of some types of cancer<br>Health claim on potassium, sodium, and reduced risk of high blood pressure<br>Health claim about saturated and trans fats and heart disease |
| Ingredient list | Check ingredients when consuming prepared foods<br>Check if vegetables and fruit are near the beginning of the list |

Dark green and orange vegetables are good sources of nutrients.

➤ **Canada's Food Guide recommends ...** *Choose lower fat milk products more often ... as a way to lower total dietary fat, particularly saturated fat.*

| CHECK THE LABEL | WHAT TO LOOK FOR ... |
|---|---|
| Nutrition Facts | Fat, saturated and trans fats, calcium, vitamin D |
| Nutrition claims | Good source of calcium, low in fat<br>Health claim on calcium, vitamin D, and regular physical activity and reduced risk of osteoporosis<br>Health claim on saturated and trans fats and heart disease |
| Ingredient list | Other ingredients, such as salt (sodium) added to cheese |

Drink 1% or skim milk more often.

➤ **Canada's Food Guide recommends ...** *Choose leaner meats, poultry, and fish, as well as dried peas, beans, and lentils more often.*

| CHECK THE LABEL | WHAT TO LOOK FOR ... |
|---|---|
| Nutrition Facts | Fat, saturated and trans fats, cholesterol, sodium |
| Nutrition claims | Low in fat, good source of iron<br>Health claim on saturated and trans fats and heart disease |
| Ingredient list | Other ingredients such as sources of added fat |

Choose leaner meats, poultry, and fish more often.

## Break the Fast
### Starting the Day Right

**W**hen you eat breakfast, you literally "Break the fast," and most experts agree that it is the most important meal of the day.

### Getting in the Mood

Our brains are fueled by glucose, which comes from carbohydrate-rich foods such as cereal, toast, fruit, and dairy products. If we don't eat breakfast, our brain cannot function optimally. This leaves us feeling lethargic, tired, moody, and irritable—and in no mood for physical activity or learning.

For those "breakfast skippers," this is why you have difficulty concentrating in your period-one class. Your brain is telling you to feed it.

### Defying the Odds

Studies show that high-school students who have breakfast do better academically, are more alert, perform better physically, and are generally in a better mood than those who don't. Yet, an alarming number of people, young and old, skip breakfast.

Worse still, breakfast skippers often turn to caffeinated drinks, foods high in refined sugars, or, at worst, smoking to give their bodies an artificial jump-start to the day. This only leads to unhealthy eating behaviors and habits that will be difficult to break in later years.

### Smart Choices

The best way to correct the breakfast-skipping habit is to start slowly. Begin your day with a piece of whole-wheat toast or half a bagel with a light spread of your favourite topping (e.g., jam or butter) and wash it down with a glass of orange juice. Try that for a few weeks and slowly build up to some of the choices below.

In a short time, you will wonder how you ever managed without having breakfast—you will feel, perform, and act better.

### Smart Breakfast Choices

- A bowl of high-fibre cereal topped with chopped fruit, with low fat milk or soy milk, and a glass of juice
- Whole grain waffles topped with fruit, a light helping of syrup or yogourt
- Toasted whole-wheat bagel spread lightly with butter, cream cheese, jam, or peanut butter
- Homemade smoothies with frozen yogourt, milk or soy milk, and a variety of sliced fruit
- Drink juice that is high in vitamin C; it will help you absorb more iron from your breakfast choices.

Consult with your doctor or a registered dietitian to find out more healthy food choices to suit your needs.

# Chapter Review

## Questions for Study and Review

### Things to Think About and Explore

1. Identify the thirteen core nutrients that must be listed in the Nutrition Facts table.

2. Describe the role that serving size information on food labels plays.

3. Define what is meant by the % DV and explain how this column on food labels can be used to help make better food choices.

4. Explain the differences between nutrient content claims and diet and health claims on food labels.

5. Distinguish between the terms "low-fat" and "fat-free."

6. Evaluate the use of the term "light," on labels. How do you think shoppers interpret this term when they read it on a food label?

### Things to Do and Practise

7. Using a sheet of bristol board, display the Nutrition Facts table and the list of ingredients from two of your favourite snack foods. Present comparisons between the two. Note the purpose of each of the components on the food label.

8. In a group, discuss how food labels can help people with special dietary needs.

9. Find two cereal boxes. Based on your understanding of % DV, determine which cereal is more nutritious.

10. Compare and contrast the information contained on the food labels of three pre-packaged meals. Present the results to your class.

11. Find three different examples of diet or health claims on food packaging and present to the class whether you feel the claims are enough to make the food a good dietary choice.

12. Make up a food schedule for the next three days that shows the essential nutrients you require each day. Indicate how you will get (and not exceed) your recommended daily intake of these nutrients. You can use a tool such as the one provided at **www.dietitians.ca/public/content/eat_well_live_well/ english/onedayatatime.asp** or simply create your own, using a spreadsheet or sheet of paper.

## WWWeblinks

Name ➢ Interactive Nutrition Label

URL ➢ www.hc-sc.gc.ca/fn-an/ label-etiquet/nutrition/ interactive/inl_flash_ e.html

A good site for more information on the government's policy on nutrition labelling, how to read nutrition labels, or how to better understand an ingredients list.

Name ➢ Vegetarian Nutrition for Teenagers

URL ➢ www.vrg.org/nutrition/ teennutrition.htm

A site offering advice to teens looking to start a vegetarian diet. Includes ways to ensure you are getting enough protein and other nutrients.

Name ➢ Canadian Council of Food and Nutrition

URL ➢ www.ccfn.ca

The CCFN is a multi-sectoral, science-based organization that focuses on food and nutrition policy information.

# 20

# Body Image and Self-Esteem: How Do You See Yourself?

**T**ake a look around and you will see images of the human body almost everywhere. These images send powerful messages about beauty, and desirable body shapes and sizes. Some of these messages promote a view of the body that is realistic and positive. However, other messages offer unrealistic ideals of how our bodies should look.

If we perceive ourselves to be as (or more) attractive as the people to whom we compare ourselves, our body image will be quite positive. If, on the other hand, social comparisons cause us to feel inadequate, we can respond in some very negative ways. Understanding the ways in which body image is shaped can help you to develop a realistic perspective that allows you to have fun and feel good about yourself.

## Chapter Objectives

In this chapter, you will:

> Investigate the meaning of the terms "body image" and "self-esteem"

> Explore the factors that may affect your perception of your own body

> Examine the "Set-Point Theory" of body weight and how it may explain weight gain and loss

> Identify the various kinds of unhealthy eating habits and their possible consequences to your health

> Examine the three main clinical eating disorders, how they are diagnosed, their consequences, and the treatments available

> Examine the serious consequences of anorexia and bulimia, and where those suffering from these illnesses can get help

> Review the steps that you and your friends can take to help you view your bodies positively

> Investigate strategies and ideas for focusing on healthy lifestyles rather than body weight

## Key Terms

> body image
> self-esteem
> Set-Point Theory
> eating disorders
> anorexia nervosa
> bulimia nervosa
> binge eating

# What Is Body Image?

Each of us has a mental picture of our own body. This mental picture is your **body image**. Body image includes how you feel about your body, what you believe about your body, how you see yourself, and how you think you look to others.

Your body image may be positive or negative. If you are satisfied with the overall mental picture you hold of your body, your body image is positive. If you are troubled by the size or shape of your body, or parts of your body, the picture you see of yourself will be negative.

## Self-Esteem

How we see ourselves plays an important role in determining our sense of **self-esteem** or our opinion of ourselves. Self-esteem describes how valued or worthy a person feels. People with high self-esteem feel confident, deserving of success and achievement, and are able to make good choices. People with low self-esteem may feel that they are unworthy of the opportunities life has to offer.

Body image is one component of a person's self-esteem. Other factors such as our relationships with others and our personal achievements also contribute to our self-esteem.

People with high self-esteem feel confident and ready to take on life's challenges.

Many factors combine to develop a person's self-esteem, including our relationships with others and our achievements.

# Factors That Influence Body Image

Body image is dynamic. How you see yourself changes over time. The way that you view your body in 10 or 15 years will likely differ from the way that you see yourself right now.

A number of factors influence our body image. These include the messages we receive from the media, the values and input of our family and friends, and our life experiences. Some of these influences are obvious, while others are more subtle.

## Impact of the Media on Body Image

Media communications often reinforce the current "ideal" body and promote the notion that anyone can attain a sculpted body simply and easily. Each day we are exposed to hundreds of advertisements featuring bodies that are "picture perfect." Many of these adverts suggest that if we looked "perfect" we would have better lives. We respond by comparing ourselves to the images we see. This process can leave people feeling dejected and dissatisfied.

While few of us will ever naturally attain the kind of body we see in advertisements, movies, and television programs, the images encourage us to keep trying. When we don't attain the body type promoted in the media, feelings of dissatisfaction and negative body image may develop.

## Family Influences on Body Image

Your family influences many aspects of your life, and body image is no exception. For example, many families do not place emphasis on their children following other people's ideals of how they are "supposed" to look in terms of body shape and size. This reduces the pressure to look or behave in a certain way.

## Friends Affect How We See Ourselves

Like family, friends influence how we view our bodies. Friends affect our body image through their actions and their words. Friends who value and promote individuality and self-acceptance, who eat well and are physically active without being obsessed with attaining a "perfect" body, can help us to view our bodies in a positive light.

## Life Changes Us

Body image is also affected by your life experiences. Experiences that demonstrate the strength and resilience of your body—such as physical activities, or overcoming an illness—can help you to see your body as a valuable asset and worthy of care.

Personal achievements help you to develop a positive view of yourself—recognizing your own valuable qualities or attributes. Involvement in pursuits that are personally rewarding can help you achieve a more rounded view of yourself.

Comparing your body to those depicted in the media can leave you feeling dejected and dissatisfied.

You only have one body, and it has to last you a lifetime. Adopt a healthy lifestyle to keep it in proper working order.

# Exploring Set-Point Theory
## Finding Your Healthy Body Weight

Chances are you know someone who has gone on a crash diet hoping to lose weight or improve his or her body shape. Extreme dieting and fad dieting may be popular but, for the most part, neither are successful.

There have been many ideas as to why this is the case. One is the **Set-Point Theory**.

### What is the Set-Point Theory?

In simple terms, the Set-Point Theory says that each of us has a weight (or "set-point") that our body is "programmed" to maintain. If we drop below this set-point, the theory says our body automatically reacts (possibly to protect itself) and we are unable to keep the weight off.

Alternatively, if we try to gain weight, the body reacts by increasing its metabolism in an attempt to maintain the set-point.

The problem with this theory is that it may be too simplistic. If it is true that our bodies regulate themselves, then why do anything to help reach or maintain a healthy body weight?

Furthermore, there have been plenty of instances of people either losing or gaining weight and, if the Set-Point Theory is true, how is that possible?

### You Can Do It

Anyone can strive for, achieve, and maintain a healthy body weight and a healthy lifestyle. If you start by accepting that your healthy body weight may not be the ideal you have seen in the media, and realize that being healthy is a lifelong pursuit and not a multi-week fad, you are well on your way.

People should aim to have their body weight fall within an appropriate range where they will not find themselves hampered by weight-related health issues .

The best way to achieve a healthy weight (as well as an overall healthy lifestyle) is not through crash dieting but rather a combination of healthy eating, regular activity, and generally taking care of yourself.

On that point, health professionals are in complete agreement.

# Unhealthy Eating Habits

Combining sensible eating habits with an exercise program that meets your individual needs (as outlined in Units 2 and 3) is the best way to ensure that you maintain a healthy body weight and positively reinforce your body image.

Sometimes, people adopt eating habits that, in an attempt to lose too much weight too quickly, can lead to serious health problems. These unhealthy (or "dysfunctional") eating habits can, if followed for too long or taken to the extreme, become what are known as **eating disorders**. It is estimated that 3 percent of women will be affected by eating disorders in their lifetime. While this is a relatively low number, it is important to realize that many more people who do not have a diagnosed eating disorder struggle with their body image and self-esteem. For example, research shows that 80–90 percent of women dislike the size and shape of their bodies.

Examples of unhealthy behaviours or thoughts include:

> Being preoccupied with food or body size/shape—having frequent thoughts about food, eating, and body size/shape

> Restrictive eating—not eating enough food to feel satisfied

> Not eating enough food to maintain a healthy body weight

> Frequently feeling unhappy with one's body size/shape

> Binge eating—eating large amounts of food in one sitting and feeling a lack of control over eating

> Purging—using various techniques to try to rid the body of calories (self-induced vomiting, laxative misuse)

> Over-exercising—exercising for the sole purpose of ridding the body of calories; becoming obsessed with exercising

## What Causes Unhealthy Eating Habits?

Usually, several factors interact together to increase a person's chances of adopting some of these habits. Some risk factors include:

> Having family members with a history of unhealthy eating

> Certain personality traits such as perfectionism, obsessiveness, negative self-evaluation, anxiety, and/or inflexibility combined with an overvaluation of appearance

> Engaging in a profession/hobby that involves pressure to be thin

> Living in a society where a thin body is seen as ideal

> Childhood adversity including abuse and death among close relatives or friends

> Being overweight and/or having people making critical comments about weight, shape, or eating

Eating behaviours and thoughts about eating can become unhealthy or dysfunctional under certain circumstances.

Eating disorders are most common among young women, but anyone can develop them.

## Digital Retouching
### Looks Too Good To Be True

**A**dvances in photo technology have allowed us to save some otherwise unfortunate photos. Red eyes can be brought back from their unearthly appearance and, if you have a few pimples on the day you're getting your graduation photos taken, a few quick clicks of a mouse will prevent you from cringing every time you see the pictures.

Unfortunately, the predominance of digital photography and retouching has also made it difficult to tell if anything we see is real.

There used to be a saying that "the camera never lies." While that may still be true, the pictures certainly do. Magazines have photo retouchers on staff who allegedly make changes to every photo that appears in their pages. Some changes are as simple as small adjustments to the colour but, in most cases, skin tone is evened out, any blemishes are removed, and teeth are whitened. In many cases, photos are also lengthened to make people look even slimmer.

Digital retouching creates unrealistic expectations for an often unsuspecting public. In response to our society's preoccupation with slimness, youth, and beauty, computer retouches can alter the shape and size of a person's body while in reality the person looks strikingly different.

Retouching can also add muscle definition to a male cover-model or transform a senior into a young woman with smooth, wrinkle-free skin.

### Speaking Out

Some celebrities have started to speak out about the unrealistic pressure to look perfect that is promoted by altered photos. Actor/singer Hilary Duff has been quoted saying "Mom always tells me to celebrate everyone's uniqueness. I like the way that sounds."

So the next time you find yourself wishing that you could look as good as someone you see in a magazine, rest assured, they wish they could look that good too.

**Before**

**After**

# What Are Eating Disorders?

Eating disorders are serious conditions that affect both physical and mental health. They are the outcome of manipulation of food and weight in an attempt by the individual to attain a sense of self control, achievement, and mood regulation. Eating disorders negatively impact every aspect of the individual's life and are life-threatening illnesses.

## Dealing with Eating Disorders

Eating disorders are complex illnesses and, as with any other illness, it is important to see a health care professional to explore treatment options. It is possible to recover from an eating disorder, but professional help is almost always needed. Since the behaviours associated with an eating disorder can worsen and become more ingrained over time, it is best to seek help as early as possible.

Different types of health care professionals sometimes work together as an interdisciplinary team to treat eating disorders, abnormal eating habits, and problems with body image and self-esteem. Each person on the team plays an important role in helping the patient recover from his or her illness:

> **Mental health professionals.** Psychiatrists, psychologists, and social workers are key members of an eating disorder treatment team. The professionals help the patient to change behaviour and deal with issues, such as poor self-esteem, that can contribute to an eating disorder.

> **Registered dietitian.** People who suffer from eating disorders often lose perspective about what a healthy diet looks like. They may restrict their food intake to a point that prevents them from meeting their nutritional needs or they may overeat to an unhealthy degree. Dietitians help people who are struggling with concerns about weight and abnormal eating habits by teaching them to choose a balanced diet that provides adequate amounts of foods and energy (calories), and encouraging them to enjoy healthy food.

> **Nurse practitioners.** Nurses with special training in eating disorder management offer mental health support and medical care to eating disorder sufferers both in the hospital and in the community.

> **Physical therapists, occupational therapists, and certified personal fitness trainers.** These professionals help people with eating disorders to be active and productive in ways that are healthy and not solely tied to weight loss.

## Types of Eating Disorders

Someone is considered to have an eating disorder when thoughts and behaviours associated with eating are so unhealthy that they interfere with their daily lives.

Relatively few people suffer from clinical eating disorders, but many experience some aspects of disordered eating. Although anyone can develop an eating disorder, it is most commonly seen in young females. It is estimated that approximately 5–10 percent of all individuals with eating disorders are male.

The three main "clinical" eating disorders are:

- **Anorexia nervosa**, which is a form of self-starvation that is characterized by drastic weight loss.

- **Bulimia nervosa** is characterized by cycles of bingeing and purging. Both behaviours are attempts to regulate feelings and weight and are counterproductive.

- **Binge eating** is much more common than anorexia or bulimia. People with binge eating disorder consistently overeat but, unlike those with bulimia, do not purge and are, therefore, frequently overweight.

## Treating Persons with an Eating Disorder

The type of treatment used to manage an eating disorder varies depending on the specific type of disorder that is involved and on the severity of symptoms. There is no single, best approach to dealing with these kinds of issues. Instead, treatment needs to be tailored to meet the needs of each patient.

Typical treatment options include:

➢ Mental Health Counselling
- Individual therapy
- Group therapy
- Family therapy

➢ Medications
- Different prescription drugs can be used to assist in treating eating disorders, depending on the needs of the patient.

➢ Nutrition Counselling
- Registered dietitians
- Family physicians

Be prepared to ask for help if you have a friend suffering from an eating disorder.

People can, and do, recover from eating disorders. If you are concerned about your own eating habits, or have a friend who is struggling with an eating disorder, do not hesitate to ask for help. Talk to your family doctor, school nurse, or guidance counsellor. All of these professionals can connect you to treatment in your community.

To learn more about eating disorders and how they are treated, visit the National Eating Disorder Information Centre's website at: **www.nedic.ca**.

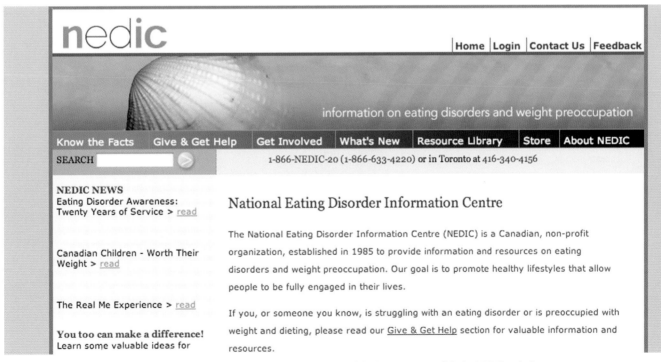

If you would like to learn more about the various types of eating disorders and their treatments, visit the NEDIC website.

# Creating a Healthy Body Image

Our society places tremendous pressure on us to be thin, fit, and attractive to others. However, only a handful of people will ever naturally attain the unrealistic type of body that is promoted in media images and valued by North American society. This gap—between what we want to look like and what our bodies naturally look like—often promotes feelings of dissatisfaction and negative body image.

Negative body image and low self-esteem can have serious consequences. People who view their bodies negatively or who feel little sense of worth often struggle to reach their goals. Their ability to form strong, healthy relationships with other people and their capacity to reach their full potential may be limited.

Gaining an awareness of the factors that influence the development of body image can help you develop the skills needed to see your body in a positive light.

A healthy body image is particularly important for young people.

Keep in mind that physical appearance is only a small part of what makes you the person that you are.

## Feeling Good about Yourself

A healthy body image promotes high self-esteem, confidence, and enhances quality of life. You cannot control or change our societal ideals, or the images that we view on TV, in magazines, or in movies. However, there are steps you can take to feel good about yourself and your body:

➤ Remember that many of the images of supposedly "ideal" bodies you see in the media (TV, the Internet, billboards, and magazins) are not in fact typical and, in many cases, are digitally altered. They do not reflect the way most people appear in reality.

➤ Remember that physical appearance is just one aspect of your being. Your thoughts, values, beliefs, and accomplishments also represent very important aspects of who you are.

➤ Instead of valuing your body simply for the way it looks, remember that it is, in fact, a very useful "tool" that can help you enjoy and take hold of life's opportunities and challenges.

➤ Learn to say "no" to experiences that you know will make you feel bad about the way you view your body. Seek out situations and friends that will help you maintain a positive image about the way you look and feel. For example, when possible, avoid "weigh-ins." Frequently hopping on the scale can lead some people to become obsessed with their body weight rather than their overall health and well-being.

➤ Eat well, be active, and love the person that you are!

## Getting Help

With so much societal pressure to look good and be perfect, some people find it very difficult to maintain their sense of self-worth and not struggle with how they look or feel.

In some cases, a negative sense of self-worth can lead not only to an eating disorder, but also to other problems. If you or someone you care about is struggling with exceptionally low self-esteem, an unhealthy body image, or depression, don't let it get out of control. Talk to someone you trust about how you are feeling. Try to find activities that make you feel good about yourself and, whenever possible, avoid activities that make you feel unhappy about yourself.

In some cases the problem may require specialized assistance. Some potential treatment options include:

➤ Psychological counselling (individual, family, or group therapy)

➤ Medications (in some instances)

➤ Support groups

Having a healthy body image can lead to higher self-esteem and increased confidence.

## Dietitians
### The Nutrition Professionals

A dietitian is a health professional trained to promote health and wellness through nutrition. To practise, dietitians must complete a Bachelor's degree in foods and nutrition, as well as a period of practical training in a hospital or community setting. Many have training that extends beyond this basic level and hold either Master's or Doctoral degrees.

In most of Canada, legislation protects the titles, "Registered Dietitian," or "RD," and "Dietitian." To use these titles, individuals must have the proper professional training and educational requirements. They must also be registered with their provincial College of Dietitians. This process helps the public identify professionals with expert training in nutrition.

### Is a Nutritionist Different from a Dietitian?

Protection of the title, "Nutritionist," varies between provinces. In some, use of this title is protected and can only be used by dietitians. In provinces where this title is not protected by law, anyone, regardless of his or her training or background, can call oneself a "Nutritionist." Recognizing this, people should contact their provincial college of dietitians or other regulatory organization to be certain that they are receiving advice from a qualified nutritionist.

### Where Do Dietitians Work?

Dietitians can be found in a variety of workplaces. They tend to practise as specialists, and the work that a dietitian does depends on the area on which he or she has chosen to focus.

- **Clinical dietitians** typically work in hospitals, care centres, or clinics. They assess the nutritional needs of their patients and develop plans to ensure optimum nutritional health.

- **Food service dietitians** manage food service operations in hospitals, other health care facilities, schools, and businesses. These professionals are experts in food safety, business management, and quantity food production and distribution.

- **Community dietitians** or **nutritionists** work to improve the health of large groups of people. They develop health promotion programs that target the specific needs of a particular community and act as a resource to other practitioners and the public.

- **Consulting dietitians** work for a wide variety of clients. Some assist in developing new products or nutritional approaches, while others focus on education or business leadership.

- **Research dietitians** are typically found at universities or colleges. Through scientific research, they strive to discover new ways to use foods and nutrition to benefit human health and well-being.

### How Can I Find a Dietitian?

Dietitians of Canada (DC) is the member services organization that represents dietitians. There are approximately 5,000 DC members and DC is recognized as a trustworthy source of reliable nutrition information. DC works to promote dietitians through programs and campaigns such as National Nutrition Month®. In addition, DC offers assistance in finding a dietitian through its website: **www.dietitians.ca**.

The DC website is a great resource for nutrition and healthy eating. The site offers a number of interactive features that allow users to assess and track their eating habits, and plan healthy menus.

# Chapter Review

## Questions for Study and Review

### Things to Think About and Explore

1. Compare and contrast body image and self-esteem. How are they related? How do they differ?

2. Assess the impact (positive or negitive) that family and friends can have on one's body image.

3. Explain the main ideas of the Set-Point Theory.

4. Distinguish between the different types of eating disorders.

5. Define bingeing as it relates to eating.

6. Compare and contrast bingeing with purging.

### Things to Do and Practise

7. How do the images we see in magazines, books, movies, and television influence our body image? Consider this question and create a collage using images that you find in the various forms of media that influence our body image.

8. Flip through a magazine targeted at women. Calculate the number of advertisements and articles that focus on dieting or weight management.

9. Make a poster emphasizing the beauty of diversity to be found in differing body types.

10. Evaluate advertisements that appear in both print and broadcast media. Discuss in a group whether the advertisements would be as effective if people with different body shapes and sizes were used?

11. Create a pamphlet that identifies three risk factors related to the development of unhealthy eating behaviours, what unhealthy eating behaviours are, what type of eating disorders can develop as a result, and what the consequences are when one is afflicted with eating disorders.

12. Prepare a two-minute speech that discusses the role that a mental health professional plays in treating eating disorders.

## WWWeblinks

Name ➤ National Eating Disorder Information Centre

URL ➤ www.nedic.ca

A non-profit organization that offers information and resources on eating disorders and weight preoccupation.

Name ➤ Real Me

URL ➤ www.realme.ca

An interactive website that explores influences on body image and self-esteem and offers strategies to strengthen them.

Name ➤ Eating Disorders

URL ➤ www.mirror-mirror. org/eatdis.htm

This site offers myths and facts about eating disorders, tips to help with recovery, and information on other disorders often found in conjunction with eating disorders.

## Table of Contents

# UNIT 8
# Physical Activities and Sports

**What this unit is about ...**

➢ Many physical activities and sports share common strategies and tactics. What are some of the basic similarities?

➢ How are the various physical activities and sports played, and what are some of the basic skills?

➢ How do I find out about getting more involved in physical activities and sports outside of school?

# 21
# Invasion/Territory Games

**I**nvasion games are some of the most common games that we play. They include sports such as soccer, basketball, ice hockey, field hockey, rugby, football, and lacrosse, just to mention a few. When Canadian Dr. James Naismith invented basketball in 1891, he did so by using his knowledge of various other invasion games. Who knows, someday we may be reading about the game that you invented.

Invasion games require many different types of manipulation skills. Players must be able to send objects away (throw a Frisbee), receive objects (trap a soccer ball), and travel with objects (stick handle a field hockey ball) with accuracy to be successful. Many of the basic strategies and skills that are used in the course of invasion games are very similar to each other—for example, carrying the ball or object, passing to a teammate, and moving to an open space.

If you understand the basic rules, skills, and tactics of invasion games, it will make you better at the particular invasion games that you already play. It will also help you learn to play new invasion games quicker.

## Invasion/Territory Games

The invasion/territory games covered in this chapter are:

➤ Soccer
➤ Basketball
➤ Ultimate Frisbee
➤ Ice Hockey
➤ Field Hockey
➤ Rugby
➤ Canadian Football
➤ Lacrosse

## Basic Strategy and Tactics

Within invasion games, there are three basic tactical problems when your team is on offence (in possession of the object), and three basic tactical problems when your team is on defence (the other team has possession of the object).

While on offence, teams are trying to (1) maintain possession of the object, (2) create space on the playing area, and (3) attack the goal in order to score points. Conversely, teams on defence are trying to (1) regain possession of the object, (2) defend space on the playing area, and (3) defend the goal in order to prevent the other team from scoring.

Solutions to these tactical problems are very similar across the different invasion games. For example, a player with the object might try to shield it away from defenders, try to deke out opponents by moving around them, or make a short pass to a teammate who is not defended by an opponent. Offensive teammates who do not have the object can provide support by moving to an open space and communicating to the player who has possession of the object ("I'm open," "Shoot," "Pass").

These solutions to the tactical problem of maintaining possession apply in almost any type of invasion game. If you understand the basic skills and the importance of providing support to your teammate in one sport, you will be a better player across all invasion-type games.

Soccer is an example of an invasion/territory game.

## Soccer

**E**nthusiasts call it "the beautiful game," and there are many enthusiasts. It is, by far, the world's most popular sport. In North America, it is called "soccer"; to the rest of the world, it is simply "football."

### History

Kicking a ball undoubtedly goes back a very long way, but what we know as modern soccer has its roots in nineteenth-century England. At a meeting of the London Football Association in 1863, the game was split into rugby football, the precursor to North American football, and association football, or soccer. Regular league play started in 1888.

British traders, sailors, and workers carried the sport with them as they travelled all over the world. Because it was easily understood, inexpensive to play, and a great workout, soccer became immensely popular internationally as a youth sport.

Today, while still rather low-profile as a professional sport in North America, soccer is the pre-eminent sport throughout the world. Few other sports even approximate it in participation and interest levels. Perhaps Scottish footballer Bill Shankly captured the sentiment best: "Some people think football is a matter of life and death ... I can assure them it is much more serious than that."

## How the Game Is Played

On the soccer field, the key to successful playing is teamwork, speed, and tactics. You can move the ball around with any part of your body except for your arms and hands. The only two players on the field who can touch the ball with their hands when it is in play are the goalkeepers, who grab, throw, or block the ball to defend their nets. If you manage to beat the goalkeeper and kick the ball through the goalposts and over the goal line, you score a point for your team.

During a game, each team has 11 players playing one of 4 basic positions—goalie, defender, midfielder, and forward. The most common layout is called a 4–4–2, with 4 defensive players, 4 midfielders, and 2 forwards (the goalkeeper's position is assumed). Defenders stop offensive attacks from the opposite team. Midfielders, some of the fittest players on the team, will travel nearly the length of the field to either stop offensive attacks, or go on the offensive themselves. The job of a forward is to score goals, or help teammates score. In junior soccer, most coaches rotate players so that each team member gets a feel for the different positions. Since soccer is a team sport, assisting others to make plays is an important part of the game.

Teamwork and speed are tactics crucial to successfully playing soccer.

## Refereeing

Referees enforce the rules of the game, and their calls must always be respected:

> **Out of bounds.** If your team kicks the ball over the sidelines, you lose possession. Play stops, and the other team gets to throw the ball back into play. If you kick the ball over your own end line, your opponents get to kick the ball back into play from the corner, giving them a great opportunity to score.

> **Free kick.** You may not kick, trip, or hold other players. The referee will award a free kick to your opponents, to be taken at the point where the violation occurred. The free kick is also awarded if a player, other than the goalie, uses his or her hands to control the ball.

> **Offside.** You are offside if, when receiving a forward pass from a teammate, there are not at least two opponents (one of whom usually is the goalie) ahead of you who are nearer to their goal line. You cannot be ruled offside when receiving the ball from a throw-in, or if you are in your own half of the field. If you are offside, an indirect free kick is awarded to the other team.

> **Carding.** If you commit very serious offences, such as continually fouling other players, you will be carded. The referee gives yellow "caution" cards to players who make several fouls. Red "stop" cards are given for offences such as spitting on another player, using really offensive language, or purposely committing a dangerous physical foul. After receiving a red card, you are ejected from the game and your team now plays with 10 players instead of 11. Two yellow cards also will result in a red card.

## The Indoor Game

Players interested in keeping their skills fresh throughout the winter months are turning to indoor soccer. The game is similar to the outdoor version with a few key differences.

- **Field.** Indoor games generally are played in either gymnasiums or inflated sports domes and sometimes even in hockey rinks.
- **Goal.** The net is smaller than in outdoor soccer and usually is about 3.5 m wide by 2 m high.
- **Team.** Indoor soccer is played with six players per side, including a goalie.
- **Offsides.** Most indoor leagues play without the offside rule.
- **Contact.** Some see indoor soccer as a slightly rougher version of the outdoor game, so referees will sometimes be more lenient with plays involving contact.
- **Walls.** Indoor games are often played on fields with walls and, in most leagues, this means the ball can bounce off the boundaries of the field without stopping play.
- **Cards.** Several indoor leagues use a third coloured card (often blue) as an additional warning before issuing a yellow card that results in a 2-minute penalty.

## Soccer: Key Terms and Basic Skills

➤ **Passing.** For a push pass, direct the ball with the inside of your foot for maximum control and accuracy. For longer distances, use an instep drive kick by locking your ankle, pointing your toes down, and driving the centre of your foot through the ball. For a lofted pass, place your kick under the ball to lift it over or past a defender. Lofted passes are also good when crossing a ball, or when taking free kicks. A chip pass—a short jab under the bottom half of the ball—allows the player to advance the ball without breaking stride.

➤ **Heading the ball.** A proper header starts at the feet. Your feet should be spaced about 25 cm apart, and staggered to provide balance when your upper body arches backwards as the ball arrives. The trunk of your body should snap forward to provide power as your forehead makes contact with the ball.

➤ **Trapping the ball.** The chest trap is used to control high kicked or bouncing balls. Use the middle of your chest, just above your stomach, to trap the ball. To trap a high ball, extend your arms for balance and lean back as the ball hits you. For a bouncing ball, lean forward, almost over the ball, to direct it back to the ground. You can use your thigh or even your head to deaden the ball and bring it to your foot.

➤ **Dribbling.** Dribbling is one of the most important skills in the game. While a pass to an open defender takes yards of territory and teamwork, a quick feint and move can spring a ballcarrier and create a team advantage in any zone of the field. The best dribblers can use either foot, quickly pivot, and simultaneously keep a view of the ball and the closest defender.

➤ **A throw-in.** Awarded to your team when the opposition kicks the ball over the sideline. Stand behind the sideline with both feet planted and throw the ball with both hands (starting behind your head and following through over your head). Most throw-ins are short throws to teammates to maintain possession.

## Innovations

Since 1970, technology has dramatically changed the appearance and sophistication of soccer balls. From a basic design with 32 stitched black and white panels, the soccer ball evolved into layers of foam and synthetic fibres which deliver better control and velocity to the kicker. In 2005, a new ball with a self-contained sensor was developed that could signal to officials when it had crossed the goal line.

## Getting Involved

Do you want to know where to play soccer in your area? Visit **www.canadasoccer.com** for a list of clubs. You will also find player tips, soccer news, and photos of your favourite Canadian players.

# The World Cup
## Playing to Win (and to Have Fun)

**BRINGING SOCCER TO THE WORLD, ONE CONTINENT AT A TIME**

Every four years, a mind-boggling number of sports fans gear up for the biggest event in men's soccer, the Fédération Internationale de Football Association's (FIFA) World Cup.

Ever since the first competition in Uruguay in 1930, the tournament's popularity and prestige have grown exponentially. More than 3.3 million spectators attended the 64 matches of the 2006 World Cup with over 30 billion more watching across the globe on television. The 2006 tournament featured 7 nations playing in their first World Cup, the most "first timers" since the 1934 World Cup in Italy.

So how did this international mania begin? In 1928, the president of FIFA came up with the idea of bringing the world's strongest national teams together to compete for the title of World Champions.

Since then, the 32 teams that pass the regional preliminaries travel to the host country where they are split into eight groups of four teams. Each group plays a mini-tournament, with the qualifiers (16 of the 32 teams) moving into elimination matches until two teams emerge as finalists. The winning team gets to call itself World Champion until the next Cup is contested.

Customarily, the event has been held alternately in Europe and the Americas, but in 2002, the World Cup broke new ground when Korea and Japan were its co-hosts. The 2006 Cup was held in Germany and tradition will break again when South Africa hosts the event in 2010.

The strongest teams usually are from Europe and South America. Brazil, Italy, Argentina, and Germany can always be counted on to perform well. In recent years however, teams from Africa and Asia have also made an impact.

Canada's team has entered the FIFA regional preliminaries 11 times since 1958, but has only qualified once to compete in the final World Cup tournament, in 1986. Luckily, many Canadians have family roots in other countries and delight in cheering for teams from their countries of ancestry during a World Cup.

In 2006, Italy beat France 5-3 in overtime to become World Champions.

## Basketball

**A**gility, accuracy and team play are some of the critical elements of basketball. Developed by Canadian Dr. James Naismith, this sport has a simple objective—to put the ball through the opposing team's basket. It requires very little equipment—which is perhaps why basketball, like soccer, is so popular around the world.

### History

Basketball was invented in 1891 by Canadian Dr. James Naismith as a way of keeping Springfield College students busy while they were waiting for the baseball season to start. The first players used peach baskets nailed to a running track and a soccer ball.

Basketball's growth spread in the United States and abroad through Young Men's Christian Associations (YMCAs), the armed forces, and colleges. By 1936, basketball was an official Olympic sport. The Canadian team won the first silver medal. The first women's Olympic basketball tournament was held in Montreal in 1976.

Having started with 18 players in a YMCA gymnasium in Springfield, Massachusetts, basketball now is played by more than 300 million people worldwide.

## How the Game Is Played

Basketball may be an invasion sport with two opposing teams, but if you ever watch a game of pick-up basketball (with the players not in uniform), you may have trouble figuring out who plays for which team. This is because if your team doesn't have possession of the ball, you spend most of your time trying to intercept it. You do this mainly by covering a player on the opposite team.

The player with the ball doesn't want to lose it. He or she tries to advance the ball towards the opposing team's basket while dribbling the ball. This makes for a court filled with players, seemingly mixed up and running around in different combinations.

You advance the ball up the court either by passing to teammates or by dribbling the ball. Once you stop dribbling, you cannot start up again. You must pass or shoot. So there are three key skills you will need to develop: passing, shooting, and dribbling.

A shot clock begins once a team gains possession. The team must make a shot that hits the rim of the basket within 30 seconds of taking possession in Olympic play, and within 24 seconds of taking possession in National Basketball Association (NBA) play.

A typical shot is worth two points and can either be taken from a standing position or achieved with a fancy and impressive slam dunk. Shots taken from behind the three-point line result in—you guessed it—three points. The one-pointer comes from getting a basket off of a free throw. A free throw is awarded when a player on the opposite team fouls you as you attempt to make a shot.

Basketball tactics build on strategy around passing, shooting, and dribbling.

## The Positions

There are five interdependent positions in basketball:

> **Point guard.** Runs the offence and is considered the coach on the floor. Also known as the 1 position.

> **Off-guard or shooting guard.** Plays are routinely run to free the off-guard for a shot. Also known as the 2 position.

> **Small forward.** Often the most gifted player on the floor. He or she should be big enough to rebound, but fast enough to run the floor on the fast break. Also known as the 3 position.

> **Power forward.** Needs to be an aggressive rebounder, both under his or her own team's basket and in opposition territory. Also known as the 4 position.

> **Centre.** Usually the tallest player on the floor. He or she will handle the bulk of the rebounding duties. Because of the centre's proximity to the basket, he or she will be expected to chip in offensively as well. On many teams, the centre is the most important offensive player. That player is also known as the 5 position.

## Basketball: Key Terms and Basic Skills

**The Three-point Shot**

The adoption of the three-point shot dramatically changed basketball. While shooting percentages dropped, smaller teams could use three-pointers to compensate for a lack of rebounding or inside game.

The three-pointer, adopted for college hoops in 1980 and in the NBA in 1981, has added a new level of excitement to basketball.

The three-point line is generally an arc at varying radii from the net depending on the level of play. In Canadian Interuniversity Sport, and in international play, the three-point line is 6.2 m (20 feet, 6 inches) from the basket. In the NBA, the line is straight along the sidelines meaning that the distance to the basket ranges from 6.7 m (22 feet) to 7.2 m (23 feet and 9 inches).

Most fans appreciate the extra drama it can add, particularly when a three-pointer is used to either tie the score or take the lead late in the game.

➢ **Shooting.** The most common shot is the jump shot, in which the player holds the ball on his or her fingertips and palms, and releases it at the top of the jump. One hand guides the ball and falls away just prior to release. Proper follow-through generates backspin and will increase accuracy. A lay-up is the most dependable shot for an uncovered player under the basket. A hook shot works close to the basket to get the ball over defenders. Players with good leaping ability can use a dunk shot.

➢ **Rebound.** Since even the best basketball teams miss as often as they score, a team's success or failure hinges on how well they rebound (gain possession of the ball after a missed shot). The best rebounders rely on positioning and determination.

➢ **Screens.** A screen or pick is a legal block set by an offensive player on the side of, or behind, a defender in order to free a teammate to take a shot or receive a pass. After setting a screen, a player often is uncovered. The "pick and roll" or "screen and roll" has been used by generations of players. A player must be stationary to set a legal screen.

➢ **Passing.** Like rebounding and shooting, passing is an essential basketball skill. Depending on the situation, players can choose between bounce passes, chest passes, and the baseball pass. A handoff, in which one player drops the ball into another's hands, is the safest and shortest pass.

➢ **Dribbling.** A properly inflated basketball will always bounce straight up at least 75 percent of the height from which it was dropped. That's why the best dribblers can watch their opponents, not the ball. To dribble, a player should push the ball down by spreading the fingers and flexing the wrist. Dribbling must be done with one hand.

### Innovations

Basketball's evolution has been accelerated not by breakthroughs in technology or tactics, but by the arrival of non-North American players.

The NBA has been graced with the skills of the top players from Europe, Africa, and Asia. Once considered invincible in international events, the U.S. men's team has recently found stiff competition from more team-oriented players. Athletes currently giving the NBA an international flavour include Germany's Dirk Nowitzki, France's Tony Parker, and China's Yao Ming.

### Getting Involved

Getting involved in basketball is easy. Most local community clubs have regular pick-up games, so you can stop in and give it a try. If your interest is piqued and you would like to know more, visit the Canada Basketball website at **www.basketball.ca**.

## Steve Nash
### Playing to Win (and to Have Fun)

*A LONG-TERM COMMITMENT TO HEALTH AND FITNESS PAYS OFF*

**M**ost basketball fans would agree that in 2004–05, Steve Nash had a breakout season in the NBA.

Nash had been an outstanding athlete in both soccer and basketball during high school at St. Michael's University School in his hometown of Victoria, BC. He continued that prowess while on a basketball scholarship at Santa Clara University in California. After being drafted into the NBA by the Phoenix Suns in 1996, Nash went on to have several solid seasons with both his original team, and the Dallas Mavericks.

However, during the 2004–05 season, Nash went from being a good NBA player to a great one. That season, he was voted the league's most valuable player, after leading the Suns (who re-signed him before the season) to the Western Conference's best record, a vast improvement after the team's dismal season in 2003–04. Individually, Nash led the NBA in several statistical categories, including most assists. Nash was also honoured back home, winning the 2005 Lou Marsh Award for Canada's top athlete in any sport.

NBA fans noted how unusual it is for a player to have such a great year so late in his career. For Nash, winning the MVP award in his ninth season was just a part of the long-term development he has been working on throughout his sporting career. Today, his mother and father (a former pro soccer player) recall the endless hours he put in on the family driveway and local courts, working to improve his skills. That determination has continued into Nash's professional career, as he has worked hard to improve both his muscular strength and his cardiorespiratory endurance (a reported personal best of 15.5 on the Beep Test).

Nash further cemented his legendary status when he was voted MVP again in 2006, becoming only the ninth player to win the honour in consecutive years.

As a relatively small player among the "giants" of the NBA, Nash has used his personal fitness regime—as well as a carefully-controlled diet—to continue to improve at an age when many players have already hung up their sneakers.

## Ultimate Frisbee

There's no sport quite like ultimate. There are no referees! Players are always expected to play by the rules, call their own fouls, and play to the best of their abilities. The "spirit of the game" encourages competitive play, but mutual respect on the playing field is most important. Just imagine if all sports worked this way.

### History

It is generally believed that this sport began as a lark at Columbia High School in Maplewood, New Jersey, in 1968 when one of the students brought a flying disc to school after playing with it at summer camp. The sport began as a free-form event with as many as 30 players per team. It was played as a replica of football, with running allowed, and a series of downs permitted for each team. It quickly morphed into something much closer to its present form.

In 1969, a parking lot with vapour lights was built at the school, and students could play long into the night. The number of possible players was limited to seven per side, a rule still in use today. Columbia High School created the sport's first formal team, and issued a challenge to all neighbouring high schools. When Columbia players graduated to university, they took the game with them and spread it through the college ranks.

## How the Game Is Played

Ultimate Frisbee, often now simply referred to as "ultimate," is an exciting, non-contact team sport, played by thousands of people in over 50 countries. It mixes the best features of soccer, basketball, American football, and netball into an elegantly simple yet fascinating game. It is played on a rectangular field with an end zone at each end. The object is to advance a flying disc over the opposing team's goal line.

Both teams start by standing on opposite goal lines. The team with the disc throws it as far down the field as possible. This is called a "pull." The offensive team then takes possession and begins to advance up the field by completing passes, while the other team seeks to obtain possession by forcing a turnover. A player who is in possession of the disc is called a "thrower."

Although you must stop running once you catch the disc, you may pivot and pass to any of your team's receivers on the field. A turnover results whenever a pass is incomplete—the disc is caught or knocked down by an opposing player, or touches the ground at any point—or is caught by a player out-of-bounds. Turnovers also occur when a player is caught holding the disc for more than 10 seconds. Teams move quickly from offence to defence on turnovers.

A goal, worth one point, is scored if you pass the disc to a teammate, and it is successfully caught within the confines of the opposition's end zone. When a team has scored, they retain the disc and wait while the opposition walks back to the other end of the field. The team that scored then throws off to start the next point. In that way, the teams change ends every point.

## The Friendly Game

For navigation purposes, players usually choose a side of the field where they put their water and bags. Calling the sides "our side" and "their side," or "home" and "away," helps you to identify the parts of the field that you want to attack or defend.

When you catch the disc, the player assigned to cover, or "check," you begins counting up from 1 to 10. You must throw the disc before the count reaches 10, or you will be called for stalling. If a nearby player does not start the stall count, you can wait as long as you like to throw the disc. Often, one offensive player stands behind the player with the disc. If all the players downfield are covered, you can dump the disc backwards to extend the possession. Offensive players often swing a pass across the field to keep their possession rolling.

In ultimate, the players govern themselves. There are no referees. Players are expected to call their own fouls.

A foul is understood to be contact that impedes another player from reaching the disc, but how loosely or tightly the game is called is left to the players themselves. If you call a foul and your opponent agrees, possession is awarded. If the two of you disagree, your teams agree to replay the sequence.

Although ultimate has only been played since 1968, it is already extremely popular and is played by thousands of people.

## Ultimate: Key Terms and Basic Skills

> **Backhand throw.** Throw the disc from the left side of your body if you are right handed, or from the right side if you are left handed. The motion is similar to the backhand in tennis.

> **Forehand throw.** This is the opposite of the backhand—throw the disc from the right side if you are right handed, or from the left side if you are left handed. The motion is similar to the tennis forehand.

> **Hammer/Blade.** Two types of overhead throws which cause the disc to arc up and away from the thrower.

> **Cut.** An attempt to get free to receive a pass. Try starting with a body fake and/or a sudden change in direction or speed. The ability to get open is one of the fundamental demands of ultimate.

> **Block.** A block occurs when, on defence, you stop the disc directly after it is released by a thrower.

> **Layout.** Dive to catch or intercept the disc.

> **Force.** Influence where the disc is thrown by positioning yourself on one side of the thrower.

> **Pick.** Yell "Pick!" if your opponent tries to obstruct your movement—this is a violation.

### Ultimate Lingo

- **Callahan.** A team's pass is intercepted in its own end zone, scoring a point for the intercepting team.
- **Catching swill.** A player manages to catch a particularly poor throw.
- **Chill** or **be chilly.** Used to urge a player with the disc to have patience and not to throw the disc too quickly.
- **Going ho.** Same as a layout; short for "going horizontal."
- **The greatest.** If an offensive player leaps from an in-bounds position, catches the disc, and releases the throw before touching the ground out-of-bounds, and that throw is caught by a teammate in the opponents' end zone, this is the greatest play possible in the game.
- **Hot.** Used to describe a good play.
- **Sky.** Leaping and catching the disc at maximum height over an opponent.

## Innovations

While offensive sets and patterns such as "The Stack" have added a level of sophistication to ultimate, defensive philosophies, built around "The Force," have more than kept pace. Teams use defensive philosophies such as Force Line, where the disc is near the sideline and defenders attempt to force throws in the direction of the sideline; Force Middle, where both sidelines are covered and the offensive player must work in a narrow strip up the centre of the field; or Force Wind, where defensive players position themselves to make the offence work into a prevailing wind. Most teams use player-to-player defences. Usually, the same players cover each other on both offence and defence. Often, one defender is designated to play deeper than the rest in the event of a long pass.

## Getting Involved

Ultimate teams are not yet common at the school level, but the beauty of this game is that it was created to be played as formally or as informally as you like. Go to **www.canadianultimate.com** to join the Canadian Ultimate Players Association, to find a league in your area, or to meet other players on the forum.

You can also follow the links to the World Flying Disc Federation's website to view the official rules of ultimate. Then you can play a pick-up game with some friends, or maybe even start a neighbourhood league.

## Toronto Ultimate Club
### Playing to Win (and to Have Fun)

**FOCUS ON THE SPIRIT OF THE GAME**

To many of its biggest fans, ultimate is something of an anti-sport. According to Thomas Meyer (left), former president of the Toronto Ultimate Club, this goes back to the first ever ultimate game, which was played in the parking lot of a New Jersey high school by the student council and the members of the student newspaper in 1968.

"The school," Meyer says, "was dominated by the jocks, so these were the kids who didn't make the team or didn't want to make the team." Unlike most sports, the game has "no referees; the players make the decisions ... ultimate came from the non-athletes, the non-jocks."

With this sense of self-empowerment to call your own fouls, players learn that how they play the game is more important than the win.

Competition still has its place in ultimate, but that isn't the aspect that many of its players appreciate about it. "The things that appeal to me about ultimate are the spirit of the game, the non-contact, and the social aspect" says Meyer. "I'm not sure why more girls don't get involved."

Indeed, ultimate is one of only a handful of sports to be completely co-ed. Since the inception of the Toronto Ultimate Club in the early 1980s, one of its primary goals has been to create and maintain an equal number of male and female members.

In Toronto, club members range in age from 10 to 50+, and leagues are formed based on how many people of each age group there are. Juniors have a league of their own—though they're always looking for more female members—and the opportunities for touring and competing are seemingly endless. There are weekend tournaments in cities throughout Canada.

At the world level, Canada has consistently been one of the top two nations, most recently winning the open, women's and junior women's divisions at the 2004 World Championships, while placing second in the other three divisions.

# Ice Hockey

I ce hockey is, by wide acclaim, "Canada's Game." It is a fast-paced sport where players must gain control of a puck, avoid penalties, and advance towards the other team's net while defending their own—and do all of this while balancing on thin blades of steel.

## History

Many historians say ice hockey's roots actually go back more than 500 years to the field hockey played in Great Britain and France. When the ponds froze in winter, players continued on the frozen surface and the game of Bandy, a form of pond hockey, began to find popularity. Bandy arrived in Canada, with British soldiers stationed in Halifax, in the 1870s and the game quickly spread.

When teams in Toronto, Ottawa, and Montreal began playing regular games, the Governor General of Canada, Lord Stanley of Preston, paid fifty pounds sterling for a trophy bearing his name to be awarded to the best team in Canada. Now the Stanley Cup is awarded annually to the champions of the National Hockey League (NHL).

## How the Game Is Played

Ice hockey is played by two teams made up of five players (two defencemen and three forwards) and one goaltender. The game is divided into three periods that last for 20 minutes with two 20-minute intermissions in between. Ice hockey players must wear a helmet at all times during the game, even if they are just sitting on the bench. Unless they are playing professionally (e.g., in the NHL), players must also wear face protection, such as a visor or a face mask.

Hockey is a game of puck possession and turnovers. The game begins with a face-off—the centre forward from each team squaring off at centre ice. Once the puck is dropped, the clock starts ticking. Players advance the puck until they can get a clear shot at the opposing goal. You can direct the puck with your stick or foot, as long as you don't kick it over the goal line. Play continues until the puck is advanced illegally (a hand pass, a stick over the shoulders, offside, or icing), the goalie "freezes," or holds on to the puck, the puck is trapped under a fallen player, the puck is shot into the stands, a player is injured, or a goal is scored.

If a team is losing late in a game, it may elect to replace its goalie with a forward player (called "pulling the goalie"), so that the offensive force will be larger.

The sheer speed of the game means the players put out a great deal of effort, and for this reason they can spend as little as 30–40 seconds (or even less) on the ice before they're substituted off.

Hockey is fast. Players can reach up to 20 km an hour, and the puck can move as fast as 160 km an hour.

## Body Checking, Line Calls, and Penalties

In some of the more competitive men's leagues, both offensive and defensive players can "check" opposing players if they have the puck. This tactic involves either stealing the puck with your stick (stick checking), or physically preventing the other player from getting into a play. In most recreational leagues, contact is kept to a minimum.

Lines that run the width of the ice are used to judge the two most common stoppages of play in ice hockey:

> **Icing.** Occurs when the puck is shot all the way down the ice, across both the centre line and the opposing team's goal line. When icing occurs, the play stops and the offending team must face off in its own end of the rink.

> **Offside.** Occurs when an offensive player crosses the blue line closest to the opposing team's goal before the puck does. When an offside occurs, a face-off is held in the central, neutral zone.

If a player takes a penalty, he or she must go to the penalty box, leaving the team with one less player. Minor penalties, such as hooking, last two minutes, while major penalties, such as fighting, last for five. A game misconduct means the offending player is expelled from the game, in addition to any other penalty the player's team must serve.

## Ice Hockey: Key Terms and Basic Skills

➢ **Skating.** Good skaters generate tremendous power by digging their skates into the ice in the first part of their stride. They use crossover strides to gain more speed than by coasting, and can stop or turn sharply.

➢ **Stick handling.** By moving the puck quickly backwards and forwards, you can keep the puck out of a defender's reach.

➢ **Passing.** You have to judge when to advance with the puck yourself, and when to pass it to a teammate who is in a better position to score. Getting the assist is as important, and feels just as good, as scoring the goal!

➢ **Shooting.** You can use a variety of shots to beat a goaltender. A slap shot, in which you draw the stick back and hit the puck, delivers great velocity but with less control. A wrist shot, in which you cradle the puck with your stick and then whip it towards the target, usually brings greater accuracy but with less speed. A one-time shot, in which you receive the pass and whip the puck forward in the same motion, gives the goaltender little chance to see what's coming.

➢ **Body checking.** In the men's game, you can use your shoulder or hip to knock an opponent off the puck, as long as the puck-carrier is facing you. It is a violation (and very dangerous) to check a player with unnecessary force or with a high stick. In women's and young men's hockey, body checking is not allowed. Some people think that this gender distinction is unfair, but others argue that women's hockey is a purer form of the sport because team tactics must rely more on skillful passing and stick handling than physical obstruction.

## Innovations

Technological improvements have allowed for one-piece sticks made from graphite and human-made compounds that resist breakage. Sticks can be made to each player's specifications and, some say, dramatically increase accuracy and the speed that players can shoot the puck.

Synthetic materials introduced in the 1990s have made goal equipment lighter and more protective. The new equipment, combined with proper coaching, resulted in steadily declining goal totals in the NHL, though recent rule changes are trying to reverse this trend.

## Getting Involved

Now that you know the basics of playing hockey, why not lace up your skates, and get out there. If your school doesn't have a rink of its own, find one nearby ... this is Canada: finding ice is never a problem.

The Hockey Canada website, **www.hockeycanada.ca** provides information on all levels of hockey—from minor league to national to Olympic level.

---

### Hockey without the Ice

**D**on't let the lack of hockey equipment and available ice stop you from playing. If you have sticks, a ball (or even a tin can), and some free space, you can play road hockey or floor hockey. You don't even have to learn how to skate.

Road hockey can be played in quiet streets, empty parking lots, playgrounds, driveways, or any other safe place you can find outside.

Floor hockey usually is played in a gymnasium or on special indoor courts, sometimes with modified sticks.

In both games there are few formal rules or specific positions and goals can be marked with whatever objects are available. Because of the lack of protective equipment, it is generally forbidden to "lift the puck" (shoot it above the playing surface) and contact is kept to a minimum.

The beauty of road hockey and floor hockey is that they can be played informally with as many or as few players as are available.

# Gold-Medal Women
## Playing to Win (and to Have Fun)

**CANADIAN WOMEN CONTINUE OLYMPIC LEGACY ON ICE**

Canadian hockey fans were expecting big things from their Olympic women's hockey team at the 2006 games in Turin, Italy, and the team didn't disappoint them. It dominated in all five games, allowing only two goals on the way to winning the gold medal over Sweden.

Nearly everyone contributed with either a goal or an assist. A few players came into the tournament with very strong credentials.

Jennifer Botterill was the youngest player on Canada's team in 1998 when it won the Olympic silver medal in Nagano, Japan. She was named Manitoba's female athlete of the year in 2001, and has helped Team Canada win four IIHF World Championships—scoring eight goals and two assists and named the tournament's Most Valuable Player—along with a gold medal at the 2002 Olympics in Salt Lake City.

Her advice to Olympic hopefuls is to find activities you like and then have fun. "It's really important for young athletes to just enjoy what they're doing, to believe in themselves, and to set their own goals." She also believes athletes should maintain a balance and strive to be great family members and friends, as well.

Hockey players often are known for playing through pain, but playing with a broken wrist? That's what Hayley Wickenheiser did in the gold-medal game.

Hayley's impressive Olympic feats don't stop there. She's been a member of Canada's national team since she was 15, and has played a huge part in Canada's four victories in the world championships as well as Team Canada's win at the 2002 Winter Olympics, where she was named that tournament's top player. She excelled again in 2006, racking up five goals and 12 assists for a team-leading 17 points.

To cap it off, Wickenheiser was the first woman ever to compete in professional men's hockey, as a member of the Salamat team in the Finnish league in 2003–04. While in Finland, she notched another "first," becoming the first woman to score a goal in a men's pro game.

## Field Hockey

**F**ield hockey—or simply "hockey," as it is known outside of North America—is played by more than three million people around the world for both competition and recreation. It is a stick-and-ball game traditionally played on grass, but it can also be played on artificial turf and synthetic surfaces.

### History

Field hockey is one of the oldest games in the world, with a lineage dating back approximately 4,000 years. The ancient Egyptians, Greeks, Ethiopians, Romans, and Aztecs all played some version of the game. It was popular because the equipment necessary to play was simple—a ball and a stick.

Modern field hockey evolved in England during the nineteenth century. The British army co-opted the game as a way of keeping soldiers physically fit and, in doing so, spread the playing of field hockey to all corners of the former British Empire. This fact partially accounts for the extreme popularity of the game in ex-colonial areas.

Today, in North America, women rule field hockey, especially at the high school and university levels. There are approximately 20,000 people playing in Canada, with the women's numbers growing and the men's staying largely the same as ten years ago.

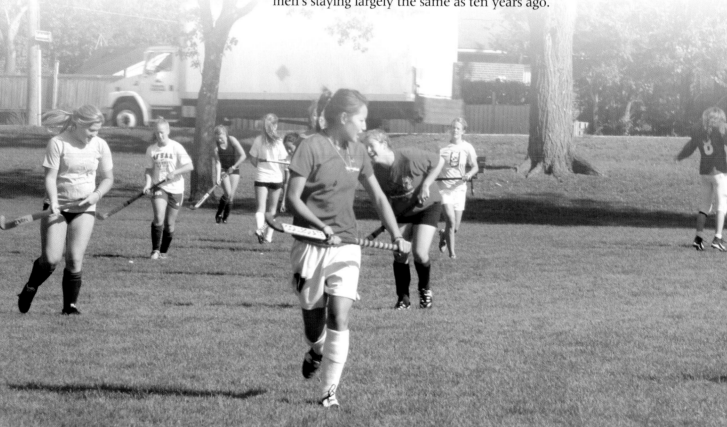

## How the Game Is Played

The object of field hockey is to move the ball across the field, or "pitch," and hit it into the other team's net by tapping, dribbling, hitting, and passing the ball with the flat side of your stick. Shaped like the letter "J," field hockey sticks are made of fibreglass or wood with a curved end, and one flat side for hitting. All field hockey sticks are right handed, and it's illegal to hit the ball with the curved side of the stick.

Field hockey is played by two teams of eleven players each—one goaltender and ten "field players." While only the goaltender has an exclusively defined role, generally the forwards score goals, the defenders protect their end of the field, and the midfielders do a bit of both. Play is continuous; there are no time outs allowed unless one of the two referees makes a call or delays the game due to player injury.

The rules are straightforward. You can only use your stick to control the ball; the exception is the goalie, who can, within his or her defensive circle, employ feet and hands to stop the ball. You can't raise your stick above your shoulders when carrying the ball, and you can't raise the ball off the ground in a dangerous manner. Field hockey is not an overtly physical game; thus, pushing, charging, and tripping are fouls.

Common strategic tactics include "calling through," where you pass straight ahead to another player, or making "drives" (hard hits that make the ball travel across long distances). You can also "flick" or "scoop" the ball up off the ground past opponents.

Unlike the somewhat genteel reputation field hockey has in the modern playground, the original versions were considered too rough for female participation.

## Scoring

Points must be scored from within the striking circle, the semi-circular area in front of each goal. A goal may only be scored from outside if the ball touches an attacking player within the striking circle.

Goals are scored in three situations:

➤ **Field goal.** You score a field goal when you beat the goalie during open, continuous play.

➤ **Penalty corner.** You are awarded this set play when your opposition's defence either commits a foul inside the striking circle, or intentionally hits the ball out-of-bounds over the end line. You take the shot along the end line at a spot ten yards away from the nearest goal post. Your teammates must stand with both their sticks and feet outside of the striking circle. Five defenders, including the goalie, stand behind the end line until you make contact with the ball. Then any player can rush into the circle to either help defend or to shoot the ball at the goal.

➤ **Penalty stroke.** This shot is awarded when a defensive infraction within the striking circle has prevented a goal. The ball is spotted seven yards from the goal, and you then go one-on-one with the goalie. You have two to three steps and five seconds to shoot. The goalie may only move off the goal line when you have touched the ball with your stick.

## The Indoor Game

So you want to play field hockey, but don't want to have to give it up once the snow hits the ground? No problem. Once winter arrives, you can just move the game inside, make a few small changes and you are good to go.

The indoor playing surface can vary considerably in size from 36–44 m in length and 18–22 m in width. At its biggest, an indoor field is less than half the size of an outdoor one. The goal is also smaller in indoor field hockey.

There are six players on each team. Because the game is played in such close quarters, the ball may only be pushed along the ground, not hit or flicked, except when taking a shot on goal.

The balls and sticks are similar between the two versions, but some players opt to use a slightly lighter or thinner stick when playing indoors.

Because of the lack of long passes and the different surface, the indoor version of field hockey is actually a slightly faster game, but both versions are exciting to watch and fun to play.

## Field Hockey: Key Terms and Basic Skills

To be a good hockey player, the ability to control the ball with your stick—"stick work" or "stick handling"—is essential. Below are some of the more common skills used to move the length of the pitch and create an open shot on goal:

➤ **Push.** Move the ball along the ground using a pushing movement of your stick. Make sure both the ball and the head of your stick are in contact with the ground.

➤ **Drive.** Use this common stroke on passes, free hits, and shots on goal. Take a hard stroke at the ball using a good backswing motion, and hold both hands together at the top of your stick.

➤ **Hit.** Strike the ball using a swinging movement of your stick.

➤ **Sweep.** Sweep the stick across the field and then follow through with a push.

➤ **Flick.** Snap your wrists to lift the ball in the air for quick passes or shots.

➤ **Tackle.** Defend your end of the field by using your stick (not your body) to take the ball away from your opponent.

➤ **Scoop.** With the blade of your stick, lift the ball up and over the front of your opponent's stick. You should use this move when dodging a tackle, or to pass the ball into open space for a teammate.

➤ **Slap Shot.** Use this most powerful stroke as either a hard, quick pass, or a shot on goal. Do a half backswing with your hands slightly apart on the stick.

## Innovations

Equipment used by field hockey players has improved substantially over the years. Field hockey sticks are made from light, durable materials that reduce vibration, and allow for better stick handling and shooting. As well, colour has been introduced widely in uniforms. For example, goaltenders can wear different coloured shirts than their teammates, and can choose from masks with customized paint jobs, similar to the ones worn by ice hockey goaltenders.

## Getting Involved

If you would like to find further opportunities in field hockey, visit the Field Hockey Canada website at **www.fieldhockey.ca**. The website has contact information for most provinces across Canada for both men and women. Click on the *Club Finder* link to locate a club near you.

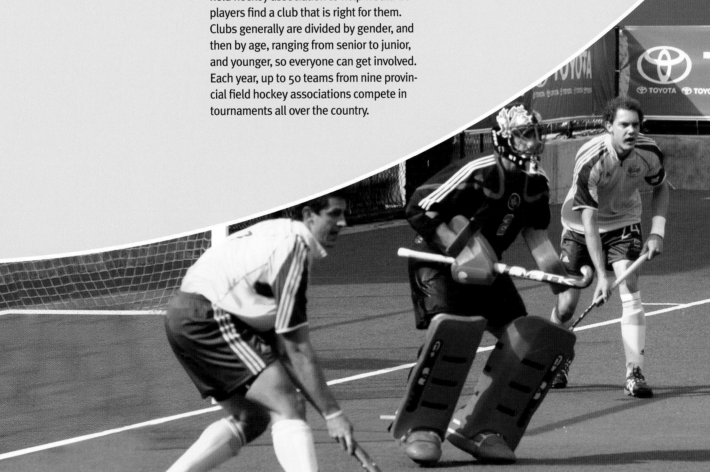

# Field Hockey Night in Canada
## Playing to Win (and to Have Fun)

In North America, field hockey has a reputation of being a woman's sport. The truth, however, is that it is the largest team sport in the world in which both men and women participate. Within Canada, there are plenty of chances for girls and guys to get involved in this sport that is definitely not for wimps.

If you are interested in joining the thousands of Canadian field hockey players, you can do so through one of the country's 400 clubs or one of the 600 school teams. Whether you want to be highly competitive, or just have lots of fun, there are certainly many opportunities to participate, and the sport is getting more popular all the time.

Almost every Canadian province has a field hockey association to help would-be players find a club that is right for them. Clubs generally are divided by gender, and then by age, ranging from senior to junior, and younger, so everyone can get involved. Each year, up to 50 teams from nine provincial field hockey associations compete in tournaments all over the country.

The mission of Field Hockey Canada (FHC) is to promote the sport and players in Canada. FHC coaches and officials are considered to be some of the most qualified in the world. With national teams for men and women, the athletes participate in prestigious competitions such as the Summer Olympics, the Pan American Games, and the Commonwealth Games.

FHC also encourages world-class competitions right here in Canada. Waterloo, Ontario, hosted the 2005 Men's and Women's Indoor Pan America Cups. Vancouver hosted the men's and women's 4 Nations tournament in 2003, and will also be host to the 2008 Women's Olympic Qualifying Tournament.

*A GROWING SPORT WITH OPPORTUNITIES FOR EVERYONE*

# Rugby

To many North American observers, rugby resembles organized chaos with un-padded players crashing into each other in uninterrupted play. This "bedlam in short pants" characterization of the sport is not far from the truth.

## History

No one can say with certainty who invented the game of rugby. The most common story told is that William Webb Ellis took a soccer ball in his hands, and ran with it instead of kicking it at the Rugby School in England in 1823. There is no real evidence of the event. However, Webb Ellis did attend the school after which the game was named, and the Rugby Union World Cup trophy is named after him to this day.

Rugby became increasingly popular over time and the first set of written rules were created in 1845. By 1870 there were over forty rugby clubs in England and on January 26, 1871, the Rugby Football Union was created to standardize and amend the rules of the game. Also that year, on March 27, the first international rugby union game was played between England and Scotland. Today the sport is played in 80 countries, including Canada, where almost 50,000 players compete.

There are several variations of rugby including: rugby union, rugby league, rugby sevens, wheelchair rugby (often called murderball), and tag or touch rugby. In this section, we will primarily discuss rugby union.

## How the Game Is Played

The forerunner to American and Canadian football, rugby is played on a large field by two teams of fifteen players each. In rugby, forward passes are illegal. To advance the ball towards the opponent's goal, you can either run with it, or pass it to a teammate as long as you are throwing either parallel to your field position or behind you. Rugby players generally pass the ball using an underhand shovelling motion, but in some cases (such as when re-starting play from the sidelines) overhand passes are used.

To move up the field, a team typically passes the ball along a string of players who are all attempting to avoid being tackled by the defensive team. If a player is tackled, he or she will attempt to throw the ball to the next player in line (often as they are being tackled) to maintain possession. The goal of this type of play is to isolate the fastest offensive players against only one or two defenders in an open part of the field. The offensive team can also choose to kick the ball up-field. You will likely lose possession, but you will be in a much better field position.

If the defensive team tackles the ball carrier, the play is not whistled dead. Instead, the carrier must immediately release the ball and the two teams engage in a struggle for possession called a "ruck." If the ball carrier is held by the defensive team, but not tackled, a different type of contest for possession takes place which is called a "maul." Both rucks and mauls have specific rules of engagement, and failure to follow these rules can result in penalties.

Unlike football, play can continue in rugby after a player has been tackled.

## The Scrum

If an accidental infringement such as a knock-on (where a player drops the ball forward) or a forward pass occurs, a scrum is used to restart the game. A scrum is made up of the eight forwards on each side who join together in an interlocking cluster formation that is three rows deep on each side. The other seven players on each team line up behind the scrum ready to either attack on offence or tackle on defence. Play starts when the ball is rolled into the middle of the scrum.

Players in the scrum each have a specific job and name:

> **Hooker.** This player is in the middle of the front row of the scrum. The hooker's job is to move the ball towards the back of the scrum by "hooking" the ball with his or her feet.

> **Scrumhalf.** This player rolls the ball into the scrum and generally retrieves it from the back of the scrum if his or her team's hooker gains possession of the ball.

> **Flyhalf.** This player usually receives the ball from the scrum half and begins the offensive charge by either running with the ball, passing the ball, or kicking it for field position.

> **Number 8.** This player has to make sure that the ball, when being "hooked" back by the hooker, doesn't leave the scrum until either he or she, or the scrum half, is ready to pick it up.

## Equipment and Positions

Unlike American football, rugby participants have a minimal amount of equipment. A mouthguard is one favourite. As well, some players wear a lightweight cap with flaps to hide and protect their ears.

Rugby is also unique because each position has a number, and that number is written right on the back of each player's jersey. As a spectator, it makes it much easier to follow along.

In rugby union, the positions and their numbers are as follows:

- Loosehead Prop—1
- Hooker—2
- Tighthead Prop—3
- Lock—4
- Lock—5
- Blindside Flanker—6
- Openside Flanker—7
- Number 8 or Eight Man—8
- Scrum Half—9
- Fly-half—10
- Left Wing—11
- Inside Centre—12
- Outside Centre—13
- Right Wing—14
- Fullback—15

## Rugby: Avoiding the Rough and Tumble

There's no hiding rugby's reputation as a tough sport. The players are passionate, and because the ball is in play even after a player is tackled, things can get rough as players scramble to get possession. If you aren't into the rough and tumble aspect, see if you can organize a game of touch rugby instead.

## Scoring (in Rugby Union)

There are several ways to score points, including:

> **A try (five points).** A player crosses the "tryline" in possession of the ball. The score is counted when the player places the ball on the ground. If they cross the tryline and then drop or throw the ball down, no points are awarded.

> **A conversion (two points).** The ball is kicked through the uprights after a try.

> **A drop goal (three points).** A player drop kicks the ball through the uprights.

> **A penalty kick (three points).** The player gets a free kick when the other team commits a penalty, and attempts to kick the ball through the uprights.

## Calling the Shots

When a referee awards a penalty, the side that won the penalty gets to restart play. Sometimes the ball is buried underneath tacklers or a minor infraction takes place. At that point, the referee blows the whistle to stop play. The referee may award penalties, call a scrum, expel a player for 10 minutes of a game, or expel a player from the game completely.

## Penalties

Rugby has a number of different infractions, including:

> Intentionally bringing a maul to the ground

> The offensive player not immediately releasing the ball upon being tackled

> A player passing the ball forward

> A player lying on the ground handling the ball

## Getting Involved

True to the rugby enthusiast's nature, Rugby Canada has an extensive website, **www.rugbycanada.ca**, with contact information for provincial clubs and unions, as well as up-to-date developments in both men's and women's rugby.

# Rugby—The U-17 Team
## Playing to Win (and to Have Fun)

In 1997, Canada's Under-17 (U-17) Boys Rugby Team swept the German tour, winning all four games. The result beat the team's record from the year before when it won three out of four games on the European tour.

Following the successful 1997 tour, the U-17 league was cancelled. The U-17 Canadian team was replaced with an Under-19 team, consisting of essentially the same players. In 2004, the U-17 team was revived with a slightly different edge.

The mandate in developing this new team was to encourage as much provincial participation as possible. Each province was given the opportunity to nominate three players (highly-populated British Columbia and Ontario were allowed more than three). Athletes who performed well at the National Festival (rugby's national championship, begun in 2003), were also allowed to try out for the team.

So, how did they do after putting together a team that only had the opportunity to practise together for three days before leaving to compete in England? Fabulously. Canada's U-17 team won all nine games. The team consisted of players from each of Canada's ten

provinces, thus fulfilling the original mandate.

On Remembrance Day, true to their Canadian nature, the boys walked from the barracks, in which they were housed for the tour, to the Aldershot train station, while discussing the sacrifices made by WWI and WWII veterans. Then they observed two minutes of silence, which ended with a sprint to catch their train to London.

Rugby Canada had another goal when reviving the U-17 team, which was to give rugby players the opportunity to play the sport at a higher level than is otherwise available in Canada. Through the adventures and international travel of the successful U-17 team, the dedication to the sport shown by these young men has really paid off.

# Canadian Football

**F**ootball is often compared to chess, with every move planned well in advance and each player having a specific role to play, like the pieces on the chessboard. Strategy is all-important in this sport, with the offensive team choosing how to advance the ball and the defensive team trying to anticipate the opponent's actions.

## History

Canadian football grew from rugby, a game invented in Rugby, England, in 1823. Rugby football spread across the Atlantic through a British Army garrison stationed in Montreal. The soldiers recruited McGill University students for games, and after a McGill team played in Boston at Harvard University, the Americans developed their own version.

The game became widely played among Ivy League schools in the United States. In 1879, Yale University player and coach Walter Camp initiated many of the rule changes that brought the game closer to the present-day version.

In Canada, the game developed through associations organized in each province. In 1884, the Canadian Rugby Football Union was created as the sport's governing body. Today, it is known as the Canadian Football League (CFL).

## How the Game Is Played

To start the game, the defensive team (made up of 12 players) kicks the ball down the field towards the offensive team. The offensive team has three tries (or "downs") to move the ball forward 10 yards (about 9 m). The defensive team tries to stop the offence's advance by tackling the ball-carrier to the ground or forcing the player to run out of bounds. The defending team can gain possession of the ball before the end of three downs by recovering a dropped, or "fumbled" ball, or by intercepting a pass.

The opposing teams face each other along an imaginary line, extending the width of the field, called the "line of scrimmage." Offensive players line up to block opponents from reaching their quarterback. The ball is "snapped" by the centre to the quarterback, who advances the ball either by running with it, passing it, or handing the ball to a teammate, who then attempts to run towards the opposite team's end zone to gain territory or to score points.

If the offensive team moves 10 yards in three downs or less, they get another three tries to move another 10 yards. If the yards haven't been gained, the teams switch offensive and defensive roles.

When the offensive team is not likely to gain the yards needed, it often kicks, or "punts," the ball on the third down.

Canadian football is a game of strategy.

## Scoring

There is more than one way for a team to score in football:

> **Touchdown (6 points).** Scored when you carry or pass the ball into the opposing team's end zone.

> **Field goal (3 points).** Scored by a drop kick or place kick (except on a kick-off) when you put the ball between the opponent's goal posts over the cross bar.

> **Safety (2 points).** Scored when you make the opposition down the ball behind its own goal line.

> **Single,** or **Rouge (1 point).** If your team tries for a field goal and misses, the defending team must return the ball out of the end zone. If the team cannot do so, a single point is awarded to your team.

> **Conversion (1 or 2 points).** After scoring a touchdown, you may attempt to add to the score by means of a scrimmage play from the opponent's 5-yard line. You get 1 point for kicking a field goal, or 2 points for carrying or passing the ball into the end zone.

Since football is physically demanding, the rules need to be enforced to ensure safety. The referee uses arm and hand signals to indicate the kind of penalty that is being called. Offending teams are penalized by deducting 5, 10, or 15 yards from their position on the field, depending on the severity of the foul. Too many players on the field will cost you 5 yards (about 4.5 m), while diving helmet-first into an opponent in a violent tackle will cost you 15 yards (about 14 m).

## Football—CFL Versus NFL

**F**ootball, as we know it in North America, was first developed in Canada and then later played and adapted in the United States. For much of the twentieth century there were large variations between the two versions. Now only a few key differences remain.

- **Field.** The Canadian field is 110 yards (100.5 m) long while the American field is 100 yards (91.4 m) long. The size of the end zone and the placement of the goalpost also vary between the leagues.

- **Line of scrimmage.** Teams line up along this line in both versions of the game but while it's a full yard (91 cm) wide in the CFL, it's only the width of a ball in the NFL.

- **Downs.** Both versions of the game originally had three downs. American football added a fourth down in the early twentieth century.

- **Players.** Canadian teams have twelve players while American teams have eleven.

## Canadian Football: Key Terms and Basic Skills

- **Passing and catching.** To throw a forward pass, grip the ball by the laces and throw it downfield. Receivers adjust to the flight of the ball when it is in the air and run precise patterns.

- **Carrying.** The first responsibility of the ball carrier is to secure the ball by creating a pocket with his or her arms into which the ball is stuffed. The carrier's—or rusher's—body should shield the ball from a tackler at all times. The ball carrier uses powerful strides and a wide stance to follow the blockers (who attempt to clear a path).

- **Punting.** The punter drops the ball from about hip level. A good punt should travel further than 40 yards (about 37 m). Precise punts that pin the opposing team back near their own goal line are an effective weapon in the battle for field position.

- **Place-kicking.** The ball is snapped from the centre to the holder who positions the ball, laces towards the target, for the kicker to boot through the uprights.

## Flag and Touch Football

Football players wear protective equipment but some of them still suffer injuries when being tackled. Those hoping to avoid injury will often play flag or touch football instead. These games are similar to traditional football but they generally allow only minimal contact.

In touch football, the tackle is replaced with either a one- or two-hand touch. In flag football, players have flags attached to their waist or belt which must be removed to end a down. Flag football has even grown in popularity enough to have its own annual world cup.

## Innovations

Football coaches and owners are always trying to stay one step ahead of the competition. Recent innovations include specialized gloves that help receivers catch the ball easier. Playing equipment today is also lighter. New artificial playing surfaces provide a softer and quicker playing surface.

At the professional level, specially designed software programs are now used to provide coaches with detailed information about their opponent's tendencies (which play the opposing team will run in a specific situation). Coaches can also communicate this information to their players through specialized two-way radios that are placed inside helmets and coaches' headsets.

## Getting Involved

Many Canadian high schools have football teams, so there are plenty of opportunities to play the game. Make sure you show up for tryouts.

You can visit Football Canada at **www.footballcanada.com** to find playing opportunities in your province or territory.

# The Grey Cup—A Very Canadian Trophy
## Playing to Win (and to Have Fun)

**THE CFL'S BELOVED CUP HAS ACCIDENTAL BEGINNING AND SUFFERS MUCH ABUSE**

**D**id you know that the Grey Cup, the famous trophy awarded to the top team in the CFL, was not originally intended to honour a football champion?

Albert Henry George Grey, Canada's Governor General from 1904 to 1911, wanted his Cup awarded to the top Canadian senior hockey team. Sir Montague Allan beat him to the punch by creating the Allan Cup. Instead, Grey donated his trophy to the champions of the Canadian Rugby Union (CRU), the precursor to the CFL.

The first Grey Cup championship was played in 1909 at Rosedale Field in Toronto, with the University of Toronto beating the Parkdale Canoe Club 26–6. The Cup was cancelled from 1916–1918 because of World War I, and then again in 1919 when an influenza epidemic swept Canada. Other than this four-year stretch, the championship game has been played each year since its inception.

In 1935, Winnipeg became the first western team to win the Grey Cup by defeating the Hamilton Tigers (now the Tiger Cats), beginning an East vs. West rivalry that continues to this day. One of the strangest Grey Cup finals occurred in 1962, when the game was played over a two-day period in Toronto after a fog rolled in and forced the game's postponement. This game came to be known as the Fog Bowl.

The Cup itself has suffered through many ordeals. It has been left behind in hotel rooms after post-game parties more than once; almost destroyed by fire; stolen, held for ransom, and then abandoned; stolen again in a bar on a dare; broken in 1987 when an Edmonton Eskimo sat on it; and broken again in 1993 by another Eskimo who gave it a celebratory head butt.

Perhaps the greatest indignity occurred in 1995, when the CFL decided to conduct a short-lived American expansion experiment. As a result, the Cup fell into the hands of the Baltimore Stallions— making them the first (and, many Canadian fans hope, the last) U.S. team ever to take home this very Canadian trophy.

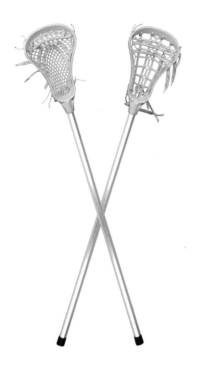

## Lacrosse

Lacrosse is the oldest sport in North America. It was originally played by Canada's indigenous people both for recreational purposes and to settle intertribal disputes. The game horrified French and English settlers. One reportedly remarked that, "Almost everything short of murder is allowable." Lacrosse now follows somewhat more restrained rules of play.

### History

Westerners were introduced to the game through the observations of Jean de Brébeuf, a Jesuit missionary. He named the game "la crosse" because the netted sticks reminded him of the Bishop's crozier or "crosse." The basic rules began to form in 1794, based on a ceremonial match between the Seneca and the Mohawks that was being used to settle a land dispute.

The contemporary game really started to take shape in 1834, when the Caughnawaga staged a demonstration match in Montreal. In 1856, Montreal dentist William George Beers founded the Montreal Lacrosse Club and formalized the rules for his club. Soon after, the National Lacrosse Association became the first national sport governing body in North America. Its motto: Our country—our game.

Parliament designated lacrosse as Canada's national game in 1859 (and confirmed it as Canada's national summer sport in 1994).

## How the Game Is Played

Though the rules of play are different for men's and women's versions of the field game (as opposed to the box game, discussed on page 368), the basic principles are the same.

Every lacrosse game begins with a face-off. The teams line up behind restraining lines with two wing midfielders in the middle of the face-off circle, awaiting the referee's whistle to draw for the ball. Face-offs also happen at the beginning of a new period and after a goal. Once the game is in action, defensive players and offensive players (attackmen) stick to their respective zones. Only mid-fielders are allowed to run back and forth.

The object of lacrosse is to fling a small, hard rubber ball into the opposing team's net using netted sticks (called crosses). Crosses range in length from three to six feet (different positions get crosses of different lengths), with a small triangular basket, called the "head" or "pocket," for carrying the ball. Players scoop the ball up with their crosses and either run, carrying the ball, or throw it to the other players.

Lacrosse typically is fast-paced, emphasizing agility and speed over pure brawn. What is different about lacrosse is that it's one of the only games where you use a netted object to try to catch the ball rather than simply smack it back at the opposing team (as in tennis or badminton). In lacrosse, perfecting the way you flick your wrist to make a pass is essential.

## The Men's and Women's Games

Men's lacrosse teams have 10 players: three attackmen, three mid-fielders, three defencemen, and a goalie. The men's version of the game is very aggressive. Body checking is allowed, but only if an opponent has the ball or is within a 2.7 m (9 foot) radius of the ball. The game lasts 60 minutes and is divided into four quarters.

In women's lacrosse, there are 12 players. The attack positions are: centre, right attack wing, left attack wing, first, second, and third home. The defence positions are: right defence wing, left defence wing, third man, cover point, point, and goalie. The 60-minute games are divided into two halves. Body checking isn't allowed, but a player can steal the ball by hitting an opponent's crosse with her own. Game play emphasizes speed and teamwork over strength and involves much less contact. The women's version of lacrosse is closer than the men's version to the traditional game played by Native Canadians hundreds of years ago.

Today, the Canadian Lacrosse Association recognizes four separate lacrosse disciplines:

> Indoor Box

> Women's Field

> Men's Field

> Inter-Lacrosse (a non-contact version of the game)

At the 2006 World Championship, the Canadian squad scored an impressive 15-10 victory over the United States, giving Canada its first world championship in 28 years.

## Box Lacrosse

**W**ith hockey being Canada's national winter sport, and lacrosse being Canada's national summer sport, it's only fitting that, when the ice and snow melt away, we fill our hockey rinks with lacrosse players. This is where box lacrosse—the most popular form of the game in Canada—is played.

This version of the sport originally was developed to promote business for ice hockey arenas. The playing area is called the box. Unlike other forms of lacrosse, it allows cross-checking and solid wooden sticks. A game consists of three periods, each lasting 20 minutes.

Box lacrosse, or Boxla, invented in the 1930s, was so successful that it replaced the field game to become the official version of the Canadian Lacrosse Association.

Canada's most prestigious lacrosse trophy is called the Mann Cup. The Mann Cup competition is played under box lacrosse rules.

## Lacrosse: Key Terms and Basic Skills

➤ **Catching.** Face the passer with your stick at ear height out in front of you. Watch the ball as it lands in the pocket and allow the stick to give a little to absorb the ball.

➤ **Passing.** Stand slightly sidewise to keep an eye on opposing players. Make sure you make eye contact with the receiver before passing.

➤ **Scoring.** Try these effective styles—overhand long shot, underhand long shot, sidearm long shot, and backhand shot (for close distances).

➤ **Stay alert.** Know where the ball is at all times, even if you don't have it.

## Penalties

Fouls in field lacrosse are either personal or technical:

➤ **Personal fouls.** slashing, tripping, checking, unsportsmanlike behaviour, unnecessary roughness, and using an illegal cross.

➤ **Technical fouls.** holding, interference, offsides, pushing, illegal screening, stalling, and warding off another player.

Personal foul penalties warrant a one- to three-minute suspension from play, and suspension from the entire game if a player commits five fouls.

Technical foul penalties lead to a thirty-second suspension or a change in possession of the ball.

## Innovations

Aspects of lacrosse have altered over the years. The equipment, issues of safety, and venues have evolved, but perhaps the biggest innovation occurred in the beginning. When William George Beers founded the Montreal Lacrosse Club in 1856, he replaced the deerskin ball with an Indian rubber ball, regulated the size of the team at 12 (later changed to 10), and devised the names of the positions.

## Getting Involved

Like hockey, lacrosse is a sport that you can discover in your high school gym class and pursue through regional, city, provincial, and national leagues. You can take it as far as you like.

To learn more about the sport of lacrosse, and where you can play, check out the Canadian Lacrosse Association at **www.lacrosse.ca**.

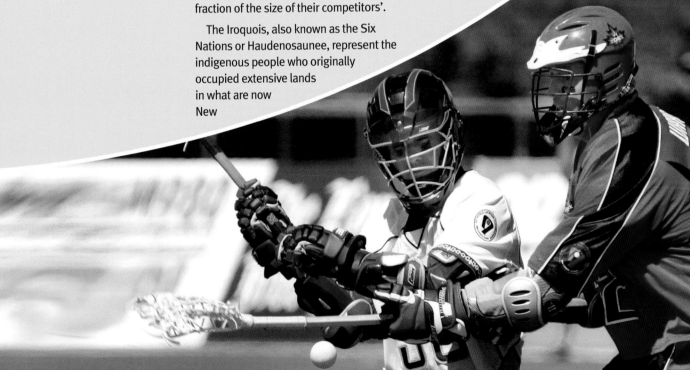

## Lacrosse—The Iroquois National Team
### Playing to Win (and to Have Fun)

The premier event in men's field lacrosse is the World Lacrosse Championship, organized by the International Lacrosse Federation (ILF). It's held every four years and takes place over nine action-packed days in July. London, Ontario, hosted the event in 2006.

The ILF recognizes 14 full-member nations: Australia, Canada, the Czech Republic, England, Germany, Ireland, Japan, Korea, New Zealand, Scotland, Sweden, the United States, Wales, and the Iroquois Nationals.

That's right—the Iroquois! They are the originators of the game, after all.

The ILF sanctioned the Iroquois Nationals as a full-member nation in 1990, making them the only indigenous national team sanctioned to compete in an international sports competition. The Nationals take great pride in the fact that they have been able to meet the challenges of competing at a worldwide level, even though they must draw from a player pool that's only a fraction of the size of their competitors'.

The Iroquois, also known as the Six Nations or Haudenosaunee, represent the indigenous people who originally occupied extensive lands in what are now New

York, Ontario, and Quebec.

The Iroquois people identify themselves as citizens of their respective nation and, therefore, the Iroquois Nationals travel with Haudenosaunee passports and see competition in worldwide lacrosse as a manifestation of their sovereignty.

Team members consider themselves ambassadors who build international goodwill and educate fellow athletes, government officials, and people around the world about their culture—in which lacrosse plays a very important part. The players also serve as role models for Iroquois youth.

Since 1990, many young Six Nations athletes have been recruited by universities and colleges, and have gone on to play professionally in the National Lacrosse League. Some have even competed at the ILF World Championship.

*IROQUOIS NATIONALS*
*DISPLAY CULTURE AND*
*SKILLS TO CANADA*
*AND THE WORLD*

# 22

# Net/Wall Games

> *...it's the mark of a great player to be confident in tough situations.*

**John McEnroe**
American tennis star and three-time Wimbledon men's champion

**N**et/wall games are popular sports that many Canadians enjoy playing. They include sports such as volleyball, badminton, tennis, table tennis, squash, racquetball, and handball. For competition or recreation—from sandy beach volleyball, to outdoor tennis, to the local squash club—opportunities to take part in these sports are everywhere.

In all net/wall games, players attempt to hit a ball or object over the net or against the wall in such a way that it cannot be returned by the opposing player. Although finding space on the court becomes more difficult with the addition of more players (six players can cover more space on a volleyball court compared to one player on a tennis court), the basic tactical problems and their solutions remain similar.

In some net/wall games, the ball is allowed to bounce once on the playing surface before it is returned (tennis, squash, racquetball). In other games, players try to prevent the ball or object from landing in their court—volleyball, badminton, sepak takraw (kick volleyball). Net/wall games can be played either as a singles game or as a team game.

The great thing about having a basic understanding of the strategy and tactics involved in one net/wall game is that many are common among all net/wall games.

## Net/Wall Games

The four net/wall games covered in this chapter are:

> ➢ Volleyball
>
> ➢ Badminton
>
> ➢ Tennis
>
> ➢ Table Tennis

## Basic Strategy and Tactics

To be successful in net/wall games, players and teams must be able to send an object over a net or against a wall into the open space. They must also be able to prevent their opposition from putting the object into the open space on their court.

The fast-paced nature of net/wall games means that players need to use advanced sending-away skills. In addition to the initial contact with the ball or object (the serve), players must also be prepared to hit a fast-moving object from an opposing player (the return).

Players use tactical skills (such as bumping, the overhand smash, the forehand, the lob, and the spike) to return objects. Players must also combine locomotor skills (such as running, jumping, diving, and blocking) with sending-away skills.

Players soon realize that there are areas on the court from which it is difficult to return a shot. These include the sidelines, corners, spaces between players, and the front and back of the court. Players can use different tactics to exploit these areas.

For example, in tennis, a player may use a drop shot to bring an opponent close to the net, which creates space at the back of the court. If the opponent is able to return the drop shot, the first player can then lob over the player so that the ball lands at the back of the court where the space was created.

The various net/wall games all use some of the same basic skills.

## Volleyball

**V**olleyball is an exciting game that develops eye-hand coordination, cardiorespiratory fitness, and agility. It is played indoors in gymnasiums and outdoors on beaches. Your skills in the gym are easily transferable to the beach when summer arrives.

### History

In the 1890s, William Morgan studied the game of basketball, which had been invented by his Canadian friend, Dr. James Naismith. Morgan blended elements of basketball, tennis, and handball and called his new game mintonette. He changed the name to volleyball when an observer noted that the players seemed to be volleying the ball back and forth.

The YMCA promoted the sport worldwide. Players in the Philippines introduced the set-and-spike style of attack that characterizes the game today. In Canada, inter-city competitions were staged during the 1920s. American soldiers played the game overseas during both World Wars, spreading the game to many regions of the world.

## How the Game Is Played

In the indoor game, each team has six players. At the time of the serve, there must be three front row and three back row players. The players rotate clockwise each time the team wins a serve.

The server starts the game by standing behind the end line and hitting the ball over the net into the opposing team's court. If you are serving, you only get one shot to get it right. It begins as soon as you toss the ball up into the air for overhand serves, or smack it with the heel of your palm for underhand serves. As long as your team continues to win points, the same player on the team continues to serve. If you make a bad serve, or your team loses possession of the ball, you don't serve again until rotating back into the serving position.

Once the ball is in play, players on opposing teams hit it back and forth over the net using their hands, forearms, head, or any part of the body above and including the waist. Play continues until one team fails to keep the ball in the air, or until a rule violation occurs.

All players must be in their service order and within the court boundaries at the time of the serve. Once the ball is in play, you may assume any position on the court (although back row players cannot attack the ball or block the opponent). This provides for a tactic called the switch play, in which the spikers and setters may trade places in order to gain a more advantageous playing position. Players must return to their original places if a side out or a point is called.

Your team must return the ball over the net after no more than three contacts, and the other team must do the same. If you receive the ball and take the first contact, it must be touched by another member of your team before you can touch it again. It is illegal to catch, hold, or carry the ball. Essentially, the ball must remain in constant motion.

Making a good return requires skill and technique. You want to make it as difficult as possible for the other team to return the ball. You also need to be sure not to touch the net when returning, or you will lose possession of the ball altogether. If you lose service, and then gain it back again, the serve must rotate to the next player on your team.

## Scoring

Once upon a time, a point could only be gained when your team served the ball. In 1999, the Fédération Internationale de Volleyball (FIVB) World Congress changed to a rally point scoring system. This system has been adopted by Volleyball Canada and is making its way through most Canadian high schools.

Under old rules, you can score a point if your team serves and the other team hits the ball out of bounds (with no one from your team touching it on its way out), fails to return the ball in three contacts or less, or violates the court boundaries in any way. In rally scoring, a point is scored on each serve, whether by the serving team or the receiving team.

Volleyball serves can be either overhand or underhand.

## Volleyball Skills

**V**olleyball players generally are classified as one of four skill groups:

- **Setter.** In many ways the leader of the offence, the setter's main responsibility is to put the ball in the air for attack.

- **Libero.** Defensive specialists who generally receive the attack or the serve, usually the player with the quickest reaction time and the best passing skills.

- **Middle blockers/hitters.** Usually tall and less skillful defensively, these players have two functions, performing very fast attacks near the setter and blocking offensive attacks by the other team.

- **Outside/power hitters.** Players from this position may attack from longer approaches and need to be skilled at passing the ball since they sometimes help the libero in receiving the opponent's serve.

# Volleyball: Key Terms and Basic Skills

➢ **Block.** A defensive play with one or more players putting their hands up above the net to prevent a spike from reaching their court. This play may be performed by any player in the front row. The hands of the blocker may reach over the net but may not contact the ball in the opponent's court until the opponent has completed the attack.

➢ **Dig.** A defensive, often diving play, to keep an attack hit from touching the floor.

➢ **Pass (bumping).** This skill requires a player to contact the ball with his or her extended forearms. The first contact after a serve is usually a bump/pass to the setter. Bumping is also used to receive a smash from the attaching team.

➢ **Set.** Usually performed off the fingertips, a setter puts the ball into a gentle arc near the net to put a teammate in position for a spike or other form of attack hit.

➢ **Spike.** A powerful attack hit over the net, playing a critical role in offence. In spiking the ball, a player jumps high in the air and hits the ball down over the net so that it's difficult to return.

➢ **Tip.** Sometimes an offensive player surprises opponents by jumping up for a spike and, instead of smashing the ball, lightly deflects the ball into an open spot on their court.

## Innovations

The International Volleyball Association introduced a new position to the game for the 2000 Olympic Summer Games. The *libero* is a defensive specialist who can be substituted in the back row for any teammate, but can't be on the court for an entire game.

Before the advent of the libero, teams with solid execution would get into nearly mechanical routines: pass—set—spike—end-of-rally. A good libero means a spike is never a sure kill and can make for some breathtaking diving saves. The libero can't serve or spike the ball over the net. He or she plays a pivotal role in serve reception and defence.

The position is best suited to a smaller, agile player, since retrieving opposition spikes is that player's role. The addition of the libero has heightened the precision of many teams' offences; they can't just blast spikes into their opponent's back court anymore.

## Getting Involved

Getting involved in volleyball is easy when you are in high school. You can play during your physical education class and you can also play for your school team.

If you love the sport and want to know what's going on around Canada and internationally, visit the Volleyball Canada website at **www.volleyball.ca**.

# Beach Volleyball
## Playing to Win (and to Have Fun)

TAKING VOLLEYBALL TO
THE BEACH BENEFITS
PLAYERS AND FANS

**B**each Volleyball has been one of the fastest growing sports in history. It can be played casually by two people on a beach or at the cottage, or more seriously as a competitive sport, or very seriously if you go all the way to the Olympics.

Beach volleyball was first played in the 1920s on the beaches of Santa Monica, California. It remained a casual beach sport until a surge in popularity in the 1990s led to its Olympic debut at the Atlanta games in 1996. Aside from a few small differences in the rules, the game is similar to court volleyball, but is played on a slightly smaller court (8 square metres instead of 9 square metres), and generally only has two players per team instead of six.

Between the 1996 and 2000 Olympics, the FIVB made an official rule change which required women to wear bikinis as their standard competition uniforms. Often referred to as "institutionalized sexism," this issue is always on the periphery when discussing the sport

Since its debut at the Olympics, the women's game has been dominated by teams from Brazil, Australia, and the U.S. In the men's game, the U.S. and Brazilian teams have been at the top. Teams from Germany, Switzerland, and Spain have also done well.

If you like volleyball and are interested in playing while enjoying the feeling of sand between your toes, don't let the fact that you don't live near a beach stop you. Indoor beach volleyball courts are popping up all over the place and currently can be found in many Canadian cities.

This way, you never have to worry about getting too much sun, and you can enjoy the sand, even if there's snow outside.

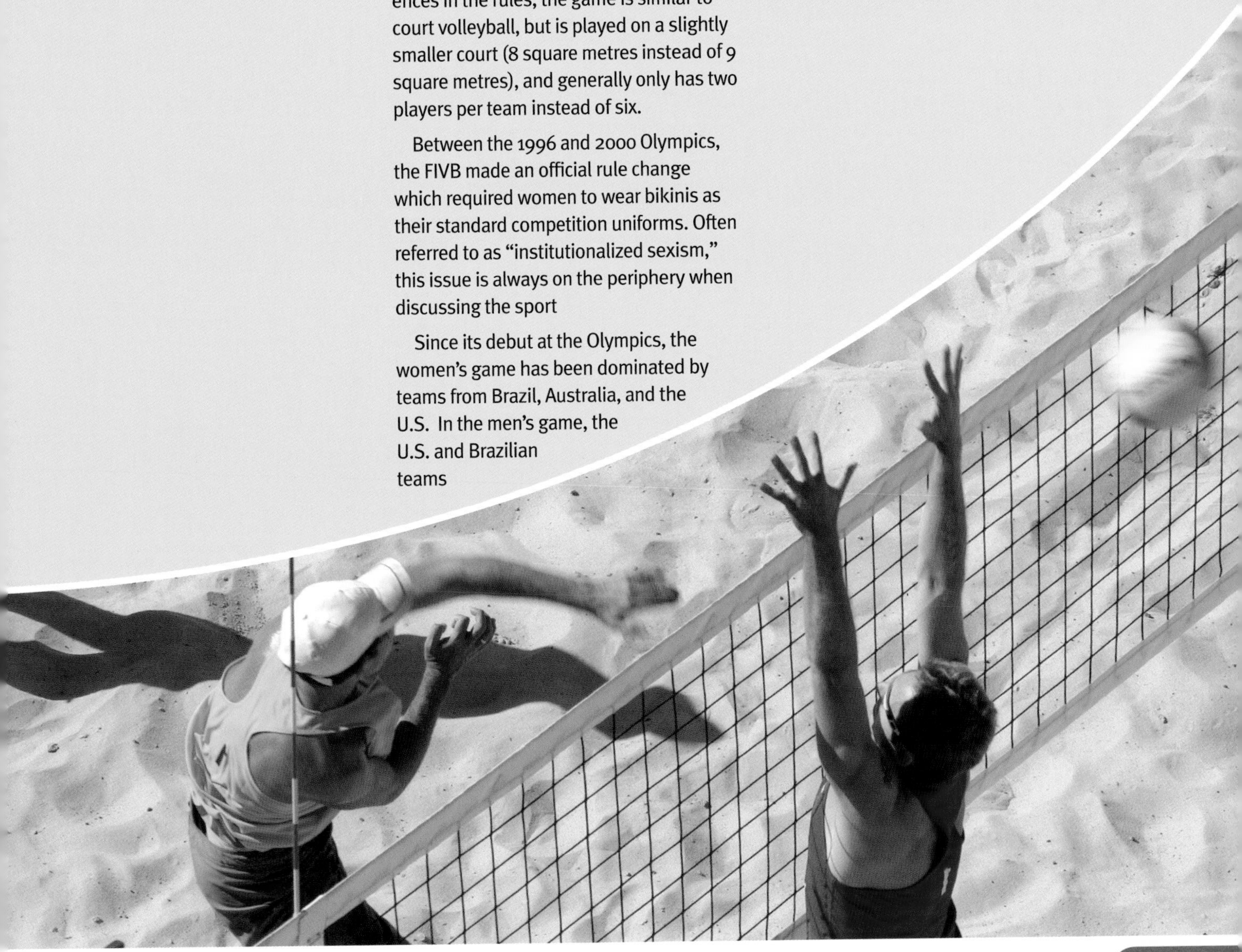

# Badminton

**S**ome consider badminton to be the world's fastest game, with the birdie sometimes leaving the racquet at speeds of up to 250 kilometres an hour. Badminton is a game that combines power, speed, endurance and tactical skill. It is one of the most widely played sports in the world.

## History

Badminton has had its fair share of names in the time it has taken to develop. It was first called Ti Jian Zi, then battledore, and shuttlecock, then poona, and finally badminton.

It is believed that some version of badminton was played as far back as 2,000 years ago in Ancient Greece. Ti Jian Zi, played in Asia in the fifth century BC, was played with the feet. Poona, which evolved in India in the mid-nineteenth century, is much closer than its predecessors to the current-day game.

Badminton clubs sprang up throughout Britain starting in the mid-eighteenth century. In the United States, the first badminton organization formed in New York in 1876. Badminton became an Olympic sport in 1992. Badminton is one of the world's most popular sports. In Canada, the popularity of the sport is growing.

## How the Game Is Played

Badminton is played both as a singles and as a doubles sport. The rectangular court is the same for both versions of the game, but the exterior lines are used in doubles matches.

To start the game in both singles and doubles badminton, one side always serves diagonally. The birdie must fall within the receiver's service court, behind the service line (the closest line to the net) for play to continue. This line is about 2 metres (6 feet and 6 inches) from the net, which means a strong serve is a must-have skill. A birdie that falls on a line is considered "in."

The basic overall strategy is to move your opponent to the baseline with a smash (a powerful overhead shot) and then use a drop shot (a tricky shot that just barely clears the net). Making the player move left and right is also effective. Essentially, the main idea is to keep the other player moving to expose an exploitable opening.

A jump smash is one of the more complicated skills in badminton.

## Scoring

The International Badminton Federation made changes to its official scoring system in May 2006. Prior to this change, you (or your team) had to be the one serving in order to win a point. Under the new rules, each rally results in a point being awarded to the player or team that won the rally.

Generally, the first side to score 21 points wins the game, but there are a few exceptions to this rule. If the score becomes tied at 20, the first side to gain a 2 point advantage wins. However, if no two-point advantage is gained before the score becomes tied at 29, the first side to get to 30 wins the game. A badminton match is "best two out of three," meaning you must win two out of three games to be victorious.

There are several ways to win a rally and gain a point. Your side wins a point if the birdie lands in bounds in the opposing side's court, or if it lands out of bounds when hit by the opposing team. Judging whether or not a birdie will land out of bounds is one of the most difficult things to assess in badminton. The best way to improve at this is to rally for fun and let it go a few times to see how good you are at judging where the birdie will land. You will get better and better as time goes on.

Another way to win a point is simply by default. If the opposing team hits the birdie into the net or hits the ceiling of the venue, you win the rally. Of course, that means the opposite is also true—if you hit the net or the ceiling, the other team will win the rally.

The net, unlike tennis, does not touch the ground. Instead, the mesh is suspended 1.5 metres (5 feet, 1 inch) above the court surface at the sidelines (2.5 cm lower in the middle). That's a fair bit of height to clear each time. Ceilings, on the other hand, generally are pretty high up, which makes hitting the ceiling the least of your worries.

## The Ever-Evolving Racquet

In an attempt to not get left behind by evolving technology, entrepreneur Minoru Yoneyama began manufacturing badminton racquets. First, in 1957, he produced racquets under other brand names. By 1961, he introduced the first "Yoneyama" brand racquet. Two years later, he established Yoneyama Trading Ltd. in Tokyo and his racquets were being distributed on an international level.

In 1969, Yoneyama produced the world's first aluminum badminton racquet (the #700). In 1973, the company presented the now-familiar yellow and blue YY logo that appears on the sides of badminton and tennis racquets to this day. In 1974, Yoneyama Trading Ltd. became Yonex.

The Carbonex 8, introduced in 1978 by Yonex, won the All-England Badminton Championship, a competition that Yonex became an exclusive sponsor of in 1984.

Today, Yoneyama's technology is used by over 80 percent of competitive players. He has extended his innovative and lightweight designs to both tennis and golf, making all three sports more precise and faster-paced.

## Basic Strokes in Badminton

Badminton emphasizes speed and agility with a dash of power. There are three basic shots:

> **Forehand.** For right-handed players, the swinging arc starts on the right side and vice versa for left-handed players.

> **Backhand.** For this shot, right-handers swing left to right, the opposite for left-handers.

> **Overhand smash.** In badminton, the most aggressive shot is the overhand smash. Here, the player hits the birdie above his or her head with the racquet moving on a north-to-south axis instead of the east-to-west direction of the forehand or backhand shot.

## Penalties

Penalties, or faults, occur in a number of circumstances:

> When the serve strikes the birdie at a point higher than the waist

> When the server fails to serve to the diagonally opposite portion of the receiver's court

> When the birdie passes through or under, or lands out-of-bounds

## Innovations

In past centuries, the cross-stringed net of a badminton racquet was made from the stomach lining of a cat or cow. Though some players still use this, technology has made things much cheaper and easier by switching to synthetic materials (plastic or nylon).

Battledore, a predecessor of badminton, was a favoured game of the leisure classes in the seventeenth century. Most often, players wore formal wear as athletic gear to play the game. It is reported that, in the early 1900s, a participant at a badminton club removed his tuxedo jacket while playing. Although this action was viewed as scandalous at the time, badminton clubs gradually accepted the need to permit special clothing and made the decision to use tennis wear as the appropriate dress for the sport of badminton.

## Getting Involved

The Badminton Canada website, **www.badminton.ca**, is filled with information of all kinds, and if you click on the *links* section, the association is happy to show you ways to get involved in your own province or city.

## Stephane Cadieux—Coach
### Playing to Win (and to Have Fun)

Stephane Cadieux, one of two coaches to the Canadian Under 16 National Badminton team, believes that keeping his athletes motivated and healthy is crucial to their success. He also believes that encouraging his players to be independent helps them reach their goals, both on and off the court.

With two of his athletes, Peter Butler and Alexander Bruce, geared towards qualifying for the Junior National team, Cadieux knows the importance of good coaching —something that, for Cadieux, doesn't necessarily mean giving all your attention to the top athletes. If Butler and Bruce have a competition in one city, but five other athletes have a tournament elsewhere, Cadieux follows the majority.

"I'm here as a motivator. I don't want to babysit them. They've been at so many tournaments, they know what to do, they know how to get warmed up, they know how to get mentally prepared, they know that they should eat certain foods, and stretch, and drink water. I'm always reminding them of those sorts of things, but I sort of want to remove myself more and more. I can't be everywhere at all times."

Cadieux's approach may seem different than what many people have come to expect from a coach. Why wouldn't you be where your best athletes are? "Because," Cadieux says, "My goal is for them to become more and more independent. I'm only there to push them as hard as they want to be pushed."

Does Cadieux think it is difficult for competitive athletes to balance school with a rigorous training schedule? Not at all. "Once an athlete gets used to working out, they need it." Cadieux says. "To be in exam mode and not have a form of release for your body is difficult. It requires discipline and it's my job to tell them when they need to go home and rest or catch up on their homework." Often, athletes are so caught up in the pressures of winning that they forget that playing badminton is a blast. Cadieux says, "it's good to just remind ourselves of why they're doing this."

*BALANCE SCHOOL AND SPORTS FOR A SUCCESSFUL AND HEALTHY LIFESTYLE*

# Tennis

**T**ennis anyone? Tennis is a great sport for beginners because it is affordable and accessible. All you need is a racquet, balls, tennis shoes, a community tennis court, and a friend ... or three. It is also a sport for a lifetime—people of all ages can play competitively and recreationally.

## History

Tennis is one of the oldest of all net/wall games. It is believed that Christian monks in France and Italy were the first to play the game that was to become tennis. As tennis moved from the monasteries to the castles of Europe during the sixteenth to eighteenth centuries, it became the highly fashionable sport of kings and noblemen and, in France, it was called "jeu de paume," meaning, "the game of the palm."

Even into the late 1960s, tennis was seen as a game only for the upper classes. Once people had television sets in their living rooms, the game was accessible to a wider audience, creating a surge of popular interest.

The professional tennis calendar centres around four Grand Slam tournaments: the Australian Open held in January and played on a hard court; the French Open held from late May to early June and played on a clay court; Wimbledon, considered to be the most prestigious tournament, held in London, England, from late June to early July and played on a grass court; and the U.S. Open held from late August to early September and played on a hard court.

## How the Game Is Played

Tennis is played on a rectangular surface. The court measures 23.77 metres in length and, for singles, 8.23 metres in width. If the game is played as doubles, the width of the court is 10.97 metres.

The length of the court is divided in half by a net. On either side of the net are areas called "service courts," which are half the width of the court. The service court on the player's right is known as the deuce court, while the one on the left is the advantage court, or "ad court."

To serve, the player must stand behind the baseline (the line furthest from the net) between the centre line and the sideline and hit the ball diagonally over the net into the service courts. You win a point when your opponent can't reach a shot, when he or she lets the ball bounce twice, or when the return falls out of bounds or into the net. After a point is gained, the server moves over and serves into the opposite service box.

Tennis is a net/wall game in which individuals or teams of two work to hit a 6.67 cm diameter ball into an opponent's side of the court.

## Scoring: Game, Set, and Match

The scoring system in tennis is a little unusual:

➢ **Game.** A tennis "game" consists of a sequence of points and is played with the same player serving. Game scoring is different in tennis than any other game. A zero score is called "love," the first game point is 15, the second is 30, the third is 40, and then one more point is needed to win (unless the score is 40-all). In other words, a tennis game basically consists of four points.

➢ **Set.** A player wins a set by winning six games —at "six all," usually a 12-point tie-breaker is played until one player reaches 7 points first or, if the tie-breaker is tied at 7-7, until one player leads by 2 points.

➢ **Match.** A full tennis match is made up of an odd number of sets, usually three or five. The match winner is the player who wins more than half of the sets.

A successful serve will usually start a "rally" in which you and your opponent alternate hitting the ball across the net. If your first service is a "fault" (hits the net or does not land in the service court), you have a second serve. A second mistake is a "double fault," and the receiver wins the point.

If there is a "deuce," meaning a tied score of 40-all, the player who wins the next point gains the advantage. If that player also wins the next point, he or she wins the game; if not, the score returns to deuce.

Players usually change ends at the completion of the first, third, and every subsequent odd game. A change of ends also occurs at the end of the set if the total number of games played is an odd number.

The doubles game—men's doubles, women's doubles, or mixed doubles—is played with the same rules but on a wider court. Teammates coordinate their efforts strategically and tactically. Much hinges on finishing a point off at the net with a decisive volley or smash.

## Wheelchair Tennis

Tennis is also one of the fastest growing wheelchair sports in the world. It integrates easily with the able-bodied game since it is played on the same courts with the same racquets and the same balls.

Wheelchair tennis follows the same rules as able-bodied tennis as endorsed by the International Tennis Federation, with the exception that the wheelchair tennis player is allowed two bounces of the ball before it must be played. The second bounce can occur outside of the field and this rule applies to both serves and returns. This means that players who use a wheelchair can easily play against friends or opponents who don't.

There are more than 100 wheelchair tennis events taking place all over the world, and it became a Paralympic sport at the Games in Barcelona, Spain, in 1992.

In 2005, a wheelchair tennis tournament was held on grass for the first time. The occasion was made more notable by the fact that it occurred at Wimbledon, undoubtedly the most well-known grass court venue in the world.

## Tennis: Key Terms and Basic Skills

➢ **Serve.** Smoothly flowing limb movements are crucial to producing a strong serve. The power should work its way up from your legs and through your upper body and shoulder until it reaches your wrist and the racquet.

➢ **Forehand.** Most players prefer the forehand as their "bread and butter" shot. For a powerful forehand, as you swing towards the ball, transfer your weight to your front leg and follow through.

➢ **Backhand.** A backhand (one- or two-handed, whichever you find easier) allows you to get to balls you couldn't easily reach if you turned and tried to "run around" your forehand. The backhand tends to be the weaker side—hence, players will often hit to their opponent's backhand.

➢ **Volley.** The volley, returning a shot before it bounces, is an essential tennis skill. A good volley is a short punch of the racquet with much of the power of the shot coming from the muscles in the legs and hips.

➢ **Lob.** You can use this shot as either an offensive or defensive weapon. It involves hitting the ball high and deep into your opponent's court, usually with top spin. The lob enables you to get into a better defensive position or to win the point outright by hitting the ball over your opponent's head and out of reach.

➢ **Drop shot.** Use this unexpected move when your opponent is deep in his or her court. Softly tap the ball just over the net so that your opponent is unable to retrieve it.

➢ **Smash.** An overhead smash is usually the final hit of a point. It is the shot used when your opponent hits a high but weak shot that is coming down in your forecourt near the net. To hit an effective overhead, keep your eyes on the ball as it drops and strive for full extension as you hit it away from your opponent on the other side of the net.

## Innovations

In recent years, the use of composite compounds in racquets and a revolution in weight training have dramatically changed the nature of tennis. Professional players are bigger and stronger, and with the new racquets, can serve the ball at speeds well over 220 km per hour!

## Getting Involved

To get involved, all you need is a tennis racquet and some tennis balls. You can play on any local outdoor court in your area, usually free of charge. Or, contact your community centre or nearby clubs if you are ready to start playing in matches.

To learn more about what's going on in Canadian tennis, visit the Canadian Tennis Association at **www.tenniscanada.com**.

## Tennis—The Davis Cup
### Playing to Win (and to Have Fun)

**A COMPETITION THAT BRINGS YEAR-ROUND EXCITEMENT**

**D**id you know that men's tennis boasts the world's largest annual international team competition? The Davis Cup is over one hundred years old, with 133 competing countries in 2006.

The idea for the tournament came from Dwight Davis (left) in 1899. He was a skilled tennis player and a student at Harvard University who wanted to hold a tennis competition between Great Britain and the United States. The American and British Lawn Tennis Associations agreed.

Davis organized the competition's format, and spent hundreds of dollars of his own money on a large silver champion's cup. The first International Lawn Tennis Challenge match was in 1900 in Boston with the U.S. victorious over the British.

By 1905, the competition had become an international success, just as Davis had hoped, and four more teams had joined— France, Belgium, Austria, and Australasia (a combined team of Australia and New Zealand). Canada first joined in 1913. After Dwight Davis passed away in 1945, the competition's name was changed to the Davis Cup in his honour.

The competition, which includes both singles and doubles games, is organized into groups. The highest is the elite World Group, made up of 16 countries. Each country's team plays to win the best-of-five matches. The winning team moves on and the losing team is eliminated, until two teams are left to compete to become the Champion Nation. Below the World Groups are the regional groups (American Zone, Euro/African Zone, and Asia/Oceania Zone) each of which are split into five levels.

Unlike some sports where fans have to wait many months for the season to begin, Davis Cup matches are played over the course of nearly a year, with the first matches starting in February, and the final match played in early December.

Although many countries have become Davis Cup Champions, including Italy, Sweden, and Spain, the United States holds the record for the most wins (31 as of 2005). Australia is in second with 27 wins.

# Table Tennis ("Ping Pong")

**C**all it "Ping Pong," "flim flam," or whatever you want, but did you know that, next to soccer, table tennis is the world's most popular sport? Around the world, more than 40 million people play competitively.

So what's the attraction? Most likely, it is because table tennis emphasizes coordination, speed, and flexibility—sex, age, height, weight, and strength are not as important in this sport. Everyone can join in, it is very competitive, and it is definitely always fun.

## History

Table tennis is believed to be of English origin. Generally, it was enjoyed by the upper class Victorians, as a kind of "miniature tennis" that was played indoors in the 1880s and 1890s. The basic rules of the game were codified in 1922 by a Cambridge University student, Ivor Montagu (1904–1984).

In 1926, five nations—Austria, England, Germany, Hungary, and Sweden—formed the International Table Tennis Federation. The World Championships began in the same year. From such humble beginnings, the modern sport of table tennis emerged.

## How the Game Is Played

Table tennis can be played as singles or doubles. To begin a game, you serve the ball such that it bounces once on your own side of the table and then at least once on your opponent's half. Experienced players can put great spins on the ball.

For the serve to be "good," the ball must be released behind and above the edge of the table, with palm up. The ball must be tossed at least six inches up and without spin. As in regular tennis, if the serve hits the net but still goes over, it is a "let" (and must be served again). If the serve is not good, then your opponent wins the point.

On the return of service, the ball must be hit before it bounces twice and must be returned directly to the server's half (without bouncing in the returner's half) of the table. If the ball is not returned, the point goes to the server. The play continues until the ball goes out of play.

After every two points, the service alternates, with the player who received last taking a turn to serve. (In recreational matches, players often still play 5 points before changing serve.)

In competition matches, games are now played to 11 points. To win, there must be at least a two-point difference. If both players reach 10 points, a "deuce" game comes into effect, and players alternate serves until one gains a two-point lead. (In recreational matches, games often still go to 21 points.)

In competition play, matches typically are best-of-five or best-of-seven games. After each game, players switch ends. In the final game, they switch ends when the first player scores 5 points, regardless of whose turn it is to serve.

You must hit the ball back to your opponent before it bounces twice on your half of the table.

## Shakehands

No conversation about table tennis passes without discussing the best way to hold the racquet. Two different grips are common—the Eastern (penholder) and the Western (shakehands). They are referred to as "Eastern" and "Western" because traditionally the penholder has been popular in Asia, whereas the shakehands has been more popular in the western countries.

The "penholder" grip is so named because it is similar to the way that you hold a pen. Because of the angle created, it gives added topspin on the forehand side, though, on the backhand, it is more awkward (requiring something of a contortion). The unique thing about the penholder grip is that only one side of the racquet face really needs to be used—in a game where a good racquet and good rubber are the main outlay, this is an important consideration.

Nowadays, competitive players tend to gravitate towards the "shakehands" grip. This grip allows good topspin on the forehand and demands less contortion on the backhand side. It also allows for mixed rubber on each side of the racquet face (smooth on one side and "pimpled" on the other, for example). Like most things, however, grip is a matter of what feels comfortable.

## Table Tennis: Key Terms and Basic Skills

In table tennis, the strokes break down into offensive (producing topspin) and defensive (producing backspin).

**Offensive strokes:**

> **Drive.** The ball is hit relatively flat and hard, creating a shot that is difficult to return.

> **Loop.** The loop is the reverse of the drive. The racquet skims the ball, resulting in a large amount of topspin.

> **Smash.** The goal of the smash is self-explanatory: hit the ball with so much force, overhead or semi-overhead, that the opponent can't return it. Spin is "optional."

**Defensive strokes:**

> **Push.** The push is used to keep a point alive and is considered a defensive measure (though in recreation play some "pushers" play most points this way).

> **Chop.** A chop is similar to a drop shot or a slice in regular tennis, with the object of dropping the ball over the net or putting so much backspin on the ball that it is difficult to return.

> **Block.** The block, which often comes in handy in response to a smash, simply involves putting the racquet in front of the ball so that it rebounds and you can get back into position.

> **Lob.** This is the most notorious shot in the sport of table tennis, and it is deceptive in its simplicity. To execute a lob, a defensive player first backs off the table 2.5–3 m (advanced players sometimes go 6 m or more); then, the stroke itself consists of simply lifting the ball to an enormous height before it falls back to the opponent's side of the table.

## Innovations

The equipment used in table tennis has evolved dramatically. As with other sports, manufacturers recognized the growing popularity of table tennis and began to make better and better equipment.

The paddle evolved from a simple wooden frame to a racquet that uses sheets of dimpled rubber, with an underlying sponge layer, allowing for greater spins and speed on the ball.

The actual celluloid ball was recently changed from 38 mm in size to 40 mm in size. This increased air resistance, thus slowing down the game, makes it more suitable for being televised.

## Getting Involved

Complete with provincial links and contact information for all of Canada, the Table Tennis Canada website, **www.ctta.ca**, tells you everything you need to know to get involved.

### The Racquet

Interestingly, table tennis is the only racquet sport that permits different surfaces (rubbers) on each side of the racquet. The different types of rubber offer different kinds of spin and speed.

International rules require that one side of the racquet has red rubber while the other side has black rubber. The type of rubber on each side may be different (smooth or pimpled, for example).

Most tournament players purchase the handle and blade (the wooden part of the racquet) separately from the two sheets of rubber used on each side. The rubber is often replaced (glued on) before each tournament, or sometimes even before each match.

Competition-level players are allowed to inspect their opponent's racket before playing so that they know what to expect during a match.

## Coach Attila Csaba
### Playing to Win (and to Have Fun)

Table tennis may be a recreational sport for most people, but it's a different story when the sport gets competitive. Attila Csaba, the Canadian Junior table tennis team's development coach, has been coaching table tennis for more than 15 years.

Team Canada competes in international table tennis tournaments such as the Commonwealth Games and the Summer Olympics. Coach Csaba says table tennis is the second most popular amateur sport in Canada, and it's becoming increasingly fashionable in places such as the Northwest Territories and Nunavut.

Attila thinks table tennis is great because "everybody can play, and everybody can play at a different level … it's never too late to start." In order to win, he says you need a strong mind as well as a strong body. Competition can be demanding, so good players need to be able to focus under pressure.

It's also a technical sport, so it's important to choose the equipment that best suits your style of play. "It will be challenging in the beginning," he says. "But the sport gives a lot." He's seen many young people who considered themselves to be "lazy"

become hard workers and hone their table tennis skills.

An all-around sports fan, Coach Csaba advises those who want to advance to a competitive level in a particular sport to concentrate their efforts. Competition-level table tennis starts, "when you control the ball, not when the ball controls you."

Coach Csaba's son, Bence, is now a member of the Canadian Senior National team, one of the top national squads in the world. Attila coached Bence when he was younger, so he can speak from experience as both a coach and a dad.

He urges young athletes to remain patient with their parents: "Sometimes parents can become stressed when their children compete, and they can be embarrassing or annoying," he explains. "But teenagers should remember that parents want you to do well because they are your biggest fans!"

*STAYING COMPETITIVE REQUIRES A STRONG MIND AND BODY*

# 23
# Striking/Fielding Games

**I**n striking/fielding games, a player on the defensive team delivers the ball to a player on the batting (or offensive) team. The batter attempts to strike the ball and score by running between safe areas (bases and wickets) without the ball being caught, or by reaching the safe area before the defensive team can deliver the ball to a specified area.

Striking/fielding games such as baseball and cricket have become synonymous with many cultures around the world. Often dubbed "The Great American Pastime," baseball, for example, is one of the most popular sports in North America. Similar games in Canada and the United States (stickball, slow-pitch, softball, and fastball) emerged because of baseball's popularity. Although gaining popularity in Canada, cricket tends to be the dominant striking/fielding game in countries such as Great Britain, Kenya, India, Pakistan, and Australia.

Although striking/fielding games are played around the world, they are all bound by many common rules, skills, and tactics that, if understood, can allow us to play them all successfully. Imagine travelling the world and being able to join in or watch a cricket game in a park in Australia. All this is possible if you are able to understand the basic rules, skills, and tactics of striking/fielding games.

## Striking/Fielding Games

The striking/fielding games covered in this chapter are:

➢ Baseball/Softball

➢ Cricket

## Basic Skills and Tactics

In addition to proficient locomotor skills such as running, sliding, and jumping, players must be able to send away objects and receive objects with proficiency when at bat and when in the field. Offensive players must be able to strike a moving ball.

Defensive players such as the pitcher or the bowler will make hitting the ball difficult for the batter by throwing it quickly, changing its speed (a fast pitch followed by a slower pitch), changing its location (close to the ground, close to the batter, away from the batter) or changing its flight pattern (in baseball, a curve ball compared to a fastball).

To score runs in striking/fielding games, players must be able to hit the ball into the open space and away from fielders. To prevent the batting team from scoring, fielders attempt to cover as much space as possible. Ultimately, fielders try to position themselves so that they are able to catch the ball in the air.

When a ball does hit the ground, fielders must decide on where to throw the ball. Sometimes this is an easy decision (no base runners, throw to first base). Other times, they may have to decide whether to attempt a difficult throw to get the lead runner out (and hence prevent a run being scored) or make an easier throw to a different base to help ensure an "out." On balls hit deep into the outfield, fielders must try to support each other by either backing up a teammate when they are attempting to field a ball or by providing a "cut-off point."

Baseball and cricket are examples of striking/fielding games.

## Baseball and Softball

**B**aseball is about more than just peanuts and cracker-jacks (as the old song goes). In the United States, if not Canada, it is referred to as the "national pastime." Among other things, it has influenced our language with phrases like "step up to the plate" and "out in left field."

### History

Most historians agree that baseball likely has its roots in the British game of rounders, with some influence from cricket. The game dates back to the early nineteenth century with the first set of rules being created in 1845 by Alexander Cartwright. Many of these rules are still part of the game today. The first amateur league was formed in the late 1850s in the New York area.

About a decade later, the first professional team, the Cincinnati Red Stockings, made its debut. The London Tecumsehs were the first baseball team in Canada, formed in London, Ontario, in 1868. Softball was invented in Chicago by George Hanock in the winter of 1887 as an indoor version of baseball, and it quickly gained popularity as an outdoor sport.

Today, the champion of the North American-based Major League is decided by a best-of-seven series known as the World Series. When baseball began, it was primarily played by North Americans. Its popularity has since spread to Central America, Asia, and beyond, leading to the creation of an international baseball tournament, called the World Baseball Classic, in 2006.

## How the Game Is Played

Baseball is played between two teams of nine players. The playing area is divided into the infield, a dirt or turf surface, where first, second, third, and home bases are set up in a diamond shape; and the outfield, which is the large grassy area beyond. Two lines extend from home plate, through first base on the right and third base on the left, and into the outfield. Any ball hit between these lines is "fair" and any ball hit outside of the lines is considered "foul."

A game has nine innings each with a top (or first) half and a bottom (or second) half. In the first half, one team bats until three of its players are called "out" by an umpire while the other team plays the field, then the teams switch places in the second half of the inning. After nine innings, the team that has scored the most runs wins. If the score is tied after nine innings, the game continues on until a team finishes a complete extra inning with a lead.

The rules of softball are slightly different than baseball (see page 392), but the basic concept of the game is the same.

It takes three strikes to strike out a batter and four balls to walk a batter.

## Scoring

In both baseball and softball, the ball is put into play by the pitcher who throws (or pitches) it to the batter. To keep the other team from scoring, the defensive team's aim is to get the batters out as quickly as possible. There are a few ways to do this:

> **Strike out.** The batter gets three strikes. A strike is either a swing and a miss or a pitch that's over the plate and between the batter's knees and armpits (the strike zone). If you have less than two strikes, a ball hit into foul territory is scored a strike.

> **Fly out** or **line drive.** The defensive team catches the ball before it touches the ground.

> **Force out.** The defensive team throws the ball to a fielder at a base that the runner must advance to after the ball is hit.

> **Tag out.** The defensive team touches a runner with the ball (or with the glove holding the ball).

The batter wants to hit the pitched ball into fair territory and run to at least first base before he or she is forced or tagged out. The batter can also walk to first base by getting four balls (or pitches that are outside the strike zone). Once on base, the batter becomes a runner.

To score a run, the runner needs to make his or her way around the diamond and touch all four bases, ending up at home base, before the third out is called. The terms "single," "double," and "triple" refer to the number of bases a runner was able to reach with one hit. If a player makes it all the way around the bases on one hit, or if the ball is hit past the boundary of the outfield, it's called a "home run."

When there are runners on all three bases, and the player at bat hits a home run, that's called a grand slam—the most runs you can score with one hit in baseball.

## What's the Difference?

**S**oftball is not just an easier version of baseball; they are different games, with different histories. After its invention in the late 1800s, softball became a popular alternative to baseball because it was played on a smaller field. Today, softball is played at the elite levels by both men and women across Canada and all over the world.

So what makes it different from baseball?

- A softball field is smaller—the distance between the bases, and the pitching distance, is about 20 feet less than in baseball.
- A softball is larger than a baseball, and a softball bat is shorter.
- The ball is always pitched underhand.
- Softball games have seven innings, not nine.
- Runners may not steal a base until after the ball has left the pitcher's hand.

Softball is generally divided into fast-pitch and slow-pitch. Fast-pitch is played at the international and professional level.

Slow-pitch is a more recreational version of softball: the ball is pitched at a very reduced speed so the hitting requires less power and accuracy. This makes it easier for people of varying skills to play.

## Baseball/Softball: Key Terms and Basic Skills

- ➢ **Pitching and throwing.** A good pitcher needs to throw a variety of pitches with varying speeds and extreme accuracy. Fielders need to be able to throw accurately from a variety of distances, sometimes over 100 metres.

- ➢ **Catching.** To catch well, either in the field or behind the plate, it's important to have a quick reaction time, excellent concentration, and the ability to anticipate where the ball will be hit. Communication skills among team members are crucial. A simple "I got it" or "take it" in the outfield can make all the difference between a player catching and missing a ball.

- ➢ **Batting.** Quick reflexes, fast decision-making skills, hand-eye coordination, and a precise, powerful swing are what separates a good batter from an average one. A good batter or hitter can also read the type of pitch that is coming and where the ball will cross the plate.

- ➢ **Baserunning.** Speed is important when running the bases, but good judgement, and an instinct to know when to run and when to stay, are just as crucial. A good baserunner takes advantage of defensive errors, such as dropped balls and wild pitches. He or she knows when to slide (drop to the ground when approaching a base to avoid a tag) and when to steal (advance to the next base during a pitch).

## The Defensive Players

- ➢ **Pitcher.** Stands on the pitcher's mound and throws or pitches the ball to home plate using an overhand style, with the goal of striking out the batter. In softball, the pitcher's circle is not elevated and the ball is pitched underhand.

- ➢ **Catcher.** Catches the ball and throws it back to the pitcher, unless the batter hits the ball. He or she also defends home plate when a runner tries to score a run.

- ➢ **Infielders.** Defend the bases and the infield when a runner tries to advance around the bases, and prevents ground balls from reaching the outfield. Four players do this job—first baseman, second baseman, third baseman, and shortstop (who plays between second and third base).

- ➢ **Outfielders.** Defend the outfield, fielding any balls hit into their territory. Three players do this job—left fielder, centre fielder, and right fielder.

## Getting Involved

If you would like to find out more about playing baseball or softball, visit the Baseball Canada and Softball Canada websites at **www.baseball.ca** and **www.softball.ca**.

# The World Baseball Classic
## Playing to Win (and to Have Fun)

**BASEBALL BOOSTS ITS INTERNATIONAL APPEAL**

**B**aseball has never held the same sort of international appeal as soccer or cricket, but those behind the inaugural World Baseball Classic (WBC), held in March of 2006, hope to change that.

The competition featured 16 teams from six different continents and was the first international tournament for national teams to feature professional players from the major leagues.

Team Canada was coached by former Toronto Blue Jay fan favourite Ernie Whitt (above). They finished in a three-way tie for first in their group in round one and scored a major upset along the way beating the U.S. team by a score of 8–6. Unfortunately, Canada did not make it to the second round due to a complicated tiebreaker system involving runs allowed.

Japan emerged from the tournament as champions, beating Cuba in the final game by a score of 10-6. Overall, the first World Baseball Classic was a success, with most games getting good attendance numbers. Although it's difficult to measure, it would seem that the international profile of the game was raised somewhat. Reaction worldwide seemed generally positive.

Tom Verducci, a writer for *Sports Illustrated* reported that: "more merchandise was sold in the first round than organizers projected for the entire 17-day event."

The second World Baseball Classic is due to be held in 2009 with subsequent tournaments being played every four years after that. The current plan is to have reigning champion Japan host the semi-final and final games in 2009, but that may change as the first round games held there in 2006 apparently did not draw a huge number of fans.

While the tournament is still in its early days, many hope that this initial positive response will eventually lead baseball and the WBC to command the same sort of fan hysteria more commonly associated with the World Cup in soccer.

# Cricket

**I**n North America, people tend to think cricket is a polite but boring game played by individuals dressed in white. In reality, cricket is fast and dangerous and played by people who are passionate about sport.

## History

The origins of cricket can be traced back to at least the thirteenth century. As the sport grew in popularity, a few different sets of rules were used until 1788 when the Marylebone Cricket Club in London, England, produced its first code of laws for the game, the successors of which still govern the game today.

In 1844, a match was played at the St. George Cricket Club Ground in Manhattan between the U.S. and Canada. It was the first match played between two teams representing their home nations, something that has come to be called a "test match." This test match lasted two days, with Canada emerging victorious.

The game spread around the world through English colonialism, and today, the International Cricket Council governs all international cricket. The ICC is based in Dubai and has several levels of member nations. The most elite are the 10 Test-playing nations (who play official test matches), followed by the 32 Associate Member nations (including Canada), and the 54 Affiliate Member nations.

## How the Game Is Played

Cricket is a bat-and-ball game, played by two teams of 11 players each. The object of the game is to score more runs than the opposition The length of a cricket match depends on the type of match. A short match lasts one day, with up to six hours of play. A longer match can last five days.

The match is divided into "innings," where one team bats and the other team takes the field and bowls. An inning generally consists of 40 to 50 overs per side in a one-day game, and occasionally as few as 20. An "over" is six consecutive throws of the ball to the batter by the same bowler. A test match takes five days, consisting of two innings per team, and requires at least 90 overs to be bowled per day.

Cricket is played on an oval grass field. In the centre of the field there is a rectangular area called the pitch, which is roughly 20 m long and 3 m wide. At each end of the pitch, there is a wicket, made up of three wooden posts called stumps. Across the top of the stumps are balanced two pieces of wood called bails. A bail will fall off at the slightest touch. There is a line at each end of the pitch about 91 cm from each set of stumps called the crease. Two players from the batting team are on the pitch at any one time, one at each crease, and a bowler has to bowl the ball without crossing the crease at the end.

To start the game, the captains flip a coin. The winner chooses whether his or her team will bat first or bowl first. The team batting has two batsmen positioned at either end of the pitch. The individual batting against the bowler is "the striker." The other is the "non-striker." The team that is bowling is positioned on the field, and is said to be "fielding." The bowler bowls the ball to the striker overhand. Bowling this way can make the ball bounce at crazy angles, so it's really difficult to hit, and sometimes difficult to avoid being hit. The wicket-keeper stands behind the wicket at the batting end and the other nine players cover the field. Cricket has over 200 fielding positions, and a large part of the game is the captain's strategy in deciding where to position the players depending on the skill of the bowler.

## Scoring

The batters are trying to score runs, stop the ball from hitting the wicket, and trying not to get out. Every time a run is scored, the batters change ends.

One of the ways to score a run is for the striker to hit the ball to an unoccupied part of the field so that the two batters have time to run to the crease at the opposite end of the pitch. They keep running back and forth so long as they can do so without the fielding team getting the ball back to the pitch and knocking the bails off the wicket.

You score four runs when the striker hits the ball and it rolls to the fence surrounding the field. You can score six runs if you hit the ball over the fence without bouncing it. Scoring runs may sound easy, but the fielding team is always trying to prevent the batsmen from scoring and to get them out.

A cricket match can last up to five days.

## Cricket: Key Terms and Basic Skills

➤ **Bowling.** Bowling well requires throwing the ball with a straight arm at the wicket. There are two types of bowlers, fast bowlers, who throw the ball in excess of 125 km per hour, and spin bowlers, who are able to put spin on the ball to make it move in different directions.

➤ **Batting.** There are batsmen with various batting skills on each team—those that can play fast bowlers, and those that can master the "spinners." All of them can hit the ball at unpredictable angles so the other team won't know what's coming.

➤ **Fielding.** Players in the field need excellent reflexes, quick reaction time, and the ability to throw accurately. Plus they must not be afraid of catching a hard, fast ball with their bare hands.

➤ **Wicket-keeping.** This position is similar to the catcher in baseball and its main responsibility is to catch the ball when it is bowled or thrown by a fielder. Unlike the other fielders, wicket-keepers can wear gloves.

## Some of the Ways to Get Out in Cricket

➤ **Caught.** A player on the fielding team catches the ball hit off the bat before it touches the ground.

➤ **Failure to defend the wicket.** This occurs when the bowler hits a bail off the stumps with the ball (bowled); or the wicket-keeper breaks the stumps while holding the ball when the striker is out of the crease (stumped).

➤ **Run out.** The stumps are broken while the batters are running between the creases.

➤ **Illegal defence of the wicket.** An example would be Leg Before Wicket (LBW)—when the umpire believes the ball would have hit the stump, but the batter's pads were in the way.

## Getting Involved

If you think you would like to try cricket but have no idea how to get started, go to the Canada Cricket website. It is filled with the latest news, articles/opinions, coaching information, and—most importantly—contact information for provincial associations throughout Canada. Visit the website at **www.canadacricket.com**.

Canada Cricket makes getting involved and finding out about cricket very simple. It even has a contact email address to which you can send new information to be added to its website.

---

**Cricket Lingo**

Here is a sampling of terms you might hear on the cricket pitch:

- **Out for a duck.** What a member of the batting team is said to be if he or she is out without scoring any runs.

- **Out for a golden duck.** When a batter is out for a duck while facing only one delivery from the bowler.

- **Maiden over.** The term used when a bowler completes an over without any runs being scored from it.

- **Nightwatchman.** A batsman who comes in to bat out of order towards the end of a day's play in a multi-day game, in order to "protect" better batters.

- **Rabbit.** A player (almost invariably a bowler, but sometimes a wicket-keeper) who is a very poor batter.

- **Century.** Also known as a "ton," when a single batter scores 100 runs.

- **Hat Trick.** When a bowler manages to get three batters out on three consecutive balls.

# The Cricket World Cup
## Playing to Win (and to Have Fun)

**C**ricket may not be widely played in North America, but that hasn't stopped the Cricket World Cup, held every four years, from being hugely popular elsewhere.

The Cricket World Cup, the premier championship of one-day cricket, is organized by the International Cricket Council. All Test-playing nations compete (Australia, England, South Africa, West Indies, New Zealand, India, Pakistan, Sri Lanka, Zimbabwe and Bangladesh), as well as a few other qualifying nations.

Cricket has long been popular throughout the British Commonwealth, but it took some time for the World Cup to establish itself. Starting in 1975, the first three tournaments were held in England, which was the only participating country at the time with the resources to host such an event. The tournament first moved in 1987, when it was played in India and Pakistan. Since then World Cup games have taken place in Australia, New Zealand, Sri Lanka, South Africa, Zimbabwe, and Kenya, and, in 2007, the West Indies.

Canada's team first participated in the men's tournament in 1979, and have qualified twice more since then.

*CRICKET IS A WORLD-CLASS SPORT THAT IS ONLY GETTING BIGGER*

In the 2003 World Cup, Canada's captain John Davison (left) scored a century (100 runs) over just 67 balls, a World Cup record.

Canada's moderate success in the tournament is a sign of cricket's growing popularity in North America. The United States even lobbied to host the 2007 tournament in order to further promote and develop cricket in the U.S.

Australia's team is the current world champion, having emerged victorious from the 2003 World Cup after beating India in the final. This is Australia's third World Cup title to date, more than any other nation.

There is also a Women's Cricket World Cup and it has actually been around for longer than the men's tournament. Like its male counterpart, the Australian women's team have won more often than any other, winning five times since the inaugural women's tournament in England in 1973.

# 24
# Target Games

**T**wo target games—bowling and golf—are among the most popular sporting activities chosen by Canadian adolescents aged 12-19. Other well-known target games include curling, archery, billiards, bocce, croquet, darts, horseshoe pitching, shuffleboard, and lawn bowling.

In all target games, players score points by projecting an object with accuracy towards a target (rolling a bowling ball towards bowling pins). Out of the four game categories, target games have the least simultaneously occurring action. Players can often focus on making their shots without having to worry about interference by opponents (as in invasion games) or having to collect or return a moving object (as in net/wall and striking/fielding games).

This is not to say that target games are easy to play. Anyone who has played or watched golf knows that it is not easy to hit a golf ball so that it avoids obstacles (trees, water, and sand traps), and eventually ends up in a hole that measures just under 11 cm.

Target games have been, and continue to be, popular among people of all ages. Not only do they require a high degree of skill, but they also challenge players to make good decisions when planning their shots. Many skills learned by playing target games can also be useful in other sports.

## Target Games

The target games covered in this chapter are:

➤ Curling

➤ Golf

## Basic Skills and Tactics

Target games require players to send an object away with a high degree of accuracy. Players can do so with their hand (deliver a curling rock, roll a bocce ball) or with an implement (hit the cue ball with a pool cue, strike a ball with a croquet mallet). Sometimes, this involves a clear shot at the target, such as in five-pin bowling or darts.

Other times, it might mean having to take an indirect pathway so that the object either bounces off another object (hitting the cue ball off the side rail in billiards) or making the object curl around an obstacle by putting some spin on it (an in- or out-turn in curling).

In target games, the athletic focus is on players mastering the best stance to send the object away effectively. Target games can still work well as team sports—players must combine their efforts to achieve victory.

In some target games, such as golf, bowling, and darts, players do not attempt to prevent their opponents from scoring. In others, such as curling, lawn bowling, and shuffleboard, strategic play is important. Players can prevent the other team from scoring by either setting up guards that protect previous shots that are in scoring positions, or by knocking away their opponent's objects that are close to the target.

Golf is one of the most popular target games.

## Curling

**C**urling is a game of finesse, extreme precision, and strategic thinking—it has rightly been called "chess on ice." The game is played by sliding large granite stones down a sheet of ice. When given a clockwise or counter-clockwise rotation, the projectile follows a reasonably predictable curving or "curling" trajectory, and this has led to the game's unique name.

### History

Who invented curling? Was it the Scots, or immigrants from Continental Europe? Evidence can be presented to prove the case for either lineage. The Scots first formalized the rules and created the game's traditions, including much of its lingo. By the eighteenth century, Scotland had become a hotbed for the chilly game. Scottish immigrants brought their curling fanaticism with them to the New World, especially to snow-bound Canada.

The first Canadian curling club opened in Montreal, in 1807, and became the first organized sporting club in North America. Today, curling clubs are important social institutions in many Canadian communities, especially in Western Canada.

## How the Game Is Played

Eight "ends," or rounds, of curling constitute a match. Each team has four players—the lead, the second, the third, and the skip.

Each curling lane, or "sheet," is 44.5 m (146 feet) from back line to back line. In Canada, its width is 4.3 m (14 feet, 2 inches) whereas international sheets are 4.7 m (15 feet, 7 inches) wide. The centre line runs the length of the surface and acts as a reference for "reading ice" and predicting the curl of the rocks.

There is also a "hog line," a "side line," and a "back line." In order for a rock to be in play, it must be completely over the hog line, not touching a sideline and not completely over the back line. The small footholds—or "hacks"—at each end of the rink is where the rock thrower pushes with his or her foot to begin the shot.

At the scoring end of the rink, the "tee" line crosses the width of the ice and passes through the centre point of the four painted circles, also known as the "house," which is the scoring area. The tee itself is a small hole in the centre of the house. When the distance between two opposing rocks and the centre of the house is too close to determine by sight, a "measure" is inserted in the tee to make the call.

The surface of the ice itself is pebbled, and its purpose is to reduce the amount of the sliding surface of the rock that is in contact with the ice. If the ice were not pebbled, it would be much harder to get a stone from one end of the ice to the other.

So how do you "throw" these rocks? First, step into the hack and squat down. Using your curling broom as a balance, push your stone slightly forward on the ice, and then pull the rock back towards you in a backswing. Now, bring the stone forward and use your foot to push off from the hack—you will end up sliding down the ice with your broom in one hand and a rock in the other.

The last part of the delivery is the release of the stone, which can be quite tricky. The type of turn that is placed on the handle is directed by the skip. The turn will influence the direction in which the stone will curl. Once the stone is released, two teammates will use their brooms to sweep the stone's path, gliding along and sweeping the ice with their brooms. This makes the rock travel farther and/or makes it curl. Good sweepers can affect the stone's eventual positioning on the ice.

## Scoring

Players throw two rocks in each end, alternating with the player on the other team who is playing the same position, until all players have thrown their rocks. Points are scored by getting more of your stones closer to the centre of the rings than those of your opponent. For example, if the two rocks closest to the centre are yours, you score two points. If the closest rock to the centre is your opponents' and yours is the next closest, they score one point.

Only one team can score points in an end; if no rocks finish up in the house, no points are awarded.

Curling is growing in popularity amongst Canadian youth.

## Curling: Key Terms and Basic Skills

➤ **Bonspiel.** A curling competition usually played over a weekend.

➤ **Brick.** A slang term for the curling stone.

➤ **Burned stone.** A stone in motion which has been touched by a member of either team.

➤ **Button.** The one-foot circle at the centre of the house.

➤ **Chip.** To hit only a small portion of a stone.

➤ **Counter.** Any stone within or touching the rings, which is closer to the centre of the rings than any of the opposition's stones.

➤ **Dead handle.** A stone that is released with little or no rotation of the handle.

➤ **End.** A portion of a curling game that is completed when each team has thrown eight stones and the score has been decided. A game usually consists of 8 or 10 ends.

➤ **Flipped out.** A stone that is released with poor technique, causing it to be wide of the skip's broom.

➤ **Guard.** A stone that is placed in a position so that it may potentially protect another stone.

➤ **Hacks.** The footholds at each end of the ice from which the stone is delivered.

➤ **Hard, hurry hard, harder.** A skip's commands to tell the sweepers to sweep vigorously.

➤ **Pebble.** A fine spray of water applied to a sheet of curling ice before play.

➤ **Reading ice.** The skill by which the skip anticipates the amount a stone will curl, according to ice conditions.

➤ **Rink.** A team. Also the building in which the game is played.

## Curling Equipment

To curl, the participant needs specialized equipment. For example, shoes are usually insulated to keep players' feet warm. Curlers will wear one shoe with a slippery sole surface (for sliding down the ice) and the other with a grip on the sole (for propelling down the ice).

Curling brooms are generally made of synthetic material, or hog or horse hair, and are usually called push brooms, or brushes. In the past, straw brooms (or corn brooms) were used but most clubs have banned them due to the debris they can leave on the ice. Some players stick to the Scottish tradition and use corn brooms for delivery, but most agree that push brooms are easier to use and more effective.

The curling stone is made from granite and has a top weight of 19.96 kilograms (44 pounds). A plastic handle is attached to the top of the stone. These handles can be engraved with numbers so that each stone can be identified.

## Getting Involved

If ever there was a sport that lets you ease your way in gently, curling is it. The Canadian Curling Association's website has a "learn to curl" flash demonstration (**www.curling.ca**). It is also well equipped with sections on youth curling, school curling, and, of course, plenty of news-worthy curling updates for the curling fanatic.

The good thing about curling is that you can start at any age, and continue to play for many years after. You can locate the provincial affiliate on the Canadian Curling Association's website, which will lead you to clubs in your area.

## Brad Gushue
### Playing to Win (and to Have Fun)

**NEWFOUNDLANDERS ARE FIRST ON THE PODIUM AND IN PROVINCE'S HEART**

The Canadian men's curling team had been playing well throughout the 2006 Winter Olympics in Turin, Italy. The five men, led by 25-year-old Brad Gushue, had made it to the gold medal match and were leading by one point when the game was suddenly blown wide open in the sixth end. Gushue's team scored an impressive six points, giving it a seven-point lead over Finland. The game continued on until the eighth end when Finland conceded the match, realizing the deficit would be too great to overcome.

It was an emotional day for Gushue who called his mother Maureen only moments after the team's victory. She had been unable to attend the games in Turin as she had recently undergone chemotherapy back in Gushue's hometown of St. John's, Newfoundland.

Despite making changes to his team shortly before the Olympic trials in 2005, everything fell into place in Turin and Gushue, along with Jamie Korab, Mark Nichols, and alternate Mike Adam, became the first Newfoundlanders ever to win Olympic gold (the fifth man on the team, veteran Russ Howard, hails from New Brunswick). Perhaps they were aided in their quest by the support of the incredibly enthusiastic Newfoundlanders back home where the Provincial Government allowed schools to close one hour before the final game was due to be shown on television.

The Canadian men did well in the qualifying round, finishing the round robin in a tie for second place. They had another big end in their semifinal match against the U.S. when they were able to turn a one point lead into a six point lead with five points scored in the ninth end.

The Olympic triumph may have been a first for both the team and for Newfoundland, but Gushue was certainly no stranger to victory; between 1995 and 2001, Gushue won six provincial junior curling titles as well as the national championship. It's no surprise that he was later able to represent Canada at the Olympics and make his country proud.

# Golf

**E**ven the most devoted golf enthusiast will tell you that golf can be a very frustrating game. It is sometimes referred to as "a long walk, spoiled." Golf is a game that requires intense concentration, great eye-hand coordination, and a steady swing. To be good, you must be able to do all three consistently.

## History

The origins of golf go back a long way. It originated in Scotland and has been played there since the late seventeenth century. The game quickly spread from Scotland through Europe and into the Americas, and has continued to be popular ever since.

The Royal Montreal Golf Club was founded in 1873, making it not only the oldest course in Canada but also the oldest course in North America.

Golf was recognized as an Olympic sport in 1900, and has even been played in outer space. In 1971, astronaut Alan Shephard hit a golf ball on the moon. His action was televised to an audience of millions around the world.

## How the Game Is Played

A full round of golf consists of 18 holes. Players begin each hole from the "teeing ground" by placing their ball on a wooden or plastic tee which elevates it and makes it easier to hit. Players aim for the area around the hole, which is called the "green," while trying to avoid hitting their ball into thick grass (the "rough"), trees, sand, or water.

"Par" is the number of shots that a skilled player should take to put the ball in the hole. Par is usually determined by the distance from the tee to the green—the farther the distance, the greater the par. Finishing a hole one stroke under par is called a "birdie," two strokes under is called an "eagle." Finishing one shot over par is called a "bogey," two shots over is a "double bogey," and so on. In golf, the lower your score, the better.

Each golfer begins play on the first hole and is allowed any number of practice swings. During the game, the ball must be played where and as it lies. As a courtesy, players should attempt to repair any damage to the course caused by their clubs and balls, and rake their footprints from sand traps.

The ball that lies furthest from the hole is played first. Every player must put his or her ball into the hole. The player with the least number of strokes on each hole tees off first for the next hole.

Two main types of hazards wait on the course to thwart a golfer's perfect game—sand and water. A "bunker" is a hazard consisting of a depression that has been filled with sand. They are most commonly found near the green, but can also show up in or alongside fairways (the area between the tee and the green). A water hazard can be a pond, the ocean, or any other body of water. If you hit your ball into one, you may play it (and risk getting soaked), or you can opt to stay dry and play a new ball, with a one-stroke penalty.

The lighter coloured grass (where the hole is located) is called the "green," the rest is the "fairway."

## The Clubs

There are three main types of golf clubs. The angle of each club head determines the loft and distance of the shot—the higher the number, the higher the loft.

> **Woods.** The wood is the longest club and is used to hit the ball the longest distances. It is broad from front to back with a bulbous head made of wood or metal. The number one wood, the driver, delivers the longest distance of any club in the bag.

> **Irons.** These have narrow heads and come in the greatest variety—low-numbered irons hit almost as far as woods, while high-numbered irons often are used for more precise shots. Wedges are a type of iron used in the sand or rough to lift the ball high out of the hazard with a little spin so that it does not roll much when it lands.

> **Putter.** This is a light metal club designed to guide the golfer's aim during short, precise shots on the green.

## Tiger Proof

The evolution of Tiger Woods from child prodigy to the game's brightest star in the late 1990s not only nudged golf to the front of the sports sections, it dramatically changed the future of golf course design.

Woods combined fantastic driving with uncanny accuracy and made a shambles out of some of the world's best and most prestigious golf courses.

Course architects responded by lengthening holes, narrowing fairways, adding extra hazards, and making a variety of other changes designed to create more challenging courses. The media dubbed this process "Tiger-proofing."

## Golf: Key Terms and Basic Skills

> **Driving.** A drive is the first shot. The object is to hit the ball a great distance with accuracy. Good golfers visualize the golf club travelling through the ball, not at it.

> **Pitching.** This is a relatively short, lofted shot designed for the ball to land softly and not roll much. This is often used when trying to shoot over a sand trap. With a proper follow-through, the ball will be carried out with a spray of sand.

> **Putting.** Accomplished players line the ball up directly under their eyes, feet shoulder-width apart or wider, and in line with the hole. The ball does not leave the ground, and should have lost most of its momentum by the time it reaches the hole.

## Golf Lingo—Talk like a Pro!

> **Back nine.** The last 9 holes of an 18-hole golf course

> **Caddy.** Someone who carries a player's bag of clubs and/or advises a player with the details of the course

> **Hacker.** An unskilled golfer whose technique often results in large divots being left on the fairway

> **Divot.** A portion of turf that is ripped out of the ground by the head of the club during a swing

> **Fairway.** The closely mown area between the tee and the green

> **Follow-through.** The continuation of a golf stoke after contact is made with the ball

> **Fore!** Yelled loudly to warn other golfers of an incoming ball

> **Front nine.** The first 9 holes of an 18-hole golf course

> **Gallery.** A group of spectators at any golf event

> **Grip.** The handle of, and method of holding, a golf club

> **Handicap.** The average difference between a player's scores and a set standard, as calculated by a specified formula

> **Hole in one.** A score of 1 on any hole

> **Sweet spot.** The centre of mass of the club, indicated by the solid spot on the clubface

## Getting Involved

Getting involved in golf used to be more difficult than it is today. With the rise of public courses, golf has changed, and now the vast majority of players do not need to be members of any particular club.

Think about caddying to learn from the pros, or, if you can get your hands on some golf clubs, you can practise shooting balls on your own. Check out **www.rcga.org** for more tips.

## Mike Weir
### Playing to Win (and to Have Fun)

**DETERMINATION AND STRENGTH OF CHARACTER HELP WIN THE DAY**

Born and raised in Bright's Grove—a small Ontario town near Sarnia—Mike Weir started swinging a golf club at age 11. By age 16, he won the Canadian Juvenile Championship and by 18, he won the Canadian Junior Championship.

Weir soon moved into the adult ranks, winning competitions both nationally and internationally, and setting new Canadian records along the way. He rose to the top with unstoppable force until he was struck with a disappointing year in 2002, finishing forty-second in the world rankings. True to his determined nature, Weir bounced back and started off his 2003 year with a bang, placing ninth at the Phoenix Open and first at the Bob Hope Classic—placements that let him walk away with $922, 000.

It looked as though everything was in place for Weir, until his competition finishes started showing reflections of his disappointing 2002 year. Leading up to the Masters—golf's biggest event—Weir had four disastrous finishes. Yet, Weir pulled it together in the end. His performance at the 2003 Master's Competition threw him into sports history as he became both the first Canadian and the first left-handed player ever to win the Master's.

With all of the emotional ups and downs and uncertainty, the strength of character that lives within Mike Weir certainly shone brightly that day.

Weir has lived in the U.S.A. since attending university in Utah; he now lives there with his wife and two daughters. However, despite the governor of Utah having declared May 12 (Weir's birthday) "Mike Weir Day," Weir identifies himself as Canadian, just as his Canadian fans do.

When he launched his own line of golf accessories, he chose to do so in Toronto. Weir has been called an inspiration to Canadians and to young people. Check out the website of one of his biggest fans (**www.mikeweir.ca**) as Mike has been known to stop by there himself.

# 25
# Body Management Activities

*It is exercise alone that supports the spirits, and keeps the mind in vigor.*

**Marcus Tullius Cicero**

Orator and statesman of ancient Rome during the first century BC

**B**ody management activities develop body rhythm, creativity, sequencing, and stability. Most people engage in body management activities to have fun and experience improvement to their health. Some turn to them for spiritual gratification, others get involved for the sheer sake of competing or seeing what their bodies can do.

Many professional and recreational athletes use body management activities to develop various elements of fitness that are dominant in their sport. For example, to increase the strength of their abdominal and deep back muscles, they incorporate Pilates or yoga into their training regimes. Those looking to develop balance and coordination enroll in dance or gymnastics. In fact, some professional athletes take ballet to increase muscular endurance, strength, balance, flexibility, and coordination.

If you are interested in doing these activities outside of your classroom, refer to the "Getting Involved" heading that appears after each individual sport or activity. Listed there is the web address of each sport or activity's governing body—check it out and get active.

## Body Management Activities

The body management activities covered in this chapter are:

- ➢ Track and Field
- ➢ Wrestling/Combative Sports
- ➢ Gymnastics
- ➢ Aquatics
- ➢ Aerobics
- ➢ Yoga and Pilates
- ➢ Dance

## Basic Skills and Tactics

Sports and activities in the body management category each have their unique skill set. Unlike target, net/wall, striking/fielding, or invasion/territory games, they don't have common sending and receiving skills, and few have implements such as "pucks" or "balls" that are used to score goals or accumulate points. Most are not team sports and do not require much specialized equipment. However, because many different sports fall into this category, it is difficult to generalize.

The skills involved in track include running, sprinting, and hurdling. The field skills include throwing weighted objects of varying sizes and shapes as far as you can. The "long," "high," and "triple" jumps, along with pole vaulting, are other field skills.

Wrestling/combative sports and gymnastics require good tumbling and landing skills. Wrestlers grab and throw their opponents to the mat, while gymnasts perform complicated tumbling feats in combination. Wrestlers receive points for throwing or "pinning" their opponent to the ground. In gymnastics, scoring is determined by a panel of judges that look for mandatory skill elements that are put together in sequence.

Aquatics are more than just swimming. Synchronized swimming, backstroke, the butterfly, and diving require dramatically different skills. At national and international competitions, swimmers rely on technology to give them a tactical advantage. The invention of full body swimsuits keeps the swimmers more buoyant and reduces drag, which enables them to go faster.

The activities most difficult to categorize are aerobics, yoga, Pilates, and dance. Although dance and aerobics competitions exist, all of these activities remain, for the most part, non-competitive. While these activities are accessible to beginners, they offer rewards for participants who take the time to gain skill and develop their strength, flexibility, and body awareness.

Whether in a race or on your own, running is a great body management activity.

# Track and Field

**M**any would say that track and field closely resembles the "athletic ideal"—participants run, jump, or throw in an effort to beat the clock, reach the finish line first, or go the greatest distance without the benefit of space-age gear.

The original Olympic sport competitions in Greece were comprised of foot races. Today, the International Olympic Committee recognizes Athletics (which includes track, field, road, and combined events) as one of its competition categories.

## History

The first recorded race was a sprint of about 92 metres that took place around 776 BC. Records show that, from very early times, local fairs in Europe included a good number of running, throwing, and jumping events. Track and field competitions gained greater prominence with the beginning of the modern Olympic movement in 1896. Competitions initially were open to men only; women started participating in 1932 when the Olympic Games were held in Los Angeles.

As the Olympic movement grew, countries began forming national athletics federations, usually comprised of provincial, state, or regional associations. In 1912, seventeen national organizations formed the International Association of Athletics Federations (IAAF), an organization that now includes 211 national track and field federations worldwide.

## Track and Field Events

Track and field is an umbrella term for a variety of athletic events in which participants:

➢ Run or walk over set distances, either short or long

➢ Heave various projectiles (e.g. shot, javelin, or discus)

➢ Jump for distance or over bars that are set at pre-established heights

Combined events, as the name indicates, are competitions that combine two or more of the above. The Olympic road events include the marathon and race walks of various lengths. Field events include both jumping and throwing competitions.

Running, jumping, and throwing are the skills used most in track and field.

## Track Events

Track events are categorized as follows:

➢ **Sprints.** Short-distance races of 100, 200, and 400 metres

➢ **Middle-distance runs.** Races of 800 and 1,500 metres

➢ **Long-distance runs.** Races of 5,000 and 10,000 metres

➢ **Hurdles.** Each runner leaps over a set number of barriers, in races of 100 metres and 400 metres for women, and 110 metres and 400 metres for men

➢ **Relays.** Races in which four runners must each run a distance of 100 metres (4 × 100) or 400 metres (4 × 400)

➢ **Steeplechase.** A 3,000-metre race for men in which participants must clear several hurdles as well as one water jump per lap

Students competing in these events will likely do so at reduced distances.

## Field Jumping Events

➢ **Long jump.** Each participant sprints to a line, jumps, and lands in a sandpit.

➢ **Triple jump.** Each participant sprints to a line, takes three successive jumps, and lands in a sandpit.

➢ **High jump.** Each participant sprints up to an H-shaped apparatus—a horizontal bar supported by two upright poles—and attempts to jump over the bar without touching it, and then lands on a large mat.

➢ **Pole vault.** Carrying a long pole made of carbon polymers, the athlete sprints down the runway and plants one end of the pole into an H-shaped hole. The pole is used to vault his or her body over a bar (2 to 6 metres high) before landing on a large mat.

## Track and Field

In addition to the pure track and field competitions, there are two combined events, both of which take place over a two-day period, and several road events.

The combined events are:

- **The decathlon.** Open only to men, in which the participant competes in 10 events—long jump, high jump, discus, shot put, javelin, pole vault, 100-metre sprint, 110-metre hurdles, and 400- and 1,500-metre races.

- **The heptathlon.** Open only to women, in which the participant competes in seven events—long jump, high jump, shot put, javelin, and 100-, 200-, and 400-metre sprints.

The road events are:

- **The marathon.** A race of 42.195 kilometres (26.22 miles).

- **Race walks.** 20 kilometres and 50 kilometres for men, and 20 kilometres for women.

## Field Throwing Events

In all throwing events, participants throw an object as far as possible within a designated area:

> **Javelin.** The participant runs up to a line and throws a javelin (a long, metal-tipped shaft made of metal or wood).

> **Discus.** The participant holds a metal-rimmed wooden plate (the discus), spins his or her body around while moving to the front of the throwing circle, and then releases the discus.

> **Hammer throw.** The participant picks up the hammer (a heavy metal ball) by the handle on the end of the wire cable that is attached to it, then completes several revolutions to gain momentum before releasing the cable to throw the hammer.

> **Shot put.** The participant throws (or puts) a heavy metal ball (the shot) using an upward pushing motion.

## The Rules

The rules of the various track and field events vary widely between levels and countries. While the specifics change from place to place, rules always govern how each competition area is to be set up, how participants must conduct themselves in every stage of a competition, and the kind of equipment and clothing that is required for each event.

The rules are intended to encourage sportsmanlike behaviour and to ensure that no competitor has an unfair advantage. Here are some examples of how rules are used to enhance competition:

> **False Starts.** A quick reaction time is crucial, especially in sprints, and rules vary on how many false starts are allowed. To minimize excessive disruptions, some events will only allow one false start without penalty, the second results in disqualification even if it is committed by a different athlete. This helps to ensure that everyone in the race is as careful as possible.

> **Lanes.** Track and lane sizes may vary but there must be enough room in each lane for athletes to be able to compete without interfering with competitors. In some long distance races, runners are permitted to leave their lanes as long as they don't bump into anyone else, while in other races, they are required to stay in their lanes until a certain point in the race.

## Getting Involved

Getting involved in track and field is easy. You have likely had exposure to the sport in school. You're probably doing some track and field in gym class—you may even be on your school's track and field team.

To find further opportunities, check out your province's track and field association or visit **www.sportingcanada.com/tf** to see where you can go with the sport after high school.

# Jeff Adams
## Playing to Win (and to Have Fun)

*AN ATHLETE READY TO BATTLE ANY CHALLENGE*

Jeff Adams is a three-time Olympian, five-time Paralympian, and six-time World Champion wheelchair racer. In addition to having been an actor and a CBC reporter and commentator, Jeff is also a motivational speaker—visiting schools, clubs, and businesses—and serves as an activist for the disabled community.

In 2002, Jeff climbed all 1,776 steps of the CN Tower in Toronto, in a specially modified wheelchair, to increase awareness of accessibility issues and to raise funds for a school outreach program. Two years later, Jeff used the international media presence at the 2004 Summer Olympic Games in Athens to call attention to the talents of athletes living with disabilities by climbing to the summit of the Acropolis in a wheelchair in about 20 minutes.

In Athens, Jeff competed in the Olympic wheelchair race exhibition events as well as the official Paralympic events. Paralympic exhibitions have been a part of the Olympics since 1984, offering spectators a taste of the Paralympic Games that take place in the host city a few weeks after the Olympics. However, the 2004 Games gave more attention to wheelchair events, scheduling them among able-bodied track and field events.

Although Jeff still supports the Paralympics, he is Canada's most vocal (and controversial) advocate of integrating disabled and able-bodied sports. He believes that the only way wheelchair racing will truly be recognized as its own sport, not just as an alternative to foot racing, is to make it an official Olympic event and to open the competition up to everyone, disabled and able-bodied athletes alike.

Other disabled athletes disagree with Jeff; wheelchair sports are often the most attention-grabbing events of the Paralympic Games, so if the top competitors go to the Olympics, the Paralympics may lose some strength.

Jeff isn't deterred. He has competed against able-bodied athletes in wheelchairs in numerous races. "It's a level playing field," he told the Toronto Star. "Sometimes they win. Sometimes they don't. It's whoever is in shape."

# Wrestling/Combative Sports

**C**ontrary to popular belief, the goal in combative sports is not to hurt or humiliate. Wrestling is the premier combative sport—you not only exercise your body, you learn how to compete in a true, sporting manner in one of the oldest of combative activities.

## History

Wrestling made its Olympic debut in the eighth century BC, when it was a much more violent, military form of combat than it is today.

In the 1896 Olympics, when organizers were looking for sports with roots in antiquity, Greco–Roman wrestling was an obvious choice. However, the style of wrestling that took place in the 1896 Olympic Games was essentially "Freestyle" wrestling (it was more violent and had fewer rules than the "Greco–Roman" style).

The first, true wrestling competition took place in 1888, followed by the first international competition for Greco–Roman wrestling in the 1904 Olympics in St. Louis.

## Freestyle and Greco-Roman Wrestling

Internationally, wrestling is governed by the Fédération Internationale des Luttes Associés (FILA). There are a number of wrestling styles recognized by FILA, the most common being Greco–Roman and freestyle, the two styles found on the Olympic program. Men compete in both styles while women compete in a modified freestyle competition that prohibits certain types of holds:

> **Freestyle wrestling.** This style of wrestling originated during the expansion of the Roman Empire (around 125 BC), making it one of the oldest sports in history. Freestyle is the world's most popular style of wrestling. Holds below the waist and the use of your legs to grab your opponent are permitted.

> **Greco–Roman wrestling.** Developed during the Napoleonic period by the French, Greco–Roman wrestling follows the same principles as freestyle, with the essential difference that the emphasis is on the upper body. You cannot hold below the belt or trip your opponent, nor can you use either your own legs or your opponent's legs in holds.

Most combative sports ensure that competitors are evenly matched by either size or ability.

## Other Styles of Wrestling

There are many cultural styles and forms based on wrestling, such as Judo (a Japanese style of wrestling using mainly throws and chokes) and Schwingen (a Swedish style). Other cultural styles include Mongolian, Turkish, Scottish, and Iranian.

## Competition Rules

At the high school level, wrestling is a sport that is practised during the winter months. Because of the very physical nature of this sport, fair competition can take place only when competitors are within certain logically divided groups.

Wrestling separates its competitors by weight. In Ontario, for example, there are 16 weight classes for boys ranging from 38 kg to an unlimited class where the minimum weight is 95 kg. There are 13 weight classes for girls ranging from 41 kg to an unlimited class with a minimum weight of 84 kg.

Currently, wrestling matches consist of three rounds, which last two minutes each with thirty seconds in between each round to towel off. You must win two of the three rounds or pin your opponent (in which case the match ends at that point regardless of the score).

A pin occurs when you or your opponent's shoulders are forced to the mat. A match can be stopped, as well, if a wrestler cries out while being pinned. If the official feels that the defensive wrestler is in pain or in danger of serious injury, he or she can stop the bout.

A wrestler's coach can also ask that the action be stopped if it seems that such a request is in the best interest of his or her athlete.

## Sumo Wrestling

**W**restling has been a major sport in Asia for at least 20 centuries. Sumo wrestling is perhaps the most well-known style of Asian wrestling. It is Japan's national sport and the wrestlers are national heroes.

In Sumo wrestling, there are no weight classes in the same way that Olympic wrestling has weight categories. Sumo wrestlers often weigh in at 150 – 200 kg.

In Japan, professional Sumo wrestlers lead highly controlled lifestyles and are encouraged to be overweight. As a result, they have a much shorter life expectancy and are prone to diabetes, high blood pressure, heart attacks, liver problems, and arthritis.

The winner of a Sumo match is determined when a competitor is either thrown to the ground or tossed off the mat.

The matches themselves usually last only a few seconds. In rare cases, they may take up to a minute.

## Wrestling: Point Scoring

The first point system was developed in 1941 by Art Griffith, a collegiate coach at Oklahoma State. The scoring system has evolved to foster certain aspects of the game—for example, more offensive action and less defensive stalling. The following are a few examples of how points can be awarded:

> ➤ 1 point for a takedown with no back exposure (the wrestler being scored on lands on his or her stomach)

> ➤ 3 points for a takedown with back exposure (wrestler being scored on exposes his or her back to the mat)

> ➤ 5 points (maximum points awarded) for a throw of grand amplitude in an arching manner

As with all combative sports, you need to concentrate and focus on technique above pure aggression to master this sport. "Wrestling teaches self-control and pride," observed Dan Gable, a champion wrestler and distinguished coach.

## Why Wrestle?

Wrestling builds speed, endurance, strength, flexibility, and coordination. In other words, wrestling teaches you to understand your body and allows you to gain a higher level of control over its actions.

In combative sports, the goal is not to hurt or humiliate your opponent. The point is to value and respect your opponent, in victory and in defeat, for allowing you to practise your moves and for teaching you some new ones.

## Women and Wrestling

Wrestling has grown in popularity over the past few years. What's more, women's presence in the sport of wrestling is growing stronger by the day. The 2006 OFSAA wrestling championship hosted 800 athletes, split evenly between the sexes.

Women's wrestling finally made its Olympic debut at the 2004 Summer Games in Athens, Greece. Team Canada participated with four women's freestyle medal hopefuls. Canadian Tonya Verbeek took silver in the 55-kilogram division.

## Getting Involved

You can join your school's team, or, if they don't have one, ask if you can start one.

Also, you can visit the Canadian Amateur Wrestling Association's website at **www.wrestling.ca** to find a list of provincial/territorial wrestling associations. Contact them to find out how you can get involved in wrestling in your area.

# Daniel Igali
## Playing to Win (and to Have Fun)

After wrestler Daniel Igali won the gold medal at the 2000 Olympics in Sydney, Australia, he gently spread the Canadian flag on the mat, jogged around it, and then fell to his knees to kiss it. Fans were touched by Daniel's patriotism, but most of them had no idea how far he had come to revel in this triumph, or how much the Canadian flag meant to him.

Daniel grew up in a mud hut in Eniwari, Nigeria. Although his parents were educated professionals, life was difficult for his family in the military-ruled country. Daniel decided to wrestle at a young age—the sport is deeply rooted in Ijaw tribal culture. By 16 years old, he was winning local tournaments. Without tuition money for university, he took a job with a wrestling team and won gold medals in two African championships.

In August 1994, Daniel's team came to Victoria, BC, to compete in the Commonwealth Games. He was then 20 years old and captain of his team. After winning only one match, he was forced to withdraw from the competition with a serious back injury.

While convalescing in Victoria, Daniel fell in love with the clean, friendly city. He decided not to return home, but this was a difficult and dangerous choice—he would have faced arrest back home if Canada had rejected his refugee status.

Daniel struggled to build a new life on his own in Canada. He worked nights as a security guard and would get only a few hours sleep before heading to wrestling practice. However, he was fiercely determined and, with the help of school grants, he entered Simon Fraser University and joined the university team. In 1999, he qualified for the Olympics by becoming the first Canadian male ever to win gold in the Freestyle World Championships.

Since the 2000 Olympics, Daniel continues to win championships. He also graduated and now is helping to build a school in Eniwari. "I want the Academy to be different in many ways from the school I attended," he says. "When I was a kid there was no opportunity to join sports programs."

*PROUD CANADIAN NEVER FORGETS HIS ROOTS*

## Gymnastics

Gymnastics has many forms or disciplines, each with its own unique appeal. Whatever your preference or skill level, gymnastics is a great individual sport, and it provides one of the best workouts your body will ever get.

### History

The word gymnastics comes from the Greek word "gymnos," which means "naked art." However, don't worry—this art form isn't, and actually shouldn't be, performed in the nude.

Greeks were doing gymnastics at least 2,500 years ago. Gymnastics first appeared in the Olympic games in Athens in 1896. The first men's team event was added in the 1906 Olympics in St. Louis, but it was the 1928 games in Paris that established the practices we know today (where men competed for both individual event winnings as well as all-around and team championships). Women joined the competition in the 1936 Olympic games in Berlin.

Because of the nature of the sport (focusing primarily on body movement, fitness, and physical conditioning), no one can pinpoint the exact moment that the sport was invented.

## General Gymnastics

General Gymnastics is the non-competitive branch of gymnastics and plays a leading role in the development of an active lifestyle. It is the lifeblood of the gymnastics community with over 90 percent of total participants pursuing this form of recreational activity.

The goals of these gymnasts may vary, but fun, fitness, and learning the fundamentals are high on the list.

## Artistic Gymnastics

Both men's and women's artistic gymnastics combine a series of tumbling, dance, and acrobatic moves on different apparatuses. Artistic gymnastics requires strength, balance, and flexibility. Although skills can be similar in both men's and women's gymnastics, the events themselves are different.

Men compete on the pommel horse, but women do not.

Women's artistic gymnastics has four events, while men's has six. Within a typical routine, there are usually similar requirements: a certain number of strength moves, and a certain number of acrobatic moves. The amount of each varies according to both the event and the level of competition.

In competition, gymnasts can win in an individual event and/or in an all-around event. The competitor with the highest individual score on a particular event wins that event. The competitor with the highest total score wins the all-around.

Male gymnasts compete in six events:

➢ Floor exercise
➢ Pommel horse
➢ Rings
➢ Vault
➢ Parallel bars
➢ Horizontal bar

Female gymnasts compete in four events:

➢ Vault
➢ Balance beam
➢ Uneven bars
➢ Floor exercise

The vault is preceded by a long runway (25 m) and requires an enormous amount of power and speed as the gymnast sprints down the runway to execute the vault. The other events involve longer and more complicated routines, each with its own set of technical requirements.

In the floor exercise, the dimensions of the 12 × 12 metre (40 × 40 feet) spring floor are the same for both men and women. They both have a number of requirements, including tumbling passes, jumps, turns, and making full use of the floor.

## Sport Starts with Gymnastics

There are many benefits to gymnastics, one of which is the fact that participation can make you an all-around better athlete. Gymnastics now is considered one of the top three sports in athletic development, along with track and field and swimming.

A resource paper published by Canadian Sport Centres, entitled *Canadian Sport for Life*, states that gymnastics provides an unmatched athletic base in areas of agility, balance, coordination, and speed.

Many consider gymnastics to be a sport that develops the all-round athlete first, and the sport-specific athlete second.

It is not uncommon to encounter successful athletes in a number of disciplines who have gymnastics in their athletic background. Blythe Hartley in diving or Clara Hughes in speed skating and biking both have gymnastics in their blood.

## Landing

Good landings are crucial in all events. Whether you are dismounting off the high bar, or coming down from a double twist on the floor exercise, it is mandatory that your two feet plant firmly on the ground. If not, major deductions will bring your score down.

Gymnastics requires power and grace. Choreographers help gymnasts with the artistic elements of routines and strength, and conditioning coaches prepare them for the physical demands of their events.

Gymnasts are among the most physically fit people you will ever encounter. Whether it is a temporary interest, a gateway into another athletic discipline, or an early stop en route to the Olympic podium, gymnastics is a great activity for almost anyone.

## Rhythmic Gymnastics

Rhythmic gymnastics differs from artistic gymnastics in that it is less acrobatic. The focus of rhythmic gymnastics is on flexibility, grace of body movement, and handling of the apparatus.

There are four possible events to compete in rhythmic gymnastics: rope, hoop, ball, and ribbon. All involve routines set to music. Gymnasts can choose to specialize in one or more events, or they can compete in all four, which also qualifies them for the all-round competition.

## Trampoline and Tumbling

Trampoline is one of the newest Olympic sports. The sport requires tremendous leg strength, endurance, and phenomenal air sense (spatial orientation). Having some daring tendencies is also a definite asset as trampolinists fly through the air, sometimes as high as 9 metres (30 feet), performing somersaults and twisting skills with grace and agility.

Power tumbling blends the exciting aspects of the floor exercise with the dynamics of the trampoline. Tumblers perform on a specialized tumbling strip, and the innovation of this specialized "floor" has raised the level of the sport to new heights. It provides the athletes with an extremely explosive "launching pad," which can propel them high into the air and allow them to perform combinations of consecutive aerial skills at levels of difficulty normally not seen in artistic gymnastics.

## Getting Involved

Often, high-level gymnasts begin the sport at a very young age. However, you don't have to be Olympic-bound to enjoy the strength and flexibility that the sport affords you. Contact your local gymnastics club and take a beginnner-level class.

To find a club near you, visit the Gymnastics Canada website at **www.gymcan.org.**

# Kyle Shewfelt
## Playing to Win (and to Have Fun)

**ALBERTAN IS CANADA'S OLYMPIC GOLDEN BOY**

**U**ntil 2004, no Canadian gymnast had ever won Olympic gold in artistic gymnastics. However, at the Athens Games, Calgary's Kyle Shewfelt changed all that.

Recording a 9.787 score in the floor event, he narrowly edged a gymnast from Romania to win the gold, putting together the finest routine of his career. "This is amazing," Shewfelt told the reporters. "I was happy to deliver the routine of my dreams in Olympic competition."

The road to gold in the floor event was not an easy one for Shewfelt. Disappointed with a 12th-place finish at the Sydney Olympics, he focused hard on improving that result, and moved up to the gold medals in both the floor and vault events at the 2002 Commonwealth Games, as well as bronze medals in both events at the World Championships in 2003.

Despite these great pre-2004 results (and a prediction of a gold medal for Shewfelt in *Sports Illustrated* magazine), there was no guarantee that Shewfelt would win in Athens, especially since the competition in the men's floor event was being described by commentators as the toughest of all time. To make things even more

difficult, Shewfelt had missed five months of competition earlier in the year because of a foot injury.

Right after his big win was announced, Shewfelt, who trains at the Altadore Gymnastics Club in Calgary, hugged his coach and family members, who had flown from Alberta for the Games.

"Coming into this Olympics, my family said they were coming and I said 'You guys, it's a lot of money, you don't have to come,'" Shewfelt told the CBC after his win. "I'm so glad right now they're here with me. I would not have wanted to experience winning Olympic gold without my biggest supporters here."

Shewfelt has also experienced success competing on the vault in men's gymnastics, and has even been immortalized by having a vault maneuver named after him because he was the first to land it successfully.

# Aquatics

**S**wimming is not only a high-profile sport for the world-class athlete, but also a popular and useful activity for the average person.

## History

From hieroglyphics in Egypt and from other visual records, it appears that the breaststroke and dog paddle were the strokes of choice at the time. The Romans popularized cliff diving as a manly activity, and this helped to advance aquatics throughout the Roman Empire. By 36 BC, Japanese Emperor Suigiu was actively encouraging his people to learn how to swim.

The Greeks did not include swimming in the original Olympics, but they did practise the sport—in fact, they incorporated swimming pools into the design of their ever-popular public baths.

The number of people who have learned swimming as a recreational or life-saving technique has exploded in the past fifty years. Swimming, which saw its first recorded championship in Australia in 1845, now is an integral part of the Summer Olympic Games. Swimmers such as Mark Spitz, Ian Thorpe, Michael Phelps, and Jenny Thompson are as big in the sports world as any amateur athletes.

## Competitive Swimming

An Olympic-size pool is 50 m long and 25 m wide. It must have at least eight lanes and a buffer lane or empty lane on each side.

➤ **Strokes.** In swimming races, participants use four basic strokes: the free style (or front crawl), the backstroke, the breaststroke, and the butterfly stroke.

➤ **Events.** Individual races can be 50 m, 100 m, 200 m, 400 m, 800 m, or 1,500 m, and relay races can be 4 × 50 m, 4 × 100 m or 4 × 200 m. In freestyle, racers may choose their stroke; the majority choose front crawl.

There are also medley events which are comprised of all four strokes in a specific order. For individual medley, the order is fly, back, breast, and free. For medley relay, it is back, breast, fly, and free.

Water provides an excellent environment for strength training.

## The Rules

The nature of the sport makes any infractions relatively self-evident. In races, the pool is divided into one lane per swimmer, and each participant must stay in his or her own lane.

Prior to the start of the race, each swimmer stands on a starting block and waits for the starter's signal to begin the race. A false start (leaving the block before the starting signal) is a violation. International and Canadian national rules no longer allow even one false start.

Each swimming stroke has specific rules designed to ensure that no swimmer receives an unfair advantage over another. For example, at turns, swimmers must touch the wall and not merely approach it in a "phantom wall touch." In breaststroke and butterfly events, swimmers must touch the wall with two hands at the turns and at the finish.

## The Equipment

Swimming requires a minimum of gear, but equipment designers have been working overtime to improve what little equipment there is.

➤ **Swimsuit.** At one time, swimsuits were woollen and covered most of the body. Later, swimmers wore synthetic suits that covered very little body area. Recently, suits have been developed that many compare to shark skin and, once again, they cover more of the body. Suits are designed to reduce drag. These changes in swimsuit technology have allowed some elite swimmers to shave hundredths of seconds off their times—often enough to break a world record.

➤ **Goggles.** Standard equipment for all swimmers, they help swimmers see better underwater, and they protect swimmers' eyes from harmful pool chemicals.

➤ **Swim caps.** Commonly made from Lycra or latex, they reduce the pool drag from long hair and also keep hair out of swimmers' eyes, and out of the pool's filtration system.

## Aquatic Aerobics and Aquatic Therapy

**A**quatic aerobics focuses on endurance, strength, weight loss, and recreation. It's especially popular with older people, pregnant women, and over-weight people who may experience joint pain or inflammation during land aerobics.

In fact, aquatic aerobics is good for everyone—it is a low-impact activity that is less fatiguing than land aerobics. It uses water resistance to:

- Strengthen and tone muscles
- Reduce stress on joints, muscles, and tendons
- Improve joint flexibility
- Increase circulation

Aquatic therapy uses rehabilitative techniques and exercises in a weightless environment to make sure your body heals properly. This type of therapy is good for treating many different types of conditions, such as the following:

- General and post-operative orthopedics
- Sports injuries
- Strokes and head injuries
- Balance problems
- Arthritis
- Amputee rehabilitation

Aquatic therapy is not just for people. Believe it or not, it is also used to treat dogs!

## Diving and Synchronized Swimming

If you enjoy being in the water but want to do something more than swim lengths, you may be interested in diving or synchronized swimming. Both are practised up to the Olympic level.

Diving has been an Olympic event for over 100 years. It requires grace, strength, and agility, as well as great precision, as divers can reach the water at speeds of about 50 km/hour.

In most cases, competitors perform dives from two categories: compulsories, which include forward, backward, handstand, twist, reverse, and inward movements; and optionals, which are much more difficult.

Synchronized swimming was developed in the 1920s by a group of Canadian women from life saving and swimming techniques. They called it "ornamental swimming," and it has evolved into what we call "synchro" today.

Synchro athletes work hard to maintain the illusion of effortless-ness during their complicated routines involving strenuous movements performed both upside-down and underwater. Exceptional breath control is needed as well as split-second timing, strength, endurance, flexibility, and artistry.

## Other Water Sports

Swimming is just one of many aquatic activities. For those who love being in the water there is a multitude of options available:

➢ **Water polo.** This sport is great for people who love being in the water and love team sports. If you're not a strong swimmer, you can try inner-tube water polo, which is less competitive.

➢ **Surfing.** This can be difficult if you don't live near the ocean, but enthusiasts are finding ways to surf away from the coastline. Rapids surfing is growing in popularity. Some devout surfers even prefer it to the ocean version because you can stay on your surfboard for so much longer.

➢ **Water skiing and wakeboarding.** These sports are very popular among Canadians with homes or cottages on lakes. Strong swimming skills are important as are balance, coordination, and a willingness to fall.

## Getting Involved

If you are interested in swimming competitively, check out Swimming Canada's website at **www.swimming.ca.**

If you are just looking to add some water-based fitness to your aerobic schedule public pools can usually be found in recreation centres and YMCAs. Many cities operate outdoor pools in the summer so you can keep fit and stay cool.

# Marathon Swimmers
## Playing to Win (and to Have Fun)

Marathon swimming favours the swimmer's endurance over speed. Individuals set records swimming across lakes and other large bodies of water.

Now known as the "Lady of the Lake," Toronto native Marilyn Bell (left) was the first person to swim across Lake Ontario at just 16 years old.

She entered the lake in New York State at 11:00 p.m. on September 8, 1954, approximately the same time as another swimmer, Florence Chadwick. Chadwick was offered money to complete the swim for the Canadian National Exhibition (CNE). Bell was not impressed that the CNE was paying an American swimmer and decided to do the swim herself for free.

Chadwick was forced to stop her attempt after a few hours, while Bell swam more than 51.5 km (32 mi.) across the lake, fighting the cold water, fatigue, and lamprey eels.

She completed the crossing by touching the break wall located just west of the area now known as Marilyn Bell Park, Toronto, shortly after 8:00 p.m. on September 9. She was greeted by a crowd of 300,000 people.

Marilyn went on to become the youngest person to swim the English Channel.

Marilyn's achievements were followed by those of Vicki Keith (below), who not only swam across Lake Ontario, but was also the first and only person to complete a double crossing. She also completed crossings of all five Great Lakes in a two-month period and set numerous other records before retiring in 1991.

Vicki mentored another swimmer, Ashley Cowan. Ashley contracted meningitis at 15 months old, and doctors were forced to amputate her hands and feet in order to save her life. At age 15, Ashley wasn't about to let that stop her from being the youngest swimmer (and the only one with a disability) to successfully swim across Lake Erie, on September 7, 2001. As Ashley told CFTO news, "You set your mind on something and just keep thinking how much you want it, and you will achieve it."

**NO DISTANCE TOO GREAT FOR MARATHON SWIMMERS**

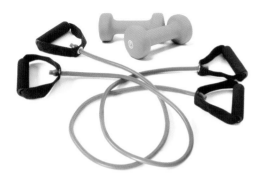

## Aerobics

**A**erobics provides a great cardiorespiratory workout (working both your heart and your lungs). It is one of the few body management activities where you can find rules and music geared towards your own personal interests. For once, you are actually supposed to listen to music in class.

### History

Dr. Kenneth Cooper, a surgeon in the U.S. Air Force, coined the term "aerobics" when he used it as the title of his 1968 book promoting exercise for the cardiovascular system. By the late 1970s, dancers and fitness experts adapted Cooper's ideas, combining them with dance moves and music to create aerobic dance routines and classes.

Why did aerobics become so popular so quickly? Because it's a fun way to exercise for people of all fitness levels, from beginner to advanced. With video and DVDs, even people who don't have gym memberships can perform the routines at home.

## Aerobics 101

Aerobics (or aerobic dance, as it is sometimes called) is a sport that is very flexible. You can do it either at home—by yourself or with a friend—or you can join a class and do it as a group activity. It's a workout with one simple concept: keep moving! Through a series of choreographed movements, set to music, you keep up a steady rhythm and, as luck would have it, your heart rate, too.

The result of all of this movement is to increase your strength and stamina and to make your body use oxygen more efficiently. The continuous motion also does wonders for most of your muscle groups. You can choose a class to specifically target almost any area. As the intensity goes up, your breathing increases and your heart beat approaches your target heart rate, which means you are getting the best health return for your efforts.

Aerobics is a fun way to exercise for people of all fitness levels, from beginner to advanced.

### The Routine

A typical aerobics class lasts 60 minutes and has three major components:

➤ **The warm-up.** This phase slowly prepares your body for the workout ahead by gradually increasing your heart rate and breathing. It is done at a slower pace than the rest of the routine. It may last up to 15 minutes.

➤ **The cardio workout.** This is the most intense phase of the routine, where you will reach your target heart rate. It may last up to 30 minutes.

➤ **The cool-down.** This is the phase where your body will gradually return to its regular heart rate. It involves deep stretches and slow movements. It may last up to 15 minutes.

### Types of Aerobics

There are two major types of aerobics. Some classes focus on one or the other, while other classes include a mixture of both types:

➤ **High-impact.** This is a very intense workout. It involves a great deal of jumping, kicking, and running on the spot at a rigorous pace. The choreography is also fairly advanced. You should be in good shape to participate in this kind of class.

➤ **Low-impact.** This is best if you are just beginning or have joint problems. You may be worried that it's only for older people, that it's too easy a workout, and that you won't get good results. This is completely untrue. You get the same benefits, but keep one foot on the floor at all times to support your weight, which means it isn't as jarring on your joints. Your heart, lungs, and muscles all are working, but there is far less risk of stress-related injury.

## Choosing the Right Apparel

**N**ot wearing the right clothes or footwear when doing aerobics can easily negate the benefits, and an ill-fitting outfit can put a serious damper on your workout.

Luckily, dressing sensibly for aerobics doesn't mean you can't be stylish. These days there are plenty of options for exercise apparel:

- **Shoes.** Make sure your shoes fit well, provide good support, and are securely tied before you work out. It's also important to replace your shoes before they wear out too much or you risk injury.

- **Clothes.** There is a huge range of styles, fabrics, and sizes available when shopping for exercise clothes. Be sure to choose a fabric that "breathes" (avoid synthetics) so that you don't overheat.

- **Socks.** Make sure your socks contain natural fabrics and are thick enough to prevent excessive friction between your feet and your shoes.

- **Outdoor apparel.** Don't let the cold weather stop you from being active, especially when there are so many good clothes available that both keep you warm and let you move freely.

## Aerobic Events

New aerobics classes, routines, and movements are developed all the time. Here are some you may want to try:

- ➢ **Water aerobics.** Usually, you will do this activity in waist-deep water. The water helps to cushion your joints. This cushioning relieves joint-stress and makes this a low-impact form of aerobics, where you get the benefit of resistance from the water to challenge your muscles.

- ➢ **Step aerobics.** This type of aerobics is easily adapted for different fitness levels. You perform the moves with the added up and down intensity you get from a step platform. Raising or lowering the platform will increase and decrease the intensity.

- ➢ **Aerobic boxing.** This is a high-impact workout that is excellent for building strength. You will punch, kick, jump rope, and jog. What a great way to get out aggression and have some fun. You will also learn a bit of self-defence at the same time. Aerobic boxing is also known as boxercise or cardio kickboxing.

## Aerobic Workout Tips

- ➢ **Stretch before every workout.** Never skip the warm-up stretches, even if you are at home or late for class. You risk injury if your muscles haven't had a chance to prepare for the extended cardio portion.

- ➢ **Work at the proper fitness level.** Start with a low-impact activity and work your way up to higher-impact aerobics. If you are taking a class that is too difficult, don't suffer in silence and definitely don't drop out. Often, instructors can modify the movements so they will be less strenuous.

- ➢ **Work out regularly.** To get the maximum benefit from your aerobics routine, you must do it regularly. Thirty minutes, three times per week will keep your heart, lungs, and muscles strong.

- ➢ **Stay hydrated.** You will sweat a great deal during this kind of exercise, so be sure to keep a bottle of water with you to avoid dehydration and keep up your energy level. When you are properly hydrated it's much easier to stay active.

- ➢ **Choose a type of aerobics that's fun for you.** If you don't enjoy the workout, you won't be motivated to keep it up. Contact your local gym, community centre, or YMCA to find out what types of classes they offer. Don't be shy. Try a few different classes to find out which is the most fun for you.

## Getting Involved

A couple of options to get your aerobics life started: join a gym that offers classes, or buy an aerobics tape and simple equipment, such as a mat, to try it at home with a friend or in a gym class.

# Aerobics Classes—Something for Everyone
## Playing to Win (and to Have Fun)

Going to an aerobics class is a great way to add activity to your routine. Aerobics classes combine music and movement in a structured workout, can be very social and, best of all, there's a class to suit just about anyone.

- **Dance Aerobics**. Dance aerobics uses varying levels of choreography to give your body a rhythmic workout. Some moves may be tricky to master at first, but most can be adapted to suit any level. Some of the most popular styles of dance being used in aerobics classes are hip hop, jazz, and salsa.

- **Exercise Ball**. Although invented in the 1950s, it is only recently that this fitness item has become a fixture in gyms and homes everywhere. Exercise balls are great for strengthening your core and can be used with many different exercises. You can sit or stand on them to improve your balance and posture, or use them as a support while lifting weights. Some people even sit on them instead of desk chairs to help improve their posture.

- **Hi-Lo**. Generally low-impact aerobic exercises are done with one foot on the floor at all times,

while high-impact involves much more movement. Some hi-lo classes include both types of exercise while others offer variations on specific exercises allowing the participants to dictate the intensity of their workout. Both high- and low-impact styles offer great cardiorespiratory workouts.

- **Belly Dancing**. While traditional belly dancing is often seen as a women-only traditional Middle-Eastern dance form, men and women of all backgrounds are discovering that belly dancing provides an intense core and abdominal workout. If you hate sit-ups and stomach crunches, this could be the class for you.

- **Boot Camp**. Another high intensity class that uses a military drill style to combine high-energy cardiorespiratory and muscular endurance training.

*USE MUSIC AND MOVEMENT TO REACH YOUR FITNESS GOALS*

## Yoga and Pilates

**W**ould you like to increase your flexibility and improve muscle tone, all while maintaining an internal spiritual balance? Yoga and Pilates have become extremely popular in North America as sure-fire ways to achieve a high level of physical fitness, to combat the negative effects of stress, and to improve overall mental and emotional health.

### History of Yoga

Yoga developed from the philosophies and spiritual practices of Vedic priests in northern India over 5000 years ago. These practices were systemized in the second century BC in a text called the Yoga Sutras, which lays out a structured plan to achieve enlightenment through meditation and action. Thus, yoga was born.

### History of Pilates

Joseph Pilates was a performer and boxer who developed a series of exercises to keep himself fit. Born in Germany but living in England when World War I broke out, he was interned in a camp with other German nationals. To promote overall health in the camp, he began teaching the other internees some of the exercises he had developed. In 1926, he moved to New York and set up an exercise studio.

## Let's Get Flexible

Yoga is a physical and spiritual practice designed to unite the mind, the body, and the spirit. People can start to do yoga at any time and essentially can continue to do it for as long as they live.

Yoga helps to promote strength, muscle control, and circulatory health, while enhancing mental awareness and concentration. Each pose or posture demands that you focus on using and correctly aligning each muscle. Don't forget about flexibility—you may learn how to bend your body into a pretzel and stretch your mind at the same time.

## Types of Yoga

There are different types of yoga, sometimes referred to as "paths. Each path its own particular emphasis or approach. Some of these paths include the following:

Yoga is an activity that works both your body and your mind.

➢ **Raja yoga** emphasizes control of mind and body. Meditation, concentration, and breathing are the main aspects of the mental practice of Raja yoga.

➢ **Hatha yoga** is the physical side of Raja yoga. Hatha emphasizes control of the body through specific exercises (poses known as asanas), combined with regulated breathing and relaxation.

➢ **Karma yoga** is the path of action. It approaches the achievement of enlightenment through an individual's actions. The goal of someone who practises this type of yoga is to act selflessly without regard to reward, and to become one with God through right action.

➢ **Bhakti yoga** means "to serve the divine," and Bhakti yoga is the path that emphasizes personal devotion. Adherents of Bhakti strive to achieve mystical union with the divine through various forms of worship, including prayers and rituals in which chanting and singing often figure prominently.

➢ **Jnana yoga** is the path that emphasizes knowledge. Its goal is to achieve enlightenment by discovering the divine knowledge that is innate in human beings. Those who practise Jnana yoga approach the world by constantly questioning and thinking about their own nature and their perceptions.

## Your Choice

Which of these yoga paths do you think might be right for you? Remember, although the different approaches to yoga have developed out of the desire for spiritual enlightenment, yoga itself is not a religion. You don't have to subscribe to a certain system of beliefs to practise yoga.

Many people take yoga up solely for its physical benefits. Regular practice of Hatha yoga, for instance, can result in a stronger, more flexible body and a deeper experience of relaxation. Many practitioners also reap the mental benefits of greater concentration and focus.

## Hatha Yoga

**A**lthough, at its roots, yoga has a very spiritual basis, it is the physical benefits of yoga that really have taken off in North America. The poses known to yoga enthusiasts today take their roots in Hatha yoga.

Hatha yoga encompasses many types or styles of yoga, including: Ananda, Ashtanga, Bikram, integral, Iyengar, Kripalu, kundalini, Sivananda, and viniyoga. Each style of Hatha yoga has a slightly different purpose. For instance, Ananda yoga concentrates on posture in order to increase the flow of energy to certain organs, whereas kundalini yoga follows the belief that the body has a natural euphoric state that can be achieved without the use of drugs.

Sound like a mouthful? Don't worry, once you have chosen the type of yoga that best suits you, you don't need to memorize the rest. In addition, while yoga poses have Sanskrit names, your instructor will probably use their English translations. Here are the English names of some yoga poses:

- Half-Moon
- Warrior II
- Swan
- Extended Triangle
- Downward Dog
- Horseman

## Pilates: Quality Not Quantity

Pilates is a body-conditioning system that strengthens and tones the muscles and promotes freedom of movement by increasing flexibility through controlled stretching. Pilates was designed to use the whole body in exercises. It involves moving fluidly from one position to the next, while coordinating your breathing with each movement.

There are two types of exercise in the world of Pilates. One is the "matwork," a routine in which you exercise on a mat on the floor, using your body as the only "exercise equipment." The other is a series of exercises you perform on specially designed equipment. Both types of exercise deliver the same results: improved posture, better balance, increased lung capacity, better circulation, and an overall sense of well-being.

If you have ever seen a Pilates class, you probably won't be surprised to learn that its inventor studied yoga. Joseph Pilates also studied Zen meditation, and he wanted his exercise system to promote the unity and the health of both body and mind. You could say he was a bit ahead of his time, considering that he developed the Pilates exercises in the early part of the twentieth century—long before the recent explosion of interest in methods that promote mind–body focus through movement.

Because there are over 500 different Pilates exercises, they cannot all be named. Essentially, the exercises are meant to support your abdomen, spine, and pelvis, thus improving your all-around level of strength and flexibility. Often, these three areas in combination are referred to as "the powerhouse," or "core."

What distinguishes this type of exercise from many other exercises is that the focus is on you and what your body is capable of doing—not what everyone else is capable of doing, not on what records have been broken in the past, and not on striving to do better than the person next to you. Everyone has a unique body type, and Pilates is specifically designed to put you in touch with your own body's issues and allow you to overcome them. Because the focus is on the quality and not the quantity of movement, you leave a Pilates class feeling recharged, rather than exhausted.

One final advantage to getting your strengthening exercises through Pilates is that it gives you strength without the bulk. Keep in mind, that muscle, whether lean or bulky, always is positive; but if you are more into the lean look, Pilates will give you that option.

## Getting Involved

Because yoga and Pilates have become so popular, classes are available at many local community centres and YMCAs. You can also check out the web for more information about the different kinds of yoga, as well as yoga and Pilates studios. If you are self-motivated, try buying an instructional video or DVD.

## Joseph Pilates
### Playing to Win (and to Have Fun)

**JOSEPH PILATES: FOUNDER OF A WORLD-WIDE EXERCISE MOVEMENT**

Born in Germany in 1880, Joseph Pilates (pronounced Puh-lah-teas) spent most of his youth feeling sick and frail. He suffered from rickets, asthma, and rheumatic fever, and generally found any form of activity extremely difficult, if not downright impossible.

From a very young age, Pilates began studying exercise physiology, anatomy, and various forms of exercise and mental training. From this research, he began developing a set of exercises that he would spend many decades perfecting—the exercises that have now come to be known as the "Pilates method" or simply, "Pilates."

A key phase of the development occurred in 1914, when Pilates was living in England. When the First World War broke out, he was deemed an "enemy alien" (Germany and England opposed each other in the war) and was sent to prison. While there, he taught his fellow prisoners the exercises he had been developing.

He was so successful at this that the English authorities enlisted his help in rehabilitating soldiers injured in battle, a process that Pilates made even more effective by attaching straps to the injured men's bedsprings, allowing them to strengthen their arm and leg muscles while bed-ridden.

After the war, Pilates further refined his exercise regimen, streamlining it to 500 exercises that he said would offer people "complete coordination of the mind, body, and spirit." Eventually, he made his way to the United States, where he began training professional dancers using his revolutionary methods.

When it came to advertising the success of his methods, nothing was more convincing than Pilates himself. He was the picture of health and strength, well into his eighties.

Joseph Pilates died in 1967, but his legacy lives on in the thousands of people worldwide who practise his famous methods of exercise.

## Dance

**W**hether it's ballet, breakdancing, hip hop, or the samba, dancing is a great form of exercise. That's right—you can have fun and keep fit at the same time. There are many different dance styles out there, so jump in and find out which is right for you.

### History

Throughout the ages, dance has been used for many different things: to tell stories and express ideas, for celebration, for religion, and for entertainment. Dances like the ballet and the waltz have their roots in Europe, dating as far back as the Middle Ages, while modern dance first appeared in the early twentieth century, mainly in the United States and Germany.

Is it really possible to pinpoint when people first started tapping their toes and moving to music? Not a chance. That's because dance— the merging of movement with music—is such a natural thing for human beings to do. As long as there has been music, rhythm, or sound of any kind, there simply must have been dance.

## Dance Styles

Types and styles of dance fall into two broad groups: social/participation dance and concert/performance dance. Many of the forms fit into both of these groups, depending on how they are performed.

➢ **Social/Participation Dance**. **Social dance** involves people getting together to dance. School dances, clubs, ceilis (Irish dance parties), square dances, dance jams, and contact improvisation sessions all offer participants the chance to dance with other people. Many social dances require a partner. Others involve participants dancing individually in a group setting, the way people do at a school dance. **Participation dance** actively encourages dancing in larger groups. Often everyone in a group will perform a set of steps together. Ever do the chicken dance at your cousin's wedding? Or the hokey-pokey when you were little? These are examples of participation dances.

➢ **Concert/Performance Dance.** In **concert dance**, also known as **performance dance**, an audience watches, but does not participate, while skilled dancers perform a routine that is usually choreographed. Almost any type of dance can be considered performance dance, provided that there is a non-participating audience present. There are, however, a number of dances that are fairly specific to this category, such as ballet or theatre dance.

Dancing can be done in large groups or whenever you feel like moving to music.

## The Various Styles of Dance

| Type of Dance | Description | Examples |
|---|---|---|
| **Social/Participation** | | |
| Historical | Variety of dances from the past | Pavane, galliard, lavolta, can-can, polonaise |
| Folk | Variety of dances where performance is governed by tradition | Square dance, Irish dance, maypole dance, Scottish dance |
| Ballroom | A huge variety of dances, mostly partnered<br>Can be formal or casual | Waltz, tango, fox trot, samba, rumba, jive, mambo, salsa, swing, polka |
| Latin | Typically refers to dances originating in Latin America | Cha-cha, rumba, salsa, merengue, mambo |
| Swing | Group of related partner dances performed to swing or rock and roll music | East Coast swing, West Coast swing, lindy hop, jitterbug |
| Street | Modern and evolve over time<br>Not bound by tradition | Hip hop, breakdancing, krumping |
| Ethnic/Traditional | Emphasizing cultural roots, which can also include folk | Belly dance, Chinese ethnic |
| Ceremonial | Ritual dances and dances for ceremonial purposes | Celebrations, peace, war, religious dances |
| Novelty/Fad | Also called "dance crazes"<br>Quirky and timely | Chicken Dance, Macarena, Limbo |
| **Concert/Performance** | | |
| Ballet | Dance form and set of techniques that can be performed alone, or as part of an opera<br>Best known for techniques such as pointe work and high leg extensions | Romantic, classical, modern, neoclassical, deconstructivist, post-structural |
| 20th-Century Concert Theatre | Includes a number of dance forms that continue to evolve<br>Combines music, songs, dance, and dialogue<br>Generally uses various forms of popular music | Free, modern, expressionist, post-modern theatre, tap, jazz |

## Dance: Getting Started

If you haven't been dancing for years, but think you would like to pursue competitive or performance dance, it is not too late. In some cases, dancing requires you to have started at a young age in order to achieve the top levels. However, you can still participate in these rigorous types of dance and find ways to perform, whether or not you are a pro.

There are other dances that you can also take up at any point in your life and still manage to get to high levels of competition. Here are a few examples:

> **Ballroom dancing.** If you are interested in performing, getting into character, and trying this out competitively, you can start at any time. You can also ballroom dance in a non-competitive, social forum. The basic ballroom dances are waltz, tango, Viennese waltz, foxtrot, and quickstep. Other styles include the latin dances (the cha-cha, samba, rumba, and jive), or swing dances (East Coast swing, West Coast swing, lindy hop, and salsa).

> **Ballet, jazz, tap, and modern dance.** If you plan on a career as a dancer in any of these categories, chances are you are already taking classes. At the performance level, these forms of dance are usually started at a very young age as they require years of training and extreme dedication. However, you can still start classes as a teenager or even as an adult, for recreation. These disciplines are great for teaching you balance, body control, grace, and flexibility. Ballet, jazz, and modern dance share enough similarities that many people try out all three until they find the pace that is right for them. Modern dance is a great way to extend the performance life of ballet dancers when standing on the tips of their toes no longer suits them.

> **Highland and Irish dancing.** Most popular among the dancers of Scottish or Irish descent, these dances are open to anyone. Classes are offered at all ages for both recreational and competitive dancing. These dances concentrate on fast and impressive footwork. Both types of dance provide a fun way to get a great cardio workout.

## Getting Involved

Just like the history of dance itself, dance organizations change and grow over time, always driven by spirit. Dance Canada's website, **www.dance.ca**, offers information about dance organizations in Canada. If you don't find what you're looking for on their website, you can email them directly by clicking on their "contact" link. Alternatively, you can search directly for clubs and classes in your area.

If you are already well on your way to the top, the Canadian Dance Assembly website, **www.dancecanada.net**, has plenty of information for professional dancers.

## Lift Your Spirits

**W**ith offices all over the United States and with Canadian contacts in Calgary, Guelph, and Montreal, the American Dance Therapy Association (ADTA) believes that when things are tough, dancing your way through them can be very therapeutic.

The ADTA is filled with instructors with master's degrees in the healing power of dance. In Canada, instructors can become certified at the Wesley Institute in Calgary, where they can take courses such as dance improvisation, therapy for children, therapy for adults, clinical skills for dance therapy, and sacred dance for healing.

The message behind this discipline of study is simple. When you're feeling down, don't hesitate to set your sad music aside, and put on something that allows you more freedom to dance, and to feel your body's natural energy.

# Swing Dancing
## Playing to Win (and to Have Fun)

If you love dancing but aren't a fan of dark rooms with loud thumping music and a huge crowd, or if the thought of dancing makes you feel self-conscious, maybe you need to look back a bit. All cultures seem to feel the need to move to a beat, and many dances survive the test of time.

One style of dance that's experienced a resurgence in recent years is swing dancing. While you may have seen swing in movies or commercials, many people are finding that this dance, danced in the night clubs in New York and Hollywood in the 1920s, 30s, and 40s, is still lots of fun.

The great thing about swing dancing is that it's very social and can be as athletic and challenging as you want it to be.

Swing dancing came about as a response to swing music, a kind of jazz identified by a distinctive rhythm, played by a strong rhythm section, and a fast tempo. It differed from previous forms of dance because the partners would "swing" away from each other rather than dancing in a closed position.

It was fast, athletic, and flashy—teens loved it, while their parents were shocked at its speed and some of the acrobatic flying flips and aerial gymnastics moves.

Over the years, swing dancing evolved in response to changes in the music. It became jive after the birth of Rock & Roll, and Western swing following the advent of Rhythm & Blues (R&B). Swing dancing has also developed regional variations over the years, so no matter what kind of dancer you are, there's likely a style of swing for you.

Swing dancing goes through waves of popularity. Dancers come in all ages, shapes, and levels of ability, and getting started is often as simple as taking a few classes at a local swing dance club.

If you are looking for a way to connect with older relatives at reunions and weddings, learning a few swing dancing moves could help you see them in a whole new way.

*GET A GREAT CARDIO WORKOUT WHILE HAVING FUN WITH FRIENDS*

# 26
# Outdoor Activities

**W**hether it's the thrill of skiing down a hill or blazing through trails in Canada's provincial parks, being outdoors affords us the opportunity to be "at one" with nature. As Canadians, we are lucky—not many places in the world have forests to hike through or hills to ski on that are located only minutes away from cities.

Many physical education programs offer outdoor education, yet few students take advantage of them. Activities such as camping, canoeing, hiking, orienteering, or skiing are fun and are also a great way to get active.

Next time your school offers a ski or camping trip be sure to sign up, especially if you have never done it before. You might discover a part of yourself you never knew existed.

## Outdoor Activities

The outdoor activities covered in this chapter are:

➢ Orienteering

➢ Hiking

➢ Camping

➢ Downhill Skiing

➢ Cross-Country Skiing

## Basic Skills and Tactics

The greatest thing about outdoor activities is that you can go at your own pace. Your level of fitness really doesn't hinder your performance or enjoyment. If you are looking for competition, both orienteering and skiing (downhill and cross-country) offer it at various levels.

> **Orienteering.** The basic skills involved in orienteering are map and compass reading. Learning how to interpret what is on a map, and visually land-marking those spots on the course, are skills an orienteer must acquire. Movement skills depend on the type of orienteering that is being done. The most common types are walking or running.

> **Skiing.** The key skills in cross-country skiing are "the classic technique" (striding and gliding) and "skating" (similar to ice or in-line skating). Cross-country skiing, according to many experts, is the best all-around cardiorespiratory exercise. All beginner downhill skiers must learn the skill of "snowplowing." It teaches how to control your speed and how to stop. Once you master the snowplow, you can try more difficult maneuvers.

> **Camping.** Many basic survival skills are practised when camping. Building a campfire, pitching a tent, cooking your own food, and sometimes even purifying water to drink. Often you must work as a team to get the campsite set before nightfall or a rainstorm. "No trace camping," which basically means leaving no garbage behind, is enforced in most areas so that others can enjoy the outdoors long after you are gone.

Always be safe and wear protective equipment when skiing.

You can engage in outdoor activities all year long.

## Orienteering, Hiking, and Camping

Orienteering, hiking, and camping are all great ways to see Canada's wilderness and get in shape at the same time. The best part is that anyone can do it! Whether you want to spend time with friends, commune with nature, or participate in competitions, here are some ways that you can "rough it."

### Enjoying the Great Outdoors

Hiking is walking, usually through trails, to explore and enjoy nature. Camping involves one or more nights spent outside, with equipment ranging from just a backpack to large recreational vehicles complete with all the comforts of home. Orienteering puts a competitive spin on outdoor activities by making a sport out of navigating with a map and compass. What you bring with you depends on which activity you will be doing.

Orienteering competitions have very clear rules about what you can and can't take with you. The equipment you will need for camping and hiking varies, but there are still some basics you will definitely want with you on a trip.

## The Outdoors as a Competitive Sport: Orienteering

Orienteering was first played in Norway, during the nineteenth century, as a military exercise. As people developed more reliable compasses, its popularity spread to other Scandinavian countries. The International Orienteering Federation (IOF), which sets the rules and principles for the game, was established in 1961, and the first world championships were held in 1966. Today, there are many different types of orienteering competitions, ranging from clubs where you can compete regardless of skill level and physical ability, to elite world championships requiring high endurance and running speed.

Players are brought to an unfamiliar area and given a map on which there are red circles to indicate control points. The object of the game is to visit each of the control points, in the correct order, in the least amount of time. The maps are created by orienteers and professional map-makers, and use an IOF-standardized system of symbols so that any reader can easily understand them.

Camping is a great way to enjoy being outdoors.

## One Step at a Time: Hiking

You will want to invest in a good backpack. Bring rain gear and extra clothing—you never know when the weather will change. You will need some sort of trail food to maintain your energy level, but the most vital item of all is water. The human body can only survive a few days without water, and it's easy to fall victim to dehydration and heatstroke during long hikes.

Make sure you bring sun protection, including sun block, sunglasses, lip balm, and a wide-brimmed hat. If you are unfamiliar with the area, a map and a compass are vital, but they won't be much use if you don't know how to use them. Matches can be used to light fires or to signal for help. Waterproof matches are your safest bet.

## Staying the Night: Camping

You will want to bring along a tent. A staggering variety of tents is available, differing in size, structure, and resistance to water. You will also want to invest in a good backpack and sleeping bag, and, if you want, an air mattress or cushion to make sleeping on the ground more comfortable.

Even if you camp by a stream or lake, the water could be dangerous to drink. If you don't want to be burdened with cases of bottled water, you can buy portable water purifiers and water stills. A pocket knife, a Swiss Army knife, or a similar multipurpose tool can be useful in a number of situations, from repairing a backpack to building an emergency shelter.

Other essential items would include: a first aid kit, which might contain adhesive bandages, medical tape, sterile gauze, soap, antiseptic, and scissors; a flashlight with extra batteries; pots, pans, and food supplies; materials to start a fire; and mosquito repellent.

Poison ivy is a common camping hazard. This woody perennial will grow almost anywhere—deep woods, clearings, sandy areas, rocks, swamps, even in your garden. Here are some tips for avoiding poison ivy:

- Watch for leaflets made of three parts
- In spring time watch for small clusters of greenish-white flowers
- In summer time watch for round berries formed on flowers
- When in doubt, don't touch any unknown plant

Oops! I did touch it. What should I do?

- Wash skin with soap and water to remove the plants' oil (the toxic part) ASAP
- Got a rash? Try antihistamines, compresses, and lukewarm baths
- See a doctor or other healthcare provider
- Avoid scratching!

Control points are marked by white and orange or white and red flags, and are placed on distinct landscape features. When an orienteer reaches one of these points, he or she registers the visit on a control card, or carries a computer chip to be scanned at every control. Basic orienteering equipment includes a compass, appropriate outdoor clothing, and a whistle for emergency use.

Orienteering variations include Relay, Score-O (competitors visit as many control points as possible within a certain time limit), Sprint (shorter events, sometimes in urban settings), Night (using a headlamp and reflective control markers), Bike-O (orienteering on a mountain bike), Ski-O (using cross-country skis), Mounted-O (on horseback), and Trail-O (for the physically challenged on an accessible course).

## Safety and Ecology

It is important to take precautions when you are out in the wild, both to protect yourself and to preserve the environment. Be aware of the rules and regulations of the trail, park, or campsite you visit, especially when it comes to garbage disposal and fire safety. Think of yourself as a guest in someone else's home—treat it with respect, and leave it exactly as it was before you arrived.

Don't place your tent in a low-lying area or under a tree. Lower ground can flood if it starts to rain. If you have absolutely nowhere else to set up camp, then dig a ditch around your shelter, and fill it in after you leave.

Be aware of wild animals. Elk and deer often travel at night over certain paths, so if you see hoof-prints, set up your shelter somewhere else. Bears are a major concern in many areas—if you are in bear territory, keep your pots and pans clean, and hang any food or perishables far away from your campsite. If possible, store your food in a cooler in your car, not in your tent.

We all know not to litter, but be especially careful about the following items:

> **Soap and dish detergent.** They pollute the water, and can damage vegetation. Environmentally-friendly products are available and easy to find. Bring them along, especially if you are camping in the wilderness.

> **Cigarette butts.** Aside from causing fires, cigarette butts are made of fiberglass and are not biodegradable.

> **Styrofoam.** Styrofoam is not biodegradable. Additionally, it is toxic if burned, so keep it away from campfires.

## Getting Involved

You can find advice, and maybe even hiking companions, at local outdoors clubs and organizations. The staff at outfitting stores—that sell camping and hiking equipment—can give you suggestions and advice. You can also check out **www.outdooradventurecanada.com** or guidebooks for inspiration.

## Sandy Hott Johansen
### Playing to Win (and to Have Fun)

*KEEP FIT WHILE SOCIALIZING, ENJOYING THE OUTDOORS, AND CHALLENGING YOURSELF*

For Sandy Hott Johansen, orienteering runs in the family. Not only is her husband a competitive orienteer, three of her five siblings compete with her on the Canadian national team. At the 2005 World Orienteering Championships in Japan, Sandy finished 9th, the best ever for a North American. The record had previously been held by Canadian Ted de St Croix (10th at the WOC in 1985).

Sandy knows that being a good all-around athlete is crucial in orienteering. "The combination of mental, technical, and physical skills is what makes orienteering challenging and exciting. It doesn't help to be a fast runner if you don't know where you're going, and vice versa."

Sandy may be a world class orienteer, but there are aspects of the sport that anyone can enjoy. "In the beginning, it was mostly being together with friends and family, being active in the outdoors, and enjoying the technical challenge that attracted me" she says.

Even the most casual participant can benefit physically from the sport, but many people don't realize that the most competitive orienteers are among the fittest athletes in the world. Their high level of endurance is similar to that of Olympic cross-country skiers, marathon runners, and Tour de France cyclists.

Orienteering can be done all over the world and by all types of people. Competitors use detailed topographical maps of the terrain to navigate their way around the course so language is not an obstacle. "I've travelled all over the world to compete," says Sandy, "from the mega-steep jungles of Japan to the lightning-fast prairies in Canada. In doing so, I've experienced so many different countries and cultures that I never would have experienced if not for orienteering."

Not many schools have suitable grounds for orienteering, but if you would like to give it a try, visit the Canadian Orienteering Federation's website at **www.orienteering.ca** for more information. They can direct you to a club, a beginner clinic, or an event in your area.

## Skiing: Downhill and Cross-Country

**W**hile some people would rather hibernate than put on a toque and go outside in the middle of a cold Canadian winter, the rest of us don't let the weather stop us from keeping fit and having a good time. Whether you want the thrill of downhill or the exhilaration of cross-country, skiing benefits people of all ages, interests, and skill levels.

### Skiing Competitively or Just for Fun

You can ski night or day, on almost any type of snowy terrain, from the steepest hills to the flattest fields. There are many types of skiing, each requiring different skills. You are sure to find one that you will enjoy.

Getting involved in skiing, either cross-country or downhill, will vary according to the province, city, and school district in which you live. Not all schools offer both sports. If you live in the prairies, chances are you have come across a pair of cross-country skis in your life. If you live near the mountains, you have likely done your fair share of downhill skiing.

## Cross-Country Skiing

If you are into hiking, try cross-country skiing. It is a great cardio exercise—you use both your upper and lower body to glide over the snow. Beginners can take it slowly and do shorter trails, while experts can ski quickly over several kilometres. There are two main techniques:

> **Classical technique.** Keep both skis parallel to each other, push back with one foot, glide forward with the other, and use one pole at a time to help propel yourself forward. The movement is called the diagonal stride.

> **Free technique/ski skating.** Move on your skis as though you were on ice skates, shifting your weight from one foot to the other with each stride. You also use a "double poling" movement, which means using both poles at the same time to go forward. This technique allows you to go faster than the classical one does, but it takes much more strength and endurance.

If you enjoy hiking in the summer, try cross-country skiing in the winter.

## Downhill Skiing

Skiing is an exhilarating way to enjoy the beautiful mountain scenery. Learn the basic techniques before hitting the slopes:

> **Snowplowing.** This technique allows you to slow yourself down or even stop by putting pressure against the snow with the edge of your skis. It is what most people use when first learning how to ski.

> **Schussing.** This is the basic method of going down the hill. With your skis pointing straight in front of you, take the plunge and make your way down. At first it will seem fast, but you will get used to the speed of downhill with practice.

## Equipment

You don't need the most expensive equipment, but you do need equipment that is of good quality to keep you safe and help you ski better. Always get advice to help you make the right choice:

> **Boots.** They should fit snugly, support your feet and ankles, and keep your feet warm and dry.

> **Skis.** They should be the right length and width for your height, as well as for the type of skiing. Downhill skis are shorter and wider than skis designed for cross-country.

> **Bindings.** They keep your boots connected to your skis, but they're also for safety. They are designed to prevent serious injury by releasing your boots when you fall.

> **Poles.** These should be light so your arms don't tire, but strong and flexible so they don't break. When buying or renting, ask for help to make sure the poles are the right length. If they're too long or too short, they will be difficult to use.

## Snowboarding

**W**hat do you get when you combine skiing, surfing, and skateboarding? Snowboarding, of course, and it's getting more popular every year.

With both feet strapped to a fiberglass board, you surf the hill all the way to the bottom, and stay balanced by shifting your weight from your toes to your knees.

One of the first snowboards was made by Sherman Poppen in 1965, when he took two skis and stuck them together to surf down a snowy hill. At first, snowboarding was only practised by a small group of people. Because it was difficult to find snowboards in stores, many of them were homemade. Because the technique wasn't fully developed and there were no instructors, many people injured themselves when they hit the steep slopes.

In 1998, snowboarding made its Olympic debut at the Winter Games in Nagano, Japan. It featured two types: the half-pipe, where the riders twist and turn in the air in a freestyle way, and the giant slalom, where the athletes go down the traditional ski hill.

The first Olympic gold medal for snowboarding was awarded to Canadian Ross Rebagliati. Today, snowboarding is a mainstream sport and can be practised at most ski hills and resorts.

## Skiing Safety

➤ **Learn from the pros.** When you are just starting out, taking a few lessons is the best way to learn the proper technique so that you don't make unnecessary mistakes and hurt yourself.

➤ **Choose the right trail or slope.** Skiing is supposed to be challenging, but if you push yourself too hard by attempting a steep slope or a long trail before you are ready, you could end up exhausted or hurt.

➤ **Don't fight the fall.** Skiing and falling down go hand in hand, so find out from your instructor how to fall properly and keep your body loose to minimize the impact. You will need to learn how to get back up, too.

➤ **Be prepared.** Before you start, learn all the basic techniques, such as how to stop. Check all your equipment to be sure it's not faulty. If you are going on a long cross-country trail, bring a backpack with water and snacks.

## Extreme Skiing

If you get really good at the sport, and you want an even bigger rush, try any of the following, but do so cautiously. Always have a buddy, and always let someone know where you are:

➤ **Mogul skiing.** As you ski downhill, you go over bumps or mounds of snow of different sizes.

➤ **Backcountry skiing.** This is only for the super-advanced skier who wants to get off the regular hill and test his or her skills. No chair lifts, no groomed slopes or trails—just you and the great outdoors. This is often a group activity and you should be careful to research the places you ski before hitting the slopes. Avalanches are a big threat to backcountry skiers.

➤ **Ski jumping.** You head down a track and soar through the air, trying to jump as far as you can. If you have seen this in competitions, it really looks like ski flying.

## Getting Involved

While some places in Canada make skiing of one kind or the other more accessible, there are still ways to try out both downhill and cross country. Join a school team, if that's an option, or go on a school-organized ski trip.

Ski equipment is expensive, but you don't have to rush out and buy the whole collection on your first time out. Rent or borrow equipment until you figure out if this is the sport for you.

Check out Ski and Snowboard Canada **www.skicanada.org** or Cross Country Canada **www.cccski.com** for more information.

## The Crazy Canucks
### Playing to Win (and to Have Fun)

**TRAINING AS A TEAM LEADS CANADIANS TO THE TOP**

Because of a seemingly reckless approach to downhill ski racing—an approach that brought many impressive victories in international races, along with an equal number of spectacular spills and crashes—the Canadian men's downhill ski team of the mid-1970s and early-1980s came to be known as "The Crazy Canucks."

On the surface, skiers Ken Read, Steve Podborksi, Dave Murray, and Dale Irwin seemed to be possessed with a burning will to zip down the massive slopes of Europe and North America, without any regard to their own personal safety, and with very little thought behind their approach to the sport as well. Nothing, though, could have been further from the truth.

As Read, Podborski, and crew notched win after win in major World Cup events (Read's victory in Chamonix, France, in 1978 was the first win by a non-European in World Cup competition), it became clear to experienced observers of downhill racing that the success of the Crazy Canucks actually was the result of some innovative training methods, originating back home in Canada.

Starting in the mid-1960s, a group of Canadian coaches decided that, instead of taking the traditional approach and placing all their hopes on a single superstar skier, supporting that one athlete with as much coaching as possible, it would make more sense to train a large group of skiers together, each working to make the other ones better.

The result was that by the mid-1970s, several Canadian skiers had reached top positions in the world ranking. At a race in Schladming, Austria, in 1978, the skiing world took particular notice when Canada put four athletes in the top ten. Read won, Murray finished second, Irwin seventh, and Podborski ninth.

The Canadians did have some detractors among fans and skiing experts. However, the Crazy Canucks, who put Canada on the world skiing map, were responsible for a huge boom in interest in the sport, both at home and in Europe, and they revolutionized ski training forever.

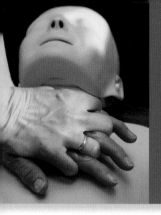

# Appendix 1
## Cardiopulmonary Resuscitation

## Key Terms

- Advanced Coronary Treatment Foundation (ACT Foundation)
- Chain of Survival
- CPR training
- High School CPR Student Manual
- heart attack
- cardiac arrest
- defibrillation
- stroke
- 4 "Rs" of CPR

**C**ardiovascular disease is the leading cause of death in Canada. Most heart attacks occur suddenly, with little warning. Many are witnessed by family members who are unprepared as to how to respond. Learning how to respond could mean saving the life of someone you love.

The **Advanced Coronary Treatment Foundation (ACT Foundation)** is a national, non-profit organization based in Ottawa. The ACT Foundation is committed to ensuring that cardiovascular disease prevention information is brought into homes across Canada.

### The Chain of Survival

Extensive medical research shows that, if present, a certain sequence of events can give victims of cardiac arrest a much better chance of survival. This **Chain of Survival** includes:

- **Early Healthy Choices**—making healthy lifestyle decisions
- **Early Recognition**—recognizing a serious developing emergency
- **Early Access**—quickly calling the Emergency Medical Services (telephone 9-1-1)
- **Early CPR**—promptly giving cardiopulmonary resuscitation when needed
- **Early Defibrillation**—having access to a defibrillator and being trained to use it when required
- **Early Advanced Care**—having access to emergency health care (paramedics)
- **Early rehabilitation**—returning to a normal lifestyle after a cardiac problem

A key component of this Chain of Survival is proper **CPR training**. CPR training is a basic "life skill" and is now included as a part of high-school education across the country.

The full text of the **High School CPR Student Manual** is reproduced in this Appendix, courtesy of the ACT Foundation.

# ACT High School CPR
# Student Manual

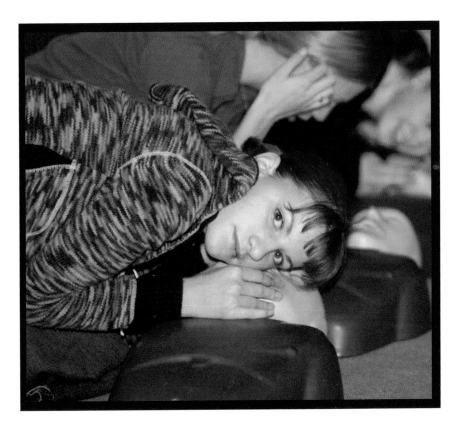

## ACT FOUNDATION

*CORE PARTNERS:*

**AstraZeneca**

**Bristol-Myers Squibb Canada**

**Pfizer Canada**

**sanofi-aventis**

*PROVINCIAL PROGRAM PARTNERS:*

**Government of Ontario**

**Hydro One**

**The Ontario Trillium Foundation**

**Shoppers Drug Mart**

# HIGH SCHOOL CPR STUDENT MANUAL
## TABLE OF CONTENTS

## Acknowledgments

This manual was written by Dr. Justin Maloney, Emergency Physician at the Ottawa Hospital and Medical Director of the Ottawa Base Hospital Program. Les Johnson and Sandra Clarke served as principal consultants, editors and guiding lights. Mr. Johnson is Director of Client Services for St. John Ambulance, National Branch, and a member of the Regional Heart Saver Committee. Ms. Clarke is Executive Director of the ACT Foundation, a national charitable foundation funded by companies in the research-based pharmaceutical industry: AstraZeneca, Bristol-Myers Squibb Canada, Pfizer Canada, and sanofi-aventis. ACT promotes CPR and improved prehospital care.

The manual was reviewed by a battery of high school teachers and students, CPR Instructors, Instructor Trainers, and hospital and Base Hospital Program staff.

The guidelines for CPR are based on guideline recommendations from the 2005 International Consensus on CPR and ECC Science with Treatment Recommendations (CoSTR).

"Tips to reduce fats in your diet..." was borrowed from The Light-Hearted Cookbook, published by the Canadian Heart Foundation. The Chain of SurvivalTM logo is a registered trademark of the Heart and Stroke Foundation of Canada. Illustrations of heart and lungs were reproduced with permission of St. John Ambulance, Canada.

This manual may only be reproduced with written permission from the author.

© 2006 Justin Maloney, M.D., c/o The Advanced Coronary Treatment (ACT) Foundation, 379 Holland Ave., Ottawa ON K1Y 0Y9

Tel.: (613) 729-3455 or (800) 465-9111; Fax: (613) 729-5837; Email: act@actfoundation.ca; Web site: www.actfoundation.ca

## THE 4 "Rs" OF CPR

**RISK**

**RECOGNIZE**

**REACT**

**RESUSCITATE**

# Hi There!

## INTRODUCTION: CHAIN OF SURVIVAL

**Welcome to the world of CPR...** Cardiopulmonary Resuscitation. You are going to learn how to help someone who chokes or someone whose heart stops. CPR is the "heart" of any first aid program. (Sorry for the pun).

### This CPR course teaches the 4 "Rs" of CPR:

**RISK:** factors in your life that predispose you to developing heart problems or a stroke;
**RECOGNIZE:** how to recognize a serious developing emergency;
**REACT:** what to do when you see a developing emergency;
**RESUSCITATE:** how to do CPR and how to help someone who is choking.

Why learn this? Don't paramedics look after prehospital cardiac arrests and other serious emergencies? Why you? Well, the key to surviving these emergencies is a chain reaction. It's the **CHAIN OF SURVIVAL,** the emergency response system we need if we are going to improve survival from emergencies:

**Early Healthy Choices:** making lifestyle decisions.

**Early Recognition:** recognizing a serious developing emergency.

**Early Access:** means calling 911 for help.

**Early CPR:** maintaining a person's breathing and circulation until help arrives.

**Early Defibrillation:** a shocking thing you are going to learn about later.

**Early Advanced Care:** paramedics racing to the side of a sick person.

**Early Rehabilitation:** returning to a normal lifestyle after a cardiac problem.

Someone's life may depend on what you learn in this course. Don't forget that for a minute. But learning it will be fun too. There is a lot of information here. It's wisdom you can take home to your family now, and carry with you through your life. So let's get into it.

**Nitroglycerin**

Many people take nitroglycerin spray when they get angina. It helps open up the circulation and relieves the pain.

# THE HEART AND WHEN IT BREAKS

## What is a Heart Attack?

Oxygen is carried by blood through a network of blood vessels, nourishing the organs of the body. Without circulating blood, without oxygen, these organs start to die.

Without oxygen, serious damage to the brain starts in 4 to 6 minutes. Other organs like the heart last longer without oxygen, but only minutes longer.

The heart is a mighty tough muscle. Like any muscle, it needs oxygen delivered to its tissues.

The heart has its own blood vessels that supply its muscle. When one of these arteries gets blocked (e.g. by plaque, which is junk like fat or cholesterol) the area of heart muscle that the artery nourishes is suddenly deprived of circulation... no blood circulating, so no oxygen... the person experiences chest pain.

If the blockage opens up after a little bit, the pain goes away (until next time). This is what is called **angina.**

If the artery stays blocked, the pain remains and the area of affected heart muscle starts to die. This is what most people call a **heart attack. (Trivia**... doctors call this an **infarction**).

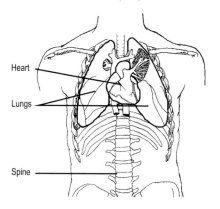

Heart

Lungs

Spine

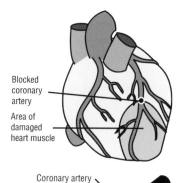

Blocked coronary artery

Area of damaged heart muscle

Coronary artery

Plaque buildup

## What is Cardiac Arrest?

When a heart stops beating, it is no longer pumping blood to the rest of the body. That heart is in "**cardiac arrest.**"

When heart muscle is suffering because it can't get oxygen, it gets irritable. (If you choke and can't get air, you'll get irritable too!) The heart's main muscles, the ones around the **ventricles**, lose their rhythmic pumping action and may start to **fibrillate**. This is a squirmy kind of muscle contraction that doesn't pump blood. It is called **ventricular fibrillation** (because it is a ventricle and it is fibrillating). This is the most common kind of cardiac arrest. It is also the most treatable.

## What is CPR?

Starting **Cardiopulmonary Resuscitation** on a person whose heart has stopped, means two things:

1. Pushing on the person's chest forces blood to flow through the body.

2. Mouth-to-mouth breathing provides oxygen to the lungs.

## What is Defibrillation?

When you call 911 and start CPR on someone, paramedics or firefighters will be there in a few minutes. They attach a small computerized device (a defibrillator) to that person. It delivers a special kind of shock to the heart, trying to kickstart it, trying to reset the heart muscle and restore its smooth pumping action. This is called **defibrillation**... ZAP!

# WHAT IS A STROKE?

If you understand heart attacks, you can figure this out. Remember how arteries to the heart can get blocked by junk, like fat or cholesterol? The area of heart muscle that the artery nourishes suddenly receives no circulation (no blood circulating, so no oxygen) and the person experiences a heart attack.

It is the same in the brain. After a lifetime of burgs and fries, an artery gets blocked up by all that cholesterol. When the area of the brain nourished by that artery has no oxygen, it gets damaged. As a result, a person may have a sudden headache, slurred speech, vision problems or sudden weakness of the face, an arm or leg. That is a **stroke**.

Someone thought, "Hmm, if it happens in the heart and we call it a heart attack why not call this a **'brain attack?'**"

One kind of stroke is different. Instead of getting clogged up like a usual stroke, a blood vessel bursts. You can't tell without tests at the hospital which kind of stroke it is. No matter which kind of stroke it is, you have to help in the same ways you will learn here.

That part was tough. You learned about blood circulation and oxygen, about hearts that stop when they fibrillate and start when someone defibrillates them. And you learned a little about strokes or "brain attacks."

Now you are ready to learn the 4 "Rs" of CPR. Knowing them lets you make the system move when an emergency occurs.

Let's tackle those 4 "Rs."

## Defibrillation A Shocking Thing!!

When you deliver the shock and the heart stops fibrillating, you have de-fibrillated it.

## "PAD" Public Access Defibrillation

Look for new small easy-to-use defibrillators soon to be hanging on the walls in lots of places, just like fire extinguishers.

Lifeguards, security guards, even hotel desk clerks and the waiter in your favourite restaurant are being trained to use them. Seriously!

These are for the general public to use. That is how they get their name.

# Risk Factors You Can Control

Cigarette smoking

High blood cholesterol

High blood pressure

Diabetes

Obesity

Lack of exercise

Excessive stress

(for some people).

# Tips to Reduce Fats in Your Diet

Eat partly skimmed mozzarella instead of cheddar cheese

Eat apple crisp rather than apple pie

Eat yogurt instead of ice cream

Remove skin from chicken

For more tips like these, look in The Canadian Heart Foundation's "The Light Hearted Cookbook."

# THE 4 "Rs" OF CPR

## I. Risk Factors — Heart Disease and Stroke

A risk factor is something that increases the chance of heart disease or stroke. If you have several relatives who have heart trouble, you may too be at risk. This, and simply getting older, are two risk factors you can't do much about.

But you can do something about most risk factors. Let's talk about these and about being **"Heart Healthy."**

## Smoking

**Smoking** causes lung cancer and stinky breath. It is also the leading cause of heart disease in Canada. It is the worst, most direct, very personal, kind of air pollution. Even if you don't smoke, those smokers around you are offering you second-hand air pollution. (Now which is worse, nice fresh air pollution or used stuff? Either way, this is not attractive!)

## High Blood Cholesterol

**High blood cholesterol** means lots of fat in the blood. Some is produced by our body, while other fat comes from our food. Too much cholesterol can cause heart disease or stroke. To help reduce your chances of having high cholesterol, eat more vegetables, fruits and grain products, limit the amount of fat in your diet and get plenty of physical exercise.

## High Blood Pressure

**High blood pressure** can damage your heart and blood vessels, increasing your chances of having a heart attack or stroke. It means your heart has to work harder to pump blood through those pipes, your blood vessels. It can run in families, but diet and stress may affect it too. Your blood pressure can be too high and you might not know it. You may feel pretty normal. But it is still dangerous. Everyone should have their blood pressure checked regularly.

## Diabetes

**Diabetes** affects the level of sugar and fat in your blood. It is a problem, but it can be managed. People with diabetes will do better and have fewer complications like heart trouble or stroke if they eat properly and follow their doctor's instructions.

## Obesity

**Obesity** is not good, because if you are obese, the heart has to pump harder all the time to move blood around.

So what's the difference if your heart works hard because you are overweight or because you exercise? Why is one good and the other not? Well, a sweaty weightlifter does a workout, hits the showers, rests a day and comes back for more. His muscles get stronger. If he had to lift weights 24 hours a day, his body odour might get stronger, but his muscles, well, they would just wear out.

## We Are Not Just Talking About Heart Attacks!

Remember, emergencies needing CPR happen for various reasons. People of all ages drown, get electrocuted, or bleed from injuries. With your CPR training you will be able to assess if a person with one of these problems needs CPR.

## Lack of Exercise

**Lack of exercise** is another risk factor. Remember, your heart is a muscle. Just like other muscles in your body, it works better if you keep fit and active. Exercise makes the heart work hard and this is good.

## Stress

**Stress** affects the body in very physical ways. If you are nervous, if your hands are shaking, you can be sure things inside of you are also being affected. If you are stressed for a long period of time, your body may break down. Heart problems can be one of the results.

## Lifestyles, Risk Factors — Some Thoughts

You never find parents **encouraging** kids to smoke. They learned the little things about smoking, like the expense and the bad breath! Some have learned about the bigger costs, about wheezing, heart disease or lung cancer.

And what overweight adult wouldn't love to be fit and thin? Yet, unlike smoking, you still find adults who don't know what a healthy diet is. Some kids are growing up with poor diet habits they pick up at home. There is more work to do here.

If some adults in your life smoke or are overweight, it may not be totally their fault. It can be really tough to lose weight or stop smoking. Now, many of those adults have health problems. You can be smarter, developing healthy living habits. You are able to learn more about what to do... and about what not to do. Set your own course.

**Well, that is one "R" out of the way. Don't be afraid to go and tell the folks at home what you have learned about Risk factors. You may help someone make wiser choices.**

**Now let's move on to Recognition...**

## II. Recognize

Recognizing that a person is having a heart attack or stroke may be tough. If it is someone close to you, it may be even more difficult.

**"Early Recognition"** means realizing someone may be having heart trouble or a stroke. You will learn the ABCs and D of that later. It means recognizing that some kinds of chest pain, weakness or choking situations may mean serious trouble. If a person is having a heart attack, there is a risk of cardiac arrest. If it is a stroke, the person may be paralyzed. **The sooner the person gets to the hospital, the better the chance that things will be OK**. People who choke may need help **right now**.

If the problem is a heart attack or a stroke, doctors now have miracle drugs called "thrombolytics" that dissolve blood clots and other treatments that open blocked blood vessels. They reduce damage to the heart or brain — but they must be given **very early** in order to work. You must recognize there is a problem and **call 911 quickly**. You can make a difference. You can help save a life!

## Signals of a Heart Attack — Look for the 5 "Ps"

**Pain** from a heart attack is often described as a heaviness, tightness, squeezing or pressure, like someone was "sitting on my chest." The pain may be severe or mild. It may spread to the neck, jaw, shoulders or arms.
**Pale skin** (that is often sweaty).
**Puffing** — trouble breathing.
**Pooped** — feeling very tired.
**Puking** — feeling sick to the stomach or actually vomiting.

## Signals of a Stroke

Signals of a stroke that paramedics look for especially are sudden **paralysis of the face, arm or leg, and/or sudden speech problems**. Other signs of stroke include **weakness, numbness, or tingling in the face, arm or leg, dizziness, and/or sudden headache**.

### Something else...

Don't be surprised if the person having trouble is also having some trouble accepting they might be experiencing a heart problem or stroke. You might see:

**Denial** — "I'm too young!" "It will go away with a little rest!" The thought, "It can't be happening to me" is pretty common.

**Fear** — the person may be terrified inside and afraid to go to the hospital.

**Be firm. If the signals are there suggesting a heart attack or stroke, the person needs to be taken by ambulance to a hospital quickly.**

**It is important that you Recognize that what is happening in front of you may be a real emergency. Remember the signals for heart attack and the signals for stroke and don't let yourself be paralyzed by Fear and Denial. Now let's learn how to React...**

**Signals of a Heart Attack**
The 5 "Ps"
Pain
Pale
Puffing
Pooped
Puking

**Signals of a Stroke**

Signs paramedics look for especially,

**Sudden:**
Paralysis of the face, arm or leg.
Speech problems.

**Suspect a Stroke?**
**Try Asking:**

Can you smile?
Can you raise both arms?
Can you speak a simple sentence?

If the Person
has Chest Pain...
What Do You Do?

Remember:

"Hazards &
Holler"

Then... stay with
your patient and
offer a little **PLT**

Position — **P**
Loosen clothing — **L**
Talk, reassure — **T**

**Alert ! Alert !**

People who have
been ill often wear
a **"MedicAlert"** bracelet
or necklace.
It will often have
information about the
person's allergies, past
medical history and
medications.

# III. React

## What if it Might be a Heart Attack or Stroke?

**Check for hazards** — make sure there is nothing around that can hurt you
(e.g. electric wires, traffic, fire, glass, gas).

**Holler for help** if you are alone. If you are still alone, call 911 for an ambulance.
If someone hears your call, get that person to call 911.

While waiting for the ambulance there are several things you can do to make a person
more comfortable:

**Position the person** so he/she is most comfortable. Usually sitting or lying down
will be best but the person will usually tell you what works best;

**Loosen tight clothing** at the neck or waist;

**Talk to the person.** Let him or her know help is on the way. Remember, as much as
possible, stay with the person. If the person becomes unconscious, he/she will need
your help even more.

## What to do Until the Ambulance Gets There

Paramedics are trying to find you. Be **Visible with Information**. Get out front. Wave
and/or flash lights when you see them.

What information should you give them about the person?

**Medications**    — Gather any medications. Bag them if you can.
**Allergies**    — Are there any? Ask. Write them down.

So, Hazards and Holler, a little PLT, and flash the paramedics. Remember that and you
know how to React when you see an emergency develop.

Now let's move on to Resuscitation...

*HOLD IT! Stop everything! Did they really just say you were supposed to
"flash the paramedics?"*

*NO! NO! They meant to say "flash the lights!"*
*...the porch lights*
*...the house lights*
*...any lights*

## IV. Resuscitate

Resuscitation is as simple as ABC & D!

**A** — **Airway.** Something in the mouth blocking air from getting in? Get it out of there.

**B** — **Breathing.** Not breathing? Do mouth to mouth. Breathe for this person.

**C** — **Circulation.** Start chest compressions to help blood circulate.

**D** — **Defibrillation.** If you started CPR, make sure help is coming, especially someone with a defibrillator.

**The purpose of CPR** is to keep alive a person who has stopped breathing and who has no circulation until either the person is breathing and circulation returns, or until medical help takes over... and how do you do that?

Well, you **remember your ABCs**, and just do what you are trained to do on the next pages!!!

## Ask Permission To Help...

Before touching a person who needs help but who is still conscious, you must ask for and get permission to help. Say you know first aid and offer to help.
Ask, "May I help you?"

If the person is unconscious or is a young child who is alone, go ahead and help; the law assumes the person wants help. Care for that person the same way you would want someone to care for you if you were in the same difficulty. Do what you are trained to do. Do your best.

# ONE RESCUER CPR — ADULT

## If someone collapses...

**1**   **Check for hazards.** Make sure there is nothing around that can hurt you (e.g. electric wires, traffic, fire, glass, gas).

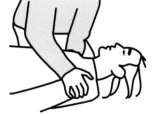

**2**   **Assess responsiveness.** Gently tap shoulders, call out to the person.

**3**   **Call 911** or your local EMS, or have someone call for you, if the person is not moving or does not respond.

**4**   **Open the airway** using the **head-tilt chin-lift** method.

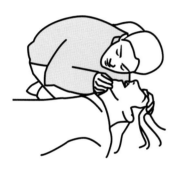

**5**   **Check for breathing** for up to 10 seconds. Put your ear over the person's mouth and nose.

*Look* at the chest for movement.
*Listen* for the sounds of breathing.
*Feel* for exhaled breath on your cheek.

*You are checking for breathing and suddenly the person takes a breath or two - a sort of gasp or sigh. Sometimes this happens, especially if a person's heart has just stopped. It will not look like normal regular breathing. The person is in cardiac arrest. Start CPR.*

## Head-tilt Chin-lift:

Place one of your hands on the person's forehead and the fingers of your other hand under the bony part of the lower jaw near the chin. Tilt the person's head back by pushing down on the forehead. At the same time, gently lift the chin up to open the airway.

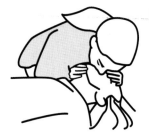

**6** **Give 2 breaths\*** if the person is not breathing normally.

Maintain the head-tilt chin-lift. Pinch the person's nose, take a normal breath and cover their mouth with your mouth (assuring a good seal at the nose and mouth).

Give 2 breaths, 1 second for each breath. Watch the person's chest to make sure it rises and falls with each of your breaths.

If your breaths do not go in, reposition the head to open the airway, check your seals at the mouth and nose, and try again.

*\*Note: You are learning how to do mouth-to-mouth breathing, but some people may be nervous to do it as part of CPR. That is OK, but it is important to do something! If you are reluctant to perform mouth to mouth, just do the chest compressions. It's better to do something than nothing!*

**7** **Landmark for chest compressions.**

Compress the lower half of the person's breastbone in the centre of the chest, between the nipples.

Place the heel of your hand on the breastbone in the centre of the chest between the nipples. Place the heel of your second hand on top of the first so that your hands are overlapping and parallel.

Interlock your fingers off the chest. Position your shoulders directly above the heels of your hands. Keep your arms straight, with your elbows locked in position. Your instructor will show you how.

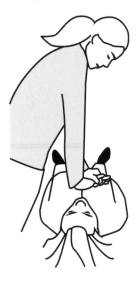

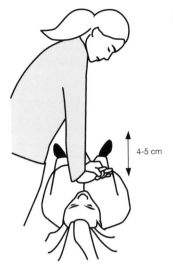

## 8 Give 30 compressions and 2 breaths.

Give 30 compressions in a little less than 20 seconds. The ideal rate is 100 compressions in 1 minute.

Compress straight down on the breastbone. Compress 4 to 5 cm (1.5 to 2 inches) at a rate of 100 compressions per minute (e.g. 5 compressions in 3 seconds). **Compressions should be hard and fast.**

It helps if you count aloud (e.g. 1 and 2 and 3 and 4 and 5 and 1 and 2 and 3 and 4 and 10 and 1 and 2 and 3 and 4 and 15 and etc. on up to 30).

Without losing contact with the chest, allow the chest to return to its normal position between compressions. Compression and relaxation times should be about equal. Find your landmark with each new cycle of compressions.

**Continue CPR** until someone brings an Automatic External Defibrillator (AED), the person moves, or Emergency Medical Service (EMS) personnel take over.

4-5 cm

### Getting Tired?

If you get tired while doing CPR and there are others around who know how to do it, ask for someone to take over. Do your best until help arrives.

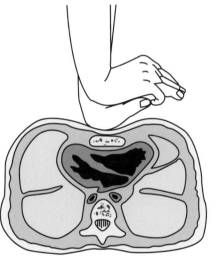

*Note: If you do it right, hard enough and fast enough, your chest compressions squeeze the heart and all the big blood vessels in the chest. That is how CPR circulates blood. It only provides about 30% of normal circulation but studies show early CPR is the most important thing to save someone whose heart has stopped.*

# Remember...

## 30 and 2

## 30 and 2

## 30 and 2

## is what you do

## Rock 'em 'till

## someone

## can shock'em...!

# CHOKING

When a person chokes on food or a small object that is lodged in the throat, air cannot reach the lungs. The person may die if help is not given immediately. **Recognize** that a person is choking by the universal distress sign of choking — hands to the throat.

When a person chokes, the throat or airway can be either mildly or severely blocked.

A **mildly blocked airway** allows some air to get in. If a choking person can still speak, cough and breathe, you know the blockage is not complete. Encourage the person to cough to try to clear the obstruction themselves.

With a **severely blocked airway**, there is no air getting in. If that person can't speak, cough and breathe, you have to **React** quickly. This is a serious emergency.

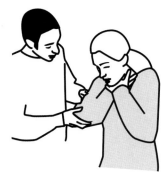

## Adult Conscious (the Heimlich Manoeuvre)

**1**  **Assess the airway blockage.** Ask, "Are you choking?"

**2**  **Holler for help.** Reassure the person and explain what you are going to do. Call 911 or your local Emergency Medical Service (EMS), or have someone call for you if the person is having difficulty breathing.

**"Are You Choking?"**

**3**  **Give abdominal thrusts** if the choking person cannot speak, cough or breathe. Stand behind the person and wrap your arms around his/her waist. Make a fist with one of your hands and place the thumb side of that fist in the belly button area, slightly above the belly button and well below where the ribs meet. Grasp your fist with your other hand and press inward and upward with a sudden forceful thrust.

**4**  **Repeat abdominal thrusts** in rapid sequence until either the obstruction is removed or the person becomes unconscious. When the obstruction is removed, the person should see a doctor to rule out complications from the obstruction or the abdominal thrusts.

## If the Choking Person Becomes Unconscious
(Carefully support the person to the ground, activate EMS and begin CPR.)

**1** **Call 911** or your local Emergency Medical Service (EMS), or have someone call for you.

**2** **Open the mouth and look for the obstruction.** If you can see the obstruction, try to remove it with a hooked finger.

**3** **Open the airway** using the head-tilt chin-lift, and check for breathing for up to 10 seconds. Even though you may not be able to see the obstruction, it may have loosened enough to let some air pass by it and enter the lungs.

**4** **Try to give a breath.** If air won't go in, reposition the head, check your seals at the mouth and nose and try to give another breath.

**5** **If the chest does not rise, landmark and give 30 chest compressions.** This may remove the obstruction.

**6** **Open the mouth and look for the obstruction.** If you can see the obstruction, try to remove it with a hooked finger. Open the airway and attempt to ventilate again. If air still won't go in...

**7** **Repeat sequence of chest compressions,** looking in the mouth, opening the airway and attempting to ventilate until you are successful, or until medical help takes over.

## Adult Found Unconscious

**1** **Check for hazards.** Make sure there is nothing around that can hurt you (e.g. electric wires, traffic, fire, glass, gas).

**2** **Assess responsiveness.** Gently tap shoulders, call out to the person.

**3** **Call 911** or your local EMS, or have someone call for you if the person is not moving or does not respond.

**4** **Open the airway** using the head-tilt chin-lift method.

**5** **Check for breathing** for up to 10 seconds. Put your ear over the person's mouth and nose. **Look** at the chest for movement, **listen** for the sounds of breathing and **feel** for exhaled breath on your cheek.

**6** **Try to give a breath** if the person is not breathing. If air won't go in, reposition the head, check your seals at the mouth and nose and try to give another **breath**. If the chest still does not rise, conclude that the **airway** is blocked by something.

**7** **Landmark and give 30 chest compressions.**

**8** **Open the mouth and look for the obstruction.** If you can see the obstruction, try to remove it with a hooked finger. Open the airway and attempt to ventilate again. If air still won't go in...

**9** **Repeat sequence of chest compressions,** looking in the mouth, opening the airway and attempting to ventilate until you are successful, or until medical help takes over.

**Recovery Position**

## Follow-Up Care *(Your Instructor will show you how)*

When the person starts to breathe, place him/her into the **recovery position** if injuries permit. The person may gag or vomit, and the recovery position will help keep the airway open and allow fluids to drain from the mouth. Monitor the breathing carefully. The person may stop breathing again. Stay with the person until medical help takes over.

For information on different rescue scenarios you may encounter, as well as new information relating to the world of CPR (including guideline updates), check out ACT's Web site at www.actfoundation.ca!

## I Know

I see you falling
I see you in pain
I see you need help
It's why I train

I see you dad
I see you mom
Sister n' brother
We help one another

I know the 4 Rs
I know the Chain
I'll save a life
It's why I train

I know the Risks
I Recognize
I will React
Resuscitate

Do you know
what it needs?
Do you know what to do?
I know what it needs
I know what to do

I know it, know it, know it
I will do it, do it, do it
Know it, do it
Know it, do it

CPR, CPR, CPR!

## It's not just about CPR !! It's about

# CP-R-R-R-R...

So you thought this CPR course was all about learning CPR. Well OK, that is understandable. But wait! Think of what you have learned. Think about the **4 "Rs."**

You now know about **Risk** factors, that a life of burgers and fries and stinky cigarette breath can be a short one. Lots of overweight adults and parents who struggle to quit smoking would have loved to know what you know when they started out.

Maybe you will never see anyone collapse. Maybe you won't ever have to do CPR. But chances are greater that you will be around someone who falls ill. You have learned to **Recognize** if that person might be having a heart attack or stroke.

Seeing someone in your family having chest pain, looking pale and sweaty (remember your Ps) should push you to help them get to the hospital. If your dad has chest pain, he may not know about clot busters. But you do. You were not trained to be shy. Step up! **React!**

The "CPR thing" is only part of this course. **Resuscitate** is only one of the 4 "Rs." Not everyone who falls sick has a cardiac arrest, but you can still help them. The sequences of CPR are important to remember. However, it is more likely you will need to remember the **"5 Ps of chest pain"** than how to do CPR. You need to remember **"Hazards and Holler and a Little PLT."** You need to be **Visible with Information** for the paramedics.

Be a champion! You have the knowledge. You know the **"Risks."** Help others avoid trouble. But if there is trouble, you know **"Recognize."** You know **"React."** And yes, sometimes you will need to **"Resuscitate"** and do CPR.

## SO, LET'S TEST YOUR 4 R I/Q...

# SCENES FROM LIFE

1 You are on a field trip to a local museum. You notice that Mrs. Jones, one of your teachers, is standing very quietly. She does not look well. Speaking with Mrs. Jones you **Recognize** her pain might be cardiac.

**(The 5 Ps of Chest Pain)**

You **React**, getting someone to look for another teacher. If there is none, you get someone to call 911. You sit Mrs. Jones down and open a window so she can get some air.

**(Hazards and Holler and a little PLT)**

Now that the paramedics are coming, ask Mrs. Jones about medications, allergies, etc... While you are doing that, ask someone else to go to the front door of the museum to guide the paramedics to where you are.

**(Visible with Information)**

2 Your allergic brother comes home from a friend's house wheezing badly. He played with a dog there and his asthma is severe. He is using his inhaler too often and not getting better. You holler for your mom, who calls 911. You reassure him help is coming. You stay right with him. You tell your mom to bag his inhalers and go to the front to wave at the paramedics as they come down the street.

**(Hazards and Holler and a little PLT)**
**(Visible with Information)**

Your brother gets sicker and suddenly you realize he is very quiet. He is unresponsive and is not breathing. You are scared, but you start CPR.

**(Resuscitate)**

3 There is a fight in the schoolyard. A boy is down. You **Recognize** his airway is OK, he is breathing. You support his neck, making sure it doesn't move.

**(ABCs)**

You **React**, yelling for someone to get a teacher and call 911.

**(Hazards and Holler and a little PLT)**

You send a friend to the front of the school to guide the paramedics. When the paramedics arrive, you point out the boy is wearing a MedicAlert bracelet.

**(Visible with Information)**

# MORE SCENES FROM LIFE

**4**    At a family dinner, you notice your grandmother is suddenly having trouble speaking. She drops a fork and can't pick it up. She looks ill. You **Recognize** she might be showing signs of a stroke.

(The "P" Sign of a Brain Attack — Paralysis)

You **React**, pointing out to everyone that Granny is sick. You note this could be a stroke. Your mom calls 911 as you help carry Granny to bed.

(Hazards and Holler and a little PLT)

While your dad checks Granny's purse looking for medications, you ask your mom questions. You write the answers down for the paramedics. Your brother moves the car out of the driveway so the ambulance can get close to the house.

(Visible with Information)

**5**    You and your dad are alone watching TV. You suddenly notice he doesn't look comfortable. He says he has pain, which you **Recognize** might be a heart problem.

(The 5 Ps of Chest Pain)

You **React**, urging him to call 911. You tell him you are afraid for him and you let him know about clot-busters. He says it is nothing, probably indigestion. He is sweaty and vomits. You decide to act on your own. You call 911. You help dad lie down.

(Hazards and Holler and a little PLT)

You leave him for a second to turn the porch light on so the paramedics can see the address number. You ask your dad where his medications are. When the paramedics arrive, you tell them dad's medications are in the bathroom.

(Visible with Information)

**6**    At a party, a girl is found unconscious in the backyard pool. Someone has lifted her to the poolside. You step up and say "I know CPR." (It scares you a little that people are suddenly listening to you and doing what you say). You **Recognize** that this person is in cardiac arrest.

(ABCs)

You **React**, yelling for someone to call 911.

(Hazards and Holler and a little PLT)

And you **Resuscitate**, starting CPR. Be careful to support her neck, because you don't know how she fell into that pool! You tell someone to get any information about this girl. Who is she? Does she have a wallet? Does it have any medical information in it? You send someone to the street to flag down the paramedics and guide them through the house to the backyard.

(Visible with Information)<br>(Resuscitate)

**There is No
"S rvival"
Without "u"**

**I know CPR**

I know **Risks**
I know **Recognize**
I know **React**
I know **Resuscitate**

I know **CPR!**
I **know!**

# LAST WORDS...
## WE WANT YOU TO RATTLE THE CHAIN

Lots of people die. They die from drowning, from heart attacks, from all kinds of things. They are someone's mom or dad, someone's brother or sister, someone's child, someone's friend... you get the picture. Maybe someone in your family died of a heart attack — someone close to you? Was everything done that could have been done? The thing is, some of them didn't have to die. If only someone had known how to help, how to rattle the **Chain of Survival.**

A person collapsing in cardiac arrest will have a much better chance if someone calls 911 fast and starts CPR fast, if someone defibrillates the person fast, and if paramedics arrive fast... all those things, FAST! These are links in the **"Chain of Survival."** The missing link? It's you! That is going to change now that you know CPR. You are never going to be helpless if someone collapses in front of you.

Not everyone is going to live just because you start CPR. But **no cardiac arrest patient lives if you don't start CPR**. The 911 system, defibrillators, paramedics... **forget it all if you don't do CPR until more help arrives**. You know how to **"RATTLE THE CHAIN."** You are the key link!

If you feel good about learning this new skill, tell your teacher. But also tell your family and friends. Show them what you have learned. Bug them to take a course as well.

You should refresh your CPR skills over time. There will be changes in the course and you will want to stay on top of things. Flashing a current CPR card might look good when you apply for a job, even babysitting.

Congratulations! Stand up and say **"I KNOW!"** No, shout it. Remember, you are CPR in your house. You are the one to make a difference, perhaps a difference between life and death for someone because of what you know. Be proud! When someone needs you, step up!

Finally, have you **"RATTLED THE CHAIN"** already? If so, turn to page 471 to learn how to tell a **"Rattle Tale."**

# GOT SOME QUESTIONS? GET SOME ANSWERS...

**1  Can I get AIDS (HIV) or other infectious diseases from doing CPR?**

You risk infection if you come in contact with someone's saliva. The risk is there, whether you kiss your date or perform CPR. Saliva has not been known to spread HIV. The real danger from HIV is from intimate sexual contact or sharing needles with an HIV-infected person.

Most people who suffer a cardiac arrest do so at home. We are talking about family. Infection? Unless you know the person has some serious infection... Comeonnnnnn! Your folks need you! Get in there!

**2  If I just don't want to do CPR on someone, do I have to?**

This course teaches you how to try to save someone's life in a resuscitation emergency. But no law says you have to. Some people worry about learning CPR. They are nervous about infection if they have to do mouth-to-mouth breathing. Don't worry. CPR is a personal skill. Resuscitation emergencies usually happen at home.

They will usually involve people close to you. Hopefully, you will react and help. If you are in a public place where some stranger collapses, you will be equipped to make a difference. Hopefully, you will jump in and start CPR if necessary. But, you don't have to. It is your decision. Remember too, if you are hesitant to do full CPR, even performing chest compressions alone is still valuable. Just making that 911 call can still save a life!

**3  Can I be sued for doing CPR?**

Some provinces have a "Good Samaritan Act" or a law like it that protects people who just try to help (visit www.actfoundation.ca for information on your province). Lawsuits just haven't happened if people meant well and tried their best to do CPR the way they were trained. Again, remember most people who suffer a cardiac arrest do so at home.

**4  You don't have to start CPR on everyone whose heart stops.**

It may be no surprise when a person suffering from a serious terminal illness, or extreme old age, has a cardiac arrest. Technically, everyone dies that way. The heart stops. Life ends. CPR is not usually meant for people whose death was anticipated and perhaps quite natural. CPR is meant for those people who have a sudden cardiac arrest — for whatever reason — when it wasn't expected.

**5  Should people with a possible heart attack or stroke take Aspirin (ASA)?**

If a person is having chest pain that might be cardiac, doctors often try to give the patient an ASA pill. It works as a sort of blood thinner, which may limit the damage done by a heart attack. You can't substitute Tylenol. It does not help for this. Also, some patients are allergic to ASA. But if the person with pain says, "ASA is no problem. I take it all the time," then OK. Just one is all that's needed. When the paramedics arrive, tell them ASA was given.

It's not so clear for patients who are suffering a possible stroke. Let the paramedics decide that one.

6   **If someone has chest pain that might be a heart pain (remember the 5 Ps?) should they take Nitroglycerin?**

Many patients take a medication called **Nitroglycerin** that helps open up those clogged blood vessels and relieves the pain of **angina**. If a person with a possible heart pain wants to take Nitroglycerin, help out. Check their pockets or purse. "Nitro" is usually in a little spray bottle. It is squirted under the person's tongue. If you see it, help the person use it.

7   **When people fall down unconscious do I have to worry about their neck?**

Sometimes when people collapse, they hurt their neck. Suspect a neck injury when the collapsed person has:

A head injury;
Fallen from a height or down stairs;
Been in a motor vehicle collision;
Bleeding from the mouth, ears, nose;
Swelling along the neck or spine.

You have learned how to assess responsiveness, the airway, breathing, and how to do mouth-to-mouth breathing. If you suspect either a head or neck injury, you must protect the head and neck from movement when you are doing these things to prevent further injury to the neck.

8   **What if it is not a heart attack? Will I look foolish if it is a false alarm?**

At the emergency department of the hospital, doctors will examine the person. They may do special tests. If there is an important problem the person may stay in the hospital. But often the problem is not caused by a heart problem and the person may get sent home. Did you make a mistake? No! It is OK to be wrong like this. Even doctors can't tell without tests. Doctors will say you did the right thing. No one should make you feel stupid. Do it again next time.

**9 What if the emergency is not caused by a heart problem?**

People who drown or choke on something have cardiac arrests, but for different reasons. They can't breathe. Oxygen can't get to their lungs and into their bloodstream. The brain stops working. Soon, they are unconscious. Other organs like the heart start to fail.

People who are badly injured and bleeding may "bleed to death." When they lose too much blood, there is no way oxygen can be delivered to various organs, which soon start to die.

CPR helps maintain the circulation and oxygen delivery for any of these people. By breathing for those people and pumping their hearts, the person doing CPR tries to keep them going until paramedics arrive.

Hearts stop for many reasons, not just because of heart problems. CPR can help in any of these cases.

**Any other questions? Check out ACT's Web site! www.actfoundation.ca (ACT has experts... lots of experts).**

## RESCUED SOMEONE? KNOW SOMEONE WHO HAS? TELL US A "RATTLE TALE"!

*Rescued Someone? Tell Us! Tell Your Teacher. Tell Your Parents to Tell Us. Or... Tell Us Yourself!*

Rattled the Chain? Someday you may use some of the skills and knowledge you have just learned.

Someone in your family quit smoking because you spoke up? You helped someone recognize they might be suffering from a heart attack or stroke? You had to call for an ambulance for someone? You helped the situation by being Visible with Information? You helped someone who was choking on food? You provided CPR for someone? Something else?

LET US KNOW! Phone (it's free!):1-800-465-9111 or email us at act@actfoundation.ca.

## CLOSING NOTES...

Your teacher will give you the ACT High School CPR Program Student Course Completion Card-Heartsaver Level at the end of this program. Wondering what to do with it? Present this card when applying for a job or put it in your portfolio! You've done a great thing by learning CPR, so don't hesitate to let others know you have the skills to save a life! Think about taking more advanced training in CPR and First Aid, and remember to take a refresher course over time!

The ACT Foundation is an award-winning national charitable organization dedicated to promoting health and empowering Canadians to save lives.

ACT's corporate health partners are companies in the research-based pharmaceutical industry: **AstraZeneca, Bristol-Myers Squibb Canada, Pfizer Canada and sanofi-aventis.**

# Appendix 2
## Contraception Chart
www.sexualityandu.ca
### The Society of Obstetricians and Gynaecologists of Canada

| | **How Does It Work?** | **Effectiveness** | **Advantages** | **Disadvantages** |
|---|---|---|---|---|
| **Barrier Methods** | | | | |
| **Male condom**<br><br>A soft disposable sheath that fits over the erect penis<br><br>Available in different sizes, shapes, thicknesses, colours, and flavours<br><br>Most are latex but non-latex condoms are also available (polyurethane, silicone, lambskin)<br><br>Available in stores and pharmacies. | Physical barrier acts to prevent direct genital contact and the exchange of genital fluids<br><br>A new condom is used for each act of intercourse | The condom is 98% effective when used perfectly<br><br>With typical use, it is 85% effective | Available without a prescription<br><br>Latex condoms protect against sexually transmitted infections<br><br>May help to avoid premature ejaculation | Must be stored and handled properly<br><br>Must be available at time of intercourse and may reduce spontaneity<br><br>May slip or break<br><br>May reduce sensitivity for either partner |
| **Female condom**<br><br>A soft, disposable, polyurethane sheath<br><br>Available in some stores and pharmacies | Placed in the vagina before vaginal intercourse<br><br>Lines the vagina and prevents direct genital contact and exchange of body fluids<br><br>A new condom should be used for each act of intercourse | The female condom is 95% effective when used perfectly<br><br>With typical use, it is 79% effective | Available without a prescription<br><br>Protects against some sexually transmitted infections | Must be available at time of intercourse<br><br>Needs to be inserted properly<br><br>More expensive than male condoms<br><br>May slip or break |
| **Diaphragm**<br><br>The diaphragm is a latex dome with a flexible steel ring around its edge that is positioned in the vagina, over the cervix (non-latex diaphragms also available)<br><br>Requires a prescription and needs to be sized by a healthcare professional. Available in pharmacies and family planning clinics | Blocks the entry to the uterus so sperm cannot enter and fertilize an egg<br><br>Must be left in the vagina for 6-8 hours after intercourse<br><br>Spermicide should be reapplied for each act of intercourse | The diaphragm is 94% effective when used perfectly<br><br>With typical use, it is 84% effective | Contains no hormones<br><br>Can be used by breastfeeding women<br><br>Some protection against certain sexually transmitted infections<br><br>Can be inserted several hours before intercourse | Must be available at time of intercourse<br><br>Requires proper insertion technique<br><br>Does not protect against certain sexually transmitted infections<br><br>Diaphragm may increase the risk of recurrent urinary tract infections<br><br>May be dislodged during intercourse<br><br>Some people may be allergic to spermicides |

| | HOW DOES IT WORK? | EFFECTIVENESS | ADVANTAGES | DISADVANTAGES |
|---|---|---|---|---|
| **CERVICAL CAP**<br><br>The cervical cap is a thimble-shaped silicone cap that fits over the cervix<br><br>Requires a prescription and needs to be sized by a healthcare professional. Available in pharmacies and family planning clinics | Blocks the entry to the uterus so sperm cannot enter and fertilize an egg<br><br>Must be left in the vagina for 6-8 hours after intercourse<br><br>Spermicide should be reapplied for each act of intercourse | The cervical cap is 91% effective for women who have not given birth (nulliparous) and 74% effective for women who have previously given birth (parous) when used perfectly<br><br>With typical use, it is 84% effective for nulliparous women and 68% for parous women | Contains no hormones<br><br>Can be used by breastfeeding women<br><br>Some protection against certain sexually transmitted infections<br><br>Can be inserted several hours before intercourse | Must be available at time of intercourse<br><br>Requires proper insertion technique<br><br>Does not protect against certain sexually transmitted infections<br><br>Cap may cause vaginal odour<br><br>May be dislodged during intercourse<br><br>Some people may be allergic to spermicides |
| **SPERMICIDE**<br><br>Spermicides come in several other forms, including creams, jellies, tablets, suppositories, foams and film<br><br>Available in stores and pharmacies | Spermicides are inserted into the vagina, and contain ingredients that disable sperm. They can be used together with other forms of contraception | Spermicide is 82% effective when used perfectly<br><br>With typical use, it is 71% effective<br><br>Spermicides are very effective when used with a barrier method | Does not contain hormones<br><br>Can be used by women who smoke or are breastfeeding<br><br>Spermicide may also provide lubrication | Does not protect against sexually transmitted infections<br><br>Some people may be allergic to spermicides<br><br>Irritation at entrance of vagina or tip of penis is possible |
| **SPONGE**<br><br>A soft foam sponge that contains a spermicide to disable sperm<br><br>Available in stores and pharmacies | Sponge is placed inside the vagina over the cervix where it acts as a barrier, absorbing and disabling sperm. It is effective for up to 12 hours | The sponge is 91% effective for women who have not given birth (nulliparous) and 80% effective for women who have previously given birth (parous) when used perfectly<br><br>With typical use, it is 84% effective for nulliparous women and 68% for parous women | Does not contain hormones<br><br>Can be used by women who smoke or are breastfeeding | Does not protect against certain sexually transmitted infections<br><br>Sponge users may experience vaginal infection or irritation<br><br>If the sponge is left in the vagina for excessive periods of time, symptoms of toxic shock may appear<br><br>Some people may be allergic to spermicides |

## HORMONAL METHODS

| | | | | |
|---|---|---|---|---|
| **ORAL CONTRACEPTIVE**<br><br>"The Pill" is the most popular method of birth control<br><br>Oral contraceptive pills contain estrogen and progestin<br><br>They come in packs of 21 or 28 pills<br><br>Progestin-only pills ("mini-pill") are also available. Discuss with your healthcare provider for more information<br><br>Requires a prescription | One pill is taken every day<br><br>Prevents the ovaries from releasing an egg<br><br>Thickens cervical mucus so sperm can't pass through it<br><br>Causes changes in the lining of the uterus | The pill is 99.7% effective when used perfectly<br><br>With typical use, it is 92% effective | Effective and reversible (not permanent)<br><br>Makes periods more regular and decreases menstrual cramping<br><br>Less acne and less hirsutism<br><br>Decreases the risk of endometrial and ovarian cancer | Must remember to take everyday<br><br>A possible side effect is irregular bleeding or spotting<br><br>Other possible side effects are nausea, bloating, breast tenderness, and headaches<br><br>May increase risk of blood clots<br><br>Does not protect against sexually transmitted infections (STIs) |
| **TRANSDERMAL PATCH**<br><br>A small patch placed on the skin on the buttocks, upper outer arm, lower abdomen or upper body<br><br>Two hormones (estrogen and progestin) are released slowly and absorbed through the skin<br><br>Requires a prescription | Apply patch once a week for three weeks and then one week without the patch<br><br>Like the OC, the patch prevents the ovary from releasing an egg, thickens the cervical mucus, and causes changes in the lining of the uterus | The patch is 99.7% effective when used perfectly<br><br>With typical use, it is 92% effective | Effective and reversible (not permanent)<br><br>Once a week<br><br>Makes periods more regular and decreases menstrual cramping<br><br>Probably similar benefits as OC but no research available | Possible side effects include irregular bleeding or spotting, breast tenderness, and headaches<br><br>Possible skin irritation where the patch is applied<br><br>May increase risk of blood clots<br><br>Does not protect against STIs |

| | How Does It Work? | Effectiveness | Advantages | Disadvantages |
|---|---|---|---|---|
| **VAGINAL CONTRACEPTIVE RING**<br><br>A flexible ring that measures 54 mm across<br><br>The ring releases two hormones (estrogen and progestin) that are absorbed through the vagina<br><br>Requires a prescription | The ring is inserted into the vagina where it stays for a total of three weeks. The ring is then removed and the woman has one "ring-free" week<br><br>Like the OC, the ring prevents the ovary from releasing an egg, thickens the cervical mucus, and causes changes in the lining of the uterus | The ring is 99.7% effective when used perfectly<br><br>With typical use, it is 92% effective | Effective and reversible (not permanent)<br><br>Once a month contraception<br><br>Makes periods more regular<br><br>Does not interfere with intercourse<br><br>Probably similar benefits as OC but no research available yet | Possible side effects include irregular bleeding or spotting, nausea, breast tenderness, and headache<br><br>May cause vaginal discomfort or irritation (but uncommon)<br><br>The ring may fall out (expelled) but this is uncommon |
| **INJECTABLE CONTRACEPTIVE**<br><br>An injection that is given in the arm or buttocks 4 times per year (every 12-13 weeks)<br><br>It contains only one hormone (a progestin) and does not contain estrogen. It can be used by women who cannot take contraceptive methods with estrogen, for example women over 35 who smoke | Prevents the ovary from releasing an egg<br><br>Thickens the cervical mucus making it difficult for sperm to get through<br><br>Causes changes in the lining of the uterus | The "shot" is 99.7% effective when used perfectly<br><br>With typical use, it is 97% effective | Effective and reversible (not permanent)<br><br>Does not contain estrogen<br><br>Only 4 times per year<br><br>May be suitable for breastfeeding women | Irregular bleeding is a common side effect<br><br>Causes a decrease in bone mineral density. This appears to be reversible when the injection is stopped<br><br>May cause weight gain |

## INTRAUTERINE METHODS

| | How Does It Work? | Effectiveness | Advantages | Disadvantages |
|---|---|---|---|---|
| **INTRAUTERINE DEVICE**<br><br>A T-shaped device that contains copper and sits inside the uterus<br><br>The copper IUD can be left in place for up to 5 years<br><br>Requires a prescription and has to be inserted by a physician | Mainly by preventing the sperm from fertilizing the egg<br><br>Causes changes in the lining of the uterus<br><br>Causes changes in the cervical mucus | The IUD is 99.2–99.4% effective | Effective and long-acting (up to 5 years)<br><br>Does not contain estrogen<br><br>Does not interfere with intercourse<br><br>May decrease the risk of endometrial cancer | Possible side effects after insertion include irregular bleeding or spotting<br><br>May increase menstrual bleeding or menstrual cramping<br><br>Perforation of the uterus may occur at the time of insertion (but rare)<br><br>May be expelled (fall out) in 2–10% of women<br><br>Does not protect against STIs<br><br>A physician must insert and remove the copper IUD |
| **INTRAUTERINE SYSTEM**<br><br>A T-shaped device that contains the hormone levonorgestrel (also called the "hormonal IUD") and sits inside the uterus<br><br>The hormone is released slowly over time and acts on the lining of the uterus<br><br>The intrauterine system can be left in place for up to 5 years<br><br>Requires a prescription and has to be inserted by a physician | Mainly by preventing the sperm from fertilizing the egg<br><br>Thickens the cervical mucus making it difficult for the sperm to get through<br><br>Causes changes in the lining of the uterus<br><br>In some women, it prevents the ovaries from releasing an egg | The IUS is 99.9% effective | Effective and long acting (up to five years)<br><br>Does not contain estrogen<br><br>Does not interfere with intercourse<br><br>Decreases menstrual bleeding and menstrual cramping<br><br>May decrease endometriosis pain<br><br>May decrease the risk of precancerous cells developing in the uterus<br><br>20–30% of women will stop having periods | Possible side effects after insertion include irregular bleeding or spotting<br><br>Perforation of the uterus may occur at the time of insertion (but rare)<br><br>May be expelled (fall out) in up to 6% of women<br><br>Does not protect against STIs<br><br>A physician must insert and remove the IUS |

## FERTILITY AWARENESS METHODS

| WHAT IS IT? | HOW DOES IT WORK? | EFFECTIVENESS | ADVANTAGES | DISADVANTAGES |
|---|---|---|---|---|
| **NATURAL FAMILY PLANNING**<br><br>Natural family planning methods rely on a woman's knowledge and awareness of her body and menstrual cycle to avoid pregnancy<br><br>They do not rely on contraceptive devices, hormones or barrier methods to provide contraception<br><br>There are several methods: Calendar, Ovulation, Sympto-Thermal, Post-Ovulation<br><br>Instructions and materials available in pharmacies. Contact SERENA Canada for expert advice | A woman monitors her monthly cycle by tracking the days on a calendar and/or by taking her temperature and/or by monitoring changes to her cervical mucus<br><br>This information helps her determine when her body releases an egg (ovulates); Ovulation is when she is most likely to become pregnant from intercourse<br><br>Intercourse is avoided during this fertile period | Depends heavily on the method used, motivation, and experience<br><br>The sympto-thermal method is 98% effective when used perfectly<br><br>Other natural family planning methods are not as effective.<br><br>The typical use failure rate is 25% | Women become familiar with their body and menstrual cycles<br><br>Information can also be used later to plan a pregnancy<br><br>Inexpensive and natural | Requires willpower, periodic abstinence, and motivation<br><br>Takes time and effort to learn to use the method properly<br><br>Does not prevent STIs<br><br>Reduces spontaneity |

## STERILIZATION METHODS

| WHAT IS IT? | HOW DOES IT WORK? | EFFECTIVENESS | ADVANTAGES | DISADVANTAGES |
|---|---|---|---|---|
| **MALE STERILIZATION**<br><br>Also called vasectomy<br><br>A surgical procedure to permanently close or block the vas deferens (the tubes that carry sperm to the penis)<br><br>Minor operation, usually done in physician's office and can also be performed in a hospital or clinic | No sperm is released in the man's ejaculate, so the egg cannot be fertilized | A vasectomy is 99.9% effective<br><br>The main reason for failure after a vasectomy is because back-up contraception was not used between the time of surgery and the follow-up semen analysis. Another form of contraception is required until that analysis shows no sperm | Does not interfere with intercourse<br><br>No significant long term side effects<br><br>Less invasive and more cost-effective than female sterilization | Difficult to have reversed<br><br>Possible short term surgery related complications include: pain & swelling, infection at incision sites<br><br>Does not protect against STIs<br><br>Not effective immediately. Need follow-up sperm analysis that shows no sperm are present in the semen |
| **FEMALE STERILIZATION**<br><br>A surgical procedure to permanently close or block the fallopian tubes<br><br>Sometimes called "having your tubes tied"<br><br>Minor operation done in a hospital or clinic, often as day surgery | Laparoscopy: A camera is inserted through a small incision below the belly button and a second instrument is inserted through a small incision just above the pubic bone. The tubes are then blocked by applying a clip or a ring or by burning them<br><br>Mini-laparotomy: A small incision is made in the abdomen. The tubes are then blocked by applying a clip, a ring, by burning them, or by cutting out a small piece of the tube<br><br>Hysteroscopy: A small camera is inserted through the cervix into the uterus. Tiny plugs are inserted into the fallopian tubes where they enter the uterus. A special x-ray is done 3 months later to make sure that the tubes are blocked | Female sterilization is 99.5% effective<br><br>Failure rates vary depending on the type of procedure<br><br>For example, female sterilization by laparoscopy is 99.5% effective while no pregnancies have been reported to date for sterilization done by hysteroscopy | Permanent<br><br>Does not interfere with intercourse | Permanent and difficult to reverse<br><br>May regret decision in the future<br><br>Possible risks of surgery include risk of anesthetic, bleeding, infection or damage to organs in the pelvis (bowels, bladder, blood vessels)<br><br>Short-term side effects after surgery may include abdominal and shoulder tip discomfort and bruising<br><br>If pregnancy does occur, there is a risk that it will be an ectopic pregnancy<br><br>Does not protect against STIs |

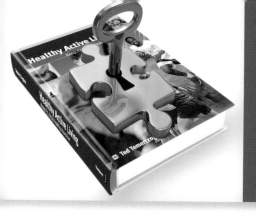

# Key Terms

**Abdominal muscles**—The two major abdominal muscles are rectus abdominis and the external obliques. Rectus abdominis is located on the anterior surface of your torso. The external obliques are located towards the sides.

**Abstinence**—Refraining from any form of sexual activity, including all forms of intercourse, that could result in pregnancy or the transmission of an STI.

**Abuse**—When someone is being mistreated either verbally, physically, or emotionally. Abuse may be direct and overt or it may be disguised and covert.

**Acquired Immune Deficiency Syndrome (AIDS)**—A medical condition that occurs when a person's immune system has become so weak that it can no longer successfully fight off infection. People who have AIDS do not normally die from it. Instead, their immune systems will be so damaged that an illness, even something very common such as a cold, can kill them.

**Action plan**—A plan that, if well thought through and carried out, can help you achieve your health and fitness goals. It can also help you achieve any other changes you would like to make happen as well—from getting good grades to developing successful relationships. An action plan involves four stages: setting SMART goals, developing action steps, identifying barriers and solutions, and identifying a final "success reward."

**Adenosine triphosphate (ATP)**—The energy molecule that provides the energy we use. This energy molecule is created from the nutrients we eat and the air we breathe.

**Adjudication**—A process where a person acting as an adjudicator (or arbitrator) listens to both sides of the story, asks each person what they think the best solution is, and considers the consequences of each solution. In the end, the adjudicator makes the final decision, which both parties have previously agreed to accept.

**Adolescence**—The period during which your body transitions both physically and emotionally from childhood to adulthood. It begins around age 13 and ends at approximately age 18.

**Advance Coronary Treatment Foundation (The ACT Foundation)**—The ACT Foundation is a non-profit organization based in Ottawa that works to ensure that information about cardiovascular disease and its prevention is brought into homes across Canada.

**Aerobic activity**—Activity that usually involves many muscles moving at the same time. Aerobic activity requires the body to burn many calories and use large amounts of oxygen.

**Aerobic fitness**—Refers to the overall efficiency of the heart, lungs, blood vessels, and exercising muscles. It is a measure of one's ability to sustain prolonged effort. Aerobic fitness results in an increase in the amount of oxygen that is delivered to your muscles, which, in turn, allows them to work longer.

**Aerobic system**—The primary way our body produces the energy we need. It involves the breakdown of food nutrients (carbohydrates, fats, and sometimes protein) in the presence of oxygen. This system allows us to perform over longer periods of time at a fairly balanced intensity.

**Alcohol**—A substance produced by fermenting or distilling various fruits, vegetables, or grains. Aside from caffeine, alcohol is the most used substance in Canada and around the world.

**Alcohol abuse**—Using alcohol in a way that causes problems for the individual or for others around that person. A person may abuse alcohol without actually being alcohol dependent, for example, when driving, during pregnancy, or when taking certain medications.

**Alcohol dependence**—A cycle of behaviour that can be very difficult to break out of without help (also known as alcoholism). It involves drinking in larger amounts or over longer periods than intended; attempting to quit drinking without success; spending a great deal of time on drinking or on obtaining alcohol; and neglecting daily activities. Someone who is alcohol dependent may deal with the many problems that result from drinking by drinking more.

**Alveoli**—Small grape-sized structures found deep within the lungs. Responsible for the exchange of oxygen and carbon dioxide.

**Amphetamine-type stimulants (ATS)**—A group of potent drugs with similar chemical structures. Most are made by illegal labs for non-medical purposes with effects similar to cocaine. ATS drugs can produce a strong dependence, making it very challenging to quit using them.

**Anabolic steroids**—A drug commonly used to treat certain medical conditions. Non-medically, steroids can help increase training endurance and build muscles, so people use them to enhance athletic performance and body image. Use of steroids is linked to a range of physical and psychological problems.

**Anaerobic system**—The system used to create small amounts of ATP, or energy, without using oxygen. The amount of ATP produced anaerobically, or without oxygen, is much less than the amount created by the aerobic system. However, anaerobic energy is especially important in short- and medium-duration activities, such as weightlifting or a shift in hockey.

**Anatomical axes**—Imaginary lines around which rotation occurs. They skewer the body in three ways: horizontally, from back to front, and vertically. The three anatomical axes are the horizontal axis (or bilateral axis), the anteroposterior axis, and the polar axis (or vertical axis).

**Anatomical planes**—Planes that are like imaginary sheets of glass placed through the body that show the dimension in which a movement occurs. The three anatomical planes are the sagittal plane, the frontal plane (or coronal plane), and the transverse plane (or horizontal plane).

**Anatomical position**—A stance or position used as a common starting point from which scientists view, describe, and analyze body parts and body movements. When standing in the anatomical position: you are standing erect with your head, eyes, and toes pointing forward; your feet are together and your arms are slightly out to the side; and the palms of your hands are facing forward.

**Anatomy**—The branch of science concerned with the bodily structure of humans, animals, and other living organisms. It is essentially descriptive—what the parts consist of and where they are in relation to one another.

**Anorexia nervosa**—A type of eating disorder. Anorexia nervosa is a form of self-starvation that is characterized by drastic weight loss.

**Appendicular skeleton**—One of the two major segments (or parts) of the skeleton. The appendicular skeleton consists of the bones that connect to the axial skeleton, the way doors do on a car's frame. It consists of 126 bones found in the arms, shoulder blades, hands, pelvic girdle, legs, and feet.

**Arteries**—Blood vessels that carry oxygenated and deoxygenated blood away from the heart.

**Axial skeleton**—One of the two major segments (or parts) of the skeleton. The axial skeleton is similar to the frame of a car in that all the major parts are attached and connected to it. It consists of 80 bones, which are located in the skull, spinal column, sternum, rib cage, and the sacrum.

**Beep Test**—A 20-metre shuttle-run appraisal developed by Dr. Luc Léger at the University of Montreal in 1982. It is a highly accurate way to measure your maximal oxygen consumption, or VO2MAX. Today, the test is commonly referred to as the "Beep Test" because of the beep sound made to tell the runners to change direction.

**Biceps**—This "two headed" muscle (bi- means two, brachii is Latin for arm) is likely the most recognized muscle in the body. The biceps, commonly referred to as "Bis" or "Pipes," rests on the anterior side of the upper arm.

**Binge eating**—A type of eating disorder. People with binge eating disorder consistently overeat but, unlike those with bulimia, do not purge and are therefore, frequently overweight.

**Bingeing**—When discussing substance abuse, bingeing is defined as using a substance past the point of intoxication. A female is considered to be binge drinking when she has four or more drinks per drinking occasion. A male is considered to be binge drinking when he has five or more drinks per drinking occasion. Bingeing is more difficult to define with drugs but, it is still defined as using them past the point of intoxication.

**Bisexual**—The term used to describe people who feel sexually attracted to both women and men.

**Blood pressure**—The force exerted by the blood against the walls of the artery. It is measured in millimetres of mercury (mmHg). It is usually stated as being systolic pressure over diastolic pressure.

**Blood-alcohol content (BAC)**—The amount of alcohol in a person's bloodstream. It is a good measure of how much a person will be affected by the alcohol they have consumed. The drinker's BAC depends mostly on the amount consumed in a given time, but also on factors such as the person's size, gender, and metabolism.

**Body composition**—The relative distribution of fat throughout the body in relation to bone, muscle, and other tissue.

**Body image**—The mental picture each of us has of our own body. Body image includes how you feel about your body, what you believe about your body, how you see yourself, and how you think you look to others.

**Body Mass Index (BMI)**—An indication as to whether your body weight (mass) is appropriate for your height. BMI is calculated by dividing your weight (kg) by your height squared ($m^2$).

**Breast cancer**—Cancer of the breast, the most frequently diagnosed cancer in Canadian women. Family history plays a role in the chances of developing it. Other factors (including smoking, diet, and possibly a virus) are also believed to play a role.

**Breast self-examination**—A procedure that can be performed at home to detect any abnormalities in the breasts. Examinations should be performed monthly, 7-10 days after the start of a menstrual period.

**Breath Sound Check**—One of two tests developed by Professor Bob Goode at the University of Toronto. The Breath Sound Check is designed to monitor the intensity of aerobic activity, based on the idea that you should be able to hear your breathing while exercising aerobically. This ensures you have reached the minimum benefit level of aerobic exercise intensity.

**Bulimia nervosa**—A type of eating disorder. Bulimia nervosa is characterized by cycles of bingeing and purging. Both behaviours are attempts to regulate feelings and weight, and are counterproductive.

**Bullying**—The act of a person or a group who holds power over someone and uses that power in intimidating, aggressive, or violent ways.

**Calorie**—A measure of the amount of energy that food will produce as it passes through the body.

**Canada's drug policy**—A strategy developed by the federal government that has the following five objectives: reduce the demand for drugs; reduce drug-related deaths; improve the effectiveness of, and accessibility to, substance abuse information and interventions; restrict the supply of illicit drugs and reduce the profitability of illicit drug trafficking; and reduce the costs of substance abuse to Canadian society.

**Canada's Food Guide to Healthy Eating**—A resource, developed by the Canadian government, to help people plan their food choices on a daily basis. It translates Recommended Dietary Allowances (RDAs) of nutrients into actual advice that people can use to change their eating habits.

**Canada's Physical Activity Guide to Healthy Active Living**—A resource, developed by the Canadian government, that sets out guidelines about how much physical activity we should strive for every day.

**Canadian Physical Activity, Fitness and Lifestyle Approach (CPAFLA)**—Standards for fitness appraisals developed under the auspices of the Canadian Society for Exercise Physiology (CSEP). CPAFLA outlines procedures for fitness assessment for people aged 15 to 69, emphasizing the health benefits of physical activity.

**Cannabis sativa**—The plant from which marijuana, hashish, sinsemilla, and hash oil are produced. Tetrahydrocannabinol (THC) is the major psychoactive ingredient in cannabis, and marijuana is its most popular form. It is the most commonly used illegal drug in Canada and around the world.

**Carbohydrates**—The body's preferred source of food energy. The body converts carbohydrates into a sugar called glucose, which it can use to fuel physical activity and burn fat. The two types of carbohydrates are simple and complex.

**Cardiac arrest**—When the heart stops beating, it is no longer pumping blood to the rest of the body. That heart is in "cardiac arrest."

**Cardiac control centre**—A specialized centre in the brain (medulla oblongata) that sends the electrical impulses to the heart. These impulses, or signals, make the heart muscle contract (squeeze) accordingly.

**Cardiac cycle**—The series of events that occurs through one heart beat. The two phases in the cycle are the diastole phase and the systole phase.

**Cardiac muscle**—One of the three major muscle types. As the name implies, the cardiac muscle is the specialized muscle tissue that comprises the heart. It is involuntary, meaning we don't control it.

**Cardiorespiratory appraisals**—Appraisals that gauge the efficiency of your heart and lungs, arguably the most important of all fitness appraisals.

**Cardiorespiratory system**—The heart, lungs, and all their supporting structures, including the blood vessels. Neglecting this system can lead to serious health problems.

**Cardiovascular diseases**—Diseases and injuries of the heart and blood vessels (veins and arteries). They are responsible for more than 35 percent of all deaths. More than 18,000 Canadians die each year from these diseases as a result of smoking.

**Cardiovascular system**—The heart, blood vessels (the network of arteries, veins, and capillaries), and blood. This system enables oxygen and nutrients to be distributed throughout the body, and for blood to be returned to the heart and lungs for replenishment.

**Cervical cancer**—A type of cancer that affects the cervix that poses a particular risk for young women. The exact cause is unknown but it's believed that a virus is likely responsible.

**Chain of Survival**—The "Chain of Survival" is a series of events that can improve survival rates from cardiovascular emergencies. The sequence includes: Early Healthy Choices, Early Recognition, Early Access, Early CPR, Early Defibrillation, Early Advanced Care, and Early Rehabilitation.

**Chin-ups**—A performance-level appraisal that measures muscular strength and endurance of the forearms, arms, and shoulders. The chin-up appraisal measures how many times you can pull your body weight up until your chin rests over a bar, and then lower it again.

**Club drugs**—A range of illegal and dangerous substances associated with nightclubs and other dance or party venues. Examples include LSD, ecstasy, crystal meth, speed, GHB, ketamine, and Rohypnol®.

**CNS depressants**—A class of drugs that include a number of prescribed medications such as barbiturates and tranquilizers. Some are also used as anesthetics.

**Cocaine**—A powerfully addictive stimulant drug processed from the leaves of the South American coca bush (variously called C, coke, snow, blow). In Canada, the most common form of cocaine is a fine white crystalline powder that is often diluted with another similar material, such as sugar, cornstarch, or talcum powder.

**Concussion**—A type of serious head injury that occurs when the brain literally bangs against the skull. This causes bruising from bleeding blood vessels attached to the brain. Nerve damage and a temporary loss of normal brain function can also occur.

**Conflict**—Any clash between two or more people or groups. It is often an essential part of learning and growing, but can be difficult to deal with and can get out of hand.

**Conflict resolution skills**—Skills and abilities (such as empathy, being clear and direct, assertiveness, active listening, patience, tolerance, and creative and critical thinking) that can help you deal with, manage, or accept stressful or conflict-filled situations.

**Continuum of drug use**—A way of measuring your potential drug use and the risks associated with it. The six levels of use are: non-use, experimental use, social use, binge use, frequent use, heavy use, and dependent use.

**Controlled Drugs and Substances Act (CDSA)**—A federal government legislation that regulates most drugs (both legal and illegal). The CDSA defines what constitutes possession and the fines or punishments associated with possession or use of controlled substances.

**Cool-down**—Light exercises or stretches that are done after participating in physical activity to return the body to its normal resting state. (See also, warm-up.)

**CPR training**—CPR training is a basic "life skill" that involves teaching about cardiovascular disease and cardiopulmonary resuscitation. CPR training is included in many high-school curricula across the country. Students receive a certificate qualifying them as a basic rescuer after successfully completing the CPR training program and the practical assessment.

**Cyber-bullying**—The use of information and communication technologies to bully others. Cyber-bullies use websites, e-mail, and phone or text messaging to threaten, intimidate, or antagonize others.

**Date-rape drugs**—A term given to any drug that is used for the purpose of getting someone intoxicated to the point where forced or non-consensual sexual activity can take place with little or no resistance. Examples include GHB, ketamine, and Rohypnol®.

**Dating violence**—Any sexual, physical, or psychological attack on one partner by the other in a dating relationship. Dating violence is often motivated by sexist stereotyping, a lack of respect for a partner, jealousy, insecurity, or an imbalance of power between the dating partners. It can happen in hetero-sexual and same-sex relationships.

**Defibrillation**—Defibrillation is carried out by means of a small computerized-device (a defibrillator), operated by trained personnel such as doctors, paramedics, and firefighters. The defibrillator delivers a special kind of shock to the heart, trying to kick-start it back to beating normally.

**Delayed onset muscle soreness (DOMS)**—Believed to be a result of microscopic tearing deep within the muscle fibres. The amount of soreness depends on the activity performed and the intensity of the activity. It can occur during any type of physical activity and at any time. DOMS can be minimized by performing proper warm-up and cool-down exercises.

**Deltoids**—A muscle located in the shoulder that is made up of three distinct parts (or heads). Each head is responsible for specific movements that allow the shoulder to move in many different ways.

**Depressants**—Substances that slow down the CNS and reduce inhibitions. Examples of typical depressants are alcohol, solvents (e.g., glue or gasoline), opiates such as heroin, pain-killers, tranquilizers, and sleeping pills.

**Diet and health claims**—A statement that appears on food packaging highlighting a relationship between diet and certain health conditions. In order to use them, manufacturers must meet the strict government-set criteria for nutritional content.

**Dietary supplements**—Products that you take by mouth, that contain a "dietary ingredient," and are intended to add to, or supplement, the foods that you eat. The "dietary ingredients" in these products may include: vitamins, minerals, herbs, or other substances.

**Dislocation**—An injury that occurs when a bone is displaced from its joint. They are often caused by collisions or falls and are common in finger and shoulder joints. Do not attempt to put the bone back into place yourself as this could cause more damage.

**Dot Drill**—A performance-level appraisal that is a part of the Bigger, Faster, Stronger (BFS) program developed by Dr. Greg Shepard. This appraisal assesses quickness, agility, and muscular endurance. It is performed on a configuration of painted dots forming a rectangle.

**Drugs**—Substances, other than food, that affect a person's mental, emotional, or physical state.

**Dynamic stretching**—Stretching while moving. Current research tells us that this is effective in preparing the body for physical activity.

**Eating disorders**—Unhealthy eating habits that become so serious that they affect both physical and mental health. They are the outcome of manipulation of food and weight in an attempt by the individual to attain a sense of self-control, achievement, and mood regulation. Eating disorders negatively impact every aspect of the individual's life, and are life-threaten-ing illnesses.

**Ecstasy**—A drug that is considered a hallucinogen, but which also has stimulant effects; made in illegal drug labs (methylene-dioxymethamphetamine, or MDMA).

**Ectomorph**—One of the three body types. Ectomorphs are a very thin, long boned body type with little muscle or fat.

**Endometriosis**—A condition that occurs when tissue normally found within the endometrium starts to grow on the ovaries, fallopian tubes, cervix, vagina, vulva, or other parts of the pelvic cavity. Endometriosis can cause abnormal bleeding, painful and lengthy periods, and pelvic pain. It is a fairly serious condition that can lead to sterility if left untreated.

**Endomorph**—One of the three body types. Endomorphs are a soft, round pear shape with excess fat around the hips and waist with little muscle definition.

**Energy balance equation**—A way to help you maintain a healthy body weight. The equation requires you to balance your "energy in" (caloric intake) with your "energy expenditure" (the calories you burn in a day).

**Erector spinae**—Three muscles comprising one of the major muscle groups of the back. The erector spinae group lies under-neath the trapezius and the latissimus dorsi and runs along the length of your spine and the back of your ribs.

**Ethnic violence**—Violence that occurs when people become violent towards other groups, based on differences of religion or culture.

**Fats**—A concentrated source of energy that is especially useful during prolonged physical activity. Fats help in the absorption of the fat-soluble vitamins that your body needs.

**Female reproductive system**—The system responsible for producing, nourishing, and transporting ova/eggs, and eventu-ally carrying and delivering babies. It includes both external and internal parts, as well as glands and tubes that connect the different parts of the system.

**Fetal alcohol syndrome (FAS)**—A condition that can occur in a fetus if women drink while pregnant. FAS can cause children to have reduced growth, mental disabilities, and a different facial makeup.

**Fitness**—A state achieved by regular exercise, proper diet, and adequate rest. The term has two dimensions, one that pertains to overall health (health-related fitness) and another which focuses more on performance and skill (skill-related fitness).

**FITT principle**—A method that can help you when designing a fitness training program. FITT stands for the four elements of any good training plan: Frequency, Intensity, Time, and Type of activity.

**Flexed-arm hang appraisals**—A performance-level appraisal that measures muscular strength and endurance of the forearms, arms, and shoulders. It is an isometric contraction (involving no movement). The test measures how long you are able to hold yourself up with your chin above a bar.

**Flexibility**—The ability of joints to bend through their full range of movement (ROM).

**4 "Rs" of CPR**—The 4 "Rs" of cardiopulmonary resuscitation are: (1) Risk Factors, (2) Recognize, (3) React, (4) Resuscitate. Knowing the 4 "Rs" allows you to help prevent cardiovascular problems and deal with cardiopulmonary emergencies when they occur.

**Fracture**—The medical term for a broken bone. The three types of fractures are simple, compound, and comminuted.

**Gang violence**—Violence committed by gang members. This is becoming a major concern in many parts of Canada, as recent years have seen many serious crimes committed by groups of young people who identify themselves as members of gangs.

**Gastrocnemius**—A muscle found on the back of the leg. Commonly called the "jumpers' muscle," the gastrocnemius is a powerful "plantar flexor" of the ankle joint. It has two major heads that resemble "tear drops."

**Gateway Theory**—A theory of drug use that proposes that someone who uses marijuana is more likely than a non-user to go on to use more serious drugs such as cocaine and heroin.

**Gay**—While this term can refer to anyone who identifies as homosexual, it is more commonly used to refer to homosexual men.

**Gender**—The condition of being female or male as defined by society. Gender differences in people arise from variations in the way they grow up—their family, education, and culture.

**Gender roles**—Sets of behaviours that project an image of femininity or masculinity. They are essentially patterns of behaviour by which women and men are expected to live.

**Grip strength**—A measurement of how strongly or tightly you can hold something in your hand. It is measured using a device called a dynamometer. Even though this test specifically measures the strength of your forearm muscles, research suggests that this is a good indicator of overall muscular strength.

**Hallucinogens**—Substances that alter a user's perception of the world around them, causing distortions in the way they sense their surroundings. While overdoses are rare, these drugs can pose a risk of accidents and injuries because they distort what the user experiences. LSD, psilocybin (magic mushrooms), mescaline, ecstasy, and peyote are examples of hallucinogens.

**Hamstrings**—A muscle group located on the back of the lower leg made up of three muscles: semitendinosus, semimembranosus, and biceps femoris. The two "semi" muscles are named after their appearance—one resembles a tendon, while the other resembles a flat membrane. Biceps femoris is named after its location (on the femur) and having two heads (bi).

**Harris Benedict formula**—A widely established way to estimate total daily caloric needs. Essentially, you use this equation to calculate the amount of energy your body uses when it is at rest (resting metabolic rate), and then multiply that amount by an activity factor (how much activity you do).

**Hate Crime**—A crime that is committed against a person or group of people because they are members of an "identifiable group," meaning any section of the public who can be distinguished by colour, race, religion, ethnic origin, or sexual orientation.

**Health Benefit Zones**—Part of the CPAFLA program, zones that provide an indication as to where you stand with respect to fitness standards for your group. The five zones are: Excellent, Very Good, Good, Fair, and Needs Improvement.

**Health-related fitness**—Assessed in five main areas: cardio-respiratory fitness, muscular strength, muscular endurance, flexibility, and body composition.

**Healthy active living**—A state where you are not just thinking about your health sometimes, but actively doing something about it all the time. It also involves learning how to develop healthy relationships, dealing with stress and difficult situations, and helping to improve not only yourself but also your community.

**Healthy lifestyle**—A lifestyle that can be achieved through good physical, mental, social, and spiritual health.

**Healthy relationships**—A relationship in which people feel good about themselves. In healthy relationships, partners respect themselves and one another. They consider and show concern for each other's feelings.

**Heart attack**—A heart attack occurs when the supply of blood and oxygen to an area of the heart muscle are blocked, usually by a clot in a coronary artery. Often, this blockage leads to an irregular heartbeat that causes a severe decrease in the pumping action of the heart and may bring about sudden death. If the blockage is not treated within a few hours, the affected heart muscle will die and be replaced by scar tissue.

**Hernia**—A problem that can occur in the male reproductive system. A hernia normally looks like a bulge in the groin area. It may occur when a portion of the intestine pushes through an opening in the abdominal wall and into the groin or scrotum. Minor surgery is required to correct this painful condition.

**Heroin**—A highly addictive opiate that is refined into a fine white or brown powder. It slows down body functions and suppresses or reduces both physical and emotional pain.

**Heterosexual**—Someone who experiences an exclusive or predominant sexual attraction towards persons of the opposite sex (woman attracted to man, man to woman).

**High School CPR Student Manual**—A training manual developed by the Advance Coronary Treatment Foundation (The ACT Foundation) and its partners that outlines the basics of cardiopulmonary resuscitation. Students receive a certificate qualifying them as a basic rescuer after successfully completing the CPR training program and the practical assessment.

**Homophobia**—The fear of, or contempt for, other people because of their sexual preference or gender identification.

**Homosexual**—Someone who experiences sexual attraction towards persons of the same sex (woman attracted to woman, man to man).

**Human Immunodeficiency Virus (HIV)**—An STI that can be transmitted through the exchange of bodily fluids passed through mucous membranes during unprotected sex or by other means, such as intravenous (IV) drug use and blood transfusions. HIV infects the cells in the blood that normally defend against infection. Over time, HIV can cause AIDS.

**Human Rights Codes**—Federal and provincial legislation that gives everyone equal rights and opportunities without discrimination or harassment on the basis of sexual orientation.

**Illinois Agility Run**—A performance-level appraisal that is a good test for sports or activities that involve changing direction and weaving around objects or opponents. It also makes for a fun obstacle course.

**Inhalants**—A dangerous class of drugs that produces feelings of euphoria and light-headedness while slowing down body systems. Examples include paint thinners, modelling glue, gasoline, and cleaning fluids. Their use can result in brain damage, suffocation, and death.

**Inter-group conflict**—When two groups (or teams) find themselves in opposition to one another. In sports, as in life, healthy competition is normal, but if this is not handled properly a dispute can have serious consequences.

**Internal conflicts**—The opposing emotions you often feel within yourself. Sometimes, it is hard to decide what to believe, especially when you can see both sides of an issue and you must choose which path to take, whom to support, or where to draw the line.

**Interpersonal conflict**—A dispute you have with someone else. You may have a completely different view on, for example, the latest current event than someone else, but it is important to understand what he or she thinks about it.

**Intra-group conflict**—Conflict among members of a group or team. Group members may take positions on either side of the argument. They may choose their position based on loyalty to the people voicing the opinion, or they may choose their position because of strong personal feelings.

**Joints**—The areas where bones connect and are held together by various connective tissue including ligaments and muscles. Elbows, knees, and knuckles are commonly-known joints. We have over 140 joints in our bodies.

**Lactic acid**—A substance that builds up inside the muscle fibres after several minutes of physically taxing activity. It is associated with the extreme pain felt on such occasions. Lactic acid build up occurs because, after 2 or 3 minutes of intense activity, the body cannot breakdown glucose quickly enough to keep up.

**Latissimus dorsi**—One of the major muscles of the back. Latissimus dorsi (the "lats") cover most of the lower back.

**Legal liability**—The issue of legal liability relates to the responsibility of individuals around an intoxicated person who are in a position to make a difference. If a bar, restaurant, or even a party host serves someone past the point of intoxication, they can be held responsible for the actions of the intoxicated person.

**Lesbian**—The term used to describe a homosexual woman.

**Ligaments**—Connective tissues that attach bone to bone.

**Liquor control regulations**—In Canada, all provinces and territories have liquor control regulations that govern the sale and advertising of alcohol. Among other things, these laws set the age at which young people are allowed to drink.

**Long-term goals**—Goals that specify what you want to achieve over a longer period. For example, long-term fitness goals could include reaching a particular body weight over a month, a semester, or even a few years.

**Lysergic acid diethylamide (LSD)**—Commonly known as "acid," one of the most common hallucinogenic drugs. It is manufactured from lysergic acid, which is found in a fungus that grows on rye and other grains. It is very powerful and its effects can be unpredictable.

**Macronutrients**—The nutrients that we need in relatively large amounts every day. In addition to water, the macronutrients are carbohydrates, proteins, and fats (these three are also known as the "energy nutrients" because they provide us with energy or calories).

**Male reproductive system**—The system responsible for producing, nourishing, and transporting sperm. It includes both external and internal organs, as well as internal glands and tubes that connect different parts of the system.

**Marijuana (cannabis)**—The most popular form of cannabis. It acts mostly as a hallucinogen, but also has depressant effects (it slows response time and affects memory) and a stimulant effect (it raises the heart rate).

**Media literacy**—The ability to sift through and analyze the messages that inform, entertain, and sell things and ideas to us. It is the ability to be a critical thinker when you consume (watch, listen, read) all forms of media—from television to billboards, from the Internet to music videos.

**Mediation**—A process used to manage and resolve conflicts that seem unsolvable. It requires a trained mediator to help the conflicting parties work out a solution. To be an effective mediator, a person needs to build mutual respect between the parties and encourage problem solving.

**Medicare**—The name of the Canadian health care system, which guarantees quality medical care to all Canadians. The fees associated with medical care are paid for through the taxes Canadian citizens pay.

**Menstruation**—The monthly shedding of the lining of the uterus if no fertilized egg is implanted. The process generally lasts between three to seven days.

**Mesomorph**—One of the three body types. Mesomorphs are naturally well muscled with broad shoulders and a narrow waist.

**Methods of contraception**—Methods designed to impede fertilization and prevent pregnancy during sexual intercourse.

**Micronutrients**—The essential nutrients needed by our bodies only in small amounts. Although we need less of each nutrient, these nutrients still play an important role in the way our bodies function. These "non-energy nutrients" help the body utilize the energy provided by carbohydrates, proteins, and fats.

**Minerals**—Inorganic substances needed by the body for good health. Minerals help make bones, proteins, and blood. They also help the body get energy from macronutrients.

**Modified Canadian Aerobic Fitness Test (mCAFT)**—A good test of your aerobic fitness. It is a "sub-maximal" appraisal, which means that you will not be going "all out" or "full blast."

**Mothers Against Drunk Driving (MADD)**—An organization whose aim is to eliminate impaired driving crashes and raise awareness of the dangers of impaired driving.

**Multiple-repetition maximum**—A method used to predict how much weight you can maximally lift at once.

**Muscle contraction**—The process that allows your muscles to move. It is a result of the filaments deep within the muscle fibre sliding over each other. This process occurs simultaneously across the entire muscle fibre and as a result the entire muscle contracts.

**Muscle pairs**—A pair of muscles that work as a team. For example, if one muscle performs a flexing action, the other performs an extending action; on the arm, the biceps brachii flexes the elbow and triceps brachii extends it.

**Muscular endurance**—A muscle's ability to perform repeatedly without fatigue.

**Muscular strength**—The maximum force a muscle can exert in a single contraction.

**Musculoskeletal fitness**—A term used to describe muscular strength and endurance as well as the flexibility of your joints.

**Neuromuscular junction**—The site on any muscle where it receives the electrical signal or impulse sent from your brain via nerves instructing the muscle to contract.

**Nutrient content claims**—Claims printed on food packaging to highlight a positive feature of the product ("high fibre," "light," "low in fat"). Manufacturers are permitted to use nutrient content claims on food labels to attract attention to their products as long as their products meet specific rules and standards.

**Nutrition**—The science behind how your body uses the components of food to grow, maintain, and repair itself.

**Nutrition Facts table**—A table, by law printed on most food packaging, that gives nutritional information about which nutrients you are getting from your food and in which proportions. It appears in a standard format so that it looks the same from one product to another, making it easier to find and use.

**Obesity**—Being overweight to the point where it is a danger to one's health. The condition may require action on many fronts, including professional intervention by a physician or other medical professionals.

**Ovarian cancer**—A cancer that affects the ovaries. Ovarian cancer can be difficult to detect because the early stages have only mild symptoms. The causes are unknown but there is thought to be a hereditary influence.

**Ovarian cysts**—Non-cancerous sacs filled with fluid or semi-solid material. They are fairly common among adult women and are generally harmless; however, they can become a painful problem if they grow large enough to push on surrounding organs. In most cases, these cysts will disappear on their own, but in some cases medication or surgery might be required.

**Overload principle**—A fitness training principle, which states that when you give your body more to do than it is accustomed to doing, you create an "overload." The overload principle underlies most of fitness activity. Unless there is some sort of overload, there can be no benefit to you.

**Overweight**—Having excess body fat for one's size and build—a condition that will lead to health problems. The main way to address an overweight condition is to choose a better diet and to be more physically active.

**Partial curl-ups appraisal**—A good test for "the core" insofar as it measures the muscular strength and endurance of the anterior trunk—specifically, rectus abdominis (the "abs"). The appraisal involves performing a maximum of 25 consecutive curl-ups in one minute.

**Pectoralis major**—A powerful chest muscle that is appropriately named after its size. It has a smaller "sibling" muscle that lives underneath it, called pectoralis minor. Pectoralis major and minor make up the pectoral muscle group. They are commonly referred to as the "pecs."

**Peer mediation**—A program used to help reduce conflict in schools. An objective third-party peer helps two conflicting parties understand one another.

**% Daily Value**—The column on a nutrition label that tells you how much, or how little, of a nutrient is contained in a particular food item or package in relation to what should be taken in on a daily basis. Daily values for carbohydrates, total fat, saturated and trans fat are based on a 2000-calorie diet. % DV values for vitamins and minerals are based on 1983 recommendations and represent the highest recommended intake for all ages and sexes.

**Performance-enhancing drugs**—Drugs that can increase lean muscle mass, and improve strength and endurance. They can be used medically to combat body wasting in patients with AIDS and other diseases that result in loss of muscle mass. They have not been found to improve agility, skill, cardiovascular capacity, or recovery time after activity.

**Performance-level appraisals**—The group of fitness appraisals that focus on specific movement skills such as speed, agility, and coordination. They are referred to as "performance-level appraisals" because they are intended for measuring and improving particular aspects of performance (as opposed to overall health).

**Physical dependence**—The state that occurs in drug users once their bodies become accustomed to the drug. They experience physical symptoms of withdrawal if they try to go without it.

**Physiology**—The branch of biology that is concerned with how the various body parts of humans, animals, and other living organisms function.

**PIER**—An acronym to help you remember the steps to take when treating an injury: **P**ressure should be administered at the same time the ice is on the affected area; **I**ce should be placed on the affected area; **E**levate the injured area while it's being iced to help reduce the swelling; **R**estrict and rest the affected area with the use of tensors or slings.

**Progression principle**—A fitness training principle, which states that fitness improvements occur gradually by progressively adding to the overload. If you are just starting fitness training, you may experience fairly rapid improvement (and probably soreness), but the rate of improvement will gradually slow down and the gains will be more evenly paced.

**Prostate cancer**—The most frequently diagnosed form of cancer in Canadian men. It occurs when cancer cells develop on the prostate. Prostrate examination and prostate tests are crucial to ensure early detection and treatment.

**Proteins**—A macronutrient that can be found in all the cells in our bodies: muscles, tendons, ligaments, hair, skin, and nails. Proteins also play a role in sight, hearing, taste, and smell. Proteins are the building blocks of enzymes that help digest food, fight infection, and build blood. If your body is short of carbohydrates, protein can also act as an energy source.

**Psychoactive drugs**—Mood-altering drugs that affect our mental and emotional state.

**Psychological dependence**—The state that can occur in drug users even in the absence of physical cravings. Users may find that drug use begins to play a larger part in their lives, and that they cannot find an easy way to quit. Psychological dependence is a serious form of addiction.

**Pulmonary circulation**—The process by which deoxygenated blood is pumped out to the lungs and newly oxygenated blood is returned to the heart.

**Push-ups**—An upper-body exercise that is also a good all-round indicator of upper-body strength. The push-ups appraisal involves performing as many consecutive push-ups as possible with no time limit.

**Quadriceps**—A muscle group located on the upper leg (the "quads"). This powerful muscle group is made up of four muscles: vastus medialis, vastus lateralis, vastus intermedius, and rectus femoris.

**Racism**—The belief in the superiority of a particular race and the prejudice, antagonism, or violence shown towards other races as a result of this attitude.

**Repetitions**—The number of times you continuously perform an exercise. If you lift a barbell once, that is one rep. If you lift it 25 times consecutively, that amounts to 25 reps.

**Resistance training**—Exercising a particular muscle or muscle group by subjecting it to additional weight stress. The weight may be an external object, such as a dumbbell, or it can involve using your body weight as a form of resistance, such as with a push-up. The objective of resistance training is to develop the targeted muscle or muscle group and to make it stronger.

**Respiratory diseases**—Diseases that attack our lungs and the other parts of the body that we use to breathe. People with these conditions often have difficulty being physically active. Each year, more than 9,000 Canadians die of respiratory diseases caused by smoking.

**Respiratory system**—The system that allows for the passage of air from outside the body to the lungs. It also allows the exchange of oxygen and carbon dioxide to occur. It is divided into two main zones: the conductive zone, which refers to the area where air enters the lungs, and the respiratory zone, which is where the gas exchange occurs.

**Resting Heart Rate (RHR)**—The number of times your heart beats per minute when at rest. The average Resting Heart Rate is between 70 and 80 beats per minute (bpm).

**Resting metabolic rate (RMR)**—An estimate of the amount of energy your body uses when it is completely at rest. It varies between individuals of different heights, weights, and ages, and can be accurately estimated using the Harris Benedict Formula.

**Reversibility principle**—A fitness training principle, which states that if you stop training for a while (a process sometimes called "detraining") you will start to lose, or reverse the gains you have made. Some strength gains may start to decrease in as little as three days.

**Second-hand smoke**—Exhaled smoke from a smoker, smoke from a smoldering cigarette or the mouth end of the cigarette that is breathed in by another person. Sometimes called environmental tobacco smoke (ETS) or "passive smoking."

**Self-esteem**—A feeling of pride in yourself and a sense of self-worth. When people respect themselves and act according to their beliefs and values, they feel positive about themselves.

**Separation**—An injury that occurs when bones separate. For example, your collar bone (clavicle) is attached to your shoulder blade (scapula) by strong ligaments. When these ligaments are torn, as a result of a collision or an awkward fall, the bones may separate. This is the most common type of separation.

**Set-point theory**—A theory that offers a partial explanation for the high failure rates experienced by many dieters. The set-point theory proposes that each of us has a weight range, or set-point, that our body is "programmed" to maintain.

**Sets**—The number of times you perform a certain number of reps. If you lift a barbell for 25 reps, then rest, then perform another 25 reps, you would have done 2 sets of 25 reps.

**Sex**—The qualities by which people are categorized by their reproductive organs and functions. Our sex is determined on the basis of our biology.

**Sex hormones**—Hormones (estrogens in girls and testosterone in boys) whose release signals the start of puberty. When the body is ready, the pituitary gland delivers messages to the ovaries and the testicles to start producing these hormones. Their release results in a number of physical changes.

**Sexual decision making**—A process that entails making conscious choices about your sexual activity.

**Sexual harassment**—Unwanted sexual behaviour of any kind. It is serious and illegal and, in some cases, can escalate to the realm of physical violence, leading to sexual abuse and assault.

**Sexual intimacy**—An aspect of intimacy that can include how much personal information we share with our partner, how we communicate, and how we want to be physically close to one another.

**Sexual orientation**—An individual's sexual attraction towards a particular group of people.

**Sexuality**—A term used to refer to a number of ideas, such as: physical development of sexual characteristics; intimacy, love, and affection; gender roles and relations between the sexes; sexual attraction; sexual contact; or sexual decision making. In other words, sexuality includes everything that defines us as girls and boys, women and men. It encompasses our physical development, sexual knowledge, attitudes, values, and behaviours. It also involves making important decisions about intimate relationships.

**Sexually transmitted infections (STIs)**—Infections caused by bacteria, viruses, or parasites, which are transmitted through semen, vaginal fluid, blood, or other body fluids, during sexual activity.

**SHARP**—A simple acronym to help you remember the signs of an injury. When an injury happens one or more of the following signs will appear: **S**welling of affected area, instantly or over time; **H**eat or increased temperature of the area; **A**ltered joint or area will not function properly; **R**edness, the area may turn red in colour; **P**ainful to move or when you touch the affected area.

**Shin splints**—Pain caused by the tearing of the connective tissue between the tibia and fibula along the front shaft of the shinbone.

**Short-term goals**—Goals that are specific and can be completed in a few hours, days, or weeks. Short-term fitness goals may involve measuring your progress in a single workout, or completing an exercise session better than previously.

**Sit-and-reach appraisal**—An appraisal that measures joint flexibility using a special device called a flexometer. The appraisal measures how far you can reach forward from a sitting-up position.

**Skeletal muscle**—One of the three major muscle types. Skeletal muscles are connected to bones by tendons. They are voluntary, meaning that we have control of them.

**Skill-related fitness**—Usually centres on the following six components: agility, balance, coordination, power, reaction time, and speed.

**Sliding filament theory**—A process that occurs during muscle contraction that involves filaments deep within the muscle fibre sliding over each other.

**SMART**—A strategy to help motivate you when setting goals for yourself. SMART stands for Specific, Meaningful and Measurable, Action-oriented, Realistic, and Time.

**Smooth muscles**—One of the three major muscle types. Smooth muscles are involuntary, meaning we don't control them, and they are automatically run by the central nervous system. These muscles do not tire easily and can stay contracted for a long period of time.

**Socialization**—Passing on the customs, attitudes, and values of a social group, community, or culture to ensure that these beliefs and customs will be passed on to new generations.

**Specificity principle**—A fitness training principle, which states that the maximum training effect comes when you mimic the effort required in the actual sport as closely as possible. In general, you improve by practising a specific activity repeatedly.

**Spermatogenesis**—The process that occurs during puberty in males that involves the pituitary gland sending a message to the testicles to start releasing more testosterone. This causes the testicles to produce male reproductive cells or sperm.

**Sprains**—An injury that occurs when a ligament is stretched or torn. Similar to strains, which occur in muscles and tendons, sprains have a grading or severity of injury classified in degrees.

**Static stretching**—Bending the joints until a slight pull on the muscle(s) is felt, and then holding that position for 15 to 30 seconds.

**Stimulants**—Substances that speed up body systems, such as the CNS and cardiorespiratory system, delay fatigue, and may produce hyperactivity. Stimulants include nicotine, caffeine, diet pills, Ritalin, cocaine, crack, speed, methamphetamine, and other drugs.

**Strains**—An injury that is caused by twisting or pulling a muscle or tendon. Depending on the severity of the injury, a strain may be the result of a muscle or a tendon being overstretched. If strains remain untreated, tears in the muscle or tendon fibres may worsen. Strains can be either acute or chronic.

**Stress fractures**—Tiny cracks along the bone that are virtually undetectable by an X-ray. They are very painful and can take a long time to heal.

**Stroke**—A stroke is caused by an interruption to the flow of blood to the brain (ischemic stroke) or by the rupture of blood vessels in the brain (hemorrhagic stroke). A stroke causes brain cells (neurons) in the affected area to die. The effects of a stroke depend on where the brain was injured, as well as how much damage occurred.

**Synovial joints**—The most common of all joints found in the body, the synovial joints provide the most movement. Some examples include: the shoulders, elbows, wrists, hips, knees, and ankles.

**Systemic circulation**—The process by which oxygenated blood is pumped out to the body and deoxygenated blood is returned to the heart.

**Talk Test**—One of two tests developed by Professor Bob Goode at the University of Toronto. The Talk Test is designed to monitor the intensity of aerobic activity, based on the idea that you should be able to carry on a conversation during aerobic activity without too much ease or difficulty.

**Target Heart Rate Zone**—The range within which you should aim to exercise your heart. It is normally calculated using the Heart Rate Reserve method.

**Tendonitis**—Inflammation of a tendon caused by irritation due to prolonged or abnormal use.

**Testicular cancer**—One of the most common forms of cancer in men under the age of forty. It occurs when cells in the testicle divide abnormally to form a tumour. If detected early, it can be cured before it spreads to other parts of the body.

**Testicular injury**—The most common problem associated with the male reproductive system. It usually results from an accidental blow to the testicles while participating in physical activities. Testicular injury can also occur when one of testicles twists around, cutting off the blood supply to the entire region.

**Testicular self-examination**—A simple process that can help men detect testicular cancer early. All men should perform a TSE regularly from the time they are 15 years old. The best time to perform one is after a hot bath or shower when your testicles have descended and the skin of your scrotum has relaxed, making lumps, growths, or tenderness easier to feel and see.

**Tobacco**—The shredded, dried leaf of the tobacco plant, which can be smoked in cigarettes, cigars, or pipes, or chewed. Tobacco is the only natural source of nicotine, one of the most addictive substances known to scientists.

**Total daily caloric need**—The recommended amount of calories you need each day, calculated by multiplying your RMR (resting metabolic rate) by an appropriate activity factor (see Harris Benedict formula).

**Transgender**—Someone with a strong desire to live as a member of the opposite sex, but who does not generally intend to undergo sexual reassignment surgery. Instead, transgendered people will often choose to dress and present themselves as members of the opposite sex.

**Transsexual**—Someone with a consistent and overwhelming desire to live as a member of the opposite sex. Transsexuals usually consider or pursue hormonal therapy and surgical changes (sexual reassignment surgery) in order to make a transition from male to female or from female to male.

**Trapezius**—One of the major muscles of the back. Trapezius, so-named because it is shaped like a trapezoid, covers the upper part of the back.

**Triceps**—Like the biceps on the front of the upper arm, triceps brachii (located on the back of the upper arm) is named after the number of heads it has (tri- means three). The triceps acts in unison with the biceps brachii—when one contracts, the other relaxes and vice versa.

**12-Minute Run**—Also known as the Cooper Test; an appraisal designed for military use by the American researcher Dr. Kenneth H. Cooper in 1968. The test is designed to determine one's aerobic capacity based on the distance completed over 12 minutes. This appraisal is suitable for all fitness levels.

**20- and 40-Yard Sprints**—One of the performance-level appraisals used to gauge one's ability to accelerate quickly. An important appraisal because, in many sports, athletes start from a stationary position and attempt to reach a high velocity as quickly as possible.

**2000-calorie diet**—The level of calorie (or energy) intake that meets the average needs of our population. A 2000-calorie diet is used by Health Canada to calculate the daily values of carbohydrates, total fat, and saturated and trans fat.

**Vaginitis**—Inflammation or infection caused by irritating substances (such as soap or bubble bath) entering the vagina.

**Vegetarianism**—A term that describes many different types of eating styles that emphasize fruits, vegetables, nuts, grains, and seeds. Most vegetarians eliminate meat, fish, and poultry from their diets, but many do not exclude all animal foods, and some vegetarians eliminate red meat only.

**Veins**—Blood vessels that carry oxygenated and deoxygenated blood to the heart.

**Vertical jump**—An action that requires the use of almost all the major muscles in the body. The vertical jump test measures "muscular power" (the ability to exert a large amount of force quickly) by measuring how high a person can reach after jumping from a standstill.

**Violence**—Acts of aggression and abuse that cause or are intended to cause injury or harm to another person. Violence can take many forms, such as physical, sexual, or psychological abuse; sexual or gender-based harassment; racial harassment or hate crimes; bullying; intimidation or extortion; vandalism; and intentional self-injury.

**Vitamins**—Chemicals that the body needs to build and maintain its cells and to release energy from macronutrients. The two types of vitamins are water-soluble and fat-soluble.

**VO$_2$MAX**—The amount of oxygen consumed during intense (maximal) effort, commonly used as an indicator of aerobic fitness. A high VO$_2$MAX score indicates that you have a strong cardiorespiratory system and your working muscles are able to receive and use more oxygen.

**Vulvovaginitis**—Inflammation or infection caused by irritating substances (such as soap or bubble bath) entering the vulva.

**Waist Circumference (WC)**—An appraisal used to predict the health risks that come with excess fat weight around your midsection. To get a pretty good indication of your body composition, combine your WC measurement with your BMI value.

**Waist-to-Hip Ratio (WHR)**—A measurement that looks at the relative proportion of fat stored around your waist and hips. It is a simple but useful measure of body fat distribution.

**Wall-Ball Toss Appraisal**—A performance-level appraisal that specifically measures hand-eye coordination. This skill is especially important in games such as tennis and baseball. It requires you to throw a tennis ball against a wall, from waist level, and catch it with the opposite hand as many times as possible for either 30 or 60 seconds.

**Warm-up**—Light exercises or stretches that are done to get the body ready for physical activity.

**Weather-related injuries**—Injuries that can result from extreme heat or extreme cold, such as frostbite, hypothermia, heat cramps, heat stroke, heat exhaustion, and sunburn.

**Wellness**—Being in "a state of good health." It is a commitment to a type of lifestyle that requires you to be health conscious, health active, health wise, and health committed.

**Wellness-awareness continuum**—A way of measuring your attentiveness to your wellness and level of activity. It is divided into four stages: conscious, active, wise, and committed.

**Yeast infections**—Monilia (commonly known as a "yeast infection") is caused by the yeast fungus Candida albicans. Candida is found in every woman's normal, healthy vagina. However, sometimes too much of it grows inside the vagina, causing an infection. Symptoms include a thick, white discharge, which can cause extreme itching and discomfort.

# Index

# Credits

### School Photos (by Tanya Winter unless otherwise noted)

Photos used with permission of Birchmount Park Collegiate Institute (TDSB) on pp. xiii, xiv, xviii (top), 2, 7, 8 (top and middle), 17 (middle and right), 19, 21, 29, 34, 37, 41 (bottom), 51 (bottom), 54, (top and middle) 56, 60 (top), 61, 63, 72, 73, 81, 84, 85, 89 (bottom), 91, 96 (top), 98, 99, (top, left, and middle), 101, 102, 103 (bottom), 104 (top), 105, 107, 108 (bottom), 113, (top), 137 (top), 138, 150 (top), 171 (top), 188, 261, 270 (bottom), 272 (bottom), 288 (top), 290, 298, 308, 309, 313 (bottom), 342 (bottom), 346 (bottom), 354 (bottom), 355, 371 (top), 372 (bottom) 373, 376 (bottom), 380 (bottom), 384 (bottom), 385, 398 (bottom), 399 (bottom), 404 (bottom), 423, 430 (bottom), 431 ♦ Photos used with permission of East York Collegiate Institute (TDSB) on pp. viii-ix, 14, 50 (top), 57 (bottom), 99 (bottom right), 103 (top), 338 (bottom), 339 ♦ Photos used with permission of Victoria Park Collegiate Institute (TDSB) on pp. 66 and 94 (bottom) ♦ Photos used with permission of Pope John Paul II Catholic Secondary School (TCDSB) on pp. 65 and 67 ♦ Top photos on p. 286 used with permission of Maplewood High School (TDSB) ♦ Photos used with permission of Northern Secondary School (TDSB) on pp. 10 (top and middle), 20 (bottom), 388 (bottom), 389 (bottom), 390 (bottom), 391 ♦ Photos used with permission of West Hill Collegiate Institute (TDSB) on pp. 303 and 366 (bottom) ♦ Photos used with permission of Malvern Collegiate Institute (TDSB) on pp. 3, 260 (bottom), 267, 274, 286 (bottom), 288 (bottom), 322, 350 (bottom), 351 ♦ Photos used with permission of York Mills Collegiate Institute (TDSB) on pp. 414 (bottom), 415, 426 (bottom), 427 ♦ Photos used with permission of Westwood Middle School (TDSB) on pp. 20 (top), and 59 (bottom) ♦ Photo on p. 52 used with permission of Sir William Osler High School (TDSB) ♦ Photos used with permission of Leaside High School (TDSB) on pp. 10 (top) and 337 (bottom) ♦ Photos used with permission of Etobicoke Collegiate Institute (TDSB) on pp. 350 (bottom) and 351 ♦ Bottom photo on p. 410 used with permission of The Country Day School (King, ON) ♦ Photo on p. 109 used with permission of Kirkland Lake District Composite Secondary School (DSB Ontario North East) ♦ Bottom photo on p. 104 used with permission of Nantyr Shores Secondary School (SCDSB), Loyola Catholic Secondary School (DPCDSB), and University of Toronto Schools ♦ Top photo on p. 183 (by Crystal J. Hall) used with permission of Cardinal Newman Catholic Secondary School (TDSB) ♦ Photo on p. 411 used with permission of Albert Campbell Collegiate Institute (TDSB) ♦ Ultimate shot on cover and top photo on p. 57 used with permission of A.Y. Jackson Secondary School (TDSB) ♦ Top photo on p. 57 used with permission of William Lyon Mackenzie Collegiate Institute (TDSB) ♦ Bottom photo on p. 358 used with permission of Westdale Secondary School (HWDSB) ♦ Photo on p. 347 used with permission of Newtonbrook Secondary School (TDSB) ♦ Photos on pp. 58 (top), 60 (bottom), 334 (top), 336, 337 (top), 343, 359, 362 (bottom), 363, 409 (bottom) courtesy of Toronto District School Board ♦ Photo on p. 323 used with permission of Mark Garneau Collegiate Institute

### Stock and Agency Photos

Photos on pp. 155 (bottom), 194 (top), 258 (top), 265 (bottom), 276 (top), 283, 341, 345, 349 (bottom), 353, 361, 365, 367, 369, 379 (bottom), 383 (bottom), 393, 397, 403, 407, 413, 417 (top), 421 (top), 425, 433 (bottom), 447: CP Images ♦ Photos on pp. 223 (top), 256 (middle), 421 (bottom): Getty Images ♦ Photos on pp. vi, x, xiii (bottom), xix, 8 (bottom), 10 (bottom), 18 (top), 49, 50 (bottom), 51 (top), 86 (bottom), 94 (top), 96 (bottom), 108 (top), 136, 145, 147, 152 (middle), 153, 155 (top), 161 (ribbon), 170 (top and bottom), 171 (middle and bottom), 175, 179, 180 (top), 181, 184 (TV and newspapers), 186, 187, 189, 191, 193, 194 (bottom), 197, 199 (top), 203 (ribbon), 210–213, 215, 217, 220, 223 (bottom), 226–228, 229 (anatomy of a cigarette images), 232, 233, 234 (top), 239 (bottom), 240, 242, 243 (bottom), 249, 250 (top), 251 (top), 253, 255, 256 (top), 260 (top), 262, 263, 265 (top), 269, 271, 272 (top), 275, 278, 279, 281, 285, 289, 291, 292 (top), 293, 296, 299, 300, 301, 302, 303 (middle and bottom), 305 (coffee and sugar), 307 (top), 309 (top), 310, 315, 318 (top and bottom), 319, 324, 330 (bottom), 334 (second from bottom and bottom), 338 (top), 342 (top), 346 (top), 350 (top), 358 (top), 366 (top), 372 (top), 375, 380 (top), 381, 384 (top), 390 (top), 400 (top), 405, 408, 419, 422 (bottom), 429 (top), 430 (top), 434 (top), 438, 439, 440 (top), 441, 444, 445, 472, 476, 486: iStockphoto ♦ Photos on pp. 5, 41 (top), 152 (middle), 165, 166, 168, 169, 178, 180 (bottom), 199 (bottom), 218, 221, 235 (top), 243 (top), 256 (bottom), 270 (top), 277 (top), 297, 325, 326, 434 (bottom): iStockpro ♦ Photos on pp. 7 (top), 15, 39, 53, 71, 87, 95, 111, 135, 151, 152 (top), 154, 162, 167, 177, 185, 195, 209, 222, 225, 229 (top and background smoke), 234 (bottom 3), 239 (top), 241, 245, 246, 250 (bottom), 251 (bottom), 258 (bottom), 259, 273, 277 (bottom), 287, 288 (middle), 292 (bottom), 307 (photos in serving size table), 311, 312, 317 (bottom), 318 (middle), 320, 321, 329, 330 (top), 332, 333, 334 (fourth from top), 377, 388 (top), 398 (top), 404 (top), 418 (top), 440 (bottom): Shutterstock ♦ Photos on pp. 418 (bottom) and 429 (bottom): Corbis

### Other Photos and Permissions

Photos on pp. iv, 10 (middle), 74–77, 79, 80, 82, 89 (top), 90, 92, 93, 96 (middle), 112, 113 (bottom), 115–133, 137 (bottom), 139, 149, 170 (middle), 184 (girl), 235 (bottom), 305, 313 (top), 327, 334 (second and third from top), 362 (top), 370 (top), 376 (top), 387, 399 (top), 400 (bottom), 401, 409 (top) by Ted Temertzoglou, Tanya Winter, Crystal J. Hall, and Paul Pacey, © Thompson Educational Publishing ♦ Photos on pp. 224, 370 (bottom) and 371 (bottom) courtesy of The Thompson Family ♦ Photos on pp. 54 (bottom), 55, 68 (bottom), 69, 83, 88 by Michelle Prata ♦ Photos on pp. 304, 316, 317 (top) by Tanya Winter with special thanks to Shoppers Drug Mart, Speros Pharmacy Care Centre Ltd., Speros A. Dorovenis ♦ Screencap on p. xvii courtesy of Canadian Health Network ♦ Photo on p. 38 courtesy of Derek Call ♦ Bottom photo on p. 58 by Rowan Greig, provided by Rees Buck ♦ Photo of heart rate monitor on p. 59 provided by Polar Canada ♦ Photo of pedometer on p. 68 courtesy of StepsCount Canada ♦ Photos on p. 70 by Tanya Winter, special thanks to Phillip Rowe, Body Pump Studio Inc. ♦ Photo on p. 86 courtesy of Nicole Tritter ♦ Photo on p. 97: Mount Royal College Recreation Centre, Calgary Alberta ♦ Photo on p. 110 courtesy of Mandi Gilles ♦ Photo on p. 134 courtesy of Sanket Ullal ♦ Bottom photo on p. 183 courtesy of Dove Campaign for Real Beauty (Unilever Canada) ♦ Photo on p. 208 courtesy of Alyson Beben ♦ Cigarette warning labels on p. 230, source: Graphic Health Warnings, www.hc-sc.gc.ca/hl-vs/tobac-tabac/legislation/label-etiquette/graph/index_e.html, Health Canada, 2000. Reproduced with the permission of the Minister of Public Works and Government Services Canada, courtesy of Environment Canada, 2006 ♦ MADD Posters on p. 238 provided by MADD Canada ♦ ESRB Graphic on p. 276 courtesy of Entertainment Software Ratings Board ♦ Image of NEDIC screen cap on p. 329 courtesy of NEDIC ♦ Top photo on p. 349 courtesy of Thomas Meyer ♦ Photos on p. 357 by Yan Huckendubler, courtesy of Field Hockey Canada ♦ Top photo on p. 379 courtesy of Stephane Cadieux ♦ Photo of Joseph H. Pilates (1943) on p. 433 *From Souvenirs of 70 Seasons*. Photo: John Lindquist, © Harvard Theatre Collection ♦ Top photo on p. 435: Jennie Worden ♦ Photos on p. 437 courtesy of Dancing with Alana ♦ Photos on p. 443 courtesy of Sandy Hott Johansen ♦ CPR Manual courtesy of the ACT Foundation

## Artwork and Tables

Artwork and illustrations on pp. xviii, 22–33, 35, 43–47, 117, 119, 121, 123, 125, 127, 129, 131, 133, 141–144, 156, 158, 163, 231, 237, 297 by Bart Vallecoccia ◆ Diagrams on p. 161 courtesy of the Canadian Cancer Society from Breast Self-examination: What you can do. Canadian Cancer Society 2005 ◆ Map on pp. 204–205 reproduced with kind permission from UNAIDS ◆ Tables on pp. 13, 64, 65, 74–78, 92 courtesy of The Canadian Physical Activity, Fitness & Lifestyle Approach: CSEP-Health & Fitness Program's Health-Related Appraisal and Counselling Strategy, 3rd Edition © 2003. ◆ Table on p. 69: Léger, L.A., Mercier, D., Gadoury, C., Lambert, J. The Multistage 20 m Shuttle Run Test for Aerobic Fitness. J. Sports Sci. 6: 93–101, 1988 ◆ Tables on pp. 81 and 84 adapted from Bigger, Faster, Stronger by Greg Shephard (Human Kinetics Publishers, 2003) and reproduced with permission of the author ◆ Table on p. 85 adapted from *Exercise Testing and Prescription* by David C. Nieman, Appendix A, Section 1, Tables 3 and 4 (McGraw-Hill, 2003) and reproduced with permission of the McGraw-Hill Companies ◆ Table on p. 107 table adapted with permission from "Ontario Health and Physical Education Curriculum Support: Grades K–10," Ophea (Ontario Physical Health Education Association), Toronto 2000, Grade 9–10, Resource Unit 2, p. 42 ◆ Table on p. 296 source: "Health Children Healthy Futures" Child Health Initiative ◆ Graphics on pp. 306 & 308 Canada's Guide to Healthy Eating and Physical Activity, Health Canada & the Public Health Agency of Canada, (1992) Reproduced with the permission of the Minister of Public Works and Government Services Canada, 2006. ◆ Chart on pp. 472–475, reproduced by permission of the Society of Obstetricians and Gynaecologists of Canada, Ottawa. Copyright © 2006 - Society of Obstetricians and Gynaecologists of Canada, www.sexualityandu.ca

## Boxes and Sidebars

Sidebar on p. 182 source: *A Barbie Who Puts Out* by Alyson Beben (Toronto: York University, 2003) ◆ Box on p. 184 source: John Pungente, S.J. From Barry Duncan et al. Media Literacy Resource Guide, Ontario Ministry of Education, Toronto, ON. Canada, 1989 ◆ Box on p. 240 source: MADD Canada (www.madd.ca) ◆ Sidebar on p. 202, *Estimates of HIV Prevalence and Incidence in Canada*, 2005. Public Healthy Agency of Canada, News Release, July 31, 2006. ◆ Box on p. 249 adapted from "Health Education and Promotion: Date Rape and Club Drugs" Copyright 2006 © York University ◆ Box on p. 271 adapted from The National Crime Prevention Center in Partnership with AESB District School, Community Mediation Services, The Mennonite Central Committee, and The John Howard Society of Newfoundland ◆ Box on p. 301 adapted from Dietitians of Canada/ American Dietetic Association, Position of the American Dietetic Association and Dietitians of Canada, www.dietitians.ca/news/highlights_positions.asp, 2003 ◆ Box on p. 310 source: reproduced from University of Ottawa, Health Services, www.uottawa.ca/health ◆ Sidebar on p. 246 adapted from "Cannabis" produced by the BC Partners for Mental Health and Addiction Information, September 2003